P9-ASL-967

DATE DUE

A HISTORY
of
AMERICAN
EDUCATION

A HISTORY
of
AMERICAN
EDUCATION

Harry G. Good
LATE OF THE OHIO STATE UNIVERSITY

James D. Teller
UNIVERSITY OF DALLAS

THIRD EDITION

Theodore Lownik Library
Illinois Benedictine College
Lisle, Illinois 60532

THE MACMILLAN COMPANY, NEW YORK
COLLIER-MACMILLAN PUBLISHERS, LONDON

370
.973
G 646h

Copyright © 1973, The Macmillan Company

Printed in the United States of America

All rights reserved. No part of this book may be reproduced or transmitted in any form or by any means, electronic or mechanical, including photocopying, recording, or any information storage and retrieval system, without permission in writing from the Publisher.

Earlier editions, by H. G. Good, copyright © 1956 and 1962 by The Macmillan Company.

THE MACMILLAN COMPANY
866 THIRD AVENUE, NEW YORK, NEW YORK 10022

Collier-Macmillan Canada, Ltd., Toronto, Ontario

Library of Congress catalog card number: 72–86503

LIBRARY OF CONGRESS CATALOGING IN PUBLICATION DATA

Good, Harry Gehman, 1880–
  A history of American education.

  Includes bibliographical references.
    1. Education—United States—History.
I. Teller, James David, 1906–   joint author.
II. Title.
LA209.G58   1973   370'.973   72–86503
ISBN 0–02–344610–2

Printing: 1 2 3 4 5 6 7 8   Year: 3 4 5 6 7 8 9

PREFACE

In the second edition of this book the late senior author reported: "These are times of great and rapid change." But he hastened to add with his typical astute historical perspective: "Change is not new. American education is always changing." Like the first two editions, this edition treats these changes in American education as a phase of the rise and progress of American culture as a whole.

Such an approach teaches that educational progress has come from the wise and skillful use of our resources, both material and human. American education can take credit for placing the first man on the moon because American teachers have recognized that even in this Space Age the most creative power present in this world is not atomic power but manpower. We Americans have always dreamed that we would find ways to discover and develop the abilities of all of our children. Thus we should heed the admonition of Francis Bacon whose words, slightly edited, were these: "Ask Counsel of both Times: of the Ancient Time, what of it is worth keeping, and of the Latter Time, what is fittest for the new day; but seek as well to create Good Precedents as to follow them."

America has created many good educational precedents in pursuing her dream of equal educational opportunity for all children, regardless of sex, race, national origin, economic level, or social background. The common community school, the junior high school, the comprehensive high school, the junior college, and the American university are all good precedents, to be improved certainly but not to be destroyed by those who would impose upon youth what they think he should have rather than what his unique individuality requires.

If we heed Bacon, we do not resist all change. Neither do we accept all proposed innovations. Each new idea must run the gauntlet of objection and opposition. Perhaps one out of every hundred new solutions will be found to be superior to the old. The danger is that the proponents of the other ninety-nine ideas will attempt to force their adoption by the use of violence, terror, arson, assassination, and other instruments of nihilism. It is at this point that historical perspective is required.

In the decade since the publication of the second edition of this book, schools have been subjected to a two-pronged attack: first they were blamed for low academic standards, lack of rigor, and too little and the wrong kind of science and mathematics; then they were accused of ignoring the emotional and social needs of the child at the expense of his intellectual development. Both groups of critics discount past achievements; both have utopian solutions. Despite the clamor of these self-appointed prophets, we would be well advised to follow Bacon's admonition.

Educational ideas and practices of the past constitute a vast historical laboratory for those who are presently concerned with the problems of education. Because these problems are persistent and perennial, one truly empirical method of solving educational problems is to analyze and evaluate the ideas and practices of great teachers. This book is intended as a historical laboratory to enable the student to do this. It is a study of present problems in the light of their past as a guide to their future solution.

As the Contents shows, we are presenting our subject in four parts; these are not merely temporal units, for each period has an outlook and character of its own.

J. D. T.

CONTENTS

PART I: TRANSPLANTATION AND ADAPTATION

1. CHILDREN IN THE NEW WORLD   3
Of Beginnings – England and Her Schools – English Settlements – Melting-Pot and Crucible – Life in Colonial America – Children and Manual Labor – Children and the Four R's – Types and Systems of Schools – Colonial Teachers – Summary – Questions – Books and Papers

2. UPPER SCHOOLS AND COLLEGES   45
Where the Latin Schools Came From – Early Latin Schools – Latin School Curriculum – The Colonial Colleges – Realist and Classical Theory – Private Schools – Franklin's Plans for an Academy – Summary – Questions – Books and Papers

PART II: AWAKENING AND CRUSADE

3. LIBERTY AND LEARNING   77
Two Theories – Founding Fathers at School – Liberty Begins in the Mind – Education in the State Constitutions – Jefferson's Plan – Statesmen and Utopians – The National University Idea – College Enthusiasm – The Older Colleges and the States – Early State Universities – Summary – Questions – Books and Papers

4. EXPERIMENTS IN LEARNING   102
Possessing the Land – East and West – Early Academies – Numbers and Distribution of Academies – Problems, Arguments, and Disputes – Organized Labor and the Schools – Opposition to Public Education – The Organs of Public Opinion – Social Reforms and Reformers – Educational Reforms – An Educational Liberal Speaks Out – Summary – Questions – Books and Papers

5. FROM PRIVATE SCHOOLS TO STATE SYSTEMS   127
Philanthropic Endeavor – Why the Lancasterian Schools Failed – An American Principle – Defining Public Education – State Systems in Outline – An Early Start in New York – Pennsylvania Beginnings – On the Western Frontier – New England Frontier – Massachusetts Indicted – Massachusetts Vindicated – Summary – Questions – Books and Papers

6. FROM SCHOOLKEEPING TO TEACHING   162
An Early Interpreter – Voices of the Profession – A Light-Bearer – Transcendental Schoolmaster – Teaching Reading – Elementary Schoolbooks – Useful Knowledge Made Interesting – Pestalozzian Principles Criticized – Teaching Aids – Books for Teachers – Summary – Questions – Books and Papers

PART III. EXPERIMENTATION AND REGIMENTATION

7. EXPANDING ELEMENTARY EDUCATION   191
The American Kindergarten – Child Study – Elementary Handwork – The Spreading Normal Schools – Oswego – Spotlight on Quincy

– Nature Study – Science-Teaching Trends – Summary – Questions – Books and Papers

8. RISE OF THE HIGH SCHOOL   219

The Meaning of Secondary Education – Another Door Is Opened – High School Origins – English High School of Boston – High Schools in Massachusetts – The Central High School of Philadelphia – Other Pennsylvania High Schools – An Early Connecticut High School – High Schools in the Middle West – Secondary Education in the South – The Worth of the High School – Standard High Schools – The Extended Secondary School – Summary – Questions – Books and Papers

9. THE OLD AND THE NEW SOUTH   246

Opinions and Arguments – Progress to 1860 – Postwar Dilemma – Reconstruction – Schools for Freedmen – The Peabody and Other Funds – Toward Universal Education – Educating Black Leaders – Summary – Questions – Books and Papers

10. COLLEGES FOR THE PEOPLE   269

Schools of a New Era – First Morrill Bill – Morrill Act of 1862 – Organization of the Colleges – College Problems – Second Morrill Act – Rural Club Work – Federal-State Cooperation; Smith-Lever Act – Cooperation, Second Phase; Smith-Hughes Act – College Growth – Summary – Questions – Books and Papers

11. EDUCATION AS A PROFESSION   294

Education as a Science – Education as a Branch of Study – Faculty Psychology – General Principles of Teaching – Methods and Management – Broader Specialties – University Courses in Education – City Supervision – Summary – Questions – Books and Papers

PART IV: ACHIEVEMENTS AND VISIONS

12. EUROPEAN THEORIES AND AMERICAN EDUCATION   325

A Great English Teacher – John Locke – Rousseau – Basedow – Pestalozzi – Herbart – Froebel – Summary – Questions – Books and Papers

13. EDUCATION FOR DEMOCRACY   349

Youth of John Dewey – At Johns Hopkins University – Diligent Professor – In Chicago – The Dewey School – Books on Education – Democracy and Education – Growth as the End – How We Think – A Colleague and Disciple – Progressive Education – Summary – Questions – Books and Papers

14. SCIENCE AND EDUCATION   389

Rice as an Educational Scientist – Toward a Science of Education – Research in Spelling Instruction – School Arithmetic – Studies of Reading – Psychology and Education – Studies of Exceptional Children – Sociology, Anthropology, and Education – Summary – Questions – Books and Papers

15. TECHNOLOGY AND EDUCATION   416

Educational Invention – Individualizing Instruction – Curricular Innovations – School and Library – Audiovisual Instruction Movement

– Language Study – Teaching Machines – Summary – Questions – Books and Papers

16. NEW DIRECTIONS FOR SECONDARY EDUCATION   446

Rise of the Junior High School – The Junior College – New Goals and Functions – General or Special High Schools? – Introducing Vocational Education – Private Secondary Education – Guidance and Secondary Education – Persistent Problems – Summary – Questions – Books and Papers

17. ADVANCES IN HIGHER EDUCATION   478

Beginning of Universities – Coeducation – Universities Breaking Old Bonds – Criticism of Universities – Trend Toward General Education – Preparation of Teachers – Adult Education – Public Monopoly of Higher Education – Exchange of Students – Summary – Questions – Books and Papers

18. GOVERNMENT AND EDUCATION   512

Education and the Constitution – The States and Public Schools – Racial Segregation – Supreme Court Decisions – Federal Support of Education – Government and Education in Emergencies – U.S. Office of Education – International Education – Unity Through Cooperation – Summary – Questions – Books and Papers

INDEX   551

Part I

TRANSPLANTATION
AND
ADAPTATION

Preview

Part I is concerned with the transplantation of European culture and education to seventeenth- and eighteenth-century America and with its adaptation to a more open and pluralistic society. The period that encompasses almost half of our history can be viewed as a giant educational experiment to determine the proper balance between schooling and the education provided by home, church, and community. We see the Colonies trying almost every variety of educational institution: parochial, sectarian, missionary, private, neighborhood, town, district, and still other elementary schools; medieval, humanist, and realist secondary schools; apprenticeship and vocational schools; and the old world colleges in the towns. In the colonial period, the foundations are laid for a secular, common, public, community school, but with a public policy that permits private schooling to continue and to compete with the public school.

Chapter 1

CHILDREN IN THE
NEW WORLD

The permanent British settlement in North America began at Jamestown, Virginia, in 1607. By 1776 the thirteen separate colonies extended along the Atlantic coast from western New Brunswick to southern Georgia. In that stretch of 1,300 miles, people from many countries and from all but the highest social levels had established their homes. In that period of 170 years great social changes occurred in the New World. In a summary such as this only the most general conditions and changes can be discussed, and in a history of education those factors should be selected that were closely related not only to the schools but also to other educational agencies; such as the home, church, and community.

Englishmen preparing to settle on the coast of America knew that they would find an uncultivated country without cities, roads, schools, banks, law courts, or the other features of a civilized way of life. They could bring the patterns of civilization with them but the institutions would have to be created. Edward Eggleston called such a removal from a cultivated to an uncultivated country "the transit of civilization."

Civilization, like the kingdom of Heaven, has to exist within people if it is to thrive outside, in society; hence, the settlers had to bring with them a supply of learning, morals, and useful skills in order to construct the schools, churches, and political institutions of a civilized community. Books could be transported but many of the newcomers could not read. The larger libraries were imported from England, a few volumes at a time, in the eighteenth century. Some books were being printed in America, such as the "Bay Psalm Book" of 1640.

The new Americans met the native Indians in council, trade, and war and learned from them in all these areas but mostly in agriculture. Indian words in the English language testify to this fact. Three of these words are names of crop-plants: *maize* (still called Indian corn), *potato*, and *tobacco*; these, with *canoe*, came from the West Indies. Other Indian words are *hickory, hominy, moccasin, opossum, persimmon, pone, raccoon, sachem,*

3

sagamore (a chieftain a few notches below a sachem), *squash, squaw, tomahawk, totem,* and *wampum.* Numerous medicines were obtained from the Indians. Tammany Hall bears the name of an Indian chief, and hundreds of Indian place-names are today scattered over the map of the United States.

The Indians influenced not only the language but the literature of America. Stories, novels, histories, and many scientific treatises have the Indian as their subject. Many of the stories and novels have been translated into foreign languages and have furnished the children of many nations with ideas for games. The doctrine of the "noble savage" even threatened to revolutionize education through the writings of Rousseau and the other Romantics.

The Indians did not educate their children in schools, which suited Rousseau very well. Among the Indians, life was the school, an idea approved by the ancient Romans, Emerson, and the American pragmatists. The Indian child learned to live in harmony with nature through his day-to-day experiences. He learned that natural resources are finite and must be used with restraint and with a view to the long-term needs of the community. In many ways the education of these "primitive" first Americans in conservation and ecology was more effective than that of the "civilized" later Americans. However, the settlers did not adopt the Indians' idea on education. Those of the settlers who were interested in education at all wanted a school separate from life and highly selective in what and to whom it taught in accordance with the European tradition.

OF BEGINNINGS

English culture was an extension of the old civilization of Europe and the very ancient East; early America was a further spur, a western offshoot, of the great inheritance that England had received, cultivated, and enlarged. All of the English colonies shared in the knowledge and beliefs of the mother country in the seventeenth century. These had changed greatly since the Renaissance-Reformation and were now transmitted through the English settlers to all of the colonies. All of early British America, not only the northeastern settlements, was truly New England, Virginia as well as Massachusetts.

Little is known of the actual beginnings of civilized life on the islands between the Atlantic and the North Sea, which now constitute Great Britain. For a long time Britain was almost over the rim of the world, the "ultima Thul," which Tennyson described as "sundered, once, from all the human race." We know about early Britons from remains and from some authors, including Caesar. Other invaders followed Caesar. The Church brought a new religion; a new language developed; and England became a compact nation, able to establish and defend her settlements against the Spanish and the French. The culture of this New England is not new at all.

American civilization grew from English seed as England had from the rest of Europe. We cannot know how old it is, it began before the invention of writing. Records were not always kept or were lost. There is a difficulty of another order. Mankind takes little notice of beginnings; they seem insignificant. Only strong movements or those that fail disastrously are recorded, and by that time their beginnings may be lost in the mists of time.

The remote sources of Anglo-American education must be sought in the valleys of the Tigris-Euphrates and the Nile. From these came the sciences of measurement, astronomy, and medicine, and the art of writing that led to the rise of schools. Newer nations stood on the shoulders of the older ones and saw farther. Chief among these older nations in our educational ancestry were three that bordered on the Mediterranean—Palestine, Greece, and Rome. From them, we gained religion, philosophy, logic, and mathematics, as well as the highly valued literature of the Bible, Homer, Plato, and Virgil. Plato and Aristotle treated education as it was and as it might be. The *Politics* and *Ethics* of Aristotle, the works of Cicero, and the *Code* of Rome, the "ruler of the nations," all show how men lived and how they should live. The ancient world had developed a high civilization, an orderly society, that was able to provide appropriate measures of justice and freedom.

By the thirteenth century, after the long feudal and medieval darkness, universities began to spring up in the chief countries of Europe. Oxford and Cambridge Universities had been established in England, and others were growing up in nearly every country. A new spirit of inquiry, travel, and exploration led to the unexpected discovery of a vast continent, a New World. This was, in part, the result of a new nationalism and international trade. The New World in turn stimulated both the wealth of nations and world commerce; cause and effect were interrelated, each reciprocal of the other. All of these were parts of the Renaissance: the rebirth—which is what *Renaissance* means—of the old forms of culture, of the ancient learning and literatures of Greece and Rome, and the birth of new art, new learning, individualism, and nationalism.

Upon the rediscovery of the great classics, Homer, the Greek tragedies, the orations, histories, and the Roman writers such as Horace, Virgil, and Cicero, an almost religious fervor seized the students of the fourteenth century. The change from the medieval to the classical outlook in a man such as Erasmus resembled a spiritual conversion. The invention of printing in the midfifteenth century helped spread the New Learning and the ideas of the Protestant Reformation.

The Renaissance and the Reformation helped to develop two types of schools: the Latin and Greek secondary school for the classes; the vernacular, elementary school for the masses. The elementary school taught the catechism, prayers, and the psalms to prepare for confirmation; and arithmetic, handwriting, and business skills. Both schools were later introduced into England and her colonies.

The classical secondary school, as well as the elementary school, was closely related to the Church in Catholic as well as in Protestant lands. By preparing pupils for the universities, the secondary school provided a necessary link in the educational training of religious leaders, and at the same time served upper class youth, many of whom went on to become political leaders. The two schools were fundamentally different and generally independent of each other, but in the primitive conditions of colonial America the two sets of pupils were often taught by the same teacher.

ENGLAND AND HER SCHOOLS

Spain and France carried out explorations and established settlements in America while England remained only an island. Spain held Florida and vast areas of the present American Southwest, and France founded Quebec and explored the interior of the continent. Navigation was developing in the sixteenth century and, for a century after Columbus landed in the New World, the Spaniards, Portuguese, and French manned the oceangoing ships, planted colonies, and sailed around the world while the English remained at home. Sir Francis Drake (ca. 1540–1596), an Elizabethan captain, was the first Englishman to circumnavigate the globe.

The advances in navigation impressed the people of the entire world, which had always been land-bound. Regions and people previously unknown became accessible, adding vast knowledge and new ideas to the European stock. The educational reformer John Amos Comenius (1592–1670) born in what is now Czechoslovakia, considered the new navigation to be one of the greatest advances of his time. He had experienced some of the dangers of sailing for he had been shipwrecked in the Baltic Sea. Comenius visited England, wrote schoolbooks for Sweden, was concerned for the conversion of the American Indians, and according to an improbable tradition preserved by Cotton Mather, was considered for the presidency of the infant Harvard College. Perhaps the most direct connection that Comenius had with America was the reprinting, in the United States, of one of his most popular schoolbooks.

The destruction of the Spanish Armada in 1588 and the subsequent decline of Spain as a naval power, helped to open the sea to English colonization. The voyage from England across the stormy Atlantic took from seven to twelve weeks, and was most frequently undertaken in summer when the ocean was calmest. To the danger from the sea, one must add vast discomfort or real hardship, and the possibility of attack by infectious diseases. But the Atlantic Ocean offered the English an escape from their poverty and unemployment, and those persecuted on the continent found an escape from the rigors of a hostile Europe, torn by religious strife and soon to be plunged into the Thirty Years War.

Great changes were taking place in the England of Elizabeth, Shakespeare, and Ben Jonson. Perhaps the greatest change was that the previous resistance to change had disappeared. The nation was no longer insular; the English now looked out upon the wide world and traversed the seas. England was again Protestant, and the Anglican Church took a middle position between Catholicism and Puritanism. The unity of the Church of England was broken by the rise of the Puritan party. The universities, and particularly Emmanuel College, Cambridge, were centers of Puritanism. Another dissenting body, the Society of Friends, arose at the same time.

The schools became conservative. The old enthusiasm for the classics had receded but no new interest had come into view and the schools continued to pick the grammatical bones. Roger Ascham (1516–1568) served as tutor to the future Queen Elizabeth and, as one would expect, his estimate of her attainments was high. Ascham's prose is admired but *The Scholemaster* contains little that was new and important in education. His younger contemporaries, Richard Mulcaster (1530–1611) and John Brinsley (c.1570–c.1630), contributed to the improvement of the English language and its teaching.

England was late in joining the scientific movement that flourished in Italy and France, and the conservative schools did not speed her progress. William Gilbert (1540–1603), a physician, performed pioneer studies in magnetism; William Harvey (1578–1657) published his discovery of the circulation of the blood in the seventeenth century; Robert Boyle (1627–1691) made important contributions in chemistry; the Royal Society was established in 1662; and the discoveries of Isaac Newton (1642–1727) in light, optics, astronomy, and mathematics placed England in the forefront of scientific development. Some of this work was done in connection with the universities, and yet had no effect upon the medieval curriculum.

By the time Elizabeth died in 1603, England had broken out of her insularity. The religious question had been settled, although not to the satisfaction of everybody. Her "singing birds" had created a great literature that gave promise of a greater one. Elizabeth was almost at the point of establishing her first permanent settlements in the territory that was to become the thirteen English Colonies and eventually the United States. These were not only her first settlements in America but the first extensive overseas dominions of the English nation and people.

Despite these signs of initiative and future greatness, England was extremely conservative socially, a land of rigid social classes, and a highly class-conscious country. The "Colonel's lady and Judy O'Grady" may have been "sisters under the skin" but they did not speak to each other except in the giving and taking of orders. Classes have always existed and always will, but the gulf between the lowborn and the highborn has been wider in some countries than in others and at different times. In England, at the settlements, the separation between the classes was rigid and clearly marked and has continued to be more so than elsewhere, more than in a new country with a shifting frontier.

Schooling was definitely tied to rank and wealth in the England of the American settlements. Those "born to be poor" needed no schooling for it was thought they would be better servants if they did not know too much. Practical skills and efficiencies were acquired through practical work. Only members of the upper classes voted or exercised any political power; the unenfranchised common people needed no understanding of, or participation in, public policy. These considerations explain why English colonizers and colonists alike were satisfied with a decadent school in the ancient languages and literatures. Not until the nineteenth century was there a revival of classical education. This was far too late for the colonial children, drilled in Latin forms and congruences; theirs was not to reason why.

The English did not lack for education counselors. The seventeenth century swarmed with school reformers: John Brinsley, Richard Mulcaster, Charles Hoole, John Dury, William Petty, William Penn, John Milton, and John Locke. Every reader will recognize the last three names but may not know what educational views they promulgated. The others will hardly be recognized even by educators and were little known in their own day. Much of what these men argued for has now been accepted, but in spite of rather than because of them. Although there are exceptions, educational philosophers are often ignored by their contemporaries; later centuries adopt their views but rarely celebrate their wisdom. It often takes people a long while to catch on.

The new age in education as in science began on the continent, and Comenius was to a degree the herald of both. The new age was to be an age of useful knowledge, practical skills, and applied science: the age of realism. Such phrases were coined as "not words but things"; "things before words"; or, "words only when joined to things." Navigation, surveying, bookkeeping, mensuration, arithmetic, and related subjects were taught in new schools called academies, institutes, or schools of industry. These were new schools for a new class of students. They were comparatively few in number and their success was not great; but in the later colonial period they multiplied in the seaport towns and larger villages of America.

The seventeenth century was the century of realism in education and the Puritan century in religion; most but not all Puritans were also realists. John Brinsley was a Puritan in whom, it was said, "we get no hint of realism," yet he urged strongly that boys should be taught English before Latin, and that this knowledge should be preserved and improved lest they come up to the university unable to write their own language. This interest in the English language is a broad hint of realism. Brinsley was interested in the religious conversion of the Indians. On the title page of A Consolation for Our Grammar Schooles (1622), he refers to Virginia. This may be the earliest book referring to education in the new settlements.

Other teacher-authors of that time, Richard Mulcaster, Charles Hoole, and John Locke, were also interested in the cultivation and teaching of English. In 1582 Mulcaster prepared a spelling-book that was to contain the 8,000 most frequently used words. It agrees surprisingly well with E. L. Thorndike's more scientifically constructed list of 10,000 commonly used words prepared in 1921. Mulcaster proposed that the elementary schools teach reading, writing, drawing, singing, and playing an instrument. He wrote a book on physical education and audaciously proposed the establishment of a college of education in each of the ancient universities, Oxford and Cambridge. Mulcaster was a conceited pedagogue yet not entirely without reason.

Like his predecessors, Charles Hoole in New Discovery of the Old Art of Teaching School (1660) developed views on the teaching of English. Attention to the national language and to the languages of the neighboring countries, was a policy strongly supported by Comenius, the greatest of the realists. The study of modern languages, native and foreign, is a touchstone, a test of realism because it proves the student's and teacher's emphasis upon contemporary subjects, nature, vocations, and politics.

The Quaker William Penn and the Puritan John Dury were both realists who placed great weight upon religious and moral instruction. There were vital differences between them and the Friends with their belief in the "inner light" and the leading of the Spirit, and the Puritans who insisted that the Scripture contained the complete revelation of the Will of God. This conflict was later to lead to tragedy in New England.

Locke was a realist whose theory included all of the previously discussed educational positions. His entire system is, however, controlled by his ruling purpose: the fashioning of an English gentleman. Locke is believed to have had a hand in drawing up a plan of government for the Carolinas, the Fundamental Constitutions, which was wholly impractical. As was pointed out earlier, the realist writers had little influence in their day. Their theories and schools were not directed to the education of men-of-leisure. The American who was most influenced by them was Benjamin Franklin.

Only the upper classes received anything more than a rudimentary education in England. Locke was typically English in this respect. The Puritans, like the Presbyterians of Scotland and the Lutherans of Germany and Scandinavia, had schools for all children. The Bible was the central study and textbook in the elementary schools. The Puritans who settled in America applied this doctrine in their Bible commonwealth and became the promoters of schools of reading and religion for all children.

Puritanism began to expand noticeably from the early years of Elizabeth to the middle of the seventeenth century. The Quakers emerged about the same time and thus began the growth of sectarianism and eventually of religious freedom in England. Under Elizabeth's predecessor Mary (1553–1558), a Catholic reaction had divided the English into mutually hostile groups, but when Elizabeth ascended the throne she turned the nation back to the Reformation settlement, the Act of Supremacy of 1535. The new queen was more interested in national unity and peace than in religion. She was measurably successful: England would not become Catholic; but this did not assure religious peace. The Catholics were not pleased and might become dangerous; the Puritans were growing stronger in the country houses, in the cities, and even in the universities; and there were the Separatists, a small but radical group.

The Puritans desired a further purification from religious practices and church services, which they associated with popery. They were opposed to the clerical surplice, kneeling for communion, using the ring in marriage, making the sign of the cross in baptism, and other less sacred matters such as fine clothes or mince pie at Christmas. But the Puritans were themselves divided on many points. Extreme Puritans no longer attended the church services, but held their meetings in dwelling-houses. The Separatists left the Anglican communion and a group of them (Pilgrims) migrated to Holland over a period of twelve years to escape persecution by the established churches. In 1620 the Pilgrims founded the American colony of Plymouth. The names of many towns in New England recall the English homes from which these settlers had come. Many came from East Anglia or London.

The number of Puritans was much smaller than the reader may suppose, but it varied greatly with time and place. Early in the seventeenth century not more than perhaps 4 per cent of the whole English population was clearly Puritan. Some of these were leading scholars, and when the King James version of the Bible was prepared, a number of Puritan university men were included among the fifty-four translators. Puritans were numerous in Parliament. In the time of the Civil Wars, Puritans and the adherents of Puritanism were in the majority, and some settlers in Massachusetts returned to England believing that Puritan rule would be permanent. At the end of the seventeenth century, Puritans numbered no more than at its beginning.

ENGLISH SETTLEMENTS

Inexperienced in foreign settlement as they were, the English sent out expeditions that were unprepared and poorly equipped for life in a wholly uncultivated land. In 1583 Humphrey Gilbert (1537–1583) attempted to colonize Newfoundland. Someone has spoken of the "murderous New England winter" that almost destroyed the Pilgrims; but Newfoundland was more rigorous and no one knows what happened to its first settlers. Sir Walter Raleigh (1552–1618) sent two expeditions (in 1585 and 1587) far to the south but the first company returned home after a year and the second perished, perhaps from hunger, disease, or Indian attack. No one has been able to solve the mystery of the "Lost Colony." Jamestown, settled in 1607, and located in a mild country named for the Virgin Queen, barely survived the calamities that had destroyed its predecessors.

Virginia was settled by Anglicans who became planters, farmed tobacco, introduced slavery (1619), and established such great families as the Carters, the Byrds of "Westover," and the Daingerfields. Three attempts to establish a college were made in the first century of settlement. In 1619 the Virginia Company held funds for Henrico College. The second attempt might have succeeded but for the Indian massacre of 1622. The College of William and Mary, chartered in 1693, resulted from the third venture. Preparatory education depended mainly upon tutors, family schools, other private schools and, in a few cases, upon education in England. The plantation system was not universal; in later times Germans, used to diversified farming and having an eye for good land, occupied the beautiful Shenandoah Valley. The German settlers, like the Cavaliers, made no effort to promote public education.

John Brinsley's A Consolation for Our Grammar Schooles (1622), which intended to help preserve the purity of the English tongue among a people far from home, has already been mentioned. No doubt Brinsley would not have approved of the borrowing of the Indian words. His book was intended to improve the "country grammar schooles," particularly those of an "inferior sort," and to extend the kingdom of Christ, especially among the heathen Indians. The author's purposes were not achieved, for there were few grammar schools of any sort and the Indians killed one-third of the 4,000 white people in Virginia before any copies of Brinsley's book reached America.

The first permanent English settlement north of Virginia was made by the Pilgrims. In their words and ways there was a certain blind, heedless urgency. The Mayflower sailed unseasonably and arrived at Plymouth Rock at the onset of a northern winter. Sickness and famine dealt harshly with the tiny company and just a little more ill luck would have extinguished all hope for Mayflower descendants. Before landing, the colonists drew up the now famous Mayflower Compact, thereby covenanting and combining themselves into a civil body politic for their better ordering and the enacting of such just and equal laws as thought best for the general good of the colony. This summary is not a copy but does contain many of the words of the Compact. In 1619, one year before the Pilgrims made their covenant, the first elected legislature in America, the House of Burgesses, had met in Virginia. These were the first steps toward political democracy in the New World. The Plymouth Colony did not achieve the leadership in education or other civil affairs that the makers of the Compact perhaps had expected.

The Puritans around Massachusetts Bay had much more influence upon education than the settlers of Plymouth or Virginia. Ten years after the founding of Plymouth, as the intolerance and persecuting fervor of the bishops increased and the Parliamentary struggle with the king became more acrimonious, the Puritans left England by the shiploads, not heeding the charge of deserting their cause at home. Immigration rose to flood proportions. Twenty thousand Puritans, including university graduates and pastors, arrived before the meeting of the Long Parliament in 1640. They came to establish a society that would conform to the Will of God, a Bible Commonwealth, and they felt certain they understood what this implied. Church and state were to be joined closely, with the church actually being superior to the civil power. In practice the government was in the hands of leading laymen and Puritan ministers and it tended to be a government of men rather than law. The outcome proved once again that without law there can be no liberty. The Bible contained the code of laws of this theocracy and the assembly also passed laws, but both were interpreted and executed by officers who felt that God was speaking and acting through them. Hence, it is difficult to understand how they could so harshly mistreat Ann Hutchinson (1591–1643) and the Quakers who also heard divine messages.

The Puritans had come to their "wintry coast" for religious freedom only for themselves. Any dissenters were to be treated even more badly than the Anglican bishops had treated them. Tolerance was almost unknown except, to a certain extent, in Holland. Samuel Willard, a leading minister, spoke for the Bay Colony when he wrote: "The design of our First Planters . . . was not Tolerance; but (they) were professed Enemies of it." Like all utopians the Puritans sought to isolate their colony against infection from without and immunize it against any germs of error from within. They failed. Ann Hutchinson and Roger Williams (1603?–1683) were driven into the wilderness, one for listening to the inner voice, the other for encouraging religious freedom. The Quakers came from Barbados or England, and the pious Puritans stripped and whipped them, put them into the stocks, cut off their ears, expelled them, and at last executed four of them. At that point Charles II, who had no love for the Quakers, stopped that ultimate brutality, but the Quakers were still whipped on bare backs as they were dragged through town after town at the tail of a cart.

Democracy, like toleration, was no part of the Puritan's design. Nothing could be more clear or more striking than the words (in modern spelling) of one of their revered and learned ministers, John Cotton (1584–1652), who said:

It is better that the commonwealth be fashioned to the setting forth of God's house which is his church than to accommodate the church frame to the civil state. Democracy, I do not conceive that ever God did ordain as a fit government either for church or commonwealth. If the people be governors, who shall be governed? As for monarchy, or aristocracy, they are both of them clearly approved, and directed in Scripture, yet so as referreth the sovereignty (God) himself, and setteth up theocracy in both, as the best form of government in the commonwealth as well as the church.

Thus, after appealing to the Bible as a textbook in political science, Cotton returned to the theocracy with which he started.

The Puritan religion was harsh. Those who say otherwise are later writers who never experienced the discipline of the sect; or they are speaking of later times when its fires were already burning low. In its prime the Puritan's religion caused fear and even anguish, perhaps especially in sensitive children. One example of this is preserved in the diary for January 13, 1696, of Samuel Sewall (1652–1730). His little daughter Betty on that day "burst into an amazing cry" because "she was afraid she would goe to Hell." This may be pertinent to a history of education and so may be the witchcraft delusion. The spirit world was very real to their imagination; it is some excuse that belief in witchcraft was widespread in the seventeenth century, and it is to the credit of the Massachusetts Puritans that they conquered it in part although only after a terrible seizure. Many of the Salem "witches" were children and other suggestible people. The belief occasioned the phenomena; people do not discover witches or see ghosts or flying saucers, unless they believe in them first. Samuel Sewall was a judge and pronounced sentence upon the Salem "witches." After the community regained a measure of sanity he had the moral courage to make public confession of his error. The beliefs that the Puritans brought with them must have influenced their schools.

Education was necessary to the Puritan scheme, for Bible-reading, and for the maintenance of church and state. What was necessary could not be left to individual desire and initiative; it had to be controlled by church and state. As there was no religious freedom, so there was no civil freedom. The people had fled from England and could not expect much Anglican help. In America they were alone in a vast forest, surrounded by savages. Education was not only a necessity, it demanded immediate attention. Soon after the settlement, and sixty years before the older colony of Virginia, the Puritans founded a college and a grammar school. Soon every town of indicated population was required to provide instruction in English for the lower classes and in Latin for the upper. In his account of Ezekiel Cheever in *Grandfather's Chair*, Nathaniel Hawthorne correctly describes the two groups as two schools taught alternately by the same teacher under one roof. The Puritans did not invent the ladder system of free public schools with a comprehensive high school and a state university.

The religious temper of the Puritans, the union of state and church, the isolation from Europe and from other colonies, and the hierarchic organization of their society, combined in promoting education beyond that of the colonies that had a mixed population. The originality of the educational arrangements of the Puritans is open to question. It is significant that as Puritanism waned, its schools declined. Except in the Eastern towns, the Latin school was not popular in colonial times.

MELTING-POT AND CRUCIBLE

The Middle Colonies were settled by a mixed population of Dutch, Swedes, Germans, English, Welsh, and Scots. They were even more diversified in religion. Colleges and schools were maintained by churches, private individuals, and boards. This has been called the region of the parochial or church schools, but the schools of the Puritans were also church schools. Private schools invaded the towns of New England in large numbers in the eighteenth century. The South has been called the area of the private school, but it had many church-connected schools as well. The regionalism of colonial education is not as clearly marked as some writers have believed.

The intermingling of many sects, nationalities, and languages made the region from the Hudson River to Georgia a melting-pot for the casting of Colonial Americans. Moravians, Huguenots, Quakers, and Germans in large numbers and of more than one religious persuasion came to America in search of religious freedom. Seventeenth-century Virginia was not always hospitable. About 1650 she refused to admit Puritans or Quakers and balked at receiving "New Light" Presbyterians, "Separate Baptists," and evangelical gospelers in general. There is a report, however, of one rector who allowed George Whitefield (1714–1770) to preach in his church on the condition that he would first read from the *Book of Common Prayer*. Eventually the English Board of Trade advised Virginia (1750) that "the free exercise of religion is so valuable a branch of true liberty" that a trading nation should preserve it.

New Amsterdam, preeminently a trading village, learned this lesson without prompting and, in fact, the Dutch had practiced it in their mother country. New Amsterdam and the entire region of the Middle Colonies formed the chief melting-pot. The village at the mouth of the Hudson was a trading post from which the furs of the Indians and the commodities of broad valleys were shipped overseas. Early in the history of the village, it is said, thirteen languages were spoken in its streets. There were hardly enough of any group of people to permit persecution. The Quakers of New Jersey and Pennsylvania were not of a mind to persecute anyone. Before the Quakers lost control, religious freedom was well-established.

Maryland, created as a haven for English Catholics, was not so fortunate after Lord Baltimore's time. The Puritans had come to outnumber the Catholics and in 1654 they dominated the Maryland Assembly, which repealed the liberal Act Concerning Religion and denied religious freedom to Catholics at that time. Rhode Island was the earliest colony founded to allow freedom of opinion and faith. Roger Williams and his successors, against the machinations of the nearby Puritans, welcomed people of many religions, including the Jewish.

The active settlement of the Middle Colonies to the south of New York was held back by Dutch claims and Dutch control of that region until 1664. After that the vacant spaces on the Atlantic coast between the southern and northern Colonies were rapidly filled up. The great increase in population that took place in the two decades following 1690 was the result, in considerable part, of the new immigration into Pennsylvania, New Jersey, and other Colonies, and of the high birth rate in Colonial families elsewhere.

The people who were coming into the Delaware Valley in those years were of many stocks and faiths. Small settlements of Swedish Lutherans and Dutch Calvinists had been there long before. Puritans escaping from the unfriendly England of Charles II, English and Welsh Quakers, and Welshmen who were not Quakers, to the number of several thousand, had come before William Penn arrived on the ship *Welcome* in 1682. Some of the Welsh moved out into the country, and Welsh names such as Brecknock and Caernarvon are found far from Philadelphia in Pennsylvania. A small number of Huguenots came in the same year (1683) as did Francis Daniel Pastorius (1651–1720) and the Mennonites who founded Germantown. Pastorius was a university-bred scholar and a Pietist. He was for several years a teacher of a Friends' school in Philadelphia and later a teacher and town officer of Germantown. The statement is sometimes made that Pastorius was the most learned man of his time in America, not excepting Cotton Mather. Among the half-dozen languages of which he had a command was English, and he prepared a little primer, *The True Reading, Spelling, and Writing of English*, which was printed by William Bradford of New York in 1697. German, Swiss, and some Dutch Mennonites came in large numbers to the counties of southeastern Pennsylvania. Twenty families of Dunkards, now the Church of the Brethren, arrived in 1719 and others followed. Influenced by the religious reformer John Hus (1374–1415), Caspar Schwenkfeld (1490–1561), a nobleman of Silesia, founded the sect that bears his name. In the first half of the eighteenth century, some Schwenkfelders settled in eastern Pennsylvania where they much later founded the Perkiomen School. The Moravians, who were the direct disciples of Hus, and who had settled in the new colony of Georgia, were aided by George Whitefield in moving to Pennsylvania where they settled at Nazareth and Bethlehem in about 1740. The

Moravians have been noted for their work as missionaries to the Indians, for their activity as founders and teachers of excellent schools, and for their devotion to music, especially the music of Bach. The Scotch-Irish, grievously oppressed in Ulster and cordially hating their English oppressors, began to arrive some time before the German and Bohemian groups, and settled in the mountain valleys of Pennsylvania and Virginia. They were mainly Presbyterians and played an important part in the Revolution and the politics and education of America. Catholics, both from Germany and Ireland, also migrated to the middle Colonies; and Maryland was for a time a haven for English Catholics. Episcopalians came in large numbers to New York and Pennsylvania. Many of these groups developed their own church schools so that the middle Colonies became a parochial school region.

Many motives served to send people across the Atlantic. Redemptioners came because they were out of work. Ship captains could sell the time of a healthy and especially skilled immigrant for more than the regular passenger fare, and even found it profitable to delay transportation, holding emigrants at embarkation ports until their savings were used up, when they could be taken as redemptioners. Some passengers were transported from English jails where they had been confined for debt, political offenses, and many more serious crimes. Others came voluntarily to escape political, economic, or domestic involvement, some for travel or adventure, and some to Christianize the Indians. Many came to escape religious persecution, especially during the horrors of the Thirty Years War; others, such as the Puritans, the Quakers, the Moravians, and Roger Williams, intended to found an ideal church. As in other conditions of human life, economic motives were usually also involved: to find gold or to work at high wages and to return; to engage in trade or to develop a new country and make a fortune. But perhaps the most frequent reason for the great migration, which to the majority meant a complete severing of all ties with the old country, was a keen desire to found quiet and comfortable homes under easier conditions than Europe could offer.

None came for educational advantages, for these were not to be found in a wilderness, except that in a negative sense the New World might help them to escape some of the disadvantages of the traditional, and at that time decadent, schools of the Old World. But apparently they had no idea of the shortcomings of the American schools of the seventeenth century. It is a striking fact that none of the Colonists were dissatisfied with the educational institutions or with the opportunities that would have been theirs in those institutions if they had remained in Europe. They were seriously dissatisfied with their religious, political, and economic opportunities, but for the schools of their mother countries they expressed the sincerest admiration by imitating them and attempting to transplant them to the new soil.

With some exceptions the Colonists were satisfied with a moderate degree of education for their children. Some of the planters of the South, some members of the official class, and those who looked forward to professional careers for their sons demanded secondary and higher schooling. But the vast majority of American settlers were less ambitious. Women and the mass of unskilled laborers were at best taught little more than reading and writing. The slaves expected no education and received none. The Puritans, the Presbyterians, the Quakers, the German sects, and all those aroused by the Reformation to a living sense of religious issues demanded literacy and a knowledge of the catechism and Bible. Some, but not all of these, also required an educated ministry. The small businessmen and skilled artisans and even the farmers needed some arithmetic, practical measurement and calculation, and elementary training in drawing up legal documents. The land surveyor was an important functionary in every community in the seventeenth century; a knowledge of navigation had to be acquired by ship captains; and handwriting and bookkeeping were required of merchants. The general effect of frontier life was to reduce both the demand and supply of schools. By 1700, or soon after, the lands nearest to the coast and the larger rivers were relatively well settled and the Indians were less menacing. The peace of Utrecht in 1713 coincided with the conquest of the Tuscarawas by the Carolinas. Soon the strong Scotch-Irish immigration was to begin. As a result of all these factors, a broad and spreading band of frontier settlements began to develop westward. In seventeenth-century America the real frontiersman, like the unskilled laborer and most women, was likely to be illiterate.

LIFE IN COLONIAL AMERICA

Some of the first settlers, most of whom were farmers, soon spread out along the rivers and through the valleys into the open country. This took place as soon as the Indians had been driven out, as in Virginia, or placated, as in Pennsylvania. Some of the first settlements remained villages for a long time; a few, in favorable locations, developed into what were then regarded as cities. On the eve of the Revolution about 4 per cent of the people lived in the five largest towns—Philadelphia, New York, Boston, Newport, and Charleston. The combined population of these five centers was only 100,000. There were also twelve or fifteen smaller towns such as Albany, Salem, Lancaster, Baltimore, and Savannah and many small places with a few score or a few hundred inhabitants. Many families in the villages and even some in the towns had some land or were otherwise employed in rural occupations. More than 90 per cent of the late colonial people, and still more at an earlier time, lived in mere hamlets or on farms and plantations.

There is a fundamental difference between the rural economy of Europe and that of America. In Europe farmers live in villages, and travel back and forth between their homes and their land daily. Most European rural villages have enough children to form a school. But the American farmer lives on his acres, in many cases a half mile or more from his nearest neighbor. Before the invention of the school bus, the one-room school was the chief educational institution for American country children.

Schools were less easily accessible in the country and more primitive than in the city. The terms were short, the interest in education was less, and during some years there was no school in a given community. Such deficiencies were greatest among the poor, the unskilled, the plantation workers, lumbermen, trappers, and frontiersmen. Both city and country life has been greatly modified since colonial times, but the countryside has undergone the greater transformation. In large sections of the country good roads, electric power, all the means of communication, modern houses, farm machinery, and the consolidated school have tended to equalize the living conditions of town and country. In colonial days there was an absolute contrast in all of these matters.

By continued immigration and natural increase, the population of the thirteen colonies reached 1,600,000 by 1760, but nearly one-fourth of this number were slaves. The total population of the colonies reached 2,500,000 before the Revolution. They supported themselves by agriculture, fishing, the fur trade, simple manufacturing, lumber and ship stores, shipbuilding, and domestic and foreign commerce. Fast Yankee-built ships carried cargoes of tobacco, flour, lumber, and fish to all ports of the world. These were bulky goods, and in the absence of similar products on the homeward voyage, the captains often brought back immigrants for ballast. Sometimes these were blacks to be sold into slavery. A portion of the foreign trade formed a nefarious triangle: the carrying of molasses from the West Indies to New England, there to be made into rum to be exchanged in Africa for slaves to work in the West Indian sugarcane plantations.

In addition to the common elementary education, some colonial occupations required a knowledge of applied mathematics and other useful subjects. Ship captains needed to understand the science of navigation. The surveyor's skill was needed to lay out cities, public subdivisions, and private tracts of land and to build canals and other large "works." There were no typewriters, and penmanship was joined to arithmetic and bookkeeping in the course of studies pursued by young aspirants to business success. Languages were in demand. Numerous teachers of these and other subjects not taught in the regular schools and colleges advertised their schools in the newspapers of all the larger towns.

English mercantile policy was partly responsible for the development of hand-industry in the colonies. The mother country thought of the colonies and too often of the colonists, as existing for the profit and convenience of

England and the English. The English tried to use the colonies as sources of raw materials to be made into usable products by English labor and manufacturers. Some of these products were to be sold back to the Americans. According to mercantilist doctrine, out of this process England was to get work and wages for her people and precious metal for her hoard.

The policy was not wholly unfavorable to America. Bounties were paid on masts and naval stores, and colonial products were often given favorable terms in the English market. Adam Smith thought British colonial policy not illiberal. But that policy was framed by the English, not by the Americans themselves; and perhaps none will accept imposed restrictions willingly. There was right on both sides. The English justly pointed to their services in building up and defending America. The Americans desired freedom to develop their own economy. England later found ways to resolve such differences; but in the eighteenth century things were allowed to drift, then suddenly checked, and a crisis resulted.

One element of the crisis was the prohibition of manufacturing by the colonists. In all of the colonies from Maryland northward, free labor and economic conditions favored handicrafts for local markets and household manufactures for home use. Even on the plantations of the South there were skilled workers, both slave and free. It was to the colonial's interest to avoid using the expensive English goods and to oppose English mercantilist policy. To dress in homespun became a matter of colonial patriotism.

Virginia began about the same time as Massachusetts to encourage the raising of wool and flax and the practice of spinning and weaving as a policy. In 1646 Virginia provided that two children from each county were to be taught at public cost the arts of carding, knitting, and spinning. Fines against the exportation of wool and laws to encourage textile production in linen, wool, and cotton goods were found in many colonies in the seventeenth century. Bounties were laid on wolves because they killed sheep.

Twice in the eighteenth century, Boston attempted to conduct a public spinning school, but neither effort succeeded. The first such school was opened about 1720 partly for the children of the Irish immigrants who were then arriving. The town selectmen voted three hundred pounds for a school for "the Instruction of the Children of this Town in spinning." The second effort was a feature of the attempt to encourage the patriotic use of homespun during the heated controversies with England before the Revolution. These premature attempts in vocational education did not add much to what the people were doing in any event.

Some colonial manufacturing could be carried on in the house or shop, and therefore during the long winter evenings and when the weather was inclement. Much of the work required only simple materials and no great skill. And children could do or help with such work using textiles, wood, and leather in making clothes, shoes, casks, hats, and other articles. They could help to boil soap made of animal fat and a lye made from wood ash; to burn charcoal; to make candles by dipping or by pouring tallow into a mold; to boil apple butter; and to work in other occupations.

There were also manufacturing activities that required the skills and strength of men. Chains, anchors, farm implements, and household utensils were made of iron that was found in most of the colonies. For fuel, charcoal was used and its production was a business in itself. Shipbuilding has been mentioned, and there were also saw, grist, and flour mills. Flour was an article of export from Philadelphia, which also had the first paper mill in the colonies, established on the brawling Wissahickon by William Rittenhouse whose son, David, later became an astronomer. Before the Revolution, the colonies had gone some distance on the way toward industrial independence. Political independence followed after, but intellectual independence was delayed.

With all the inventiveness and mechanical skill of the Colonists, travel and transportation remained slow, costly, and laborious for Americans throughout the colonial period. Water travel with boats, canoes, or the clumsy dugout was the cheapest mode of travel. Canoes were useful where portages were required. The dugout was made, as the word indicates, by hollowing out a large log and "was fashioned like a trough for Swine." Fishing smacks, sloops, and larger sailing vessels were used on the ocean.

On land, men walked or rode on horseback and used packhorses or heavy wagons to transport goods. For wheeled vehicles, roads were necessary. The Conestoga wagon was a later invention that became common in the eighteenth century and continued in use until about 1850 when the settlements had reached the Pacific coast. The deep sag in the bottom of this "covered wagon" kept the freight from sliding back and forth on mountain roads.

Light, four-wheeled vehicles such as coaches were not often used until after the Revolution, because the roads were too bad and too few. In 1767 it still took two days for a fast coach to travel the ninety miles from Philadelphia to New York. An early turnpike extended sixty miles from Philadelphia to Lancaster, and the Mohawk Valley had another turnpike. But generally, roads, bridges, and taverns providing lodging for travelers were only found in the vicinity of large towns.

As a result of such conditions, most of the people were rooted in one spot and isolated from the life of the outside world. Men lived an entire lifetime without ever going to the nearest city, although it was only twenty or thirty miles away. It was more difficult to arrange for a trip within the colonies than for one across the ocean. This was one of the reasons why early America faced toward Europe and not toward her own West. News—"intelligence," as it was called—was transmitted mainly by word of mouth. A weekly post was established between Boston and New York in 1692, but there was no public intercolonial postal system until 1707, and that only reached a few of the larger towns. The few newspapers had a very limited circulation.

The "mental outfit" that the colonists had brought with them was largely drawn from a superstitious past. "If there was much lack of book learning in the generation of English people that sprung up first in American soil, there was some gain in a life in which exigent wants compelled a habit of shrewd observation." So Edward Eggleston (1837–1902) wrote, and so it might seem; but let us see. The people after a century of shrewd American observation still believed that if a long hair from a horse's tail were left in water, it would turn into a snake. It was long held that some birds grew on trees and that some birds wintered at the bottom of ponds or retreated from the cold blasts of earthly winds to the moon. Witchcraft, Indian medicines, ghosts, and the terror inspired by comets and eclipses long survived the most careful observation of the average American.

Children were more useful in colonial days than in later times because there was work for them to do; but children valued for the work they can do are likely to be exploited, as were the children in the factories of the Industrial Revolution. In the colonies children's tasks were not purely routine and did not so easily lead to exploitation. Yet overwork was certainly common. The stern religious views of their parents deprived many New England children of opportunity for play and companionship. Parents of many sections felt that children should be docile and quiet, speaking only when spoken to. Many children were frightened by the harsh Puritan theology. Nearly all books were religious works.

Even in England the newspaper was in its infancy when the first American settlements were being made; and in the colonies there was no successful paper before 1704 when the Boston *News-Letter* was established. During the remaining seventy years of colonial dependence, the newspaper developed into an institution that was to play a great part in the struggle with Great Britain and eventually also in the development of education.

It is evident that the school and the press are interrelated. When the school has taught the elements of reading, the newspaper provides a means of further education not only in reading but in topics and fields of general interest as well, and is often brought into the classrooms of even elementary schools. The colonial newspaper performed a special service for education in the private school period. It was through newspaper advertisements that the private schools were able to present the public information about their facilities, subjects taught, terms, and dates of opening. Through newspaper reports on school "exhibitions," plays, examinations, and other public events, the schools received a great deal of free advertising. School news is now an important part of the content of the daily paper, and through the "readers' letters" the public can express its views on the conduct of the schools. The newspaper as an instrument in the public relations policy of the school was not so highly developed in colonial times, but it is today one of the most important means of communication between school and people. It is also one of the chief reasons why the school is much concerned with the freedom and fairness of the press.

The early colonial newspapers were not free, but were published "by authority" of the government, or were controlled by a Puritan oligarchy as in Massachusetts, or by the Friend's Monthly Meeting as in Philadelphia. Freedom of speech and the press, essentials in democracy, had to be won gradually in a number of dramatic lawsuits. One of the most exciting was that against John Peter Zenger of New York.

Zenger (1697–1746) was the publisher of the *New York Weekly Journal*, founded in 1733 with the help of merchants, landowners, and lawyers who were opposed to the English governor, William Cosby. Cosby, who had been driven from a government post in Minorca by charges that he had been involved in irregular financial practices, tried some of the same schemes in New York. Zenger's backers used the *Journal* to attack the governor and the court, which he controlled; and when the grand jury would not indict Zenger on a charge of seditious libel, the governor had him arrested "on information." When the case was tried, the governor had the attorneys for the defense disbarred and Zenger was recommitted to jail.

The issue was whether the freedom of the press could be maintained against the opposition of an arbitrary royal governor. The leaders of the popular party sprang a surprise at the second arraignment. They had engaged Andrew Hamilton (d. 1741) of Philadelphia to defend Zenger. Hamilton argued, against the actual law at the time, that the jury had the right to determine whether the matter that Zenger had published was libelous. He convinced the jury that "the truth published from a good motive" cannot be considered libelous, and this principle has since been incorporated in law. The jury, at some risk to themselves, brought in a verdict of acquittal.

Andrew Hamilton's advocacy in the Zenger case has been compared with the speech of James Otis (1725–1783) against the writs of assistance. Hamilton was not only a very astute lawyer but was also a successful administrator as well as the architect and selector of the site for the old Pennsylvania State House, which is now known as Independence Hall. But the victory in the Zenger case for the freedom of the press is Hamilton's highest title to fame.

Although the Zenger case ended auspiciously, freedom of the press, like freedom of speech and teaching, must be continuously guarded and maintained if it is to be safe. In the dispute that preceded the Revolutionary War the royalist authorities attempted to secure an indictment for libel against Isaiah Thomas (1749–1841), famous printer and the publisher of a patriot paper, the *Massachusetts Spy*. As in the Zenger case, the grand jury refused to return a true bill and a suit was lodged on "information." When it became evident that no jury would convict, the case was dropped.

The newspapers played an important part in the pre-Revolutionary debate. They had increased in number from a single paper in 1704 to about fifty in 1776, and many took the side of the patriots. One of the mistakes made by the British in their plan to tax the colonists was the choice of a stamp tax with the requirement that newspapers and legal documents such as deeds and contracts had to be stamped. This aroused the opposition of two of the most vocal groups in the colonies, the newspaper owners and the lawyers. Only a tax on sermons would have been more ill-advised.

The rapid growth of newspapers had another influence that had a bearing upon the spread of information and education; it stirred up the demand for a better postal service. The need for such service was felt in the colonies from earlier times, and various suggestions and practical efforts were made as the population increased and spread. To meet this need was difficult for obvious reasons. Governor Lovelace of New York took an interest in the problem in 1673, and eleven years later it was again taken up by Governor Dongan of the same colony. Both efforts were premature, but in 1692 the British government assigned the monopoly of a weekly postal service between New York and Boston. So bad were the roads between these cities that a week was actually required to complete the journey. It was the practice of the post riders to start toward each other from two termini of the route and to exchange mailbags somewhere near the midpoint.

Early in the eighteenth century, regular post routes were established between Philadelphia, New York, and Boston with a few short spurs and some irregular service to New Hampshire and Virginia at the ends of the main route. The early postmasters were almost invariably newspaper publishers who sometimes used their office to distribute their own papers and prevent the circulation of competing sheets.

The colonial service became a branch of the British postal system in 1707, and American postmasters general were thereafter appointed by the Crown. The need for a means to send official communications to the governors and to receive their reports was a reason for British interest in the matter. Postage on private letters was still collected on delivery, and the charges were proportioned to the distance. To carry a single sheet from London to New York cost one shilling; from New York to Charleston the cost was one shilling ninepence. There were no postage stamps. The carriers had a way of defrauding the department by carrying letters in their pockets instead of in the sealed post bags and collecting the charges for their own use.

Benjamin Franklin was appointed Postmaster General in 1753. Contrary to his claim that he never sought an office, he worked hard and used influence to obtain this one, but he greatly improved the service, extended it to cover the whole coastline, and made it yield a profit to the government. Franklin established a rate for newspapers that was fair to all and required carriers to accept and deliver all papers for which carriage was paid. In 1774 he was removed after years of absentee operation, but the new American government reappointed him. This time Franklin held the office for only one year and then secured it for his son-in-law, Richard Bache.

The circulation of newspapers and the transmission of letters, magazines, books, and all means of communication are educational agencies. There would be little use in learning to read if reading matter were not available. The publishing business, the post office, and the public library serve and are served by the public schools.

CHILDREN AND MANUAL LABOR

The occupations of the people and their domestic arrangements affect education and culture in every society. Men, women, and children all had to work in colonial society merely to live, and to work hard if they desired to live in a civilized manner. Child labor laws were not even considered; children began to work at an early age and soon became accustomed to employment and were skillful at it. In their teens boys did the work of men and girls assumed the jobs of women. They matured early. "With us," Franklin said, "marriages are (consummated) in the morning of life; our children are educated and settled in the world by noon."

Such arrangements left little time for schooling, reading, music and other arts, or any leisure activities. There was little to suggest such activities and diversions in a land that had few libraries, theaters, musical organizations, and no athletic facilities. Some notice must be taken of the various "bees," quilting, husking, singing, barn-raisings, weddings, and consequent "bellings," housewarmings, hunts, horse races, and other country amusements. There were lecture-days and training days in New England. Customs and facilities varied with time and place. In the course of the colonial period some deprivations were remedied in the cities. Books, libraries, and leisure increased and the theater and musical organizations were accepted and established, but few were able to enjoy their productions. Schools and colleges were founded early but developed slowly. A number of men could be named who under unfavorable circumstances created for themselves opportunities for self-education. Among them were Benjamin Franklin, John and William Bartram, and David Rittenhouse.

Poor lighting and lack of privacy and leisure made the evening hours unfavorable for study. Candles were made of tallow, bayberry, or wax, and making them cost time that should have been spent in using them for study. Windows were small, so that even in daytime the houses were dimly lighted. Heating was another difficulty. To supply the wood and tend the fire in one of the great open fireplaces added much to the labor of a household. Phosphorus matches were unknown, and the ancient habit of covering up the fire to keep it alive through the night gave us the word *curfew*, the sign for children to leave the streets. Because of the cost and labor involved in keeping up a great wood fire, only one room of the house was heated or even partly heated. Diarists reported that in the cold northern winters the ink sometimes froze on their pens as they wrote within a few feet of the fire. With the whole household gathered around the fireplace, there was no opportunity for quiet and sustained mental work.

In spinning and weaving, mending and cobbling, in making splint brooms out of soft yellow birchwood and dozens of other useful implements, many carved out with a jackknife, there was a kind of education. Boys and girls learned to be cooperative, to take responsibility, and to be unbelievably industrious. They acquired many skills and learned the uses and possibilities of many kinds of materials. In our day the school tries, not always successfully, to "make work," to develop skillful hands and active brains in the youth. In earlier times the teacher did not need to invent such forms of industrial arts education.

Children did not always have a family to look after them. Some were brought to America in their teens without their parents. These, along with children whose parents had died, were known in common speech and in law as orphans. Court records show that some of them were mistreated. Those who were apprenticed were to be educated and put on the road to become useful citizens. A successfully completed apprenticeship brought the young person the rights and privileges of citizenship that were denied to the poor and unskilled youth.

The law and the custom of apprenticeship came from the mother country, but it had been a form of education in the oldest societies from the dawn of history and apparently before there were any records. The essence of apprenticeship consists of a combination of education and skilled industry by which the master of a trade teaches its "mysteries" to a novice. Specific directions, observation, and imitation are the methods. The moral conduct and behavior that an artisan must exhibit are instilled along the way. At the time of the American settlement it was often customary to permit the apprentice to attend school long enough to acquire the arts of reading and writing.

Learning to do by doing has been employed in the oldest arts and sciences from early times. It is not something that our contemporaries have a right to gloat over as if it were their discovery. And although it has become the habit of many to speak of it in hushed tones, it has no magical powers. Those who merely imitate, without theorizing and experimenting, learn to do only what has been done before. And this was the usual result of an apprenticeship. But the system had real value, as one would infer from the fact that it lasted so many centuries. The work was concrete and measurable. It was easy to tell whether the craftsman's level of skill and knowledge had been attained. It permitted no bluffing. It produced salable products and transformed boys who had no "influence" into useful men. It helped to solve two social problems by reducing the number of possible vagabonds and by supplying society with necessary goods and services. Unfortunately, girls, who were usually excluded from the schools, were also excluded from apprenticeship.

The colonists were not wholly dependent upon apprenticeship for their supply of skilled workers. Many artisans came from abroad. Edward Johnson (1598–1672) in his *Wonder-Working Providence* listed about thirty trades that were practiced in Massachusetts in the middle of the seventeenth century. He reported that the coopers and the shoemakers had formed guilds. Some of these craftsmen may have learned their craft in America but many others continued to come from abroad. Some came as redemptioners permitting the ship captain to sell their skill and time for four years or more to pay for their passage across the ocean. Among them were schoolmasters, bookkeepers, bookbinders, gardeners, carpenters, and blacksmiths.

In colonial life, apprenticeship served to replenish the skilled labor force, but it was also a police measure to prevent vagrancy, idling, and begging. The Massachusetts Bay Colony Law of 1642 mentioned the great neglect of parents and masters in training their children in "learning and labor and other employments which may be profitable to the Commonwealth." To remedy this defect the selectmen of each town were required to attend to the "calling and employment of children" and "especially of their ability to read and understand the principles of religion and the capital laws of the country." Children who were not receiving such an education were to be apprenticed to masters who would teach them. The town was to provide materials and tools for vocational instruction, but books are not mentioned.

This was an educational law that did not mention schools. It required the parent or master to teach his child or apprentice, but permitted this to be done in the home or shop. It required the selectmen to watch over the behavior and the habits of the young. The whole tenor of the act shows that its purpose was to promote not only the welfare of the children but also the general welfare of the colony and people as well. The tendency for the state to enter the family and to assert a public interest in the upbringing of the children may be thought to have had its beginning in the English-speaking world in this law. Town records show that it was enforced, although we do not know how universally it was enforced.

If the Law of 1642 did start a new trend in the relation of the state to education, it will be desirable to fix its antecedents more exactly. The Massachusetts law can be traced to the English Reformation, which, by the stress it laid upon the Bible, led many, especially the Puritans, to insist that children must be taught to read. There were accompanying economic factors. The hard lot of the poor was doubled and their number was increased by the closing of the monasteries, the enclosing of the common lands to make sheepwalks, and the currency inflation from the influx of South American silver and gold. The economic distress in England in the sixteenth and seventeenth centuries was a prime cause of the rapid peopling of the colonies. It was also a cause of the English poor and apprenticeship laws.

Laws for the relief or public support of the poor began before 1540 and were gradually strengthened by successive enactments. It was soon seen that if the poor youth were taught trades they would be less likely to require public alms. The Statute of Artificers of 1562 was in part a compulsory apprenticeship law. This was a beginning. The climax of this movement was the Poor Law of 1601, which was a code on relief, apprenticeship, and punishment for the lazy and recalcitrant. This law was enacted just before the founding of the English settlements in the New World where the law was duly copied.

The other colonies were slow in following the lead of Massachusetts Bay in adding the teaching of reading, religion, and the colony laws to apprenticeship. An early law of Virginia published the English Statute of Artificers and another in 1642 conferred upon justices of the peace the power to bind out and apprentice children. But not until 1701 did the law require the teaching of reading and writing. In Pennsylvania the earliest laws required that all children must "be taught some useful trade or skill that the poor may work to live, and the rich, if they become poor, may not want." A Maryland law charged the judges to inquire whether the masters were teaching their apprentices or merely employing them at common labor. The northern colonies approached the example set by Massachusetts Bay, but enforcement was a problem everywhere and especially where the masters were themselves unskillful and illiterate. But such as they were, the apprenticeship laws were the first attempts by American governments to compel the education of children.

CHILDREN AND THE FOUR R'S

As with the children of the American Indian, children in colonial society learned the manual arts that were essential for living by working in their homes and communities. However, to complement the learning of religion in the home, more formal training in reading the Bible was required. For this reason, next to religion, reading became the second greatest task set for schooling in Colonial America, after which came 'riting and finally 'rithmetic. The original elementary school was the school of the Four R's. This was the school valued by those Protestants who settled in the English colonies because it taught their children to read the Bible.

But this was a goal and not the beginning. The hornbook or battledore was the first instrument put into the hands of the little children when they entered the dame school. The hornbook was a small, wooden, paddle-shaped implement. A sheet of paper, with the alphabet, numerals, the Lord's Prayer, and other reading matter printed on it was pasted upon the blade and the entire implement was covered with sheets of transparent horn—hence the name. The battledore, which was made of stiff paper, contained similar materials. In the dame school, kept by a woman in her home, the youngest children learned to read.

Schools of the period were dull and often grim. About the middle of the colonial period, John Locke wrote that he "had a fancy that learning might be made a play and recreation to children" so that they would "desire to be taught." Many Americans in the eighteenth century read Locke's *Thoughts,* but there is no record of any who put his "fancy" to the test. To do that they would have had to discard the hornbook and the rod.

The primer, which came after the hornbook, can be traced from the later Middle Ages. It was, as its name indicates, intended for use as a first book. Many different primers were in use at different times, but the one that was most commonly used in the early American schools was *The New England Primer.* Its history has been written by the historian and bibliographer Paul Leicester Ford, who estimated that 3,000,000 copies of it were printed. Although it was in common use for a century and its range extended far beyond New England, this number seems too great to have been purchased by the small populations of colonial times. This primer set the pace for such widely used schoolbooks as Noah Webster's spelling book, Lindley Murray's grammar, Warren Colburn's arithmetic, and William Holmes McGuffey's readers. Crudely printed and illustrated with rough woodcuts, its appearance did not recommend it. Its best-known feature is the rhymed alphabet that began

> *In Adam's fall*
> *We sinned all*

There was also an outline of Puritan theology including the *Shorter Catechism,* John Cotton's *Spiritual Milk for Babes,* and other pieces. An examination of the book reveals better than many words could how the philosophy of childhood education has changed since the seventeenth century.

After the primer and catechism it was the custom to introduce the Psalter or Book of Psalms and then the New Testament and the complete Bible. Locke criticized this sequence and advised the use of stories; but except for the Bible stories of Joseph, Locke could remember only two that seemed suitable for children, *Aesop's Fables* and *Reynard the Fox.* The day for children's literature did not dawn until the latter part of the eighteenth century. Meanwhile, the spelling book came into use.

The spelling book is as indicative of an era and the changed temper of American education as The *New England Primer.* It signifies the growth of secularism or at least of a neutrality in religion that permitted the establishment of common schools without a particular confession of faith. A spelling book was printed on the first American press at Cambridge, Massachusetts, before 1650. The book is thought to have been Edmund Coote's *English Schoolmaster,* but no copy of this imprint remains. It was not a secular book. In addition to the alphabet and spelling exercises, it had a short catechism, prayers, psalms, writing copies, and a list of "hard words alphabetically arranged and sensibly explained." This idea of teaching little children "hard words" out of context and before they were needed was an almost universal teaching error of those and later days. In later days "helps" in the study of English print became common, but before 1600 there was not even a dictionary. An early hint of an English dictionary was called a list of "hard usual English words" and came out in London in 1604, just three years before the settlement at Jamestown. When the great dictionaries of the eighteenth century appeared they were too expensive for use in the schools.

George Fox (1624–1691), Quaker founder, prepared a schoolbook, *Instructions for Right Spelling and Plain Directions for Reading and Writing True English,* which was, like many later spellers, a sort of omnibus book having spelling-words, catechism, proverbs, scripture selections, and some arithmetic lessons. Thomas Dilworth's *A New Guide to the English Tongue* continued to be used in American schools even after the Revolution. William Perry, an Englishman like Dilworth, tried to improve upon the title and contents of the *New Guide.* He called his book *The Only Sure Guide to the English Tongue, or New Pronouncing Spelling-Book.* It was issued in America (1785) by the famous printer and historian of American printing, Isaiah Thomas (1749–1841), who reported that in the course of thirty years he had sold about 300,000 copies.

Two years before the appearance of Perry's *Only Sure Guide,* Noah Webster (1758–1843), an American compiler, prepared the most famous speller and most widely sold of American schoolbooks, *The American Spelling Book* (1783), which in popular speech was called "the blue-backed spelling book." It was the first of a three-book series—speller, grammar, and reader. For the series, Webster, who was a pedant as well as a businessman, invented the grand title, *A Grammatical Institute of the English Language.* The spelling book continued in use for more than a century and the numbers of the book that were reported sold reached an astronomical figure. Not too much dependence should be placed upon such figures, for they are often estimates, and usually not underestimates. It is, however, certain that Webster's spelling book and its competitors put an end to the importation and reprinting in America of English books of this kind.

The extraordinary vogue of spelling in colonial and later schools may have been caused, in part, by mistaken notions of the nature of language and of the way one learns to spell. The science of language was in its infancy and Americans knew little of what there was to be known. The great mistake of colonial Americans was the failure to understand that speech is the real, the living language, and that writing and print are only its lifeless symbols. A related error was the choice of separate words as the elementary units of language. The true elements are expressed thoughts, that is, statements, questions, or commands, or even ejaculations, for example, "Well, I never!" meaning "I am astonished." This emphasis upon separate words led them in turn to spelling, as if one could not recognize a word without spelling it.

From all this came the mistaken pedagogy of reading, which had for centuries deceived teachers including Pestalozzi. The first step in that old method was to teach the names of the twenty-six letters; then to have the children spell and pronounce several hundred two- and three-letter syllables; and then, to have them spell words syllable by syllable, such as "*sat-is-fy*" thus "*s-a-t, sat; i-s, is, satis; f-y, fy, satisfy.*" After this had gone on for many dreary weeks, the child was taught to read, and he learned, by recognizing phrases and words and sentences without spelling, exactly as he would have learned in the first place without knowing the names of the letters. To learn those names in proper order is a very simple matter when the time comes to consult the dictionary. Some training in phonetics is also given. Those who criticize newer methods of teaching beginning reading do not always take the trouble to understand what the problem is. A little knowledge of the history of education would be useful to them.

Beginning reading was, in colonial times, often taught in the dame school, and the schooldame had no knowledge of pedagogy or the science of language. She invariably followed a dead routine, but better educated teachers for long years did no better. If in some corners the old methods are still in use, that is unprofessional conduct.

Quill pens were used throughout the colonial period and fifty years beyond. They were cut with a penknife from goose quills, and had to be mended and repointed from time to time. There were no lead pencils, crayons, chalk, blackboards, or unsanitary and noisy slates and slate pencils. Writing was not taught in the dame school because the little children could not manage pen and ink. Inexpensive and handy paper tablets were not available, but foolscap could be stitched together at home and used for writing material. Copybooks and ciphering books were made in this manner. Much of the teacher's time was occupied with the making and mending of pens, the setting of copies, and the supervising of time-consuming writing exercises.

Except for arithmetic and handwriting, all subjects were taught through oral recitations. Reading, spelling, grammar, and when they were later introduced, history and geography, were recited orally. This was partly a result of the high cost of paper.

The almost exclusive use of the oral method had an unfortunate effect upon the entire curriculum. When pupils had mastered the simplest mechanics of reading, the recitation was conducted by having each one read a paragraph or stanza aloud until the entire lesson had been read. Often there was no attention to the meaning of the passage or even of the new words. Only the pronunciation of the words was important. This was word-calling, not reading. It tended to restrict the amount of material that could be covered and to forestall the development of silent reading. Its bad effect upon the teaching of spelling is evident. Subjects such as grammar and geography were taught by an oral question-and-answer method based upon the words of the book. Nearly everything that was taught in the old school was taught from a book, and taught not by discussion but by question and answer; the questions often taken from the book by the teacher, and the answers in the words of the book by the pupils.

The Hindu-Arabic numerals were introduced into Europe in 1202 if Leonardo of Pisa was, as is believed, the first to use them in a Latin book. That was four centuries before the English settlements in America, and all that time was required to secure acceptance of this new method of calculating "with the pen." In earlier times a "manual method" of calculating with calculi or pebbles or counters on a counting-board or abacus was used, and it probably continued in use because so many people were illiterate and unable to use the pen. By the seventeenth century the battle had been won. People continued to count on their fingers and to calculate without calculi, "in their heads," but there is no known case of the use of the abacus and "manual arithmetic" in early American schools. This was an important change. Older European arithmetic books often promised to teach both methods.

Today teachers have gone back to the manual method of using beans or other small objects in teaching beginners to count and to make simple combinations of numbers. This is an example of the principle that the way in which a process was first developed in practical life may be a guide to the intelligent teaching of it to beginners. The teaching of a language through its use in speaking and writing rather than through grammar is another example of this principle. The idea is suggestive but not universally applicable.

In arithmetic the use of objects was reintroduced after it had long gone out of use. There is a story that Napoleon's soldiers brought back some examples of counting frames or abaci from Russia. Edward Brooks (1831–1912), an American teacher of arithmetic, in his *Normal Methods of Teaching* (1879), strongly recommended the constant use of the abacus in arithmetic. The kindergarten also aided in revolutionizing the beginnings of number work. The colonial school rarely hit upon such enlightened ideas of teaching.

Only the business uses of arithmetic and bookkeeping and the geometry and trigonometry used in surveying and navigation were much valued by early America, and these practical applications were often taught in special schools advertised in the newspapers. Mathematics as an intellectual pursuit had only slight appeal in colonial days. Young Benjamin Franklin wrote a characteristic essay on the usefulness of mathematics. But even scientists or promoters of science such as the younger John Winthrop (1714–1779), David Rittenhouse, and Thomas Jefferson cannot be called exceptions as they also considered mathematics as only a useful tool. No original work in mathematics was produced, and the colleges taught no courses in mathematics that would now be considered advanced. The Boston Latin School appears to have taught no mathematics before the Revolution. In the Middle States, Benjamin Rush (1745–1813), the physician and founder of the first free dispensary in the United States, went through a Latin School and Princeton College without coming into contact with the subject.

In early times, skill in even the common measurements and simple calculation was not thought to be necessary for everyone. Such skill, however, was essential in commercial life and most trades, and it could be acquired in special writing and reckoning schools. In New York and other commercial and seaport towns, private teachers of these subjects were common after 1700. Philadelphia had many schools offering instruction in arithmetic and applied mathematics, and the Penn Charter School and the later Academy of that city each had a separate mathematical department. Isaac Greenwood (1702–1745) of Boston wrote *Arithmetic Vulgar and Decimal* (1729), the first separate arithmetic text by a native American, but it was too advanced for beginners. The Dutch schools of New Amsterdam gave attention to the arithmetic needed in that trading post, and Peter Venema of that city prepared an arithmetic text in the Dutch language. But until the Revolution nearly all textbooks were written in England and imported or reprinted in the colonies. After the Revolution a large number of American textbooks appeared. There were several reasons for this, and the adoption of the American decimal monetary system was one.

Arithmetic was an extremely complicated subject in early times. It has been much simplified, and the teaching of it has been much improved. In earlier days the books began with abstract definitions. Then followed rules for writing and reading numbers; the four fundamental operations including five or more "cases" of multiplication; common and decimal fractions; and weights and measures in profusion, often to the confusion of the pupil. Under the last-named topic one had to learn what a firkin, a puncheon, and a quintal were, as well as the difference between a Flemish and an English ell. There was also the "rule of three" in several cases and a number of different "rules for the calculation of interest. This list could be continued, but enough has been given to show that the old arithmetic was composed of many special topics and technical processes. The new arithmetic omits unnecessary topics and attempts to make all processes understandable. In a later chapter we shall come back to this topic.

The study of English grammar, which was to occupy so large a portion of school time in the nineteenth century, had barely begun in colonial schools. But propaganda for the teaching of grammar had started early. As early as the winter of 1734–1735, a writer in the *American Weekly Mercury* advised parents "to decide early whether their children are to become scholars or clerks and tradesmen, in order that they may receive their Education accordingly." Even if they were to become scholars it seemed to him best to have the children begin with the English rather than the Latin grammar. Both the views and the language of the *Mercury* article point to Franklin as the probable author.

In grammar as in arithmetic, English textbooks were used at first. Robert Lowth and Thomas Sheridan were among the authors whose books were reprinted in America. About the time of the Revolution, Anthony Benezet, a teacher of the Penn Charter School, published *The Pennsylvania Spelling-Book* and an "easy introduction" to English grammar. The *Grammatical Institutes* prepared by John Ash was intended to prepare children for the more difficult work by Lowth. The grammar prepared by Noah Webster has been mentioned. As in the case of arithmetic, the Latin schools neglected English grammar and many private masters offered to teach it. Literature, geography, history, and other subjects were rarely taught before 1800 or 1850.

TYPES AND SYSTEMS OF SCHOOLS

Colonial school arrangements were casual and the result of mere custom when not specially adapted to local peculiarities. Many schools were not permanent or located in one place, or were so located that all the children could have access to a school. School terms were short, the most frequent terms being three months. The attendance was irregular, and there was no established curriculum in the lower or common schools. Teachers had no formal preparation in regard to how or what to teach, and they made the curriculum from what they knew and what books were at hand.

There was a general lack of a system, or rather one may discern the faint outlines of several systems. At least two kinds of schools were in the mind of the author who wrote the article on the study of grammar published in the *American Weekly Mercury* in 1735. He spoke of preparing children to become clerks and tradesmen or scholars, thus drawing a line between common school education or, if a little more advanced, what was called "a good English education" and, on the other side of the line, a classical education in Latin school and college for "scholars." On one side were the dame school, elementary school, apprenticeship, and the private schools in the cities that taught practical subjects and advertised their offerings in the newspapers; on the other side stood the preparatory Latin school and the college, ready to prepare future ministers, lawyers, and doctors, or, as the writer of 1735 more briefly and less accurately said, "scholars."

The dame school was held in the narrow and perhaps untidy quarters of a kitchen or bedroom. The teacher, ordinarily a housewife, sometimes a widow, collected a small fee for teaching very young children "their letters," syllables, spelling, and reading. The hornbook and primer were the usual teaching materials.

When the child had learned to read a little and was ready to learn to write, he had to be removed from the dame school to a district, a neighborhood, a subscription, an "old field," or a parochial school. These are merely different names for the ordinary elementary school under various forms of management. The district school was controlled by an elected board and the neighborhood school was run by a committee or informally selected trustee. The subscription school was a private school conducted in accordance with a contract subscribed to by the teacher and patrons; and generally the "old field" school was merely a variety of the subscription school. The name was derived from its location on waste or exhausted land. Parochial schools were connected with a church. Literally taken, a parochial school is the school of a parish, and the term is most frequently applied to Catholic schools connected with parish churches; but other Christian bodies also established and maintained local schools. Lutherans supported many parish schools. The Monthly Meetings of the Friends, which have advisory and to some degree directive functions in relation to local meetings, established schools. The Anglican Society for the Propagation of the Gospel in Foreign Parts, that is, outside of England, established schools in America. All of these schools were generally elementary schools that taught spelling, reading, writing, arithmetic, religion, and often sewing to girls. They were ungraded, poorly equipped, and some were unsupervised schools. As will be appreciated from this discussion, there was no fully developed system of elementary schools in the colonies.

A few examples existed in which the beginnings of a system may be seen. In its educational management, Holland had devised a form of cooperation between church and state that was carried into New Netherland. The Dutch West India Company had almost complete control of the government of this colony and appointed the schoolmaster and paid his salary. He had other income as well. The schools were not free, except to the poor. Town rates or compulsory contributions were exacted, and in the village of Bergen, in what is now New Jersey, and apparently in other towns as well, these rates became a school tax. A house was provided for the schoolmaster, and the school was maintained in the same building. Thus the government, which was exercised by the Dutch West India Company, provided for the "prudentials," that is, the finances and equipment of the schools.

The church looked out for the qualifications of the schoolmaster including his piety and orthodoxy. New Amsterdam had a school in 1638 that became the still functioning School of the Collegiate Dutch Reformed Church. Other schools were opened as needed in a score of nearby villages and in settlements on Long Island and along the Hudson River to Albany and beyond. These schools were modeled upon the parochial schools of Holland. The ruling body of the mother church in Amsterdam selected and certified the schoolmasters for competence, character, and doctrine. They were rated as minor officials of the church and served the church by carrying announcements, ringing the church bell, and, in the minister's absence, taking charge of the services on the Sabbath. This system of state-church cooperation could not become a permanent arrangement in a country that was to reject the state-church principle. But in any case the English came in and established a new government.

There were also private schoolmasters in New Netherland as in other colonies where there were towns. They taught penmanship, arithmetic, bookkeeping, and other useful subjects. Some conducted evening schools for apprentices and others who were employed in the daytime. In the Dutch period even these private schoolmasters were licensed to carry on their occupation.

The Dutch language continued in use in the family, church, and school of the descendants of the original settlers for many generations after the English assumed control of the colony in 1664. For example, Peter Venema's arithmetic was published in 1730. For a long time many communities had to support schools in two languages. This is merely the first example of this situation that later occurred wherever there were large bodies of non-English citizens.

Some of the English governors of New York continued the practice of licensing only those schoolmasters who had been approved in the home country. In this case the home authority was the Church of England working through the agency of the Society for the Propagation of the Gospel in Foreign Parts. This missionary body founded in 1701 at once became active in the settlements and trading posts in the West Indies, throughout the Middle and Southern colonies where there were Anglican churches, and especially in New York. They maintained schools, and their missionaries exercised a watchful interest over the teaching of religion. The charity school established by the Society in New York City in 1710 became the School of Trinity Church and still survives. This body supplied and directed schoolmasters, set up school and parish libraries, provided textbooks, and attempted to invigorate inactive congregations, to convert Indians, and in every way to promote the growth of the church. The teacher's pay was provided in part by the Society and in part by the community. The schools were mainly elementary charity schools charging fees to those who could pay but admitting poor children free. Sometimes they taught more advanced subjects. This is another example of a tentative system of elementary schools, but the influence of the Society came to an end during the Revolution.

New England was the home of the town as a political unit, the annual town meeting, and the town school. From English custom and for worship and defense, the settlers centered their homes in small villages. Also, nature cut up the surface of the country into valleys, meadows, and hills and supplied the land with many small streams that once supplied water power to mills and factories. At first the land about a village was parceled out in strips, in the fashion of the Middle Ages. The region lacked the deep, rich soil of more level sections and had no staple crop such as the tobacco, cotton, and rice of the South or the wheat and flour of Pennsylvania. For these reasons New England became a land of villages, small farms, family industries, and local governments by towns, that is, township units.

The government of New England was as significant for its educational arrangements as were its physical and economic features. The Massachusetts Bay Colony, not Plymouth, set the pattern for its political and educational development. At first all those who had the right of suffrage voted in Boston. When the distances of Salem, Dorchester, Cambridge, and other towns made voting in the capital inconvenient, a representative system was introduced. This took place in 1634, but Virginia had taken such action before. Each town then sent its representative, or a number of representatives if the town were large, to the general court or legislature to make laws for the colony. The general court was also a judicial body at first and gave directions for the enforcement of the laws it had enacted. All civic matters in each town were decided in the annual town meeting of the voters. One of such civic matters was the choice of representatives in the general court; another was the maintenance of public services, such as roads and schools. Not everyone could vote in a town meeting. For sixty years following the settlement only men who were members of the church and had a certain amount of property were allowed to vote.

The government and the church were closely united in New England. And in harmony with its system of local government by each town was the fact that New England was the land of the Congregational Church in which each congregation was a semi-independent unit. The Calvinist theory also held that the state is the arm of the church. The general court legislated for both town and congregation. Each of these managed its own internal affairs, but the agents were the same people.

In Europe the church and school had been intimately connected for more than a thousand years, and this connection was retained in most of the schools in all the colonies. Apprenticeship and the private schools in the cities were at least partial exceptions to this pattern tending to develop in a secularist direction. But the usual elementary school, Latin school, and college were all religious schools teaching the doctrine approved by the parents of the children. This was not new. From early times when the church had been surrounded by the pagan world and in much of the medieval period when the church was set in the midst of barbarians, the school was a natural and necessary ally, or rather instrument, for the church conducted her own schools and frequently there were no others.

The Puritans, even more than most Christians, were convinced of the necessity for Christian schools. They demanded that the children should be taught to read and to know the principles of their faith as stated in the catechism and confession. Unlike some Protestants, the Puritans also demanded an educated minister for every pulpit. This made necessary an elementary school for all, boys and girls alike, and a Latin school and college for the education of leaders in church and state. This was the exact demand of many of the reformers beginning with Luther. Thus state and church and school were brought into an intimate union. As a result the Bay Colony provided by law for all three in less than twenty years from its founding.

Some Massachusetts towns established schools of their own accord but not all did so. In 1647 the general court passed the act, which from the language of its preamble is known as "the old deluder Satan" law, and which required all towns of fifty families to maintain an elementary school, and towns of one hundred families to provide a secondary school to train boys for college. The law set a fine for failure to comply. A single teacher, qualified to teach both English branches and Latin fully satisfied the terms of the law. Even so, some towns found it cheaper to pay the fine than to maintain the school.

The law was not always obeyed. In many towns the number of pupils preparing for college was often very small and some of this small number were prepared under private tuition by the minister. At a given time a town school might not have a single pupil of Latin. Some towns evaded the law quite deliberately and skillfully. Teachers were employed while the general court was in session and dismissed when it adjourned; or a teacher shuttled back and forth between neighboring towns as frequently as was necessary to delude the authorities into believing that each town was maintaining a school. The larger and richer towns maintained the schools more continuously, but even in these the number of Latin pupils was often small. In the seventeenth century all the New England colonies except Rhode Island enacted laws similar to the Massachusetts Law of 1647.

Gradually the town schools declined. As the Indians were driven west and the settlers took their lands, the homes became more widely and thinly scattered over the townships. Hamlets began to dot the countryside. The people in the outlying parts of a town found the distance from the school too great for their children. To serve the more isolated families the teacher began to move from place to place within the town, teaching a few months in one village and a similar time in another. Sometimes the school was held for short periods in as many as six places in a single town. In 1710 in the town of Malden the teacher was required to teach in three places; in 1737 in Lunenburg in four places; and in 1725 in Harwich in six. In this last-cited case the lengths of the terms at each stand varied from four months to almost nine, and three and one-half years were needed to complete one round. Obviously, some of the children would attend only a single term in three or four years, but this was an extreme case. This phase in the decline of the New England schools is known as the moving-school phase.

In the next phase the townships were divided into independent school districts, each with a separate board and each maintaining a simple elementary school for a term as short as three months. This was the district school of tradition, the school of the little red schoolhouse celebrated by romantic former pupils, a poor thing indeed but suitable for thinly settled sections. Like the similar neighborhood school of the Appalachian valleys in Pennsylvania and Virginia, the district school grew up without legislation. In Massachusetts it was legalized in 1768 and 1789, and in New Hampshire in 1805.

Another device of the district system was the provision of two terms in a year, a winter term for the older boys and girls who were released from much of the farm work at that season and a summer term for the younger children. The winter term was likely to be rough, not only in regard to the weather, and the teacher had to be a strong and resolute man. In the summer terms the girls were given an opportunity to teach. As the schools in New England declined, those parents who could afford to do so sent their children to private schools. Even in Boston there were at times more pupils in the private schools than in the city public schools; this was true as late as 1820.

The district school and system were important in our history, and the term should be defined. There are several kinds of school districts. Townships, counties, cities with vast populations, special areas formed *ad hoc*, and indeed any bounded areas may become school districts by merely setting up agencies to erect, direct, and maintain schools for the people within its borders. In this most general sense of the term, each of the states is a school district enclosing many subordinate districts. But when the "district system" is mentioned, the reference is to a particular size of districts, namely, the smallest possible administrative school units, those with a single one-teacher school and a board to direct it. The essence of the district is in the separation of each school and board from all others. Although it is a misuse of words to call these adjoining educational atoms a system, this is historically the sense of the word.

The so-called district system spread from state to state across the country with the frontier settlements. Having been formed to meet the needs of thinly settled regions where only a handful of children could come together in one place, the system was also carried into cities where each ward had its one-teacher school and special trustees. When city school boards were formed they were composed of these ward officials who represented their wards rather than the city as a whole.

As the population in more recent times grew more dense, the district system was abandoned and larger units and schools with several or many teachers were substituted. The process is not yet completed. An urgent problem in many states is that of creating larger and fewer districts to equalize costs; promote secondary, technical, and special education; place schools in the best locations; facilitate supervision; and enlist capable personnel. This problem is being slowly and painfully solved.

COLONIAL TEACHERS

Just as there is no single description that will fit all present-day teachers, so there is none for all colonial teachers. Everyone is an individual, and in characterizing a whole class or profession of people much allowance must be made for the variations that will exist in any large group of people. Colonial teachers were of several kinds as can be demonstrated from the records. There were teachers who absconded, got drunk, were cruel, or committed financial irregularities. But several considerations must be kept in mind in passing judgment. Standards of conduct vary with time, and we should not too severely condemn errors that were overlooked when they were committed. We should not judge the innocent by the guilty or the accused who may not have been guilty.

Those who appointed teachers in colonial times no doubt tried to secure good men. No doubt they looked for character, education, manners, and whatever other qualities were demanded at the time. Sometimes they were unable to properly judge the applicant, particularly his educational qualifications. Sometimes there was not much choice because of the small number of candidates. Sometimes special qualifications, such as church membership or an ability to play the organ, were overvalued in comparison with the applicant's knowledge or teaching ability. Modern authors sometimes criticize our forefathers because they demanded church membership or conformity in doctrine, but this is a wholly unhistorical position. Of course, Friends' schools were taught by teachers who belonged to the Society, and Lutheran schools were taught by Lutheran teachers. Taking an analogous example from the present day, American communities do not want their children taught by Communist teachers.

The teachers of Puritan New England were frequently, and in some towns almost always, college graduates. The Society for the Propagation of the Gospel took great care in selecting prudent, learned, politically loyal, and pious teachers who conformed to the doctrine and discipline of the Church of England. The teachers in the Friends' schools were generally of good repute. Some of the teachers of private schools in Boston, Philadelphia, and other towns were honorable and distinguished. The teachers of the district schools and many of the subscription schools probably did not always meet the highest standards of education and character. Some colonial teachers, even in that day when corporal punishment was approved, were known for their brutality and tyranny, but they were exceptions.

One curious custom of that time was called "boarding 'round." The teacher in the district school was lodged and boarded for a week at a time in the family of one patron and then of another. By this system the school money was made to last a little longer than it otherwise would have. The practice did not enhance the dignity of the profession or make it easier to secure good teachers. The short terms made teaching a part-time employment. The wages were low, about equal to those of a good farm hand. The lack of equipment, the limited curriculum, and the irregularity of attendance further reduced the desirability of the profession. One cannot feel any surprise that few remained in the vocation more than a few years.

Teachers in the Latin schools and tutors in the colleges stood in the highest ranks of the occupation. Perhaps the most famous teacher in the Latin schools of New England was Ezekiel Cheever (1614–1708) of New Haven and Boston. Cheever taught for seventy years and has been celebrated in verse and story, such as by Nathaniel Hawthorne in his *Grandfather's Chair*.

SUMMARY

The colonial population grew rapidly, the settlements became denser in the East and spread toward the West, and some wealth was accumulated and comfort was attained. The colonial period covers one-half of the time that has elapsed since the settlement of Jamestown; the changes that occurred during that time must be kept constantly in mind. Only slight intimations of that development can be given in a brief summary. Ninety per cent of the people were still engaged in rural and outdoor occupations and one-fourth of them were slaves at the end of the period. To supply themselves with good schools would have been a very difficult task.

Home manufacturers gave employment to many, including children. Living conditions in the homes were not conducive to the intellectual life. Superstition played a greater role in many minds than science or literature. Children matured early and received only a rudimentary education. Mathematics and its practical applications were taught to young adults in private schools.

The means of communication improved. Roads and an intercolonial postal service to distribute newspapers and letters helped to spread ideas. A great victory for the freedom of the press was won in the Zenger case.

The apprentice system gave vocational training. Skilled artisans and trained young workmen from abroad kept coming, and thus the system was to a degree self-maintaining. There were also guilds, but they played a minor part. The colonies also had to deal with young vagrants, orphans and neglected children. Apprenticeship laws were passed partly as police measures and partly as relief steps. The "learning and labor" law of 1642 in Massachusetts was one of these laws, but there were also comparable laws in other colonies.

Standards of teaching and learning in colonial schools were low because frontier conditions did not permit or demand anything better. The different school systems varied slightly in administration but hardly in purpose. Subscription, neighborhood, and "old field" schools were adaptations to local conditions. Some of the neighborhood schools had a community or democratic basis but no legal status. The highly lauded town schools were anticipated by similar school legislation and church regulation in several European countries where Lutheran or Calvinist principles prevailed. The town schools of early New England were sectarian, controlled by the church and partly administered by the state as the arm of the church.

The common judgment that this was a period of transplantation is correct; but as schools were multiplied to meet the needs of a growing population, they were adapted but not always improved. And indeed some of the changes introduced into American education were changes for the worse. The moving and district schools, the backwoods schools in the log schoolhouses, the custom of "boarding 'round" for three-month terms, and the multitude of small schools competing with one another in the cities were not improvements.

QUESTIONS

1. Why were the differences between urban and rural schools greater in early times than they are today? The differences between these two

groups of schools should be studied for every period. It is a persistent problem.

2. Why did schools and educational attitudes differ in the several sections of colonial America? These sectional differences are continuing features and should be studied for every period.
3. How did the elementary education of boys differ from that of girls in the colonies? Why?
4. Did the practical education acquired from the ordinary activities in living and working in colonial times provide for the full development of human capacity and adequate preparation for service to the community and colony? This question will require full consideration. A short answer will not do.
5. Consider the suggestion that old things must have merit and compare it with the freely expressed view that the newest idea, invention, or institution is best. What is your statement on the relation between the merit and the persistence of ideas or other human achievements?
6. How are freedom and ease of communication related to education?
7. What are the merits and defects of an apprenticeship type of education? What part does high skill play in life?
8. What is the definition of education as it was carried out in colonial schools?
9. What is civilization? How does it differ from culture, as anthropologists use these words? Did the American Indians have either civilization or culture?
10. By what principal old and new means is civilization transmitted (spread)?
11. Why were social classes less powerful and less stable in English America than in England?
12. How does social stratification affect the spread of civilization and education?
13. What social (economic, religious, distribution of population, occupational, and other) factors affected education in early colonial times? More briefly, what did education have to begin with?

BOOKS AND PAPERS

Among the books on children and home life in colonial times are several written by Alice Morse Earle. Of these, *Child Life in Colonial Days* is perhaps most pertinent to the present chapter. For bibliographical help one can go to Monica Kiefer's *American Children Through Their Books, 1700–1835* (Philadelphia, 1948). Along with the description of the books there is much information in this volume on the manners, religion, discipline, and medical treatment of children. Some sources on the childhood of persons who became prominent may be gathered by using the bibliographies in the *Dictionary of American Biography* and from Barnard's *American Journal of Education*.

In this and following chapter-bibliographies, short titles are used; and except in the case of university presses and institutions of learning, the names of publishers are generally omitted.

Anonymous, "Some Thoughts of Education," *American Weekly Mercury*, December 31, January 7, 1735. Also in R. F. Seybolt, *The Private School*, University of Illinois, 1925.

BAILYN, BERNARD, *Education in the Forming of American Society*, University of North Carolina Press, 1960.

BARKER, ERNEST, *Church, State and Education*, paperback, University of Michigan Press (1957). First published, 1930.

BEVERLY, ROBERT, *History and Present State of Virginia*, edited by L. B. Wright, University of North Carolina Press, 1947. Treats of eighteenth-century conditions.

BRUMBAUGH, M. G., *Life and Works of Christopher Dock*, Philadelphia, 1908.

CUBBERLEY, E. P., *Public Education in the United States*, Boston, 1934; also, *Readings in Public Education in the United States*, Boston, 1934.

CURTI, MERLE, *The Social Ideas of American Educators*, New York, 1935.

DRIVER, HAROLD E., and W. E. MASSEY, *Comparative Studies of North American Indians*, Philadelphia, 1957. *Transactions*, American Philosophical Society.

EGGLESTON, EDWARD, *The Transit of Civilization from England to America in the Seventeenth Century*, New York, 1901; *The Hoosier Schoolmaster*, *The Hoosier Schoolboy* and other novels.

FICHTER, JOSEPH H., *Parochial School, A Sociological Study*, University of Notre Dame Press, 1958.

FLEMING, SANDFORD, *Children and Puritanism*, Yale University Press, 1933.

FORD, P. L., *The New England Primer*, New York, 1898.

JAMESON, J. F., ed., *Johnson's Wonder-Working Providence, 1628–1651*, New York, 1910.

JERNEGAN, M. W., *Laboring and Dependent Classes in Colonial America, 1607–1783*, University of Chicago Press, 1931.

JONES, RUFUS, *The Quakers in the American Colonies*, London, 1911.

KARIER, CLARENCE J., *Man, Society, and Education*, Chicago, 1967.

KILPATRICK, W. H., *Dutch Schools of New Netherland and Colonial New York*, Washington, D.C., U.S. Government Printing Office, 1912.

KNIGHT, E. W., *Public Education in the South*, Boston, 1922; *A Documentary History of Education in the South Before 1860*, University of North Carolina Press, 1949–1953, five volumes.

———, and C. L. HALL, *Readings in American Educational History*, New York, 1951.

KONWISER, H. M., *Colonial and Revolutionary Posts*, Richmond, Virginia, 1931.

KRAMER, SAMUEL NOAH, *From the Tablets of Sumer*, Indian Hills, Colorado, Falcon Wing Press (1956). A more popular version of this story, with good illustrations is by Edward Chiera, *They Wrote on Clay*, edited by George G. Cameron, a Phoenix paperback, University of Chicago, first published in 1938 but frequently reprinted.

LEACOCK, STEPHEN, *The Boy I Left Behind Me*, New York, 1946.

MAURER, C. L., *Early Lutheran Education in Pennsylvania*, Philadelphia, 1932.

MILLER, PERRY, and THOMAS H. JOHNSON, *The Puritans*, New York, 1938.

MONROE, PAUL, *Founding of the American Public School System*, New York, 1940; also *Readings in the Founding of the American Public School System*, New York, 1940 (microfilm).

NIETZ, JOHN A., *Old Textbooks*, Pittsburgh University Press, 1961.

RICH, W. E., *History of the United States Post Office to 1829*, Harvard University Press, 1924.

RUTHERFORD, LIVINGSTON, *John Peter Zenger, His Press, His Trial*, New York, 1904.

SEYBOLT, ROBERT FRANCIS, *Apprenticeship and Apprenticeship Education in Colonial New England and New York*, New York, Teachers College, Columbia University, 1916.

SCHLESINGER, ARTHUR M., *Learning How to Behave, A Historical Study of American Etiquette Books*, New York, 1946.

SCHUYLER, L. R., *Liberty of the Press in the Colonies*, New York, 1905.

THAYER, V. T., *Formative Ideas in American Education*, New York, 1965.

TRYON, R. M., *Household Manufactures, 1640–1860*, University of Chicago Press, 1917.

TUER, A. W., *History of the Hornbook*, New York, 1896.

WARFEL, HARRY, *Noah Webster, School-Master to America*, New York, 1936.

WICKERSHAM, J. P., *History of Education in Pennsylvania*, Lancaster, Pennsylvania, 1886.

WOODY, THOMAS, *Early Quaker Education in Pennsylvania*, New York, Teachers College, Columbia University, 1920.

———, *Life and Education in Early Societies*, New York, 1949.

WRIGHT, LOUIS B., *The Colonial Civilisation of North America, 1607–1763*, London, 1949.

YOUNG, ROBERT FITZGIBBON, *Comenius and the Indians of New England*, London, 1929.

Chapter 2

UPPER SCHOOLS
AND COLLEGES

Chiefly boys and young men attended the upper schools and colleges of the colonies. Private schools taught girls needlework, penmanship, music, and even languages, but these were lower rather than upper schools. Girls did not go to college and therefore did not prepare for college. The Latin grammar school and the college were the uninvaded preserves of the male sex; and the college remained to them inviolate until 1838 when Oberlin opened her regular college course to girls.

The colonial upper schools and colleges were for a select class of youth. Some were the ambitious sons of struggling but sacrificial farmers, for the poor boy in America has always found ways to go to college. What will happen if fees, especially in public institutions, continue to rise is not to be predicted. Others were the sons of the wealthy and professional classes. All hoped to become the ministers, teachers, lawyers, civil servants, doctors, and businessmen of their generation. Some became architects and erected the fine buildings of the larger colonial towns. The numbers of these students were limited, but then so were the suitable positions.

Their teachers, their parents, and they themselves when they thought about it believed that a classical education would help to provide a solid foundation for such elevated careers. That these studies had little to say about the particular problems that they would meet in life was considered a positive merit. Direct and specific preparation for many of the unpredictable and infinitely diverse problems of life being impossible, they had recourse to a general education that would help to solve all problems. This was their belief and decision two centuries ago. Today, and now that the ancient classics have been dislodged from their privileged position, educators with the support of engineers, physicians, and scientists are returning to the theory and practice of general education.

The upper schools of the colonies were of two kinds, the Latin grammar schools and the practical schools in the commercial cities. Only the former prepared pupils for college and were traditionally recognized as secondary

45

schools. The practical schools offered what was then called an English education, that is, not a classical one. This is the kind of education that Franklin valued and tried to promote in Philadelphia. The mathematical and English subjects of such schools formed an upper story based upon the studies that had been begun in the elementary schools. The integration between elementary and practical schools was loose, or rather was lacking, but the two were of the same kind and belonged together.

In the same manner the college formed the upper story of the studies that had been begun in the Latin grammar school. The connection between these two was close, having formed centuries earlier. They formed a single system. By undertaking the study of Latin, a boy by this beginning announced his choice of a career that would take him away from the shop, the farm, or the accountant's desk to a professional or managerial occupation. Not much time could be spared for preparation. Active life for both the student and the apprentice began at about the same early age; and this age was eighteen years, which was the normal age for graduation from college. Americans, as Franklin said, matured young and married early. But in such matters there are always many exceptions; and in respect to early marriage, Franklin himself was an exception.

WHERE THE LATIN SCHOOLS CAME FROM

Like other institutions, the Latin grammar school is best explained by its history. Only by examining its origin, nature, and purpose and its role in early times and foreign countries can an understanding be gained of the American imitation. Our examination must be brief. The speech of ancient Rome was carried through all the Mediterranean countries of three continents, to the shores of the Black Sea and the valley of the Danube, where the name of Romania still testifies to its ancient use, and in the north and west to the British Isles. It was carried by merchants, government officials, soldiers, and from the first Christian century by the Roman Catholic Church and its indefatigable missionaries.

In all this area in which a score of nations now find room, Latin was the language, not of peasants but of governors, traders, students, and the church. Hundreds of dialects were used in this area. Many of them were only spoken, because they had no literature. Many were lacking in the words needed to discuss all general or abstract questions. Because Latin had this vocabulary and was a cultivated language it became the universal language of educated Western Europe. It was used by those who had business beyond the narrow limits of a neighborhood or who wished to convey general ideas.

Of the changes that the Latin language suffered in the long centuries of the Middle Ages we shall not speak. There are good reasons for this omission. One reason is that it was not the medieval Latin of business, law, or the church that was studied in the later schools. The schools, from which the colonial teachers borrowed, taught the literary language of the ancient Roman poets, orators, historians, and moralists, the language of Cicero, Virgil, and Livy. These writers and others who resembled them were judged to belong to the highest class of writers and are therefore called classical.

The meaning of the word *classical* is not precise like that of a mathematical term. But it is of such importance in our account that some explanation of its meaning must be set down here. The classical writers dealt with universal topics that concern all men, simply as men. They wrote of travel and adventure, of fate and unseen powers, of war and danger, of love, courage, loyalty, and their opposites, especially when they can be seen embodied in the actions of persons. Cicero, for example, wrote of "traitorous Catiline," eulogized Roman culture, and, among a hundred themes, wrote on friendship, old age, and the education of an orator-statesman. Classical writings are generally marked by restraint, clearness, and regular form in contrast with the formless and exuberant manner of the romantic writers. The language of the classical writers of whom we are thinking was modeled upon the speech of the best-educated Romans of the two centuries following 100 B.C. This definition of the word *classical* will have its uses, but it should be received as only the beginning of wisdom in respect to the topic.

The secondary schools of Europe had become classical before the Enlish settled in America. Their medieval textbooks of grammar, rhetoric, and logic had been put away, and the classical writers had been substituted. But as we have indicated, it was the language rather than the matter of these writers that was studied. They were studied as models of style, construction, and diction, not for their philosophies of life. But usually only selections from their works were read; and therefore the boys frequently failed to get a clear impression of the whole mind and personality of an author. Nor was there much effort to teach the place of a writer in the history of his time, or to consider the problems that he faced and his purpose in writing. Thus authors became the texts for "exercises" in grammar.

In the seventeenth century there was no real understanding of Greek civilization or of its relation to Roman culture. War and politics formed the main content of historical study, and these activities were treated as the work of individuals. Ancient economics and science were unknown, as was the archaeology of the classical civilizations. The Germans were only beginning to study these subjects, and the period of the new humanism was still in the future. The enthusiasm for classical learning that had marked the Renaissance was dead; the interest in the history of civilization was unborn when the settlers transplanted the English type of grammar school to American soil.

From John Locke's *Thoughts* we may learn something, most of it unfavorable, of the English grammar schools. He was a Westminster pupil at the exact time when the Puritans of Massachusetts were enacting the "old deluder Satan" law. His main criticism is directed against the rude manners and bad conduct that impaired the schools; but he also held that the intellectual work was inferior. If so, these conditions were not caused by any sparing of the rod, for the school was then under Busby, the floggingest headmaster of them all. We cannot go into it here, but Locke's estimate may not have been entirely just. In any case the American schools could not even come up to their English models.

The English grammar schools of the seventeenth century were day schools. So were the American. The English schools were small, having perhaps fifty to one hundred boys; the American were smaller. The Boston Latin School, however, had 147 pupils in 1767; and between 1744 and the outbreak of the Revolution its numbers never fell below one hundred. It was probably the largest in the colonies. The North Latin School of Boston was only one-third to one-half as large in the same period, and those in smaller towns had very few Latin pupils along with many taking English studies. The curriculum was more extensive and the exercises more numerous in England than in America; but to this important matter we shall return.

EARLY LATIN SCHOOLS

Two of the earliest efforts in America to establish schools were made in Virginia, and one of these was an endeavor to found a Latin school. About 1620 funds were collected and plans were made to teach a "convenient number" of Indian youth the art of reading, the principles of the Christian religion, and a useful trade. This is a group of ideas resembling those of the Massachusetts Bay Colony law of 1642 and they came from the same general sources, namely, the Reformation and the practice of apprenticeship. About the same time plans were made to erect a building for a Latin school, a master was appointed, and it was proposed to have an usher, that is, an assistant, to teach writing and arithmetic. The Indian massacre of 1622 ended these efforts.

Two Virginia schools that may have taught Latin at an early date were the Symms School endowed by a will of 1634 and the Eaton School by a somewhat later bequest. Very little is known of these institutions, but they were not in operation for any extended time. A connection is claimed to exist between the early foundations and the twentieth-century Symms-Eaton School of Hampton. There were private Latin grammar schools in colonial Virginia such as the two conducted by clergymen in which Thomas Jefferson prepared for college. Others are known to have existed, but their history is often hard to trace. A Latin grammar school was connected with William and Mary College. Other colonies in the South had private schools. One of some note that was in existence before 1750 was conducted by Samuel Finley, later president of Princeton College. It was located at Nottingham in Cecil County, Maryland, and an academy at this place, as the custom of schools is, claims a connection with Dr. Finley's old school.

The reasons why the South had difficulty in developing and maintaining large numbers of good schools in colonial times are well known and were known then. The unnamed author of "An Advisive Narrative Concerning Virginia" (1662) asserted that from "the sparse population" there has resulted "their almost general want of Schooles for the education of their Children"; and that this lack caused their youth who were "beautiful and comely Persons . . . [to be] unserviceable for any great Employments either in Church or State," as it also obstructed the "Conversion of the Heathen." This "advisive" account declared that towns were a necessity, as were funds from England, English workmen to erect buildings and clergymen for the service of the church and the catechizing and teaching not only of children but of parents and masters as well. The author seems to have feared a return to barbarism in the colony. He proposed the creation of "Virginia Fellowships" at the English universities for the aid of those who would prepare themselves for service in the churches of the colony. The "Narrative" was submitted to the Bishop of London but apparently nothing was done to carry out its suggestions.

Many Southern planters' sons were educated abroad and others in family schools on the plantations, whereas some were sent to Northern schools. But it was not only the planters' sons who attended English and European schools. From all or nearly all of the colonies and from city and plantation, some of those who could afford to do so sent their youth to study and travel in older countries. The "grand tour" was still an institution in Europe where for educational purposes boys of the higher classes were conducted by their tutors through the leading countries. Catholic parents were likely to patronize church establishments in France or Belgium. Other young gentlemen might go to one or another of the classical schools of England, as did Edgar Allan Poe at a later date. Some went to study law at the Inns of Court in London, for in the South especially, as in South America today, a legal education was considered particularly appropriate for a gentleman. Classical learning was also highly favored in the South. And no part of the country sent more students of law and classics to England than Charleston, South Carolina.

Charleston also had classical schools of her own. The Society for the Propagation of the Gospel, private interests, and the state legislature cooperated in erecting a Latin school about 1712. In consideration of grants from the state treasury it was to educate twelve boys free. In Charleston and elsewhere, those who could afford to pay for a foreign education were a small minority. Some important Americans, like the Carrolls and the Pinckneys, were educated abroad, but the total number formed only a small proportion of the youth.

The best account of a mansion-house or family school on a plantation is that of Philip Fithian. He was a Princeton graduate and taught in the Carter family of northern Virginia. He left an account of the social life of the time (1773) and of his work as a teacher. A more modest example is that of John Harrower, an indentured servant, employed as a teacher in the Daingerfield family of Fredericksburg. One of his achievements was the instruction of a deaf boy from a neighboring plantation. In general, the fact is that Latin grammar schools were not numerous in the South, and many that were opened did not continue permanently. Parents could not assume that as their children developed, a secondary school or any school would, as a matter of course, be within easy reach.

In New England the Latin school flourished in a modest sort of way. For fifty years Boston had no other town school than its Latin School, which may have taught English also. Doubtless there were private schools. Other towns followed the example set by the capital city, and five—Charlestown, Salem, Dorchester, Cambridge, and Roxbury—did so by 1645. The passing of the law of 1647, noted in the preceding chapter, probably indicates that many of the town fathers in other places were not as fervent in their zeal for schools as the colony fathers desired. Some schools were opened but did not "succeed" or were operated intermittently. Some had difficulty in finding a master. Some employed means of evading the provisions of the law. About one-third of the towns of Massachusetts had schools by 1700. Of the remaining towns, many were too small to fall under the provisions of the hundred-family law.

There is more direct evidence that the Latin school was not popular in all parts of the commonwealth. One example is found in the history of the town of Woburn. While the General Court was in session in a particular year the teacher of the town of Andover was engaged to teach also at Woburn, and his appointment was certified to the General Court. Then this Andover teacher, who bore the doubly famous name of Dudley Bradstreet, took a day off from his regular duties to open the school at Woburn. But, as he no doubt expected, no pupils came and without pupils there were no duties. Yet the town had a master and therefore a school. Collecting his fee for the day's attendance as master he returned to his regular duties in Andover. Thus it appears that absenteeism was not entirely confined to church administration but appeared, if rarely, also in the schools.

Towns sometimes directed the selectmen to hire a teacher at the cheapest rate possible. One town reported that its people favored "common learning" but that few wished to become scholars. The small number of college students in the colonial colleges shows that this distaste was widely shared. During her first sixty years Harvard was the only college in the colonies, and yet the average number of graduates for each of those sixty years was only eight. And most of these students had come from five towns, namely, Boston, Cambridge, Charlestown, Dorchester, and Roxbury, the same five named previously except that Boston takes the place of Salem. Some Latin schools in Massachusetts did not prepare a single student for college in ten or even in twenty years. W. H. Small, who was a careful student of the whole subject, came to a radical conclusion on the unpopularity of the Latin grammar school in Massachusetts. He wrote: "The whole [eighteenth] century is marked by indifference to the law [of 1647] or open defiance of it. More and more the conviction is forced upon us that this form of school existed not by popular will but by force of law."

Although Connecticut was "out West" in the early seventeenth century, there are records of several Latin grammar schools in the colony before 1650. It seems probable that there were such schools in New Haven and Hartford in 1639, and the latter town made an appropriation for a town school in 1642 when the noted master, Ezekiel Cheever, was appointed to teach in it. The Connecticut school law of 1650 was an almost exact copy of the Massachusetts law of 1647.

Within a year after his arrival in Philadelphia, William Penn and the council (1683) engaged a teacher of reading, writing, and bookkeeping; and it was proposed, but perhaps not carried out, to open a school of an academic character, teaching the sciences. After years of silence the record was resumed. From this continuation it appears that the Friends' Monthly Meeting established a "Public School" in 1689. By-and-by the city council of Philadelphia claimed the right to pass upon the qualifications of the teacher. Perhaps the friction growing out of this conflict over jurisdiction led the Friends to petition for a charter for "their" school. The Monthly Meeting asked for the right "to choose and admit" and "to remove and displace" the trustees, masters, and pupils in any way they pleased and "as often as said meeting shall see occasion." The request was granted, the charter issued (1701), and thus began the William Penn Charter School.

Among its early teachers before the charter was granted were men educated in German and Scottish universities and therefore capable of teaching the classics. One was the German scholar Francis Daniel Pastorius (1651–1720), and associated with him was a teacher of writing and arithmetic. At that time (1699) the school seems to have had two departments, one the classical, and another the English and mathematical. Pastorius did not stay long. Probably there were few pupils in the classics, and that department may have lapsed for a time. The teaching in other branches was certainly continued. By the methods frequently employed to secure the earliest credible date for the founding of schools, it might be possible to push the origin of the Penn Charter School back to 1683 when a school was first opened in Philadelphia, but the connection is doubtful. The William Penn Charter School became the center of a system of charity schools located in different parts of the city. Support for the school and its pendent charity schools came from rents, gifts, legacies, and fees but, from the first, instruction was free to the poor.

Friends' children were often a minority and this caused concern in the Monthly Meeting over the bad manners and morals of some others, which tended to corrupt those who had been more carefully reared. This has been a problem of Friends' schools in many times and places, for the desire to promote the Friends' way of life is the primary reason for their schools. One method of coping with this problem consisted in the selection of the pupils to be admitted and the employment of teachers who were members of the Society. This practice is, no doubt, the source of the term *select school* used by the Society. The matter has a special pertinence at present when several other religious bodies that have been sending their children to the public schools are deserting them and establishing their own denominational schools.

Several other Latin grammar schools were established in the Middle Colonies before the Revolution. They were usually religious in tone without being controlled or supported by a church. The "Log-College" at Neshaminy (1726–1742) was conducted by Presbyterians but not officially connected with the Presbyterian church, and the same statement applies to four or more other Pennsylvania schools where ministers taught languages and some theology to those who aspired to the same vocation. Lutherans and others also conducted Latin schools. There were some efforts to establish an Episcopal Latin school in Philadelphia before the Revolution, but they did not succeed until 1787 when the Episcopal Academy was incorporated.

LATIN SCHOOL CURRICULUM

To prepare boys for college was the task and purpose of the Latin grammar school. An early statement of this assignment is found in the admission requirements of Harvard College in 1642. At that time boys were to be admitted when they were able to read Cicero at sight, speak Latin, make Latin verses, and give the forms, the declensions and conjugations of the Greek nouns and verbs. The close connection between the Latin school and college is also indicated by some phrases from *New England's First Fruits*, a pamphlet published in London in 1643. It said that a "fair grammar school" had been erected by the side of Harvard College "for the training up of young scholars" in "academic learning" until they were judged ripe enough to be received into the college. The reference is to the Cambridge Latin School.

There are no records for a detailed study of the curricula of the different schools. Perhaps it is a warranted inference that few or no colonial schools had a more complete and extended offering than that of the Boston Latin School. Even this school has no clear record of its curriculum before the year 1712. At that time the first three years were spent upon the elements of Latin, the declensions, conjugations, simple agreements, and vocabulary. In the fourth year Erasmus' *Colloquies* and Ovid were read. In the fifth year these were continued and Cicero's *Epistles* were added. Cicero, Ovid, Lucius Florus, and Virgil were studied in the sixth year. And in the seventh and last year a whole flock of authors, for the first time including Greek writers, were read. They were Cicero, Justin, Virgil, Horace, Juvenal, Persius, the *Greek Testament*, Isocrates, Homer, and even Hesiod. It is to be particularly noted that according to this curriculum, which was written out by Nathaniel Williams, the successor to Ezekiel Cheever, the boys seem not to have begun the study of Greek until the last quarter of the sixth year. And the following year they were expected to read not only the *Greek Testament*, which might be considered possible, but also difficult authors such as Isocrates and Hesiod.

Various required exercises were included in this curriculum of 1712. Master Williams wrote that in "the fourth year, or sooner if their capacities allow it" they were to translate Erasmus with the help of dictionary and grammar. Each made a copy that was corrected by the master, and after several days they were required to translate it back into the Latin of the author. Other exercises were explained by Williams, but this one is of special interest because it shows that the famous method of double translation recommended by the Spaniard Juan Luis Vives and the Englishman Roger Ascham was introduced into an American school. This was a true case of transplantation. A plan very similar to this plan of double translation was used by Franklin in the effort to acquire a good English style. He paraphrased passages of good prose and after some time, working from the paraphrase, he tried to write in the manner of the original.

Although the young Latin scholars of Boston were something more than mere beginners, they did not accomplish as much as was expected of the contemporary schoolboys of Old England. We may compare the Boston Latin School with England's Westminster. Several of the authors commonly read in England were neglected in Massachusetts. Such authors were Sallust, Livy, Caesar; and of the Greeks, Lucian and Demosthenes. Terence is not named in the Boston curriculum of 1712, but we learn that Cheever had used this author. The authors and subjects taught in both schools appear later in the Boston course than in the Westminster schedule. Thus the *Colloquies* of Erasmus were introduced in the second year at Westminster but not until the fourth year in the American school, and this two-year difference in favor of the English boys is uniformly maintained. The following table shows this uniform difference. The Roman figures indicate years of the course in each case.

WESTMINSTER-BOSTON CURRICULUM TABLE (1712)

Books				Westminster	Boston
Erasmus' *Colloquies* appears in year				II	IV
Cicero's *Epistles*	"	"	"	III	V
Greek *Grammar*	"	"	"	IV	VI
Cicero's *de Officiis*	"	"	"	IV	VI
Justin	"	"	"	V	VII
Isocrates	"	"	"	V	VII

This comparison is incomplete because in many cases the two schools used different books, and the school exercises also differ. But it seems clear that the English schoolboy was expected to cover far more ground than the American. The disparity is only increased when we recall that after making slow progress for six years the Boston school attempted to redress the balance by introducing ten new authors in the last year. For the later curricula of the Boston Latin School the *Tercentenary History* by Pauline Holmes, as listed in the chapter bibliography, may be consulted.

Little is known of the curricula of the other colonial Latin schools. Something can be inferred from the college entrance requirements, but unfortunately we do not know how strictly they were interpreted. The Princeton requirements of 1748 were about the same as those of Harvard in 1642. Except that Yale had recently added arithmetic (1745) to its requirements, college admission studies had remained practically unchanged for a century. Translation from English into Latin and Latin versification were sometimes expected. In some colleges the president and two tutors had to certify the candidate's fitness. Much less emphasis was laid upon Greek than upon Latin in both Latin school and college course.

Few boys acquired such a mastery of Latin as would have enabled them to read and enjoy the ancient authors without the help of lexicon and grammar. Yet there were other benefits. John Adams, Jefferson, Madison, Hamilton, and others had somehow, partly from secondary sources, acquired a knowledge of the politics of the Greek democracies and the Roman republic, knowledge that served them well in the Revolution, in the Constitutional Convention, and in public life in general. Jefferson and perhaps a few others lived with and loved the ancient literatures to the end of their days. Now great literature is functional, in a noble sense of this slippery word, in the life of anyone who has the capacity to respond to it. This is a constant argument for the study of Latin and Greek by such persons. But American conditions did not stimulate enthusiasm for classical studies. The time available for study was short, the need for practical skill was great, and doubtless many college graduates never looked into their Virgil or Homer in later life.

THE COLONIAL COLLEGES

The first American colleges were small, conservative, widely scattered and isolated, and six of the first nine were less than thirty years old when the colonial period ended. The other three were ancient by comparison. The foundation dates of all are indicated in Table 2–1. Harvard, the

TABLE 2–1
THE COLONIAL COLLEGES

Present and Early Names		First Charter	First Degrees
Harvard University	Harvard College	1636	1642
William and Mary College	William and Mary College	1693	1700
Yale University	Collegiate School, and Yale College	1701	1702
Princeton University	College of New Jersey	1746	1748
Columbia University	King's College	1754	1758
University of Pennsylvania	College of Philadelphia	1755	1757
Brown University	College of Rhode Island	1764	1769
Rutgers University	Queen's College	1766	1774
Dartmouth College	Dartmouth College	1769	1771

oldest, had been founded in 1636, and after a bad beginning graduated its first class in 1642. We have already noted that for sixty years it remained the only college in British America. William and Mary was merely a grammar school at first and conferred its first degrees in 1700. A third college, Yale, was chartered as a collegiate school the year following (1701), but had difficulty in finding a permanent home. Its very existence was endangered by the struggle between three towns, each of which wanted the school. It was not finally located at New Haven until 1717. Hartford, one of the contestants, was promised the State House to compensate it for the loss of the college; and for many years Connecticut maintained two capital cities, Hartford and New Haven. The other six foundations had hardly come into full operation when the Revolutionary War broke out and in several cases seriously interrupted the work of the colleges.

Although most of the American colleges were young in 1776, higher education was already hoary with age. Higher education was the daughter of the church, and the oldest universities in Europe are older than any existing institution except the church. In the Middle Ages, as the universities began to take form, residence halls for students were founded. The residents of the halls gradually formed organized bodies, with laws, property, officers, and corporate rights and powers. The Roman word for such a body was *collegium*, whence the English word "college." In the universities, professors, tutors, students, and officials were expected to live a communal or collegiate life, eating at a common table, lodging in college buildings, and conforming to college laws.

Upon such a plan the colleges of Oxford and Cambridge were set up, and this was the plan followed also in America. But in England each university included and exercised certain controls over her several colleges, and only the university had the power to confer degrees. An analogy with the American government will be illuminating. The colleges of Oxford, for example, may be taken to correspond to the states and the university to correspond to the federal government. As in the United States, each student is a citizen or member of his college and also of the university. But the English system of congregating a score or more colleges in one place under the control of a university could not be followed in the new world. In early America, owing to the dispersion of the people, each college was chartered as an independent degree-granting institution that in England would have been considered a small university.

The medieval universities had a medieval curriculum. It was composed, on one side, of professional studies, law, medicine, and divinity, and on the other of logic and other so-called liberal arts. The Renaissance brought in a new conception of liberal education based upon a classical curriculum, critical methods, and a modern individualistic spirit. Some religious reformers, such as Erasmus, John Colet, Sir Thomas More, and their successors, accepted this outlook and introduced the "new learning" into Oxford and Cambridge. By the seventeenth century, Emmanuel College, Cambridge, whence many of the founders and supporters of Harvard came, had become a center of the Puritan religion. To the classical impulse the reformers added the study of the Scriptures including the Greek New Testament, the Hebrew of the Old Testament, and theology. The American colleges, therefore, began with a curriculum that had been laid down in somewhat separate strata by three great movements, the medieval university movement, the Renaissance, and the Reformation. From the first had come logic, rhetoric, some scraps of ancient mathematics and science, and the constant exercises in academic disputation; from the second, the Latin and Greek classics; and from the Reformation, the Hebrew and other Semitic languages, the Old and New Testament studies, and Protestant theology. Of modern science, history, or literature there was hardly a trace, certainly no more than a trace. Such rigid systems based upon the past are the natural result of strict orthodoxy whether it be in religious, civil, or economic affairs.

As the first European universities were the children of the church so the first American colleges were the children of the Protestant churches. Although some were not legally bound to any denomination, all had moral and customary religious bonds. The exception, if there was an exception, was the College of Philadelphia. Its founders ruled out sectarianism, claiming that the trustees were selected "without regard to religious persuasion." They were selected, as the historian Edward Cheyney believes, for their wealth, liberality, and social influence. Nevertheless, three-fourths of them were Episcopalians, the provost was an Episcopal clergyman, and "an Anglican tinge colored the institution during the whole colonial period." But this college did not have the preparation of ministers as its purpose, an important difference.

The education of ministers was the primary purpose at several of the colleges, never the only one. Many things besides divinity were taught in all of them and for several reasons. Ministers were expected to have a general as well as a theological education. And the colleges needed students and did not wish to exclude boys who belonged to other than the ruling denomination or who were preparing for other secular professions. Nor did these have any other choice, for all the colleges except the one in Philadelphia were denominational. Only the medical school of the College of Philadelphia offered professional education outside the ministry and this for only ten years before the Revolutionary War began. In the senses here indicated it is true, as Samuel Eliot Morison is anxious to maintain, that early Harvard was not a divinity school; but it is also true that its primary purpose was the preparation of ministers because the founders dreaded to leave "an illiterate ministry" to the Puritan Congregational churches when those ministers who had come from England "should lie in the dust."

Although the colleges were church institutions, they had to appeal to the state for legal rights and powers, such as the right to receive and hold property and the power to grant degrees. Harvard was founded "to supply the publicke with fit Instruments principally for the work of the Ministry." A new college, Yale, was created in Connecticut partly through the machinations of the Mathers, who had lost their hold upon Harvard, and partly because, for some, that institution was becoming too liberal in its theology. The founders of Yale required the "Westminster Confession to be diligently read in the Latin Tongue and well studyed [sic] by all the Schollars," "for the upholding of the Christian protestant Religion by a succession of Learned and Orthodox men." The State of Connecticut in the Yale Charter of 1701 asserted its desire to support "so necessary and Religious an undertaking."

As indicated, the colleges did not exclude students because they came from a denomination other than the one controlling the college in question. They never followed the English practice of setting up religious tests in the charters or college laws. But such matters can also be managed by consent and common understanding without legal warrant. In their public statements the denominational attitudes of the later colleges were liberal.

The charter of Brown University (1764) opened all offices except the presidency and all staff positions to Protestants of any denomination. The youth of all denominations were assured of equal advantages. The members of the board were taken from four denominations in fixed proportions, but the Baptists retained a large majority. The Dartmouth charter (1769) had no religious tests for students, president, or trustees, and no person was to be excluded on account of "speculative sentiments in religion." And seven of the eleven trustees were to be laymen. This board was remarkable also on account of its small size.

The charter of Queen's College (1770) was granted in answer to the petition of the ministers and elders of the Reformed churches among the people who had come from the United Provinces, that is, from Holland. The purpose was stated in the most general terms to be "the education of youth in the learned languages, liberal and useful arts and sciences, and especially in divinity, preparing them for the ministry and other good offices." The president was to be a member of the Dutch Reformed Church, but there was no test for the thirty-eight trustees. Although no religious requirement for the professor of divinity was stated, his membership in the Dutch Reformed Church was taken for granted. The most extraordinary requirement of the Queen's College charter was that there was "always to be one professor" whose duty it should be to instruct the students in the use and grammar of the English language. This was necessary because Dutch was the native language of many students. The college had trouble in maintaining itself, and at the turn of the century was closed for several years.

The colonial colleges were small. To discover how incredibly tiny they were in comparison with small-college enrollments in the twentieth century we must go to the records, not the college historians. Harvard had about twenty students in 1642 and sixty in 1670. But a decade later the college enrollments again dropped to very low levels. Better times followed and about 1690 the annual number of graduates over a ten-year period averaged thirteen. The enrollment moved upward until 1725, downward to another low about 1750, and again reached a new high just before the Revolution. In 1775 Harvard graduated forty, Yale thirty-five, Columbia thirteen, Dartmouth eleven, and Pennsylvania eight. At Princeton the graduates numbered twenty-seven in 1776, seven in 1777, and an average of six for the following five years. The war was no doubt responsible for the decline. Most of the colleges maintained preparatory Latin schools or departments, and the enrollments in these were often larger than those in the colleges themselves. The colleges did not issue annual catalogues, but one may estimate that the total enrollment in the nine colleges on the eve of the Revolution was 750 students and had probably never exceeded that figure. This number of college students out of a population of nearly 2 million white persons—for slaves did not go to college—is only one-fiftieth of the numbers that come from a similar population today. It was as though a whole state such as Kansas were sending only 750 students to college.

The colleges were small and correspondingly poor. They did not have the noble architecture, the velvet lawns, the well-stocked libraries, or the abundant leisure that surrounded the university students of England. The buildings were mere shells, and even when the outside was made of stone, the inside—the floors and partitions—was of wood. This helps to explain the frequent college fires. Students normally entered at the age of fourteen and were required to live "in college" in bare, uncomfortable, and un-adorned study-bedrooms and to subsist on the food furnished at the college commons. Bad and insufficient food was one of the chief causes of the numerous college riots carried out by students. Arbitrary government was another, and so was the poor teaching of a barren curriculum. Standards of work doubtless rose as the colleges became better established, but they were not high. In the early years of one now famous university, a student reported that all they did was to "construe poorly" five or six orations of Cicero, five or six books of Virgil, and most of the Greek Testament and to gain "a very superficial knowledge of part of the Hebrew Psalter." Everywhere the formal classwork consisted of recitations from a textbook. There were no electives. All students of each year recited from the same books, usually to a tutor who was himself a recent graduate without advanced education.

The English universities were operating upon one of the lowest levels of their whole history when the American colleges were rising. Edward Gibbon, Adam Smith, and others testify to that. The frontier conditions in America depressed still further that low-level education, borrowed from England. Yet great men, the founders of the Republic, came from those poor institutions. It is possible to gain an education under untoward circumstances. And those poor institutions had the capacity to grow with the country and to become the large and great universities of the present. This development did not begin in colonial times. In that period the realist private schools gave the best example of educational enterprise.

REALIST AND CLASSICAL THEORY

The realist conception of education and the older classical scheme were like oil and water—they would not mix. Not until the nineteenth century did the older Latin schools introduce English, modern languages, and science into the classical course. At the Boston Latin School the change was made gradually between 1814 and 1829. In colonial times and after, some of the Latin schools had a form of "released time" when the boys or some of them were excused for part of the school day to take lessons from another school or a tutor in handwriting, arithmetic, bookkeeping, or English.

The other comparable colonial device was the two-course plan such as the Penn Charter School employed. But this was after all different because the two courses, the classical and realist, were taken by different groups of pupils. It may be compared with the practice of many Latin schools that gave classical instruction to boys who were to go to college and elementary teaching in reading and arithmetic to others who were intended for business or the farm. Such facts reveal the contrast, even the opposition and conflict, between the older form of education and the new.

The conflict grew out of psychological and historical causes. A classical education was the avenue to the old professions and especially the ministry. For the clergy the ancient languages were a necessary instrument. Their pertinence in the study of law and medicine was less evident; but it was easy to assume that what was good for the highest profession was also good for those of somewhat lower degree. And the desire of the professional class to maintain their standing as a class apart was one reason why all regularly educated men insisted upon the preeminence of that kind of education.

There was, secondly, the belief in the disciplinary value of classical studies. This belief was hardly even scrutinized in colonial times, but the basis for it has since been severely shaken. It is true that language instruction was better organized, and equipped with better books and aids than English and science instruction; but it is somewhat ironical and yet a fact that the belief in automatic transfer and the dependence upon prepared exercises should have tended to dampen the enthusiasm and to lessen the industry of Latin teachers. In the third place, in education as well as in business, possession is nine parts of the law. The classics held and had long held the field and it was much easier for them to continue in possession than for the new subjects to invade it.

Private schools were the early dispensers of realist education and from these, pulled this way and that by educational and social forces, the hybrid American academy developed. But the realist movement did not originate in America and was no longer new when it was introduced. In the earlier half of the sixteenth century, traces of such ideas were to be found in the works of Luther and Vives. In the following century John Amos Comenius, "that incomparable Moravian," became a missionary for these principles and some of his books were brought to America, but if they had any influence, it cannot be made out now. Nor can we now prove or disprove the belief of Cotton Mather that Comenius was considered for the presidency of Harvard. Bacon and Locke were better known in the new world, and the stimulating effect of their views was acknowledged. There was the Puritan academy of England, which one might have expected to find copied in Puritan New England, but clerical and classical influence was too strong. Realism was more acceptable in the Middle Colonies and in busy commercial cities everywhere. It was encouraged by the founder of Pennsylvania, himself a product of classical Oxford.

William Penn recorded his enlightened views in his *Frame of Government* (1682), written in England. He taught that government should actively promote good as well as repress evil. That is a free government where the people make their own laws; and that will be a good one where the people are wise and virtuous. But virtue and wisdom do not come by inheritance; they must, he claimed, be propagated by education.

The *Frame* provided that the governor and council were to establish and direct all public schools and to reward authors and inventors. At the age of twelve, children were to be taught a trade or useful occupation, that "none may be idle, but the poor may work to live, and the rich, if they become poor, may not want." He demanded that the government should look after this because "it is a sort of trustee of the youth," and they in their turn are soon to be the rulers. He would spare no cost for the education of his own children but urged that they should be taught useful knowledge, "consistent with truth and godliness." He recommended mathematics applied to shipbuilding, navigation, surveying, and other crafts; but he especially praised agriculture, "which is an occupation, industrious, healthy, honest, and of good example."

Penn's realism, partly revealed in the preceding sentences, is more fully developed in his *Reflections and Maxims,* a work of his old age. Penn wrote that the physical world is what youth ought to study; children can best understand sensible things; but we fail to include these in their education. Instead "we press their memory too soon." We load them with words, rules of grammar, rhetoric, and a foreign language or two. We are at great pains "to make them scholars but not men."

There is, however, no necessary opposition between scholarship and manhood, and Penn's sharp antithesis is false. But many of the more radical Reformation groups, Friends, Moravians, Pietists, Anabaptists, agreed with his main position. And all of these sects were well represented in Pennsylvania. Education, they held, should promote piety, practicality, industry, and business success.

For the higher learning they had no high regard; but in the seventeenth and eighteenth centuries some of them did not see how one could get along without Latin. Penn's *Reflections* spread the view of Comenius. He admitted that languages should not be neglected but thought "things are still to be preferred." He pointed out that children love to use their hands in making tools, playthings, and useful objects and thought that this hint should not be overlooked by teachers. But there should be books in Latin for children; and these should deal with nature and mechanical subjects so that at school "they might learn things [together] with words." It is too bad that gardeners, farmers, and artisans so often do not understand the science of their calling. Besides, from nature we may learn to admire the wisdom of the Creator. This may, indeed, be a paraphrase of some passages by Comenius. These views, like the theory of classical education, came from Europe, and they were well suited to the immediate needs of middle-class America.

PRIVATE SCHOOLS

Private adventure schools, unsupervised and without any connection with other schools, were numerous in colonial times. They were conducted by individual teachers who earned a living by this means. For support the teachers depended upon fees paid by the pupils whom they were able to attract; for regulations they relied upon custom or invented their own new ones. Such schools were as private as a grocery store, and their success, like that of a store, depended upon their ability to supply and sell a product, namely, instruction in knowledge and skill. Many private schools were found even in the New England towns where there also were town and district schools. Thirty-five years after the close of the Revolution in the city of Boston there still were as many children in the private schools as in the public ones. Everywhere a large proportion of the private schools taught only the rudiments to children. The consideration of these was taken up in Chapter 1, but there were also some advanced schools that will be treated here.

By 1700 the larger towns had become important centers of trade. In these towns there was need for those who had acquired a more advanced education, those who could write a good business hand, and were quick and accurate at figures and the various kinds of weights and measures; those who could keep a set of books; and those who could apply the elements of astronomy, geometry, and trigonometry to navigation and surveying. In a new country the work of the surveyor had a special importance. He served as the engineer in road building, laying out towns, erecting public works, and plotting farms and larger tracts of land. The schools taught the mathematics, basic science, and business practice needed in such work, and the other skills were acquired in an informal apprenticeship. There were no developed schools of engineering in America until long after the colonial period had ended; but the private schools laid the foundations of a practical engineering profession and thus of a new class of skilled people performing necessary functions.

The nature of these schools and the quality of their teachers can be more concretely shown by means of a few examples. For comparison we shall also include some teachers of the classics and other subjects. Most of our examples will be drawn from Philadelphia and surroundings because it was the early center of science and realist education. Good examples could be drawn from New York, Boston, and other places. Because Philadelphia was a new city in the first half of the eighteenth century and growing very rapidly, most of the teachers came from other colonies or from England or Germany. And we shall not be able to exhibit many typical teachers. The very fact that these teachers made enough of a mark in the world to get into the historical record stamps them as somewhat unusual.

The teachers of secondary school subjects and conductors of private schools were men. At the end of the colonial period many women were engaged in teaching elementary schools, but nearly all the teachers of classics, modern languages, mathematics, and English grammar were men. Indeed, there were few places where women could have learned these subjects. We offer brief accounts of some Philadelphia teachers and a few others as evidence of the character of the private schools and schoolteachers of the eighteenth century.

Theophilus Grew (d. 1759) was a teacher of mathematics who first came into notice at Annapolis in 1732 as a successful almanac-maker. Two years later Grew was in Philadelphia offering to teach mathematics from arithmetic to trigonometry with many practical applications; and except for one brief absence he remained in that city and calling. His general repute is indicated by his work as a consultant in the long contest over the boundary-line between Pennsylvania and Maryland. If he was largely self-educated, as seems probable, this fact would be another proof of his ability. In 1750 he was appointed mathematics master in the Philadelphia Academy, but he continued to carry on his evening school as well. This again shows that some of the colonial teachers were men of quality.

There were many private schoolteachers of many subjects in the colonies, especially in the eighteenth century. In his work on *The Private School* in the colonies, Seybolt compiled a list of the private teachers in Philadelphia between the years 1722 and 1783. Most of these names were taken from newspaper advertisements. Seybolt's list, admittedly incomplete, contained ninety-seven names; and to these Professor James Mulhern has added sixty-five others with the statement that the total of 162 names does not yet account for all the private teachers of the city in the period designated.

One of the names omitted by Seybolt is that of Thomas Godfrey (1704–1749) who advertised for mathematical pupils in 1740. Godfrey was also a maker of mathematical instruments. He was a member of Franklin's club, The Junto, and when he died, Franklin in an obituary notice said he had "an uncommon genius for all kinds of Mathematical

Learning, with which he was extremely well acquainted. He invented the new Reflecting Quadrant used in Navigation." So he did, but Edmund Halley had made the same invention independently and the Royal Society divided its prize of about eighty pounds equally between the two men.

We turn now to New England for an illuminating example. For about a decade, Isaac Greenwood was Hollis Professor of Mathematics at Harvard College (1727–1738), and when he was dismissed from that position he went back to his earlier business, the private teaching of mathematics. He offered subjects ranging from the elements to the calculus, and his language shows awareness of both Newtonian and Leibnitzian methods. It is probable that some advanced subjects were occasionally advertised merely as "good business" without the intention or ability to teach them, but this remark does not apply to Greenwood.

Throughout the eighteenth century, Boston, New York, Philadelphia, and other cities had private teachers of mathematics and its applications to dialing, gauging, mensuration, navigation, surveying, and bookkeeping. This tendency to emphasize practical applications is what one should expect in a new and undeveloped country. Andrew Lamb, who taught in Philadelphia for forty years, was one of those who featured the teaching of navigation. He claimed knowledge of both the science and art. In his advertisements he said: "Sailors, take a friend's advice, be not cheated by land-men that pretend to navigation for they know nothing of a sea-journal, which is the principal thing you want to know, and the use of sea-charts." He declared that his pupils were qualified to go as mates on the first voyage. He may be compared with Christopher Colles of the same city who offered to teach "land-men's crafts," especially the building of all kinds of mills and waterworks, such as dams, canals, docks and bridges, and military branches including gunnery and fortification. Colles' reputation was good enough so that John Fitch considered asking him for technical assistance in constructing what was to become the most extraordinary "waterwork" of its time, namely the first successful steamboat. In the end, however, Henry Voight became Fitch's assistant.

The most practical, because it is universally needed, branch of mathematics is arithmetic, the first and simplest. With independence, American arithmetic books began to appear, not slowly and timidly but in great profusion. One of the first was by Nicholas Pike (1743–1819), his *New and Complete System of Arithmetic* (1778). He was the master of the Newburyport, Massachusetts, grammar school and also carried on a private evening school. His book explained the then new federal money. According to L. C. Karpinski, he made in this and other respects "an enduring contribution to American education."

Arithmetic and grammar books for the elementary schools were considered in the preceding chapter. English composition, grammar, and public speaking were not often offered in private schools until late in the colonial period. Reading and writing were taught in elementary schools, and German, French, Portuguese, and Spanish as well as the ancient languages in the private day and evening schools; but grammatical and practical instruction in English "as a science and as a language" was rare before 1750. A notable teacher of these branches was David James Dove (c. 1696–1769), who was installed in 1751 as the English master in the Philadelphia Academy. His mathematical colleague, Grew, had been in office for a year at that time. Dove, like Grew, although possibly lacking collegiate education, was highly competent. He was a native of England and was fifty-four years old when he arrived in America.

At the Academy he attracted so many pupils that he was given two assistants. As Franklin was quick to realize, he was a find for the new institution, but in less than three years he fell out with the board. After that he taught in a private coeducational school and had two boys who were to be famous, Richard Peters and Alexander Graydon, among his pupils. From the *Memoir* left by Graydon we learn that it was Dove's practice in his school to substitute disgrace for corporal punishment. This took the form of sticking the rod under the collar and part way down the pupil's back while the other end projected above his head. Thus decorated, the culprit had to stand on a bench for a period supposed to be proportionate to his offense. After a time Dove accepted the position of English teacher in the Germantown Union School, which had been founded to compete with the Philadelphia Academy; but he soon resigned to set up his own school next door to the Union School in order to better compete with that rival. Dove was also a forceful, sarcastic writer and a skillful etcher, but with all his talents he lacked one talent, that of cooperating with others.

At the close of the colonial period, John Poor (1752–1829), a graduate of Harvard, became the head of "the justly famous Young Ladies' Academy" in Philadelphia where he worked from 1787 to 1809. This school, according to Professor Thomas Woody, drew pupils from several states and foreign countries and received a charter in 1792, "the first encouragement of the sort given to girls' education in the United States." It was at this school in 1787 that Benjamin Rush delivered his address, "Thoughts on Female Education."

While these and other immigrants from England and New England and from the continent of Europe were creating the beginnings of a new education in Philadelphia, a devoted elementary teacher in the country nearby was writing an early book on education, one of the first to be composed in America. This was Christopher Dock (c. 1698–1771), "the pious schoolmaster on the Skippack." He came to Pennsylvania about 1710 or later, from Germany; and sometime in the following decade he opened a school among the Mennonites of Montgomery County. Part of the time he had two schools, teaching three days of each week at Salford and the

other three at Skippack. As a device for motivating work in composition
he had the pupils of each school write letters to those of the other school.
He served as the carrier. His book on education, called *Schulordnung*
(1770), deals with manners, morals, piety, and schoolkeeping. He was himself noted for simplicity, piety, and a gentle disposition. In regard to discipline he had the arresting thought that the teacher should find the cause
of misconduct and should treat that rather than the symptoms. The early
schoolmaster on the Skippack has as secure a place in the educational
history of that time as the teachers of applied mathematics and the
languages.

The preceding paragraphs on a few teachers of the private school era
will be of some help in finding the answer to questions raised in Chapter
1 about the characters and qualifications of colonial teachers. But not too
much weight must be placed upon a few examples; and the collection of
all possible information would not provide the data for wide and safe
generalizations. It must always be remembered that most teachers were
"humble folk," like most farmers, housewives, mechanics, and other people
of the lower middle class. They left little information about themselves
and attracted little attention from others. Some things, however, we may
infer and a few things we may know.

We know that teaching was a highly competitive business without
regulating legislation or supervision, and without any great number of
endowed or chartered schools to set standards for the emulation of the wise
and honest. The first colleges in the four middle colonies of New York,
New Jersey, Pennsylvania, and Maryland came into operation in the
middle of the eighteenth century. Before that time there were few good
grammar schools in these colonies. Neither colleges nor grammar schools
had considered any change in method or curricula to meet the needs of
the people more adequately. It was the private schools such as those named
previously that attempted to prepare youth for an active life in a new
country. The chief controlling and directing force among these was competition. Teachers in their advertisements exploited their advantages of
experience and education; offered a far greater number of subjects than
they could teach in any one term; and claimed to be the inventors or the
heirs of new methods capable of performing miracles of facile instruction.

Long experience as a teacher and practical experience on Atlantic voy-
ages were reasons advanced by Andrew Lamb why the public should continue to patronize his teaching of navigation. His statement that his pupils
"could go as mates on their first voyage" seems questionable. Others made
more extravagant claims. At a later period N. G. Dufief claimed to have
a method by which he could "teach French" in thirty-six lessons. Others
in other subjects reduced the needed hours. The somewhat notorious James
G. Bennett advertised as follows: "It is now well-known that a complete
knowledge of bookkeeping as applied to the various branches of commer-

cial business can be acquired in twenty private lectures of one hour each. Terms, twenty dollars." Some claimed that they had enjoyed the patronage of famous persons, even that of King George II. Occasionally a letter was written to a newspaper to ridicule the extravagant claims of those who were designated as "quack teachers," or the "48-lesson man."

The usual term in the private schools was about thirteen weeks, or a quarter of a year. Fees were often collected in advance, but occasionally a teacher lost his pay because he did not hold to this rule. Seybolt quoted one man who gave as the reason for strict enforcement of the prepayment rule that he had been committed to debtor's prison because previous pupils neglected to pay their fees. One object of the society of private school-teachers founded in New York City in 1794 was to aid members in collecting delinquent bills.

Many teachers were to some extent specialists. The largest number taught the rudiments only, reading and perhaps writing and arithmetic. But there were those who taught mainly mathematical subjects, or one or more languages, or the various kinds of spoken and written English, or perhaps only penmanship. The teaching of penmanship was almost a profession in itself. The number of different "hands" was legion. One man offered to teach the Round Text hand, the ledger, the plain or ornamental Italian, the ordinary running hand, and also the Roman, Italic, Old English, German Text, and other hands, as well as embellishing and flourishing. Fancy penmanship was an "accomplishment." The academic subjects and especially mathematics and its applications were divided into many subdivisions. In a single announcement, a teacher might offer to teach as many as twenty-five separate subjects. It is not known how large the classes were, how many classes a teacher undertook to meet in one term, or how many times they met each week. The academy inherited many of the characteristics of the private schools that had prepared the way for it.

FRANKLIN'S PLANS FOR AN ACADEMY

The academy was a transitional institution bridging the differences between the Latin school, the private school of the colonial cities, and the public high school. It shared some of the characteristics of each of these. This transition was to a large extent accomplished by 1876 when the National Centennial was celebrated. A hundred years earlier there had been very few academies. In 1876 there were thousands, but many were yielding to the encroachments of the high school. Meanwhile, the academy had also become a preparatory institution and helped to transmit to the high school its twofold function of preparing pupils for direct entrance upon life or for admission to college. Thus there have been three main types of American secondary schools: the classical or Latin grammar school from the settlements to the Revolution; the academy from the Revolution to the Civil War or somewhat beyond, perhaps to 1876; and the high school to the present. Schools of all of those types are still in operation.

When fully mature, the academy was a middle school that was governed under a state charter by a board of trustees, with a broad realist curriculum loosely held together. But common usage does not always follow this definition. Many schools called academies were never chartered, and many taught Latin and Greek as well as realist subjects. Many preparatory schools attached to colleges were also called academies. One might say that in popular speech any semiprivate or wholly private secondary school is an academy, and in New York and a few other states several public high schools still retain their former title of academy. This is an example of the loose use of terms in education; and for this there seems to be no easy cure. The conclusion is that ideally an academy is the kind of institution defined at the beginning of this paragraph, but that practically it may diverge in various ways from the ideal.

Several new educational opportunities were provided by the private schools and academies. They offered instruction above the elements to girls of the middle classes. This was a real advance, and in this America was a pioneer. Elementary home economics was taught in an early girls' academy. Some schools gave instruction in methods of teaching and school management, providing professional preparation for teaching to boys and girls before there were any normal schools. Handwriting, commercial arithmetic, and bookkeeping were taught to young business people. Some academies were established by religious denominations. Some were boarding schools. It is evident that the academy was an experimental institution tending to become an all-purpose school, but developing without overall planning.

One attempt to provide a reasoned design was made by Benjamin Franklin about the middle of the eighteenth century. His *Proposals Relating to the Education of Youth in Pennsylvania* (1749) came out several years before William Smith's *Mirania* and long before Dock's *Schulordnung*. The *Proposals* was only a pamphlet but it was a significant publication on education as a special subject; and it led to a practical result, the founding of the Philadelphia Academy. This was its object.

Franklin had already founded a reading club, the mother, as he claimed, of those subscription libraries that formed the reading tastes of his countrymen, "and made tradesmen and farmers as intelligent as the gentry of other countries." Out of his junto the American Philosophical Society grew, a learned body on the order of the Royal Society of London. This has shown the vitality of several of Franklin's creations. Thirty years ago this Society, which was organized by Franklin in 1743 "for the promotion of useful knowledge among the British plantations in America," celebrated the completion of its second century. It is a scientific rather than, in the present sense of the word, a philosophical society. It has always had famous names on its rolls; and among the earliest were Doctor Thomas Bond, who was a pupil of John Kearsley; John Bartram, botanist; and Thomas Godfrey, mathematician and maker of astronomical instruments. In the promotion of his reading club, library, and learned society, Franklin did not meet the opposition that dogged his academy project.

The *Proposals* was not intended to be original in idea, but only in its demand that the idea should be put to work. Franklin's chief purpose was to show that the idea was not new but was reasonable, widely accepted as an idea, and should be acted upon. He named and quoted the great writers who had supported his views, particularly John Locke, no doubt because he was read and approved in America. All this was to show that this idea was not the effect of a chance inspiration, nor the plan of an educational amateur, but was one developed by experienced teachers and educational philosophers. He stated the realist as opposed to the classical position in education, but he could not point to many institutions such as he had in mind. The first German *Realschule* had been opened in Berlin only two years earlier, but of this he was unaware. He did not refer to the Puritan academies in England, perhaps because his plan differed from their practice.

What was to be taught was the main topic of the pamphlet. Twenty or more subjects were proposed. Most of these can be placed under three major heads and their subdivisions, English, mathematics, and history. Franklin's concern with history is the outstanding fact here, for English and mathematics were the leading subjects in the private schools. The proposal to teach history was new; and the history was to be the "new history" of morals, customs, commerce, practical arts, and religion, not merely the old history of war and politics. He supported the realist demand for concrete teaching aids. The subjects may be set down in semitabular form as follows:

Physical exercises, running, jumping, wrestling, swimming
Handwriting, drawing with perspective
Arithmetic, accounts, geometry, astronomy (no algebra)
English as a language, grammar, literature
History, ancient, modern, English, the new universal history
Geography with maps
Oratory, debating
Logic
Morality, "benignity of mind, religion, studied historically . . . the
    excellence of the Christian religion and proofs of Divine Providence"
Natural history, gardening, agriculture, and, according to individual
    taste and need, languages ancient and modern.

This is a realist curriculum. Franklin meant to provide an educational program suitable for the commercial and productive classes. Bacon had said that knowledge is for delight and power. Franklin attempted to increase the delight and power, especially the latter, of merchants, mechanics, and active men in general. He placed great emphasis upon skill in the use of the English language, a lesson that he had learned in his work as a printer and in his experience in persuading his fellow townsmen to good works.

To administer the program he urged the formation of an academy with a charter and a board of trustees. The *Proposals* dealt with the location of the building, the grounds and lands, and the equipment and apparatus. Not all of his proposals were accepted. The academy did not, as he had intended, become a boarding school, nor did it adopt a school uniform for the pupils. The trustees may not have taken the personal interest in the pupils that Franklin desired. Educational tradition was too strong for him. His associates insisted upon a classical course in the academy parallel to the realist program. After instructor David James Dove left, the English course faltered. The institution became mainly a Latin school to prepare students for the College of Philadelphia, which was opened in 1755. Franklin's exposure of the bad faith, as it seemed to him, of the trustees in devitalizing his realist program was one of the last acts of his life, and shows how dear to him that program was.

While the academy was still in the formative stage Franklin distributed his *Idea of an English School*, a paper of ten or twelve pages. This was an exposition of Franklin's central idea. In it he outlined the work to be done in each of the six years that he proposed for boys eight years old who had already acquired the arts of reading and writing. No place was given to foreign languages. In the *Proposals* they had been named at the end for those who should need them; from the *Idea* they were omitted. In this period Franklin still believed that he could win general support for his English school by making concessions to the Latinists. This was a mistake to be expected of an inexperienced person, and Franklin should have known better.

The *Constitutions* of the Philadelphia Academy provided for both a classical school or department and an English-mathematical one. The classical master was made rector of the entire institution, thus placing the English-mathematical master and his school in subordinate positions; and his salary was set at double the amount paid the English master. The fate of the English school has already been indicated. When the academy became an appendage to the college, it was felt by some that an English School was wholly out of place in the collegiate environment.

Just before the college was established, the Reverend William Smith was chosen to teach in the classical school of the academy in May, 1754. He had been educated at the University of Aberdeen and had been a schoolmaster in Scotland. In America he published a pamphlet called

A *General Idea of the College of Mirania*. In this essay he gave considerable support to Franklin's scheme for an academy; but it does not appear that he tried to promote the English school, especially after March, 1755, when he became head of the college with the title of provost. For whatever reasons, the English school became an elementary school for little children. The chief reasons were not the absence of Franklin, the connection with the college, the appointment of the classically trained provost, or the higher salary of the classics master in the academy. The chief reason was one that even Franklin could not overcome. People just did not believe that an education without Latin was real education. An English education might do for shopkeepers and mechanics who, it was thought, were probably not capable of taking a high polish anyway. It required a hundred years to convince the larger public of this error.

SUMMARY

Education above the elementary grades was not often open to girls in the colonies. Advanced education was to be broad and liberal. Only the private schools aimed to teach what was directly useful in practical life. Classical education was based upon those ancient literary works that scholars considered the best of their kinds because they deal with universal topics, in a restrained and logical manner, and in elevated language.

Latin schools and colleges, coming out of a long European history, supplied this kind of education. When they were transplanted, the early enthusiasm for the "new learning" had already declined; and the later interest in ancient culture, philosophy, art, and economics had not yet arisen. In the interval these institutions were largely grammatical and stylistic institutes. The Latin schools were most numerous in New England, where they were town schools, but even in New England they were not popular in the more rural parts. In the rest of the colonies the Latin schools were usually private and often temporary. The curriculum everywhere consisted mainly of Latin grammar and authors and the elements of the Greek language.

The colonial colleges continued these studies and added Hebrew, academic disputation, medieval mathematics and science, and theology. Their primary purpose was the preparation of ministers, but a majority of the students followed other vocations. The students lived a meager collegiate life under the close supervision of the college officers. Disorder was common, in reaction to the close surveillance, poor teaching, and unattractive living conditions.

The conflict between the older classical and the rising realist education grew out of various causes. There was social discrimination favoring the classically educated professional classes and against those in the practical vocations. The belief in the superior disciplinary effects of classical studies was met with skepticism. It was pointed out that many college men were impractical theorists and dreamers. The needs of a new country were set against the long and honorable history of classical education. Realism was brought in from abroad in the ideas of Comenius, Locke, and William Penn. Penn in several ways anticipated Franklin who, however, cited other authorities.

Private realistic schools were numerous in the cities in the last colonial century. They taught modern languages, practical knowledge and skills, and the applications of mathematics to navigation and engineering. A few examples illustrate the nature of these schools and also illustrate what is well known, that some of the teachers were both able and eminent. These private schools prepared the way for the American academy; and Franklin's creation must be considered an example of an institution that was too far ahead of the time for success.

QUESTIONS

1. Why did the colonists transplant classical schools instead of creating new upper schools more appropriate to American needs?
2. What kinds of schools should they have established for those able to stay in school to age fourteen? until age eighteen?
3. Why were girls excluded from all education except the most elementary? Consider traditional reasons and taboos, economic factors, notions about family government, health, the distribution of intelligence, and any others.
4. Would you argue that education for women is more important on the frontier than in a developed country?
5. Prepare a report on the teachers of the Boston Latin School. What general conclusions may and what may not be drawn from your report? Use the *History* by Pauline Holmes and other books.
6. Why did American Latin schools fail to reach the standards of those in England?
7. What factors aided and what retarded the development of realist schools? Consider among several others the scientific activity of the Middle Colonies.
8. Compare the early William Penn Charter School with Franklin's academy. Use James Mulhern's *History of Secondary Education in Pennsylvania,* Thomas Woody's *Educational Views of Benjamin Franklin,* Wickersham's *History of Education in Pennsylvania,* the *Dictionary of American Biography,* and other books.
9. What were the salient features of Franklin's plan? How original was his scheme?

BOOKS AND PAPERS

There are many histories of individual colleges but there is space to list only one of the better ones, Morison on Harvard. Some college histories are poor because they include much trivial material, are badly written, or are too distended, running to so many volumes in some cases that no one will read them. We have at least one good history of a Latin school, that by Pauline Holmes, listed as follows.

BRIDENBAUGH, CARL, *Cities in the Wilderness, 1625–1742,* New York, 1938.

BROWN, E. E., *Making of Our Middle Schools,* New York, 1905.

COON, C. L., *North Carolina Schools and Academies, 1790–1840, A Documentary History,* Raleigh, 1915.

ELSBREE, W. S., *The American Teacher,* New York, 1939.

FITHIAN, PHILIP VICKERS, *Journal and Letters . . . 1773–1774, A Plantation Tutor of the Old Dominion,* edited by H. D. Farish, Williamsburg, Virginia, 1943.

FORCE, PETER, ed., *Tracts and Other Papers,* Washington, D.C., 1938. The "Advisive Narrative" is No. 15, Vol. III.

HOLMES, PAULINE, *History of the Boston Public Latin School, 1635–1935,* Harvard University Press, 1935.

HORNBERGER, THEODORE, *Scientific Thought in the American Colleges, 1638–1800,* University of Texas Press, 1945.

KRAUS, MICHAEL, *Intercolonial Aspects of American Culture,* Columbia University Press, 1928.

MIDDLEKAUFF, ROBERT, *Ancients and Axioms,* Yale University Press, 1963.

MORISON, SAMUEL ELIOT, *Three Centuries of Harvard, 1636–1936,* Cambridge, Harvard University Press, 1936.

POTTER, DAVID, *Debating in the Colonial Chartered Colleges, 1642–1800,* New York, Teachers College, Columbia University, 1944.

ROACH, HELEN P., *History of Speech Education at Columbia University, 1754–1949.* New York, Bureau of Publications, Teachers College, Columbia University, 1950.

SMALL, W. H., *Early New England Schools,* Boston, 1914.

SMITH, WILLIAM, *The Works of William Smith, Late Provost, College of Philadelphia,* Philadelphia, 1803, containing "A General Idea of the College of Mirania."

THWING, C. F., *History of Higher Education in America,* New York, 1906.

UHL, W. L., *Secondary School Curricula,* New York, 1927.

WERTENBAKER, T. J., *The Puritan Oligarchy,* New York, 1947, containing a somewhat more favorable view of Puritan institutions than that expressed in the same author's *The First Americans* (1927).

WOODY, THOMAS, *History of Women's Education in the United States* (2 vols.), Lancaster, Pennsylvania, 1929; and editor of *Educational Views of Benjamin Franklin* (New York, 1931), which contains the chief educational writings of Franklin, but his paper "On the Usefulness of Mathematics" is reprinted in D. E. Smith and J. Ginsberg, *History of Mathematics in America,* Chicago, 1934.

Part II

AWAKENING
AND
CRUSADE

Preview

In Part II we see the Awakening of the American people to education as
a legitimate function of government and the beginnings of a Crusade for
independent state systems of education comprising the kindergarten, the
elementary school, the high school, and the university. This American
dream was to provide an equality of opportunity for all pupils to climb an
educational ladder rung on rung extending from the gutter to the university at public expense. This was necessary because a republican state
requires an enlightened public opinion, as Washington expressed the need;
and to maintain individual liberty and civil rights as Jefferson maintained.
By the close of the Civil War most of the northern states had developed
the outlines of their unitary systems of public schools, and the southern
states had made similar progress toward parallel systems of public schools,
one set of schools for the white and another for the black children.

Chapter 3

LIBERTY AND LEARNING

Contemporaries noted that the American Revolution began before the Revolutionary War and continued after the peace. Some attempted to trace its origins from the Reformation or from the "glorious revolution" of the English Whigs in 1688. Whatever the origins, its effects were felt in Britain, in France, even in Russia, and it promoted freedom for most of Latin America.

The greatest effects of the Revolution were felt in British America where it led to the founding of an independent nation, the United States of America. The adoption of the federal principle was a happy inspiration, for instead of exploiting the territories it gave them the assurance and the method of becoming states equal to the oldest in the Union. The federal court provided for a single system of justice in the entire land. The separation of church and state forestalled all fear of religious wars.

National unity was increased by the free movement of goods and persons from state to state. Jefferson proposed the decimal system of coinage, and Nicholas Pike's *Arithmetic*, "for the use of the citizens of the United States," introduced it into schools and won the praise of Washington. Noah Webster proposed the use of an American language instead of the English, but since the two were nearly identical this had no very momentous results. He did produce *An American Dictionary of the English Language*. The painters began to use American subjects and writers tried to create an American literature.

The educational thinkers of the Revolution and the following years were led by Jefferson, Benjamin Rush, Robert Coram, James Sullivan, Noah Webster, Pierre Samuel Du Pont de Nemours, Samuel Knox, and Samuel Harrison Smith; and many of these and of the founders of the nation saw the problem of education as a political question and treated it as a phase of public policy. Education in their view was a means of preserving liberty, securing unity, promoting good citizenship, and developing the resources of the land and people. Education would help maintain the union of states, a united people, and a republican government.

77

Not all of the writers of the early years were wise, and some of their thought was ill-timed. There was abroad a wrong idea that a national system of education under centralized federal control was both feasible and desirable. There was inadequate understanding of the principle that successful school-systems must grow in intimate connection with the societies that they serve. This generalization is illustrated by many con- temporary national systems, the English, the French, and even the Russian, each of which has conformed to the social conditions of its country. Recent Russian history does not contradict the principle. It was the liberal educa- tion of the early 1920's that conflicted with Russian history; it is the present authoritarian system that agrees best with Russian autocracy, past and present. In the new United States with its individualism, localism, states' rights, and denominationalism, a centralized school system should not have been so much as thought of.

Many new trends revealed themselves and old ones continued in the Revolutionary and early national periods. Numerous colleges were estab- lished by the religious denominations. Efforts were made during the war and afterward to change some of the older colleges into state institutions. A new state university movement led to the creation of twenty or more such institutions before the Civil War. But even with the support of George Washington the national university idea could not be realized in an actual institution. The federal government began to make grants of land to the states for state universities and for elementary schools. Local efforts and state constitutions and laws made provision for public elemen- tary education in the early national period; and the public high school began to dispute the ground occupied by the academy. Several of these topics are discussed in the next section and the others will be taken up in the following chapters.

TWO THEORIES

For some time after the Revolutionary War, activity in higher education far exceeded that in the development of the common schools. There are several reasons for this. The children of the poor did not have time to attend school for extended periods. The colleges appealed to the well-to-do, they had a fixed curriculum, and they prepared professional people. Work- ingmen's sons would be workingmen and, it was thought, they needed little schooling. The population was scattered and it was difficult to gather small children into schools. Colleges and academies were often boarding insti- tutions. Finally, those most active in school promotion were college-trained and naturally favored the kind of education that they themselves had enjoyed.

Another phenomenon of the post-Revolutionary and early national periods that needs to be explained is the feverish American borrowing of foreign ideas and practices. This seems to be in conflict with the prevailing nationalism. Before the Civil War the United States introduced French military education at West Point, French methods in civil engineering education, and with British help the new French mathematical methods. French systems of teaching the deaf and the blind were borrowed. England supplied the monitorial schools; but these were shortly superseded by the Pestalozzian doctrines from Switzerland and Germany. Another Swiss, Fellenberg, contributed the manual labor system, which had a brief vogue. The American normal school, largely a native development, was influenced by various European examples. This list could be made longer.

No doubt there are several reasons for this American receptivity. The new nation was educationally underdeveloped and there was need for institutions to cope with growing requirements. With the struggle for independence and its achievement came greater exposure to foreign practices. The alliance with France, a country with a highly developed special and technological education, was a factor. Travel and books contributed. Educationally the mother country was in one of her most unprogressive periods at the time when the colonies revolted. The mere fact of separation may have been a positive influence toward borrowing from Europe rather than Britain.

FOUNDING FATHERS AT SCHOOL

One way to build a bridge from the colonial to the national period is to answer the question: What schooling was received by those who lived during the transition? This will be to leave abstractions and to turn to facts. Our bridge will not be a very wide one because the known facts about the individual farmers, frontiersmen, workers, and housewives are not abundant. We do know something about the education of many of those who were leaders in the Revolution and in the framing of the government. But these were not average men. They were all unusual at least in this, that they were in positions of national importance at critical times. We shall examine the schooling of those who signed any one of three political documents, the Declaration of Independence, the Articles of Confederation, and the Constitution of the United States.

Two men, Robert Morris and Roger Sherman, signed all three of these documents and a number signed two of them. There are 117 different names attached to the instruments. All of the colonies were, of course, represented. With few exceptions these leaders were born in the first half of the century of decision and none later than 1760. The oldest was Benjamin Franklin, born in 1706, and the youngest was Jonathan Dayton of New Jersey who was only twenty-seven when he served in the Constitutional Convention.

The educational opportunities of the period from about 1712 to 1782 have been considered in a general way in the preceding chapters. The particular information about the education of these signers comes from the *Dictionary of American Biography* and similar sources. Their opportunities ranged from almost none to the best that America and Europe together could offer. It probably is significant that the signers of the earliest document, the Declaration, had received appreciably less schooling than either of the other groups. The movers for independence were not mainly upperclass people. Franklin recorded that he attended school for two years. About one-third of his colleagues in the Congress of 1776 had attended only country schools or had been mainly self-taught. There were some such in each of the other groups but in smaller proportions. Those with little formal education came from every section and had used their opportunities in various ways. Stephen Hopkins of Rhode Island, a farm boy, became a practical surveyor and learned politics as moderator of town meetings. Roger Sherman of Connecticut was apprenticed to a shoemaker and became successively a writer, publisher, and lawyer. John Penn of North Carolina attended a country school and read law in books borrowed from a friend. Others read medical books and helped a doctor in his practice. Mercantile careers, especially when they were not too successful, gave leisure to read.

At the opposite end of the range there were thirty-eight graduates of American colleges, the larger numbers from Harvard, Yale, Princeton, and Pennsylvania. Jefferson graduated from William and Mary and Gouverneur Morris from Columbia. The ages of the whole group at graduation ranged from fifteen to twenty-four years. James Madison stayed at Princeton for a year after graduation to study ethics and theology under Witherspoon. Two of these college graduates went abroad to study medicine, Benjamin Rush at Edinburgh and Hugh Williamson at Utrecht.

Others of the founding fathers had studied in the secondary schools or the ancient universities of England, or had read law in the Middle Temple, which was in effect a law school. Most of these, as noted before, were Southerners, chiefly South Carolinians. Few were given such extended opportunities as came to Charles Cotesworth Pinckney of Charleston. After working at home with the aid of a tutor, he was sent to Westminster School, matriculated at Oxford where he heard Blackstone, entered the Middle Temple, and wound up in France where he studied botany and chemistry under leading scientists, and military science in a royal military academy at Caen. Charles and Daniel Carroll of Maryland, Richard Henry Lee of Virginia, and William H. Drayton of South Carolina also were educated in Europe. Two famous Scotsmen who belong to the signers, John Witherspoon and James Wilson, were educated in their native land.

Our bridge is narrow and somewhat frail, and we must resist the temptation to draw a heavy load of conclusions over it. It is safe to say that many of these 117 signers were exceptional. Such men create opportunities. Schools are useful even to the most gifted, more useful than to the less gifted; but they are not indispensable. One of every three of these statesmen had only a few months of schooling, usually in poor schools; and one in four had a college education.

LIBERTY BEGINS IN THE MIND

The principles of liberty and of public education in a free country are complementary. To study the origins of public education in the United States one must examine the American doctrine of liberty. Thomas Jefferson always declared, whenever the subject came up in his later years, that in writing the Declaration of Independence it had been no part of his purpose to aim at originality. That would have defeated his purpose. The sentiment of the document, he said (with considerable exaggeration) to one who had asked, "was the sentiment of all America." Men would certainly not have risked their lives and honor upon that sentiment if it had not been their own.

The Declaration is, therefore, a primary source for the principles of liberty that the Americans of 1776 intended to maintain. The fundamental principle was this, that governments derive their just powers from the consent of the governed. The patriots considered self-government a natural right, guaranteed by the law of nature. This Jefferson asserted.

Two years before the Declaration, Jefferson had written a *Summary View of the Rights of British America*, and its contents may help to explain why he was chosen to write the Declaration of Independence. In the *Summary View* he held that the king was only the chief officer of the people and that he had only those powers that the laws gave him. For the people he claimed the "natural right" to emigrate and to establish a new society with such laws as they believed would conduce to their happiness.

The ruling political theory of the time was that of the law of nature and the social compact. Early man was thought to have lived in a state of nature without organized society or government or public order. Men maintained themselves by craft and force. They overcame the brutishness of such a condition by a compact in which the many promised cooperation to each other and loyalty to a ruler in exchange for the promise of orderly processes of security and justice. Thus was a political society created in which all were in a sense equal. Rulers governed by consent and, according to John Locke, remained rulers only as long as they kept their part of the compact. If either party failed to keep the compact, mankind, it was held, would revert to a state of nature and a new beginning would be in order. There was discussion both in 1776 and 1787, each a revolutionary era, whether the country was not then in a state of nature.

These ideas were current in the ancient world and some of them may be found in Plato's *Republic*; but they were developed for England and America by John Locke and later in Europe by Jean Jacques Burlamaqui (1694–1748), a Swiss jurist whose *Principles of Natural Law* was translated into English in the last year of the author's life. A Philadelphia historian, Sidney G. Fisher, wrote "To this day anyone going to the Philadelphia Library and asking for No. 77 can take into his hands the identical, well-worn volume which delegates to the Congress read with earnest, anxious minds." The reference is to the library of the Philadelphia Library Company, of which Franklin was the leading founder.

These exponents of natural law held that the pursuit of happiness and therefore of self-development is a right inherent in all men; that civil equality, equal standing before the law, and equal treatment by the courts are simple attributes of citizenship; that the people themselves have the right to frame a government and laws that will promote these great ends. And they held that these principles were not invented but were discovered in the nature of men and written on the human heart.

The application of this philosophy to education is not difficult. It declares that social institutions must preserve and not infringe upon the natural equality of human beings. That equality is infringed when the wealthy and the well-born are given opportunities to mature their talents that are denied to poor children, lacking an address and a name. Schools cannot make people alike in attainment; but they must open to all every opportunity for growth and acquirement.

The founders of the United States realized that the liberties of the citizen are jeopardized if he does not early acquire the understanding of those rights and the intelligence to maintain them. They say that it is through education that he must gain this knowledge and training. They understood that unless the rule of the people leads to prosperity, happiness, and justice, that unless they rule wisely they will lose the chance to rule at all. With such a philosophy the nation's stake in a sound and freely accessible education is obvious.

How gradually this political philosophy was transmitted from the leaders to the people and applied to education is a great part of the following story. Only slowly did it become clear that this doctrine not only justifies but requires a complete system of public schools equally open to all. Eventually it was admitted that this places upon the legislature the duty "to provide by law for a general system of education ascending in a regular gradation from township schools to a State University, wherein tuition shall be gratis and equally open to all." This is the language of the first (1816) constitution of Indiana; but its demand was not soon to be achieved and has not yet been achieved everywhere and for all.

The federal Constitution does not deal with education, but its indirect influences upon education have been manifold and profound. Most profound has been the doctrine of reserved powers stated in the Tenth Amendment. This has not only left education to the states as a reserved power but it has served to warn off the federal government from interference with education in the states. It has not served to prevent Congress from distributing aid to education in the states, chiefly aid in vocational fields. This power to distribute educational funds implies the power to withhold them and thus to control education in the states by indirection. The First Amendment, dealing with religion and with freedom of communication; the Fourteenth Amendment with its "due process" clause; the power to maintain a postal system and to promote science and the useful arts; the powers assigned to the Supreme Court or developed by it; the general welfare clause (I, 8) and the taxing power—all and sundry have been used in ways that have influenced education in the states. Attention is to be given also to the provision of the Constitution that "the United States shall guarantee to every State in this Union a republican form of government" (IV, 4). The question arises whether such a form of government can be maintained without a system of public education. This question that may have seemed academic earlier may yet become practical. The racial desegregation decision of the Supreme Court of 1954 may make it so. But in the past and in the main, public education has been a state function, based upon state constitutions and laws.

The states have allowed considerable freedom to the local divisions. Communities that desire to go beyond the minimal requirements of the state law have an open road. But there are strict state requirements and controls. On the other hand, the whole system is gradually becoming more uniform over the nation. The trend toward a national school system is persistent. Whether direct federal requirements and controls will eventually be developed cannot be known now.

EDUCATION IN THE STATE CONSTITUTIONS

The new state constitutions contained the earliest official statements on education in the evolving nation. Two months before independence was declared the Continental Congress advised the people of the colonies to form their governments. In ten of the colonies, this was done promptly. Connecticut and Rhode Island merely altered their charters; and Massachusetts, delayed by partisan struggles, adopted a new constitution in 1780.

Provisions on education were included in six of the eleven new constitutions. These paragraphs were moderate in their demands; but to have included them at all was an advance upon the thought of earlier times, when the state, which speaks for all the people, was not expected to speak or act in regard to education. Educational provisions in the new constitutions are evidence that the political philosophy analyzed previously was at work in this field. They are evidence that the states were beginning to sense the necessity of education for citizenship and public service.

Those beginnings were moderate. Pennsylvania in 1776 adopted one of the most radical of the new constitutions. It provided for a unicameral legislature and assigned to it the power to elect the governor. But the educational clause, Section 44, provided only that "a school or schools shall be established in every county by the legislature, for the convenient instruction of youth with such salaries to the masters, paid by the public, as may enable them to instruct youth at low prices; and all useful learning shall be duly encouraged and promoted in one or more universities."

By adopting this section the state acknowledged a duty to promote education but it did nothing more. One school in each county, the minimal demand, would have served only a minute fraction of the people; and the legislature could choose its own time to act. It did; it chose not to act. The schools were not to be free but the constitution did not say whether the salaries were to be paid by the state, county, or other unit. The last part of the clause may have given warrant for the seizure of the College of Philadelphia, to be described as follows. This timid educational section was copied by other states. Omitting a few unimportant words, it was incorporated in the North Carolina constitution of 1776; in substance in the constitutions of Vermont and Georgia in 1777; and it may have influenced the Missouri constitution of 1820.

The central idea of all these provisions was that the state should supplement private facilities. There was no thought of universal public schooling. And before the end of the war the people began to grow more conservative, a trend that frequently shows itself in the later phases of a revolutionary movement. As the early constitutions were revised toward the end of the century, provision was made for the education of the poor only. The second constitution of Pennsylvania (1790) asked the legislature to provide free education for the poor, and the constitutions adopted in 1798 by Georgia and Delaware were even less explicit.

The financial stringency and the mounting state debts in the war and afterward made the legislatures even more cautious. There was a tendency for constitutional provisions on education to become long, eloquent, and indefinite. This is notably the case with the constitution adopted in 1780, after a heated struggle, by the state that led all the rest in education, Massachusetts. John Adams wrote the educational sections. He began with a historical introduction celebrating the "wise and pious ancestors" who had founded Harvard, and "divers persons" who had added to its endowment, and he praised the constitution and powers of the corporation and the overseers of the college. The rights and powers of Harvard are duly confirmed. The next section declares that "wisdom and knowledge as well as virtue" are necessary to self-government, and finally it calls upon the legislatures and magistrates to cherish "literature and the sciences and all seminaries of them. . . ." Four years later New Hampshire, which had omitted education from its first constitution in 1776, incorporated in its revised instrument some of the ideas just quoted from the constitution of its southern neighbor.

The flowing phrases of Adams have sometimes imposed upon historians of education the belief that these provisions were far "ahead of the general conceptions of the time." This is a mistake. Adams himself in a letter written twenty-five years later said with truth and candor that the words had come from his heart rather than his head. A more compact and eloquent but possibly derivative statement of the same general thought was incorporated into the Northwest Ordinance of 1787, and was admired and copied into legal documents in various states. It read: "Religion, morality, and knowledge being necessary to good government and the happiness of mankind, schools and the means of education shall forever be encouraged" by the legislatures. Few or none would doubt that this is a good sentiment; but as law it leaves out the essential elements.

JEFFERSON'S PLAN

The Virginia "bill for the more general diffusion of knowledge" that Jefferson prepared in 1779 provided for a primary school in every "hundred," a unit comparable to a township. These schools were to be publicly controlled and in part publicly supported. Children could attend without charge for three years, and longer by paying tuition. Reading, writing, arithmetic, and the history of Greece, Rome, England, and America were to be the subjects of instruction. The Bible, commonly read in schools at that time, was not mentioned, and Jefferson was against putting the Bible "into the hands of children at an age when their judgments are not sufficiently matured."

Because, in his view, the reasoning powers did not develop much before the age of fifteen, Jefferson considered memory work most appropriate for children. All free children, boys and girls, living within a given hundred were, as we have seen, to receive free instruction in its school for the term of three years and afterwards at private expense as long as might be desired. For every ten schools there was to be an overseer, "eminent for his learning, integrity, and fidelity to the commonwealth." He was to appoint the teachers and supervise the schools. In the bill the space for the teachers' salaries was left blank.

The bill of 1779 provided for twenty secondary schools distributed throughout the state. Bright boys selected from the primary schools were to be given two or more years of free education in the classics, English grammar, geography, and arithmetic through cube root. Capable pupils were to be retained for the full six-year course of secondary schooling. From those who were culled out, teachers for the primary schools were to be chosen. Those who attained the highest distinction in the secondary schools were to be sent to William and Mary College for a complete education, free. This selective scheme was to apply to the scholarship pupils only. Those able to pay could send their sons to school and college at their own cost and without meeting the competitive tests. The secondary schools were to be controlled by public boards of visitors.

Jefferson has been both praised and condemned for this plan of secular and public education. One opening for criticism is provided by the fact that the great Virginia democrat, who was violently anti-Platonist, devised an educational plan that has a resemblance to Plato's own. And then he provided for only three years of free education. On the latter point it is to be kept in mind that Virginia had no system of schools nor any effective public opinion in favor of establishing one. Three years of free schooling was not all that Jefferson might have desired, but as a skillful politician he knew it was unwise to ask for more. Even the selective feature can be defended. In extending educational privileges to new classes, some kind of selection has throughout history been very often used. Too often selection has been based upon wealth or family or influence; Jefferson agreed with Plato in basing it upon merit. This defense does not meet the fundamental objection that the bill proposed class legislation in conflict with the political principles of its author. Doubtless Jefferson meant it to be the first step on the way to a system of universal public education.

It was too long a step for Virginia to take at that time and for many years. The legislature did not consider the bill in 1779; and when it was taken up in 1796 it was passed in an optional and therefore ineffective form. For thirty years after writing the bill Jefferson was engaged in politics and public service, but education became his chief public interest after his retirement. His leadership in forming the University of Virginia was exercised in this later period of his life.

Political, practical, and intellectual motives led him to devote so much attention to education. He held that education while not the only need was, in his words: "essentially necessary" in a republic. Education was useful, he saw, for increasing production, saving labor, preserving health, and especially for the improvement of agriculture, "a science of the very first order." Beyond the ever-present political issues and practical needs, Jefferson was devoted to intellectual interests. He possessed these in greater variety than almost any other American of his time. He knew by experience that learning is good not only for use but also for itself alone, that is, for personal satisfaction.

From Paris in 1786 he wrote to a friend that only an educated people could preserve their freedom and promote their own real happiness. This education, he said, "it is the business of the state to provide and that upon a general plan." To John Adams he once said that his bill of 1779 was intended "to defeat the competition of wealth and birth for public positions."

Because "the people are the best judges of local issues" and "the safest depositories of freedom," Jefferson favored local control of the primary schools. The people themselves, he said, do incomparably better than a central government what they are competent to understand. Of compelling attendance at school there was no question in America then. Once, indeed, he revealed a more urgent temper. He proposed to withhold the ballot from those who, given the opportunity, did not learn to read. John Adams disagreed.

STATESMEN AND UTOPIANS

Many of the statesmen in the new republic gave expression to their views upon education, frequently to their views on its political importance. Washington gave personal attention to the schooling of his foster children and grandchildren and even of the children of relatives and friends. He contributed to the support of schools in Alexandria and elsewhere. He urged Congress to aid in the promotion of science and literature; to establish a national military school; and to consider the proposal to create a national university. His fundamental view was stated in his first message to Congress and again in similar language in the Farewell Address in the now familiar words: "Promote, then, as an object of primary importance, institutions for the general diffusion of knowledge. In proportion as the structure of government gives force to public opinion, it is essential that public opinion should be enlightened." These we know were Washington's sentiments even though the words were supplied by Hamilton.

Education as public policy was a frequent topic with John Adams. He had a special distinction among the greater statesmen. He had been a teacher. The small town where Adams was born and where he always lived was noted for the number of students it sent to Harvard College, of which number he was one. He graduated in 1755. Undecided with regard to a profession, he became the master of a Latin school and taught for three years, but unwillingly. At twenty-three he became a lawyer and began the hard, laborious climb to eminence as an attorney, political scientist, and statesman.

Among his early publications was his study of the canon law and the feudal law, "the two great systems of tyranny" since the beginning of Christianity, so he declared. In this dissertation he asserted the rights of the poor, "for such they have, undoubtedly, antecedent to all earthly government . . . rights derived from the great Legislator of the universe." This is the concept of a higher law to which the provisions of the social compact had to conform if they were to be valid. Now Adams makes the application to education. The great, he said, keep the poor from the knowledge of their rights; and it is knowledge alone, diffused through the whole body of the people, that can preserve them from tyranny. Jefferson would not have disagreed.

The "happy condition" of Massachusetts Adams ascribed to four institutions, the town meetings, the congregations, the schools, and the militia. In his *Defence of the Constitutions of the American States* he spoke particularly of education, declaring that under a free government it is more indispensable and must be more general than under any other. All the people of every rank and class must be educated in a republic; and schools must be conveniently located and maintained at public expense. If nations ever become wise no human being will be allowed to grow up in ignorance.

That John Adams thought the educated class should rule will not surprise anyone who knows him; but he also believed that they in fact do rule. He made a little calculation on the latter point. Massachusetts, he wrote, "has probably educated as many sons to letters, in proportion to numbers, as any state in the union, perhaps as any nation ancient or modern." He calculated that over the whole period of nearly two centuries since the founding of Harvard, about one in 750 of the whole people had been graduated by the college. If this calculation is correct the proportion in Massachusetts was about three times that of all America. And what did these graduates do? They governed the province and state, they were the ministers, lawyers, physicians, and teachers, the bankers, scholars, and leaders in all lines. And they still, he declared, govern and lead. "I hope, then," he wrote to John Taylor of Caroline, "you will acknowledge that 'abilities' form a distinction and confer a privilege, in fact, though they give no peculiar rights in society."

Other political leaders expressed their views on education. Samuel Adams wished to have children in early youth taught the art of self-government and the doctrines of religion. John Jay considered "knowledge to be the soul of a republic." Madison declared that "knowledge will forever govern ignorance; and a people who mean to be their own governors must arm themselves with the power which knowledge gives." Over and over this theme is repeated. Thus Benjamin Rush: "To conform the principles, morals, and manners of our citizens to our republican forms of government it is absolutely necessary that knowledge of every kind should be disseminated through every part of the United States."

In our times of troubles before the new government was firmly established, many men who had faith in republican government and in the power of education to fit men to govern themselves became obsessed with the fear that time was running out. Men of experience in public affairs, lawyers, and public officials, such men as James Sullivan (1744–1808) of Massachusetts and Nathaniel Chipman (1752–1843) of Vermont feared that disaster might overtake the country before citizens were made aware of the dangers. They feared disunity and insurrection and the loss of public and private credit because of the general ignorance. The remedy, education, they feared would not arrive in time. It was, to borrow a twentieth-century phrase, a race between education and catastrophe.

Yet no one had a workable plan. Many plans were proposed by Robert Coram, Samuel Knox, Samuel Harrison Smith, Pierre Samuel Du Pont de Nemours, and others. But the planners did not show how the schools could be supported or administered or how the teachers could be secured. Several proposed a national system for this highly decentralized country. Many years of thought and trial were required for the solution of these essential practical problems. Meanwhile the country survived and even prospered.

THE NATIONAL UNIVERSITY IDEA

"The idea of a national university," wrote Professor Edgar B. Wesley, "has one marked characteristic; it persists." On this it would not be unfair to remark that it is only the idea that persists. The idea is old, but contrary to the opinion of some there is no trustworthy evidence that it was expressed before 1787. And there is no present indication that such an institution will be established.

The *American Museum* for January, 1787, contained an article entitled "Address to the People of the United States," written by Benjamin Rush. He favored a number of political measures that were intended to increase the power of the federal government. And he proposed, as far as known for the first time, the establishment of a "federal university." Rush defined his idea more fully in the same magazine (November, 1788) in an article that was widely copied, "Plan of a Federal University." Between these two appearances of the idea, Madison had moved in the Constitutional Convention to include among the powers of Congress the power to establish a national university; but his motion was lost. Washington took up the idea and urged it upon the attention of Congress. He bequeathed stock in a navigation company for the future endowment of the school, but this property proved valueless. Four of the first six presidents recommended the consideration of the idea to Congress. After John Quincy Adams retired, nothing more was heard of it in the national councils for forty years.

Renewed agitation began in Grant's administration and continued for many years. But again the efforts failed of reaching their object. And in the course of the century the Library of Congress, the Smithsonian Institution, the several departments of the government, and other public and private institutions have made the City of Washington a great educational and research center. Independent and state universities, the country over, perform the legitimate functions that Rush and the early leaders assigned to their proposed institution. During the height of the agitation in the latter part of the nineteenth century, several leading presidents of the larger universities were in opposition to the whole idea. Such an institution would not, however, be unique. Many Latin-American countries have national universities. But the Anglo-Saxon countries and the other nations that have influenced American education strongly do not. At present the need for federal aid to primary and secondary schools and to higher education is far more urgent than the need for a federal or national university.

COLLEGE ENTHUSIASM

No new colleges were founded in the heat of the Revolutionary struggle, but with the approach of peace many were established as if to make up for lost time. None of the oldest colleges was more than a few miles from salt water, but the people were now moving into Kentucky and Ohio. American distances were great, travel across the mountains was difficult, college expenses in Eastern towns were high, and, not least in importance, the East was becoming too liberal in its theology for the West. If the Western people were to have adequate college opportunities and the Western chuches an orthodox ministry, new institutions were needed.

New foundations were created with such speed, one after another, that President Ezra Stiles of Yale, borrowing a word from the religious vocabulary of the time, was led to speak of "college enthusiasm." Counting only the viable institutions, seventeen colleges were founded before the end of the century and twelve more by 1820. And this was only the beginning of what became a race, for, by 1860, 182 of the country's "permanent" colleges had been established. Nine out of every ten had some connection with a religious society.

Not all of the forces of that time were favorable to the colleges. On the contrary, these 182 were the survivors of a much larger number. For lack of students or funds, by reason of dissension in the faculties or the constituencies, because of bad management within or competition without, those colleges that had been unwisely established, with more zeal than calculation, died. Perhaps half of the colleges of this middle period did not survive their twentieth year.

There was also another cause. As later in the French Revolution, when the *sans culottes* thought scholars unnecessary, so in our own Revolution and afterward there were some who were against all but the most elementary education. The opposition was in part caused by a false notion of equality. Not all people could go to college; and it was held that those who did go obtained an unfair advantage over others. Robert Coram called it "a scandal to civilized society that part only of the citizens should be sent to colleges and universities to learn to cheat the rest of their liberties." John

Adams, replying to a letter from a New Jersey correspondent, J. D. Sergeant, admitted that there was everywhere "a spice" of prejudice against liberal education. "But," he said, "liberty has no enemy more dangerous" than this. Some found the reasons for this opposition in the impractical curriculum, in the vanity and pride of collegians, or in the destructive effect of a college education upon the religious faith of the students.

Fom the standpoint of the objectors there was merit in these objections. Orthodoxy was in particular danger in the late eighteenth century. The views of the Enlightenment were almost universal in some of the older colleges. Deism and materialism were widely affirmed by the students. Yale, which had been founded less than a century before because Harvard was becoming liberal, had hardly any professing Christians among her students. This was, however, a passing fashion; and to its passing the new president inaugurated at Yale in 1795 made a contribution. This president was Timothy Dwight (1752–1817).

Table 3–1 contains the names of seventeen colleges, now reduced to sixteen, founded between the close of the Revolutionary War and the end of the century. Most of these were frontier institutions. They were located on the second American frontier beginning in Maine, passing through western Vermont and Massachusetts, touching a few points in central New

TABLE 3–1
COLLEGES OF THE EARLY NATIONAL PERIOD

Earlier Names	Present Names	First Charter	First Degrees
Washington College	Washington College	1782	1783
Liberty Hall Academy	Washington and Lee University	1782	1785
Hampden-Sidney College	Hampden-Sidney College	1783	1786
Transylvania Seminary	Transylvania College	1783	1790
Dickinson College	Dickinson College	1783	1787
St. John's College	St. John's College	1784	1793
University of Georgia (Franklin College)	University of Georgia	1785	1804
Franklin College, 1787 Marshall College, 1836	Franklin and Marshall College	1787	1853
University of North Carolina	University of North Carolina	1789	1798
University of Vermont	University of Vermont	1791	1804
Williams College	Williams College	1793	1795
Bowdoin College	Bowdoin College	1794	1806
Greeneville College	Tusculum College	1794	1808
Blount College	University of Tennessee	1794	1806
Union College	Union College (Schenectady)	1795	1800
Middlebury College	Middlebury College	1800	1802

York and Pennsylvania, and spreading out into a great Appalachian triangle with its base in Georgia and Tennessee. This pressing of the colleges upon new and newer frontiers was to be repeated again and again as the people moved westward. Because the institutions founded in decades before and after 1800 were small and poor in their early years they did not maintain high standards; but instead, in America, "the spontaneous impulse to general culture was widely diffused" among the people. And this wide diffusion of a moderate culture was both more useful and politically wiser in a new republic than the creation of a small class of savants would have been. The course taken was not because of careful planning, however, but was the natural result of the social and material conditions.

THE OLDER COLLEGES AND THE STATES

None of the colonial colleges were state schools, but Harvard and William and Mary were partially endowed and supported by the government. A majority of the Visitors of the latter were publicly appointed. Yale, or a Yale faction, at least, desired to have the state represented on the board and this was achieved in 1792. In other cases the Revolution brought on criticism and attacks from the outside because the colleges were considered insufficiently patriotic. A plan to have the State of New York take control of Columbia failed; but instead a board, the University of the State of New York (1784, 1787), was created and given general powers over all secondary and higher institutions.

The most radical change wrought by the Revolution overtook the College of Philadelphia in 1779, which, though a temporary result, is as instructive as the Dartmouth College case, to be considered later. The college operated under charters of 1753 and 1755. In the former year, William Smith was appointed with Franklin's approval to a teaching position and soon became provost or head. By the latter year he was already thick in Pennsylvania politics. He was an Anglican clergyman and, together with some of the trustees, was accused of Tory sentiments. We have seen that the college was considered to be under church influence. By 1756 the incautious provost was writing to a brother clergyman in England that more than half of the trustees were favorable to the church which, he said, "by soft and easy means daily gains ground" in the college. The honored historian of the University of Pennsylvania speaks of the institution's "Anglican tinge," but this looks like pretty full color.

In the Revolution Doctor Smith rejected all part in the movement for independence, while the state of Pennsylvania had become democratic and in 1776 adopted the most liberal of the new constitutions. That instrument, as noted, proposed the creation of "one or more state universities." The party that had come into power was not favorable to the college with its loyalist and Anglican connections. A legislative committee was appointed to prepare a report. They found in attendance twenty-two college, forty medical, and about eighty preparatory students. The finances were not in a satisfactory condition and, of course, the committee and the legislature did not wish to be pleased. Their minds had been made up to reconstruct the school on patriotic and more modern lines. It will not be necessary to make direct comparisons with recent legislative investigations.

The board of trustees and the faculty were dissolved. Rules conformable to the new state government were laid down. Additional funds were voted. A new board of twenty-four trustees was named. The charters of 1753 and 1755 were retained but, in harmony with the change in academic language that was developing, the institution was rechristened the University of the State of Pennsylvania.

The new trustees and the new faculty were able men and some of them, for example, John Dickinson of the trustees and David Rittenhouse of the faculty, were eminent. The program of studies was expanded and greater attention was given to the sciences. Four parallel courses were set up for the students' choices. There is here a slight anticipation of specialization and the elective systems; and this was the year when Jefferson was proposing his new plan of education and modernizing the college of William and Mary. The great difficulty at the new university in Pennsylvania was financial. The depreciation of the Continental money, the commercial debacle, and the difficulty in collecting the rents from the confiscated Tory estates assigned to the university kept the institution poor.

The old College of Philadelphia with the old board and staff had not ceased to operate in the meantime but was carrying on its work in new quarters. Its officers and friends regarded the legislature's action as illegal and as an unjust and vindictive expropriation. After ten years, with the winning of independence and the peace, the cooling of tempers and a shift in the political forces in the state, a majority of the legislature had come to hold similar views. In 1789 the funds, as far as possible, and the powers of the old College were restored to it. Two years later the two institutions were joined to form the present University of Pennsylvania, an independent institution. This curious episode was a rehearsal for the Dartmouth College dispute, forty years later.

The famous lawsuit over the control of Dartmouth College arose out of the political conflict between the Jeffersonians and Federalists in New Hampshire. In 1816 the Jeffersonians had control of the legislature while Federalists still controlled the college, a close parallel to the Pennsylvania situation of 1779. Personality difficulties were involved in both cases but these may be neglected here. In New Hampshire the Democratic-Republicans so changed the charter that its original provisions were practically annulled and then set up a new institution, the University of New Hampshire. The board of the college, in turn, brought suit to retain their rights and privileges; and this cause eventually reached the United States Supreme Court. The highest court's decision, written by the Federalist jurist, Chief Justice John Marshall, and handed down in 1819, declared that the college charter was a contract and that under the Constitution the binding force of contracts could not be impaired (I, 10). This restored the board and the college to their earlier status and ended all serious efforts to transform independent colleges into state institutions by legislative expropriation. This is an example of influence upon education growing out of the Constitution. The present University of New Hampshire is the outgrowth of a land-grant college established in 1868. It has no connection with the earlier institution bearing the same name.

Some writers have tried to assess the influence of the Dartmouth College decision upon education. One student found "convincing evidence" that the decision helped to delay the state university movement by as much as fifty years. But he did not present the evidence. The state university movement had begun long before and several such institutions were in active operation when the Dartmouth case arose. Usually a different view has been taken of the educational effect of the decision. Charles and Mary Beard in their *Rise of American Civilization* claimed that the decision cleared the way for both private and state institutions. It made the church colleges "secure from popular storms" and notified the states that public universities would have to be created and could not be fashioned out of existing colleges against their will. Both of these statements are clearly true. But *post hoc non ergo propter hoc*. It does not follow that the rapid establishment of both types of institutions that followed the decision was caused by the decision to any important extent.

The political character of the attack upon the charter is one of the facts that should not be ignored in an attempt to understand American education. That the motive was political is indicated by the message of the governor to the New Hampshire legislature in 1816. He argued that the charter of 1769 contained monarchical principles, especially the cooptation principle by which members of the board were empowered to fill vacancies in their own body. This principle he declared to be "hostile to the spirit and genius of a free government," and advised a change in the "mode of election." All governments, he added, have exercised the right to amend and improve acts of incorporation.

The governor sent a copy of the message to Monticello, and Jefferson replied in a letter of July 21, 1816, which became famous. He wrote that a monarch might have to be restrained from interfering with a trust or charter but such a restriction "against the nation itself" he thought "most absurd." All laws should be alterable, otherwise "the earth belongs to the dead, and not to the living." This letter raises fundamental questions. One such question may be whether the party in power in 1816 in New Hampshire was the state "itself" and was competent to express the state's true and permanent will. All laws and constitutions should be alterable but not for transient causes, as Jefferson himself had said, or in the heat of passion for partisan purposes.

EARLY STATE UNIVERSITIES

Forty years separated the attack upon the College of Philadelphia and the verdict in the case of Dartmouth College. In that interval the first nine of the present state universities were begun, two in Ohio, one in Vermont, and six in the South. The University of Virginia, the last of this group of nine, was chartered in 1819 but not opened until 1825. It was the only one that from the first maintained high standards, but even so Jefferson complained that they had accepted "shameful Latinists" at first. It was a collection of academic "schools," very different in plan from the usual American state university; but it aimed to do advanced work at a time when the typical college was conducting textbook recitations.

The first of the nine to be named and chartered was the University of Georgia. It was granted a charter in 1785 and an endowment of 40,000 acres of wild land. It was provided with an academic senate composed of a board of trustees and a board of visitors. The trustees were the active policy-making and governing body, and the visitors had power to examine the students and to review and even veto trustee action. The early Americans, possessed of a dread of irremediable tyranny, resorted to such checks and balances; and such a dual government is still operating at Harvard University. The University of Georgia was to be composed of a number of colleges and the first of these, Franklin College, was opened not in 1785 but in 1801 and remained small and mediocre for many years. Georgia, like other states, provided some financial aid in the early years, then completely neglected it, and commenced to supply regular support only in 1875. Thus the University of Georgia, in its financial history, resembles most of the early state universities. It was not till after the Civil War that the states began to see the necessity and to assume the obligation for continuous support of their universities. The University of Georgia now comprises senior colleges, junior colleges, an extension division, and the experiment stations, all under a Board of Regents and a Chancellor for the whole system.

Although the University of Georgia was the first state university to be chartered, the University of North Carolina was the first to be opened. This means that we must rule out such controlling boards as the University of the State of New York and such temporary institutions as the University of the State of Pennsylvania, both earlier than either Georgia or North Carolina.

The University of North Carolina received its charter in 1789. The proudest feature of its early history is that, like the Mecklenburg Resolutions, it was a result of a people's pursuit of independence and self-govern-ment. Otherwise it had a humble origin. The charter of 1789 made the board self-perpetuating by cooptation. Each judicial district was to have one representative on the board, but distances and travel difficulties made this an unwise provision. The framers also provided that there should be no regulations that would interfere with the rights of the students as men and citizens. This was 1789. To the students this meant freedom; to the faculty, police duty. The mandate against unrepublican laws did not pre-vent the promulgation of the usual rules against profanity, firearms, liquor, absence from chapel and from divine service on Sunday, and others taken from the college books of laws of the period. The university set up a court to try offenders and instituted five degrees of punishment ranging from a reprimand to expulsion; and in the application of these and other laws the administration managed to provoke a first-class riot and rebellion before the school was five years old.

Financially the young university was as poor and as completely neg-lected by the state as other such institutions. No appropriations were voted. Indeed, the first legislative appropriation for current expenses was secured by the then just elected president of the university, Kemp P. Battle, in 1876. Some funds were realized in the early years from escheats, from unclaimed warrants of Revolutionary soldiers, and from lotteries. Attacks were leveled at the institution because it brought professors from other states, especially Northerners whose politics did not please the South. There were few schools in the state able to prepare students. The univer-sity was formally opened on January 15, 1795, but the first student did not arrive until February 12. The cost of board was fixed at $30 a year. On the faculty was Dr. David Ker, a classical scholar who had recently come from Ireland.

A simple course of study consisting of common school and secondary school branches was offered. There were forty students by the end of the first term. At the opening of the second term the preparatory classes were separated from those of college rank and a plan projected that required six professors, the president included. Latin and Greek were required for the bachelor of arts degree; but students were also allowed to select any studies for which they were prepared and upon completion of these they were given a certificate stating what they had accomplished. The author of this sensible scheme soon left the university and the new president, who was American-born and educated under President John Witherspoon, made the University of North Carolina as nearly as possible into a Southern Princeton. In its small equipment, its primitive surroundings, and its lack of state support, the University of North Carolina was like a great many of the early institutions of its kind. From such origins many justly re-spected state universities have developed. To understand more fully that present institutions have not always been what they are, that they have grown to their present state from small beginnings by overcoming difficulties, and that success is not accidental are some of the objects of historical study. State universities provide excellent illustrations.

Further examples of early state universities that began as poorly equipped seminaries or preparatory schools are numerous. We may summarize several of the unfavorable conditions. Sometimes the schools were located in small, comparatively inaccessible towns without adequate lodging and board and without foot or street pavements. The people often lacked understanding of the nature and objects of advanced education and tried to compel institutions to meet their uninformed ideas. Interference by unlawful means in the internal affairs of a frontier state university was not unknown. Preparatory schools were often lacking in new states and the university was compelled to establish such a school. We have seen that the University of Virginia, although it had the finest campus of its time, suffered from lack of qualified students. The University of Michigan established "branches" in various towns to provide itself with freshmen able to do college work. At the same time most of the early state universities did not have the library, laboratories, or staff to meet the needs of strong collegians.

Everywhere relations with the state were unsatisfactory. Legislatures chartered institutions under the title of state university but provided them with cooptative governing boards. There were early so-called state universities that were merely independent colleges. And like other independent colleges they received no sustaining appropriations or other help from the state. Many of these schools were under the tacit control of religious denominations, usually the Presbyterians, Congregationalists, or Methodists. There was no conception of the service functions of a state university or of its present relations to the public school system. The state university idea like the institution itself has been a gradual, often painful, growth.

This survey may properly close with a few further examples to accompany that of their leader in time, the University of North Carolina. The University of Vermont, with a self-perpetuating board, was created in 1791. Some state universities were formed from previously founded colleges; but in most of these cases there was no opposition to the action. Blount College was given a charter by the state of Tennessee in 1794. It was a Presbyterian school. By a series of legislative changes and recharterings it became the state university in 1879. The process required eighty-five years. In the course of a similarly long and bewildering series of changes of name and purpose, South Carolina College, created in 1805 as a state school, became the university of the state, for the second time, in 1906. It should be plainly said that, as already intimated, authorities do not always agree on all these dates. Colleges usually try to select the earliest defensible foundation date. Tewksbury's *Founding of American Colleges* has been generally but not invariably followed in this account.

Indiana University uses 1820 as its natal year, but Tewksbury dates the charter of Indiana College in 1828 and of the university in 1838. Before the school became a college it had for some years been known as Indiana Seminary. The first teacher of the school, Baynard Rush Hall, has himself written a pungent, often humorous account of the primitive conditions surrounding this pioneer college in the woods and of the quarrels within the school and between it and the townspeople.

Ohio was the first of the states to profit from the new land-grant policy of Congress. That plan, followed consistently as new western states were admitted into the Union, assigned two townships of land to each state for a university. Ohio, however, received three townships and established two universities. These were Ohio University at Athens (1804) and Miami University at Oxford (1809). They received their charters and grants of land and then were completely neglected by the public authorities. For long periods they were carried on more under denominational than state care.

The South and West became the state university sections. New England and the Middle States were late in creating similar institutions. New York began to develop her state university after World War II. Only yesterday, Pennsylvania changed the name of her state college to state university but without changing the nature of the institution.

SUMMARY

Political and educational ideas generated in the struggle for independence continued to influence Americans for a long time after the peace. A new kind of education suitable for a republican people was seen to be necessary. Some impatient individuals proposed a national system that would have imposed upon society the schools they thought needed. Fortunately, democratic processes were followed even though they were slow. Whether from success in the war or for some other reason, there was greater interest in higher than in primary education. The new era was marked also by great attention to foreign educational developments.

The times clearly called for the expansion and the improvement of education, since it appears that only one-fourth of the Revolutionary statesmen had received what was then regarded as a finished schooling and the lowest third had received very little schooling. Equal political privileges in the new nation clearly pointed to a need for equal educational opportunities. Political liberty and citizenship necessitated political education because, so it was declared, men who do not know and value their rights will lose them.

The federal Constitution does not mention education but it has had great educational influence. Its greatest influence in this field comes from its doctrine of reserved powers. Upon this is based the doctrine of state control of education, and this in connection with the doctrine of states' rights has been a determining influence in American education. The early state constitutions made only weak references to education when they made any, showing that even the states were not ready to pursue a vigorous educational policy. Most of the eloquent passages in the early state constitutions were ineffective sentiment.

Realistic criticism of Jefferson's selective plan must be based upon the actual and backward condition of education and educational sentiment in Virginia in 1779. On the other hand, Jefferson's greatest interest was in advanced education and he was, like lesser contemporaries, too much under the influence of the Renaissance tradition. Few or none at that time saw what Pestalozzi was just then developing, namely the liberalizing possibilities of vernacular education in the elementary school.

The national university idea arose in this period but never became embodied in an institution. A host of new church colleges were established, especially in the South. The state university movement was growing and Jefferson regarded the University of Virginia as the crowning achievement of his life; but the true greatness and real function of the state university was a later discovery.

QUESTIONS

1. What conclusions may be drawn from the facts in the second section of this chapter? And do you agree with the one stated in the chapter summary, beginning with "Equal political privileges"?
2. Does liberty begin in the mind? How would the application of your answer affect schools? Why is liberty to be prized?
3. Why was all direct reference to education excluded from the federal Constitution? How and when has the constitution affected American education? This question will be pertinent at many points of the following history.
4. Would strong educational provisions, even mandatory ones, in the early state constitutions have been (a) possible and (b) useful?
5. Can the selective features of Jefferson's plan be explained? Justified? Is not all effective education selective?
6. Was John Adams correct in the claim that the educated class held the power in society? In this connection consider the facts in the second section of this chapter.
7. What could a national university do that is not done now and what could it do better than what is now done by other universities?
8. Why did both hostility to higher education and greatly increased promotion of it show themselves after the Revolution? Was there any

relation between the two? Did its enemies stimulate its friends to greater exertions?

9. What would have been the effect upon college education if the attacks upon Pennsylvania and Dartmouth had been permanently successful?

BOOKS AND PAPERS

The definitive edition of the papers of Thomas Jefferson is by the Princeton University Press. A complete edition of the papers of George Washington has been published. And there have long been available extensive published collections of the works of these and other statesmen. President Eisenhower endorsed the report of the National Historical Publications Commission, which recommended, as part of an extensive program of publication, the inclusion of the papers of Mann, Barnard, Emma Willard, and other educators. Such a program should include the papers of the eighteenth century writers who urged the promotion of national education as an aid to the national unity that the new Constitution was to secure.

BOORSTIN, DANIEL J., *The Americans, the Colonial Experience*, New York, 1958.

CAJORI, FLORIAN, *Teaching and History of Mathematics in the United States*, Washington, D.C., U.S. Government Printing Office, 1890, Circular of Information, No. 3.

COUSINS, NORMAN, ed., *In God We Trust: The Religions Beliefs and Ideas of the American Founding Fathers*, New York, 1958.

DU PONT DE NEMOURS, PIERRE SAMUEL, *National Education in the United States*, translated by B. G. Du Pont, University of Delaware, 1923.

ERIKSON, ERIK M., and D. ROWE, *American Constitutional History*, New York, 1933.

GOOD, H. G., *Benjamin Rush and His Services to American Education*, Berne, Indiana, 1918; and "Who First Proposed a National University?" *School and Society*, March 11, 1916.

HANSEN, A. O., *Liberalism and American Education in the Eighteenth Century*, New York, 1926, containing summaries of documents and extensive bibliographies; an important book, half of which (pp. 45–199) is concerned with plans for national education.

HINSDALE, B. A., Compiler, "Documents Illustrative of American Educational History," *Annual Report* of the U.S. Commissioner of Education, 1892–1893, Vol. 2, pp. 1225–1414, Washington, D.C., U.S. Government Printing Office, 1895.

HONEYWELL, ROY J., *Educational Work of Thomas Jefferson*, Harvard University Press, 1931.

HOYT, JOHN W., *Memorial in Regard to a National University*, Washington, D.C., U.S. Government Printing Office, 1892, Miscellaneous Senate Document, No. 222, Fifty-second Congress, First Session.

LYON, HASTINGS, *The Constitution and the Men Who Made It*, Boston, 1936.

RUDOLF, FREDERICK, ed., *Essays on Education in the Early Republic*, Harvard University Press, 1965.

SCHUYLER, R. L., *The Constitution of the United States*, New York, 1923.

TEWKSBURY, D. G., *Founding of American Colleges and Universities Before the Civil War*, New York, Teachers College, Columbia University, 1932.

WALSH, JAMES J., *Education of the Founding Fathers*, Fordham University Press, 1935.

WESLEY, EDGAR B., *Proposed: The University of the United States*, University of Minnesota Press, 1936. This paper does not show how it is known that "the idea of a national university was widely current in 1786," as stated (p. 3*n*.).

Chapter 4

EXPERIMENTS
IN LEARNING

The spirit of young America as it spread in the valley of democracy was celebrated by the youthful Emerson. His America was still a country of open frontiers, the land of the pioneers, conquerors of the West. Every person stood alone there, and counted as a unit. Assistance or protection could be secured if there was need, but there were few civil associations or laws to help or to hinder.

In the East, people depended more upon each other and upon government. Industry was flourishing, population was becoming dense, and cities were breeding slums and political and social diseases. People united to instruct the young, aid the weak, and raise the distressed. They tried to reform prisons and asylums, reduce intemperance and poverty, and to teach the deaf and the blind. A movement looking toward the abolition of slavery was arising. Private schools and public education were parts of this many-sided reform effort. To educate the children of everyman was the greatest reform of all.

Private education may be interpreted as either an obstacle or as an aid to the acceptance of public education. In different ways it was both hindrance and help. Without private schools and their teachers and patrons, public education could never have come into being. Temporarily good private schools delayed the transition, but in the end the greater the services they rendered the more they served to increase the desire to extend these advantages to the whole community.

The movement for public education began in the private schools, where the spirit of the pioneer penetrated. Experiments in education were numerous in the period of the academy, the country college, the manual labor schools, seminaries for girls, lyceums, mechanics' institutes, the educational plans of organized labor, and the introduction of phrenology and other crotchets.

We shall see that the people demanded a wider educational opportunity than the private, tuition-supported schools could provide. This demand, although there was serious opposition and conflict, was favored by people of every class and profession. The lyceum and a large part of the newspaper press supported the movement. This chapter deals chiefly with the private phases of the whole movement and Chapter 5 with the rise of state systems. No one state or section can claim exclusive credit. Emerson was indulging in hyperbole when he said: "Europe extends to the Alleghenies; America lies beyond." In time "the sentiment of all America" favored public education but without proscribing private schools.

POSSESSING THE LAND

When the new Constitution and the government had come into operation, the next event in the history of the United States was the expansion and settlement of its territory. The passes and valleys of the Appalachian highland were the open gateways into Kentucky, Tennessee, and Georgia, where the new colleges mentioned were established. This settling of the earliest Southwest was the beginning of the migration that was to span the continent. To occupy the coastal strip and the adjacent valleys had required two centuries. All the remainder of the vast area between the two oceans was acquired, settled, and organized into forty-five states and three territories in one century. With the opening of Oklahoma in 1890, the last physical frontier in the Old West disappeared. Before this, however, still another new frontier, separated from the rest of the country, had been acquired in 1867 through the purchase of Alaska. This increased the continental area to be governed from Washington to about 3,500,000 square miles.

In making the peace of 1783, the Whig government of Great Britain ceded the whole region from the mountains to the Mississippi. If there was any calculation that the western lands would prove a cause of dissension between the states, it was an error. The western lands had already in fact been ceded to the national government; and the public domain tended to unify rather than to divide the country and was one of the chief means to increase the power of the government.

Distances and the snail-pace travel of those times was a matter of great concern. Madison discussed this problem in Numbers 10 and 14 of the *Federalist*. He argued that with such improvements in roads and interior navigation as he could foresee, the territory to the Mississippi River was not too large for a republican government; that the representatives from the most distant parts would be able to reach the seat of government in time to perform their duties. He did not anticipate the steamboat, railroad, or telegraph (1844); but neither did he have any prevision of the territorial expansion that was soon to begin.

The Northwest Ordinance for the government of the territory north of the Ohio was adopted in the year when the Constitution was framed. In the preceding chapter its clause on education was mentioned. Its most celebrated clause, apparently written by Nathan Dane (1752–1835), of Massachusetts, excluded slavery from the territory. This, no doubt, deterred planters, but it did not prevent the entrance of others from the South. Settlers came from all sections, as is shown by the names of such towns as Richmond, New Albany, New Philadelphia, Lancaster, Springfield, Princeton, Akron, and many more. Many came from that earliest Southwest mentioned before. These were up-country people who owned no slaves. They were backwoodsmen who built their log cabins out of sight of any neighbors and who were compelled to move again and again because the settlements were becoming too dense around them. Abraham Lincoln's people in Kentucky were of this type. Others came across the mountains from western Virginia and Pennsylvania into Ohio and Indiana and later to the forests of Wisconsin. Pioneers from New England and New York came to the southern shores of Lake Erie but also to Cincinnati and many other parts of the territory. These were the times and places of the subscription schools and other private enterprises described by Doctor Daniel Drake, and illustrated by the occasional manuscripts of teachers' contracts that have escaped destruction.

EAST AND WEST

Two new classes that worried the men of property in the East were the pioneers, woodsmen, and small farmers in the West, and the new labor organizations in the cities, the two groups that contributed most heavily to the election of Jackson in 1828. To the latter group we shall return in a later section. The old colonial antipathy between the seaboard and the back country was repeated in the old Northwest and flared up again and again as in the eighties in Populism, and in 1896 in the free silver campaign under Bryan. By 1820 Ohio was fourth in population among the states, exceeded only by New York, Pennsylvania, and Virginia. In that year Ohio and Kentucky together had well over 1 million people in a nation of less than 10 million.

The migration from the East tended to retard the growth of the older states while accelerating that of the new ones. This population shift made it difficult to provide schooling for the children of the pioneers. Frequently they did not get any. As Lincoln has recorded, the people did not take it for granted that those to whom they were talking were able to read and write. The movement toward the West was to continue a long time while the West itself was growing into a great giant. The country east of the Mississippi had not been fully settled when the area of the United States was more than doubled by the Louisiana Purchase (1803).

Soon afterward Florida was added, then Texas, California, the Oregon country, and in 1867, Alaska. The writers of the *Federalist* would have had great difficulty to show that so large a republic was possible. Mechanical invention solved the problem. Incidentally, the airline distances of Juneau and Seattle to the national capital differ by only 500 miles; and Hawaii is far closer in travel time than Boston was in 1787.

Invention helped to weld the far-flung republic into a unit. Once more we must return to 1787. The successful operation of a steamboat on the Delaware River by John Fitch while the Convention was in session was an event worthy to be chronicled with the stories of the Constitution and the Northwest Ordinance. Twenty years later Robert Fulton renewed the effort to develop steam navigation; and by 1820 river and coastal steamers were numerous. The ocean-crossing steamship was almost ready. The railroad era began in Jackson's administration and led at once to the development of civil engineering courses and departments in academies and colleges.

Along with the political came the industrial revolution. Slater's spinning mill (1791) and Whitney's cotton gin (1793) together with steam power began the transformation of the textile industry. From these mechanical changes important social results flowed. One was the formation of an unskilled urban working class; and another was the growth of the plantation and slavery under the rule of King Cotton. Manufactures stimulated the growth of northern cities. This was not only a result of the industrial development but also of the growth of immigration and the invention of farm machinery, which reduced the number of farm workers needed on a given number of acres.

Industry and the prairies supported each other in soliciting immigrants from the Old World. Between 1820 and 1860, 5 million came through the Atlantic ports to live in the United States; and these numbers were to swell to much greater ones after the Civil War. The illiterate peasants from southern Europe, the freeing of the slaves, and the thin population on the frontier created difficult educational problems.

EARLY ACADEMIES

Signs pointed to the growth, in the early nineteenth century, of a new social order with a closer approach to the political equality of man with man. The newer states gave up the custom of requiring property qualifications for voting and the older states lowered theirs and then abandoned them entirely. Various devices were used to prevent small groups of the wealthy and well-born from remaining in power. The caucus with local committees to sound out and to create sentiment was used by the supporters of Jefferson. The two-party system, each party harboring men from all ranks and conditions, was either the finest achievement or the best luck of American politics. The party convention to select national candidates; shorter terms; and rotation in office—these were intended to distribute political power. Like other political devices they had their bad effects and could be perverted to evil uses. By 1824 eighteen of the twenty-four states had provided that the presidential electors were to be chosen by the people, not as formerly by the state legislatures. Educational campaigns for democracy and also attempts to suppress it were contemporary with the rise of the workingmen's organizations and the campaign for the rights of women instituted in 1845 by Lucretia Mott and Elizabeth Cady Stanton. It was noted, especially by foreign visitors, that an extraordinary number of societies, conventions, publications, and platforms poured forth their propaganda. New educational agencies arose. The academy, a private enterprise institution, was such an agency.

The American academy, as noted before, was a transitional institution. In general a private school, it was in some instances at least semipublic. It gave opportunity to that middle class of pupils who could afford the time and cost of some schooling above the elementary but who were in many cases not preparing for college. It was the second of the three American middle schools and formed the bridge from the Latin school to the public high school. Its period of dominance extended from the Revolution through and beyond the Civil War. By the decade of the eighties, educators who noted contemporary trends predicted that the high school would win in the competition. In that period many academies were turned into public high schools under local elected boards.

Another change took place toward the end of the century. As the old academy with its village associations and its local and middle-class patronage declined, a new kind of academy developed. Many of these new institutions were boarding schools. Some were both expensive and socially exclusive, drawing their pupils from widely separated places. Some were military academies, or provided other facilities not found in public schools. Others were church-connected, often Catholic, schools. Not a few catered to pupils who did not do well in public schools. Most of them had this common characteristic that they served those whom the public school system failed to satisfy. A well-known handbook of private schools, prepared and published by Porter Sargent of Boston, lists several thousand such secondary, or both elementary and secondary, schools. More recently some have added junior-college work.

Some of the early academies were merely modified Latin schools teaching also some modern subjects. This was true of the Governor Dummer Academy incorporated in 1782. One of the early pupils that this school prepared for Harvard was Samuel Phillips of the family that founded and endowed the Phillips Andover (chartered 1780) and Phillips Exeter (1781) academies to instruct youth not only in academic subjects "but more especially to learn them the great and real business of living." A school founded in Virginia in 1776 was appropriately called Liberty Hall Academy. It has since become Washington and Lee University. Erasmus Hall and Clinton Academy were founded in the state of New York in 1787. Thus it is evident that the academy movement gathered strength in different parts of the country before 1800 and, as the table in the following section shows, schools of this type were endowed in considerable numbers in that early period. They were not always called academies but often seminaries, institutes, halls, lyceums, and by still other titles.

NUMBERS AND DISTRIBUTION OF ACADEMIES

As the people increased and formed new towns, the academies multiplied without becoming larger or notably better equipped and more efficient. In New York State the average enrollment in the incorporated schools was less than seventy-five in the early period and did not reach two hundred at any time in the nineteenth century. The uncharted academies were at all times far more numerous than the incorporated ones and, in the first half of the century at least, much smaller. Although these statements are based upon the known facts concerning New York State academies, it is probable that they have a wider application also.

A somewhat expanded discussion of New York developments may be justified because in that state these institutions were especially strong and numerous. The number, as Table 4-1 shows, was nearly one and one-half times as great as that of the next most populous state.

For incorporation by the Regents of New York, the academies had to meet certain standards with regard to the amount of property owned, the number of books in the library, and the number of students in attendance. Here we see the introduction of those quantitative measures of school efficiency later used by the regional associations for standardizing high schools. The incorporated academies of New York could expect a measure of financial support from the state. Although the amount was never large, there is evidence that it tended to encourage the founding of new schools, perhaps to the disadvantage of existing ones.

No restrictions upon the founding of academies were written into law. On the contrary, the law of 1784 that first created the Board of Regents plainly said that no person or persons should be deprived of the "right to erect such schools or colleges as to him or them shall seem proper." This was clearly meant to keep the field free from state interference and almost asserted that school founding is a natural right. It is a good example of the pioneer attitude. This attitude on the part of government, not by any means obsolete, permits the operation, occasionally, of schools that may endanger the health, waste the time, or possibly pervert the morals of pupils.

In other states where there was no state board of education, charters

TABLE 4-1
NUMBER OF ACADEMIES INCORPORATED IN SEVERAL
STATES DURING CERTAIN PERIODS

	Va.	Md.	Pa.	N.Y.	Mass.	O.	Ind.	Totals
1775–1800	20	7	11	19	17	0	0	74
1801–1820	32	31	36	25	19	16	3	162
1821–1840	33	64	34	101	78	97	72	479
1841–1860	40	55	101	139	40	86	84	545
1861–1870	1	3	38	30	10	8	30	120
	126	160	220	314	164	207	189	1380

The above table has been compiled from figures found in Heatwole on Virginia, Slaybaugh on Maryland, Mulhern on Pennsylvania, Miller on New York, Walton on Massachusetts, Burrell on Ohio, and Boone on Indiana. The Maryland and Ohio figures are taken from manuscripts prepared under the sponsorship of respectively Professors James Mulhern of the University of Pennsylvania and R. H. Eckelberry of the Ohio State University. Official records being what they are, it is not likely that the figures are entirely trustworthy. The figures for Ohio, to take one example, do not agree with those given by E. A. Miller in the *School Review* for June, 1920.

were granted by special act, or this power was vested in a state officer, usually the secretary of state. In Pennsylvania the county courts had this power from about 1840 and exercised it freely. Some of the Pennsylvania academies—the Bedford Academy is an instance—came close to being public schools in that the charters provided for the annual election of trustees by the voters. But many academies in that state were controlled by private stock companies, another example of free enterprise in education. Land was freely voted by the legislature of Pennsylvania and other states for academy endowment. At the time when the present concept of public education was still cloudy and in process of formation, these schools were associated in the public mind with the public schools if not actually considered as a link in that system.

Massachusetts was one of the states that attempted to control the founding and location of new academies. The report (1797) of a legislative committee, which it is claimed was written by Nathan Dane, recommended a general scheme of state endowment upon three conditions: (1) that each academy must have a constituency of thirty to forty thousand people not already served by a similar school; (2) that all parts of the state must be served equally by state endowments of land; and (3) that no grant should be made to an academy unless it already had in hand permanent funds to maintain its buildings and equipment and pay part of its salaries.

Not many states attempted to regulate the academies founded within their limits; and the institution spread to all or nearly all parts of the country. Late in the eighteenth and in the following century, girls' and coeducational academies began to flourish. Greenfield Hill in Connecticut was a private school for both boys and girls conducted with great success by Timothy Dwight until he was chosen president of Yale College. Sarah Pierce had a well-patronized school for girls at Lichfield where she had Catherine Esther Beecher for a pupil. And Miss Beecher in turn established the Hartford Female Seminary, incorporated in 1827, where her sister Harriet taught some of the English and perhaps also some of the sentiment that helped to make her *Uncle Tom's Cabin* popular. Incorporation, good equipment, and specialist teachers with a departmental organization were among the notable features of the Hartford Female Seminary.

Emma Willard was even better known than Catherine Beecher as the founder of an early school for girls; and her sister, Almira Lincoln Phelps, was a close second. After serving her apprenticeship in her home state of Connecticut and at Middlebury, Vermont, Mrs. Willard moved to New York State. In 1819 she established her seminary at Troy and this school became a permanent institution. Although the preparation of teachers was one of her objects, she did not forget that many of her girls would marry and become homemakers. She taught an elementary form of practical home economics, and this has caused some to consider her as the founder of that field of study. She at least held the conviction that homemaking could be developed into a teachable science and art. Many of her graduates taught in the girls' academies of the Southern states. She also traveled widely, wrote textbooks, and engaged in the promotion of education for peace.

In the older portions of the South, academies had appeared as early as they did anywhere, and they spread rapidly soon after the Revolution. Many were established by the Baptist, Methodist, Presbyterian, and other denominations. In state after state, academies bore such Methodist names as Wesleyan, Cokesbury, or Asbury, and Bible names such as Bethel or Ebenezer. Virginia and the Carolinas were much under the Princeton influence exerted by the graduates of the New Jersey college. Some of the Presbyterian academies in the South were, however, taught by Scotch-Irish teachers from overseas. One example was William McWhir who has a certain distinction from the fact that at Alexandria, Virginia, he had two of George Washington's nephews as pupils. One of the Southern states known for the strength of its academy movement was North Carolina. In his *Public School Education in North Carolina*, Professor Edgar W. Knight gives a list of about 175 academies; and for the year 1840 about 140 with 4,400 pupils were reported in operation. This would indicate an average enrollment of little more than thirty.

The South was the region of the county academies also. Maryland, Georgia, and Louisiana tried the county academy system with land endowments provided by the state. The lands were not very productive and the plan was not often successful. Tennessee may serve as an example. On the same day in one act, on September 13, 1806, the legislature of Tennessee incorporated twenty-seven county academies. Public lands were set aside for their support; and from 1840 to the Civil War the legislature annually appropriated $18,000 to be divided equally among the county academies, which had by that time increased to seventy-four. This sum of $250 to a county in addition to student fees made the difference between survival and extinction to many schools. But it had another effect, that of delaying the development of the public high school.

In Iowa, organized as a territory in 1838, high schools were formed before an extensive academy movement had time to develop; and a great many of these schools never got beyond the paper stage. Catherine Beecher as the agent of the Women's Educational Association was active in founding a girls' school at Dubuque. It went into operation in 1855, but four years later it was sold to the public school district of the city. In contrast was Howe's Academy of Mount Pleasant, which was aggressively coeducational. The founder asserted that "this is God's plan, in the establishment of families," and insisted that educationally boys and girls must be treated exactly alike. The school lasted until 1916 when, no longer able to compete with the now universal high school, it had to close.

The old academy was succeeded after 1890 by the new. Many are church schools maintained by the Roman Catholic, Lutheran, and other religious bodies to instill their doctrines in the youth. A considerable number are military schools, which put boys into school uniforms and subject them to military discipline. Some are ranch schools, which offer life in the open with horseback riding and outdoor sports. The military and ranch schools are boarding schools. There are, on the other hand, country day schools in the suburbs or in the outskirts of the great cities. Many of these were established after World War I when the Progressive movement was growing. A few are coaching schools for slow learners who are to be prepared for college. The varieties are numerous and the student can gain further information from Porter Sargent's *Handbook of Private Schools* to which reference has already been made.

PROBLEMS, ARGUMENTS, AND DISPUTES

Laissez faire in regard to private schools opened the way to the establishment of many weak institutions. They must have been badly located or inefficient or both because they did not long survive. Up to the year 1870 the New York Regents had incorporated 314 academies, but the largest number reporting in any single year was 190. This was in 1865. What had happened to the rest? One of every twelve incorporated academies died in its first year, half of them survived for fifteen years or less, and only one in eight lived for half a century. The average life span of the schools established in the successive periods, moreover, became progressively shorter. The earliest group lived an average of sixty years before they were closed or were transformed into some other kind of institution. A middle group incorporated between 1800 and 1827 survived forty-eight years. And those founded in the next period ending in 1857 were merged with public high schools, sold, or otherwise eliminated from the list of accepted academies in twenty-five years. The rise of the public high school is one cause of the early demise of many, but other academies were closed before the high school became a factor.

The mortality rate of the private, select, and other unincorporated schools and academies is not known. But the general reason why they were not recognized was that they were weak. They were far more numerous than the Regents' academies, in 1870 at least eleven times as numerous. Many were the purely personal ventures of individual teachers. For all of these reasons it is unlikely that they were a dependable source of secondary education of good quality. In these respects New York seems typical. In 1837 the South Reading, Massachusetts, academy building was sold for use as a public school. Two years later the Lexington academy building was used for the first state normal school. After the middle of the century every decade saw several Massachusetts academies turned into public grammar or high schools. Not only one but six Pennsylvania academies became state normal schools; many in this state were sold to pay debts or to save the investment of stockholders; and forty or more were donated to public school boards. The same processes occurred in other states.

Laissez faire and improvisation ruled also in the department of the academy curriculum. Many academies, like their predecessors, the private schools, did not establish orderly sequences of studies but organized instruction in those subjects for which there was a demand and for which teachers were available. When more definite requirements were set forth they often included an English, a scientific, and a college preparatory curriculum. Each school had its own policy in permitting substitutions and in allowing pupils to take extra subjects. Work in methods of teaching was an occasional extra. In girls' academies a special charge was often made for instruction in piano or French. Fees for elementary branches were lower than those for secondary subjects.

One circumstance that strongly affected the offerings of any given school was the enrollment and the consequent number of teachers. Since the academies depended so largely upon fees and therefore desired to attract many pupils, it is understandable that they should have attempted to teach too many subjects. Many classes, heavy schedules, and superficial work would seem to be the probable results. But in one of the few cases where this opinion can be checked it is seemingly incorrect. The case is that of the Moravian school, Nazareth Hall in Pennsylvania. In 1793 six of the regular teachers taught respectively fourteen, fifteen, sixteen, nineteen, twenty and twenty periods a week, assignments that would not be considered excessive by high school teachers today. But this was a large school and it is probable that many academy teachers taught not twenty but thirty periods a week.

The academies, considered all together, offered many subjects. The list of all the branches found in the New York academies contains 154 entries. But in this list the English language is divided into six subdivisions, from spelling to rhetoric, and physics into ten, from acoustics to statics. But however we combine, rearrange, and count them, the number of branches was large. And the range extended from the most elementary branches to advanced studies usually taught in colleges. There were academies that promised to teach analytic and descriptive geometry, Oriental languages, psychology, and metaphysics. They entered the fields of business, theology, engineering, and teaching; and occasionally one offered a counterfeit subject. One such subject was called "phreno-mnemotechny."

Like the fabled horseman riding off in all directions at once, the academy attempted too many services to achieve any of them without lost motion. For this reason it came into conflict with the supporters of more specialized schools. Academies and private schools enrolled far more elementary than secondary pupils, and in their own neighborhoods often seriously weakened the public schools. Public school superintendents were not slow in calling attention to this; and they also denied the claims of the academies that they were better equipped to prepare boys for college. Because the academies prepared teachers, the proponents of normal school education were offended. The rising business colleges claimed superior capacity to prepare bookkeepers because their teachers were specialists. The academies suffered the usual fate of the path-breaker. They had pioneered in many fields, and the specialists whom they had trained now turned to the creation of institutions that would supersede them.

For a time the academies benefited from public hostility to the school tax. It is true that they also received lands and money from the states. Perhaps every state in the first half of the nineteenth century provided endowments and current funds for the use of its academies. But these, although really contributed by all the citizens, were a hidden tax that if noticed was not felt. Such gifts, therefore, aroused little opposition as compared with a tax, however reasonable, that had to be paid out of money in hand.

The private and semipublic status of the academies that had once been a virtue was later considered a vice. George Clinton (wealthy governor of New York but elected by the people, at least by those who had the vote), in his message to the legislature in 1795, declared that the advantages of the academies "are principally confined to the children of the opulent, and that a great proportion of the community is excluded from their immediate advantages." It was the sentiment that the greater proportion of the community should not be excluded from the immediate advantages of education that led America to prefer the high school to the academy. The cities with multiplying jobs for well-educated youth, the laboring classes demanding opportunity, the equalitarian sentiment on the frontier, manhood suffrage, and all that is meant by "the age of Jackson" spelled out the spread of public and the decline of private education; but the change required decades.

ORGANIZED LABOR AND THE SCHOOLS

The coming of the factory and the new industrial system led to the development of a wage-earning class of people who did not own the tools they used or work in their own shops or need any great skill. Today these people form the great body of the members of the Congress of Industrial Organizations (CIO). The older American Federation of Labor (AFL) (1886) has a larger proportion of craftsmen, highly skilled workers, and it was these who formed the first labor organizations. The comparison is still a good one even though the two bodies were united in 1955 (AFL–CIO).

The coming of the factory also caused the rise of new classes at the other end of the economic scale. In addition to the rich farmers and planters and the merchants and land speculators, there now developed manufacturers and financiers who provided capital for the industries. In early times farmers, small manufacturers, mechanics, and craftsmen had much in common and formed the economic opposition to the bankers, merchants, importers, and speculators. The former class, joined by the frontiersmen, were supporters of Jefferson and later of Jackson, and opponents of Hamilton and Biddle and their centralizing financial policies.

The boundaries between the common occupations were easy to cross or to erase completely. Farmers were in many cases small manufacturers or skilled workmen, operating grist or saw mills, blacksmith or wheelwright shops. Journeymen craftsmen owned their homes and frequently developed a small business. Laborers acquired land and became farmers. But the factories and the cities disrupted this simple, rural economy. Factory workers became a separate class. Without tools or home ownership they became dependent upon the managers and foremen of large plants and were interchangeable like the parts of the machines that they tended.

Organization, beginning in Washington's administration, developed slowly. At first the unions were local bodies in which the workers in each craft, the tailors, printers, shoemakers, were organized separately. One of the most surprising of these was the Society of Associated Teachers of New York (1794). They united to help the members collect overdue tuition bills, relieve distress among the members and their widows, and promote the interests of their vocation. Their Jeffersonian outlook is proved by a public letter of welcome to Joseph Priestley, chemist, teacher, liberal preacher, and refugee from political persecution. The membership was not large in comparison with the number of teachers in the city and the bargaining power of the society was weak. As public education developed, teachers in public schools organized to secure favorable school laws and also to gain higher pay; but they have generally hesitated to use the strike as a weapon because they regard themselves as public servants and the stoppage of their work as against the interests of the children. In recent times a group affiliated with the AFL–CIO, the American Federation of Teachers, has favored and sometimes employed more aggressive action.

Artisans and factory workers made a different kind of union history. City-wide unions were formed after the depression of 1819, and in the latter twenties they began to take an active part in politics. A Workingmen's party was organized in New York and Philadelphia in 1828. Its tangible demand was for shorter hours, but they supported this demand not upon whim or the mere desire for ease and comfort but upon political grounds and the familiar doctrine of natural rights. They understood Jefferson's declaration that all men are created equal to mean that every man whether employer or laborer was entitled to one vote, to even-handed justice, and to educational opportunity. Only with leisure and through education can a man develop his talents and inform his mind so that he will be able to carry out his duties as a citizen. Some of the early leaders impetuously declared that if the legislators had done their duty these ideals would have been realized in the first years of the Republic.

A minor success along these lines was achieved by the nameless author of a labor pamphlet published in Philadelphia in 1827. He urged the establishment in every larger town of a newspaper not controlled by special interests and a library with reading rooms and a place for lectures and debates to be open every evening and holiday. These things were done. An early labor paper, the *Mechanics' Free Press*, was founded in Philadelphia and proved the forerunner of many such journals established in 1830 and the following years; and the Mechanics' Library Company of Philadelphia was formed in those years.

The Workingmen's party of the same city conducted a campaign for public schools. An 1829 committee report was published, setting forth the lamentable conditions then existing. They rejected the pauper system that provided free instruction only to those who testified that they could not pay the low fees of the elementary schools. They asked for free and universal infant and elementary schools in which the teaching was not to be restricted to "words and figures" but would also attempt to form rational self-governing character. They favored a manual labor school in each county of the state. They proposed the creation of local school boards elected by the people and responsible to them. This was a highly significant demand and an attack upon the current practice of frittering away public money by appropriating it to private school societies.

The report, as one would expect, excited both favorable and hostile comment. It is easy to believe that it had an influence in forming the body of opinion that came to the support of the fundamental school law of Pennsylvania that was enacted a few years later. But in 1834 when that law was passed the Workingmen's party was no longer active. It is not correct to say, as some writers have said, that organized labor was the chief artificer of public education. This is a point in our history that is sometimes disputed, and influence is hard to measure; but there are solid facts that bear upon the issue. The early unions were small, and the movement was destroyed by the financial panic of 1837. Until the middle of the century the suffrage was restricted in several of the most populous states. Public education was favored, and propaganda for it was supported by men and women of many classes including some of the rich, the governors of the states, editors, ministers, doctors, lawyers, and even some of those who taught and many who were taught in private schools. There were also opponents in many classes, but the movement for public education was not a class movement. It is to be remembered that the laboring people had much to gain from public education, but even they were divided upon the issue.

Not all of the early labor leaders were of the same mind; and the Workingmen's party, especially in New York City, developed a socialist wing. These ascribed their distresses to the unequal distribution of the land and of private property. The main body, however, disclaimed such "agrarianism," but opponents accused all workingmen of secret sympathy with it. Among the radical labor editors was Robert Dale Owen, son of the socialist Robert Owen, who had established the New Harmony colony (1825) in Indiana. Absolute equality, the elimination of all class differences, was the younger Owen's object. To reach this object he proposed a system of free, public boarding schools for all children. He was not the first to think of this, or the last.

Owen's plan was explained in six issues of a labor paper that he edited. The essays were copied by several newspapers and also distributed as a pamphlet. His schools were to be supported by taxation at a time (1830) when the school tax was in many states nonexistent. But the main object was not merely free education but uniform education, clothing, food, and lodging for all children in the effort to develop a classless social order.

This plan of a socialist pioneer received no support from the individualistic pioneers who then formed so large a part of America.

OPPOSITION TO PUBLIC EDUCATION

Workingmen argued that the civil equality that a republican government implies brings with it the necessity for free and universal education. It was this equalitarian principle that roused the opposition of some members of the privileged classes. Their spokesmen ridiculed the idea of education for laboring people. The New York *Morning Herald* said that the long apprenticeship in youth and long hours of labor in manhood made universal education impossible. The Philadelphia *National Gazette* declared that the "peasant" must labor in order that the rich might cultivate his mind. "No government, no statesman, no philanthropist can furnish what is incompatible with the very organization and being of civil society." The editor saw the school tax above the horizon, still small "like a man's hand," in the day of Elijah, but large enough to cause alarm. He wrote that "the scheme of universal Equal Education at the expense of the State is virtually 'agrarianism,' an arbitrary division of the property of the rich with the poor."

Other editors tried to convince their readers that public schools must be inefficient. The *Connecticut Courant* pointed to the decadent system of its own state as evidence. The *Courant* showed that the funds from the sale of the lands in the Western Reserve had kept the state from levying a school tax. The results were low salaries, poorly prepared teachers, ungraded schools, and short terms. "When the money is used up, the school term ends," the editor reported; and this was true. But from these premises he drew the false conclusion that public schools are always poor schools. Henry Barnard was soon to show the people of Connecticut how they could improve their schools and they did so, although they might have done more.

Some newspapers found the idea of advanced education for women highly amusing. Hundreds of academies and a few colleges had proved that it was entirely feasible, but some editors were hard to persuade. They found the dream of grand republican seminaries "ridiculous." Perhaps the reference to the "Roman matrons" that the schools were expected to produce was a sneer at classical studies for young women. The whole series of arguments against opportunities for labor, the poor, and women, against the school tax and against the possibility of efficient public schools was intended to preserve entrenched selfishness and special privilege. The history of public education has shown how erroneous these editorial opinions and arguments were.

THE ORGANS OF PUBLIC OPINION

With the ballot came the need to spread knowledge more quickly and widely. The newspapers became means to this end. They numbered about 800 in the nation in 1830 and increased to 1,400 in a decade. Circulations were still small but were increasing; and the distribution was local but growing wider. After the telegraph came into use, the papers were able to report the debates and votes in Congress, the actions of conventions, and the speeches at public meetings. Every city now had its newspapers, and larger cities sometimes supported a dozen. Some of the distinguished papers were the Washington *National Intelligencer*, which had been founded at the suggestion of Thomas Jefferson, the Richmond *Enquirer*, and the New Orleans *Picayune*. In New York, Horace Greeley was editor of the *Tribune*, William Cullen Bryant of the *Post*, and Henry J. Raymond of the *Times*. A weekly edition of the *Tribune* that carried stories, poems, book reviews, and travel letters was sent to places as far away as the Midwest. Before the Civil War 400 daily papers, ten times as many weeklies, and several hundred magazines were being published in the United States.

Some magazines were regional in their appeal. The *Knickerbocker* of New York and the *Southern Literary Messenger* of Richmond are examples. The latter was edited for a short time by Edgar Allan Poe as was *Graham's Magazine* of Philadelphia. There is educational significance in the growing circulations of the women's magazines. Most popular in 1830 was Sarah J. Hale's *The Ladies' Magazine;* and Mrs. Hale also edited the highly successful *Godey's Lady's Book. Godey's* developed the permanent formula for magazines of its class when it added the multiple departments of fashions, fiction, housekeeping, recipes, education and child care, with many pictures. Different in kind, intended for both sexes, and national in their circulation were the *North American Review*, founded in 1815 and continuing far into the next century, and *Niles' Register* of Baltimore. The *Review* was a critical journal, and the *Register* a collection of information and opinion in part clipped from other papers, still a popular type.

Specialized journals in law, medicine, religion, and education were also established. The *American Journal of Science*, founded in 1818 and edited by Benjamin Silliman, and other scientific and scholarly journals were published in the period. The *Academician* (1818), an educational magazine, was edited by Albert and John W. Picket, and the *American Journal of Education* (1826) by William Russell. A new editor, William C. Woodbridge, changed the name of the *Journal* to the *American Annals of Education*. Other educators, Horace Mann, Henry Barnard, and J. Orville Taylor, also founded magazines devoted to the improvement of teaching.

Next to the press, the lyceum became the means of developing educational sentiment and opinion. The lyceum was a lecture system of which Josiah Holbrook became the promoter. The *American Journal of Education* in 1826 published an outline of the plan; and the institution spread from city to city and state to state until most of the North and West were well supplied with lyceum centers. In less than a decade from the beginning, 3,000 local lyceums were reported. Lectures were not new. Amos Eaton had been delivering courses of scientific lectures in Massachusetts and New York for many years before 1826. The novelty consisted in setting up permanent local and state organizations to promote lectures, engage lecturers, and administer the programs. The whole system was a voluntary form of adult education without public support or regulation. The speakers brought to the communities, often isolated places, ideas and views on science, history, politics, education, morals, or civic improvement. Committees arranged for the sale of season tickets, and the patronage determined the number of the lectures and the fees paid for them.

The lyceum movement was not only a system of adult education but also a means for the advancement of public education. Local lyceums held meetings on school improvement but it was the state lyceum organizations and the national body composed of delegates from the states that made the greatest efforts to secure the passage of good school laws and the establishment of state education departments. The American Lyceum, which was the national body, held nine annual meetings to consider the best means of organizing and supporting public schools. The last meeting was held in 1839. It may have been a casualty of the economic depression.

Other societies to a certain extent paralleled this second function of the lyceum movement. The Pennsylvania Society for the Promotion of Public Schools, the American Institute of Instruction, and the Western Literary Institute were devoted to the improvement of schools and the development of public school systems. The first of these with Roberts Vaux as president was organized in 1827 and the other two soon after.

The Pennsylvania Society had a share in creating the supporting opinion for the general school law of 1834, which became the foundation for the Pennsylvania public school system. The American Institute of Instruction usually met in Boston and was in the main a New England association. But many educators of national reputation appeared on its programs and its annual reports reflect the history of educational opinion for many years. The Western Literary Institute met in Cincinnati and received delegates from most of the Western and Southern states. It was influential in securing the passage of "the great school law of Ohio" in 1838 and in suggesting the report on European education by Calvin E. Stowe. And as the early teachers' society of New York City had given encouragement to the publication of *The Academician* so the Western Literary Institute helped to form a public for *The Western Academician and Journal of Education and Science* (1837–1838).

The transitional character of these three and similar societies is shown by the fact that they were not confined to teachers alone. The membership included men from many walks of life, businessmen, lawyers, ministers, college professors, and physicians. All who were concerned with education as a public service were welcome. After the public schools were established in the form of separate state systems, it became advisable for the teachers to form state associations, and these became professional groups without many members from the general public. Much later the parent-teacher associations were devised to bring the two parties together once more.

SOCIAL REFORMS AND REFORMERS

The establishment of free schools for all the children of all the people forms one of the greatest of social reforms, but this was accompanied by many others that gave further substance and character to this experimental age. Sentiment and support for any given kind of reform often worked to the advantage of other kinds. Emerson indicated one of the types when he alleged that every young man was carrying about with him some plan for an ideal society. The socialism of Robert Owen and Fourierism, which for a little while expressed itself in Brook Farm, Oneida, New Harmony, and other community projects, were some of these utopian plans. Successful special efforts in education were made to teach the deaf, the blind, and those of low mentality. Humanitarians tried to secure decent treatment for the insane, the criminal, and the indigent. Societies were formed to reduce the lessening but still widespread evils of intemperance.

Slavery, however, produced the most violent public agitation of the years between Jackson and Lincoln. It was in 1831 that Garrison founded *The Liberator*. A leading abolition center and a station on the underground railroad were created two years later when Oberlin College was founded. For thirty years the South met agitation and argument by counterargument. The Constitution accepted the fact of slavery and it gave Congress no power to interfere with it. Slaves were to enter into the reckoning of the number of representatives that any state was to send to Congress. For twenty years the slave trade was to be protected. By a clever use of language all this was said without once naming slaves or slavery, and this doubtless indicates a certain sensitiveness on the subject as early as 1787. In 1861 the whole debate burst into flame and slavery disappeared in a terrible war. The slaves were freed. But the freeing of 4 million illiterate slaves and the sectional hostility and the destruction caused by the war set for the country some of the most perplexing educational problems of its entire history.

The evil lot of some other unfortunates was partially alleviated about the same time, in one case by a teacher. This was Dorothea Lynde Dix (1802–1887), who taught school for many years. At the age of thirty-three she was the head of a school for girls in Boston and a writer of didactic books for children. One of these, her *Conversations on Common Things* (1824), went through many editions. But her great achievement was the improvement of the treatment of the insane and the change that she produced in the public attitude toward those hapless sick people. Her success was the result of her thorough investigation of the conditions and her full reports revealing mistreatment of the insane in prisons, alms-houses, and asylums. Her work as a nurse and nursing administrator in the army during the Civil War would have made her famous if that work had not been overmatched by her services as the "apostle to the insane." But even today mental patients are sometimes mistreated or neglected and there is need for care lest practice in some hospitals slip back to the intolerable conditions revealed by Dorothea Dix more than a century ago. The battle against inhumanity, like that against ignorance, is a constant and continuing one.

Another battle was that for prison reform, which began in the work of John Howard and Elizabeth Fry in England. This did not go unnoticed in America, where such reforms were also needed, and where two reform systems competed with each other. One was the Auburn plan providing small cells, complete isolation, and no work, and the other the Pennsylvania plan with larger cells, and exercise space, and work with pay. The latter was more expensive but also more humane. How humane imprisonment should be was a problem. The penology of the time had not fully overcome the notion that the purpose of imprisonment was retribution; but the best thought of the time was that its purpose should be reform, reeducation, and the return of the offender to orderly, civil society.

The inclusion here of these examples of social pioneering may be questioned. But they are in each case examples of adult education, of the deliberate promotion of a public opinion that would lead to action. They involved the reeducation of public servants, of police officers, prison wardens, turnkeys, guards, nurses, hospital attendants, even physicians. And they posed educational problems, those of educating the freedmen, the mentally ill, and the criminal. But these examples also have a larger relation to educational movements. Like public education movements they illustrate the growth of a social conscience and of a sense of the need to strengthen weak links in the social chain. By social osmosis any one reform tends to suggest others in nearby domains.

EDUCATIONAL REFORMS

Early in the nineteenth century, schools were established for the deaf and the blind. Thomas Hopkins Gallaudet, who is otherwise known as the promoter of normal schools, learned the French methods of teaching the deaf by means of the sign language of gestures and the manual alphabet. Under his direction the school at Hartford was opened about 1817 and its methods were widely accepted by later schools of its kind. Nearly all the early schools for the deaf were founded by state action and were residential schools. When Horace Mann and Samuel Gridley Howe on their tour of Europe in the middle forties discovered the lip-reading and voice methods in use in the German schools for the deaf, they jumped to the unwarranted conclusion that manual methods were out-of-date and should be discarded. Present educators of the deaf and deafened use both manual and vocal methods.

About 1832, schools for the blind were opened almost simultaneously in Boston, New York, and Philadelphia. The head of the Boston school for the blind was Samuel Gridley Howe, who made his institution known, by voice and pen, and by touring the country with his best pupils and persuading state legislatures to establish similar schools. He did much to provide books for the blind, but the alphabet that he used has long been discarded for the now almost universal six-point Braille. Laura Bridgman, a blind deaf-mute from New Hampshire, was Howe's most famous pupil and his success with her was his greatest triumph. It was also a great triumph for the art and science of education. We shall return to this topic in Chapter 14.

Both Gallaudet and Howe established classes for children of low intelligence in their schools—Gallaudet about 1820 but Howe not until much later. It was, however, gradually discovered that the training of mental defectives is a special task requiring teachers with special preparation; and separate schools and classes were established for them. Provision for them and for deaf, blind, and crippled children is now made by many cities; and in some cases the national service clubs provide funds for such education.

Of the numerous communal societies, each proposing to teach mankind how life should be lived, the only one that made much use of the school in that task was New Harmony in Indiana. It was established about 1825 by the British utopian socialist, Robert Owen, the founder of the well-advertised infant schools of New Lanark in Scotland. During its brief period, New Harmony was the home of a remarkable group of scientists. The schools were planned by the geologist, William Maclure, who had brought Joseph Neef from Europe where he had been, in his own words, "a coadjutor of Pestalozzi." Neef was placed in charge of the New Harmony schools. Manual training and instruction in the sciences were given a larger place there than they were to have in the schools of the country for many years. What effect this might have had upon schools in general is unknown, for Owen was soon compelled to withdraw his support and the New Harmony community came to an early end.

Other schools of the period were more successful in teaching manual training, science, agriculture, and engineering. The Gardiner Lyceum in Maine was opened in 1823 and has been called the first school of agriculture in America. It had some success in teaching the practical applications of science to agriculture, but when the state withdrew its support this school also was closed. The Rensselaer School, now the Rensselaer Polytechnic Institute, was likewise founded (1825) to aid the farmer by preparing science lecturers who were to serve the rural schools. In its original conception it was, therefore, a kind of normal school, but many of its graduates found positions in higher educational institutions and in the service of the various state governments. In harmony with its early plan the methods used in the school emphasized skill in teaching as well as investigation.

The techniques of the school were devised by the head teacher, Amos Eaton. On his plan, the students, some of them college graduates, were divided into small groups of five or six persons. Each group took some chemical, physical, or other problem, usually one of technological importance, and made experiments, carried out field studies, read the pertinent literature, and made a report to the rest of the school. The report was not to be merely verbal. The group had to go through the physical processes and demonstrate their methods and results. Many of Eaton's pupils attained high rank in scientific investigation and in teaching. After 1835, with the coming of the railroad, the Rensselaer School developed into a school of civil engineering.

AN EDUCATIONAL LIBERAL SPEAKS OUT

Workingmen wanted free public schools; so did farmers, businessmen, and many others. But they were not clear about the kind of schools they desired and therefore could not agree. And even if they had been better prepared to say what kind of schools they desired, they might have been divided over the best way to secure them. The average citizens of 1830 wanted better school buildings but they were not keen to pay for them. They desired to have new subjects introduced, such as geography, United States history, and English grammar, but they were less eager to have a longer school term. They wanted to have their children get on in life. To do that the children needed arithmetic, reading, and writing. Good English was important and also good manners; but about the general aims of education the pioneers had not thought a great deal when Emerson began to write on such matters.

Emerson was a philosopher, not a school founder like Franklin or an administrative leader like Horace Mann. Ideas were his specialty; and confidence in the power of education and faith in the free individual were his basic ideas. Education, he declared, has produced civilization, and civilized man is as far above savage man as the savages are above the wild beasts. The universe exists to produce men. It produces men by answering their questions, and we must believe that it will eventually answer all the questions that men can ask. The perfect man when he appears will be produced by education. It follows, does it not, that the universe is a school and all the men and women merely students?

Every person, Emerson said, is a new Will. He is not to repeat the experiences of others—or to obey them. He is an original, not a copy, and men must let him be himself. The secret of right education consists in respecting the pupil. He has the right to say to the State: "You shall educate me, not as you will, but as I will," and not in elementary branches only but extensively in the arts, sciences, languages. Emerson, the individualist, considered this the basic premise of education in a democracy.

In method and content, Emerson's plan resembled those of the realists. Learning should proceed by means of experiment and self-activity. Books were to be used only "when the boy is ready for them." We might with advantage follow the Roman rule, he thought, and teach only what does not require the use of chairs and desks and the equipment for listening, as John Dewey was to say. Emerson, the thinker, writer, and lecturer, was scornful of books and lectures. Our education is an education of words, he cried. After fifteen years spent in classrooms we come out with a bag full of—wind. Thoreau in a canoe is the best pedagogue. The true school is one that collects about a natural teacher such as Socrates or Jesus. When we leave the natural method, and adopt a fixed program, and insist upon uniform required subjects, and draw in large numbers of students, then we are tempted to introduce rules, organization, discipline, and bribes. Then education, as was to be said afterward, becomes a ritual, not an adventure.

The tradition to which Emerson's philosophy of education belongs was developed by Rousseau and more recently has been carried forward by John Dewey. Something may, of course, be said in opposition to Emerson's views. It will seem to many that the child is less free, less an individual, and more dependent upon the family, society, and the long past than Emerson thought. Originality and freedom are not absolute any more than obedience and cooperation are. The child may not have a clear idea of the kind of education that he wants now or will later wish for; and the state that collects and dispenses tax money may have a notion of its own regarding the kind of education that it is willing to support. Emerson's confused attitude toward books and direct experience might serve as topics for further homilies.

Emerson, like Milton, was a kind of Platonist and humanist, each of his own kind to be sure. Each took a realist position in education, scorning the philosophy on which they had nourished their souls. Man wills to have what he lacks and thus mankind progresses on a zigzag course that cannot be read unless one studies a long section of it. Hence one of the uses of the history of education. And hence, also, it may be admitted, Emerson's emphasis was needed in the formal, repressive schools of his time. It may be that universal and suitable opportunity, in a sense, does imply that the free individual must be educated as he wills and not as others will.

SUMMARY

The people acquired the land west of the Great River and they occupied it, all in the nineteenth century. This was their greatest achievement, one that brought on the Civil War and determined its outcome; and it made the United States a powerful, and for a time a largely self-contained, nation. Invention made possible the extension of representative government to the vast new areas, and the creation of new states on the pattern of the old. The pioneering spirit that marked the physical and political development was active also in education.

Pioneering in education was necessary if provision was to be made for the children of the frontiersmen, of the laboring people in the cities, and of the new immigrants. This part of the story will be told in the chapter which follows this one. The age was also interested in the education of men of technical skill and practical affairs, and in the education of girls. A great number of private and semipublic academies were founded to serve these wants and needs of a middle class which, although not rich, was able to pay for its education. The academies were noted for the diversity of their subject-offerings. In their effort to meet all demands and even to anticipate them, the academies frequently became superficial; and a fierce competition for students led to the closing of many of the weaker schools. The academy was a transitional institution; and when the high school overtook it, the academy became a supplementary institution fitting into niches not well filled by the public schools.

People of all classes worked for the creation of public school systems, but there were also some who were strongly opposed. Some of the large newspapers ridiculed the aspirations of the masses and attacked the efforts of organized labor, of educators, state governors, and other public men to promote school systems. The lecture system known as the lyceum spread rapidly over the country. The American Lyceum was a strong promoter of state school systems; and support was given by educational magazines, teachers' societies, and promotional associations formed by leaders in business and public affairs.

Social reforms were paralleled by new educational efforts and the two kinds of activity reinforced each other. Among the new activities in education were the schools for the deaf, the blind, and the mentally retarded, schools emphasizing science such as Neef's at New Harmony, and schools of agriculture and engineering. Amos Eaton devised a scheme of activity instruction that is in the best educational tradition. Samuel Gridley Howe originated a plan that was effective in teaching a deaf and blind girl, Laura Bridgman, the first such case in history. The same methods, improved by Anne Sullivan, succeeded even more brilliantly with Helen Keller, as we shall see later.

Emerson expressed the spirit of the pioneer. His views on education have the virtues and the defects of the extreme individualist. With increasing tendencies toward social control and the welfare state, his views may become even more challenging in the future than they were in his own time, for the individualist has a part of the truth about human nature.

QUESTIONS

1. Why did the South permit the exclusion of slavery from the Northwest Territory? How may this have affected the development of education in the Territory and in the states carved out of it?
2. Evidently invention was economically and politically important. How, if at all, was it important to education?
3. How would the high school have been different without the academy, that is, if it had directly followed the Latin school?
4. Why were academies numerous in the South where there were few Latin schools and few high schools before 1900?
5. Why do governments that supervise public schools fail to take steps to protect the children in the private schools?
6. Why did organized labor favor and some great newspapers oppose the extension of education?
7. Why did educational and social reforms tend to develop together?
8. Compare Eaton's plan of teaching with other activity methods, such as the seminar, project, problem, and "workshop" plans.
9. Why is it useful to study Emerson's educational philosophy and perhaps most useful for those to do so who tend to disagree with it?

BOOKS AND PAPERS

On the growth of the population, consult E. B. Greene and Virginia Harrington, *American Population Before the Federal Census of 1790* (New York, 1932), and Bureau of the Census, *A Century of Population Growth* (Washington, 1909). Among the books elsewhere mentioned which will be useful for this chapter are one by E. E. Brown, another by James Mulhern on secondary education, and three by Thomas Woody on Quaker education, Franklin as educator, and the education of women.

ABBOT, EDITH, *Some American Pioneers in Social Welfare*, University of Chicago Press, 1937.

Anonymous, *Historical Sketches of Education in Michigan, Office of the Superintendent of Public Instruction*, 1880, Lansing, 1881.

CARLTON, FRANK T., *Economic Influences upon Educational Progress in the United States, 1820–1850*, Madison, Wisconsin, 1908.

COON, C. L., *North Carolina Schools and Academies, 1790–1840, A Documentary History*, Raleigh, 1915.

CUROE, P. R. V., *Educational Attitudes and Policies of Organized Labor in the United States*, New York, Teachers College, Columbia University, 1926.

DAVIES, JOHN, *Phrenology, Fad or Science*, Yale University Press, 1955.

DRAKE, DANIEL, *Pioneer Life in Kentucky*, Cincinnati, 1870.

FINEGAN, T. E., *Teacher Training Agencies, A Historical Review*, Albany, University of the State of New York, 1917. Treats of New York State and has matter on the Society of Teachers of New York City; but for the minutes of this early teachers' association, see the State Superintendent's *Annual Report* for 1891.

FOLGER, JOHN K., and CHARLES B. NAM, *Education and the American Population*, Washington, U.S. Government Printing Office, 1967.

FUESS, CLAUDE M., *An Old New England School, Phillips Academy, Andover*, Boston, 1917.

HAYES, C. B., *The American Lyceum*, Washington, U.S. Government Printing Office, Bureau of Education Bulletin, 1932, No. 12, with bibliography.

HODGEN, MARGARET T., *Worker's Education in England and the United States*, New York, 1925, with bibliography.

JACKSON, SIDNEY L., *America's Struggle for Free Schools*, Washington, D.C., 1941.

JONES, HOWARD MUMFORD, ed., *Emerson on Education, Selections*, New York, Teachers College Press, 1966.

KNIGHT, E. W., *Public Education in the South*, Boston, 1922.

LEOPOLD, R. W., *Robert Dale Owen*, Harvard University Press, 1940.

LOCKWOOD, G. B., *The New Harmony Movement*, New York, 1905; and see a paper by C. A. Browne, "Science at New Harmony," *Scientific Monthly*, June, 1936.

McALLISTER, ETHEL M., *Amos Eaton, Scientist and Educator, 1776–1842*, University of Pennsylvania Press, 1941; and see a paper which deals with Eaton's students, by H. G. Good, "Amos Eaton, Scientist and Teacher of Science," *Scientific Monthly*, November, 1941.

MANSFIELD, E. D., *Personal Memories, 1803–1843*, Cincinnati, 1879.

MILLER, G. F., "Academy System of the State of New York," *Fifteenth Annual Report* of the Education Department, Vol. 2, pp. 76–246, Albany, 1919.

REICHEL, L. T., *History of Nazareth Hall*, Philadelphia, 1855.

RICKETTS, P. C., *History of the Rensselaer Polytechnic Institute, 1824–1934*, third edition, New York, 1934.

STEVENS, NEIL E., "America's First Agricultural School," *Scientific Monthly*, December, 1921.

THAYER, V. T., *Formative Ideas in American Education*, New York, 1965.

WALTON, GEORGE A., "Report on Academies," *Fortieth Annual Report* of the Board of Education [of Massachusetts], Boston, 1877.

Chapter 5

FROM PRIVATE
SCHOOLS TO
STATE SYSTEMS

Until far into the nineteenth century most elementary schools were private schools. Most of them, whether they were public or private, were ungraded and unsupervised; and nowhere did they form a regular system or articulate well with the schools above or below them. The terms were short, frequently lasting only three months. Horace Mann in his boyhood never attended school for more than ten or twelve weeks in any single year. Henry Barnard had slight regard for the dame and district schools that he first attended. Barnard will be noticed in the following chapters.

Country schools were the poorest, often being only makeshift subscription or district schools, teaching little besides reading, writing, and simple calculation, and that little, not well. School buildings were as poor as the schools and often were unfit for use. Many of the well-to-do families sent their children to private schools and thus lost interest in the public schools and weakened their support. Those who were unable to pay were admitted free in public schools as charity pupils. Public schools were widely considered as schools for the poor.

The movement for the improvement of public education developed slowly before 1830 but more rapidly thereafter. New York had created her Board of Regents, and had made a state appropriation for schools before 1800 and established the first American state superintendency of common schools in 1812. Other states followed this example. Pennsylvania (1834), Ohio (1837), Massachusetts (1837), and about the same time Michigan and Kentucky were laying more or less firm foundations for their future systems.

By then the private school tradition was giving ground to the public school movement. The pauper school and the rate bill were becoming odious to the generation that had elected Jackson. The workingmen, frontiersmen, many professional men, and men with political insight demanded a closer approach to equality of educational opportunity. They were resolved to create a common school for rich and poor, and they understood that only the states could provide universal, free education.

The Lancasterian schools, which will be more fully considered, formed a middle term between the ungraded private and the graded public schools. The Lancasterian schools were private, but they showed the way to a school so moderate in cost that the public became willing to assume its support. Also the Lancasterian or monitorial schools were established in cities where a large number of children could be educated together. And the cities became the leaders in developing public education and state systems of support and regulation. For rural people, especially, the state system was the only solution of the problem of universal education.

PHILANTHROPIC ENDEAVOR

Many cities established public schools under special laws before the state as a whole was ready to take so advanced a step. Philadelphia, Lancaster and other cities of Pennsylvania, Baltimore in Maryland, Cincinnati in Ohio are examples. Many special laws were passed in the several states to permit cities to go ahead of the country districts in their educational provision.

In the cities also there were many philanthropic societies that established schools for special classes of children. There were schools for free Negroes, for the children of particular religious denominations, for poor boys; there were Sunday Schools and evening schools; and in 1806 the Lancasterian schools of England were introduced into New York City. They spread to other cities like a brush fire, but in many places, like such a fire, they soon died out. In New York City they persisted, and to support and promote them there was chartered in 1805 the Society for Establishing a Free School in the City of New York for the Education of Such Poor Children as do not Belong to or are not Provided for by any Religious Society. This title was to prevent opposition from church charity schools by showing that the new society would not trench upon ground already occupied.

The Free School Society was later known as the Public School Society but it was actually a private organization and its schools were private schools. The first school, opened in 1806, was followed by others, and the society remained active until 1853, when it transferred its property to the city Board of Education, which had been created eleven years before. For nearly fifty years the society rendered useful service but it failed, as philanthropic efforts were bound to fail, in the effort to enroll all the unschooled children of a city.

WHY THE LANCASTERIAN SCHOOLS FAILED

The Free School Society used the Lancasterian system, more descriptively called the monitorial, or mutual instruction, system. This system had been developed in England by Joseph Lancaster (1778–1838). Although he developed faults of character, he was a good teacher and successful promoter. The essential idea of mutual instruction was not his own. It had apparently been borrowed from Andrew Bell (1753–1832), who had obtained it from schools in India. The Jesuits, Comenius, and others had anticipated Bell and Lancaster. In Lancasterian schools, a part or all of the teaching was done by the more advanced pupils, those who knew a little more instructing those knowing a little less. This was the essential feature. The schools were called mutual instruction schools because the pupils taught each other, or monitorial schools because the pupils appointed to teach or help in other ways were called monitors. There were teaching monitors, monitors of discipline, monitors of this and that, and inevitably a head-monitor in charge of the monitors.

The Lancasterian schools had a more than halfway military organization. Pupils rose, marched, wheeled, sat down, and took up their books at a word of command. They were minutely graded into those who were studying words of one, two, three, or more syllables and so in other subjects. Classes were to be kept very small. Every monitor and child was to have something to do every minute and a motive for doing it.

Many of the motives that were used were not the best. Extensive use was made of punishments and of rewards and rivalry. For punishment, Lancaster even made use of shackles and of the dunce cap; for rewards, there were badges, offices, and orders of merit. By such means he avoided the use of the strap; but they tended to make the children conceited and priggish and did not increase their love of knowledge or their desire to cooperate with others.

The system was intended to educate the poor and the cheapness of it was its chief recommendation. The cost per pupil was low when the schools were large because they required only one salaried person, the principal. With 500 or more pupils the expense for each might be as low as $2 or $3 a year. Many ingenious ways were used of saving expense on books, supplies, and equipment. Writing with the fingers on sand tables, the use of slates, of wallcharts instead of books, and memorizing from dictation were some of these ways.

The curriculum and aims were narrow and mechanical. No such lofty purposes as education for citizenship or the liberal education of the poor entered into Lancaster's plans. These were the ideas of Pestalozzi. Lancaster, aiming chiefly at literacy, began with the alphabet, spelling, reading, the catechism, and Bible verses, and added some arithmetic and geography. Practically all of it was memory work, for that was all that the child monitors were able to conduct.

From the Lancasterian school opened in New York in 1806 as a beginning, the plan spread to the cities and towns of the entire country. In New York funds to the amount of several thousand dollars were collected preparatory to the opening of the first school. But later the city council and the state legislature also appropriated funds in support of the expanding system. The society began to build its own schoolhouses. The first one provided for 500 children in one room, 150 in another, and also living quarters for the head-teacher. Girls were admitted to the schools after 1819.

In 1826 the society began to charge fees for the tuition of those able to pay, although still admitting the poor free. This brought on dissension and loss of patronage and the fee system was abandoned six years later. Meanwhile, various religious groups had demanded a share in the public funds that had been given the Free, or Public, School Society. The educational deficiencies of the method were also becoming clear and the legislature withheld further funds. Through the years the society enrolled more than 500,000 childen and expended $3,500,000. When its work was done, it turned over to the board of education more than one hundred schoolhouses and other property. As in other such cases, the transfer should have been made much earlier.

The transfer occurred in 1853, but the blow that was to destroy the Public School Society was struck in 1842. It came about in the following way. The society's schools used the King James translation of the Bible, a version to which Catholics have always objected. Some of the reading books also were offensive, but at first the Catholics lacked the numbers and leadership to effect a change. State and city school funds were distributed to the Public School Society and sometimes to other teaching bodies. But in 1831 the Common Council made the mistake of assigning some funds to the Protestant Orphan Society and refusing aid to the Catholic Orphan Asylum when equal treatment was requested. From that time there was no peace in New York City school affairs until a genuine public system was created.

That was a period of strong and mounting nativist sentiment and of particular opposition to the Irish Catholic immigration that was increasing. By 1840 two new personalities, Governor William H. Seward and Bishop John Hughes of the New York diocese, had become active in the controversy. The governor was willing to use public funds to aid parochial schools and the bishop would have accepted this settlement; but the Common Council supported by the Protestant churches and the newspapers rejected the plan. The able secretary of state, John C. Spencer, who also served as the state superintendent of common schools, proposed to extend the state school laws to the city, a simple and logical solution, but one that was not accepted at first.

Speakers who discussed the problem abused the Catholic minority and they in turn broke up the meetings. In the fall of 1841, the bishop and his aides put up a Catholic party ticket in the city and it polled enough votes to give the victory to the Whigs. This taught the Democrats that in the city, at least, the Catholics held the balance of power. The Democratic legislature that assembled in January, 1842, was anxious to regain Catholic support in New York City. On the school question it adopted the solution that had been proposed by Superintendent Spencer, a solution that neither Democrats nor Whigs, neither Catholics nor Protestants in the city, really wanted. It, however, passed the Maclay bill (1842), which simply applied the state educational law to New York City. The law provided for a board of education, its members to be elected by wards, and forbade the payment of public funds to schools that taught or favored any sectarian religious doctrine. The Public School Society did not long survive the loss of public funds. The courts were to be called upon to decide whether the English Bible used by Protestants is a sectarian book, whether it might be studied as literature rather than as religion, and other related questions.

The struggle in New York was peaceful and polite in comparison with the violence that broke out in Philadelphia over the same question. That city had long had a public school system when the Catholic Bishop Francis Patrick Kenrick in 1842 addressed a letter to the Controllers of the Public Schools. He asked that Catholic children might be permitted to read from the Douay Bible instead of the King James, and the board agreed. But Protestant religious papers, speakers, pamphleteers, and secular newspapers so worked upon the people that rioting, the destruction of two Catholic churches, and several fatalities resulted. This happened in May and again in July of 1844 and may have been induced by the rapid influx of Irish mill and railroad workers and the disturbance to the economic, political, and religious life of an old American community with strong nativist convictions.

The most important legal case in this period, which involved the reading of the Bible in schools, was *Donahoe v. Richards*, 38 Maine 376 (1854). The Supreme Court of Maine decided that a board had the legal and constitutional right to expel a child from school for refusing to read the Bible used by the school even though the child or its parents had religious scruples against doing so. This case also led to a great uproar in the small community where it originated. The rule was considered decisive until the Supreme Court of Wisconsin in 1890 reversed it in *Weiss v. District Board, City of Edgerton*, 76 Wisc. 177 (1890). The court in this case held that reading the Bible, a sectarian book, is worship, and declared: "It is believed that Wisconsin is the first state whose constitution contains a direct prohibition of sectarian instruction in the public schools." The question of religion in public education will come up again and we must now return to the spread of the Lancasterian system.

A free school begun by a group of Quakers who called themselves the Association of Friends for the Instruction of Poor Children introduced the monitorial system into Philadelphia about 1807. The system was also introduced into some of the charity schools founded earlier. Both New York and Philadelphia established Lancasterian model or teacher-training schools, and when Lancaster came from England to the Quaker City he was employed as head of the model school that then had over seven hundred pupils. These model schools were among the earliest American institions to attempt the training of teachers. The one in Philadelphia was opened in 1818. The training consisted merely in teaching young men how to organize and operate a Lancasterian school. Lancaster's *Improvements in Education* (1803), which went through several editions and republications, was a practical manual. He had no new—or old—psychology or philosophy of education.

From New York and Philadelphia the monitorial system spread to Albany, Poughkeepsie, and Schenectady, and to Harrisburg, Lancaster, Erie, and other places. In the West, monitorial schools were established in Cincinnati and Detroit. Lancaster's pupils, and their pupils, spread the schools far and wide. In many cities, the Lancasterian system prepared the way for the establishment of public education. This occurred in New York, Philadelphia, Baltimore, and elsewhere. Newspapers and public men favored the plan. When its defects—superficial teaching, mechanical administration, appeal to wrong motives—became apparent, it was abandoned even more rapidly than it had been introduced. Before Lancaster's death in 1838, his movement had become a lost cause. But significant results had been achieved. Many had been convinced that the cost of universal education would not be prohibitive. Schoolmen had learned lessons in the organization and grading of schools.

Contemporary estimates were, however, sharply divided. William Dunlap, theatrical manager and playwright, was favorably impressed when he heard Lancaster speak, but after a second lecture he called him "a quack." Others thought him a charlatan. But DeWitt Clinton, twice governor of New York, called him a benefactor of the human race, the creator of a new era in education, a blessing sent down from heaven to redeeem the poor of this world from the power and dominion of ignorance. There was some truth in every one of these apparently conflicting views. Lancaster was vain, extravagant, a poor manager, and something of a mountebank, as Sir Walter Scott charged; but his system, which was not wholly his own, rendered valuable service in the promotion of education.

AN AMERICAN PRINCIPLE

When the Lancasterian schools and the whole philanthropic system were gradually discarded in the early nineteenth century, a new principle was substituted. This was the principle of free education for all in public, common schools. Because the monitorial system had provided schools and some education, however defective, for many, a more complete education was now to be offered to all. But there was a further reason for this expansion in new political conditions that had nothing to do with the whimsies of Joseph Lancaster. The new principle was one that fitted in with the rise of the common man to power. The common man demanded schools that were common in the sense that children were admitted free and without regard to social class.

This was an American idea. Europe with its dual system did not have it and therefore the United States could not borrow it. This idea was the cornerstone of educational democracy, and it must be emphasized that it was laid in the time of Horace Mann and Henry Barnard, and that later philosophies merely built upon it.

True, it has had to be reinterpreted from time to time. It was gradually recognized that the principle meant that country children shall have as good an education as city children; Negro children, Mexicans, and Nisei as good an education as Anglo-Saxons; children in the South equal opportunity with those in the North; and those with mechanical aptitudes as careful nurture as those who are apt in the use of pen and tongue. The principle has had to be interpreted, and applied. This has been much of the task of education in the last hundred years. Those who accepted the principle a hundred and more years ago were too often satisfied when they had provided equal opportunity in a one-room school, which offered little opportunity as best.

Emerson, who had given vigorous expression to the principle, had a broad and deep conception of education; but he lacked in understanding of the means. He did not understand the function of the state as provider of opportunity. Public education meetings, even when Horace Mann was the speaker, drew from him only a yawn. His one-sided individualism needed tempering with social responsibility, cooperation, and a dash of conformity. Such individualism had long gone hand-in-hand with philanthropy, offering a full meal to a fortunate few but only crumbs to the many. This is just what was wrong with the philanthropic arrangements that were to be superseded.

And some of Emerson's praise of the old New England plan of education was not deserved. The first schools, it has been shown in earlier chapters, were transplanted. They taught merely the elements of literacy and religion. The chief purpose of the early laws was to provide for the neglected portion of the youth, the poor, orphans, and children of neglectful parents. It is a pertinent comment that the level of education among the dependent classes began to decline soon after the settlements and continued on its downward course for a century. Evasion of the law of 1647 was frequent. Even in New England, the region of so-called state activity in education, the church was far more active than the state in promoting and controlling schools. The principle that boys and girls, all the children of all the people, should be educated in free, public schools, under the direction and with the aid of the state, was a later idea.

DEFINING PUBLIC EDUCATION

To draw a correct definition of public education from students would be a difficult task for any modern Socrates. The task is made difficult by the qualities that private and public schools have in common, and by the habit of people to use general descriptive words instead of exact, scientific ones. If they are questioned, students will say that public schools are common, free, open to all, supported from taxes, and controlled by elected boards. In the class of private schools there are, it will be replied, church, military, preparatory, and country day schools, while public schools show less variety. But such arrays of casually chosen similarities and differences can hardly be made the basis of a definition.

Even the courts have found it difficult to draw a clear and simple distinction. They have sometimes held that a public school is "a common school, one that is open to all, belonging to the public." Mo. Court of Appeals, *Roach v. St. Louis,* 7 Mo. App. 567 (1879). These phrases are neither synonymous nor exact. By "common" the court doubtless meant inclusive rather than inferior. And "open to all" is too broad. Both private and public schools limit attendance in many ways such as by age, ability, preparation, or place of residence. No school is literally open to everyone. We may take the third phrase as the best, although the statement that a public school belongs to the public is not very informative.

When the problem has come before the courts, which has very frequently occurred, they have generally considered only the elementary public schools; and this has been one source of their difficulty, for there are public high schools, universities, and schools for the deaf, to take a few examples. High schools are public and now fairly common in all states, but they were public before they became common. State universities and state schools for the deaf are public but not common. Public schools are not always free, which is probably what the court meant by "open to all." Free, private schools are now rare, while of public schools the reverse is the case. Thus we see that historical changes as well as the various levels of public education make it difficult to frame a simple definition.

The sources of a school's support have been held to determine its public or private character. The courts have generally rejected this criterion. Legislatures have granted lands and funds to private schools as a sort of "protection" of an infant and not lucrative industry; public schools have accepted gifts or bequests; and neither school has been changed in character thereby. But if a school received all or nearly all of its support from public sources, it is a question whether it could resist the pressure to become a part of the public system.

We shall not reach a definition on these inductive lines. A decision in 1869 by the Supreme Court of Massachusetts will be more helpful. The

Court declared that to be public, a school must be "under the order and superintendence of the public"; and that this is not the case when the trustees have to be chosen from the membership of certain churches. This decision bears upon the question whether the Massachusetts school laws of the seventeenth century, including that of 1647, formed the beginning of public education in America. By this test it seems that the town schools established under the law of 1647 were not public. But we may ask: Does not the fact that everyone belonged to the same church alter the whole case? And did the coming of many sects into the colony, a historical change in the population, transform public schools into private ones?

We shall briefly recapitulate. It is difficult and may not always be necessary to make a sharp distinction. But when it is necessary, the criterion of control should determine whether a school is to be considered as a public school. In a democracy, at least, a school is public when its control and management are vested in the civil electorate, the body of the voters. But public schools have many characteristics. They are usually tax-supported, relatively free, open to a wide public, often nonsectarian, and integrated into a state system of schools. They have these additional characteristics because they are controlled by the people.

STATE SYSTEMS IN OUTLINE

Recent state constitutions direct the legislatures to establish systems of public schools. Earlier constitutions often omitted the subject or spoke in vague terms. Later instruments have become more explicit.

The Constitution of Illinois of 1870 provided that the legislature should "provide for a thorough and efficient system of free schools **whereby** all the children of this State may receive a good common school **education**." A few years later the state supreme court held that this was a minimal requirement that did not operate against the establishment of high schools. Other state constitutions have demanded the establishment and maintenance of "a general, suitable, and efficient system of free schools" (Arkansas, 1874); "a general uniform, and thorough system of public, free, common schools" (Idaho, 1890); or "a liberal system of public schools throughout the State" (Alabama, 1901). Evidently it is not considered sufficient to order the formation of a public school system; but the language of the constitutions is largely rhetorical, and often it is copied from similar documents in other states.

State systems have evolved slowly and experimentally and are the results of constitutional and legislative provisions. Much of the legislation has been of a piecemeal nature, and in the early laws moral, religious, and eleemosynary purposes are evident. From the first the colonies and later the states were independent and, as a result, so were their educational systems. This is a noteworthy feature of American educational organization. The "reserved powers" clause of the federal Constitution preserved this independence.

The variety of the state systems is increased by the economic and population differences between the states and sections. The greatest difference among the systems has been the segregation of Negro from white pupils in separate schools in the South. Northern cities sometimes separate the races, but this has not been required by state law. There are great differences in the degree of state control of schools. New York, Maryland, and New Hampshire are examples of strict and detailed control, whereas many of the states on the plains, such as Kansas, Nebraska, or the Dakotas, and some in the South permit the locality to exercise broad powers. It is important to know that the states can control the local schools completely if the legislature so votes. Even the school units, the cities, townships, and districts are creatures of the state and derive all their powers from the state. It is important to know this when men argue for the preservation of local autonomy in school matters and when it is proposed "to give the schools back to the people." Only by permission of the state legislature or power delegated by it can the local school district control its own affairs.

The differences between the state control systems are lessened by the constant migration and free communication between the states and within each one of them. They are also lessened by the influence of the federal Constitution. The Supreme Court in the so-called Oregon case (1925), for example, denied the right of any state to abolish private schools just because they are private, or to require all children to attend public schools. Federal aid to education in the states has done a great deal to promote similar developments in the different states in vocational and higher education. States also copy each other. Almost all states now have a state board of education, although the constitution and powers of these boards differ widely. All states have school systems, elementary, secondary, and higher, that are similar but not equally fully developed or equally well supported. It is readily possible to exaggerate the differences, great as they still are, between the state sytems. The outlines of a national pattern are clear.

AN EARLY START IN NEW YORK

The remaining sections of this chapter examine the early history of state systems. The educational history of colonial New York did not give promise of the rapid progress that was to take place under the federal Constitution. A law of 1784, revised in 1787, started the movement by creating the Board of Regents to have direction of secondary and collegiate education. A law of 1812 created the first American state superintendency of common schools. In 1834 New York began to support the academic education of teachers. Some of the academies set up classes for the study of educational problems, such as teaching methods or school organization. These events are enough to show that New York began early in developing a state system; but no state has been able to lead in everything, or all of the time.

There was no reference to education in the first New York constitution as passed in 1777 or as amended in 1801. The governors and a committee of the Regents urged the importance of universal education and pointed to the progress of neighboring states. But the Regents had no money for elementary education. It is not clear what progress they had observed in neighboring states in 1787; and it is perhaps surprising to find a board charged with the care of secondary schools and colleges concerning itself with elementary schools.

The first concrete step in the state system of elementary education was not the law of 1812 but the granting of land for school support. About the time when the old Congress in its Survey Ordinance of 1785 set aside Section Sixteen of each western township for schools (see the section On the Western Frontier), New York, which did not share in that plan, enacted a corresponding law based upon its own "wild lands." The second step was taken ten year later (1795) through the passage of "An Act for the Encouragement of Schools." The encouragement was in the form of an annual appropriation, to be continued for five years, of $100,000 for schools.

The quotas of this sum for the counties and the formula for the distribution to the towns were stated in the law; and each town was required to raise by property tax one-half as much as it was to receive from the state. This principle of conditional giving has been widely followed by the states, by the national government in its dollar-matching-dollar requirements, and also by private donors. The schools were not made free but the New York law was mandatory. Each town was required to elect school commissioners to certify the teachers and supervise the schools. The attempt to extend the act in 1800 failed, although by only a few votes, and state aid ended for the time.

If the Regents had been charged with the administration of the common schools, New York would have begun with a more complete system. But the contrast between elementary and secondary-higher education which at that time existed in the minds of men forbade this. Unfortunately, the separate administrations built up special interests that were to prevent unification for more than a hundred years.

The administration of the lower schools, separated from that of the Regents, was instituted, as indicated above, by the appointment of a superintendent of common schools under the law of 1812. The appointee was a young lawyer, Gideon Hawley (1785–1870); his duties were to be primarily fiscal. After the effort to renew the treasury grants for schools failed in 1800, the legislature laid the foundations of a common school fund that was to produce twice the sum of $100,000 a year. The proceeds from the sale of 500,000 acres of state lands were to be accumulated until the amount of $4,000,000 was attained. Local school units, in order to participate in the proceeds, were to be required to raise a specified tax. For the accomplishment of these purposes an official was needed, and in this way there appeared in the United States the office of state superintendent of schools.

The first duty of the first state superintendent was to digest plans for the management of the common school fund; and the second was to improve the organization of the common schools. He was to supervise the collection of school moneys, to accumulate moneys from the sale of lands in the school fund, to report the expenditure of school funds, and "to give information to the legislature respecting all matters referred to him by either branch thereof, or which will appertain to his office; and generally to perform all such services relative to the welfare of the schools as he shall be directed to perform. . . ."

Americans of those times, still shuddering over the memory of the tyranny of George the Third, feared all executive power whether of the governor or of the lowly school superintendent of the state. Hawley, however, had somewhat more power than the usual state superintendent was to be granted for a century afterward; and he made the most of what he had. In his administration was begun that concentration in his office of judicial influence over education that has made the New York department one of the strongest in the nation. Hawley served as superintendent for nine years, until 1821, when by a political maneuver the office was abolished. His duties were added to those of the secretary of state. The same process was followed in other states. The first superintendent's office in Maryland continued two years (1826–1828), in Ohio three years (1837–1840), in New Hampshire four years (1846–1850). There were shorter or longer interruptions in the continuity of the office in almost half of the states. Hawley, it is pleasant to report, was promptly chosen secretary of the Board of Regents.

New York began to experiment with the public preparation of teachers in 1834. In that year a new law provided aid to one academy in each of the eight judicial districts for the maintenance of a special class for teachers. Ten years later the normal school at Albany was created and others followed after the Civil War. Both plans of teacher-training were maintained for many years. A union free-school system providing for the public support of high schools was begun by a permissive law of 1853. But the rural schools of New York did not become entirely free until 1867 and after a great political fight. Cities had earlier abolished the rate bill, a method of assessing the costs of a school upon the patrons in the proportions of the total number of days attended by all the children sent by each patron. The separate state school office to provide supervision over elementary education was restored in 1854; but the two branches, one dealing with elementary and the other with secondary and higher schools, remained separate until 1904. Then they were combined under a single officer whose dual title is reminiscent of the old division. He is the president of the University of the State of New York and commissioner of education. The first to hold this office was Andrew Sloan Draper (1848–1913), who had for a decade been president of the University of Illinois.

PENNSYLVANIA BEGINNINGS

In Pennsylvania, as in other states, the cities secured special legislation giving them permission to form their own school systems. To pass general school laws for a state was more difficult, especially if the laws were to be mandatory. Most states, therefore, started with permissive laws and set up fixed requirements only when favorable sentiment had been formed.

In Pennsylvania as elsewhere there were many arguments against public education. It was new and it was expensive. Radical democrats tended to oppose all grants of executive power and all new offices if they could be avoided. Some thought public schools socialistic. Country people were opposed to schools because the children were needed on the farms. Schooling made them lazy and vain, it was claimed. Many Germans wanted their own language taught in schools. Some Germans were Lutherans, some were Catholics, and both favored parochial schools. Some German sects were opposed to too much schooling as tending to change their views and way of life. Much of the opposition to public education in Pennsylvania came from the German and the mountain counties.

Before the 1830's most states depended upon subscription schools and public schools supported by tuition fees, rate bills, and proceeds from school lands. The school tax was almost unknown. Pennsylvania had done almost nothing. Its constitution of 1790 enjoined the legislature to establish schools in which the poor would receive free instruction. The legislature did not act for almost twenty years; and then it passed the pernicious law of 1809, which established no schools but asked poor parents to confess their poverty to private schoolteachers who would then be reimbursed by the state. There cannot have been many worse forms of school legislation.

For more than forty years after 1790, the state, outside of the towns, was without public schools. This was not wholly owing to lack of effort. A bill providing for a county system of free schools was actually passed by both houses in 1794, but was lost in conference committee through a disagreement over details. A general public school law was passed in 1824. This included the provision that the poor should be given free tuition. But the attack upon even this weak law became so violent that the legislature hastened to repeal it before it came into operation.

Ten years later the public school forces were more determined and successful. George Wolf, a former teacher, was governor; Samuel Breck who had entered politics expressly to work for public education served as chairman of the joint committee of the two houses upon education; and Roberts Vaux led the Pennsylvania Society for the Promotion of Public Schools. The committee in presenting its bill took care to say that they had omitted the word *poor*. They said: "Let all fare alike in the primary schools and imbibe the republican spirit." After the long hard campaign, the bill, to the surprise of many, was accepted almost unanimously. The fight came afterward but the campaign to repeal it failed.

The act of 1834 should not have aroused such bitter opposition, for it was an optional law. It made cities, boroughs, counties, and townships the administrative units. Except for a brief period, Pennsylvania escaped the district system. The law instituted the school tax and gave state appropriations to those units in which the tax was collected. This was a means to encourage the acceptance of the law. In all units that accepted the law, the schools were made free; and in 1848 the law became mandatory. Each local unit was governed by six elective directors. The secretary of state was made superintendent of common schools, *ex officio*, until 1857 when a separate office was created. A law of 1854 had established the county superintendency and permitted the grading of the schools. Several other states, Maine, Vermont, New York, and Ohio, established or reestablished the state superintendency in the fifties; and several also passed permissive school grading laws at this time.

ON THE WESTERN FRONTIER

Several states in the old Northwest enacted general school laws and created state systems fairly early. Those states had the benefit of the Congressional school lands; but these proved less valuable than the people had expected. The Survey Ordinance of 1785 reserved Lot. No. 16 of every township "for the maintenance of public schools within said township." In the survey plan each township was a square, six miles on a side, and was divided into thirty-six sections each one mile square and numbered as in Figure 5–1. As the diagram shows, the sixteenth section was the third from the northern and the third from the western boundaries of the township. The reservation of this square mile of land (640 acres) in every township for the schools did not apply to the older states. Ohio, admitted into the Union in 1803, was the first state to receive the grant. Later states in some cases received two sections and even four sections in each township for school support. The legislature of each state had the duty to conserve and manage the school lands. Some states managed them well, collecting the rents and applying them to the schools. Others sold the lands

6	5	4	3	2	1
7	8	9	10	11	12
18	17	**16**	15	14	13
19	20	21	22	23	24
30	29	28	27	26	25
31	32	33	34	35	36

Figure 5–1

early, usually at low prices, and in some cases dissipated the money. Ohio belongs to the latter group.

The Ordinance of 1787 asked the legislatures of the Northwest Territory to encourage schools and the means of education; but the legislature of Ohio did not heed this admonition until the session of 1812, when the first general school law was adopted. It was weak, like most early school laws. It proposed the division of the townships into school districts at the option of the voters and the election of district school committees of three members. Two-thirds of the householders of a district had to consent before a schoolhouse could be built. A tax could be laid to make up the deficiency caused by the inability of some to pay their school fees. Thus was the district system imported from the East to become the basis of public education in Ohio. The next legislature had a majority of both houses opposed to public education, and in the words of an early historian of the state, "They broke up in a row and went home." The first great forward steps were taken in 1837 and 1838.

The office of superintendent of common schools was created in March, 1837, and Samuel Lewis, a successful, self-educated lawyer was chosen to fill it. His duties were to collect information, to promote interest in, and to report on common schools. His first report was a progressive statement. He urged the establishment of school libraries and of high schools. He laid bare the scandalous mismanagement of the school lands; and he showed that even with competent administration the income from these lands would be inadequate to support the schools. He proposed an increase in the state school fund to provide an annual income of $200,000. He recommended laws giving districts power to borrow money for buildings;

providing for local school supervision in city and country; and requiring full educational and financial reports. He proposed a state school journal, and *The Ohio Common School Director* (1839) was established.

The law of 1838, which followed this report, provided for a school census, a common school fund, and a county school tax of two mills. It established county and township supervision, although by *ex officio* personnel. It gave local boards the power to control the curriculum but required that all schools must be taught in the English language. This provision was aimed at the German schools that had been established in Cincinnati. But there were already so many influential Germans in that city that they were able to secure the repeal of this clause. In 1840 the office of state superintendent was abolished, and his duties were assigned to the secretary of state. Some of the ground thus given up was not recovered until 1853, when the state office was reestablished, a state tax levied, the rate bill abolished, the schools made free, and a beginning made in the curbing of the district system.

In Michigan, as in many other states, the chief city first developed schools. The trading post of Detroit is said to have had schools in 1755, and there were a number of Catholic missions among the Indians when Father Gabriel Richard arrived in 1798. He established schools for both races and obtained recognition for education from the territorial legislature that passed the general school law of 1809. The town had a newspaper in 1817 and a Lancasterian school a year later. Detroit was a westerly outpost of the Lancasterian movement and about the same time the home of the curious university named Catholepistemiad, or institution of universal knowledge, chartered in 1817. The name was based upon the old idea that a university teaches all knowledge, a misconception that probably will never die. Detroit entered upon the main-traveled road of educational progress in 1838 by establishing public schools, making them free in 1842 when the city board of education was instituted.

The first general school law (1809) of the territory provided for the creation of school districts, the conducting of a school census, and the laying of a school tax. This early legislature knew what must be provided first in framing a new school system, but the time was not ripe and the law was stillborn. A second general school law (1829) was modeled after the Massachusetts law of 1789. The kinds of schools, whether elementary or secondary, and the length of the terms were to be based upon the number of people in an area. The voters of a township were permitted to divide the area into districts, each with one teacher and three elected trustees. The law was optional. Support was to come from school lands and taxation but the rate bill was soon substituted, and was used until 1869, longer than in New York.

Michigan was the fourth state carved out of the Northwest Territory and was admitted into the Union, as the twenty-sixth state, in 1837. She profited from the mistakes of her sister states in managing school lands. Michigan, while still a territory, appointed a superintendent of common schools to administer her school lands and managed them as one property; and also applied the proceeds as needed by any part of the state instead of applying the income from a particular section only in the township whence it was derived. The state constitution of 1835 made education a branch of the state government and provided for the establishment of a state school office. The law of 1837 created the office of superintendent of public instruction and gave the officer supervisory power over the schools and the management of the school lands. The law provided for state and local taxation and local boards, but it assigned strong supervisory powers to the superintendent. These were the ideas of the framer of the law, John D. Pierce, who had read Victor Cousin's report on the schools of Prussia. From that document he gathered that centralized power was essential. As a matter of practical politics and as it applied to the formative period of American education, this was an overstatement. If one considers the history of the colonies, the early conditions in the Union, and the people and their manner of life, it is easy to arrive at the opposite conclusion, that the district system and local control were unavoidable.

Indiana is an excellent example of a state that long suffered from an excess of localism and frontier democracy. The constitution of 1816 required the legislature to establish a general system of free schools equally open to all. This was the voice of enlightened people, but there were too few of them. For many years the state suffered under the most virulent forms of the district system and the rate bill. The school law of 1833 was one of the weakest of such instruments, and the kind of schools that resulted is described in Edward Eggleston's *The Hoosier Schoolmaster*. Millard F. Kennedy in his *Schoolmaster of Yesterday* shows a more recent picture of the Indiana pioneer school and teacher; and Jesse Macy's *Autobiography* paints the vocational versatility of the pioneer. Macy's family, about 1850, had a farm with a tannery and sawmill, and raised wool and flax and made them into cloth and clothes. A sugar-maple "orchard" necessitated a coopering business. Most of the farmers were also carpenters, builders, joiners, and cabinetmakers, or blacksmiths, or shoemakers. Teaching was also such a part-time trade; and the results were equally crude.

The Indiana Constitution of 1851 repeated the mandate of 1816 and the general school law of 1852 was to fulfill its demands. Unfortunately, as it turned out, the new constitution demanded the erection of a "general and uniform system of common schools." The state supreme court thereupon pronounced all local school taxes unconstitutional, since they would vary from district to district and thus destroy the uniformity of the system. The state common school fund was able to provide for public schools for only two months annually at a "uniform" salary of $55 for the term. Districts that had a sufficient number of paying pupils used the rate bill to extend the term. Not until 1867 did the schools of Indiana become free for a longer term than two months.

The discovery of gold caused a rapid increase in the population of California at a time when large areas east of the Rockies were unoccupied. There was only one cabin on San Francisco Bay in 1835, but upon the admission of the state into the Union in 1850, California had 90,000 people, most of them in the general region of the Bay. People came from all parts of the East and foreign lands. They continued to come. The census of 1860 showed that the population of the state was more than four times as great as it had been ten years earlier.

The first constitution provided for an elected state superintendent and for the preservation of the school lands, and required the legislature to establish a common school system. At its first session no such action was taken by the legislature; but in 1851 it created a primitive district system similar to those of the preceding century in the East. The elected district trustees were empowered to build schoolhouses but not to levy a tax for this or any other purpose. They were to examine teachers and give certificates good for one year only. The law was based upon the supposition that there was a common school fund, which was contrary to fact, and it provided for the distribution of the nonexistent proceeds, not only to public schools but also to church, orphan, almshouse, and any other private schools according to the number of children in each. The third session of the legislature authorized a small county tax for schools, and made the county treasurer *ex officio* superintendent of schools, as had been done in eastern states earlier. It all sounds as though school systems in their evolution were bound to begin in the same way and to traverse the same inexorable steps in a series comparable to the culture epochs; but in fact the sparse and shifting rural population was the reason for such laws, here as elsewhere.

Nor was religious controversy lacking. In San Francisco at first Bible reading in the schools was a requirement; and over some objections this was carried out. In 1854 the offices of the school trustees and superintendent formerly chosen by the council were made elective. Church and other nonpublic schools were amalgamated with the public schools. To share in the public funds, teachers in Catholic, Methodist, and other schools now had to be examined by the public agency. In this merger the religious controversy again broke out and the discord was promoted by the Know Nothing party of that time. The issue was not settled until many years later when all religious exercises were banned from the city schools and from the public schools of the state.

The city schools were far ahead of those in the rural parts of the state. In California, as in New York or Pennsylvania, the city schools operated under special charters that provided for both funds and freedom. Cities developed graded, free schools, whereas the ungraded schools in the country limped behind with short terms, maintained by tuition charges and assessments.

In California, as in other newer states, the new day in education came quickly. In the 1860's the state developed a progressive system that deserved and gained the praises of Henry Barnard and other national leaders. In 1862 John Swett, a teacher from New Hampshire and Massachusetts, was elected state superintendent. If he was not the author of the slogan that "the wealth of the state must educate the children of the state," he used it skillfully. He had the touch of a master politician. Calling a state teachers' institute, he had every teacher who attended take back to his district and circulate petitions to the legislature for a state school tax and better schools. The response was universal and effective. He secured legislation providing for a state board with power to set up a curriculum and to select textbooks, a state school tax, increased county and local taxes, free schools (1867), school libraries, a state educational journal, *The California Teacher*, a longer term, and the professional preparation of teachers. Henry Barnard said: "There is nothing so liberal in the way of taxation in any other state in the world." William Russell, founder of the old *American Journal of Education*, who had been one of John Swett's teachers, sent his warm commendation.

Before turning to the New England frontier, it may be noted that in several states the schools did not become free until the 1860's. Such states were California, Indiana, Michigan, New York, and in New England, Connecticut and Rhode Island. In Massachusetts, Delaware, and Pennsylvania (a few districts excepted) the schools became free before 1850. Vermont made its schools free in 1850, Ohio in 1853. There is no apparent regional trend here, nor any clear line between older and newer states.

NEW ENGLAND FRONTIER

Education in early New England lacked central guidance and a general plan. Each town was an independent school district. Soon the unity of the town as a school district was impaired by the moving school and shattered by the district system. The extreme decentralizing trend of the section was most evident in the thinly settled portions such as the northern states and the western part of Massachusetts.

Take New Hampshire, for example, which became independent of Massachusetts in 1679. School developments resembled those of rural Massachusetts. The moving school and the district system began to appear about 1700. One town, Londonderry, in 1736 voted that the town schoolmaster should teach for two months in each of five places in the town and for one month in each of two others. According to the last royal governor, nine-tenths of the towns had no school or had one kept by an ignorant and immoral itinerant. The governor's statement may have been prejudiced, and it is doubtful that he had any detailed knowledge of the conditions. But we know that in 1805 the district system was made legal, an action that had already been taken in Massachusetts. This system satisfied the law of New Hampshire until 1885, when it was abolished.

Long before 1885 a new age had dawned in much of the country. Of high importance among the changes that affected schools were the rise of industry, the growth of towns, the opening of the West, and the invention of farm implements. The people of New Hampshire moved to the cities or left the state. Many farms were abandoned. The immigrants who moved in settled in the cities and worked in factories. The census of 1870 showed a decline in the population of the state. Fifty years before, in 1820, eighty of every hundred persons in New Hampshire lived on farms; but fifty years after 1870, in 1920, only twenty-five of every hundred remained on farms. In many cases the rural leaders had been the first to leave. The district schools were left with few pupils or none. The turning point in school administration occurred in 1920.

There had been several efforts to create a state school office in New Hampshire. A law of 1846 provided for a state school commissioner to be appointed by the governor with the consent of the council. But his duties were few and his powers negligible. He was merely to visit schools, gather statistics, and make an annual report. As in other states, even this insignificant office was abolished in 1850. After a period of county supervision, in 1867, the office of superintendent of public instruction was created, but again without the powers implied by such a title. This lasted fifty years. And then, in 1919, partly as a result of the revelations produced by World War I, a highly centralized department of state school administration was created.

The new law provided for a state board "with the same powers of management, supervision, and direction over all public schools in this state as the directors of the ordinary business corporation have over the business of the corporation, except as its powers may be limited by law." This means that the board could do anything that was not contrary to common or statute law. New Hampshire at last had a powerful state organization. But the business corporation, engaged in making and marketing consumer goods, is hardly a fit model for a state school board. The law of 1919 has been modified. But we have gone far enough to see how persistent the small pattern organization was in this rural and mountainous state.

Before we turn to the awakening in Massachusetts we shall briefly notice the state school offices of the present day. All fifty states now have a chief school official and a state board or department of education. In the majority of the fifty states, the chief state school officer is called Superintendent of Public Instruction, but in others he is named Superintendent of Schools, Commissioner of Education, or other titles.

The qualifications of the chief officer vary from state to state. In some states he must be a college graduate; in some he must have had educational experience; or the law may demand a special kind of certificate assuring his possession of both education and experience; but in other states there is no specified qualification. He is elected by popular vote in about two-thirds of the states, and in the rest he is appointed by the governor or chosen by the state board. Most states have fixed terms of two to four years, but in some the tenure is indefinite and the incumbent may serve for many years. In those states in which the term is only two years, and when the two major parties are evenly balanced the chance for reelection is precarious.

Now and then in one state or another the office attracts and holds men of the highest caliber, and not always by paying a high salary. Horace Mann endured the labor and abuse of the office for twelve years at $1,500 a year. There have been other great superintendents of public instruction or commissioners of education, such as John Swett of California, Newton Bateman of Illinois, and Andrew S. Draper of New York, but the average capacity of the holders of the office has not been high.

Early state boards, like the early state superintendents, were given little power. This has been changed in several states, but in many cases they have neither the legal responsibility nor the staff to perform the functions that are or should be devolved upon them. In the majority of states the members are appointed by the governor or are members *ex officio*. But the worst of the situation is that the qualifications for membership are low, and in some of the states there are no special requirements.

With the advice and recommendation of the chief school officer, the state board should formulate the state educational policies, submit the budget, and propose needed legislation. In many states, the state department inspects schools and enforces the laws. In addition to these major duties, many minor ones must be performed. The staffs of the departments are often inadequate, and half of the personnel may be concerned with vocational education. The conclusion is that although the central agencies in the state systems have seen great development since 1850, they have not kept pace in qualifications, members, and delegated powers with the need of the present. However, with the present trend to channel increasing amounts of federal funds through the state departments of education, the power of chief state school officers probably will expand in the future.

MASSACHUSETTS INDICTED

"The newer Western States," wrote Francis Adams, "enjoy one great advantage over the people of Massachusetts. They have been exempted from the immense labor of forever boasting of their ancestors, and so have more time to devote to their posterity." Adams was born and educated in central New York, but by 1875 when he wrote these ill-tempered sentences he had become an expatriate and lived in England. But the reformers of education in Massachusetts actually were in a position of some difficulty.

The schools of that colony had soon begun to decline from the standards set by the early laws. Their defects continued to grow and multiply until they led to the public school movement and controversy in the first half of the nineteenth century. The reformers of this period had to rouse Massachusetts from her educational slumbers; and they tried to do this by praising the educational wisdom and enterprise of the colony fathers while castigating the irresponsibility of their degenerate sons. But apparently such schools as most native-born historians ascribe to early Massachusetts never existed except in the first years and the wealthy eastern towns of the state.

In any event the reformers could not propose a return to the conditions of 1647 and therefore had to explain why the bright prospects of the Bay Colony had been dimmed. There was a sound judgment underneath the Adams sarcasm. Others also noticed that some newer states were more ambitious and less bound by the past than the East, but the West lacked the wealth and concentrated population of parts of New York and Massachusetts.

Three Massachusetts reformers gave comparable accounts of the short-comings of the contemporary schools. These were: James Gordon Carter (1795–1849), Samuel Read Hall (1795–1877), and Horace Mann (1796–1859). Carter had been a district school teacher before he prepared his two series of influential newspaper articles on education. These were also published in pamphlet form as *Letters . . . on the Free Schools of New England* (1824) and *Essays upon Popular Education* (1826). Elected to the legislature, Carter prepared a bill to establish normal schools, which failed, and one to create a state board of education, which succeeded (1837). Thus he opened the way for the career of Horace Mann, who continued to work on the lines proposed by Carter. Hall published his *Lectures on School-Keeping* and this contained a criticism of contemporary schools.

Although Carter praised the early schools of the colony, he admitted that they had not been free from bigotry and intolerance. He condemned the law of 1789 for its "alarming relaxation" of standards, but conceded that this law merely ratified what had long been common practice, the district organization and the neglect of the Latin schools. He charged that the people in his time were satisfied with short terms, irregular attendance, a narrow curriculum, ungraded schools, and untrained teachers. "Thus," he wrote, "we have departed more and more widely from the principle assumed by our fathers in the establishment of the Free Schools, viz., to provide as good instruction in all elementary and common branches of knowledge for the poorest citizen in the commonwealth as the richest could buy with all his wealth." But the early elementary schools were not free; the public high school became free in Massachusetts only in 1891; and Carter's statement tacitly admits that the purpose of colony action in education was to provide for the poor. He also agreed that the Latin schools were "always viewed with prejudice" as "an institution for the accommodation of a few at the expense of the many."

Good schools, said Carter, who was most effective when dealing with the positive side of his subject, will be expensive, for the district system must be abandoned. The schools must be graded, supplied with well-prepared teachers, uniform books, and a broader curriculum that must include physical education. He was not deceived by the Lancasterian schools, which he called "a hollow mockery." His outline of the normal school was almost a blueprint of the institutions later established under Mann. He favored Baconian inductive methods, knowing little of Pestalozzi. Before long the legislature, partly as a result of Carter's agitation, took action, restoring town control, establishing a common school fund, requiring the teaching of advanced subjects in large towns, and eventually creating the state board and a state education office.

The opening lectures in Hall's book on teaching also deal with the defects of the schools of New England and set down eight separate causes of their low condition. Some of these stemmed from scanty support resulting in poor buildings, a lack of teaching aids, low salaries, and teachers with only a district school education. But Hall believed that there were more fundamental causes. The communities were rent by sectarian controversies and the people refused to perform their Christian duties toward the schools. These conditions led to the establishment of private schools and the drawing off of still more support from public education and thus to the forming of a vicious circle.

As critic and reformer, Mann agreed with his contemporaries on the wisdom of the educational plans of the Bay Colony and, in contrast, on the bitterness of their present fruits. But the early laws were not as good as the reformers claimed. The early laws set no standards of support, or of teacher competence, and were silent on other vital matters. The famous law of 1647 merely said that "there shall be schools"; and the fine for noncompliance was so low that it constituted an invitation to evasion. Enforcement of the law depended upon the chance that some citizen would report the delinquent town to the general court.

In his *Tenth Report* as secretary of the Massachusetts Board of Education, Mann declared that it would be easy to write a history of popular education in Massachusetts. The cornerstone of this facile history was to be the declaration that the law of 1647 had made education both universal and free. Mann was mistaken. Girls were not regularly admitted to the common schools until after the Revolution. A school tax was first required by the law of 1827, and the schools were made free by the law of 1834.

Education is not universal when one-half of the children are excluded and the other half attend irregularly; and it is not free while rate bills are levied.

At the beginning of his term of office, Mann charged that the towns and visiting committees were not obeying the law. They did not, he declared, select uniform textbooks, employ qualified teachers, make the required reports, or even maintain the schools that the law enjoined. He did not fail to notice the poor support given to the public schools and the large amounts expended for private instruction. Absence from school, up to half the enrollment, was a major evil. The attendance of children was sometimes equally or even more disastrous. Every year from three to four hundred school rebellions resulted in the closing, before the end of the term, of one out of every ten schools in Massachusetts. This information comes from Mann's *Second Report*, not from a school novel. Bad school buildings were a contributing factor to bad conduct.

The teachers were not satisfactory. The solution of this problem was to be found in improved preparation, higher salaries, and better working conditions. And although there has been great improvement in all of these areas, this is just what is recommended now, more than a century after Mann. In his time the wages of a male teacher in Massachusetts were about equal to those of a farm hand. (See Table 5–1) Women earned less than men by one-half or two-thirds. Board was added to the money wage; but it had to be secured by boarding 'round. This Mann considered an indignity to which no teacher should be subjected.

The curriculum seemed poorly adapted to the needs of farmers, railroad builders, and factory operatives. Mann was a utilitarian and a moralist.

TABLE 5–1
TEACHERS' MONTHLY WAGES,
EXCLUSIVE OF BOARD, ABOUT 1847

	Men	Women
Massachusetts	$24.51	$ 8.07
Pennsylvania	17.02	10.09
Connecticut	16.00	6.50
Ohio	15.42	8.73
Maine	15.40	4.80
New York	14.96	6.69
New Hampshire	13.50	5.65
Michigan	12.71	5.36
Indiana	12.00	6.00
Vermont	12.00	4.75

From Mann's *Eleventh Report*. The states in the table are arranged in the order of the wages paid men teachers. Note that the rank order for women teachers is not the same.

Perhaps he was a utilitarian even in his ethics, but he was no professional philosopher and he may not have been clear on this point in his own mind. But he did believe that knowledge should be practically useful and that utility outranks artistic elegance and philosophic wisdom. This set for him the problem of selecting the most useful knowledge, a topic upon which Herbert Spencer also was to write.

In the report for 1839, Mann studied the knowledge needed by engineers, artisans, and machinists, namely, knowledge of materials, of power and its transmission, of mathematics; and for navigation, a knowledge of astronomy also. In citizenship and government, a sound judgment must be based upon knowledge of social organization and social forces. He said that all this applied with force to the manufacturing and commercial state of Massachusetts. He returned to this argument again and again. He urged the teaching of physiology, by which he meant both "the laws of life" and the preservation of health. He ended his curriculum theory with the conclusion that "caprice rather than intelligence has presided" over the selection of subjects.

To show how capricious the selection seemed to him, Mann raised such questions as the following: Do the numbers of the pupils who study the several subjects correspond to the relative importance of the studies? Why should algebra, which not one man in a thousand ever uses in the business of life, be studied by twice as many pupils as bookkeeping, which everyone, even the day laborer, needs? Is there a single subject more necessary than physiology? The conclusion was that a sound and practical treatise on the relative value of school studies was much needed. Such a book would show what studies should be taken up and in what order. It would enable students to pursue studies "for periods of time proportional to their respective utility."

We shall see that several writers have attempted to fill this need but without distinguished success. We shall note, for example, that Charles W. Eliot, president of Harvard University, thought bookkeeping, as taught, was a useless subject and algebra of great value; but in another connection he thought all subjects of equal value when seriously pursued for equal periods of time. Herbert Spencer, the English philosopher, and Edward Brooks, superintendent of the schools of Philadelphia, agreed more or less closely with Mann. That educators are unable to solve this basic curriculum problem is an educational misfortune if not a scandal.

MASSACHUSETTS VINDICATED

The vigor of the effort put forth by Massachusetts to improve education corresponded to the greatness of the need. Improvement depended upon the public mind and conscience. To gain the moral and financial support of the public for his proposals was Horace Mann's task in Massachusetts, as it was the problem of other reformers in other states as well. Mann, a lawyer, legislator, and politician, developed into a missionary, a public relations expert, and an educational field general. Against angry opposition on more than one front he won a series of campaigns if not the war. Final victory in this war, with lasting peace, is probably not possible. Men do not agree upon the kind of schools they want. Some do not want public schools at all. Unless the fight is constantly pressed, it will certainly be lost. This was one of Mann's axioms.

Mann was driven by the conviction that education is the certain means to prosperity, security, happiness, and salvation. It was no mere job that he had undertaken. It was a call, his vocation to make a better world. He did not invent but he used the suggestion to "open a school and close a jail." He was not alone in this faith. In 1830 all America hoped for a new social order and many were certain that education was the means to produce it. Much of this heady optimism has given way to a sounder, more moderate estimate of the power of education.

Mann used several means to reach the people. His annual report was his message on the state of public education in Massachusetts. In the reports he also considered large questions of theory and practice. He founded the *Common School Journal* (1839) to deal with issues as they arose and to reach the teachers, members of school boards, and the public. He was tireless in traveling over the state and addressing meetings. He regarded the normal schools as the most effective means to carry the new methods and ideas of good education to young teachers who would apply them. Unfortunately, they enrolled only a small minority of the state's teachers. Although it was no part of his official duty, Mann answered many calls from Southern and Western states for addresses and advice. Late in life, when president of Antioch College, he seems to have been asked to aid in framing a school code for the state of Iowa. He visited Europe and the resulting *Seventh Report* was one of his most famous publications. He entertained visiting educators who came for help, including Domingo Faustino Sarmiento from Chile.

School improvement had begun in Massachusetts before Mann became secretary. Even the law of 1789, which was the radical Samuel Adams' idea of radical democracy in education, had one progressive feature. It provided for the admission of girls to the district schools. A new epoch began in 1818. The primary schools and the high school of Boston may have influenced the enactment of the law of 1827, but this is not stated as a known result. An act of 1826 began to undo the errors of 1789 by partially restoring the control of the towns over the school districts. Each town was required to elect a school committee with the duty to choose the textbooks and to examine the teachers. The districts employed the teachers and managed the school property. Mann charged that two-thirds of the towns did not examine the teachers or did so merely perfunctorily; and he suspected collusion between town and district authorities to enable any district to employ any teachers whom the district wanted even though they could not qualify. One-third of the towns did not select the books; and as a result the textbooks were not uniform. In these and other cases, Mann's task was that of inducing local authorities to obey the laws.

A state school fund was established in 1834. Towns were to receive a proportionate share in the proceeds on the condition that they would annually raise $2 per child and would make the school reports required by the law. Thus the towns were to be remunerated for doing their duty. Mann's first report showed that in 1837 the annual cost of teaching a child in the district schools was $3.35 and in private schools, $12.

Everywhere in the nation there were groups of people who were against public education. In Massachusetts there were those who opposed school improvement because it would increase taxes; tend to centralize control; interfere with farm work, family discipline, or religion; and foster socialism. The economic upset of the panic of 1837 raised a tension that was increased by Mann's effort to have the laws obeyed and his success in establishing the state normal schools. The opposition declared the public schools godless, the normal schools useless and expensive, and the state board an example of Prussian centralization. The opposition to Mann is evidence of his influence. It may have been the state board that saved the state school office, which in some other states was at least temporarily abolished.

For one reason or another, Mann was under attack during much of his whole term of office (1837–1848); and some of the shafts were directed against him personally rather than against his policies. We shall not repeat these. But there were three particular controversies that filled most of those years. They were the attack upon the normal schools and board of education that came to a head in the legislature of 1840, the pamphlet war with the teachers of Boston, and the controversy over the teaching of religion in the common schools. The first two of these, Mann may be said to have won in the sense that he had the better of the argument and the opposition was silenced. The third was a running battle that continued for years, and although Mann may have won a tactical victory the question was not finally settled and the last of it has not yet been heard.

Mann and the board, not being satisfied with the condition of the schools, tried to improve them. This was their first offense. In 1839 the legislature passed a law that required every district, including those that maintained schools for only two or three months, to extend the annual school term to six months. In the same year the legislature accepted, from Edmund Dwight, public-spirited citizen and friend of Mann, a donation of $10,000 and added to it an equal amount for state normal schools, the first in America. One was opened at Lexington, the same year, in an academy building that stood facing the town common. Three were established in Mann's term, and two others later.

In the winter of 1840 a well-planned assault was made upon the board of education and its "Prussian" policy of state control of education. Actually the board had no important powers of control. The committee on education in the lower house split over the issues. The majority report was an itemized attack upon the board and also upon the whole idea of professional education. This again is a matter that has not been settled in a hundred years. The hostile majority in the committee addressed themselves to the interests of private teachers and their influential patrons, to the taxpayers still wincing from the effects of the panic of 1837, to religious sectaries, and to the pride of self-made teachers. The weakness of their attack was in its lack of any positive plan to improve the common schools; and the people and legislature had come to believe that the common schools needed improvement. The legislature voted to support the board and to develop the normal schools. But such questions can rarely be settled permanently and today the content and value of the professional education of teachers is again an issue.

The *Seventh Report* of Mann contained his account of his European journey and his conclusions upon what he had observed. He was favorably impressed with much that he saw in German schools, the knowledge, teaching skill and unobtrusive management shown by the teachers, the curriculum, and the friendly relations between teachers and taught. Mann's praise of Europe was taken by some Boston teachers as disparagement of their own knowledge, skill, and discipline. Thirty-one principals started a pamphlet attack, and Mann replied. The shrill tone of his rejoinders has been criticized. Outsiders joined in the fray, which lasted for a year and a half and attracted the attention of the whole country.

The subject of corporal punishment, against which Mann expressed decided adverse opinions, irritated the masters most of all. Mann did not propose to have physical chastisement completely banned but he wanted all other available means of reform tried first. In the Boston schools it is said to have been administered freely and with great severity. Edward Everett Hale considered the Boston masters "inferior men" and believed that "cowhiding" and "thrashing" were their chief accomplishments. He reported in A *New England Boyhood* that his father would not send him to such schools as the Boston grammar schools were but did send him to the Latin school, "a civilized place." At a somewhat earlier time, however, if not when Hale was a pupil, there was a good deal of flogging even in the Latin school, with all its civilization, and also a robust school rebellion that drove the teacher from his post.

The sequel to this controversy with the Boston masters was a city-wide written examination of the pupils of the grammar schools. This was arranged by Mann and his friend Samuel Gridley Howe, who had conveniently been elected at the proper time to the Boston school board. As a result, four of the grammar school principals were dismissed from their positions.

The most sustained of the controversies in which Mann was involved grew out of the demand by fundamentalists for doctrinal religious teaching in the schools. This would have been contrary to a law of 1827 that was reenacted in principle in 1835. Mann was not to be blamed for the law itself, but he had interpreted it and urged compliance with its provisions. And he was a Unitarian at heart, although not a member of any denomination at the time, and his personal religion was brought under attack. Those of the opposition understood that he would make no concession to their demands.

The controversy could have been anticipated. In the circumstances it was almost inevitable. Dogmatic Calvinism had been taught in the schools of Massachusetts from the settlement for almost two centuries. The *New England Primer* and the *Westminster Catechism* had been in daily use. The minister regularly visited the schools to teach religion and to see that it was taught.

Meanwhile, two religious changes were taking place. With the acceptance of a policy of toleration many sects came in; and secondly, orthodoxy was losing ground to a growing liberalism. Within two generations of the settlement of Boston, the liberal religious trend at Harvard became one of the reasons for the founding of Yale. In his youth, John Adams, born in 1735, became aware of the growth of Unitarian sentiment among his friends and neighbors. In a well-known educational clause of the Massachusetts Constitution of 1780, which was written by Adams, the legislature is enjoined to cherish humanity, benevolence, charity, and other virtues, but religion is not mentioned. Before the time of Horace Mann the orthodox Calvinists had become a minority in the state and it had become impossible to find any sectarian creed that everybody, or even a majority, wanted taught.

All this led directly to the prohibition of sectarian teaching by the law of 1827. But there was remaining a large body of Calvinists, both Congregational and Presbyterian, in the state and outside of it, who felt in conscience bound to try to turn back the clock. Mann was caught between two irreconcilable parties.

Mann proposed to have the schools teach what was common to Protestant creeds, to have the Bible read without comment, and to have teachers by word and life illustrate nonsectarian Christianity. Even though Roman Catholics and unbelievers did not enter the fight, Mann did not satisfy his opponents. They called his proposal a "godless scepticism." The Presbyterian Synod of New Jersey in 1845 expressed the fear that it would develop "infidel youth who will not be fit to maintain our free institutions." The editor of a Protestant Episcopal church paper accused him of "watering down" Christianity. The worst result of the controversy was that it led to an attack upon the whole concept of universal, free education. Mann was not to bear the blows unaided. Many papers came to his defense. Many orthodox as well as liberal Christians, including the governor of the state, who was a Baptist, supported him. For many years a solution similar to the one proposed in Mann's time was widely accepted but, as every newspaper reader knows, the question of religion in relation to public education is again a problem today.

In spite of all the opposition and indeed partly because of it and through it, Mann succeeded in powerfully stimulating public education in Massachusetts. The opposition drew to his side many supporters, and there were also many who had from the first been his friends and friends of the cause. Such were Edmund Dwight, who gave $10,000 for normal schools, Governor Edward Everett, Josiah Quincy, then president of Harvard College, Charles Brooks, a promoter of normal schools, Senator Charles Sumner, George B. Emerson, author and teacher of note, and numerous others. Mann promoted too many improvements to have all of them named here. He aided in bringing back the town government of schools in place of the district system; in the formation of school libraries with books useful for morals, health, agriculture, and other practical interests; in developing instruction in vocal music and drawing and improved methods in teaching primary reading; in developing a sane discipline; in urging the construction of decent schoolhouses and the introduction of blackboards; in forming teachers' institutes that in Massachusetts were able to enlist the genius of Agassiz; in establishing the payment of school board members for attendance at meetings; and, dearest to his heart of all his improvements, in the creation of the state normal schools. His reputation extended far beyond Massachusetts to all parts of the United States, to South America and Europe. Many people from the Southern and Western states applied to him for help with their school problems. In France and England tribute was paid to his talents and achievements.

He said: "I regard normal schools as a new instrument of progress for the improvement of the human race. I consider that without them the public schools would lose their strength and power for good and become mere charity schools." Much as he disliked to admit it, that is what the public schools were when all the wealthier families patronized private schools and when even in the public schools those able to pay were asked to do so. "Neither the art of printing," he wrote, "nor the freedom of the press, nor free suffrage could long subsist for useful and salutary ends if schools for the education of teachers ceased to exist."

Before the expiration of Mann's period in office (1837–1848) the cause of public education and the development of state systems had made great progress in Massachusetts and the nation. By 1848, twenty-four of the thirty states of the Union had a state school office, although some offices were directed by *ex officio* chiefs. The local school tax and state aid were widely accepted and formed the fulcrum and lever of school improvement.

In Massachusetts during Mann's secretaryship, the annual state appropriation had doubled and local taxation had grown even more rapidly. More than $2,000,000 was expended in improving schoolhouses. Salaries had increased by more than 50 per cent. The average school term had been lengthened. Much of the progress, however, had occurred only in the richer parts of the state. By 1847 Mann had been converted to the principle of compulsory attendance, and in 1852 Massachusetts passed a law requiring children to attend school. As this was the first such law in the nation, it was, as one would expect, a weak one. The state normal schools, also the first in the Union, had become fairly well established, and three states, New York, Connecticut, and Michigan, had established similar institutions.

It would be difficult to assign the proper share of credit for these achievements to the chief movers. Certainly Mann was a powerful force, a great promoter, a devoted servant. But many of the ideas had been proposed before his time. The normal school idea had been urged for fifty years and recently by two great governors of the state, Levi Lincoln and Edward Everett. Finally, the donation of Dwight, the management of Mann, and the teaching skill of Cyrus Peirce brought them into existence and then saved them from threatened destruction. In this and other ways Massachusetts became an educational leader and example in the time of Horace Mann.

SUMMARY

The Lancasterian schools prepared the way for the transition from private to public education; and this transition took place in the period preceding the Civil War. The new idea was to provide free education for all children in public schools, open to all classes and to rich and poor alike. This principle was favored by the democratic trends in the country. The early tendency was to interpret the principle to cover only elementary schooling for white children; but a much broader interpretation is now accepted.

Public education is variously defined, but the key fact is this, that it is controlled and administered by those who are appointed by and accountable to the civil electorate, the voters. Public education is developed in state systems that vary from state to state; but there are powerful influences that tend to direct the development of the state systems along parallel paths.

The state that first developed a present-day type of system was New York. In that state a Board of Regents for secondary and higher education was created in 1784 and the first common school superintendency in 1812.

New York used the method of stimulating local effort by rewarding units that raised their own contribution, by granting them state appropriations. The state began to aid the preparation of teachers in 1834, established a normal school in 1844, and gave public support to high schools in 1853.

After nine years the state superintendency was abolished and the duties of the office added to those of the secretary of state. This plan was continued until 1853, when the state superintendency was restored. Half a century later the secondary-higher and the primary systems were united into one state school administrative agency (1904).

Because of the diverse nationalities and religions in the state, Pennsylvania found it hard to pass a general school law. Even so she was the next state after New York to create such a law (1834) but on an optional basis only. It was in 1857 that the state established a separate state superintendency. Until that time the secretary of state had performed the duties of such an office.

Ohio was admitted in 1803 and was the first state to receive the federal land grants for public schools, commonly called Sixteenth Section grants; and additional grants for a university. The other states west of Ohio shared in this distribution of land for schools. In Ohio as in New York the office of state superintendent was abolished and not restored until after the middle of the century. In Michigan and Massachusetts among the early states this office was permanent from the first, although efforts were made to destroy it. Indiana is a good state in which to study the influence of the frontier upon education. The public schools of Indiana, California, and New York did not become free until after the Civil War, but later states provided for free education from the first and in some cases even while they had only territorial status. This is an example of older states influencing the practice of newer ones. California was much influenced by New York.

New England was famous for good schools in its cities, but there were many children not in school even in the cities and many poor schools in the country districts. Excepting Massachusetts, the states in this section were not especially prompt in developing state systems nor were these highly developed at first. Massachusetts was in the van and profited from the promotion work of several governors and from that of James G. Carter, but especially from the leadership of Horace Mann. Many who migrated from Massachusetts to the West helped to develop public education in distant states.

QUESTIONS

1. What part can philanthropy play in a nation served by public education? Consider the individual donors, the campaigns for funds, the

wealthy foundations, contributions to colleges by business corporations.

2. Did the Lancasterian method of mutual instruction rest upon a true insight into education and psychological processes? In what ways could the method be usefully employed today?

3. How much of the history of American education could be treated under what is here called "an American principle"?

4. Why is it difficult to define *public education?*

5. Why did many states retrace their steps in the development of their systems of education? Study cases.

6. What are the essential parts of a state system?

7. Why were permissive laws frequently enacted and with what results? What national education acts were permissive? What further use could be made of this strategy?

8. Outline the somewhat conflicting, at least contrasting, effects of the frontier upon educational development. Do these tend to support the "Turner thesis"?

9. Would it have been better tactics for the Massachusetts reformers to assert that they were proposing a radically different educational program than the one initiated by the founders of the colony? How was it different?

10. What was the "vicious circle" in the fact that both private and public schools existed in large numbers in Massachusetts? What is the probability of a return to this condition in the United States?

11. How does one reconcile the common belief in a century of progress with the fact that the schools are now, as then, suffering from low salaries, uncongenial working conditions, teacher shortages, many partially unqualified teachers, and so on?

12. In Chapter Two of *A New England Boyhood* by Edward Everett Hale, it is said: "It will be hard to make boys and girls of the present day understand how much was then expected from reforms in education." Collect and analyze the evidence; and compare it with the hopes of 1900 and after.

13. Why did Mann become involved in more than one man's share of educational controversy?

14. Why do you judge the controversies to have been favorable (or unfavorable) to the improvement of education?

BOOKS AND PAPERS

A literature of school reminiscences exists in several, perhaps in all civilized, languages. Such memories are frequently worked into novels such as *The Hoosier Schoolmaster,* which is an eminent example of a large class. In his *American Journal of Education,* Barnard prints many reminiscences, and Professor Thomas Woody transmits one such account in the *History of Education*

Journal (Winter, 1954). For documents, such as teachers' contracts, see Cubberley's *Readings in Public Education;* Knight and Hall's *Readings in American Educational History* (New York, 1951). The National Education Association provides reprints of Mann's *Reports* at a modest price.

ADAMS, FRANCIS, *Free School System of the United States,* London, 1875.

BILLINGTON, R. A., *The Protestant Crusade, 1800–1860,* New York, 1938.

BISHOP, E. A., *Development of a State School System: New Hampshire,* New York, Teachers College, Columbia University, 1930.

BOURNE, W. O., *History of the Public School Society of the City of New York,* New York, 1870.

BRUBACHER, JOHN S., *Judicial Power of the New York Commissioner of Education,* New York, Teachers College, Columbia University, 1927.

CARTER, J. G., *Letters on the Free Schools of New England,* Boston, 1824; *Essays on Popular Education,* Boston, 1826.

COMPAYRÉ, GABRIEL, *Horace Mann and the Public School in the United States,* New York, 1907. The translation from the French is by Mary D. Frost, and the book is evidence of the esteem in which Mann was held abroad.

CUBBERLEY, E. P., "The School System in San Francisco," *Educational Review,* April, 1901.

CULVER, R. B., *Horace Mann and Religion in the Massachusetts Public Schools,* Yale University Press, 1925.

HAMILTON, O. T., *The Courts and the Curriculum,* New York, Teachers College, Columbia University, 1927.

HAMILTON, ROBERT R., and PAUL MORT, *The Law and Education with Cases,* Chicago, 1941.

HINSDALE, B. A., *Horace Mann and the Common School Revival,* New York, 1898.

JACKSON, SIDNEY, *America's Struggle for Free Schools,* Washington, 1941.

KENNEDY, M. F., *Schoolmaster of Yesterday,* New York, 1940. Written in collaboration with Alvin F. Harlow.

McCADDEN, JOSEPH J., *Education in Pennsylvania, 1801–1835,* University of Pennsylvania Press, 1937, with bibliography.

McVEY, F. L., *The Gates Open Slowly, A History of Education in Kentucky,* University of Kentucky Press, 1949.

MANN, MARY, ed., *Life and Works of Horace Mann,* in five volumes, Boston, 1867. Volume I is a life of Mann by his wife and the other volumes contain his writings and official reports.

MONROE, PAUL, *Founding of the American Public School System,* New York, 1940.

NORTON, A. O., *The First State Normal School, The Journals of Cyrus Peirce and Mary Swift,* Harvard University Press, 1926.

REEDER, W. G., *Chief State School Official,* Washington, U.S. Government Printing Office, Bureau of Education Bulletin, 1924, No. 5.

REIGART, J. F., *Lancasterian System in New York City,* New York, Teachers College, Columbia University, 1916.

RIPPA, S. ALEXANDER, *Educational Ideas in America,* New York, 1969.

SPAULDING, F. E., *One School Administrator's Philosophy*, New York, 1952, containing an account of rural education in New Hampshire about 1875.

STEWART, W., and W. M. FRENCH, "The Influence of Horace Mann on Sarmiento," *Hispanic-American Historical Review*, February, 1940.

SWETT, JOHN, *Public Education in California*, New York, 1911.

WILLIAMS, E. I. F., *Horace Mann, Educational Statesman*, New York, 1937.

Chapter 6

FROM SCHOOLKEEPING TO TEACHING

The adoption of the principle of free education for all in a public school common to all led to the adoption of new principles of teaching. These principles were compounded of parts of political equality, democracy, and practicality, with the idealism, scientific method, and child psychology that stemmed from Comenius, Francis Bacon, John Locke, and Rousseau. To assign particular items to individual authors would be difficult.

The great mediator through whom the foreign ideas were transmitted was Pestalozzi, who has been called the founder of the modern elementary school. It is modern because it offers a liberal education instead of teaching merely the literary skills to which the old school mainly restricted itself. But Pestalozzi worked in Switzerland, wrote in German, which few Americans could read, and his career closed in 1827. These factors, added to the wide difference between the American and European societies, made an exact translation of his program impossible. But an American version of his principles together with native ideas changed schoolkeeping to teaching.

The ideas of Pestalozzi had their period of greatest influence in the educational awakening. But it was his ideas also that at a later date formed the closest alliance with the kindergarten and child study ideas to form what was called the "new education," and served, still later, as the opening phase of Progressive education. Teachers and textbook writers frequently indicated their debt to Pestalozzi, but not all of them. This was perhaps in the nature of things for, as Horace Mann said, many shared Pestalozzi's views and applied his principles who had never heard his name. Many also must have independently developed views and practices similar to his. It is by no means safe to equate similarity to a source with derivation from it.

AN EARLY INTERPRETER

Joseph Neef, who had been one of Pestalozzi's assistants at Burgdorf in Switzerland, was brought to Pennsylvania by William Maclure, a philanthropic Scotch-American who was also a leading geologist. The purpose was to introduce Pestalozzi's methods; in a few years Neef published his *Sketch of a Plan and Method of Education* (1808) and opened a school near Philadelphia. The school had to meet the competition of the Lancasterian system at the time of its rising popularity; but Neef obtained pupils, some from great distances. One of his pupils was David Farragut, later an admiral but then a young midshipman. The admiral gave a good report of his early schooling, of the useful knowledge gained, the oral instruction, the collections of minerals and plants gathered on long excursions with their hatless teacher, the swimming, climbing, and military drill. This was evidently no Gradgrind's school. Neef also taught at New Harmony, Indiana, in Robert Owen's community and at other places, but he failed to make any deep impression.

The book by Neef is a first-hand account of the Pestalozzian program and the first such account given to Americans. He proposed to have his pupils learn by inquiry and investigation. They would learn old things in a new way. Arithmetic was taught in very short steps, using objects and by having the pupils work out the number combinations. Drawing was to come before writing, and a great deal of oral work before reading. Books were not to be used until after the pupil had made much progress through conversation. In geography the pupils were to measure gardens and fields and draw plans to scale. The book shows Pestalozzi's work in his earlier rather than his Yverdon period.

VOICES OF THE PROFESSION

Early educational journals gave educators a chance to discuss the principles of teaching. One such paper, *The Academician* (New York, 1818–1820), published interpretations of the views of Locke, George Jardine, Scottish professor and author of *Outlines of Philosophical Education* (1818), Richard Edgeworth and his daughter, Maria Edgeworth, the authors of *Practical Education* (1798), and Pestalozzi. An anonymous contributor who had collected books on Pestalozzi by French and German authors was convinced that these views, already well known in Europe, should also be published in the United States. He described Pestalozzi's object lessons with their use of observation, description, and drawing; and he devoted space to the Swiss educator's *Mothers' Book*. In the second installment of the series, he wrote as though he were reporting a personal observation of the routine of the Yverdon school, and indeed as though he had taken part in a first lesson of the day. This lesson was a walk before breakfast to study nature and to collect objects for further study. The author identified himself only as "a native of Clinton County." This county occupies the northeastern corner of New York state.

At this time (1818) John Griscom, chemist and teacher, was touring Europe and he visited Pestalozzi; but being unable to speak German he had to depend upon the account given him by J. P. Greaves, an Englishman then living at Yverdon. Griscom attended classes in arithmetic, languages, and drawing, and observed an exercise in which Pestalozzi, as Griscom understood, taught religion. He made some observations on the teacher's earnestness and the pupil's close attention. Griscom reported that there was nothing mechanical in Pestalozzi's school, as there was in Lancaster's, and he professed to believe that the Swiss teacher's life and labors were forming "a most important epoch in the history of education." But this favorable view did not prevent him from shortly establishing a private Lancasterian high school in New York City. Not in this case alone were the practical realities of America more powerful than an ideal. In Emerson's words "Cripple Practice" could not overtake "Winged Theory."

A second teacher's magazine, the *American Journal of Education* (Boston, 1826–1830) was founded by William Russell (1798–1873). Russell was educated at Glasgow, Scotland, under George Jardine. In the first number of the *Journal*, Russell recommended the teaching of history to small children by means of stories told by the teacher, and urged that the stories should deal with local happenings so that the children could be taken to visit the places where they had occurred. He argued for home geography also. He urged the use of supplementary reading material so that the children would not be compelled "to plod their weary way again and again over the same lessons." These ideas, if they were not his own, may have come from the Hill family, which employed such methods at the Hazelwood School near Birmingham, England; or they may have been diffused in the educational atmosphere from the writings of Locke, Rousseau, and the Edgeworths.

The early numbers of Russell's *American Journal* treated American topics and reported American news. In its pages appear the men and measures that were changing education. The abortive effort of 1825 to establish a state school of agriculture in Massachusetts, as recommended by Governor Levi Lincoln, is reported. There were articles on physical education, mutual instruction, the education of girls, and the infant school, the newest thing on the educational horizon. Russell published the "Faculty Report" of 1826 directed to the trustees of Amherst College in which there was proposed "a department of the science of education" for that institution; and the Massachusetts law of March 10, 1827, which provided a legal basis for the public high school in that state. There is a description of the Gardiner Lyceum in Maine, with a particular account of the plan of student self-government followed in that school.

The *Journal* did not print much on Pestalozzi, and this may have been because of lack of information about him. In the July number of 1827 there was a favorable review of *The Pestalozzian Primer* (Harrisburg, 1827). The compiler of this schoolbook was John M. Keagy, a Swiss-American physician who was conducting a Pestalozzian school in Harrisburg. In the November number there is an obituary paragraph on Pestalozzi, then recently deceased. More than a year later Russell compiled from *The Academician* of the preceding decade an article on Pestalozzi's principles of instruction. This came out in 1829 in the March–April number of the *Journal*, which had recently been changed from a monthly to a bimonthly magazine. This is evidence that it was not prospering, and after two more years its place was taken by the *American Annals of Education* with William C. Woodbridge as editor.

In a candid footnote to the article taken from *The Academician*, it is explained that Russell had no knowledge of the earlier paper when he started the *Journal*. Russell declared that he had thought of himself as an absolute pioneer in American educational journalism. Was this error because of the obscurity of *The Academician*, to the lack of libraries and infrequent communication between educators, or to the provincialism of Russell and his associates? We do not know. The fact may be evidence of nothing more than a faulty memory. Twenty years later Russell in an address again erroneously referred to his *Journal* as "the first enterprise of the kind in the English language."

How much of Russell's mature doctrine was because of Pestalozzi also remains in doubt. The content of his *Intellectual Education*, prepared about 1850, has many points of agreement with the Pestalozzian system of ideas. He emphasizes the training of the perceptive faculties. He would encourage the child's curiosity and the kindred element of wonder. He extolled the advantages of novelty and variety in teaching and proposed the study of insects to develop habits of attentive observation. He tried to find an ABC of observation, almost certainly a Pestalozzian idea; and chose color, form, number, weight, and sound for his alphabet. He urged the use of teaching aids. He would not have teachers ask questions prepared in the textbook but proposed instead the use of questions asked by the children themselves. The purpose of all this was the development of the mental powers to compare, classify, and generalize.

Pestalozzianism "by association" is indicated by Russell's selection of the faculty of the private normal school that he founded at Lancaster, Massachusetts, in 1853. The group included Lowell Mason, Hermann Krüsi, Jr., Dana P. Colburn, Louis Agassiz, and Arnold Guyot. Of these the first three were avowed disciples of the Swiss master. Agassiz and Guyot paid no attention to pedagogy, but in their teaching methods they fitted in with the others.

The conclusion is that before 1830 little was known of Pestalozzi in New England and not a great deal in the rest of the country. The Fellenberg manual labor system, which had a Pestalozzian origin, was introduced in 1816 and began to spread about 1830. Some of this was because of William C. Woodbridge, who had traveled in Europe and who continued the work of the *American Journal* in the *American Annals of Education*. He did much more than Russell had done to publish the doctrines of both Fellenberg and Pestalozzi. Other educational journals are listed in Table 6–1.

TABLE 6–1
EDUCATIONAL JOURNALS OF THE AWAKENING

1. *Academician*	New York	1818–1820
2. *American Journal of Education*	Boston	1826–1830
3. *Teachers' Guide and Parents' Assistant*	Portland, Me.	1826–1828
4. *American Quarterly Register and Journal of the American Education Society*	Andover	1829–1843
5. *American Annals of Education*	Boston	1830–1839
6. *Common School Assistant*	Albany	1836–1840
7. *Common School Advocate*	Cincinnati	1837–1841
8. *Western Academician and Journal of Education and Science*	Cincinnati	1838–1839
9. *Journal of Education*	Detroit, etc.	1838–1840
10. *Connecticut Common School Journal*	Hartford	1838–1842
11. *Common School Journal*	Boston	1839–1852
12. *District School Journal*	Albany	1840–1852
13. *Common School Journal of the State of Pennsylvania*	Philadelphia	1844
14. *Journal of the Rhode Island Institute of Instruction*		1845–1849
15. *Ohio School Journal*	Kirtland and Columbus	1846–1850

Note.—Although none of the above journals was permanent—and only three survived for more than a decade—these were among the most important magazines of the teaching profession during the first quarter century of the awakening.

A second instrument of publicity was the official report on education in foreign countries. In later times and more academic circles, this type of reporting came to be known as a form of comparative education. Three reports on European, chiefly German, education had a special importance. Victor Cousin made a study, for the French government of Louis Philippe, of the organization of the Prussian schools (1831). At the request of the Ohio legislature, Calvin E. Stowe in 1837 reported on elementary instruction in Europe, and this study was reprinted in the official documents of six states in addition to Ohio, namely Pennsylvania, which provided both an English and a German text, Michigan, Massachusetts, North Carolina, New York, and Virginia. And the third example was by Horace Mann, whose observations of 1843 were included in his *Seventh Report* to the Massachusetts board. It was this that touched off the controversy with the teachers of Boston; but its real importance lay in its account of the teachers, teaching, and spirit of the German schools.

Among the topics treated by Stowe and Mann were many that were new, or new to Americans, at that time. Instead of beginning with the alphabet on the children's first day of school, the German teachers prepared them for instruction in reading by conversation lessons; and when reading was begun it was taught by a combination of word and phonic methods. Mann fought hard for better methods in primary reading, and although his influence prevailed in some schools, the alphabet was still taught first in many schools at the end of the century.

The German schools had an "enriched" curriculum. Object lessons, nature study, home geography, music, and drawing, common subjects where the influence of Pestalozzi was felt, were not often found in America in 1840. Arithmetic taught by analysis instead of by rule aroused Mann's admiration, whereas Stowe, referring to the books by Warren Colburn or Joseph Ray, thought this method was already in common use in the United States. Stowe was right about the books but may have been mistaken about their wide use and influence.

German teachers were active. They did not sit down, they moved about. They knew their material, needing no book in the hand while teaching. They did not hear lessons, they taught children, taught them knowledge, ideas, skills, and subjects. They held the attention and were kind and considerate. Mann saw no evidence of the use of corporal punishment. It is just possible that he was not shown everything. There is no doubt that these two reports, widely read, made an impression upon the teaching and conduct of schools in favored places. But we must not forget the angry retort of the Boston masters, nor fail to notice that cities farther removed from Mann in space and mental outlook did not bother to reply. In the open country the ideas may have had little immediate effect.

Mann was critical of the autocracy of the German rulers and the submissiveness of their people and he was not, perhaps, unaware that schools can be used to produce slaves. But he waxed enthusiastic over the German schools and their teachers. He came back more than ever convinced that the normal school held the key to the improved education of the future. Massachusetts had opened a state normal school four years earlier, in July, 1839. It followed the programs developed by T. H. Gallaudet and J. G. Carter and was actually provided by equal amounts of private and public money. But it was Mann's persistence and the generous contribution of his friend, Edmund Dwight, that made the school a reality. Two others were added soon after. In 1844 New York also founded one in Albany. A total of about a dozen state normal schools were in operation by 1861.

The early normal schools reviewed the common branches with their teen-age pupils, added a few secondary school studies, taught two or three courses in methods, school management, and elementary psychology, and conducted a primary school for observation and practice teaching. The normal schools formed a third means of turning schoolkeeping into teaching and by far the most effective one in the case of those whom they reached. But they reached so few. For every teacher who had graduated from a normal school, or even attended one for part of a year, the typical state had to employ many with less preparation or none.

Other means were also used to reach more teachers. The teachers' institute, meeting once a year for only a week, and the normal institute with a term of four to six weeks were invented in the forties. High schools introduced a teachers' normal course. County and city normal schools were established. City superintendents conducted Saturday classes for professional study. Teachers' associations, presenting speakers on educational improvement, became active about 1830. That is when the American Institute of Instruction in the East and the Western Literary Institute and College of Professional Teachers of the Midwest were organized. The state teachers' associations followed. All of these brought books, magazines, educational leaders, information, and ideas to the teachers. Of great importance was the summer school, but that developed after the Civil War. Not all teachers heard the call of these voices, or, hearing, caught the vision of a new school; but what they heard and gathered was a gain. No one had even spoken to their predecessors of a better way.

A LIGHT-BEARER

Those who prefer to have their history presented in neat, separate periods might find three eras in the nineteenth century. These would be the academy movement, the educational awakening, and the "new education." Mann and Henry Barnard (1811–1900) both began their lifework in the awakening. Mann's career closed early at Antioch College; but Barnard, who lived to the age of almost ninety years, continued on through the new education of William Torrey Harris, William H. Payne, Francis W. Parker, and their contemporaries.

Although Mann and Barnard agreed upon many questions, they were very different personalities. No great controversies are associated with Barnard's name. His opponents rarely attacked him and he attacked no one. He had the temperament of the student and it was owing to him that educators had the information to form considered opinions upon the educational questions of his time. Some, at least, of the light that he shed was his own. He was a source as well as a bearer of educational wisdom.

Both Mann and Barnard were drafted for work in education. Neither chose it, but Barnard had unconsciously made some preparation for it. At Yale he had successfully cultivated the art of public speech. He took several trips in the United States and in 1835–1836 he made the first of several extended tours of Europe. On this first European visit he became acquainted with the Pestalozzian movement and met the educational statesman Henry Brougham in England. He thought highly of travel as a means of education, and doubtless gained that benefit from his own journeys; but the most useful result for others came from the ideas and knowledge of education that he gathered.

He has been called an interpreter of Pestalozzi, but he was much more. He also interpreted Froebel, the kindergarten, the normal school, and other means for the professional education of teachers. He recognized the favorable effect of the high school upon the lower schools. He had as great an interest in the practical problems as in the theory of education, and he provided full knowledge on many topics in place of the scattered information that alone was available before.

When the Connecticut legislature provided for a state board to promote the common schools, Barnard was chosen its secretary. After four active years he found himself without an office because party politics had caused the repeal of the law of 1838. The same sort of attack had succeeded, as noted previously, in Ohio and elsewhere, but had failed in Massachusetts. Until the political wheel in Connecticut turned full circle, Barnard was appointed to the state education office in Rhode Island and then, with the Whigs again in power, he returned to his own state as state superintendent and principal of the new state normal school. Barnard claimed that he made fifteen hundred speeches on education in the course of his life, most of them in his fifteen years as state school officer. He visited schools, advised and encouraged teachers, founded and edited state school journals in the two states in which he served, answered a heavy mail, and made out his annual reports.

In his first annual report, Barnard gave an account of his observations on European education. In 1850 the Connecticut legislature asked him to prepare two books for teachers. He prepared a work on school architecture, the first systematic treatise on the subject. It created a new branch of professional study. The second book was on the professional education of teachers and covered the whole subject as it existed at that time. A few years later he issued a third book, a work on comparative education with the title, *National Education in Europe*.

Barnard's greatest literary achievement was his *American Journal of Education*, the second educational journal to use this title. It was started in 1855 and continued for thirty-one volumes. It has been called an encyclopedia of education, but it lacks organization and is rather a thesaurus or treasury of educational materials. Its value was increased when, after Barnard's time, an index to the *Journal* was prepared.

In practical administration Barnard was not successful. Such was his fame that extraordinary numbers of city superintendencies, state university presidencies, and normal school principalships were offered him. He was for brief periods president of the University of Wisconsin and of St. John's College, and was for three years (1867–1870) the first United States commissioner of education. But he was no politician; his administrative practices were loose; and he expected everyone to be discreet, honest, and loyal, and was, therefore, if for no other reason, a bad judge of men.

The whole range of education received the attention of Barnard. He favored infant schools and was apparently the first native American to notice the kindergarten, an example of which he saw in London when he was a delegate to an international exposition. This was the kindergarten conducted by a sister of the German-American Mrs. Carl Schurz, who opened a little private kindergarten in her home at Watertown, Wisconsin, in 1855. He was an earnest promoter of high schools and adult education. And although he had only the briefest experience as a teacher, he turned a bright light into and over all the schools of his time.

TRANSCENDENTAL SCHOOLMASTER

A list of home-grown educators of the early national period includes the names of Ralph Waldo Emerson and Bronson Alcott (1799–1888) and places these men in the same idealist and transcendentalist bracket. As educational philosophers they belonged to the school that regards individual growth as the end, and self-expression and creative activity as the great means, of education. The members of this school differ among themselves at many points, for the group includes Rousseau, Froebel, Tolstoi, and Dewey. In their educational philosophy, Emerson and Alcott were bold and enterprising. But in practice as a young teacher Emerson was timid and conventional. Alcott supported his brave words with deeds and took the unhappy consequences.

In a letter Alcott explained that whatever children themselves do becomes a part of them; and that he did not measure progress by the number of pages covered. He declared that instruction should not be drawn from books alone. It is absurd to believe statements just because they are found in print. How to escape such a silly plight? His answer, worthy of Emerson, was that children should learn to be independent and even eccentric if their reason approves. This was not copied from Emerson but anticipated him. It shows that the author did not mean to be a docile disciple. The course here recommended is a discipline for heroes and martyrs.

Alcott's preparation included the peddling of tinware among the planters' families of the South, who taught him gentility, an initiation in North Carolina into the Quaker doctrine of the inner light that blended with his native mysticism, and the reading of Milton, John Bunyan, William Penn's *No Cross, No Crown*, the *Journals* of George Fox and John

Woolman, and many other books, including some about Pestalozzi but none by him. His cousin and friend, William A. Alcott, was acquainted with William C. Woodbridge, and Woodbridge, who made several tours of Europe, was able to tell the Alcotts about education in foreign lands. This was not the usual preparation of country school teachers.

At the age of twenty-four Bronson Alcott began, and for five years continued, to teach in district schools near his home in Connecticut. From his home he went to Boston to teach in an infant school, then to Germantown, Pennsylvania; and finally he conducted the Temple School in Boston (1834–1836) until its sudden debacle permanently ended his career as a teacher of children.

His teaching became progressively freer and more untraditional as he gained in experience and suffered from opposition. Of opposition there was no lack. In his first school he introduced light gymnastics including exercises that to the eyes of his Puritan patrons resembled dancing, and the children dramatized stories. Even these mild innovations disturbed some of the parents, but they did not interfere. There was carping because there was not enough memorizing and because the children were encouraged to express their own ideas on questions they did not understand.

Alcott, like the noted English headmaster, Edward Thring, of Uppingham School, thought the "almighty wall" a great teacher; and he tried to make his walls and his entire schoolroom beautiful, spending his little sum of money somewhat lavishly for works of art and fine furniture. Mystic and neo-Platonist that he was, he considered nature a symbol of the divine reality. Under the influence of Wordsworth's *Ode* he came to believe that inborn truth, the ideas and sentiments of the children's minds, were proper objects of introspective study by the children.

The curriculum of the Temple School has been published. In the twenty-two lessons that made up the work of a week, two dealt with arithmetic, two with geography, one was a drawing lesson, and the other seventeen were devoted to word study, conversations on soul and body and on the Gospels, and to writing in the pupils' personal journals. The absence of science is to be noted. Not the senses but the "inner sense" was what Alcott was bent upon cultivating.

The final explosion at the Temple School was occasioned by the publication of the *Conversations on the Gospels*, exercises that he had conducted with the children. There were other causes. Alcott was an abolitionist in an era when Boston was wildly antiabolitionist; his faithful and very capable and sensible wife was Abbie May, the sister of a noted abolitionist, S. J. May; the Alcotts had made a friendly visit to William Lloyd Garrison when he was confined in city prison. Alcott had admitted a Negro girl as a pupil of his school. But it was the *Conversations* that started the withdrawal of pupils until only his own children and the young Negro were left.

The offending book, like Alcott, was religious, but its religion was not that of Boston. Its inquiring, Socratic method, based upon the view that all truth is implicit within the soul whence it is to be drawn out by questioning, offended many, including some teachers. W. E. Channing, a liberal, and generally friendly to Alcott, doubted that the mind of a child should be so much turned inward. The book dealt in a very delicate way with sex in an age that allowed no one, not even a physician, to speak publicly of such matters. Alcott had gone too far along these lines—and on borrowed money. The sheriff sold the statuary, the furniture, and the library, all the property that Alcott had in the school; and he could not secure a teaching position elsewhere. The people preferred less transcendental teachers for their children.

TEACHING READING

New ways of teaching reading came to be used in the educational awakening. Before 1800 the spelling book had taken the place of the primer as the pupil's first book, and Noah Webster's *Spelling-Book* had been started on its ominous course through the schools. Webster was born in 1758 and he has told us that when he was young the books used in school were "chiefly or wholly, Dilworth's Spelling Books, the Psalter, Testament, and Bible." Others have reported that in the dame school the children were called up one by one; and the teacher with a penknife pointed to the letters of the alphabet, one at a time, and asked, "What's that?" Learning the alphabet might take three to six months and then spelling was begun. Reading came later. Although better ways were known, this incredibly dull and wasteful method was followed in American schools long after 1800. A French professor-politician, Joseph Jacotot (1770–1840), had devised a "universal method" by word recognition, and he was not by any means the first nor was he wholly unknown in the United States.

Samuel Worcester may have been familiar with Jacotot's method when he published his *Primer* in 1828. Bache in his *Report* said the system of Jacotot was well known. Worcester explained in his book that a child may learn to read words by seeing them and hearing them pronounced and explained, without knowing the letters. This idea did not meet with the universal favor that it deserved to obtain. Ten years later, Horace Mann in his *Second Report* attacked the old method with vigor, argument, and examples, and he returned to the subject upon his return from Germany. He based his claim for the word method not upon common sense alone but also upon the good results obtained in Boston where it was in use. In 1842 George B. Emerson proposed for discussion at teachers' meetings this question: "Have you tried the experiment of teaching" children to read before they know the letters and with what result? On a later page of *The School and the Schoolmaster* he described the method in a lesson based upon Worcester's *Primer*. Other teachers and textbook writers continued the campaign, and the new method slowly gained ground over the old custom and against the wishes of many parents. In the last century other methods have been devised; the experiments and the books and articles on the teaching of reading have multiplied and are still increasing.

The content of the reading books was also changing in the educational awakening. Noah Webster's three-book series consisted of a speller, reader, and grammar. Webster's aims were moralistic, patriotic, and linguistic. He tried to unify America by inculcating common sentiments and a uniform language. Others also purposed to foster Americanism, and this sentiment was sometimes fed upon anti-British prejudice. William Russell protested against the use of pictures or words that would tend to arouse animosities against foreign nations. This is a universal problem not confined to America or to schools; but schools have been flagrantly used by many governments to inculcate not merely a necessary patriotism but chauvinism and national hatreds. The United Nations and UNESCO, in trying to control these trends, have to meet the opposition of superpatriots and demagogic politicians.

Closely related to the moral and political purposes of the reading lessons was the emphasis upon oral reading and public speaking. School reading books often had an introductory section giving advice upon accent, phrasing, stress, pauses, stops, and gestures. Even in country schools, Friday was speaking-day. The great fault of this elocution, as it was called, was its affectation of elegance. This is the fault of those who, having little to say, yet feel impelled to speak, perhaps by the hope of applause. Real oratory or serious public speaking is a different matter, and it is surprising to find an artificial elocution in the schools in the great period of American oratory. Careful exposition and serious argument would have been more appropriate.

Republics have been noted for their oratory. We may think of Greece, Rome, France, England, and the United States. The orator, said Quintilian, is a good man speaking; and Emerson said the man behind the speech gives it weight. Perhaps these words imply what should not be forgotten, that the orator speaks on matters of general interest and importance. Politics is the most frequent subject. The deep and powerful stream of American political oratory had its source in the fateful issues of revolution and independence, and was fed by the debates on the Constitution, the tariff, slavery, secession, and reunion. It began with James Otis and John Adams, flowed from the lips of Webster and Clay, and ended for the time with Abraham Lincoln. The period after the Civil War had few great speakers in Congress and none in the Presidency.

The educational awakening was a period of warm political debate, torchlight and log-cabin processions, and great and small orators. In common school and college, bright young people were seeking to become public speakers, and often valued what they gained in their literary societies more highly than the work of the classroom. The lyceum movement was in its more flourishing era. The leaders in the movement for public education were notable public speakers in many cases, and as an orator among the educators Horace Mann was preeminent. Today, owing to a change in taste, his reports read much better than his speeches. Living in the time of Daniel Webster and Edward Everett, his long sentences, unusual words, and far-fetched analogies seem not to have attracted any special notice; but before his death in 1859 people had come to prefer the plain style of Lincoln.

Meanwhile those who compiled school reading books began to choose selections that would convey useful knowledge and serve the purposes of practical life. Upon his return from Europe, Horace Mann complained that American reading books were literary when they should have been informative and utilitarian. The reading books that he had examined over there and approved dealt with the phenomena of nature or with food, utensils, the qualities and uses of materials, and with houses and their construction. In the process of learning to read, the child should also gain useful knowledge. This utilitarian aim was gradually added to the patriotic, moralistic, and other earlier tendencies; and there was even a slight trend to encourage supplementary reading and the formation of school libraries.

ELEMENTARY SCHOOLBOOKS

New principles of teaching can be spread by means of lectures or by books on educational theory intended for teachers. These are the means used in schools, study classes, and meetings attended by teachers. A more direct way to introduce changes in instruction is followed when the new principles are embodied in textbooks. Both methods, the instruction of teachers and new textbooks, were used to improve elementary education. New or unusual subjects such as geography, nature study, and music were introduced, and old ones such as arithmetic were transformed.

The older geography textbooks had been summaries of information that the pupils were asked to memorize. This was not worth doing, for it would not be retained; and, outside of schools, such information would be found as needed in a reference book. In some of the older books, rhyme was used to aid the pupil in his distasteful task. For example, one such rhyming geography was written about 1785 by Robert Davidson, a professor in Dickinson College. Sometimes a tune was added and the list of the states, their capital cities, and the rivers on which they were located were repeated in singsong. This was the *reductio ad absurdum* of geography instruction, and evidently needed to be reformed.

The reformed method consisted of the selection of more interesting material, appealing to the children's understanding, and whenever possible, showing them the objects with which they were dealing. The authors of the newer textbooks began with the phenomena of the locality and after some explorations taught pupils to draw plans and maps of the schoolroom, the schoolyard, and the surrounding region. These were steps in the right direction. Among the writers of such books was W. C. Woodbridge, who collaborated on a widely used elementary text with Emma Willard; and another was William B. Fowle. Much more might have been done in developing exercises to be carried out by the children and in connecting geography with studies of weather, the action of wind and water, and with life on the farm; but a beginning was made in developing a rational study of the earth. The Swiss geographer Arnold Guyot lectured to teachers and wrote textbooks; and after the Civil War a more pronounced effort was made to improve the teaching of geography.

Music was added to the elementary school course in the educational awakening. Except for literature, which was administered in small snippets in the reading books, music was the first of the fine arts to be taught in the lower schools. Drawing, modeling, and dramatics were not added until the latter half of the century. It was not until after his return from Germany, where every teacher was able to read music and to play an instrument, that Mann took occasion to recommend the teaching of music; and he felt that he should apologize for his previous neglect. Boston had added music to its curriculum in 1838 and had engaged a music supervisor. Several cities in New York had introduced the art even earlier, about 1830. Lowell Mason was the music supervisor in Boston and he developed a superior program. He was also engaged by the state of Massachusetts as a lecturer on music education at the annual series of teachers' institutes. His exercise books and musical collections were widely used. His principles of music teaching followed those of Pestalozzi. But Mason did not hesitate to compose and improvise in the middle of a lesson, and he varied the application of his principles so frequently that he can hardly be said to have followed any system strictly. Others may assign him to his rank as a musician, but there is excellent evidence that he was a master teacher.

The principles of Pestalozzi were also applied in the teaching of arithmetic and, in the first instance, by Warren Colburn, whose *First Lessons in Arithmetic on the Plan of Pestalozzi*, completed in 1821, opened a new era in the teaching of the subject in the United States. Before publishing the little book, Colburn took the precaution to have it tried out in the classes of the newly opened high school of Boston, the English Classical School. The principal, George B. Emerson, used it while it was still in manuscript and gave a highly favorable account of it. He called it "our only perfect school-book." In a later edition Colburn explained that he had not seen any work of Pestalozzi "but only a brief outline by another." This other one may have been Joseph Neef, whose *Sketch of a Plan* contains twenty pages on the teaching of arithmetic with a plate showing Pestalozzi's Table of Units. Colburn's claim that his problems were his own must be admitted. He was indebted to Pestalozzi for some indispensable ideas such as the following.

Beginning with the counting of objects, the child must be led to understand each step. There must be no learning by rote, no rules, and no appeal to authority but only to reason, that is, the child's reason, not the teacher's. Arithmetic is the art of comprehending numbers, not the manipulation of figures. In the beginning, therefore, the numbers must be both small and concrete. The early work must be done without writing, that is, "in the head." This is the origin of mental arithmetic, which lasted for almost a century as a distinct branch of study in the schools. Another principle is that school arithmetic should be applied in many fields, such as travel, sport, kitchen recipes, population, sizes of hats or shoes, and not, as formerly, to commercial topics only. Colburn's book had an extraordinary success. In the first quarter century after publication more than forty editions came from the presses. It was translated into foreign languages and imitated at home.

The new and more inductive geography books, music exercise books, and mental arithmetics made great changes in the schools where they were used. The books, in fact, changed not the teaching only but the subjects themselves. Other subjects or activities were beginning to come in—a little history, physiology, health and physical education—but progress was slow and unevenly distributed.

USEFUL KNOWLEDGE MADE INTERESTING

School terms gradually became a little longer, attendance a little more regular, and printing much cheaper and faster. As more children learned to read with ease and pleasure and as families acquired the means to indulge the taste for reading, schools, teachers, and writers set about the task of satisfying the demand. The process called into play one of the leading functions of teachers in all times and places, the business of simplifying knowledge and ideas so that more people might be able to acquire and understand them.

The lyceums, which began in 1826, were one agency exercising this function. They sprang up, as we have seen, in all parts of the northern and western states where there were enough people with easy access to the meeting places. The task of the lyceum lecturer was that of spreading knowledge and ideas by putting them into the common speech without, as Matthew Arnold advised, debasing either.

There was a great and rising interest in the sciences both as pure knowledge and ideas and as useful applications to practical life. There was a marked interest in the relations between science and religion. Much of this centered upon a comparison of the teachings of geology and Genesis. The evolution controversy was still in the future. There was keen interest in the application of science to agriculture partly because the old lands of the East now had to compete with the black soil of Illinois and Wisconsin. Agricultural geology, chemistry, and botany and economic entomology were developing and were raising the belief that the farmer would gain great help from them. This hope was not to be realized at once but it affected schools and lyceums hardly less because of that.

The naturalistic movement in the schools of Europe was in full swing. It had begun with Basedow and Rousseau and was continued with variations by Pestalozzi and Froebel. The school movement there, as in the United States, was part cause, part effect, of the rise of a children's literature. One model for children's books had been furnished by DeFoe, and everywhere men had written and children had read the extended Robinson literature, mostly imitations that lacked the power of the original; but the tastes—of writers, adults, not children—had now changed and in the United States children's books had become practical, informative, and moralistic.

There is no good reason, some educators of the period said, why elements of useful knowledge should not be acquired in every district school in addition to the present limited course. They argued that good supplementary reading books would accomplish this end and would be interesting besides. This was not wholly new. Even the *New England Primer* began with a natural history alphabet, as in "The Whale's the Monarch of the Main as Is the Lion of the Plain." But the rest of the book does not fulfill this early promise.

A change took place about 1800. In 1794, for example, Isaiah Thomas published *The Natural History of Beasts, Which Are to Be Met with in the Four Quarters of the Globe*. But most of the beasts, such as the lion and tiger, lived in quarters of the globe with which American children were not familiar. Perhaps the purpose was to arouse the imagination of the children or to stimulate their interest by presenting things new and strange. Other books with comparable titles presented more accessible animals, birds, plants and trees.

Some authors tried to make factual material more appealing by throwing it into a conversational form. *Conversations on Common Things or Guide to Knowledge* was prepared by "a teacher" who furnished questions for other teachers to ask. This book soon reached a second edition, and some books of this sort went through many editions. One of the most popular authors was Jane Haldimand Marcet (1769–1858). Beginning early in the new century when she was thirty-two years old, she wrote many books for children and several of them in conversational form. One was

her *Conversations on Political Economy*, which won the praise of Jean
Baptiste Say and T. B. Macaulay. Although her book on economics was
praised, her *Conversations on Chemistry* was popular. It appeared in 1806
and in half a century sold 160,000 copies in the United States alone. Also
popular was the companion volume, *Conversations in Natural Philosophy*
(1819).

Mrs. Marcet's *Natural Philosophy* was revised in 1826 by Thomas P.
Jones, a competent scientist who in this same year (1826) founded and
long edited the *Journal of the Franklin Institute* of Philadelphia. A reviewer of this edition considered the book suitable for supplementary
reading in common schools. He deplored the shortcomings of a system of
education which allowed children to go out knowing nothing of the
simplest operations of nature. Another reviewer preferred his science full
strength, undiluted with conversation. "Leave out," he commanded, "all
the twaddle by Caroline and Emily, present the science in plain didactic
form, and you will have one of the best textbooks in the language."

There were also early how-to-do-books. One was written by Samuel
Read Hall, who is known only for his *Lectures on School-Keeping* (1829).
Hall may have been the first American to write a how-to-do book for chil-
dren. His book was called *The Child's Friend;* or *Things Which Every Boy
Can Do* (Boston, 1833). Some of the suggestions were exercises in elemen-
tary science and were intended to cultivate the child's ingenuity.

Stories that dealt with nature, travel, crafts, and juvenile science were
written in great numbers. Two of the writers whose books are still remembered, although no longer read, were Samuel Griswold Goodrich (1793–
1879), better known as Peter Parley, and Jacob Abbott (1803–1879). Both
were prolific and often wrote on subjects that had to do with nature and
morals and manners.

The Tales of Peter Parley About America (1827) was followed by more
than a hundred volumes in which the same fictitious character, a kindly
and omniscient old gentleman, answers the curious questions of excessively
polite children with an unnatural appetite for knowledge. Literally millions
of copies of Peter Parley books were sold. Many were not written by
Goodrich but by collaborators including, of all people, Nathaniel Hawthorne. Goodrich was really like the Peter Parley of his books, a kind of
stream of consciousness writer, as his *Reminiscences of a Lifetime* (1856),
in two garrulous volumes, shows. This book is also a source on the schools
of about 1800.

Jacob Abbott was a minister and a teacher. He founded the Mount
Vernon School for Girls in Boston and wrote an early book on teaching.
But he was best known as a writer for children. His series of Rollo books
ran to twenty-eight volumes; and he also wrote a series on "science for the
young," a Lucy series, and others. His characters are very good, not the
mischievous rogues of daily experience. Abbott also wrote a large number

of biographies for the young, and these were still read fifty years later. His subjects were captains and kings, like Alexander and Julius Caesar. This may imply a "great man" view of history, but although he attempted to teach history, geography, and elementary sciences, he was neither a historian nor a scientist. That such didactic, moral, and superficial books as those of Goodrich and Abbott were read by young adolescents of several generations, raises questions about the nature of American education.

PESTALOZZIAN PRINCIPLES CRITICIZED

Although some forms of Pestalozzian education gained wide approval in America, there were those who thought they had detected flaws in it. This critical response became more marked in the latter part of the century when the English version of Pestalozzi's system was imported; but it must be recalled that few Americans had direct knowledge of the system at its source. Few Americans saw Pestalozzi or his schools. They came into the movement too late. What Woodbridge, Stowe, Mann, and the rest studied was a series of imitations. This American Pestalozzianism was in great degree an imitation twice removed. Therefore, what was criticized was something attributed to Pestalozzi and was not always true to his principles. Here we shall give some early criticism only, leaving the discussion of the imported English Pestalozzianism to a later chapter.

A critical article appeared in the *American Annals of Education* for January, 1837. It seems to bear the stamp of William A. Alcott's writing, but it is unsigned. The writer claims that in his zeal for the development of the faculties, Pestalozzi tended to undervalue positive knowledge. His pupils were encouraged to investigate and reflect and they sometimes had a surfeit of practice, but they did not obtain a sufficient body of correct information. If for "development of the faculties" we substitute "power of thinking and problem-solving," the criticism of Pestalozzi in 1837 will be similar to what is sometimes said of Progressive education now. One hears it said that Progressives do not teach knowledge except as it helps in thinking and in solving problems. Although Pestalozzi sought to develop many faculties—observation, imagination, reasoning, and others—the Progressives reduce all of them to one, the thinking that solves problems. This parallel between early critics of Pestalozzi and late critics of Progressive education suggests that the two movements may be of the same species.

The numerous studies that Pestalozzi really favored, it was said, would not be needed to achieve the objects of his disciplinary theory. Pestalozzi had greatly enriched the curriculum, adding many skills, arts such as music, and naturalistic studies such as home geography. If one assumes wide and easy transfer of training, as Pestalozzi did, a much simpler curriculum would have been sufficient. There seems to be a conflict in his own principles; or perhaps we should tolerantly say that his practice was better than his principles.

He did not indiscriminately favor all subjects and this provided a foothold for a further criticism. He discounted history and any subjects that depend upon the testimony of witnesses and participants. He is said to have called history "a tissue of lies." One may ask how this can be known if historical truth is unattainable, for it is only by means of true history that false history can be detected. Napoleon, whom Pestalozzi held in abhorrence, declared history to be "a fable agreed upon"; but one suspects that this opinion reflected his fear that it would tell the truth about him. No such suspicion can apply to Pestalozzi, who was the soul of truthfulness; and this is a truth attested by history.

The critics of Pestalozzi's attitude toward history claim that moral education must be based upon the study of man and of moral conduct. The same remark would apply to other social studies, for all of these, including psychology and education, are to a great degree historical studies. Whether the principles of Pestalozzi have been generally useful and successful is itself a question that only history can settle.

In the 1830's Pestalozzian influence was effective when it supported existing educational trends, but otherwise it was not, or at least not always. For example, Pestalozzi worked along philanthropic lines and his schools were private schools. In America the demand for universal education in public schools was becoming strong and continued to grow. The introduction of new studies such as geography had preceded Pestalozzi's influence. His example affected textbooks and methods in geography in this early period but more especially after the Civil War. In spite of Pestalozzi's attitude, American history was introduced and gradually became a regular study. In the improvement of elementary reading instruction his methodic work was wholly mistaken and his practice was not helpful. Thus the American response to the Pestalozzian principles was itself a criticism of them.

TEACHING AIDS

Great as the Swiss master was, his success was limited by the lack of equipment. In the absence of books, laboratory supplies, and well-equipped shops, he somehow got along without them. And this was the state of all schools until the nineteenth century and in fact until late in that century. How bare the American schools were can be seen in the pictures and descriptions that have come down to us.

The general tradition and practice of the schools was against self-activity and investigation by the pupils. In this respect at least, Pestalozzi was on the side of the future. He promoted investigation and he improvised physical means. In America, as long as the spelling book dominated instruction, there was no need for teaching aids, but this situation changed when new studies and methods came in. The Lancasterian movement had done something to supply simple physical materials, such as sand tables, wall-charts, and even blackboards.

About 1817 the blackboard was introduced at West Point, Dartmouth, and other colleges. Twenty years later it was still unusual in the primary schools of Massachusetts, and Horace Mann exerted himself with considerable success to urge its introduction. George B. Emerson in 1842 spoke of the blackboard as if it were standard equipment, but this was not true in the rural schools. A curious article on "Black Tablets" by Gallaudet appeared in the *American Journal of Education* in 1830. He explained that large slate slabs were hard to obtain and proposed a mixture of lime, plaster of Paris, and lampblack to be spread on the wall of the schoolroom. He recommended the use of such a writing surface in teaching handwriting, arithmetic, and map-drawing. Such suggestions for improvising aids are rare in the school publications of that time.

Commercial makers of school equipment were also few. It was fifty years later, in 1884, that the National Education Association, meeting at Madison, Wisconsin, in its resolutions took especial note of the "excellent displays of school products and appliances." Those who examine the large present-day exhibits of the thousands of "school products and appliances," extending from pencil sharpeners to school buses, have some difficulty in "thinking away" this wealth of aids and "thinking back" to the bare walls and desks of early times.

One of the early suppliers of elementary school equipment was Josiah Holbrook (1788–1854), promoter of the lyceum movement. He offered for sale "an apparatus," that is, a collection composed of geometrical forms, a numeral frame, a globe, two maps, an orrery, instruments to illustrate the seasons, and simple equipment for the teaching of physics and chemistry. A Boston instrument-maker offered air pumps, model steam engines, and machines to demonstrate the simple mechanical powers. He offered to manufacture orreries on commission. Probably few schools had the means to purchase such equipment in the 1830's and 1840's, but in time demand and supply increased together. The normal schools were helpful in this improvement by showing young teachers how to use teaching aids. Most of the materials remained quite simple until after laboratories, shops, and kitchens were installed and electric current was supplied. The growth of invention and industry and the larger funds that became available to school boards were corresponding factors in the equipment of the modern school. In the 1830's a school was comparatively fortunate if it had a blackboard.

BOOKS FOR TEACHERS

The multiplication of educational writings was an element in the general movement known as the educational awakening; and it was especially connected with the rise of teachers' classes and normal schools. There were the reports on education in Europe by Calvin E. Stowe, Alexander Dallas Bache, and Horace Mann, which gave extended consideration to curricula and methods. The Bache report was not the result of a hurried trip. Whereas Stowe and Mann each spent a few weeks or months on the ground, Bache prosecuted his inquiries for two years. The ideas of the time were spread by numerous published addresses also. Such were those issued by the American Institute of Instruction, which usually met in Boston, and by the Western Literary Institute and College of Professional Teachers of Cincinnati. The latter society expired in 1845 but published its annual proceedings until that time. The American Institute of Instruction proved a more permanent body and continued its meetings and publications until 1908. Some thirty educational journals were established by 1840, but only nine continued publication for two years or longer. Reports, proceedings, and addresses of societies, journals, and educational textbooks were the chief printed means for disseminating ideas and information in the awakening.

The early books for teachers attempted to treat the whole field of education, including school management, curriculum, and methods, within the compass of one small volume. Sometimes they also considered the equipment of schools, the preparation of teachers, and the problems of a general educational philosophy.

A list of these early books will include at least the following:

Schulordnung, by Christopher Dock	1770
Sketch of a Plan . . . of Education, by Joseph Neef	1808
Method of Instructing . . . in the Arts of Writing and Reading, by Joseph Neef	1813
Lectures on School-Keeping, by Samuel R. Hall	1829
The Teacher, by Jacob Abbott	1833
The School and the Schoolmaster, by Alonzo Potter and George B. Emerson	1842
Theory and Practice of Teaching, by David P. Page	1847

The first of these books to have any great influence was Hall's *Lectures on School-Keeping.* It deals with discipline, method, and curriculum and includes the natural sciences among common school studies. The teacher should explain the how and why of common natural phenomena. In this field the recommended methods were taken from Bacon and Pestalozzi.

The teacher was advised not to take "yes" for an answer when pupils say they understand. It is the teacher's duty to find out for himself whether they do.

The *American Journal of Education*, established after Hall began teaching in the academy at Concord, Vermont, where he wrote his book, is the main source cited by him. As this magazine furnished some of the materials so it may also have been the stimulus that called out the book. The *Academician* is not mentioned. Hall's volume attained a considerable circulation. In the year of publication it was used as a textbook in a teacher's class at Canandaigua Academy, New York, and perhaps at other places. By special arrangement, 10,000 copies of the third edition were printed in 1832 and bound in paper to be distributed to the schools of the State of New York. This distribution gave one of the participants, James Wadsworth, the idea of district school libraries in New York. These, as we shall see, became a reality. The fourth edition of Hall's book came out in 1833 and the fifth about twenty years later. A centennial volume containing a reprint of the first edition is included in the bibliography of the present chapter.

The boys and girls in their late teens who were enrolled in normal schools and normal classes in academies and high schools needed simple textbooks. Hall's was such a book and in 1833 another appeared. This was Abbott's *The Teacher*, "a book full of ingenious devices." It is a book on school management suggesting ways of meeting or forestalling many of the petty but distracting problems that beginning teachers have to solve. By anticipating the pupils' difficulties and making careful assignments, questions about lessons may be anticipated and answered before they are asked. Teaching pupils how to study is one of the teacher's duties. Pupils may help in distributing and collecting papers and may be encouraged to carry on a limited form of self-government, with a court to handle minor offenses. There is an account of the origin and conduct of the system of self-government used in the Gardiner Lyceum, but for common schools Abbott preferred a less elaborate constitution.

Whether the self-government system at the Gardiner Lyceum had an independent origin there, as Abbott seems to have believed, or was borrowed may not be known; but it was not unique. Experimental schools had long used it. Fellenberg had such a scheme operating at Hofwyl and this is a possible source of the Gardiner Lyceum plan. Froebel at Keilhau, the Hazelwood School in England under Thomas Wright Hill and his family, and Thomas Jefferson at the University of Virginia made various efforts to operate school republics. In all ages this has been a natural thought of people who value freedom. As George B. Emerson said, Abbott's *The Teacher* was "a book full of ingenious devices"; and it has excellent advice on the daily tasks of the teacher, along with a good deal of moralizing.

Other early books for teachers were *The Teacher Taught*, by Emerson Davis who was known as a textbook writer; *The Teacher's Manual*, by Thomas H. Palmer; and *Suggestions on Education*, by Catherine Esther Beecher. More important and more comprehensive than these was *The School and the Schoolmaster* (1842), by Potter and Emerson. Alonzo Potter was a teacher who became a bishop of the Episcopal Church, and George B. Emerson was the first principal of the Boston high school of 1821. Their book is in two parts evidently written without sufficient collaboration by the authors. The first part, by Potter, discusses the school as a social agency and insists that public education must be directed toward the public interest. It deals with the duties of school trustees and once again reviews the defects of the common schools and the proposed remedies.

In the second part, Emerson deals with the organization and management of schools and the best modes of instruction. In dealing with instruction he offers some general principles: that the teacher should follow "the order of Nature"; that instruction should be so thorough that the pupils can go through the lesson without hesitation; and that the teacher should help pupils with their difficulties, just enough and not too much. Although vague, as most general principles of teaching are, these call attention to the need at important points for tact and judgment. They also reveal an emphasis upon high standards.

In dealing with special methods, Emerson is much more exact. Although he considers eleven common school branches, he devotes more than half of the whole treatment to three: reading, grammar, and arithmetic. He took a decided stand upon one of the questions then very prominent at teachers' meetings, namely, the use of emulation. He was against all use of prizes, rivalry, and marks of distinction as incentives in school.

In his demand for high academic standards, Emerson makes a statement, almost a proposal, that foreshadows future practice. We may premise that in 1842 college standards were neither high nor fixed and that Emerson had been a tutor in mathematics at Harvard. He wrote that "every college examiner who lowers the standard of requirement does a wrong to all youth who are looking in that direction," that is, who desire a sound education. And he adds that "if all the colleges of the Northern and Middle States could be induced to unite," they could at once raise the standard of all preparatory schools. This idea became a fact fifty years later with the formation of the regional accrediting associations, the Carnegie units, and the College Entrance Examination Board. The question of standards is one of the crucial questions not only in secondary education but in all education; and it spawns many further questions. It is also a question for which there is no generally accepted solution. It may be a "persistent problem," since the answer would depend upon philosophy.

The School and the Schoolmaster was written at the invitation of a man already mentioned, James Wadsworth, wealthy agriculturist and philanthropist of New York. He paid the authors for their work, and paid also for the manufacture of an edition of 15,000 copies, so that one copy might be placed in every school of New York and one given to each school official. The governor of Massachusetts at the time was Martin Brimmer, who was Wadsworth's son-in-law, and he paid for the distribution of a copy to each school district of Massachusetts. When the school journal, *Common School Assistant* (Albany, New York, 1836–1840), was established, nearly 40,000 copies of the paper were distributed each month during the first year through the aid of several "philanthropic gentlemen." All of these distributions were sequels to the circulation of Hall's book with which we remember Wadsworth was also concerned.

A somewhat similar sequel was the founding of district school libraries in New York. Wadsworth, who had enough political influence to be a factor in the decision to build the Erie Canal over the opposition of the Hudson River counties, worked upon Governor Marcy and others to secure the passage of a school library law. And a law was enacted in 1835 that permitted the districts to tax themselves for the purchase of books; but few did this. When the surplus revenue deposit was made in 1837, Wadsworth and others secured the allocation of a part of New York's share to the school library project. With this money and a further donation by Wadsworth, books for children were added to the books for the teacher of every district school in the state. The results were not as happy as had been expected, as we shall see in a later chapter.

SUMMARY

An early indication of the coming awakening came in the introduction of Pestalozzian ideas through the agency of a private citizen who brought Joseph Neef to Philadelphia. Neef was considered "an odd fellow" and not the best choice as the ambassador for strange new ideas, for which the new world was hardly prepared. The publications that were to make those ideas known were themselves little known. No one can say how much influence Pestalozzi's doctrines exercised in the early United States, but it is clear that they did not spread quickly and that native practices incorporated and adapted them to suit American needs. Apparently there was no direct imitation of Pestalozzi.

Teachers found means of expressing themselves in the newspapers, as J. G. Carter had done, in the new educational magazines, in their reports upon foreign school systems, and in the meetings of the rising educational associations. The normal schools helped teachers to improve their own schools and also made them missionaries of general school improvement. School publicity was essential to the awakening.

A test case of the effect of foreign ideas might be made of the change in Alcott's views and practice. When he began teaching he knew little if anything of European schools, yet the superiority of his school over the old district school was noteworthy. Meanwhile, he learned much of Pestalozzi but became less rather than more like him. At the summit of his teaching career, no one could call him a Pestalozzian unless his appeal to the conscience of children makes him one.

New methods of teaching children to read were developed before 1830, methods whose superiority is unquestioned, but they were not quickly adopted. The content of the reading books became less political or literary and more practical. Great attention was still given to oral reading and public speaking. Schoolbooks in several subjects were changed to appeal to the senses, the active powers, and the reason of children. A considerable children's literature of common and practical knowledge developed; and conversational and story forms were used in the effort to make useful knowledge interesting.

Although new teaching aids were introduced in the period of the awakening, they were few and, except for the blackboard, of minor importance. Such aids were used first in colleges and secondary schools and became available to primary schools only in recent times. Books for teachers multiplied and were greatly improved in this period. But at the end of the period, about 1860, they were still brief and comprehensive summaries, single volumes, that contained what it was considered necessary for every teacher to know.

QUESTIONS

1. Was the growing interest in European schools an effect or a cause of the educational awakening?
2. Why do you agree (or, as the case may be, disagree) with the rather common view that Alcott was "the American Pestalozzi" or an American Pestalozzian?
3. How may the dependence of one person or a group upon another be proved? What specific cases of Pestalozzi's influence upon American education can be proved?
4. How may one account for the slight influence of Joseph Neef? In developing your answer, consider the Lancasterian schools, the War of 1812, the existing views of elementary education, and other factors.
5. Why were the normal schools less effective in improving teachers and teaching than their promoters hoped?
6. Do you agree that textbooks affect teaching more strongly as well as more directly than theories about teaching? Why, or why not, and under what circumstances?

7. What were the values of the teaching of "mental arithmetic" and how can they be preserved, or again introduced?
8. Why have none of the children's books of the period covered in this chapter retained their once great popularity?
9. Apply the analysis used in your answer to No. 8, or a similar one, to the books and journals for teachers.
10. Periodically books and articles attacking current methods of teaching beginning reading appear. After reading one of these, evaluate the paragraph on reading and reading books in the summary of this chapter.

BOOKS AND PAPERS

Professional books, journals, reports on foreign education, and private and public normal schools were among the means that aided in transforming schoolkeeping into teaching. The book by Joseph Neef, although somewhat erratic, was more progressive than S. R. Hall's *Lectures*, which came twenty years later. Albert Picket founded a teachers journal, the *Academician*, which was followed by better ones, edited by William Russell, W. C. Woodbridge, and their successors. Reports by Cousin, Stowe, Bache, and Mann gave Americans some knowledge of European schools; but private and public normal schools were the most effective means to improve teaching. Arthur M. Schlesinger's *Learning How to Behave*, which is mentioned in the bibliography of Chapter I, could be appropriately listed in the present bibliography also.

BARNARD, HENRY, *School Architecture*, Hartford, 1842; and many later revisions, with slightly different titles, the sixth edition 1855; *Normal Schools and Other Institutions for the Professional Education of Teachers*, Hartford, 1851, reprinted, Greeley, Colorado, 1929; *National Education in Europe*, Hartford, 1854.

BLAIR, ANNA L., *Henry Barnard*, Minneapolis, 1938.

BRUBACHER, JOHN S., *Henry Barnard on Education*, New York, 1931.

DAVIS, S. E., *Educational Periodicals During the Nineteenth Century*, Washington, U. S. Government Printing Office, Bureau of Education Bulletin, 1919, No. 28.

DIEKHOFF, JOHN S., "The School Conspiracy," *Educational Research Bulletin*, November 11, 1959.

FLUECKIGER, S. L., *Lowell Mason's Contribution to Music Education*, Columbus, Ohio, 1936, an unpublished dissertation at the Ohio State University.

HINSDALE, B. A., "Notes on the History of Foreign Influence upon Education in the United States," *Annual Report* of the U. S. Commissioner of Education, 1897–1898, Vol. 1, pp. 591–629.

MONROE, WILL S., *History of the Pestalozzian Movement in the United States*, Syracuse, New York, 1907. A useful but incomplete treatment, not free from positive errors.

NEEF, JOSEPH, *Sketch of a Plan and Method of Education*, Philadelphia, 1808; and, on Neef as a teacher, see Charles Lewis, *D. G. Farragut, Admiral in the Making*, Annapolis, 1941.

POTTER, A., and GEORGE B. EMERSON, *The School and the Schoolmaster*, New York, 1842. Emerson, who contributed the more important sections of this book, wrote his *Reminiscences*, Boston, 1878. See also Barnard's *Journal*, Vol. V, pp. 389 *ff.* and 417 *ff.*

RICH, ARTHUR L., *Lowell Mason*, University of North Carolina Press, 1946.

RUSSELL, WILLIAM, "Intellectual Education," in Barnard's *Papers for the Teacher*, First Series, New York, 1860.

SANBORN, F. B., and W. T. HARRIS, A. *Bronson Alcott, His Life and Philosophy*, Boston, 1893. There are several recent books on Alcott by Dorothy McCuskey, Odell Shepard, and others. Elizabeth Peabody prepared the *Record of Mr. Alcott's School*, Boston, 1874.

SULLIVAN, MARK, *Our Times*, New York, 1932. Vol. 2 contains matter on school elocution.

SUNDERMAN, L. F., "History of Public School Music, 1830–1840," *Educational Record*, April, 1941.

THURSFIELD, RICHARD E., *Henry Barnard's American Journal of Education*, Johns Hopkins Press, 1945.

WRIGHT, A. D., and G. E. GARDNER, *Hall's Lectures on School-Keeping*, a facsimile reprint, Dartmouth Press, 1929.

The following recent books are more general than those listed in the specialized "Books and Papers" for the chapters in Parts I and II. However, they provide additional interpretations, sources, and studies of the issues discussed in these chapters:

BAYLES, ERNEST E., and BRUCE L. HOOD, *Growth of American Educational Thought and Practice*, New York, 1966.

BEST, JOHN H., and ROBERT T. SIDWELL, eds., *The American Legacy of Learning*, Philadelphia, 1967.

CALHOUN, DANIEL, ed., *The Educating of Americans*, Boston, 1969.

FRASER, STEWART E., ed., *American Education in Foreign Perspectives*, New York, 1969.

FULL, HAROLD, ed., *Controversy in American Education*, New York, 1967.

FULLER, EDGAR, and JAMES B. PEARSON, eds., *Education in the United States, Historical Development and Outlook*, Washington, 1969.

GUTEK, GERALD LEE, ed., *An Historical Introduction to American Education*, New York, 1970.

HILLESHEIM, JAMES W., and GEORGE D. MERRILL, eds., *Theory and Practice in the History of American Education*, Pacific Palisades, California, 1971.

KOLESNIK, WALTER B., and EDWARD J. POWER, eds., *Catholic Education*, 1965.

NOLL, JAMES WM., and SAM P. KELLY, eds., *Foundations of Education in America*, New York, 1970.

PARK, JOE, ed., *The Rise of American Education,* Northwestern University Press, 1965.

PULLIAM, JOHN D., *History of Education in America*, Columbus, Ohio, 1968.

TYACK, DAVID B., ed., *Turning Points in American Educational History*, Waltham, Mass., 1967.

Part III

EXPERIMENTATION AND REGIMENTATION

Preview

In Part III we see acceptable types of elementary, secondary, and higher schools evolving after many decades of experimentation *and then their* regimentation *into a mammoth school machine. In forming a ladder system, children were classified and graded according to their progress up the rungs of the ladder; then the lower rungs of the ladder were articulated into the elementary school and the higher rungs into the high school and university. As schools became fully though variously graded, there arose a chorus of opposition to the system. Teachers and citizens protested against the regimentation, the close grading, and the lock step. They demanded more flexible organization to provide greater individualization of instruction. Innovations within the system are thus proposed, tried out, and accepted or rejected.*

Chapter 7

EXPANDING ELEMENTARY EDUCATION

A famous ancient teacher once explained that, in his country, education began with the earliest years of childhood and lasted to the very end of life. We shall appropriate the first part of this explanation by defining elementary education so that it will begin in early childhood. The years that follow after childhood may be left to other forms of education but the whole of childhood belongs to the elementary school.

The teacher of the ancient time continued, saying that as soon as the child was able to understand what was spoken, parents and nurses taught him to say what was true and to do what was right. Later there was instruction in reading and writing, learning songs and playing a stringed instrument, and games and sports. Knowledge can be taught in play according to this writer, who lived more than two thousand years ago. The music, games, and dances, he believed, would mold the manners of the children and would form their character. Altering the plays and songs of a people, he continued, will in time change their customs, laws, and the constitution of the state. In his country, as children increased in years, they trained in the gymnasium and they learned the laws in order to become courageous in war and wise in council. This teacher was Plato (B.C. 427–347) of ancient Athens.

Some of the founders of American education had a less generous conception. Education was not to begin in early childhood and it was not to continue long. Little time could be spared for schooling. That little was to be devoted to the four R's, and no time was to be wasted on "fads and frills" such as music, games, and dances were thought to be.

We have seen that a change was taking place in the 1830's. Horace Mann was attempting to introduce practical subjects. Informational books for children were being written. The methods of teaching were undergoing reformation. Buildings and equipment were improving. But there is no accurate information on the extent of these changes, no census of the number of schools that were improved or the exact degree of that improvement. There was a trend and that is all we can say.

191

Two thousand years earlier the ancient Greeks, of whom Plato spoke, had been much concerned with the activities of children, less with the accumulation of knowledge. It was the kindergarten, music, handwork, nature study, and elementary science that introduced activities into the elementary school. A new period began after the Civil War. This is the time of the so-called "new education." A new institution, the kindergarten, which we shall consider part of elementary education, was introduced. Child study and the normal schools, also, brought new light and a new spirit to elementary education.

THE AMERICAN KINDERGARTEN

The term *American kindergarten* has two different connotations. Some kindergartners in the United States, with authentic knowledge of Froebel's doctrine and complete devotion to his purpose, felt free to accuse their American colleagues of ignorance and heresy. They lashed out at those who seemed to promote spurious and degenerate forms of the kindergarten, forms that did not follow the founder's precepts and exercises. They were equally hostile to those who were attempting to make money out of the movement. Both educational malpractice and greed were charged. It will not be profitable to rake over the ashes of these old fires; but it may prove useful to know that the American was sometimes regarded as a spurious version of the true German kindergarten.

The words *American kindergarten* are also used simply to designate the kindergarten as it existed and developed in America. And in this process it slowly but steadily diverged from the Froebelian model. Americans certainly knew less about Froebel than some of the German experts, felt less piety toward him, and, for these reasons, were more willing to question his ideas and to take an experimental attitude toward his institution. It is intended here to use the words *American kindergarten* in this neutral sense but without denying that there may have been some bogus kindergartens and mercenary kindergartners.

The child study movement that paralleled the introduction of the kindergarten was not without effect upon the new institution. The kindergarten was one of the reasons for the developing interest in child study, but it was in turn affected by what was learned about child development and behavior. Before 1870 little was heard in America about the kindergarten, but in a decade it became a subject of frequent consideration at educational meetings. In 1884 the National Education Association recognized a separate kindergarten department.

The creator of the kindergarten, Friedrich Froebel (1782–1852), was part religious mystic but also part scientist and lifelong observer of the ways of children. His writing is frequently cloudy but the key idea is clear. It is this: "What one tries to represent or do he begins to understand."

We understand what we make, and through making it we also learn to value it. It becomes for us a standard. Therein lies a danger. The small-town banker who wrote a book about his trip around the world confessed that he read his own book more than any others.

The child is characterized by his activities, so Froebel teaches. And as every child is an individual, different from all others, and is self-active, every child's activities are creative. Yet these activities must be called out by suggestion, example, and material facilities. Early in his career, Froebel was a teacher of boys and only afterwards did he teach little children. Thus the activities that he selected and devised for children of different ages range from pat-a-cake to group self-government.

The recognition that creative activity is educative led Froebel to collect a wide range of individual and social plays, games, handwork, projects of building and constructing, collecting, gardening, music and the plastic arts, storytelling, and so on up to the already-mentioned self-government in a school democracy. These activities demand, and therefore develop, skills, and from skills come the enrichment of life and, indeed, civilization. It is to be noted that Froebel was not wholly original, for he had among his books a well-thumbed copy of J. H. Heusinger's *On Using Children's Strong Urge to Activity*, which taught similar doctrine.

The histories of philosophy do not mention him, but Froebel was something of a philosopher. The key to his philosophy may again be found in a sentence. He wrote: "In all things there lives and reigns an Eternal Law, based upon an all-pervading, power-filled, living, self-conscious and hence Eternal Unity which is God." And as God is the Creator so the self-active child is a creator in a small sphere, but in its own right.

No proof of these insights is offered, and the relation of creation to law is not explained. But it should be made clear that human creation is of an entirely different order from that of the Biblical conception of the creation. Man "creates" neither the matter nor the laws of nature. He discovers, obeys, and uses them as best he may. Froebel assimilates man's creation to God's. Since Froebel's day this ambiguous use of double-edged words has become all too common in educational discussion. And, in the second place, the introduction of this religious concept had important effects upon the history of the kindergarten and not least in the United States, where the reformers, philanthropists, and the churches became its early promotors.

We have called Froebel something of a philosopher. Perhaps he was rather a poet looking at the stars as compared with the astronomer with his proofs and figures in the lecture room. At least he continued to speak in symbolic terms. The round ball, without separate parts, was to symbolize, even to the little child, the unity of the world. The other "gifts" also had hidden meanings that were supposed to influence even the unconscious or subconscious mind.

The kindergarten itself was one of the symbols of this symbolical thinker. It was a symbol of society, a soul-garden that was also a school for the "education of man." The word signifies that children, whom Froebel correctly considered as organic beings, are to grow as plants grow in a garden. The teacher's work, like the gardener's, is to improve the soil and protect the plants from weeds that might choke them. That is all. The creative activity of the child will do the rest. Froebel interpreted this activity as the unfolding of something that was "preformed" in the child. With respect to preformation, symbolism, and some other ideas, Froebel was the victim of the immature philosophy and science of his day.

Symbolism is, however, a necessary means in all education. Symbols are means of communication. They communicate both ideas and feelings.. Words are symbols of ideas, and ideas are symbols of things. Many things such as the flag or the fire bell are symbols. Symbols may suggest or connote as well as denote. The flag stands for the nation and it suggests, and by suggesting may call out, patriotism. Froebel's mistake was that he thought the little child could by himself discover the meaning of an arbitrary symbol. Some things, to be learned, must be taught, by teachers, books, social experience, or otherwise, but certainly taught.

The American kindergarten gradually eliminated Froebel's immature science and much of his mysticism. But this took time. Henry Barnard published an early kindergarten notice. His more extensive publications on this subject came much later. Elizabeth Peabody studied in Germany in the later sixties; but most Americans were taught by Germans in the United States and only gradually did they form their own more critical views of the Froebelian theory. The disciples of the master long tried to hold to the very words, and "gifts" and exercises that had been transmitted to them. Matilde Kriege and her daughter established a training school for kindergartners in Boston in 1868. Others soon followed in New York, Washington, San Francisco, and elsewhere. The California Kindergarten Union (1879) had for one of its purposes the preservation of the "pure doctrines" of Froebel; the American Froebel Union was formed to protect the name of kindergarten from "ignorant imitations and perversions." The struggle between conservative and liberal views continued for a long time. It was partly for this reason that John Dewey was unwilling to admit the kindergarten, by name, into his experimental school; but he was also opposed to much of Froebel's theory.

One may hope that what was called American ignorance and perversion yielded to study and honest effort. But there were other factors. The attempt to keep the kindergarten unchanged was bound to fail. School supply houses provided new materials. The exercises increased in number and variety. Small movable tables and chairs, not made "merely for listening," were used, and the children helped with the housekeeping. Attention was given to health habits, rest and sleep as well as activity were found useful, and free lunches were supplied. The use of English instead of

German made changes in the verbal material, and substitutes were found for the crude early translations of the original songs, stories, and poems. The American took the place of the Froebelian kindergarten. It followed Froebel's spirit rather than his set form.

Many of the early kindergartens were established for the children of the poor. Philanthropists who were interested in developing manual skills, which might later prove useful to mechanics or factory hands, took a long chance in donating funds for kindergarten education. Churches and groups of church and school people established "free" or "charity" kindergartens as missionary institutions. The Young Women's Christian Association took an active part. So did the Society for Ethical Culture in New York under the leadership of Felix Adler, who also played an active part in introducing the kindergarten in California. Adler stressed the educative value of work, which, he said, is not something added to education but is an organic part of it. It cultivates hand and brain, making the hand "wise and cunning" and the brain "clear and vigorous and enlightened." Under his direction the Ethical Culture Schools were developed as a continuous ladder without the clash between the kindergarten and the primary grades that long afflicted some school systems.

The kindergarten was made a part of the public school system of St. Louis in 1873. This was the achievement of a philanthropic kindergartner, Susan Blow, and a capable superintendent of schools, William Torrey Harris. Seven years later there were more than fifty public kindergartens in the city. Other cities followed slowly, but after 1890 progress became more rapid. Until that date there were about as many children in private as in public kindergartens, but by 1900 the latter were forging ahead and the combined enrollment of both had increased from about 30,000 in 1890 to about seven times that number in 1900. Kindergartens have been common only in cities and towns. The growth of cities and the recent increase in the birth rate have raised attendance to new high levels.

Many special problems have interested American kindergartners. Such were handwork and industrial education; and the manual training movement was connected with the kindergarten philosophy. The kindergarten was integrated with the primary grades and both benefited. Parental education and child study were often considered in meetings of the organized kindergarten teachers.

CHILD STUDY

Child study, like the kindergarten, began in Europe and in part through the kindergarten effort. Froebel collected "mother plays and nursery songs" in his native Thuringia, and one could have predicted that the new institution would further the study of children's interests. But the ideas are older than Froebel. Rousseau had urged teachers to study their pupils for, as he said, it was clear that they knew nothing about them. Comenius' little book on infancy revealed his kindly attention to child traits and activities. Pestalozzi for a short time kept a diary of his small son's development. This biographical method was also followed by H. A. Taine in France and Charles Darwin in England. Many later students followed this plan.

A teachers' society in Berlin about 1872 investigated schoolchildren's knowledge of their surroundings. It was found that children had not observed the most familiar objects, had not visited the monuments of the city, and thought a forest would be like a park. Boys were compared with girls, city children with those from the suburbs and the country. It was found that those who had attended the kindergarten made the highest scores.

The Berlin report stimulated G. Stanley Hall to probe the *Contents of Children's Minds upon Entering School*. The study was made in September of 1880 by four trained kindergarten teachers who asked the children for their understanding of about one hundred terms ranging from the names of common objects and animals to moral and religious words. A little later J. M. Greenwood, superintendent of Kansas City, made a similar study. Hall discussed the scores, referring to sex and social group differences. He also found kindergarten children "knowing" more than others. He explained that one sees not what is presented but only what is attended to; and he remarked upon the high ratio of ignorance, tradition, superstition, and emotion in the minds of children entering school. Country life seemed to him to have great educational value. He had been a country boy. And, no doubt, country life does educate for country living.

The report of Hall's investigation was published in the *Princeton Review* (1883), in the *Pedagogical Seminary* (1891), in Hall's book, *Aspects of Child Life and Education* (1907), and elsewhere. In old age, Hall wrote of it: " 'The Contents of Children's Minds' attracted more comment, was translated into more languages and set the pattern for more similar studies than anything else that I have written." The study has been called the beginning of the child study movement. This, Hall considered an error. But associations for child study were founded in several states and the National Education Association formed a special department for it. Much of the early work was done by Hall's graduate students including Earl Barnes, Henry H. Goddard, J. E. Wallace Wallin, Arnold Gesell, Lewis M. Terman, and other now well-known psychologists. The investigation of 1880 was not made by paper questionnaire, as some books say, but by direct questioning.

The Clark University group in many studies did employ the paper questionnaire and has been severely criticized for it. The editor of the

Educational Review (November, 1896) spoke of "the silly question-papers sent out at haphazard to be answered by persons of little scientific training or none." This "raking together of an undigested mass of alleged facts" should not, he said, be called research. In his *Life and Confessions of a Psychologist,* Hall admitted grave faults of method in some of the studies, but claimed that many of his students had done good work. There is truth in each of the statements. The field of the questionnaire as a scientific instrument is a limited one.

Since Hall's time the methods of child study have changed. A meeting of those interested in the field was held at the Columbian Exposition in Chicago in 1893. Hall was a participant and urged the importance of the study as an aid to education. This meeting seems to have stimulated James Sully in England and Alfred Binet in France, both of whom made important contributions. In Germany, Ernst Meumann developed an experimental type of child study and educational psychology. This is an example of the way in which different countries contribute to the promotion of a common interest. Twenty years after the Chicago meeting, Edward Lee Thorndike published his *Educational Psychology.* It is evidence of the changes that had taken place since the work of Bain and Hall.

Even when Hall was beginning his work, studies of a wholly different kind were being conducted and he rejected the title of "father of child study," which has been applied to him. He considered H. P. Bowditch as the pioneer. In 1879 Bowditch began the measurement of the height and weight of the Boston schoolchildren. Large numbers of such measures were reported in the following decades, and a bibliography of 1920 listed more than nine hundred of these anthropological studies. The physical measurement of college students was begun by Edward Hitchcock of Amherst in that period. The mental inventory and physical measurement that may be taken as the two poles of child study thus appeared about the same time (1880). The mental inventory has developed into a study of behavior and achievement development, "child growth and development." The anthropologists gradually devised standard procedures, such as the measuring of many dimensions, the use of X-ray pictures to determine skeletal development, and the construction of tables and curves of growth.

A most important phase of child study was developed in connection with the education of mentally deficient children. This was the invention by Simon and Binet in Paris of the intelligence test, its translation by one of Hall's students, H. H. Goddard, and its revision and improvement by another, Lewis Terman. Terman has used the tests in the study of superior children. In World War I, group tests were developed and used to classify recruits. Mental or intelligence tests have proved of great use in educational and vocational guidance, particularly since their capabilities have been more fully understood and when they have been used by trained psychologists. Recently they have led to the better, but still far from complete, understanding of the nature of intelligence. It appears that it consists of a number of special factors or aptitudes such as the verbal, numerical, and others, or of several special factors and a general one. The first of these views is L. L. Thurstone's and the second is that of the English psychologist, Charles Spearman. It is not a unitary aptitude as Binet was inclined to believe.

Many biographical studies of children were made before and soon after the end of the century. These often had the same defects that also vitiated the questionnaire results. Some were made by doting relatives and the several studies followed no common system. Children's speech and drawings were frequent topics. Studies have been made of learning and reasoning ability in relation to age; of the sequence, development, and permanence of child interests; and of the growth of moral and social concepts. When early in the present century children's drawings were studied, it appeared that they tended to parallel language development.

Many students hold that physical and mental child growth follows a general pattern; and their purpose is to draw a complete map of the process. It is also obvious that the environment influences development and that one must not expect such a map to consist of precise outlines. Indeed, the environment is often so powerful that we may have to draw special maps for children of different classes or in different locations. One incidental illustration of environmental influence comes from studies of language development. No sure way has been found of correcting speech errors if the child constantly hears "incorrect" speech. This shows that the out-of-school experience may be more effective than the school; and that it not only directs but thwarts and limits the child's language development. It dooms him, if he is a Milton, to remain "a mute inglorious Milton."

ELEMENTARY HANDWORK

The kindergarten paved the way for handwork in the primary grades and thereby helped the children to go beyond the four R's. This connection was noticed by a New York City curriculum committee in 1887. Perhaps they did not know that, long before, Froebel had made the same comment and had indeed used simple activities such as stick-laying, less simple ones such as gardening, and exacting work with tools. The superintendent of Jamestown, New York, was a pioneer in the introduction of activities into each of the grades. The Society for Ethical Culture in both its kindergarten and its school for workingmen's children developed a continuous course of graded activities with vocational elements in the upper grades.

Felix Adler (1851–1933), who was the founder of the Society for Ethical Culture and the director of its schools, had been educated in Germany.

He returned during the depression of the 1870's, able, learned, and filled with a reforming zeal that found much work to do in the slums of his native New York. He was an exponent of education by activities and work; and he drew a parallel between experiments in the sciences and invention and creativeness in the arts and industry. "As experiment conjoined with observation is necessary to the discovery of truth," he wrote, "so object-creating must supplement object-teaching in the rediscovery of truth, which it is the purpose of all education to facilitate." We shall repeat what was stated previously. He held that activities are not something added to regular instruction but are an organic part of it. He meant that a course of study that does not develop "a wise and cunning hand" as well as a clear brain is an incomplete course. In his report for 1882, Adler told of inquiries that he was receiving. State and city superintendents were seeking information about the Workingmen's Kindergarten and School because they hoped to introduce similar programs in their home cities. Some had already done so. This was shown by a children's industrial exhibition that was held in New York a few years later. Exhibits were shown from Midwestern as well as Eastern cities; and they contained work by children of all the grades.

Many of the teachers of those children may have had little specific preparation for their work. At any rate the need for a teachers' school or college to prepare for such work was becoming clear. In the East also, as well as in the Middle West, the professional preparation of high school teachers, for work in all fields, was coming under consideration. The subject had been raised at Columbia University as early as 1858. In 1881 President F. A. P. Barnard devoted a section of his report to the presentation of a strong argument for action. But what he recommended was a series of evening lectures on the history, philosophy, science, and art of education. This was to be especially addressed to the teachers of the city. In the course of his argument, Barnard revealed that although he knew that two educational professorships had been created in Scotland and that work was to start at Cambridge University in England, he did not know that William H. Payne was occupying such a chair, about five hundred miles away, in the University of Michigan. His views were not to be speedily accepted in such an old-line and provincial institution as Columbia College then was. Progress was to come in another way.

An Industrial Education Association was formed in New York in 1884. Its purpose was "to study and devise methods and systems of industrial education and to secure their introduction into schools." They were especially concerned for New York City, which had no public high schools until almost the end of the century, about sixty years after Philadelphia and seventy-five after Boston had developed these institutions. The association became active in the preparation of teachers of industrial arts. It was the active power in the creation of the New York College for the

Training of Teachers. With the prodding of Nicholas Murray Butler (1862–1947), this modest school for the preparation of home economics and industrial arts teachers developed into the Teachers College of Columbia University, and began to prepare teachers and educational workers in all fields. It was almost twenty years after President Barnard's proposal when Teachers College became affiliated with Columbia.

Closely connected with the industrial arts and the sciences is the art of drawing. As a language it has many uses, and like other languages all normal people can acquire the essentials of it. The smallest child above infancy can begin, but practice and maturity are needed to perfect it. Drawing was one of the educational skills that Horace Mann wished all teachers to learn; but economic and industrial purposes were more effective than Mann in introducing drawing instruction into the schools.

For artistic, economic, and educational reasons, drawing was introduced into some schools about the middle of the nineteenth century. In Cleveland an enthusiast, John Brainerd, guided and supervised the classroom teachers in teaching drawing. In Syracuse, New York, the schools became known in this field about 1858. The state of New York in 1875 made the teaching of drawing compulsory in state normal schools. But Massachusetts had already in 1870 introduced drawing into the common schools and required the large towns to provide free instruction in drawing to adults. The national expositions in Philadelphia in 1876 and Chicago in 1892–1893 gave evidence of national progress in drawing, design, and all graphic and plastic arts. Progress in elementary drawing was important in the teaching of handwork, nature study, geography, and other subjects.

THE SPREADING NORMAL SCHOOLS

Twenty years after the state normal schools had been founded in Massachusetts, schools of this kind were still few in number, small and weak, but were beginning to multiply and grow. In 1860 there were twelve state normal schools, one city normal school, and an indefinite number of normal classes or departments in high schools, state universities, and other institutions. Before long the school at Oswego, New York, was to be opened. It began in 1860 as a city school but was adopted by the state. In five years the number of state normal schools almost doubled. There were twenty-two in operation by 1865. They were thinly scattered through half the northern states from Massachusetts to Kansas. They were able to prepare only an insignificant fraction of the teachers for a nation of 35,000,000 people.

There was little that the earliest normal schools could teach beyond the reviews of the common branches and practice teaching. There were no specialized books on school administration or on the psychology, the philosophy, or the history of education. The not uncommon belief that the history of education occupied a large place in early teacher education is a mistake. The two best books, Potter and Emerson's *The School and the Schoolmaster* and Page's *Theory and Practice of Teaching* were comprehensive and general treatments of the whole subject of education within the compass of a few hundred pages. But 1860 was the hour before the dawn of 1865.

The rapid increase in the number of state normal schools began before 1865 and continued at the rate of about twenty-five new schools each decade to the end of the century and after. The institution was adopted in the Southern states. A specialized literature on education developed. Curricula were extended from one to two, three, and four years. But in the main, the state normal school continued its close connection with rural education, receiving its pupils from and returning its graduates to the country schools. This connection caused the low entrance requirements. In the cities the high schools maintained pedagogical classes and prepared elementary teachers. Some cities began to establish their own normal schools. St. Louis had taken this step in 1857, creating a school that was later named after her famous superintendent, W. T. Harris, the Harris Teachers' College.

To its formal inquiry in 1871, the United States Bureau of Education received official replies from 114 schools for teachers. These had an average enrollment of less than one hundred students in each. Only fifty-one of the schools were state institutions and the rest were a mixed group of county, city, and private normal schools and normal departments in colleges and universities. By 1900 there was a threefold increase of state normal schools over the number of 1871. But meanwhile the population had doubled; and compulsory attendance laws had further multiplied the enrollments. The result was that the state normal schools were no nearer their goal, that of providing rural teachers with an adequate preparation for their extremely difficult and lonely task. All the books point to the rapid expansion of the normal schools after the Civil War, but actually they had to multiply rapidly in order to maintain their position. At the end of the century, most rural teachers still obtained their licences upon examination after attending a school for teachers for a short time or even without any professional training.

The early state normal schools in many cases lacked the facilities and the qualities that such an institution should have. Their equipment was often meager; they were badly located and received insufficient support; their loyal staffs were overworked and underpaid, and many of their staff members were insufficiently prepared. From the first there were exceptional teachers and exceptional schools. Among the latter one would place the schools of Normal, Illinois; Ypsilanti, Michigan; Bridgewater, Massachusetts; Albany and Oswego, New York; and doubtless others.

OSWEGO

The Oswego Normal School became famous for its system of object-teaching. As practiced at Oswego, object-teaching was the stepchild of the Pestalozzian movement, which had been precariously maintaining itself in the United States for half a century. We have noted the work of Joseph Neef, the arithmetic text of Warren Colburn, the doctrines of Horace Mann, the normal schools of Massachusetts, and other traces of Pestalozzi's influence. Object-teaching came to Oswego not from Switzerland directly but by way of England. It was presented in a highly formal manner that made it easy to transmit, and its spread was further aided by a strong personality, Edward Sheldon.

Edward Austin Sheldon (1823–1897), the leader in organizing the public schools of Oswego and the state normal school and of object-teaching in both, had some of the qualities of Pestalozzi himself. Sheldon, like Pestalozzi, was a man of self-denying spirit that did not exclude a keen desire for recognition; like Pestalozzi he revealed great sympathy for the poor and the power to enlist the assistance of the rich and to hold the attention and interest of the young. Like Pestalozzi he conducted a "ragged school." But unlike him, Sheldon was a country boy with an almost fanatical love of fine trees. When a workman contrary to instructions cut down a great elm at Sheldon's home, "Shady Shore," he "mourned as for the loss of a friend."

At midcentury the city of Oswego had 12,000 people, several private schools, the ragged school that Sheldon directed, but no public schools. A public school party was forming in the town, and of this Sheldon became the spearhead. When the party became a majority he became, in effect, superintendent of schools. In this position he revealed organizing skill of a high order, and in the history of the years following 1853 we find one example of the ways in which public education came into existence in many places.

In his own life-story he has told how, closing the ragged school, he created a graded system of schools offering thirteen years of schooling to rich and poor. There were three divisions in the lower schools, called primary, junior, and senior, and each had a three-year course. Above these he provided and opened a four-year high school. Attendance laws were lacking, and with twelve primary schools only two senior schools were needed. He also found that many boys and young men between the ages of eleven and twenty-one who were employed needed and desired further education. For these he opened an evening school; and for children moving into Oswego from the ungraded country schools, he organized an unclassified school to fit these newcomers for the regular classes. For the teachers he held weekly staff conferences lasting three hours on Saturday mornings.

The school day was fully and strictly laid out, and frequent factual examinations of the pupils were demanded and the results reported to the board of education. Although Sheldon had attended Hamilton College, he did not finish and had no professional preparation. Of Pestalozzi he had never heard. But whatever one may think of his solutions, it is clear that he did not need to have the educational problems pointed out to him.

Good members of the school board he considered next in importance to good teachers. It was for this reason, he wrote, in the *Autobiography*, edited by Mary Sheldon Barnes, that "I felt it incumbent upon me as far as possible to run the elections. . . . Sometime before an election I was on the alert, picked out a good man and spoke to my friends about him. . . . On election day I was not idle but went the rounds to see that they did their duty. . . . By this eternal vigilance we succeeded in keeping a good board. Occasionally, the opposition was too strong for us and a 'kicker' would be elected. In such a case I was careful to give him every possible attention, taking him around from building to building, showing him conditions and pointing out needs. As a result he sometimes became the most liberal man on the board and moved to advance the budget beyond what the board were willing to approve." It was in such ways that he "gained the reputation of winning over to the interest of the schools every man, however serious his opposition when elected . . . 'they gave me *carte blanche* . . . I got the title of 'Pope Sheldon.' " This was written long after, when the memory of his difficulties had grown dim but that of his success, as is the way with memories, was still bright.

Our brief narrative indicates how a small city system was started a century ago. The mechanical arrangements and the exacting discipline of teachers and pupils would not be approved now and indeed Sheldon himself later disapproved of them. "My tendency was," he wrote in 1897, "to restrain the activities and impulses of children, while now I would encourage and cultivate them by giving them proper direction." He should have applied to pupils and teachers some of the clever "management" that he bestowed upon board members. Some of his teachers must have lacked experience. Sheldon kept the schools under his constant surveillance. He felt that he had "to be everywhere." The lessons, it is no wonder, seemed dull and lifeless. It was these conditions that led to the Oswego object-teaching system.

In a Toronto museum, not in use in the schools of Toronto, Sheldon found a collection of pictures, color charts, and other visual materials. These had been acquired by Egerton Ryerson (1803–1882), chief school official for the province of Ontario, Canada, on his educational tour of England and Europe, and he now sold them for $300 to Sheldon, who was making an educational tour of Canada. Sheldon put the "objects" to work. The materials had come from the stock of an English Pestalozzian group, the Home and Colonial School Society. From them he also obtained a teacher, Margaret Jones, who came for one year to introduce the new methods; and when her term expired he was able to engage Hermann Krüsi, Jr., the son of Pestalozzi's first assistant. Krüsi, however, voiced some criticism of the formalized type of object-teaching that had been developed in England and that was now applied in Oswego. Before we consider the criticisms we shall examine a sample lesson.

A "lesson on plants" from Sheldon's manuscript has been published. In Dearborn's *The Oswego Movement* it reads, in part, as follows: "1. Require the children to look at some flowers and say in what they are alike. (They all have leaves; they all have stems; nearly all have the *outer leaves* [calix] of a *green* color.) Let the children smell the flowers—they all have some kind of smell. Ask how they are produced (from slips or seeds). If a slip or seed be put into the ground and gets proper nourishment, what takes place? (They grow [*sic*.]) All flowers are grown. . . . Who made the flowers?

"2. Having found out in what flowers are alike, lead the children to discover in what they differ. . . .

"3. Let the children say of whom we should think when we *look at flowers?* . . . Why flowers are made of different colors? . . . Whom they should thank when they gather flowers?"

From this incomplete sample one infers that cut flowers were used and were passed from pupil to pupil. But flowering plants have roots and these have important functions which were neglected. On the other hand, such a lesson may go in any direction, ending up not in science but in religion as this one did. It was standard practice to have the pupils name the qualities of objects. "This apple is large, firm, red, wholesome," and so on. But the discussion might wander off into horticulture or history. Apples have, according to tradition, played various parts as, for example, in the drama of William Tell, and of Newton, and of a notable couple in an ancient garden. All this raises the vital question of the purpose of object-teaching.

The usual answer to this question was based upon the faculty psychology. This does not call for special remark because the faculty psychology was so generally accepted. Using its terms we may say that object-teaching was intended to develop accuracy of observation and perception, to lead pupils to form correct concepts, and to grow in reasoning power. The Pestalozzian principle was accepted that the materials and lessons were to be adapted to the stages of the children's mental development. And also following Pestalozzi, the lessons were to promote vocabulary growth and skill in describing objects both orally and in writing. There was an alphabet of observation. This was an expansion of Pestalozzi's number, form, and language, and it included also size, sound, odor, color, and ideas of relation such as part and whole.

The true idea of school education, said Sheldon, is not so much to impart knowledge as to prepare the mind to acquire knowledge and to convey it to others. The teacher, he said, must be ready in speech and skilled in drawing so that he will be able to supplement real objects or in their absence to use sketches in place of things. He must be on easy footing with children and have the power to hold their interest and direct it. To this set of teaching qualifications we may add a sentence from Hermann Krüsi, Jr., one of Sheldon's able and loyal assistants. He said: "In the acquisition, or teaching of any branch of study, I have always tried to penetrate to the principle, in order to render the subject clear to myself before presenting it to others," which is a most commendable practice for teachers to follow.

Object-teaching had to face hostile criticism. It will be fairest to begin with the "wounds of a friend." Krüsi thought the lessons often had no connection with each other, followed no overall plan. There seemed to be too much crude analysis, children being asked to name the parts of the human body, the parts of a plant, as in the above example, or of an animal, perhaps the horse. In the third place, too many unfamiliar words were taught, such words as "fetlock," "pastern," and "withers," or, in other connections, used to name qualities such as "porous," "transparent," and "opaque." An outside critic listed "chalybeate," "imbricated," "amorphous," and many more. Thus the object lesson became a senseless vocabulary lesson. The teachers' questions did not stimulate but instead, as Krüsi said, restricted the pupils' responses. Good answers might be considered wrong because they were not the ones demanded by the lesson plan. Lastly, there was often only one object, an apple or a cube, held up before the class who thus found "observation" difficult. Krüsi thought the best examples of object-teaching were found not in the lessons from which the name was derived but in arithmetic or drawing where pupils were encouraged to develop their own ideas, illustrations, and experiments. All sciences are based upon realities that have to be observed before symbols and abstractions can be useful; but he recognized also that nature studies should lead to ideas and principles that are indeed "real" and "clear" or "true" but not "concrete." He was pleased when H. H. Straight introduced into Oswego a more flexible and intellectual course of nature study that by no means neglected contact with things. But there were difficulties, for some teachers in the normal school were wedded to object lessons and opposed nature study just as their predecessors had opposed object lessons because they were wedded to the book.

The most sensational criticisms of Oswego object-teaching came from outside the school and were made by H. B. Wilbur of Syracuse. His attacks, called "vindictive" by some, were made first before the state and later before the national educational associations. Replies were made by Sheldon, by committees appointed to investigate, and even by some English Pestalozzians who were drawn into the debate. This became one of the long drawn-out (1862–1865) controversies of American educational history.

Controversy broke out on the home front as well as abroad. In 1872 the school board of Oswego discontinued object-teaching in all grades above the three primary years. But there had been trouble earlier, and when Sheldon wrote his autobiography in 1897 he had forgotten his long-past difficulties. With all of his management and his political activities in school board elections, he was not always the master of events. It was partly for this reason that in 1863 he sought and secured state aid for the normal school, which had been a local institution. In 1867 it became a state normal school, and two years later Sheldon gave up his position in the city schools to devote all his time to the preparation of teachers. The teaching profession had in the main supported his program and the publicity was of the greatest service to the school.

If one may judge the influence of the Oswego normal school by the distribution of its graduates, it must have been far-reaching. In the first twenty-five years there had been in attendance between five and six thousand students of whom more than two thousand graduated. The graduates were to be found teaching in the schools of nearly all the states and territories and in several foreign countries. The largest numbers were employed in New York and adjoining states and in the old Northwest Territory states. Such facts do not, however, tell us much because there is no way of telling how well the Oswego methods were received. The greatest deficiency of the teachers lay in the lack of a thorough scientific education. "It is a great mistake," said Agassiz, "to suppose that just any one can teach even the simple elements of science. To have a smattering of something is one of the great fallacies of our time."

SPOTLIGHT ON QUINCY

Almost as soon as Oswego had reached the height of its celebrity, the crowds of educators began to turn toward Quincy, Massachusetts. Superintendents, teachers, and reporters came and also some who were intent merely "either to tell or to hear some new thing." They came to see the change that had been worked in a sleepy school system by a new superintendent, Francis Wayland Parker (1837–1902), who had in earlier positions experimented with Sheldon's object lessons. Another part of this book tells more about him; but here we shall deal mainly with the "New Departure," the "New Education," or the "Quincy Methods," as the change was variously called. Colonel Parker always denied that there was in the Quincy methods anything that was entirely new. After we see what there was we may perhaps judge whether any of it was new.

Both the Oswego and the Quincy methods were applied only in the elementary school and mostly in the primary grades. They were alike in the use of concrete materials. To observation both added forms of expression and reporting, such as language, drawing, and modeling in clay. The best-known report on the Quincy methods even calls these activities "object lessons," but there is in them a clear approach to what we shall in the next section call nature study. Some of the lessons were carefully prepared and others were called impromptu exercises. There was an impromptu lesson on the horse, "the beginning of zoology." In Quincy in 1880 all pupils had seen horses, and except for the drawing of a horse by the teacher on the board this was simply a conversation lesson. It was an object lesson; but at Oswego the range of the lesson subject would have been out of the ordinary.

There was a plant lesson, an "introduction to botany," in which the children planted seeds in a box filled with earth brought in by a pupil. There was some conversation on what will grow and what will not. A lesson upon hills was to introduce the pupils to the study of geography. After making hills in the sandbox a pupil poured water on them. This illustrated erosion, but the teachers at Quincy resisted the tendency to use big words. As the lesson ended, the children were told to notice the shapes of the hills on their way home and to prepare to model them in school the following day. This, said the reporter, "may be made the first step to that grandest of all sciences, Geography."

In the primary school years covered by Lelia E. Patridge in her report on the Quincy methods, there are lessons on form, color, number, language, and all the school rudiments. One reporter declared that the children of Quincy wrote English earlier and better than anywhere else. The compositions reprinted by Miss Patridge and the pupils' drawings that she presented in her book are excellent. According to a third commentator, the work was a "tremendous success" so that "a surplus of volunteers" offered to teach in the schools without compensation in order that they might thoroughly learn the Quincy methods.

At Quincy there was an effort to combine subjects. Every lesson was to be made a lesson in the language arts of speech and writing. The spelling book was wholly discarded, and spelling was taught in writing and reading. Parker favored the use of many reading books in each grade, not just one. Every language lesson could also be the beginning of science instruction. Lessons on color involved form. Number work could use both form and color. All lessons were to teach good manners and morals. History and geography were to be combined quite after the manner of Herbart; and Parker in some passages seems to hold that history is determined by geography.

All the accounts declare that at Quincy teachers and pupils worked together joyously and harmoniously. From Charles Francis Adams, Jr., who was most responsible for bringing Parker to Quincy, comes the testimony that in both primary and grammar grades the new superintendent created a new spirit. "It was certainly most pleasant to go into the rooms," wrote

Adams, "and feel the atmosphere of cheerfulness, activity, and interest which pervaded them."

Three related attempts to improve the quality of elementary education were made in the nineteenth century. Each effort was based upon the improved preparation of teachers. The three leaders were Horace Mann, who led in the creation of state systems of schools and the founding of state normal schools; Edward Sheldon, who spread object-teaching and founded the Oswego State Normal School; and Francis Parker, who made of Quincy an object lesson in good teaching and became head of the Cook County Normal School in Illinois. Thus the professional preparation of teachers was a leading interest of each of these.

All of these efforts were based upon the principle that the elementary school should provide a broad, general education, a truly liberating experience. Such a program, reaching far beyond the four R's and also beyond the so-called professional areas, required teachers who were themselves educated persons, knowing what and why as well as how. Nature study was to be a contribution to this program, but such teachers were not easy to develop in the normal schools.

NATURE STUDY

To tell when nature study began in the schools we should know what it is—a question that presents some difficulty. If it is merely a variety of object-teaching, or if, on the other hand, it is science, we had better call it by the appropriate one of these names. The *Nature Study Review*, which began publication in 1905 when the movement was well advanced, defined it as the simple observational study of common natural objects just because they are interesting. Simple observation is here contrasted with the processes of technical science, such as analysis, dissection, quantitative work, and the search for scientific laws. The phrase "common natural objects" is not entirely fitting. The objects of object lessons were often colors, an egg, a piece of glass, and similarly unrelated things. But the usual objects of nature study are plants and animals, and these are observed in their natural habitat. This study of life histories, adaptation, and distribution includes the observation of such matters as soils, weather, bird migration, animal cover, hibernation, and other surroundings and habits of living things. This kind of study comes under what the scientist calls ecology. Nature study is different in matter and method from both object lessons and science. It resembles the activities and interests of the old-fashioned naturalists. The words themselves may have been taken, as has been supposed, from the German *Naturkunde*, which is literally nature knowledge rather than the study of nature. It is certain that the phrase quickly came into wide use about 1889.

Within the field thus indicated there were several kinds of interests. Some naturalists and nature study exponents tend to gush over the "dear" things that they find in the woods or garden, or they sermonize on the "spirit of nature" that to them "seems to hover like a fairy around the waterfalls." At a great distance from this is the nature study that prepares for the study of agriculture, hygiene, or botany and zoology. And to be found between these extremes is the custom of correlating nature study with geography, or drawing, or composition, and sometimes with local history. The latter practices do not necessarily indicate that the observation of nature is lacking in intrinsic interest; but they do tend to affect the materials selected and the methods. With these reservations and illustrations the *Review's* definition may be accepted. Little equipment is needed. Except for a simple microscope and a field glass, the needed apparatus can be made in the school shop or by the pupils at home.

Like other such movements, nature study did not have a noticeable beginning. Here and there in academies and normal schools and even in the common schools, there were teachers who taught children about trees and animals, who took them on trips or brought nature into the schoolroom. The majority did none of these things, but there was an increase in the number of helpful books and materials for those who wished to introduce the study of nature.

In his annual report for 1871 William T. Harris published A *Syllabus in Nature Study* for the schools of St. Louis. He gave economic reasons for this step. Science, he said, explains the processes of nature and thus enables industry to create the products that improve the living conditions of the people. This is evidently not the voice of a mere theoretician. Natural science was recommended because it is an instrument of civilization. The syllabus gave advice on teaching. The lessons were to be largely oral, and experiments and demonstrations were recommended as well as books. The material reached beyond biology and included some physical geography, meteorology, and astronomy, and touched the "human sciences" of economics and pedagogy. The program, which was to occupy one hour a week, did not have the rich variety of organisms and phenomena that later courses introduced; but it was an improvement over object-teaching.

Within a year after coming to Boston, Louis Agassiz (1807–1873) was to be found lecturing to teachers in their institutes in Massachusetts. These meetings were held in late summer, and the lecturer appeared with a jar of live grasshoppers. It was one of his devices to have nature herself lecture for him. Each teacher had to hold a grasshopper while Agassiz explained its structure and habits. When his wife opened her school of sixty or more girls, he helped out with daily lectures on natural history illustrated with specimens, models, and drawings. It has been said that he never had a more responsive audience, and it was usually augmented by some of the mothers of the pupils. Although he had the expert's dislike of books by amateurs, he helped his wife, Elizabeth Cary Agassiz, prepare *A First Lesson in Natural History* (1859), a little book for children somewhat in the tradition of Mrs. Marcet. It soon attained a second edition and was also revised for a third.

Agassiz and his students had to do with the creation of many natural history museums. One of his students, Albert Smith Bickmore, "created the design" for the American Museum of Natural History established in New York, known around the world, and in later years long presided over by Henry Fairfield Osborn. Bickmore was one of the pioneers in the movement to bring schools and museums together for nature study. Osborn has told how Bickmore in 1880 started lectures at the museum for teachers; in 1904 for children; in 1902 began to lend nature study collections to schools; and in 1914 sent the museum lecturers with the collections out into the schools. All this began with Agassiz. No one can say how much would have happened without him or how soon. To secure nature's help in teaching was not new when Agassiz used it, but his charm, his scientific reputation, his theism, even his anti-Darwinism, and the intellectual and economic conditions of the nineteenth century increased his influence in the United States. But he was not the father of nature study; its original ancestor may have been Pestalozzi, or Aristotle, or even before these two men

> *That shepherd who first taught the chosen seed*
> *In the beginning how the heavens and earth*
> *Rose out of Chaos;*

and in fact N. S. Shaler's *Autobiography* (p. 298) suggests that this latter farspun guess may have had the support of Agassiz himself.

On the list of Agassiz's students at Penikese, the name of H. H. Straight (1846–1886) stood first; and this, although accidental, is symbolic of his rank as "probably the outstanding elementary science teacher" of the group. That he who made his own way and wrote nothing should by the age of forty acquire such a reputation is astonishing. Straight early became an orphan, worked on farms in western New York, and began teaching in his middle teens. His salary was $13 a month for a three-months' term. He entered the preparatory department of Oberlin College, hoping to find a way to go to Germany to study languages. To earn the means for this, he again turned to teaching, and at Galena, Ohio, he introduced some object lessons into the work of his classes. Whatever the effect of this upon his pupils, it changed his own life. Instead of Germany he studied at Cornell and Harvard, assisted Shaler in his geological surveys in Kentucky and neighboring states (1875), and the following year was appointed by Sheldon to teach science at Oswego.

We have seen that Straight was not fully understood at Oswego. He was repelled by the formality of the object lessons, their pretentious vocabulary, the lack of connection between lessons and the failure to relate them to the rest of the work of the school. To Straight, Parker gave the credit for his own interest in the correlation of studies; but it is hard to believe that after his years in Europe Parker had to come back home to learn about that Herbartian idea.

At Oswego, Straight taught from living plants and animals in their natural environment. He had learned from Agassiz and Shaler, and at Cornell from Burt G. Wilder to stress the unity of nature. He took his classes to the shore of Lake Ontario and to swamp, forest, and field. There they learned by direct observation and inference how living things depend upon natural conditions. In 1882 he taught in the summer school at Martha's Vineyard, and Hermann Krüsi, Jr. visiting the school, found that Straight's "educational wisdom" was receiving greater recognition there than at home. The following year he joined Parker in the Cook County Normal School for the last few years of his short life.

The work that Straight was compelled to lay down was taken up and more fully developed by Wilbur S. Jackman (1855–1907). He was appointed to the science department of the Cook County Normal School in 1889. When Parker joined the University of Chicago, Jackman accompanied him. He also had been a farm boy with few early opportunities, but he managed to complete a normal school course and at the age of twenty-nine graduated from Harvard College. His sound preparation in science kept him from diluting nature study with romantic sentiment, and his practical administrative skill enabled him to develop a course that carried the students regularly through the seasons. His *Nature Study for the Common Schools* (1894) and his book on fieldwork followed the succession of nature phenomena through "the rolling year." His teaching and writings helped to give nature study an assured place in the elementary grades. When the normal school was united with the University of Chicago, he also served as principal of the University Elementary School. In later years Elliot Rowland Downing and other scientists continued to maintain the position of Chicago as a nature study center.

The two decades from 1890 to 1910 and the two states, Massachusetts and New York, were preeminent for their contributions to the nature study movement at the height of its influence. Massachusetts was at that time still reaping its harvest from the work of Horace Mann and the normal schools and of Agassiz and his disciples. Penikese and the Martha's Vineyard Summer School have been mentioned. In New York the agricultural depression of the nineties brought together at Cornell University a number of prominent nature study leaders; and the teaching and publication that were begun at that time have been continued by their successors.

In Massachusetts the teachers' association of Plymouth County in 1890 prepared for the schools a series of nature observations and asked the members to report on the work at the following meeting of the association. Observations on plants, animals, and minerals were proposed, and the following year the outline was expanded. This is the county in which the Bridgewater Normal School was located, and the former students of this school had long been given an introduction to science. Many of these responded eagerly to the suggestion of their association and reported the adoption of supplementary reading books in natural history or the correlation of nature study with drawing and language lessons.

In New York the movement had a less academic beginning. In the agricultural depression of the early 1890's, many rural people flocked into New York City and the relief agencies began to ask why the land should have become unable to sustain its people. This question led naturally to an inquiry into the condition of agriculture and the formation of a citizens' committee for its improvement. It was proposed to interest country children in farming by teaching them about nature; and the legislature was induced to make an appropriation for this purpose. The money was made available to the college of agriculture at Cornell University, and the work was directed at first by Professor Isaac Roberts (1833–1928) and then by Liberty Hyde Bailey (1858–1954).

Bailey became an eminent writer, editor, and teacher of agriculture and horticulture and the founder of the Bailey Hortorium at Cornell. He was also an effective promoter of nature study. In this he was putting to use the lessons he had learned from a rural teacher in Michigan. After graduating from the Agricultural College of his state, he became an assistant to the great botanist, Asa Gray. His numerous publications include both technical and inspirational books, elementary textbooks on botany, and a famous essay that he called The Nature-Study Idea (1903). This sensible and charming little book was written for teachers, but it does not, as the title might suggest, deal mainly with the philosophy of nature study. It answers many practical questions such as, "How shall I start in teaching nature?" or, "Is nature study thorough?" It has a chapter on the school garden with an account of the gardens at the Hampton Institute, and another chapter on the agricultural phase of nature study. From the way the Cornell movement was initiated one would expect a strong emphasis upon agriculture, but this was not Bailey's idea. He had been a farm boy; and he believed that a flower garden would do more than a bumper wheat crop to keep a boy on the farm. And it is a fact that the Cornell nature study publications did not greatly stress the economics of agriculture.

There is in The Nature-Study Idea this discouraging interpretation of educational history, as follows: "We have failed to reach the farmer effectively because we still persist in employing old-time and academic methods. Historically the elementary public school is a product of the university and the college. 'The greatest achievement of modern education,' writes W. H. Payne, 'is the gradation and correlation of schools, whereby the ladder of learning is let down from the university to secondary schools, and from these to the schools of the people.' This origin of 'the schools of the people' from the university explains why it is that these schools are so unrelated to the life of the pupil, and so unreal; they are exotic and unnatural. If any man were to find himself in a country wholly devoid of schools and were set the task of originating and organizing a school system, he would almost unconsciously introduce some subjects that would be related to the habits of the people and to the welfare of the community. Being freed from traditions, he would teach something of the plants and animals and fields and people. Yet, as a matter of fact, what do our rural schools teach? Nothing of this kind." Some of the facts in this useful lesson, as Bailey attempted to teach it, require correction. The elementary school, independent at first, was drawn into the secondary school and university orbit. More recently this trend has been reversed.

To increase the vitality of rural education by bringing it into close connection with farm life, Cornell University used a part of its special appropriation to promote nature study in the schools. In this work Anna Botsford Comstock had already shown expertness. She and Bailey visited many rural schools to learn what human and material resources were available. They found that the object and nature teaching of the Oswego Normal School graduates formed a good beginning. Others of the group that collected around Bailey were George T. Powell, director of farmers' institutes, and John W. Spencer, a fruit-grower from Chautauqua County. The New York Experiment Station gave aid. Lecturers were sent into the rural schools to give illustrative lessons and to aid teachers in forming study programs.

Rural school leaflets written by this staff were distributed in hundreds of thousands of copies to the schools. Mrs. Comstock, who was an entomologist and artist, wrote many of them. Out of these and her experience and that of her colleagues she wrote her *Handbook of Nature-Study*. Her preface written in 1911 contains an account of the Cornell movement. E. Laurence Palmer, who has succeeded to the leadership of nature study at Cornell, has prepared many of the later leaflets. In one for September, 1944, he has listed the subjects of nearly one hundred such pamphlets beginning with one of January, 1920, on "small winter mammals." Each year there is one intended for teachers. Several of these deal with elementary science books.

There has been an opinion in some quarters that the multitude of nature books has been harmful to nature study. Some schools have made nature study a literary pursuit. Having pupils read about "wild folk at the pond" or about "nature hobbies" is not nature study. But the observational study of nature was not crushed by the mounting pile of publications that have come from the presses yearly since about 1900 or 1910; and wisely used, the better books can be stepping stones to better observation and wider knowledge of nature than the unaided pupil could attain. Some of the opposition to nature study came from those who wished to replace it with vocational agriculture. Others, supplementing Liberty H. Bailey's opinion, thought nature study could be made practical. But it must be admitted that most work in nature study has been and is general and liberal, noc really vocational in nature. The study has held its place in some school systems but not in all, not in any large proportion in fact. From two postcard investigations it appears that in the schools of half a dozen states there was no trace of nature study, and in each of such large and populous states as California, Illinois, New York, and Pennsylvania, only twenty-five or thirty cities and school systems reported nature study courses. Some of the actual work may not have been reported, some may have been done under another name, perhaps in connection with geography. But this, or something like this, is the outcome of the work of scientists, institute lecturers, normal schools, and authors over a period of three-quarters of a century.

SCIENCE-TEACHING TRENDS

The greatest difficulty in improving nature study and in even maintaining it in the schools is to be found in the inadequate scientific education of the elementary teachers; and no curriculum can be effective without knowledge, intelligence, and enthusiasm in those who administer it. The second difficulty grows out of heavy schedules, large classes, and lack of administrative support with which elementary teachers must somehow cope.

With the rise of the junior high school and the development of general science about the same time, there has been a tendency to make the nature study of the fifth and sixth grades more systematic than nature study has sometimes been. The elementary teacher seeking help from the teachers in the junior high school has tended to follow their ideas and methods. This is merely a single example of a two-way movement between lower and higher schools that has always been in existence. Not only have the high school and the college been mutually influencing each other but this is also true of the elementary and the high school. Subjects, methods, and purposes have moved up and down on the ladder as need arose. And the junior high school, partaking of the nature of the school below and the one above, became an easy pathway for ideas. In this interchange there is danger as well as benefit. The danger to elementary school science is that it will become too systematic and logical and that there will be presented generalizations that the elementary schoolchild cannot grasp.

The great benefit that may come to elementary science from the junior high school is in the emphasis that will be placed upon the solving of problems. But the problems must be easy enough and not too easy; and this point cannot be readily determined. They should also lead to further questions and to useful applications. How to find a supply of such tasks and to provide the background and materials to set the inquiry in motion is one of the urgent and largely unsolved problems of elementary education. For help we are entitled to look to the specialists in elementary education and elementary school science teaching.

The main current trend in the field is one in the direction of elementary science. If this seems to take us back to William T. Harris and the seventies of the last century, we shall be only partly correct. The new elementary science movement is much richer in ideas and better adapted to the children's interests than the St. Louis efforts of long ago. Teachers and teaching have improved in this area, and the nature study movement deserves much of the credit for the change. But problems may be too easy as well as too hard. In teaching children to think by means of science, we should, indeed we unavoidably must, teach science.

A major trend in elementary education has favored the enrichment of the course of study or, in the current speech, of the experiences of children. A great many activities have been introduced as well as much new knowledge and many kinds of problems. The school has gone beyond the four R's.

SUMMARY

After the Civil War a movement developed to enrich the elementary school program and to extend and improve the preparation of the elementary teachers. The kindergarten with its play activities and games, its group exercises and informal manner, became an object lesson to the elementary school and especially so when it became a part of the public school system. Both the discovery that children learn through inventive and creative work and that activities could be educative without being based upon books and formal lessons were of the greatest importance in the reform of elementary education.

The liberal wing of the kindergarten movement did not continue Froebel's "gifts" and exercises or accept his symbolism; but other American kindergartners, under the influence of German fundamentalist trainers, continued the strictly Froebelian practices and theories. The struggle between the two parties continued into the twentieth century. John Dewey after 1896 did not want to admit that the University School had a kindergarten.

Child study was closely related to the kindergarten movement. Froebel himself had carried out studies of the play, games, songs, and constructions of children. The psychologists took up the study of children's growth and development and introduced new methods involving questionnaires, continuous records, physical measurements, mental tests, and controlled experiments. Information was gathered on language development, drawing, reasoning, skills, interests, and other phases in the effort to learn how children mature and what influences affect their development.

Educational and industrial influences led to the introduction of handwork and drawing into the elementary schools. Felix Adler was an eloquent and distinguished spokesman for the education of the hand. He urged that school activities and handwork served a purpose in learning analogous to that of experiment in science. This Froebelian doctrine has had great influence upon child psychology and curriculum practice and theory.

The spread of the normal schools was a major feature of the development of elementary education after 1860. They increased in numbers and also in facilities and power, yet they were hardly able to keep pace with the increasing numbers of teachers and the demands made upon them. Oswego was one normal school that made a definite impression upon American education. But the sort of impression it made was not wholly favorable to progress. Its formalized methods were not adapted to develop the initiative, originality, and self-education of the pupils. The Quincy schools took a step in this direction, and nature study when well directed followed what was later to be known as the Progressive tradition.

QUESTIONS

1. What do children learn by doing—to do, to know, to reason, or to invent and create? What apparently are the educational values to be derived from these several outcomes?

2. What are the positive values and what the limitations of the concept that the teacher is to be merely a child-gardener rather than one who instructs, warns, and controls his pupils?

3. Froebel, it is known, thought that democratic America would be highly favorable to the kindergarten and so it proved. Why, then, in adopting it was it changed?

4. Why was it necessary to create a new separate institution, the state normal school, to prepare teachers when there already were many colleges with capable faculties and not too many students? Find other examples illustrating the same principle.

5. If we truly observe only that to which we actively attend, what success in forming able observers was to be expected from object lessons?

6. Why is the organization of ideas and of knowledge important?

7. Would scientists approve the definition of nature study given by the *Nature Study Review?* Ask several. What do scientists think of "nature study"?

8. What evidence may show that Straight independently discovered correlation of studies? What is the probability that Parker learned it from Straight and not in Germany?

9. Is the account by Payne a true account of the origin of "the schools for the people?"

10. Why has nature study as a separate discipline declined while "nature

books" remain popular, for example, Rachel Carson's *The Sea Around Us* (1951)?

11. Why, in the expansion of elementary education, was more attention devoted to knowledge than to activities?

BOOKS AND PAPERS

Each of the chief subjects in this chapter has an independent literature of its own, and some had the support of special magazines such as G. Stanley Hall's *Pedagogical Seminary* for child study and the *Nature Study Review* for the subject indicated. On safeguards to be observed in questionnaire studies, see an article by G. M. Whipple in *School and Society*, August 27, 1927. There were numerous books, historical, expository, and critical, on these subjects. W. H. Kilpatrick's criticism of Froebel is listed. Agassiz, for all his reputation as a teacher and teacher of teachers, became a controversial figure, the occasion as well as the author of many books and papers.

BAILEY, LIBERTY H., *The Nature-Study Idea*, New York, 1904.

BARNARD, HENRY, *Papers on Froebel's Kindergarten*, Hartford, 1890, being selections from the *Journal*. The date of the first issue of the *Papers* is in doubt. This revised edition has a critical paper by I. H. Fichte (1797–1879), who, like his more famous father, was a philosopher.

BOYDEN, A. C., *History of the Bridgewater Normal School*, Bridgewater, 1933.

COMSTOCK, ANNA B., *Handbook of Nature Study*, Ithaca, New York, 1941, a printing of the twenty-fourth edition, revised in 1939.

CREMIN, LAWRENCE A., *The American Common School*, New York, Teachers College, Columbia University, 1951.

DEARBORN, NED H., *The Oswego Movement in American Education*, New York, Teachers College, Columbia University, 1925.

DOWNING, E. R., *Our Living World, A Source-Book of Biological Nature-Study*, University of Chicago Press, 1919.

FOSTER, JOSEPHINE C., and N. E. HEADLEY, *Education in the Kindergarten*, New York, 1948.

GORDON, EVA L., "Elementary Science Library," *Cornell Rural School Leaflet*, Vol. 43, No. 1, Ithaca, New York, September, 1949.

HALL, G. STANLEY, *Life and Confessions of a Psychologist*, New York, 1923.

HARRIS, W. T., "Relations of the Kindergarten to the School," NEA *Proceedings, 1879*, pp. 142–158; and *How to Teach Natural Science in Public Schools*, Syracuse, New York, 1895.

KILPATRICK, W. H., *Froebel's Kindergarten Principles Critically Examined*, New York, 1916.

KRAUS, JOHN, "The Kindergarten; Its Use and Abuse in America," NEA *Proceedings, 1877*, pp. 186–207, an accusatory address.

PALMER, E. L., "The Cornell Nature Study Philosophy," *Cornell Rural School Leaflet*, Vol. 38, No. 1, Ithaca, New York, September, 1944.

PATRIDGE, LELIA E., *Quincy Methods Illustrated*, New York, 1886.

REISNER, EDWARD H., *The Evolution of the Common School*, New York, 1930.

RUSSELL, JAMES E., "Organization and Administration of Teachers College," *Teachers College Record*, January, 1900.

SHELDON, E. A., *Autobiography of Edward Austin Sheldon*, New York, 1911. Edited by a daughter, Mary Sheldon Barnes, teacher and writer, with an introduction by Andrew Sloan Draper.

STRICKLAND, CHARLES E., and CHARLES BURGESS, eds., *Health, Growth, and Heredity, G. Stanley Hall on Natural Education*, New York, Teachers College, Columbia University, 1966.

TELLER, JAMES, D., *Louis Agassiz, Scientist and Teacher*, Ohio State University Press, 1947.

UNDERHILL, ORRA F., *The Origins and Development of Elementary School Science*, Chicago, 1941.

WELTER, RUSH, *Popular Education and Democratic Thought in America*, Columbia University Press, 1962.

Chapter 8

RISE OF THE
HIGH SCHOOL

The high school, although it is far younger than the English, French, and other great secondary schools of Western Europe, has undergone much greater changes than these schools have. It began as a school for boys but soon admitted girls also. It began as a specialized and has become a comprehensive school. It began as a terminal school similar to the realist academy, early assumed classical college-preparatory functions, in midcareer undertook to give vocational education, and should now, in the opinion of some, become a universal school for all American youth.

The greater part of this revolution has occurred since the closing decades of the nineteenth century, when it was transformed into a higher common school whose chief task is not the preparation of selected young people for college studies but the preparation of young people for "the real business of living." It is significant that the quoted words are taken from the early documents of one of the earliest academies, Phillips **Andover.** But the real business of living and the means of preparing for it have changed since 1787; and the high school has contracted its classical and expanded its realist studies and added the vocations and activities to its program. It has become the center of community activity and the pride of its community. Of many a town and city it can be said that the high school building is the finest building in it. It has spread from the cities to the country districts and is coming to be within reach of all the children.

THE MEANING OF SECONDARY EDUCATION

The public high school is not the only American secondary school. Secondary education is a broad term covering private as well as public schools for adolescents. Among these are military academies, expensive and exclusive preparatory schools, and the numerous church-controlled academies and high schools. In earlier times, and in many countries even now, only the preparatory schools, which generally are for a selected portion of the upper classes only, were and are called secondary. In France, for example, the high school would be considered a mixed secondary and higher primary school, secondary in so far as it is preparatory, and higher primary in so far as it continues the work of the elementary school.

An informative passage in Alexander Dallas Bache's *Report* (1839, p. 450) reveals his own liberal American position on this definition and thus shows disagreement with leading French educators. Bache wrote as follows: "It is usual to confine the title of secondary schools to those which prepare for the learned professions, and in this view the only secondary instruction in Prussia is given in the gymnasia," in which the ancient classics received the main emphasis. But Bache, disagreeing with this view, held that the "Real Schools (*Realschulen*)" were equally entitled to be called secondary because the ages of the pupils and the level of their attainment were the same as those of the gymnasial pupils. The objection to the *Realschulen* by some educators was based upon their exclusion of the classics and their stress instead upon modern languages, mathematics, and sciences. They arose in Germany in the eighteenth century, and the English and American academies had much in common with them.

The graduates of the *Realschulen*, Bache said, go to schools of architecture, engineering, and manufactures, and these professional schools maintain as high a standard as the universities. For this reason Bache regarded the *Realschulen* as secondary schools even though many of their pupils did not attend any higher schools but went directly into the business of life. He even included the higher trade schools in the secondary class because they had a standard comparable to that of the classical gymnasium. Bache reported that F. P. G. Guizot, French historian and educator, agreed with him but that Victor Cousin did not. French officials and administrators certainly did not. Perhaps Bache came to his liberal conclusions because he was educated at West Point, not at an old-line classical college. The well-developed American high school came fully within Bache's conception of secondary schools.

The high school had many characteristics that distinguished it from the secondary schools of Europe. Chief of these was its relation to the common schools. The common, normal, and high schools developed together and were intimately related; but the common school was basic to the other two because it furnished them their pupils. The high school was from the first a higher common school, but as time passed it came to a considerable extent under the control of the colleges. Sometimes only those high schools that had the approval of the colleges were considered worthy of the name "high school." It was resistance to this trend, the expansion of its program, the reestablishment of its earlier alliance with the elementary schools, that has made it the unique American institution that it has become.

About 1890, which might be taken to divide the early period from the later, the average enrollment was fewer than one hundred pupils to a school; and only three per thousand of the whole people were attending high schools. The movement to consolidate rural schools gained strength at the turn of the century, and many rural high schools were established. This tended to keep down the average enrollment because the rural schools were often very small. But in the cities attendance rose higher and higher, often creating the necessity for several schools in a city; and by 1930 not three but more than forty per thousand of the population were in attendance. This prodigious growth, more fully indicated in Table 8–1 on page 237 has been a surprise to professional and lay people alike. It must be because of strong educational and economic forces.

ANOTHER DOOR IS OPENED

Until recent times, in many parts of the civilized world, secondary schools were for boys alone and for those boys only who belonged to the wealthy, genteel, professional, or official classes. These privileged children were separated from the offspring of workingmen and peasants and were kept separate through the remainder of their schooling and throughout life. In this way the secondary schools, in the older sense of that term, shutting the door against the common people, helped to maintain the class structure of society of which they were an expression.

American society has also had and still has its classes, but these have been less permanent and less widely separated from one another than those of older countries. Wealth has been easy to acquire but, without the ancient law of transmission to the eldest son, hard to hold in the family. The changing economic currents have created many new fortunes and dissipated the old. And on the other hand, there have been many opportunities to acquire a competence. Such have been the results of inventions, of the exploitation of natural resources in land, coal, oil, and the like, and of the competition in an expanding domestic market. The number of families who could do without the labor of their children increased in the nineteenth century; and many of these children attended the new high schools.

There were other reasons for the extension of education. Such were universal suffrage and the spread of the elementary schools. The high schools prepared teachers, and as the schools were better articulated with the elementary schools they opened new vistas to the pupils of the upper grades. In many instances, not in all, the press favored the high school. There is an obvious reason why publishers should favor the spread of education. Organized labor had good reasons to favor not only the common but also the high school. The growth of equality between the sexes and the Christian and democratic emphasis upon the dignity of the human being favored universal educational opportunity.

The year 1890, which has been named as the time when the great expansion of the high school began, should not be taken in an absolute sense. The school has always been in transition; but 1890 is near the half-way mark of its entire history, and in the latter half the changes were greater and followed each other more rapidly than in the early years. Take numbers alone. There are ten times as many high schools today as there were then and thirty times as many pupils. The high school door has been opened wide.

The year 1890 curiously synchronizes with the closing of the frontier. The most valuable public lands had been taken up by that time. Farm machinery and farm chemistry were coming into use. The agricultural revolution had begun. Farmers produced a succession of increasing crops with a diminishing labor force. The rural high school soon arrived to prepare rural youth for better farming and better living on the farm; but it also prepared the oversupply of farm youth for careers in the city. In the city, also, jobs for teen-age children were becoming fewer. And an extraordinary rise in high school attendance occurred in the depression of the thirties when there were hardly any jobs. To get children off the streets in that period, legislatures passed more stringent school attendance laws and raised the attendance ages.

From this it might seem that the increased enrollments were wholly the result of unusual conditions. But this would be a wrong conclusion. Attendance had been growing ever since 1890 and except during the war period it has continued high. For this there are underlying social reasons, some of which have been mentioned. One of these should be especially remembered. It is the fact that the high school is a continuation of the elementary school. Its main task is to educate more completely the citizens of a free society. It accepts the challenge of Lincoln at Gettysburg to prove that Americans are capable of living as free men, and it hopes to educate all American youth so that they will scorn to become slaves.

This chapter reviews the beginning and early history of the high school. To do this it will be necessary to keep in mind that from the beginning the high school was dependent upon the common school. In many cases the high schools grew directly out of common schools; and in all cases high schools could become mature only as the common schools nourished them.

HIGH SCHOOL ORIGINS

The early high schools arose in three or more ways: by establishment according to a definite plan; by the transformation of an academy into a public high school; and by the gradual development of advanced work in an elementary school until a separate organization was formed. The last-named, evolutionary process appears to have been a common and natural development. An ambitious teacher with eager pupils would introduce advanced classes into the program of his school. This frequently occurred even in ungraded schools, in which cases perhaps nothing further happened. In larger schools such an effort might be the beginning of a complete high school. Algebra, natural philosophy, and Latin were favored subjects. They were taught in most academies, and many teachers had studied them. Additional subjects could be added until a year of high school work was offered; then two years in a separate room occupying one teacher's whole time, and finally a full course would be given.

Official reports by state superintendents of schools show this process taking place, but in many cases the movement began before the state offices were established. Two superintendents who made such reports were Henry Barnard in Connecticut and Thomas Burrowes in Pennsylvania. Both gave accounts of the teaching of secondary subjects in common schools. The same facts were also noticed in Iowa and California and such conditions must have existed in many other states.

An example of the process in San Bernardino, California, was described by Porter Sargent (1872–1951) in his *The Handbook of Private Schools*. As quoted in the volume for 1951–1952, he wrote as follows:

My only secondary schooling was seven months with six other pupils in a room of an eight-room grammar school in a California town in 1887. It was the first year of a new high school, which was a not too welcome innovation due to the initiative of the principal of the grammar school. He was a rather crude Kansan, with normal school training, but he was alert, lithe, Lincoln-esque, with a sparkle in his eye and tremendous energy.

We read Shakespeare aloud, which was all new to him, and he got a tremendous kick out of it. "By golly! That *is* good stuff!" As we went through geometry he kept about two lessons ahead. It was undiscovered territory, so he imparted his interest to us. He knew no science, but he was hungry for it, and with enthusiasm we went through Steele's "Fourteen Weeks in Geology," in "Zoology," in "Chemistry," with a box of apparatus in a little side room. He would stamp his foot in exultation and delight. It was contagious. He was the best kind of a teacher because he was teaching himself and carrying us along on the wave of his enthusiasm.

In Pennsylvania and Ohio special laws were passed to permit particular towns to establish high schools. About 1850 a large number of states were enacting legislation to allow the formation of union districts and union schools or to allow the teaching of advanced branches. Precise information is often lacking but in some of these cases high school work had been started before the permissive legislation was adopted. In Ohio evidence shows that a score of high schools had been started before the Akron law of 1847. Massachusetts took the unusual step (1827) of requiring towns of a certain size to teach secondary school subjects. The law did not mention the high school but its intent was to provide high school instruction including, in the largest towns, college-preparatory work.

The most complete and best-equipped high schools were formed according to plans worked out in advance. The best examples were found in such cities as Boston (1821), Philadelphia (1838), and Chicago (1856). As the movement developed and as the high schools became more standardized, outright establishment became common.

ENGLISH HIGH SCHOOL OF BOSTON

Boston, as the custom was, distinguished between boys' and girls' education and also between education for boys who were going to college and for those other boys who were not going to college. For boys who were to receive a college education, the city had almost from the beginning maintained a public Latin school. Both the boys who were not going to college and, after 1789, girls received an elementary education in reading and writing schools where the instruction included English grammar, arithmetic, and bookkeeping. Because they were not intended for college and the professions, secondary education was not called for or considered appropriate for them. This was the old idea. In addition to the public schools there were numerous private schools in the city. Some were dame schools teaching reading, for no boy or girl could be admitted to the public reading schools until after he or she had attained the age of seven years and had learned to read, not before. Some of the private schools were upper-class schools for girls. Many Boston children also did not attend any school. Educationally speaking we have here four groups of children; those, fewer than two hundred in number, who were in the Latin school, the 2,300 pupils in the public reading and writing schools, the 4,100 attending private schools, and not fewer than five hundred who were not in any school.

This was the situation about 1818 when the story of the first public high school in the United States may be said to begin. At that time after considerable agitation, Boston created a system of public primary schools to teach reading to children under seven. Having thus extended the system downward, the question arose whether it should not be extended upward as well. A committee was formed to consider this question, and it reported that boys could finish the elementary school course in five years instead of the seven allowed them. Not only loss of time but also, they said, loss of training in application and industry were the results. And in the second place, they reported that the elementary course did not give a sufficient preparation for their future responsibilities in either mercantile or mechanical pursuits. Many who pay taxes for the support of the existing schools, they said, have to send their sons out of the city to academies in order to prepare them for their lifework. The committee, therefore, recommended "the founding of a seminary to be called the English Classical School."

They proposed a three-year course of study to be normally completed between the ages of twelve and fifteen. Pupils were to be admitted only once a year and upon "strict examination" in reading, writing, English grammar in all its branches, and in arithmetic as far as simple proportion. The teachers were to be university graduates. The course that was proposed included the study of English, mathematics, social studies, and science and was, therefore, a liberal rather than a vocational course. No foreign languages were included and it did not prepare for the colleges of that day. The weight of emphasis fell upon English, especially composition, and mathematics including trigonometry, navigation, and surveying. Both English and mathematics were studied throughout the three years. It is easy to see a resemblance between this course and that of the Philadelphia Academy founded seventy years earlier.

In accordance with this plan the school was opened in 1821. The first name chosen for the school is confusing. It was called the English Classical School. Perhaps this was to convey the idea that instead of the ancient classics this school would stress the great English writers. Actually the school placed far more emphasis upon writing and speaking than upon literature. Perhaps the word was used in the sense of *excellent* and the purpose was to show that the school was of a higher order than the common schools. Whatever the intention the name was soon changed to English High School. It is claimed that John Pierpont, the secretary of the Boston school committee or board, proposed the new name, perhaps in imitation of the well-known high schools of Scotland. From Boston, as we know, the name was carried to every city, town, and large village and community in America. Few chance ventures in nomenclature have been equally successful.

The first principal was George B. Emerson, who became a noted educator but was in 1821 a very young man for so responsible a place. He personally examined the applicants, admitted 100 boys, and organized the school, not along departmental lines but according to year-classes and rooms as shown in Figure 8–1. All subjects were required. Each class worked as a unit for a whole year. There were two sections for each of the two lower

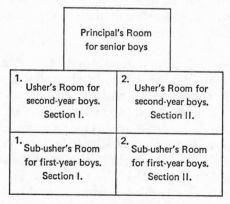

Figure 8–1. English Classical School Plan

classes and one section for the third or highest class. Each pupil was as-signed to a particular teacher from whom he received all his instruction for that year. The principal had charge of the room for seniors. It was evidently supposed that many entering boys would not remain to complete the course; and the curriculum was so arranged that those who had to leave early would be able to gain as much as possible from their interrupted studies. This was an idea that might have important effects upon curriculum-making.

Since this is considered to be the first American high school, we shall recapitulate several of the important differences between it and the usual high school of the present time. The Boston school of 1821 was not co-educational and the ages of the boys, twelve to fifteen years, corresponded to the ages of present junior high school pupils. Admission was by examina-tion. The school was organized by grade-rooms like a present-day elemen-tary school. This plan had been in use also in the early colleges. As in the colleges, any given teacher had a fixed group of pupils. Although the school was to prepare the pupils for "mercantile and mechanical employments," the subjects were of the kind now called academic, and not vocational. There was only one curriculum without electives or foreign languages and, therefore, it did not prepare for college. It was a terminal school, not, like the present high school, a middle school between common school and col-lege. It corresponded to the free academy of the time.

Why the committee decided upon a three-year school is not clear; nor do we know why the later high schools adopted a four-year course. The Boston Latin School had a five-year course at that time and European sec-ondary school longer ones. American boys were apprenticed at fourteen or earlier and it was probably thought that few middle-class boys would remain at school after fifteen. The colleges had adopted a four-year course that normally took in the ages between fourteen and eighteen. And since the more elaborate of the early high schools aspired to become people's colleges, and actually attained a standard equal to the colleges, it is possible that the four-year high school was formed by imitating the colleges. Such conven-tions once accepted tend to become fixed for long periods. It is certainly not clear that all high school curricula should be just four years or just six years long.

Another development of that time will further illustrate the state of opinion in a city known for its progress in education. In 1826 Boston estab-lished a girls' high school under a noted teacher, Ebenezer Bailey. In two years the school became so popular and so many applied for admission that the city refused to vote the funds needed for its maintenance and it had to be closed. The mayor, Josiah Quincy, later to become president of Harvard, was hostile to the school and declared it a failure; but many people did not share this opinion. Not until 1855 did the city again provide secondary education for girls. At that time a "high and normal school" was opened.

HIGH SCHOOLS IN MASSACHUSETTS

The industrial revolution, by increasing the number of positions in management and in office work, must have had a great influence upon the rising high school movement. That there was such a movement is shown by the figures. Six towns besides Boston established high schools in the 1820's and about sixteen others in the 1830's. By the close of the Civil War there were slightly more than one hundred high schools in Massachusetts. The second such school in the state was a high school for girls established by Worcester in 1824. The mill town of Lowell made two innovations. In 1831 that city established (1) a coeducational high school that (2) offered both an English and a classical course. Lowell is an excellent example of the influence of the new social and economic forces. Not all of the one hundred high schools of Massachusetts were full-course schools, and almost forty towns that should have had high schools according to the law of 1827 were delinquent.

In the early nineteenth century, New England, and especially Massachusetts, were entering upon a great period of textile manufactures and railroad development. The growth of cities and taxable wealth provided the pupils and the dollars for advanced education and employment for the graduates. The population of Massachusetts increased from slightly over 500,000 in 1820 to 1,250,000 in 1860. The first factories were established along the fall line of the rapid New England streams, but the high-compression steam engine designed by Oliver Evans in 1802 enabled the new industrial capitalists to establish their mills in cities without water power.

By the end of the War of 1812 there were 75,000 industrial workers in the cotton factories of New England and the numbers grew steadily. The war had been so extremely unpopular in that section that secession was advocated and nullification practiced. The "free, sovereign and independent state" of Connecticut refused to honor the nation's call for troops. But in the end the section benefited from the war. By preventing the importation of British goods it gave the American manufacturer a time advantage that the tariff of 1816 was designed to hold for him.

Many of the early high schools taught the subjects of an English education that were supposed to have some use in business. In this group were included bookkeeping, composition, public speaking, drawing, and mathematics including surveying. The aims, topics, and ground to be covered in these and other fields were indicated only by specifying the number of years, or terms, or quarters to be devoted to each or by naming the textbooks to be used. There were no real courses of study. As late as 1890 the president of Harvard University declared that a large proportion of the 230 so-called high schools in Massachusetts were not secondary schools in fact. He certainly meant that they were not effective college-preparatory schools.

And in small towns the high school was often a department of an elementary school. In larger centers separate Latin and English high schools were maintained for a time, but eventually the two curricula were almost everywhere united in a single school.

Of the 160 or more high schools in New England by 1865 slightly more than one hundred were, as we have seen, in Massachusetts. It was to be a long time before any other state had so many. The movement gradually spread to other sections, but some of the schools in the Middle and Western states followed an independent course. One of these, the Central High School of Philadelphia, was for many years an outstanding institution known for the breadth of its curriculum and the wealth of its equipment.

THE CENTRAL HIGH SCHOOL OF PHILADELPHIA

Pennsylvania had no long tradition of public education such as characterized the Eastern states and for a time adopted no general high school law like that of Massachusetts. For these reasons the state's legal battles over the high school question resemble those of Michigan and other Western states. The Pennsylvania litigation has not received the attention given the Kalamazoo case, but because it came early it possesses a particular interest.

By special legislation, Philadelphia was in 1818 made "the first school district" of the state. It will also be recalled that a state system was created by the laws of 1834 and 1836. The right to establish high schools was implicit in these acts, but the school board of Philadelphia felt the need for an explicit grant of power to establish a "central high school" for the city. This was granted in a special act of 1836. The general elementary school law remained permissive until 1849 when public education became mandatory, but by that time all but a small minority of the townships had already established it. This act of 1849 was contested, and in 1851 the supreme court of the state passed upon a suit to outlaw the schools. In that decision (*Commonwealth* v. *Hartman*, 17 Pa., 118) the court ruled, as other courts have done, that the state constitution and the school laws fix only the minimum provision that districts must provide and not the maximum that they may establish. But in 1887 Pennsylvania, after all, passed a general high school law.

A windfall from the federal government gave Philadelphia the means to provide its new high school with a building that was luxurious for that time. The windfall was the surplus revenue distribution of 1837. A small part of the state's share was applied on the building of the new Philadelphia Central High School. This building cost $72,000 at a time when city school buildings were constructed for a third of this amount or less. "Imposing in appearance, convenient in its location, and equipped with all the devices that an acute and interested Board could secure, it was one of the prominent buildings of Philadelphia." The most conspicuous of its "devices" was the astronomical observatory with a telescope by a famous German firm, made to specifications prepared by a committee of the American Philosophical Society. This was the fourth observatory to be erected in the United States and perhaps the only one ever erected for the use of a high school. W. H. Wells, superintendent of the schools of Chicago, admitted that the Philadelphia Central High School was without a rival "in the completeness of its appointments and the extent of its course of instruction."

The school was fortunate in securing the help of Alexander Dallas Bache to develop a complete and logical system. Bache, a great-grandson of Franklin was, as stated previously, a graduate of West Point. In 1836 he became president of Girard College and spent two years in an examination of European education. This study resulted in his *Report on Education in Europe to the Trustees of Girard College for Orphans*. It is the most extensive of the well-known reports on European education; and a noteworthy feature is the attempt to use the comparative method. Bache's hope that he might find the time to extend the comparisons to all the countries which he had visited was not fulfilled.

Bache was impressed by the thorough work of the Prussian classical and realist schools. The latter prepared some boys for the higher engineering schools and others for immediate entrance upon practical life. Upon his return the Philadelphia board elected him president of its new high school to serve until the opening of Girard College. At the high school he organized three courses. A "principal course" of four years included studies in English, French, geography, history, mathematics through trigonometry and descriptive geometry, mechanical and natural philosophy, natural history, morals and evidences of Christianity, writing, and drawing. This course resembled that of the German *Realschulen*, but these had a much longer course and included both chemistry and Latin, which Bache omitted. His omission of chemistry from a realist course is conspicuous and hard to explain.

In the four-year classical course, Latin and Greek replaced the French and the amount of required mathematics was substantially less than in the principal course. For the remaining subjects the two courses were practically identical. The third course omitted all foreign languages but included English and the other subjects of the courses described. It was a short course, occupying only two years, and it never became popular. The classical course was taken by those who were preparing for college, but the largest numbers enrolled in the principal or modern language-mathematics-science course.

Admission to the school was by examination as at Boston. The year was divided into semesters and new students were admitted at the beginning and in the middle of each year. The discipline was based upon the West Point system with its demerit marks. Included in the first graduating class (1842) there was one, L. Hall Grandgent, who was to be for many years a teacher in the English High School of Boston.

The new school with its fine building and high standards pleased many

Philadelphians; but there were also dissenting voices. The period beginning about 1840 formed a critical time in education when it was difficult to hold the gains of the previous decade. The awakening had aroused the enemies as well as the friends of public education. Of this we have already seen evidence in Ohio and Massachusetts. By 1842 Philadelphia had spent her share of the surplus revenue distribution, the country had not entirely recovered from the crisis of 1837, and there was mounting opposition to the school from some of the taxpayers. Some objected to the nature of the courses. They wanted the school to teach applied chemistry, surveying, bookkeeping and other "practical" courses. Others complained that the school in the center of the city was inaccessible from the outlying sections. Apparently no one objected to the entrance examinations or the exclusion of girls. Philadelphia continued for a century to build separate high schools for boys and for girls as did many other eastern cities.

OTHER PENNSYLVANIA HIGH SCHOOLS

Public high schools began to appear in Pennsylvania in the middle thirties and there is evidence that the developments in New England had been observed. The name was, however, sometimes applied to private institutions such as the High School of the Franklin Institute, which was carried on in Philadelphia from about 1824. Priority among the public high schools of the state would not be easy to establish. Each of the three cities, Honesdale, Carlisle, and Norristown, claims to have had a high school by 1836. More complete institutions, it seems, were organized within a few years of that date by Harrisburg, Lancaster, and York. In large towns it was the custom, as in New England, to set up separate schools for boys and for girls.

There were many cases of academies in both regions that deeded their property to the public school board. Many Pennsylvania academies served a whole county and had received state aid upon the condition of admitting all the eligible children of the county. Pennsylvania law provided that a local high school that accepted an academy's property must also assume its educational obligations, a requirement that must have prompted many school trustees to look into the mouth of any such gift horse that was offered to it. There were cases in which the law placed an excessive financial burden upon local districts.

There were over one hundred high schools in the state by the end of the century, most of them in larger towns. But by that time the day of the rural township and centralized high school was dawning. A law of 1901 authorized the creation of township and union high schools. Such schools had already been organized by friendly agreement. But there are even now rural and mountain sections in Pennsylvania where neither the law nor public sentiment has been effective in providing adequate high school accommodations.

AN EARLY CONNECTICUT HIGH SCHOOL

Middletown in the south-central part of Connecticut was a town of about 3,500 people in 1840 when its high school was started. The schools of the town were still ungraded. Henry Barnard, recently appointed chief state school official, had declared in 1838 that there were hardly any graded schools in the whole state. Ambitious teachers introduced advanced subjects to the detriment of the younger pupils. Barnard urged the towns to grade their schools and to found high schools for pupils who wanted to study algebra, physics, or Latin. This would allow the teacher in the lower school to give proper attention to reading, writing, and spelling.

A special law of 1839 gave Middletown permission to grade her schools. A high school was voted but it was at first more elementary than high. There was no entrance examination, and all of the 252 children in the schools of the city who were between the ages of nine and sixteen were assigned to the high school. The census of 1840 shows that there were about five hundred children between these two ages. This indicates that half of the children above the age of nine years were in private schools, at work, or on the street. Middletown was not unique in this respect.

The new high school was conducted in a church basement. There was a department for boys and another for girls. The school charged a fee of $4 a year. It became free in 1861, twenty-one years after the founding. There was no fixed curriculum at first, but the school aimed to prepare some pupils for college and others for practical life. In a period of about ten years, three curricula were organized, an English, a classical, and a mathematical curriculum. Later a normal curriculum was added, with practice teaching, professional subjects, and reviews of the common school branches. For lack of sufficient staff, some use was made of pupil-monitors. Courses varied from one year to five years but the school eventually adopted the standard four-year course. Evidently this small-town school without adequate resources had to experiment and to some extent to improvise its organization, curriculum, and methods. It illustrates unusually well the experimental and tentative nature of the first high schools. One certain fact about the high school is this, that it is largely a native growth.

HIGH SCHOOLS IN THE MIDDLE WEST

In the West as in the East the high school was at first a city institution that was instituted when the schools were graded. In Ohio, as we have seen, a number of high schools were opened before 1850. Both Cleveland and Columbus began high school work about 1846. The Cleveland school was notable for early work in the teaching of science. The first high school in Columbus was opened in a church basement by Asa D. Lord, who had been for a decade the head of a private normal school at Kirtland, Ohio, called the Western Reserve Teachers' Seminary. Meanwhile, he had become prominent in school affairs in the state and was elected the first superintendent of the Columbus city schools. The establishment of the high school followed almost at once. We now move to Illinois.

The first public elementary school in Chicago was opened in 1834, and for ten years the schools were conducted in rented quarters. In 1844 the city built its first schoolhouse and in 1854 appointed its first superintendent. Meanwhile, a period of astonishing growth had begun. The city which in 1840 had less than 5,000 people had well over 100,000 by 1860. A public high school in a "spacious and elegant" building was established in 1856 under William Harvey Wells, who came from the principalship of a Massachusetts normal school to serve as Chicago's superintendent of schools.

This first high school of the city may have been in part modeled upon the Central High School of Philadelphia. The obvious differences were that the Chicago school was coeducational and offered a normal course. There were three courses in the beginning, classical, English, and normal. Having been engaged in teacher preparation with Henry Barnard and at the Westfield Normal School in Massachusetts, Superintendent Wells placed great emphasis upon professional training including in-service work. In this he was following a current trend of that period. Many city high schools offered a normal course.

Admission to the high school was by examination; and of almost four hundred applicants during the first year only 176 passed and were admitted. The school offered them high academic fare in languages, mathematics, and the sciences. There were no laboratories before 1874. But in most respects and for its time this was a well-equipped school.

A collection has been published of the programs offered at different times between 1856 and 1906 by some of the high schools of Iowa. These show some variations from school to school and some changes from time to time during that half-century, but the outstanding facts are that the offerings were generally similar and the changes slight. From time to time more languages, sciences, mathematical branches, and additional kinds of history were offered; but there was no change of type. Like the country academies, they devoted a large part of their energies to reviews of the common branches. One school in 1856 taught reading, spelling, mental and written arithmetic, geography, and physiology. Several of the early Iowa high schools watered their curricula in this way but not always to the same extent. And Iowa was not unique in this respect. Many New England high schools and Ohio high schools in the same period followed the same practice.

Material facilities and teaching aids were also wanting. Textbooks were the only tools. Many of the early schools were begun in rented rooms, church basements, or public halls. The first high school in Burlington occupied a church building for ten years. The one in Dubuque was opened in 1856, closed because of financial distress in 1860, and again opened in a rented room in 1866. These pioneer conditions have long since been overcome in the rich and populous states; but there still are many small and poorly equipped high schools in isolated rural sections of the country.

As the high schools in Iowa became larger, it became possible to offer two or more parallel curricula and to allow some electives. But in this great agricultural state there was not a trace of agricultural instruction in the forty selected curricula that are exhibited in Aurner's history. The preparation of teachers was, however, stressed. The historian of the Iowa schools asserted that in the beginning the preparation of teachers for the common schools was the primary purpose of the high schools. As late as 1900 two-fifths of the Iowa high schools were preparing teachers.

This development was perhaps general, and it certainly was not peculiar to Iowa. In Cincinnati educational subjects were included in a regular high school course. In Chicago, it has been indicated, the high school offered a normal curriculum. In Boston a "high and normal" school for girls was established soon after the middle of the century. The Central High School of Philadelphia in 1896 extended its "course in Pedagogy" to two years and made it a regular department of the school. This became a post-high school department, called the School of Pedagogy, for young men who were preparing themselves for service in the city schools. While the state normal schools prepared rural teachers many cities prepared their own staffs in the local high schools.

SECONDARY EDUCATION IN THE SOUTH

Education in the South may be interpreted in its own terms by comparing its present condition and recent past with the situation that existed at some earlier time such as 1870 or 1900. In such a study we should consider also the resources that were at different times available to promote education and what hostilities and perversities worked against it. Studied and judged in this way, the progress has been great, especially during the last half-century. But it is customary to compare the South with more highly industrialized and more densely populated sections. This also is allowable if the student will keep in mind the differences between the sections, differences that are never merely economic but also social and that may cause the people of one region to desire educational outcomes quite different from those approved elsewhere.

The latter of these two methods will yield almost a complete contrast with northern conditions if we consider public high schools in the South before 1900 as the base of the comparison. There were few high schools in the section at that time and some of these were incomplete. The upper social class preferred the private school; the lower did not expect secondary schooling for their children. At a much earlier period the North had been of the same mind. Since then the urban high school had spread and grown in the North; but in 1900 neither section had many rural high schools.

The South still had many private schools and academies where boys prepared for college and girls finished their school education. In this assortment of private schools one finds a main reason for the slow development of the public high school. There were enough schools of several kinds to satisfy the existing demand for secondary education and to block any decided efforts under the hard economic conditions to foster new public high schools. This balance between supply and demand was broken by a new force, the campaigns of the Southern Education Board, which began to raise the demand far above the available means of satisfying it.

The South was not entirely without public secondary schools before the twentieth century, although some states were almost in that condition. In 1887 Tennessee had only four public high schools that were recognized as competent to prepare students for the state university. The complementary fact is that the state at that time had enough private schools to warrant the closing of the university's preparatory department. Twenty years later in 1906 the state of Virginia had about seventy incomplete high schools but only ten free public high schools that offered four years of work. In that year (1906) the state university had only eight students who had been prepared at these ten schools. This may be a comment on the policy of the University of Viriginia at that time as well as a reflection upon the standards of the high schools. Their graduates may have preferred to attend other colleges. About the same time there were only seven accredited high schools in Georgia; and in South Carolina two and one-half times as many pupils prepared for college in private as in public schools. About 1900 Alabama had a considerable number of high schools but many must have been incomplete schools.

In the first decade of the new century the rapid expansion of the high schools in the South began. Several of the state universities were becoming interested in the public high schools as a source of students, especially of those who could not afford to attend private schools. Administrators realized that more students would require bigger budgets but also that larger enrollments would help to persuade the legislatures to increase their appropriations. Whereas Illinois and other northern agricultural states had thousands of boys and girls preparing for college, those in Georgia or Alabama could be counted in hundreds. The difference lay in part in the greater encouragement given the free public high schools in the northern states. In those states the public elementary and secondary schools and the state university, land-grant colleges, and teachers' colleges formed a single system, a highway from the lowest grade to the professional school.

In the South, Georgia led out. In 1904 the University of Georgia appointed a professor of secondary education and assigned to him the task of encouraging the establishment of high schools with local support, aiding them to become efficient preparatory schools, and relating them to the schools below and the university above. By a law of 1906 Georgia provided for agricultural high schools and South Carolina and Virginia soon passed similar laws. Agricultural high schools had been created in Alabama even earlier but they did not become effective vocational schools until the early years of the present century. Boys' and girls' clubs began in the South in the same decade and spread rapidly. The Smith-Hughes Act and the organization of the "Future Farmers of America" began to put new life and spirit into the teaching of vocational agriculture in all parts of the country, and in the South they have been particularly effective. Finally, the consolidation movement has not only multiplied the rural high schools but has promoted better rural elementary schools and helped to secure better-prepared teachers for rural schools of every grade. The average term of the rural schools began to lengthen with the campaigns of the Southern Education Board. The General Education Board aided with funds and skilled advisers in the fight against poor schools, poor farming, and poor health among rural people.

Although a main aim of the early high schools in the South and North alike was to prepare the pupils for college, the Southern schools developed farm-life and rural vocation and homemaking curricula very early. The work of Seaman A. Knapp was first accepted in the South and marked progress was made in adapting the high school to the practical needs of the people. The land-grant colleges and experiment stations were making themselves felt. Appropriations were made by state legislatures for state normal schools and for departments of education in the state colleges and state universities. In all this the high school was a key institution. If this summary seems to resemble the account of the advances made in the North at an earlier time, the simplest explanation is that the educational awakening had now come to the South.

THE WORTH OF THE HIGH SCHOOL

The Kalamazoo case, already mentioned, was a friendly suit at law, brought to determine whether the city had the legal right to establish a high school, to employ a superintendent of schools, and to collect taxes to support these services. Other such suits were brought in other states and, like this one, were carried up to the state supreme courts for determination. The Kalamazoo case has become historic, perhaps chiefly because of the eloquence of the decision pronounced in 1874 by Chief Justice Thomas M. Cooley. The decision (30 Mich. 69) agreed with that in Pennsylvania in 1851 and in every other state where the matter has come up. It was to the effect that the legislators in establishing a system of public or common schools did not set any limit to the number of years that were to be embraced by it or restrict the offices and officers that might be necessary to its proper functioning. But Cooley went into an account of the history of public education and argued that the legislature in establishing the common schools and a state university must have intended thereby to create a complete system of schools, hence the necessity for a high school to complete the path to the university. This argument has always had a special appeal for educational historians. In Illinois and at least seven other states, similar cases were decided in the same way; but perhaps in none of them by an equally eloquent jurist.

It was doubtless no accident that the Kalamazoo litigation occurred in a time of financial scandals and stringency. Few people bothered about the high school as long as it was small and confined to opulent cities, and for a long time it was, as stated before, mainly a city school. Poor roads and the thin population long tended to keep it out of the rural sections. Missouri, the twenty-fourth state, and the first American high school were born in the same year, 1821. Half of the United States was Indian country. Entrance examinations, academic studies, and high standards kept many children away from the schools that existed. The district system impeded the establishment of the high school. It was true as charged that all the people paid for the public secondary schooling of a few. Was the high school worth what it cost; and who received the benefits it conferred? This question is often asked in times of business recession when dollars are scarce. The 1890's, just when pupils began to flock to the schools, were such a time. High school attendance doubled during that decade, and staffs had to be increased at a time when boards of education were in financial straits. Several large city boards dismissed their principals, and proposed a shorter school year and the dropping of the more expensive studies. The old charges were renewed: the high school is not necessary, is undemocratic, and, most important, is too expensive. Europe began to say that the American public could not continue to meet the mounting costs of its broadening program of secondary education. (See Table 8–1.)

The 1930's also, the period of the Great Depression, were such a time. Between 1910 and 1930 the high school enrollment doubled and then doubled again. And in the course of the depression it increased by another 50 per cent. The irony of the situation lay in the fact that financially the schools became most burdensome in the slack times when they were most needed. At such times the young people who cannot find work remain in school in addition to those who would normally be there.

In the history books, the great depression has overshadowed the crises of the nineties. But in the nineties, Coxey's tattered army of the unemployed marched on Washington and Bryan campaigned for free silver. The high school was attacked as it had been in the populist eighties. Again it was affirmed that the high school had been no part of the original plan for

TABLE 8–1
TOTAL PUBLIC AND NONPUBLIC SECONDARY
SCHOOL ENROLLMENT

Year	Enrollment Grades 9–12 and Postgraduate	Population 14–17 Years of Age	Number Enrolled per 100 of Population 14–17 Years of Age
1889–1890	359,949	5,354,653	6.7
1899–1900	699,403	6,152,231	11.4
1909–1910	1,115,398	7,220,298	15.4
1919–1920	2,500,176	7,735,841	32.3
1929–1930	4,804,255	9,341,221	51.4
1939–1940	7,123,009	9,720,419	73.3
1941–1942	6,933,265	9,749,000	71.1
1943–1944	6,030,617	9,449,000	63.8
1951–1952	6,596,351	8,525,000	77.4
1959–1960	9,599,810	11,154,879	86.1
Fall, 1967	13,700,000	14,618,000	93.7

From the *Biennial Survey of Education in the United States*, U.S. Department of Health, Education, and Welfare, Office of Education.

public education and this in spite of the fact that there had been no original plan. The high school was becoming expensive because it was reaching larger numbers of pupils; but even then it was argued that the public should not be asked to pay for a school that reached only a minority. In some cities the newspaper press aided in protecting the schools from unjustified retrenchment.

It was in this period that the state of Massachusetts raised its high school requirements. Dissatisfaction with this policy led Frank A. Hill, the secretary of the state board, to express (1898) his conviction that the high school returned to the public all that it cost. The state had in 1891 taken certain important legal steps. A new law of that year made every high school tuition-free to the children of its town; it required every town that did not have a high school to pay the tuition of any of its children attending the high school of another town; and it abolished the category of second-class or incomplete high schools. Another law passed in 1896 made graduation from high school or its equivalent a condition for admission to a state normal school. These laws placed the high schools of Massachusetts in a more advanced position than they had occupied under the law of 1827.

Secretary Hill stressed the stimulation that a high school gives to the elementary school and its pupils. By the mere presence of the advanced school the elementary pupils, he said, gain a more elevated conception of education and begin to work toward these higher ideals. The high school in 1896 became a factor in the preparation of elementary teachers. Until that time they came to the professional school with only an elementary school preparation, knowing only what the schools in which they were to teach had taught them. The secretary was certain that the elementary schools would benefit from the advanced preparation and the pupils would profit. Henry Barnard had expressed the same view.

To those who attended the high school it offered a choice of studies. Thereby, Hill pointed out, each pupil was able to gain a better understanding of his own capacities as well as a somewhat specialized training. He declared that the high school was offering a better preparation for life than ever before. And yet he proposed further improvement. He said the worth of the high school could be increased by closing the gap between it and the elementary school. Better preparation for life and greater continuity between the primary and secondary stages of that preparation were to become leading themes in the years that followed. Secretary Hill had skillfully selected two critical problems to bring before the people.

Better preparation for the real business of living was to be furthered by the new subjects that were being introduced. Manual training was brought into view by the Russian exhibit at the Centennial Exposition of 1876 in Philadelphia; and manual training high schools were opened in Baltimore (1883) and in a hundred cities by 1900. An agricultural high school was opened in connection with the University of Minnesota in 1888. Others were established in the North but they spread much faster in the Southern states. Drawing and other plastic arts, music, and homemaking courses were added in many places. High school commercial courses had to meet the severe competition of the private business colleges, which were often better equipped and had the motive of large profits to urge them forward. It was in the period after the Civil War when the Bryant and Stratton chain of business colleges attempted to gain a monopoly of commercial education. The war with Spain, the resulting introduction of Spanish into the high school ostensibly to prepare for business with Latin America, and the introduction of business administration departments into universities, all furthered the development of commercial courses in high schools. By 1900 the public high school was gaining on the private business schools. All these are examples of the effort to develop what may be considered better preparation for expanding occupations. These changes and the junior high school, which was intended to provide the second of the proposed improvements, will be treated in Chapter 16.

STANDARD HIGH SCHOOLS

No other country has as many secondary schools as the United States. The comparison, if it is to be valid, must take into account that European schools are standardized by officials who enforce national laws. In the United States the state requirements have been lenient, and many incomplete and substandard high schools have been established. Such schools may give a wide variety of courses, many of them elementary and vocational, in commerce, agriculture, industrial skills, music, fine and practical arts. These may be of real value to the children of a community, but the colleges of the later nineteenth and early twentieth centuries refused to give entrance credit for them.

In most communities some of the young people want to prepare for college, and the local high school is expected to offer the required courses. This the substandard high school was often unable to do. In these circumstances a widespread demand for standard high schools arose, schools whose graduates would be accepted by the colleges without examination or who, if examinations were required, would be prepared to pass them with creditable marks. People wanted an answer to the question: What is a standard high school? That answer can be found only in the history of the school.

Colleges have tried to answer this question by emphasizing the schools' preparatory functions. Now college requirements have always weighed more heavily upon the small high schools that could offer only a few courses and perhaps only one curriculum. Small schools were compelled by public sentiment to make provision for college entrance work and could do little more. As a result the small school has often been prevented from serving the youth of the village community. It had to prepare a few boys and girls for college, even though in consequence many were denied a high school education.

One of the early ways in which colleges determined the real meaning of the term *high school* was that of the accrediting system. The University of Michigan in 1871 began the practice of sending committees of professors to visit high schools, and the graduates of those that they approved were then admitted to the university without examination. Other universities began to accept the accreditation of state education departments. This plan quickly spread because it lifted the entrance examination burden from the backs of the faculties, and the college was not risking very much because the students could be received on probation. Successful high schools considered it an honor to have their names on the list of accredited schools. At the same time accreditation was usually recognized only within a given state and it did not remove the necessity of preparing pupils in the particular studies required by the colleges of their choice. It was declared in the *School Review* for October, 1898, that a tabulation of the entrance requirements of almost five hundred colleges showed that the demands of no two were identical.

An effort to promote greater uniformity and to improve secondary education in general was made by the regional standardizing associations. These are voluntary unions of colleges and secondary schools holding meetings for the consideration of common problems and making rules for the guidance of their member institutions. The New England Association was founded in 1885, that of the Middle States and Maryland in 1892, and others as follows: North Central, 1894; Southern states, 1895; Northwest, 1918; and West, 1930. Schools that upon inspection met the standards of their own regional associations were accredited and the colleges of the association accepted their graduates. The standards vary from region to region and there is no complete cooperation between the associations. Further, by far the larger proportion of high schools in the country are not accredited by an association.

A third way of determining the effectiveness of the high schools in preparing pupils for college was developed by the College Entrance Examination Board founded in 1899 by the Middle States Association. A suggestion of this kind had been made by George B. Emerson in 1842 and more recently by President Barnard of Columbia University and by others. The board soon became an independent organization; and it has long conducted subject examinations for college admission in all parts of the United States and in foreign countries. Pupils from both public and independent secondary schools take the examinations.

The National Education Association also took an interest in the relations of the secondary schools to the colleges and in 1892 appointed the Committee of Ten with President Charles William Eliot of Harvard as chairman. Since the committee and its subcommittees were heavily staffed with college presidents and professors, private school teachers, and no women, it is surprising to find that they concluded that it is not the chief business of secondary schools to prepare pupils for college, but to prepare them for life whether they go or do not go to college. They agreed to this because they believed in formal discipline and the general transfer of training. They believed that the same subjects taught in the same way provide the best preparation for both college and life. It is not surprising, therefore, that these academic people stressed academic subjects. The report was too narrow in its outlook for some members of the committee, and President James H. Baker of the University of Colorado wrote a dissenting minority report. The main report received great acclaim and was the subject of much discussion, but it seems to have had little practical effect. The schools continued to expand their programs, increase their electives, and make very decided differences in their treatment of college and non-college youth.

THE EXTENDED SECONDARY SCHOOL

A movement to reorganize large areas of the educational system gave a new answer to the question about the nature of the secondary school.

The movement to standardize the high school was a step in this reorganization and the next one was the effort to define the relations between the elementary, secondary, and higher schools and, as one might say, to tighten the joints between them. The desire to produce this closer articulation was one of the reasons for the junior high school and the junior college.

A few illustrations will indicate what the problem was. In earlier times many academies were doing elementary work, many elementary schools had several advanced pupils studying algebra, geology, or Latin. Many high schools were not capable of preparing pupils for college or for a vocation, nor even of providing a good English education; and others were equal to the colleges of that day. At the same time some colleges were academies or high schools in all but name, whereas others maintained high standards. Such conditions existed as late as 1900 and even later.

When the cities had developed a standard elementary school, when the associations of secondary schools and colleges had defined the nature of the high school, and when the Association of American Universities after 1900 had produced a list of approved colleges, the stakes were set. It could no longer be said that the basic terms of American education were undefined. The meaning of the words *secondary school* and *secondary education* was becoming clearer.

The definitions brought into sharp relief the differences between the education of children, of youth, and of mature men and women. Evidently in a sequence of three schools the gaps would appear at the bottom and the top of the second member. A bridge to make the transition easier was needed between the elementary school and the high school. The junior high school was created for this purpose. By that time, in 1910 or 1920, it had come to be believed that as many children as possible should attend the high school, hence the need for the bridge.

At the upper limit of the high school, a different solution was proposed. It was believed that many high school graduates should not attempt a four-year college course but would benefit from two years of college work. At that point, therefore, a spur was needed to prepare young people for an occupation or to complete two further years of liberal studies. This indicated the need of a junior college.

Many leaders in universities considered the end of the sophomore year as the point of greatest difference in advanced work. These regarded the first two years of college as secondary school work. Only men and women who were able to proceed under their own power, without close supervision, should on this view be encouraged to proceed into the upper division of the college. The junior college, like the junior high school, would be a bridge; and like the junior high school, it would be a secondary education unit. Secondary education would in this case continue from the ages of twelve to twenty years. In connection with a study of "New Directions for

Secondary Education" in Chapter 16, we shall return to the junior high school and junior college movements.

SUMMARY

The high school is a secondary school but it is also, in contrast with European secondary schools, a common school, not the school of any privileged classes. The history of the high school may be treated in two periods, with the year 1890 as the dividing point. In the earlier period those schools that had the means to do so tended to overstress college-preparatory work or themselves tried to become people's colleges.

The high school has been preserved as a common school because the great middle class supports it and there is no sufficiently powerful and permanent class of wealth and privilege to preempt it. The school, Antaeus-like, has renewed its strength by contact with the common people. Early high schools were often outgrowths of the common schools, or were academies made over, or in a few striking cases were deliberately planned. In 1827 Massachusetts passed a law compelling certain towns to teach secondary subjects and by 1850 many states had enacted laws that could be applied in favor of high school establishment.

A study of the formation of several of the early high schools illustrates the above statements and reveals the great diversity of standards and means. Two purposes were recognized almost everywhere, preparation for college and for life; and to these, a third, preparation for teaching, was included. The study of cases also shows that early high schools were improvised and that standardization came about slowly and is even now incomplete. The urban and industrial revolution had a powerful effect upon the movement and upon the nature of the schools. Later high schools have been modeled upon the earlier ones.

A new period opened about 1890 or earlier. The program of studies began to expand, and the old academic barriers were broken and so were all enrollment records. Each of these is both cause and effect. Vocational education became common, but it is curious that in an agricultural nation, agriculture was late in making its appearance.

The high school had to meet great opposition; and it conquered its enemies by meeting the needs of their children. This may be called the Great Change. Opposition still flares up now and then especially in times of financial stringency.

High school standardization was attempted by the colleges in the 1870's. Later the colleges and secondary schools combined to form regional standards and these have had some success, but it is still true that only a minority of the high schools are able to meet the standards. Committees of the National Education Association tried to define the purpose and function of the high school. The Commission on the Reorganization of Secondary Education (1918) had great influence. But the actual reorganization of secondary educational institutions into the junior and senior high schools and the junior college has had the greatest effect in redefining secondary education in those parts of the country where these institutions have been successfully introduced. The total effect has not been to make secondary education more uniform. Rather it has accentuated the differences that have been from the beginning inherent in the process of free development.

QUESTIONS

1. Why did early secondary education have greater prestige than elementary or common school education? Was this partly or entirely justified?
2. What evidence goes to show that the formation of the high school was the unforced and unpremeditated expression of the common people's desires?
3. Why did the high school movement begin with apparent suddenness in the second decade of the nineteenth century? Will the same factors explain the even greater burst of speed after 1890?
4. Why did academic subjects carry greater prestige than vocational ones? Compare the older emphasis upon Latin, Greek, and mathematics with the current demand for more general and humanistic education.
5. Why did (and do) girls attend high schools in such large numbers? Compare the numbers of boys and girls in attendance and the numbers of each sex graduating in some high schools that you know.
6. People were long opposed to public education, to compulsory attendance, to high schools. Why has this opposition declined? Because of custom propaganda, experience and conviction, or other reasons?
7. Why would it be fortunate (or unfortunate) if high schools were rigidly standardized by regional associations (or by the state) and after some years all nonstandard schools closed?
8. Why would you favor (or oppose) the extension of the public junior college?
9. What is a high school?

BOOKS AND PAPERS

The complete history of the high school has yet to be written. Brown's *Making of Our Middle Schools* did not bring the story down to the date of its publication, seventy years ago. Krug treats the period from 1880 to 1920 during which the high school assumed its familiar shape and characteristics. In Vol. II, he carries the story to 1941. Kandel wrote on a vast subject, the *History of Secondary Education*, and could devote only a hundred pages to that of the high school. There are some good monographs and state histories by Gifford, Grizzell, Hertzler, Inglis, and Mulhern. Barnard's *American Journal of Education*, histories of education in particular states, histories of individual high schools, doctor's dissertations, and articles in magazines such as the *School Review* contain material that should be assembled and critically treated.

AURNER, C. R., *History of Education in Iowa*, Iowa City, 5 vols., 1914–20.

BOYNTON, F. D., "High School Attendance," *School Review*, September, 1922.

BRIGGS, THOMAS H., *Junior High School*, Boston, 1920; *Curriculum Problems*, New York, 1926; *The Great Investment*, Cambridge, Massachusetts, 1930.

BROOME, E. C., *Historical and Critical Discussion of College Admission Requirements*, New York, 1902.

BROWN, E. E., *The Making of Our Middle Schools*, New York, 1902.

BURRELL, B. JEANNETTE, and R. H. ECKELBERRY, "The American High School Question Before the Courts in the Post-Civil War Period," *School Review*, April and May, 1934; "The Free Public High School in the Post-Civil War Period," *School Review*, October and November, 1934, with bibliography for each topic.

CORNOG, WILLIAM H., *School of the Republic, 1893–1943, A Half Century of the Central High School of Philadelphia*, Philadelphia, 1952.

DEXTER, E. G., "Ten Years Influence of the Report of the Committee of Ten," *School Review*, April, 1906.

EDITORIAL, "The College Entrance Examination Board," *School Review*, November, 1902, an account of the first two years of the board.

EDMONDS, F. S., *History of the Central High School of Philadelphia*, Philadelphia, 1902.

GIFFORD, W. J., *Historical Development of the New York State High School System*, Albany, 1922.

GRIFFIN, O. B., *Evolution of the Connecticut State School System with Special Reference to the High School*, New York, Teachers College, Columbia University, 1928.

GRIZZELL, E. D., *Origin and Development of the High School in New England Before 1865*, New York, 1923.

HAHN, ROBERT O., and DAVID B. BIDNA, eds., *Secondary Education, Origins and Directions*, New York, 1970.

HERTZLER, SILAS, *Rise of the Public High School in Connecticut*, Baltimore, 1930.

HILL, FRANK A., "How Far the High School a Just Charge upon the Public Treasury," *School Review*, December, 1898.

INGLIS, ALEXANDER, *Rise of the High School in Massachusetts*, New York, Teachers College, Columbia University, 1911.

KANDEL, I. L., *History of Secondary Education, A Study in the Development of Liberal Education*, Boston, 1930.

KRUG, EDWARD A., *The Shaping of the American High School*, New York, 1964; Vol. II, University of Wisconsin Press, 1972.

MULHERN, JAMES, *History of Secondary Education in Pennsylvania*, Philadelphia, 1933.

SARGENT, PORTER, ed., *A Handbook of Private Schools, An Annual Survey*,

Boston, 1942, has the passage quoted, by permission of Mr. F. Porter Sargent, in the Section above, at p. 82f. The number issued in 1952 has a portrait and other biographical material on the founder and editor.

[SCHEFFY, C. C.], *One Hundred Years of the English High School of Boston*, Boston, 1924.

SHOEMAKER, FOREST LEROY, *Public Secondary Education in Ohio, 1875–1933*, Columbus, Ohio, 1936, an unpublished dissertation at the Ohio State University.

SPAULDING, F. T., et al., *Reorganization of Secondary Education*, Washington, U.S. Government Printing Office, being Monograph No. 5 of the National Survey of Secondary Education, and Bureau of Education Bulletin, 1932, No. 17.

STOUT, J. E., *High School Curricula in the North Central States, 1860–1918*, University of Chicago Press, 1921.

STUART, MILO H., *Organization of a Comprehensive High School*, New York, 1926.

WASHBURN, CARL DEWITT, *The Rise of the High School in Ohio*, Columbus, Ohio, 1932, an unpublished dissertation at the Ohio State University.

Chapter 9

THE OLD AND THE NEW SOUTH

The new government of the United States came into operation in 1789 under a Constitution based upon compromise. There was reasonable doubt about the nature of the Union. Was it now indissoluble or was it still a federation of states as it had been under the Articles of Confederation? Able men disagreed. During the intersectional struggle later, compromise also followed compromise until by 1860 the issue had acquired so keen an edge that further union seemed impossible to many.

Dissension over the nature of the government had arisen early. Even among the founders there was speculation about the permanence of the Union. Some of their successors from time to time suggested, proposed, or defended the idea of secession. There were the Virginia and Kentucky resolutions, the Hartford Convention, nullification in South Carolina, and the agitation of radical abolitionists who denounced the union of free and slave states with all the violence that language can convey.

None of these attacks resulted in a decisive test, but Calhoun taught that a sovereign state, such as he conceived South Carolina to be, had the right to forbid the enforcement of federal law within its territory. By threat and bargain, Jackson stilled the controversy of 1832. A group of resolute Southern states at that time or later might have broken up the Union. By 1861 the North had become too strong. Her population was four times that of the white people of the South, her industry, railroads, and shipyards were too fully developed, and Lincoln was president. The preservation of the Union was the principle to which Lincoln was most completely dedicated.

The South was not without advantages. She was the invaded section and her people were fighting for their own institutions, their way of life, and their homes. She had the inner lines of movement. Her armies were well led and many of her soldiers were accustomed to the use of horse and gun. Each of the combatants underestimated the resources and the determination of the other. The Northern soldiers had more schooling than the Southern but it was of a sort not directly useful in war. We no

246

longer believe that Waterloo was won on the playing fields of Eton or that the schoolmaster decided the Franco-Prussian War in 1870. Neither section had much formal training in engineering except that of the military schools.

By 1863 it seemed to many observers, foreign and American, that the question how long the Union would last was about to be answered; but in the middle of that year, Gettysburg and Vicksburg showed that the question was to remain open. The war ended in 1865 and after a harsh "reconstruction" the South first acquiesced in the result and then after bitter years learned to welcome the reunion. Rarely after such a war have the opposing sides, even after fifty years, been able to unite in applauding the outcome. Educational philanthropy, extended by the North, was at least of some help in the achievement of this result.

Before the war, Southern senators and congressmen generally opposed federal activity in education. The states' rights argument delayed the creation of the land-grant colleges, and the Morrill Act was adopted in 1862 while the South was not represented in Congress. The Federal Department of Agriculture was voted in the same year. The Bureau for Refugees, Freedmen, and Abandoned Lands was created in 1865. Two years later the United States Department, later Bureau, of Education was formed. The Hoar Bill, a punitive measure intended to impose a federally controlled system of education upon the South, was introduced in 1870 but fortunately it did not pass. The conciliatory Blair Bill to provide federal funds for education to be carried out by the states was also lost but it is significant that many Southerners favored it. Most of such measures, including the two just mentioned, are treated later in this or in the following chapter. The list will serve to suggest the trend which came with the war and reconstruction. Even education became somewhat more national in outlook.

As the country was recovering from the war, the vast plains, mountains, and valleys of the great West called for settlers and the enterprising young men responded. Cities and towns grew up and schools were needed. The war had increased the proportion of young women in the teaching force and this was especially true in the towns. Salaries were higher in the West and there teaching also acquired a distinct glamor. The heroine of more than one Western novel and picture was a young schoolmistress who could choose her man in that man's country.

In the North the graded school, high school, normal school, and college became widely distributed and firmly established. Public education far outdistanced the private school. Enrollments and attendance in the primary schools were stabilized by the attendance laws. City systems developed, with superintendents, increased support, trained teachers, and regular courses of study. The country was in the process of making education universal in fact.

Public education was much less fully developed in the South than in the most advanced states of the North. Some Southern states that had paper systems had few schools, especially in the country districts; and the South was largely rural. The war and the waste and corruption of the reconstruction governments further depleted the material and moral resources of the people. And yet new beginnings were made, laws passed, and public school systems established. There was a great lack of means and the Negro schools did not receive their proportionate share of the funds. Help was given by the Peabody donation and other gifts, but full educational awakening did not come to the South until the end of the century.

OPINIONS AND ARGUMENTS

Educational opinion in the South resembled that held farther north at an earlier time. What was believed in New York or New Jersey in 1790 was still affirmed in many parts of the South in 1860. In both places and times education was considered a valuable attainment for those who could get it; but like health or fortune its acquisition was a personal and private matter. This was not mere theory. The sparsity of the population, slavery and the unproductiveness of slave labor, the depletion of the soil, the poverty of the small farmers, and the destitution of the poor whites formed a condition in which public education could not thrive. Even the planters were not as prosperous as they seemed. In the cities free schools were possible and some cities were actually engaged in promoting public schools.

There was great opposition to the principle of taxation for public education, and other means of support were diligently sought. Such means were the state school funds, land grants, and the surplus revenue distribution. Special imposts were levied on institutions that were unpopular with many people. Banks and theaters often came within this class, and therefore bank taxes and licenses to operate theaters were approved. Lotteries were a frequent source, as they had been in all parts of the country in earlier times. The use of such sources shows that the people's representatives hesitated or refused to vote a school tax.

Behind the financial difficulty there was the deeper reason that many, poor as well as rich, were opposed to universal public education. In this respect, also, the South held the views that had been held in the North only one or two generations earlier when many of the "best people" preferred and supported private schools. Some families wished to select their school instead of having it provided for them. Many preferred a church school to a secular or a religiously neutral one. Many of the planters did not want their children to associate with those whom they considered trash. Many of the upper classes did not see why the poor should have an education and many of the poor agreed with them. Those in the mountains and the backwoods who had little or no education were not easily convinced of the need for it. Colyer Meriwether reported that there was opposition to public schools "in retired places" and there were many such places in the old South. All this goes to show that the thoughts of the prewar South, although affected by its social and economic system, differed from those of the North mainly in timing.

After the war Southern opposition to public education continued and it did not come mainly from the cabins of the poor. It came instead from former slaveowners, business and professional men, politicians, and professors in colleges and theological seminaries. Some of these, adhering to a *laissez-faire* theory of government, expressed a genuine dread of state paternalism. They professed to believe that public schools might become the means of the absolute control of the thoughts and opinions of the people. Who would now say, after looking about the world, that their fears were wholly groundless? But neither was there safety in the policy that they approved. Popular ignorance would have given false prophets an equal chance with those whom they regarded as the true ones. Looking ahead, they argued that free schooling would be followed by compulsory schooling. And this was hardly a prediction at a time when state after state was enacting compulsory attendance laws.

Some of these opponents insisted that universal education was both impracticable and undesirable. That it was in operation a few hundred miles away did not deter them. They simply denied that it was successful or could be made to succeed. They argued that the greater part of mankind must work for bread and denied that "real mental culture" can coexist with daily labor. They held that state education would be mere smattering, mere reading and writing, which would soon be lost by the laboring class through disuse. But to their minds the worst of the matter was that those who did retain these arts would be likely to become dangerous agitators turning every factory into a debating society.

The opponents of public education did not fail to propose a solution of the educational question. It was to continue the existing practices without change. They claimed that the truly kindly and philanthropic way to serve the genuine interests of the working people was to educate, not the workers themselves, but the higher classes who would then in turn lift the submerged multitudes. By this procedure, it was claimed, all portions of the social organism would be raised together, the true relations of class to class would be preserved, and the lower class would receive by association with its superiors the only real education possible to it.

This might appear to be a parody; but it is a summary of the views of Robert L. Dabney, clergyman and seminary professor, expressed in a newspaper debate in 1876 with William H. Ruffner, the superintendent of public instruction of Virginia, and it is taken from a work by Dabney's son, Charles William Dabney (*Universal Education in the South*, I, 154*ff.*). And this line of reasoning was not unique. It was used in other aristocratic societies. But in 1876, in a state that revered the memory of Thomas Jefferson and in a country that had not formally repudiated the principles of the Declaration of Independence, it was an anachronism. One is bound also to reflect that under slavery the education of the superior class did not raise the submerged classes, black or white, to any dangerous elevation.

The times were, however, out of joint. In the opposing camp were the Republican politicians and their partisans, former abolitionists, soldiers of the Union armies, and all who wanted to be assured that having won the war they would not lose its fruits. As early as 1863 Lincoln had written to General Banks that "some provision should be made for the education of the blacks." The radical section of Northern opinion was determined to secure not only some but equal provision for the education of blacks. In 1874 General Butler's Civil Rights Bill in its early form included a compulsory demand for mixed schools. But before the bill came up in the Senate, its sponsors became convinced that, if adopted in that form, it would destroy the newborn public schools of the South because nearly all the white children would be withdrawn from them. All public schools, it was said, would then be attended only by blacks and the white people would refuse to support them. This would leave many white children without schools of any kind, whereas the rich would establish and patronize private schools as they had done before the war. The racial coeducation clause was therefore stricken from the bill. But the fight that it had occasioned may be a partial explanation for some of the reactionary theories of the time. Nor is this even now merely ancient history, as all those know who have read of the present state of educational opinion in parts of the South.

PROGRESS TO 1860

No close comparison is needed to show the difference in the stages of educational progress that had been reached by the two sections before the war. The North had accepted the school tax and demanded the public elementary school, but it was not yet free everywhere. Many of the Northern public schools were graded and the public high school had been established in cities and many small towns. State appropriations allotted by the chief school official enabled the Northern states to enforce regulations on the qualifications of teachers, course of study, length of term, and other items. Rural schools were less efficient than those in the cities but these also were improving, and the principle that they must be regularly maintained was accepted.

The Southern states before 1860 had made only a slender beginning upon such a program. Some states had a body of school law but few good schools. The want of a dependable source of sufficient funds was the primary want. In a number of states the distribution of the surplus revenue aroused great hopes of educational improvement. In some states it was thought that by adding the federal money to the common school fund a system of public schools could be supported without a special tax. It was this idea that led the legislature of Georgia to send a committee to the North to investigate school arrangements and to report a plan for a school system for that state. But it became clear that the available income would be insufficient and the economic recession of 1837 made an end of the proposed plan. The financial distress had a bad effect upon the program of other states also.

One Southern state, North Carolina, was an exception to the general rule. This state, which in 1789 had chartered a state university, also organized a public school system long before her neighbors and about the same time as many of the Northern states. The first effort did not succeed. A legislative committee in 1817 studied the schools of New England but the plan that resulted could not be put into effect. More than twenty years later a second effort was more successful. Until that time the suffrage in North Carolina was limited to landowners, but a new and more liberal constitution extended the right to the ballot. About the same time the state's share of the surplus revenue was added to the school fund. But the main reason for the favorable attitude on public education is to be found in the people.

The western portion of the state lies in the hills and valleys of the Blue Ridge Mountains and is suited to a diversified agriculture on farms of small or moderate size. As this section filled up with independent farmers, the population of the central and western parts of the state began to over-balance that of the eastern part where the plantation economy limited the landowners to comparatively small numbers. These wealthy planters were defeated by the western democratic elements in the election of the legis-lature and the constitutional convention of 1835. The "back country" won over the seaboard region; and the new constitution laid a broader base for suffrage, provided for equal representation, and required the election of the governor and other state executives by the direct vote of the people, not as formerly by the legislature.

The second event was the receipt by the state of almost $1,500,000 from the surplus revenue. This was applied to education and to internal im-provements, which, by increasing the state's taxable wealth, later also benefited education. The state now became one of the group of common-wealths that were enacting comprehensive school laws: Pennsylvania, Ohio, Massachusetts, Michigan, and in 1839, North Carolina.

The North Carolina statute was a county-option law; but after a vigorous campaign all but seven counties accepted its provisions. It provided for county boards and the districting of the counties. Each district had a local board, not elected by the people but appointed by the county court. For the support of the schools the law required the county tax in the amount of $20 per district and the appropriation by the state of double this amount. Free blacks were not taxed, and their children were excluded from the schools. That the schools were needed is made clear by the returns from the census of 1840 when one-third of the adult white population admitted that they were unable to read or write.

There was no effective state agency to promote, unify, and report upon the local efforts, but in 1853 the state superintendency was instituted. Calvin H. Wiley became the devoted and efficient incumbent and remained in office until 1866. The period, 1853–1860, is known as the educational awakening under Wiley. His methods and achievements resembled closely those of the best midcentury promoters in other states.

Wiley made his last report, the seventh, for the year 1860. It gave the returns from eighty-one of the eighty-six counties. It showed that about 70 per cent of the children of school age were enrolled, that 90 per cent of the teachers were licensed, that the schools averaged about fifty pupils, that the average term was four months, and that more than $100,000 had been paid in school taxes. This with the "two for one" appropriation from the state fund provided about $100 for each of the 3,000 schools and an average monthly salary of about $25. If this wage was actually received, the North Carolina teachers of 1860 were somewhat better paid than those of most Northern states. However that may be, the school system of North Carolina was the best in the South.

With North Carolina we may compare her neighbor, Virginia. The legislature of the Old Dominion passed "an act to establish public schools" in the early year of 1796. This act, based upon Thomas Jefferson's bill of 1779, was an optional law; and this feature nullified the law. A literary fund, the usual resource of a people not ready to consent to a school tax, was established in 1810 and was increased by large sums owed the state by the national government. By 1816 it amounted to $1,000,000, and the next legislature passed Virginia's second school law. This was a charity school measure, hardly intended as a step toward free public education.

Nor was the literary fund reserved for the benefit of the children and protected against encroachment. Even the Visitors of the University of Virginia with Thomas Jefferson at the head borrowed for the use of the university from the literary fund that had been formed for the support of elementary schools. After thirty years (1820) the fund was providing some schooling for only half of the indigent children of the state. The governor said the law should be repealed and a better one enacted in its place. Unfortunately, the new law, Virginia's third, adopted in 1846 and intended to provide free education for all white children in schools to be supported from the literary fund and a county tax, was another optional law. Only nine counties accepted it. And this was the extent of Virginia's efforts for universal public education before 1860.

Little progress was made in the other states of the section. South Carolina adopted a free school law in 1811 but it was for orphans and poor children only. The schools served a useful purpose in Charleston, but over the state they reached only a small fraction of the children. County systems of free schools without taxation or state supervision were established, more in law than in fact, in Maryland, Tennessee, and Kentucky. The history of education in Kentucky by Frank L. McVey places "the real beginning of public education in Kentucky" in the year 1870, "when an act was passed by the legislature implementing the paper system set up by the legislature of 1838." A similar statement would apply to most of the South and even the dates would need little adjustment.

The educational awakening of the thirties that roused the Northern states merely caused those of the South to stir in their slumbers. They would not vote the school tax and effective state supervision. Texas, Mississippi, and Florida made little progress. Of all the states in the deep South, Louisiana came the nearest to a working system. As in the North, some of the Southern cities, New Orleans, Mobile, and Atlanta, were ahead of their states. Also in the later prewar years some progress was made in Georgia and Alabama. It is possible to believe that if the economic, social, and religious facts were available in sufficient detail, the educational differences between the sections could be fully explained. One fact that includes a good many others is this, that an efficient common school system because of its power to dissolve social caste would not have been in harmony with the planters' way of life.

POSTWAR DILEMMA

In absolute numbers of men killed and dollars spent, the cost of the war weighed more heavily upon the victors than the vanquished. One hundred thousand more Union than Confederate soldiers lost their lives. The North expended $2 billion more upon the conflict than the Confederacy. Yet the South suffered more from its smaller losses because it had fewer men and dollars upon which to draw. And whereas shiploads of immigrants came into the North to work in mine and field and factory and the Northern bondholder got his money back, the South, instead of immigrants, had only carpetbaggers, and the debts of the Confederate state and central governments were never paid. The state school funds disappeared with the rest of the resources. The paper money of the South depreciated until it became worthless.

The destruction of property by the Northern armies was a serious loss for a nonmanufacturing region. In Atlanta, which did have some factories and was a railroad center, Sherman destroyed or carried off everything of any value. The burning of Columbia, applauded by the North, was condemned by the South as the act of barbarians; and accusations and recriminations on account of it continued for decades. The march to the sea had laid waste a belt across Georgia "sixty miles wide." The Shenandoah Valley was devastated by contending armies and finally swept clean by Sheridan. The Union armies marched through the South, camped in it, and foraged on it, while only one great battle was fought on Northern soil.

Such facts have an abstract meaning for those of a later day but to the people of that time they translated themselves into present sorrow and suffering. Grant at Appomattox, at one of the high moments of an uneven career, permitted Lee's soldiers to keep their horses because they would be needed in the spring plowing. But when they arrived at their homes some found that there was no plow, that missing or worn parts could not be replaced, or that seed corn was lacking. The labor system was ruined. Manufacturers, banks, railroads, and the state governments were prostrate. A fresh beginning had to be undertaken.

The educational problem was as difficult as any that faced the South during the reconstruction. The upper classes had to develop respect for a more democratic society and for the educational instrument that would help to maintain it. The rural South had few good schools and in many places no schools at all. The poor whites in the pine barrens were isolated from many civilizing influences and suffered from endemic disease. Four million blacks, more than 90 per cent illiterate, were now free and were to be prepared for the responsibilites of citizenship decreed by the new amendments to the Constitution. As slaves they had been kept in ignorance on principle by laws with severe penalties.

Every meeting to teach blacks to read and write was, in prewar Virginia, "an unlawful assembly." Participants if they were blacks were flogged. For the same offense, whites were given a jail sentence and were also compelled to pay a fine. Every Southern state had a law of this type. Teaching slaves to write was especially obnoxious because it might aid them in forming combinations and conspiracies.

Oral religious instruction of slaves was approved as favorable to morals and good order. Southern churches spent considerable sums to Christianize the blacks and their efforts were effective. Free blacks sometimes acquired financial means and were able to send their children to the North for schooling. They were a frequent reminder that the race did not lack capacity, as the slavocracy preferred to claim. One objection to the presence of free blacks near the plantations arose from the likelihood that they would present ideas of freedom to the slaves.

After the war the white people had to be convinced that the education of the blacks was possible, desirable, and indeed necessary. Before the war the white South had not succeeded in providing schools for all its own children. Military rule, the conflicting activities of the Freedman's Bureau, and corruption in the handling of funds did not simplify matters. More than a hundred years have elapsed and the problem is still occupying the attention of the section and the nation. This is evidence of the difficulty of the social problem that faced the South. But we must also say that great progress has been made and much of that progress has been due to the blacks themselves as we shall see in Chapter 18.

RECONSTRUCTION

Peace did not return at once when the fighting stopped on the battle-fields. Reconstruction had to begin in an era of mutual hatred and suspicion and continual recrimination, and it is not surprising that some of its measures were considered vindictive. Besides, there was not a single accepted and well-planned reconstruction policy, but two, the Presidential and the Congressional, neither fully developed.

The Presidential policy begun by Lincoln and, with important changes, followed by Andrew Johnson was conciliatory; and by the end of 1865 all the seceded states had formed governments acceptable to the President, had renewed their allegiance to the Union, and had ratified the Thirteenth Amendment abolishing slavery. Presumably they had now again become full members of the Union.

There were, however, many unresolved difficulties. Now that the blacks were free they became competitors of the poorer whites for work and land, and a hot wave of racial antagonism flared up. The great land-owners had no money to pay wages and could offer the ex-slaves only sharecropping opportunities. Often the agreements seemed to institute a new form of slavery worse than the old because the white owner now had no responsibility for feeding, clothing, or housing his workers. And the new freedom went to the heads of some of the blacks and they loafed and wandered about without working. These became a disturbing element of society. Southern legislatures thereupon began to adopt "black codes" designed to compel the blacks to work and restricting their freedom of movement and contract. To many in the North this seemed intolerable. The idea grew that the South was trying to reenslave the freedmen.

Congress had never conceded to the President the right to set the terms of reconstruction. The elections of 1866 gave the Radicals, led by Thaddeus Stevens in the House and Charles Sumner in the Senate, the power to undo Johnson's work. They proceeded to secure the passage of laws to enforce their own terms. The laws of 1867 reestablished army rule in the South, set up five military districts, and provided for universal black suffrage. From that time the reconstruction of the seceded states was in the hands of Congress.

Under Presidential reconstruction, attempts had been made to establish public schools but without providing for the education of blacks. This last, we know, was contrary to Lincoln's instruction. It is doubtless pertinent to remember that Andrew Johnson had been a slaveholder. The case of Arkansas may illustrate the policy. It will at least show that those are mistaken who teach that Presidential reconstruction made no contribution to education.

In Arkansas the Union armies, driving the Confederates before them, were able by 1863 to occupy the northern half of the state, including the capital, Little Rock. By Presidential proclamation the citizens were permitted to form a new government. The elected governor had once been a teacher, and in the state convention of 1861 had been the only man to vote against secession. On his recommendation the legislature, composed mainly of former Confederates, voted a tax for free schools and a full complement of state, county, and local school offices. They opened the schools to all white children but made no provision for the education of blacks.

Military rule and Congressional reconstruction annulled the Arkansas school law before it became effective. A new constitution with a long section on education was adopted and a new school law was enacted. This provided for separate schools for the children of the two races. An outburst of extravagance from which the reconstructionists themselves recoiled exhausted the limited funds, and teachers were paid in scrip. A third constitution and school law were adopted in 1874, and new officers did much to moderate the prejudice against the education of blacks in this border state. The new law was an excellent one but factors that the law could not reach held back progress.

When it became clear that progress would come very slowly, if at all, some in the ruling party decided upon radical measures. Representative George F. Hoar of Massachusetts in his bill of 1870 provided for the appointment by the President of a superintendent of schools for each delinquent state, the appointment by the Secretary of the Interior of division and local school superintendents for each such state, the prescription by federal officers of all textbooks, and the collection by federal agents of an annual direct tax for schools. The measure was contrary to all American educational history, and the Hoar Bill never came to a vote in Congress.

The introduction of the Hoar Bill may have had one important result. Argument over the bill directed the minds of many in Congress and in the country to the subject of federal aid for education. Bills were introduced into Congress to create a national school fund from the sale of public lands. When these failed to pass, Senator Henry W. Blair of New Hampshire in 1881 introduced a federal aid bill that provided for the distribution of $77,000,000 to the states in the proportion of the number of illiterates in each state. The money was to be appropriated in specified annual amounts over a period of years. The Senate repeatedly passed the Blair Bill, but every time it failed in the House. The last defeat occurred in 1890, the year that saw the passage of the second Morrill Act for agricultural and engineering education in land-grant colleges.

After World War I there was a great revival of interest in federal aid; and these efforts became prominent again after World War II. The National Education Association has worked for such legislation. Congress, the parties, and the sections have been divided. There has been opposition from some Catholic organizations and from the Chamber of Commerce of the United States. Educators and businessmen have not been united in favor of the policy or have opposed particular features of the several bills. These have in very few instances reached the floor of either House. Meanwhile the heavy burden that school support places upon the poorer states and the disparity in educational provisions that obtains among the states seem to many to provide a sound argument for federal aid.

Under Congressional reconstruction all of the Southern states established public schools not only for whites but also for blacks, and this has been a permanent gain. It is possible that the fear that the army would order the establishment of mixed schools was one of the reasons for the alacrity with which the South accepted the segregated public school for blacks. The black schools were not given proper financial support, but under Presidential reconstruction the states did not even propose to educate the former slaves. The new state constitutions included mandatory educational provisions and the laws provided for a school tax, state supervision, and universal education. In time, teacher preparation, certification, minimum terms, and expanded curricula were demanded. Compulsory attendance was long delayed.

SCHOOLS FOR FREEDMEN

When schools were opened for blacks, the young and many adults came to learn. For this there were all the usual reasons but also an unusual one. Knowledge may be both pleasant and valuable, but to the ex-slave it was also a symbol of his new status, a privilege formerly monopolized by his masters. But it was soon discovered that getting an education is a long, laborious process, however great the interest may be. Meanwhile, the learners had to live, which was sufficiently difficult for many. They lacked understanding of the best line to take and, without guidance, frequently aimed at impossible goals. Probably their teachers, often Northern idealists, did not provide proper guidance. Many became discouraged and gave up.

From the early months of the war, efforts were made to teach the blacks who were within the Union lines. The American Missionary Association, formed by the Methodist and other Northern churches, gave aid to a free black, Mary L. Peake, who began to teach refugees at Fortress Monroe in 1861. This little school is claimed as the seed-grain from which Hampton

Institute grew. And Hampton, under Samuel Chapman Armstrong, did not make the mistake of offering a purely literary education to those who would have to live by manual work. The American Missionary Association also supported schools in cities along the coast, and these were later absorbed by the school systems of Norfolk and other towns. Other organized groups engaged in the support of schools in Southern localities.

Some thousands of teachers and more than $1,000,000 were contributed by the North to aid in such programs. Many teachers came from the old abolition centers and way-stations such as Oberlin on the Underground Railroad. The white people of the South were frequently hostile to this new invasion and refused to rent living quarters or furnish board to teachers whom they regarded as their enemies. Schoolhouses were burned down and malicious reports were circulated in the effort to drive out the Yankee educators.

The Army and the federal government undertook to teach as well as protect the freedmen. General Grant in 1862 appointed Colonel John Eaton, later a general and in peacetime the second United States Commissioner of Education, to act as commissioner for freedmen in Arkansas. In 1864 General Banks from the New Orleans headquarters of his military district laid down a detailed educational directive. This was to provide for the "rudimental instruction of the freedmen" under his protection. The directive, really a military order, provided for a board of education with power to tax and in fact to requisition, to build, to hire, and to regulate and discipline. The army supplied books, set up courses of study, and set the school hours. The teachers had to make returns and reports on all of these matters. This was a form of compulsory education previously unknown in the United States.

The government also created a special agency to care for the interests of the blacks, the Bureau for Refugees, Freedmen, and Abandoned Lands, always known as the Freedmen's Bureau. It became a government within the government and served as legislature, court, tax collector, and executive, ranging through the whole extent of civil organization and control. It had a superintendent of freedmen's schools who took over and extended the work begun by Eaton. Grants were made to the missionary societies especially for schoolhouses. There was an educational supervisor for each state. In the five years of its existence it gave some elementary education to almost 250,000 pupils. Many now well-known black colleges were aided by it, among them Morehouse, Fisk, and Howard. Berea received aid from the bureau and taught the two races in the same classes until Kentucky forbade this by a law of 1904. The bureau was abolished in 1870, many of the Northern teachers went home, and the obligation to blacks in the South became the obligation of the states where they lived.

In carrying on its work, the bureau disbursed millions of dollars and exercised extralegal controls. Its agents were accused of graft and of devious political activity to promote the Radical scheme of reconstruction. The bureau was an arm of the United States government, controlled by the Radicals. Its head, General O. O. Howard, was honest, but no administrator or judge of men. There were several official investigations of his military and official conduct but he was "exonerated."

THE PEABODY AND OTHER FUNDS

George Peabody was a pathmaker for the great American educational philanthropists such as Andrew Carnegie, John D. Rockefeller, and the Henry Ford family. Stephen Girard, founder of the Girard College for Orphans, was almost the only predecessor who could be ranked with him. He provided for others what he had failed to get for himself, the chance to go to school. His formal education was all obtained in four terms in a village school. When his birthplace celebrated its bicentennial, he sent as his toast: "Education: a debt from the present to future generations." This sentiment was chosen by the Peabody Education Board for its seal. This board was chartered in 1867 by the State of New York and received from Peabody more than $2,000,000 to be applied in aid of the education of "the entire population" of the South. The board's first general agent was Barnas Sears, who had followed Horace Mann as Secretary of the state board of education in Massachusetts.

The major policy of the board, apparently the work of Sears, was to give substantial aid to a few well-located schools that would serve as examples and models instead of spreading the money in small amounts over a large number without much benefit to any. The aim was to stimulate permanent improvement, not to give relief. A few well-placed, efficient, permanent schools seemed to be stronger arguments for an improved public education than the slight and temporary improvement of many. This principle proposed by Sears has had great influence and has been given extended application by the numerous educational foundations that have followed and imitated the Peabody Fund and Board.

Sears also advised giving aid for the better preparation of teachers. Some subsidy to girls' normal schools was proposed, and scholarships for young men who would agree to teach in the public schools. He thought teachers' associations and educational journals should receive aid as being means toward better public relations. He advised that all of the board's contributions should be distributed through the offices of the state school officers or other public officials, for a main purpose of the board was to stimulate state activity in public education. Considering that the money was to be applied in a dozen states, the income from the fund was not large; but by following the policies indicated, its publicity value was far greater than its purchasing power.

The Peabody Board in forty-six years disbursed about $3,500,000 in twelve states. The general principle was followed that the board would not underwrite more than about one-fourth of the cost of a particular operation. Every Peabody dollar thus attracted $3 extra from taxation or philanthropy. After 1880 the general agent of the fund was J. L. M. Curry, a Southern planter, legislator, and gospel minister. One of his achievements was the development of the George Peabody College for Teachers. Sears had succeeded in opening a normal school in connection with the old University of Nashville. After some years and much effort the state began to make small appropriations, and almost a generation later the Peabody Board appropriated to its endowment $1,500,000 of the fund principal. The school was chartered in 1909 and opened in new buildings in 1914.

The experience of the Peabody Board in the application of its policies was of the utmost value to the Southern Education Board and the General Education Board when at the turn of the century these bodies came to the aid of the educational movement in the South. Earlier and smaller agencies also gained from that effort. A second trust for education in the South was established in 1882 by John F. Slater of Norwich, Connecticut. He gave $1,000,000 for the education of freedmen and their descendants and especially for the preparation of black teachers. The Slater trustees conferred with Curry in making their plans and eventually what was left of the Peabody Fund was united with the Slater Fund.

The policies of these early boards tended to concentrate their aid upon the larger schools in the cities where they would be seen; and as a result the smallest, most isolated, and destitute schools for blacks in the rural South failed to get the needed stimulus. A Philadelphia Friend, Anna T. Jeanes, in 1907 created a fund of $1,000,000 to help these forgotten people. The managers of the fund introduced a new force, the Jeanes teacher. They selected the most successful black teachers of a community to spend a part of their time in helping other teachers to improve their work and their schoolhouses and particularly in introducing industrial and domestic education. This scheme of the Jeanes supervisors was suggested by Virginia Randolph, a black teacher in Henrico County, Virginia, and the Jeanes teacher idea spread not only in the South but also to the schools of several sections of Africa.

All of these funds later cooperated with the General Education Board. They accomplished much in starting and establishing public education in the South, but the income from a million or even $400 million was not sufficient to educate the children of twelve states. Those states reaching from Virginia to Texas had 17,000,000 people in 1890 and twice as many fifty years later. Only an efficient tax system together with the help of the federal government could have provided the funds that would have been needed and are needed to educate all the children of this large section.

TOWARD UNIVERSAL EDUCATION

The school laws of reconstruction days demanded equal school opportunities for white and black alike, but this promise faded early. For a time after the war the white farmers and the blacks cooperated in politics in opposition to the planters, but economic competition soon broke up the union. Many whites thought the blacks should pay for their own schools. The blacks were more and more deprived of political power; and the tax receipts from the property of blacks were so low that they also lost whatever chance they may have had for equal school opportunity. Without help from the white people, the blacks in large areas would have had no schools whatever.

The question of mixed schools for the two races, if it were pressed, was recognized as an insuperable difficulty. But Barnas Sears unaccountably considered this an unrealistic issue. He reported a case in which blacks admitted, or perhaps he should have said "claimed," that they were demanding mixed schools merely to secure equal, not common, facilities. This may well have been the fact in a given instance, but it is hard to believe that Sears could have taken this as a typical case. Black leaders knew that separate facilities for a poor, ignorant, and until recently, enslaved people, to be paid for by the money of a dominant class, would not be equal. Some of the Northern reconstructionists clearly intended to force mixed schools upon the South, perhaps rather to chastise "the rebels" than to aid the freedmen. After the Southern white people regained control of their state governments, they established separate public schools for the two races but until recent times there was no real attempt to make the black schools "equal" to the white schools.

And even equal opportunity would not have been any great opportunity. Ten years after the end of reconstruction, North Carolina had a shorter school term and a higher illiteracy rate than before the war. For a generation the white public schools, although helped by some Northern funds, made little progress. Every state had created a public school system, but the schools themselves, especially in the country, were not well attended, well housed, or well taught. Reports show that in some of the Southern states more than half of the children were not enrolled in the public schools. How many were in private schools is not known. Most of the progress had been in the cities. Lack of money was one great difficulty and the separate schools for the two races made education expensive, especially in the country where enrollments were small.

For a time in the 1880's it appeared that the federal government might help in the support of public schools. The Blair Bill, mentioned previously, was introduced for this purpose in 1881 and passed by the Senate of three successive Congresses, but each time it was rejected by the House.

By 1890 the South had become convinced that there was no prospect of early national aid. They had also seen the educational progress of the North and, at home, the influence of the Peabody and other funds in selected areas. Unfortunately, the latter had not spread as far and as rapidly as had been expected. The South was beginning to look more to her own resources. The closing decade of the century was one of financial stringency, but in 1898 the first of a series of annual conferences on education in the South was called at Capon Springs, West Virginia.

This may be taken as the beginning of a new educational awakening. It was, however, different from the awakening that had come to the industrial North long before. That was a movement to establish state school systems. The South in 1900 had long had the basic laws, officers, and machinery of public education, and this was an effort to provide the machine with fuel and lubricants and to get it to run.

The original idea of the meetings had come from a Northerner, Edward Abbott, the son of the Jacob Abbott mentioned in an earlier chapter. Abbott's interest, like that of many Northerners, was a philanthropic and missionary interest in the education of the blacks and mountain whites; and the first conference was called to promote Christian education. Later meetings broadened this reference to stress the general literary education of both blacks and whites and, one may safely say, of white people especially.

The public response to the discussions revealed people who saw little good in any kind of education for blacks except industrial education. Booker T. Washington had succeeded only too well in teaching his lesson that the black must literally work his way upward. There were many, also, who believed that if the whites were educated first, the education of the blacks would follow almost automatically. This was an alluring but untenable idea. Although they received much help from their white neighbors, not always cheerfully given, the fact is that the blacks to a great extent educated themselves, as all people must do if they are to be educated.

The meetings soon came to be known as the Conference for Education in the South, and they were largely in the hands of the Southern people. The programs glow with the names of Southern men who already were or were to become famous, men such as Curry, C. W. Dabney, C. B. Aycock, Edwin Alderman, Charles D. McIver, and many others. To effect a more permanent organization, the Southern Education Board was formed in 1901. An agent was employed to work during the year in the intervals between the meetings. But the conference and the board had no great amount of money to use and none to distribute. Two years later John D. Rockefeller was brought into the movement and the General Education Board was organized and received national incorporation. This body still further expanded the scope of the work. It was to promote the education of all the people not only in the South but in the United States. The South, however, shared extensively in its benefactions.

The chief value of the whole movement to the South was the arousal of interest in education. Educational campaigns were organized in state after state and some were continued for several years. Every phase of public education was discussed—support, longer terms, illiteracy, teacher preparation, buildings, libraries, rural consolidation, high schools, and a great many phases now included under the recent term, *fundamental education*. Among these later activities there were the farm demonstration work of Seaman A. Knapp, club work by boys and girls, sanitation and health work, and the campaign against the hookworm and malaria. The various funds, Peabody, Slater, Jeanes, Phelps-Stokes, and Rosenwald, cooperated with the Southern and General Education boards.

The interest aroused by this movement also increased the amount and the proportion of public money for education. But as a Southern leader pointed out at the beginning, the wealth to support universal education must be produced before it can be used. The rural South has not had the wealth to provide the schools that its children deserve. Philanthropy, even the philanthropy of the largest fortunes and the richest foundations, it may be repeated, will not educate all the children. And ways must be found to increase the prosperity of the South, to keep at home the wealth that is now siphoned off by the great Northern corporations, and to secure federal aid. Only by such means can the children of the rural South be given the opportunities provided for children in New York or California.

EDUCATING BLACK LEADERS

The various funds, Peabody and others, aided both blacks and whites or, in several cases, blacks only. But with the whites in undisturbed control of public education, the black schools were even less adequately supported than those for white children. Statistics reported in percentage gains show that black education made rapid progress, but the figures will be deceiving unless it is remembered that slaves had received no education. Thus the original base was close to zero and the total enrollment at any time was also the increase in enrollment since 1865.

There were some special schools for blacks, such as the Hampton Normal and Agricultural Institute, the Tuskegee Normal and Industrial Institution, Fisk and other smaller colleges and universities, and after the second Morrill Act (1890), the seventeen land-grant colleges. All of these have prepared teachers, journalists, bankers, farmers, and leaders in many lines among the black people. Some of these constitute other cases of philanthropic aid for black education.

The founder and first head of the Hampton Institute was Samuel Chapman Armstrong (1839–1893). He was the son of American missionaries in Hawaii and early learned the methods of industrial and intellectual education used at the Hilo Manual Labor School in Honolulu. He graduated from Williams College in 1862, commanded a black regiment in the Civil War, worked in Virginia under the Freedmen's Bureau, and in 1868 founded Hampton Institute for blacks. Later, Indians also were admitted.

It is sometimes said that Armstrong's Hawaiian upbringing fitted him in a special manner to deal with primitive people, but the American black of 1868 was not primitive. He had had a long apprenticeship of labor for others. Social conditions and prejudices and the short time the black could remain in school made it advisable to teach him to use his hands. He had to work to survive and working skills were likely to be useful. The idea of industrial education for the young blacks and Indians appealed to employers and men of wealth and both Hampton and Tuskegee received contributions from such sources. Hampton Institute, as the school is now called, has over 2,500 men and women students and is recognized by the Southern Association as a Grade A college. Without question its most famous graduate is Booker T. Washington (1858–1915), the founder of Tuskegee.

Tuskegee was founded in 1881, and Washington always ascribed much of its and his success to the education he had received at Hampton. But great as that contribution may have been, his rise "up from slavery" was in large part because of qualities that schools cannot teach, intelligence and a remarkable warmth of personality. His power of effective public speech and his social and political wisdom may have been increased by his education. Much of his philosophy of education was developed by his experience at Hampton. His political wisdom is shown in his policy expressed in his famous speech at the Atlanta Exposition in 1895. He said: "In all things that are purely social we [of the two races] can be as separate as the fingers, yet one as the hand in all things essential to mutual progress." This pleased white people as did the policy of Tuskegee in teaching industrial and trade arts and skills, thrift, and honesty, and in campaigning against the one-room cabins in which, Washington said, 6,000,000 blacks were living. These were Washington's ways of elevating the black.

White people did not all press for much black elevation but they wanted capable workers. And Northern capitalists were willing to contribute to their training. The capitalists were a major source of the support needed by Tuskegee. Some blacks attacked the vocationalism of Washington. W. E. B. DuBois (1868–1963), a graduate of Fisk University with a Ph.D. degree from Harvard, was one of these critics. He said the black race could be elevated only by its exceptional men, leaders trained not in manual vocations but in intellectual and liberal arts. He thought the Tuskegee work-education was unduly restrictive, tending to keep the black in a servile position.

The issue thus joined had already been decided not by theory alone but by the force of broad educational trends. The period when Hampton and Tuskegee were developing was the era of the new land-grant colleges, of the introduction of manual training, and of the spread of the normal schools. Their success in teaching trades and vocations was reinforced by the ongoing work of American industry in the postwar period. But trade training was not as permanently successful as it seemed to be at the time. Mass production by the great manufacturing corporations and the rise of the labor unions were changing the world's work and the social relations of the workers. These trends were not foreseen, and in view of the industrialists' opposition to the unions it is doubtful that Washington would have been willing to introduce special ourses for labor leaders into Tuskegee.

Tuskegee has developed into a college of over 3,000 men and women. It started as an elementary and high school and became a college after Washington's time. One of its great teachers and scientists of recent times was George Washington Carver (1859–1943). It offers a great variety of courses in agriculture, education, home economics, institutional management, nurses' training, and others. There are cooperative work-study courses and many of the students earn all or part of their expenses.

In the seventeen states of the South that have traditionally separated the two races in schools, there are 17 black land-grant colleges of "agriculture and the mechanic arts," although in many cases they do not use these words in the title. In the same states there are about fifty other black colleges including Howard University, Fisk University, Morehouse College, and the two, Hampton Institute and Tuskegee Institute, already described. There are also hundreds of small struggling colleges and schools. The land-grant colleges for blacks now enroll about 25,000 students; but for a long time they were treated in stepmotherly fashion by the states and the quality of their work was poor. All of these public and private institutions together with some normal schools prepare the teachers of the black elementary and high schools of the South. This whole phase of educational development will be changed by the Supreme Court decision against segregation as shown in Chapter 18.

SUMMARY

The cold war between the sections began with the founding of the Republic; and when compromise was no longer possible and war broke out, each side could honestly claim that it was fighting for the right, and could believe that it, being in the right, would be victorious. And great as was the loss of life and material possessions in the debacle of the South, it did not, perhaps, exceed the moral and spiritual damage that she suffered. To this the horrors of reconstruction must be added.

There were causes in nature and society for the slender developments in public education before the war. Included among the latter were the class structure of Southern society, the depressed condition of the lowest classes, and the lack of wealth to pay a school tax. Also family and church control of education was strongly rooted. For these reasons public education made little progress before 1860. A few states and a number of cities had, however, made a beginning; but it does not seem likely, as has been claimed, that an effective system would have developed quickly if the war had not come.

The war left the South prostrate; the planters continued in opposition to public education; there was now a black problem; and there was also a drastic reconstruction policy. All these hindered educational efforts. Presidential reconstruction under Johnson might not have done much for the black. The Congressional plan, though harsh and vindictive, did at least make some attempt to start the education of the freedmen. Many of the efforts by the missionary societies, military agencies, and the Freedmen's Bureau had only moderate success.

After reconstruction the states took up what was their proper task, the developing of effective state systems. They were greatly aided in the effort to provide for universal and improved education by the boards and funds created by Northern philanthropists. Beginning about 1900 the Southern Education Board initiated campaigns in state after state to inform and arouse the citizens. The work was really done by the Southern people themselves. In regard to education this was the beginning of the new South.

As will be shown in a later chapter, the public high school in the South is also a result of the awakening in the present century. There were few high schools in the section before 1900 and practically none outside the cities. Whereas the first effort was an attempt to develop standard college-preparatory schools, the South became the pioneer in the development of agricultural high schools teaching also home economics, health, and housing.

Teachers for the elementary and high schools are prepared in public and private colleges. A special feature of Southern education is the large number of black colleges, great private universities and small substandard colleges, and the black land-grant institutions, only now beginning to go forward.

QUESTIONS

1. What would have been the effect of the enactment of the Blair Bill? Was its failure fortunate or unfortunate for the United States? For the children of the South?

2. Evaluate the Southern arguments against public education. We may assume that public education is not perfect.
3. How may we account for the shortcomings of the prewar school law and educational efforts in North Carolina?
4. Compare the Northern postwar educational efforts in the South with those of the United States in Germany after World War II.
5. Why do you agree (or disagree) with the view that the educational differences between North and South had little influence upon the Civil War?
6. What may be learned from the Southern experience concerning educational promotion?
7. Would Booker T. Washington have been more successful if he could have foreseen the present labor organizations, the status of the leading trades, and other conditions bearing on black education? Why or why not?
8. What conclusions useful in American education can be drawn from a comparison of black education and race relations in the American South and South Africa?

BOOKS AND PAPERS

Some of the shorter papers by Edgar W. Knight of the University of North Carolina may be located through the *Education Index*. He was a leading student of the educational history of his section, and his *Documentary History* contains many of the sources for a study of the earlier developments in the South. Eleven or more of the Circulars of Information published by the Bureau of Education deal with the Southern states and cover education in the reconstruction period. A list of the Circulars may be conveniently found in Tewksbury's *Founding of American Colleges*, p. 253. The reports of the General Education Board deal with a later period.

ALDERMAN, E. A., and A. C. GORDON, *J. L. M. Curry, A Biography*, New York, 1911; and Jessie Pearl Rice, *J. L. M. Curry, Southerner, Statesman, and Educator*, New York, 1949.

BOND, HORACE MANN, *The Education of the Negro in the American Social Order*, New York, 1934.

BOYD, W. K., "The Antecedents of the North Carolina Convention of 1835," *South Atlantic Quarterly*, January and April, 1910.

BUCK, PAUL H., "The Poor Whites of the Ante-Bellum South," *American Historical Review*, October, 1945.

CLIFT, VIRGIL A., ARCHIBALD W. ANDERSON, and H. GORDON HULLFISH, eds., *Negro Education in America*, New York, 1962.

CURRY, J. L. M., *George Peabody and a History of the Peabody Fund Through Thirty Years*, Cambridge University Press, 1898.

DABNEY, C. W., *Universal Education in the South*, University of North Carolina Press, 1926, two volumes.

EBY, FREDERICK, ed., *Education in Texas: Source Materials*, University of Texas, 1918.

KNIGHT, E. W., *The Influence of Reconstruction on Education in the South*, New York, Teachers College, Columbia University, 1913; *Public Education in North Carolina*, Boston, 1916; *A Documentary History of Education in the South Before 1860*, 5 vols., University of North Carolina Press, 1949–1953.

KONKLE, B. A., *John Motley Morehead and the Development of North Carolina, 1796–1866*, Philadelphia, 1922, with specially drawn maps to show political history.

LEE, GORDON C., *The Struggle for Federal Aid: First Phase*, New York, 1949.

McVEY, FRANK L., *The Gates Open Slowly, A History of Education in Kentucky*, University of Kentucky Press, 1949.

ORR, DOROTHY, *A History of Education in Georgia*, University of North Carolina Press, 1950.

PARKER, FRANKLIN, *George Peabody, A Biography*, Vanderbilt University Press, 1972.

RYAN, W. CARSON, et al., *Secondary Education in the South*, University of North Carolina Press, 1946, a collection of papers by several authors.

SWINT, HENRY L., *The Northern Teacher in the South, 1862–1870*, Vanderbilt University Press, 1941.

WALKER, N. W., "Joseph Spencer Stewart: An Appreciation," *The High School Journal*, January, 1935.

WASHINGTON, BOOKER T., *Up From Slavery, An Autobiography*, New York, 1900.

WOODSON, CARTER G., *The Education of the Negro Prior to 1861*, New York, 1915.

Chapter 10

COLLEGES FOR
THE PEOPLE

The new college of agriculture and the mechanic arts was proposed for the people of the farm and shop who had small interest in purely academic education. Although it was not a wholly unique institution, it was modeled upon no other particular one and it is native to the United States. Efforts to establish similar schools had been carried on for two generations, at least ever since Thomas Jefferson had attempted to include agriculture among the studies of his university; but they had not succeeded for lack of a definite plan, financial support, and the interest of those who were to be benefited.

Undergraduate colleges of agriculture were not unknown in other countries. It was in 1856 that McGill University in Montreal created a faculty or school of agriculture and later one of engineering. Similar provisions were made in Australia and other British dominions that have an undergraduate college. Europe, lacking such an institution, has created separate specialized schools of agriculture, engineering, and other vocations. Latin America combines the technical and higher vocational faculties in its universities, but these are specialized divisions, not providing a general education. It is in educational systems which stem from the British schools that one finds the combination of general or liberal and special vocational studies in the same curricula.

This characteristic also marks the American high school, with which, as we shall show, the new colleges were to be closely connected. The high school also is different from the schools of its type in other countries. The difference is found particularly in its comprehensiveness. Proposing to enroll "all American youth," it attempts to provide a program of courses that will serve every large interest group. The new college was a similarly liberal-vocational school that combined many of the functions of the old college and the technical school; and it has prospered because it has succeeded in opening new doors to youth.

The original name was fairly descriptive. It was a college of agriculture

269

and mechanic arts. Neither of these subjects was well developed in 1860, and the term *engineering* was not much used in early days. More recently the name *land-grant college* has gained in favor, but its brevity is its only recommendation, for it does not indicate the nature or the functions of the school. In view of the prodigality of the government of post-Civil War times, one might with equal appropriateness speak of land-grant railroads. Still later the schools have in many cases adopted the name *state college*, which at least indicates that they are public institutions. We shall use these titles interchangeably.

Both the high school and the new college had from the first, or they have developed, a decidedly vocational purpose. Education in the United States became pragmatic long before the word was chosen as "a new name for an old way of thinking." The philosopher merely tried to justify a program that had already commended itself to the active portion of the community. The pragmatic, vocational purpose provided a powerful drive for educational experiment. From ancient times to modern, vocations had been acquired by the conventional, unimaginative method of apprenticeship. The development of schools that joined science and practice marked a new educational epoch. In the nineteenth century such schools were still new, and the land-grant college, especially, was founded upon the view that science could become useful in agriculture and industry.

It was not a doctrine that could be easily made acceptable to the working farmers and mechanics. We shall trace several of the efforts to develop schools of agriculture and engineering prior to the Morrill (land-grant) Act of 1862. Private schools and academies in the colonies and the young nation, as we have shown, taught surveying, navigation, bookkeeping, and other vocational activities. Such training, with some practical experience added, prepared young men to build roads and canals, to lay out towns, and to perform other construction work. Fairfield Academy in New York was known for its elementary engineering courses. The Erie Canal, which was opened in 1825, was built by young men whose schooling was obtained in an academy. Here we have a beginning in the teaching of one of the main fields of the land-grant college, namely, what the Morrill Act called the mechanic arts.

SCHOOLS OF A NEW ERA

The opening of the Erie Canal may be taken to mark a new epoch in the life of the United States, the beginning of the age of the canals, railroads, and mass transportation inland. At that time there were no schools of civil engineering in the United States; but the national Military Academy at West Point, which had been established in 1802 and reformed in 1815, prepared military engineers. In times of peace some of these young lieutenants, having resigned their commissions, turned their training to the building of railroads and public works, and some to the teaching of engineering in colleges and academies. Joseph G. Swift, the first West Point graduate, taught such courses at Hobart College. Captain Alden Partridge, when he was dismissed from his position as superintendent of the Military Academy, established Norwich University, where he developed an engineering course. At the old Cincinnati College another West Point graduate began a course in civil engineering in 1836. He was Ormsby M. Mitchel, who made a fortune not by teaching engineering but by practicing it and investing in the railroads that he built.

The supply of engineers from the Military Academy was, however, limited and the demand was increasing. With the growth of cities and the large factories, needing streets, water, power, and other facilities, with the westward expansion of the nation redoubling the need for transportation, with the Civil War and the economic expansion that followed, the demand for engineers increased in a geometrical ratio. And this is where the land-grant colleges came in.

Experiments in the teaching of agriculture proceeded in step with the first attempts to teach engineering. There was no logical necessity for the union, and today, when the two are taught in the same institution as they are in the land-grant college, they are administered in completely separate departments. The reason for their more intimate union in early days is the historical one that the farmer in earlier times had to be a jack-of-all-trades. This may account also for the early designation of the land-grant institutions as colleges of agriculture and mechanic arts.

The idea of a school of agriculture and related skills had occurred to several men, including Thomas Jefferson, before 1800. Further interest in the matter may have been created by the introduction of the Fellenberg manual labor education, but this proved to be an unfortunate effort, partly because it favored practice without science. Several academic colleges undertook to teach agriculture and failed for the opposite reason. They were unable to apply their sciences to practical life. And experience seems to indicate that new kinds of instruction to serve a new clientele are more successful in specially designed schools. A radically new departure is likely to be emasculated if it is made a part of an old school with a successful tradition. To receive fair treatment it must be put into the care of its friends. This is part of the reason why the land-grant colleges succeeded after much travail when other attempts had failed.

Two specially designed schools that were as successful as their resources permitted were the Gardiner Lyceum of Maine and the Rensselaer School of New York. Robert Hallowell Gardiner owned large tracts of land on the Kennebec River. These he donated about 1820 to found a school "to prepare youth by a scientific education to become skillful farmers and mechanics." He had found surveyors and millwrights working by rule-of-thumb, wholly ignorant of the principles underlying their work. "Our farmers were still less intelligent," he wrote. The school was incorporated with six trustees in 1822, received aid from the two-year-old state of Maine, and prospered through the ministrations of a succession of remarkable teachers. Three of these, Benjamin Hale, John H. Lathrop, and Ezekiel Holmes, left their mark on education in several states. The program of studies in 1824 included English but no foreign language, chemistry, agricultural chemistry, physics, mathematics, and navigation; but the courses were largely individual and elective, the students working on experiments and special topics. This highly flexible plan and the fact that the school had a system of student self-government, already mentioned in an earlier chapter, raises the question whether its founder and teachers were acquainted with the work of the Hill family at Hazelwood School in England. The Gardiner Lyceum has been called "America's first agricultural school"; but after it lost its state subsidy, about 1831, it became under uninspired teachers a humdrum New England academy.

The second specially designed and temporarily successful school of applied science was founded in 1825 at Troy, New York, by Stephen Van Rensselaer and named for him, Rensselaer School. The founder was one of the feudal landlords, deriving from the Dutch patroon system of the early settlements. Since he collected rents from vast estates, one reason for his interest in agricultural prosperity is obvious. The Rensselaer School used laboratory and field-experience methods in teaching chemistry, physics, geology, natural history, and other sciences useful to farmers. The purpose was the indirect one of preparing teachers "to instruct rural youth in the application of science to the common purposes of life." The school educated many men who became eminent as college professors, state geologists and entomologists, or consulting chemists, but, as in the case of the early land-grant colleges, few of the graduates became teachers of farm children. In 1835 a brief course in civil engineering was offered and became so popular that the school quickly became a technological institution. It is now called the Rensselaer Polytechnic Institute.

A number of other agricultural schools were projected or established. The Cream Hill School in Connecticut and the Farmer's College near Cincinnati were actually opened and maintained for some years. In New York Simeon DeWitt's plan for an agricultural college and the People's College proposed by Harrison Howard and in Virginia the farm school proposed by Richard Kidder Meade were unrealized projects. With a little more skill and management the People's College might have succeeded. There were also efforts to establish state colleges. It was the failure of the New York legislature to follow the lead of Jesse Buel about 1823 that caused Van Rensselaer to create his private school. The Massachusetts legislature debated the question of a state school about the same time but also refused to act. With all this interest and these "near misses" it was clear that some state would soon hit the target at which so many had aimed. And this actually happened. Michigan, Maryland, and Pennsylvania almost simultaneously about 1857 established state schools or colleges of agriculture that proved to be permanent institutions. The movement had been growing for several decades, and Justin S. Morrill, who had such a large part in furthering it, became a congressman just in time to capitalize upon the interest created by the propaganda.

FIRST MORRILL BILL

Morrill was the author of the land-grant bill. This is not denied. But after the colleges had become successful and the original moves had been forgotten, a debate arose over the origin of the idea. There were many direct anticipations of the land-grant act. A call for a federal land endowment for state schools of science, agriculture, engineering, and business was contained in a memorial to Congress submitted by Alden Partridge in 1841. He had even proposed that the proceeds should be distributed to the states in proportion to their representation in Congress. It is possible that Partridge was Morrill's prompter in regard to these ideas. It is even probable, for they lived in the same part of Vermont, and Morrill's business partner was a trustee of Partridge's school, Norwich University. Indeed, Morrill himself had been proposed for a place on the board but refused the invitation. It is known that the two men met and Partridge was not one to conceal his ideas; but yet actual demonstration of Morrill's debt to Partridge is lacking.

The attempt to link Morrill with Jonathan B. Turner of Illinois College at Jacksonville ends in a similarly indefinite conclusion. A number of farmers and industrialists in Illinois attempted to obtain federal aid for vocational education. This so-called "Turner Movement" persuaded the Illinois legislature in 1853 to adopt a resolution asking Congress for a donation to each state of half a million acres of public land for a state industrial university. Turner proposed to have these institutions formed to prepare teachers of agriculture and industrial subjects in high schools and lyceums. It was Turner's view that the higher institutions would reform the lower, making them practically useful to farmers, mechanics, and the working people in general. But as in the case of Partridge, the debt of Morrill to Turner has not been proved. There has been some tendency to minimize Turner's ability and to consider him a blunderhead; but his idea that the colleges should prepare teachers of agriculture and engineering has proved sounder than Morrill's program.

One may believe that Morrill must have learned about the proposals for agricultural schools that were so widely published. Many men for many years had been trying to devise a workable scheme. Yet Morrill claimed that the ideas in his bills were his own; but he freely admitted that some of his colleagues in Congress helped him in getting the legislative approval which gave the ideas all their importance. Some present-day students have concluded that the exact opposite was the fact, that the basic ideas of the legislation were gathered from various sources, but that it was Morrill's parliamentary skill and his persuasive advocacy of the proposals that secured the passage of both the agricultural education bills introduced by him.

The first of these bills was passed by Congress in 1859. It provided for the appropriation to each state of 20,000 acres of public land for each of a state's members in Congress. This endowment was to support colleges of agriculture and the mechanic arts. The bill permitted the teaching of the usual academic subjects but the vocational branches were to be especially emphasized. In the debate Morrill declared that his purpose was simply "to do something for the farmer"; but it has been conjectured that his original idea, not publicly acknowledged, was to attach the farmers and industrial workers to the new Republican Party. The debates and the voting on the bill were strongly partisan in complexion, the Whigs and Republicans generally voting for it and the Democrats against it, Northerners generally favoring and Southerners opposing it. It was the time of the Kansas-Nebraska Act, the Dred Scott decision, and the John Brown raid. Instead of considering the educational purpose and probable effect of the law, the debate ranged over questions of states' rights and constitutionality and the probable effect of the dispersal of a quantity of public lands, which was, however, a mere trifle compared to the vast empire donated to the railroads.

According to the bill the land was to be unequally distributed, the largest amounts going to the most populous states. Some argued that this was, on a per capita basis, an equal distribution. These ignored the fact that certain basic expenditures may be just as great for a small as for a larger college. This same question of what constitutes a just and equal distribution was to reappear again and again in the consideration of subsequent educational legislation. The members from the large and rich states are usually reluctant to share their funds with the poorer states. The same broad, humanly selfish attitude that troubled the Constitutional Convention in 1787 frequently appears in educational administration. It was this trait that was revealed in the claim that the state has no right to tax a man for the education of another man's children. Cities do not willingly help in the support of rural schools. Federal aid bills have a difficult time in Congress for several reasons, but one of them is that rich states want to reserve all their wealth for their own use. The author of the land-grant bill certainly saw that it would be difficult to secure its passage unless the states with many votes were given the greater prizes. He reported that his colleagues to whom he appealed for advice applauded the purpose of the measure but doubted that it had any chance of adoption. The bill was passed in February, 1859.

The debate had provided the chief topics for the veto message that

President James Buchanan sent to Congress. The President said that the bill showed disregard of the financial needs of the government in a time of stringency. This was a reference to the economic distress of 1857. The land market would be glutted by the offer of so many million acres for sale at one time and the government would lose millions. He predicted that the states would soon ask for further aid from the Treasury and this prophecy did indeed come true. He thought the government had "no power and should have no power" to follow the donation into the states to make sure that it would be applied to its intended object. This statement incidentally reveals that there was no real substance to the argument that this law would infringe upon the rights of the states. If the government was helpless in the case it could not at the same time interfere with "state sovereignty." But what the President seemed to imply was that the states could not be trusted. Measures have since been taken to guarantee that federal funds granted to the states for education will be properly applied. The laws that serve this purpose would not have been approved by extreme advocates of states' rights.

The President also held that the law would injure the existing colleges, many of which, he incorrectly believed, were already teaching agriculture. There were only a few efforts in that direction, and these were feeble. Without federal aid it is unlikely that they would have soon succeeded. The argument of the message may be largely specious, but as it restated the proclaimed views of almost half of the members of Congress, the supporters of the bill did not have the power to override the veto. The Civil War and the political and economic forces of later times completely changed the opinion of the country in this matter. Congress has passed several bills providing federal aid to the states for vocational education. Beginning with Lincoln, half a dozen Presidents of both major parties have signed these acts without vetoing or probably even contemplating the veto of any one of them. One cannot miss the significance of this centralizing and nationalizing trend. We shall take up the first and most fundamental of these federal laws, fundamental because it created the institution through which the later laws are administered.

MORRILL ACT OF 1862

Outside of Congress the agitation for a land-grant college law continued after the veto as before. In Congress, Morrill made what he later acknowledged to have been a rather fretful speech; but in December, 1861, he gave notice to the House that he intended to introduce a bill similar to the previous one. This new bill, after a debate that dealt mainly with public land questions and, as in the former case, hardly at all with educational objectives, was passed and became law through the signature of Lincoln in July, 1862. Two months earlier the Congress had enacted another law that was to have the most far-reaching influence upon the real purposes of the Morrill Act. By that earlier law the Congress had created the United States Department of Agriculture.

In his new bill Morrill had made two major changes from the earlier version. The law as enacted raised the amount of land per member of Congress from 20,000 to 30,000 acres; and it provided that the new colleges were to teach military tactics. According to the new multiplier, New York, with thirty-three members in both Houses, would and did receive eleven times as much free land as Kansas, a new state, with its two senators and a single representative. There were several states that received the smallest possible amount, but we may continue our comparison between New York and Kansas. New York obtained 990,000 acres, or forty-three townships, and Kansas was to have 90,000 acres. The amount actually bestowed was about 97,000 acres. There was no discrimination. The comparison only shows the inequality resulting from the fair application of a bad principle.

The total amount of the grants to all the states under the Morrill Act was 16,000 square miles. This seems like a large amount when one compares it with the areas of the smaller states. There are eight states each with an area of less than 16,000 square miles. But the public lands at one time and another held in trust by the nation comprised about two-thirds of its whole area. Of this vast expanse the agricultural college grant was a small fraction. It is still a small fraction when the comparison is made only with the lands that were granted to various railroads. The government made its first grant of public lands to encourage railroad building in 1850. But in 1862 Congress chartered the Union Pacific Railroad and in less than a decade it chartered, and out of the public lands endowed with more than royal munificence, a whole group of great railroad corporations. Also in 1862 Lincoln signed the Homestead Act, which gave a quarter-section of land without cost to any citizen who would improve it and live on it for five years. These and other historical facts are pertinent to any consideration of the grants for education by the Congress of 1862.

The other change made by Morrill in his second bill, the military training requirement, has sometimes been taken to mean that although the colleges are enjoined to teach military tactics, this training may be made optional to the students. Some of the colleges have at times followed this course. But it may be doubted that this was the intent of the framer of the law or of the Congress. We were at war when the bill was passed. Morrill, arguing for the clause, said that the training would improve our preparation against possible foreign enemies. It may be noticed also that Morrill and his colleagues could have known little by report and less by experience of elective systems and optional exercises in college. Such practices were still rare in 1862. In practice, as indicated, some of the colleges have at some time made military training optional with the students. But in nearly all, state law or college regulation has made it a requirement for graduation. Conscientious objectors have in some cases been excused.

According to the Morrill Act each state that accepted the grant was required to apply the proceeds "to the endowment, support, and maintenance of, at least, one college, where the leading object shall be, without excluding other scientific and classical studies, and including military tactics, to teach such branches of learning as are related to agriculture and the mechanic arts, in such manner as the legislatures of the States may respectively prescribe, in order to promote the liberal and practical education of the industrial classes in the several pursuits and professions in life." This language may upon a first reading seem clear; but it proved puzzling to the founders of the colleges, who attempted to use the wording as a guide in developing new institutions. The extreme positions were occupied by opposing groups: those who preferred a broad, inclusive construction of the sentence and those who insisted in placing a narrow and strict limitation upon the studies that could be considered as related to agriculture and the mechanic arts.

The broad constructionists argued for the study of the necessary mathematics, science, and language that would enable the student to understand the principles of his business. The strict constructionists took a "practical" and at the extreme a trade-school view. In the end the broad constructionists won the argument, but since their plan required thorough preparation for entrance and the early students were not well prepared, the victory was delayed for many years. At last it became clear that without a sound scientific and scholarly foundation there can be no collegiate teaching of agriculture or engineering.

ORGANIZATION OF THE COLLEGES

Many of the states hesitated to accept the grant. Each had the right to decide upon the location and, within the terms of the act, upon the character of the college. Broad and narrow construction were both within its terms. State legislatures normally set up committees or outside boards to solve these critical questions, and these bodies sometimes split into warring factions. Existing colleges also, without ever having thought about the matter before, suddenly discovered their fitness and asserted their eagerness to serve as land-grant colleges. Not only sectarian colleges or struggling little schools but proud state universities entered into the contest for the federal funds. Evan Pugh of Pennsylvania, who was an able promoter of this type of "new education," referred to the undignified haste of the literary colleges to grasp for resources to which they had no legitimate claim. In Michigan, Maryland, and Pennsylvania the grant was given to the state schools of agriculture that had recently been founded. In Ohio a college of agriculture and mechanic arts and in Illinois an industrial university were created, but these within a few years were transformed into state universities that included the teaching of agriculture and the mechanic arts.

In fifteen states, where the state university had become well established, the land-grant institution was made a part of it, whereas in twenty-eight others it was established as a separate "A. and M." college. Later other states accepted the former of these two plans. In Morrill's home state of Vermont, when an effort was made to separate the land-grant college from the state university, he opposed the proposal. Massachusetts founded a separate college of agriculture over the opposition of Harvard, Amherst, Williams, and other colleges. This has now become the University of Massachusetts, but it still devotes most of its strength to agriculture, horticulture, and home economics. In this state, however, one-third of the Morrill Act grant was assigned to a private school, the Massachusetts Institute of Technology, for engineering education.

In several other states the grant was assigned to private institutions with results that were not always happy. In four of these the federal grant was afterwards withdrawn from the private institution and applied to a newly organized land-grant college. One of the cases occurred in Connecticut, where the Sheffield Scientific School of Yale University was at first selected to receive the grant. To many this seemed an admirable choice, because Yale had an excellent record in science instruction dating from the early years of the century when Benjamin Silliman joined her faculty. More recently a school of applied chemistry had been developed. And the Yale authorities took special care to assure themselves that they had the facilities needed to meet the demands of the law. They invited its author to a conference at the Sheffield School and Morrill informed them that a farm was not absolutely necessary to fulfill the law's requirements. It had been his purpose, he said, to establish schools of science rather than agricultural schools. The title of the bill, Morrill declared, was not his but was assigned to it by a clerk and was not altogether appropriate. This is one more example of Morrill's vacillation when dealing with educational questions. It is hardly profitable to argue about the source of his ideas when he could not remember what they were.

The farmers of Connecticut had other and more settled ideas. They thought Yale treated agriculture as a secondary interest. They objected to the high admission requirements and the theoretical nature of the teaching. The Grange began to agitate for the removal of the grant to a school that would be closer to the soil. In the Cream Hill School of Agriculture they thought they had an example of what was needed. The Storrs Agricultural School was founded in 1881. It became the Storrs Agricultural College in 1893, and the federal funds were transferred to it after the state had indemnified Yale for their loss. The Storrs School was renamed Connecticut State College in 1933 and the University of Connecticut in 1939. It seems probable that this title will still be in use when the centennial year rolls around in 1981. Other unfortunate unions that ended in divorce occurred at Transylvania University in Kentucky and at Dartmouth College. In a few cases, as at Cornell and Rutgers Universities, the affiliation with a private institution became a permanent arrangement.

The colleges did not find it easy to live within their means. Their lands were mismanaged in some cases or sold at bargain prices. More than half of the states sold them at less than the customary $1.25 per acre, and three states received less than fifty cents per acre. The funds were not always safely invested. The same political and financial irregularities that had led to the dissipation of the federal grants for common schools reappeared in the management of the college. To this there were exceptions. The Cornell lands, for example, were selected and managed by Ezra Cornell, and the university realized an average of just over $5.50 per acre on its almost 1,000,000 acres.

Some clear conclusions may be drawn from this history. Because most American colleges were financially poor they grasped for the "new money" of the federal grant without considering how well they were qualified to carry out the program. But also there was no definite understanding of the program. Even Morrill had no developed plan. Local and state pressure groups exerted undue influence in locating and organizing the schools. And the states failed to secure the services of experts on the conservation and management of their lands and trust funds.

COLLEGE PROBLEMS

Other perplexing discoveries came to light. One was that the much advertised demand for the colleges did not come from working farmers. This is shown by the epithets they used and the scorn they heaped upon the schools. After all the clamor about the urgent need for agricultural education, it was found that the men who followed the plow and fed the cattle had little respect for the "book farming" taught in the "cow colleges." And what was worse, there was little scientific agriculture to be taught because the science was in its infancy. Partly for this reason the long exploded manual labor scheme was tried and rejected again. At the Michigan State Agricultural College the students were required to work three hours a day doing ordinary farm work and chores. And this was not unusual. Manual labor, after it was given up in the arts colleges and theological seminaries, was revived in the colleges of agriculture and in time again discarded.

It was found that the young people from the country schools could not read, write, and figure well enough for the work the colleges attempted to do. One-fourth of the students who applied for admission did not have "a good common school education" and the colleges found it necessary to establish preparatory departments. And this was true in Massachusetts as well as in Iowa and Kansas. This evidence in regard to the state of common school education in the country districts is supported by the fact that it was the universal practice of normal schools to review the common branches in regular classes. It also has bearing upon the present controversy over the past and present effectiveness of the schools in teaching the four R's.

In technical matters the early professors were not well prepared. They were, without question, educated men, but educated in classics, theology, or, best of all, in medicine. One early professor, whose later success and reputation permitted him to be candid, has described his own beginning practice. He said: "I began to tell the students what I knew about farming. It did not take me long to run short of materials." There was nothing in the library to help him. "One might as well have looked for cranberries in the Rocky Mountains." And "thus fortunately," he concluded, "I was driven to take the class to the field and farm. . . ." This was the tactic of Isaac Roberts, later professor at Cornell University, who obtained practical teaching materials by having students collect weeds from the nearby farms. In other classes the pupils had to recite not merely the ideas but even the words of the textbook.

Every new curriculum departure raises a similar problem: Where to find those who can teach what they have not been taught? On the nonsensical theory that everyone has to be taught everything that he will be called upon to do, there could be no progress whatever. The answer is that a few men of talent will invent new methods, organize materials, and devise equipment. When the new schools become better established, they can supply each other with capable teachers; and this is what the land-grant colleges did. They were aided by the experiment stations, as we shall see.

Step by step the schools developed new policies. Women were admitted almost from the first at several colleges, and at Kansas State College from the very beginning. At Iowa State College about one-third of the students in the first quarter-century were women. Michigan and Illinois admitted women in 1870, Nebraska in 1871. They were not better prepared than the men, and many were placed in the preparatory departments. Kansas established a "kitchen laboratory" in 1874, and early forms of home economics teaching were introduced in a number of the colleges. Manual training was taught to men. Winter short courses on the campus and farmers' institutes off the campus were undertaken. The long vacation was placed in midwinter to permit students to earn money teaching in country schools. Some schools attempted to arrange their courses so that those who would not graduate could obtain the greatest practical value from their studies.

Everything possible was done to attract students, but to little avail.

Enrollments remained low until about 1900. In the early decades engineering attracted more students and proved itself more teachable and more useful when acquired than agriculture. Only one-third of the early graduates had been enrolled in agriculture, and most of these did not engage in farming, but entered government service, or became scientists or teachers. This condition changed as the applications of science to agriculture became better developed and the colleges became able to offer more useful and specialized courses in agronomy, animal husbandry, horticulture, and other fields.

Among the several agencies for the creation of a scientific agriculture, the experiment stations had a leading role. Such institutions were well known in Europe and their value was demonstrated before they were introduced into America. Evan Pugh, the first head of the Pennsylvania State University, after obtaining a doctor's degree in chemistry in a German university, undertook a research project in plant physiology at the famed experimental farms at Rothamsted in England. After or even before the land-grant colleges were established, provision for experimental farms was generally made. At least seventeen states had created such farms or stations before federal assistance was given. But in 1887 Congress passed the Hatch Act appropriating $15,000 annually to each state for agricultural research. This amount was increased by the Adams Act of 1906 and the Purnell Act of 1925. These laws recognized that the improvement of teaching in the colleges waited upon the advancement of knowledge. The experiment station became the research arm, coordinate with the teaching function of each land-grant college.

SECOND MORRILL ACT

The colleges had early learned that they could not thrive on their endowments. Much of the land, as we have seen, had been sold at low prices, the proceeds had not always been well invested, and as a result the annual income was often small and uncertain. One state reported an annual income of less than $7,000. The institutions, mindful that they were to be the institutions of the poor, had a tender conscience and also a sober wisdom that restrained them from setting high rates of tuition or piling fees upon fees. But they needed money. Within a decade after 1862 they were back, as President Buchanan had foreseen, knocking upon the door of the Treasury.

Morrill, whose interest in the schools never flagged, initiated a campaign for an annual money grant to colleges that had been "permanently endowed" by a land grant. This bill proposed to provide equal amounts to the small and the large states. It was repeatedly introduced into Congress in 1872, 1873, 1875, 1879, and so on until 1890, when it finally overcame the long-continued opposition. With the signature of President Benjamin Harrison the second Morrill Act became law.

During the years while the bill had been under consideration, several states had come to understand that their state universities could not prosper without regular support. The land-grant colleges, on the same ground, appealed to the Congress. The second Morrill Act provided for an annual appropriation from the national Treasury to each land-grant college of $15,000 for the first year, the amount to rise by $1,000 each year to a maximum of $25,000 a year. This maximum was to become the regular and permanent contribution of the government to the current expense of each college.

The law had another provision. It required that the annual appropriation of the act should be withheld from states that required the segregation of the races unless they provided agricultural and mechanical colleges for blacks. Thus the law in effect required the establishment of the 17 such institutions that are now in operation in the Southern states. These have been noticed in the preceding chapter.

In the debates on the bill some echoes of old disputes were heard and early experiences of the college recited. It was reported that speculators had resold college lands purchased at a fraction of the government price for a hundred times the amount paid for them. At one time Morrill had proposed joining his forces with the supporters of the Blair Bill, mentioned in Chapter 9; but when he discovered that this bill would not pass, he concentrated upon his own objectives and succeeded. The old confusion between broad and narrow education plagued the debates. Really there still were three main views: that the colleges should teach rule-of-thumb farming and shopwork; or that they should teach the application of science to agricultural, engineering, and related interests; or that they should aid the poor, the children of farmers and industrial workers, to obtain a college education. Morrill himself said in 1890 that the colleges should teach "all the learning demanded by any portion of the American people." With this somewhat ambitious phrase we may compare Ezra Cornell's desire to "found an institution where anyone may study anything."

The land-grant institutions may not be able to meet such inclusive demands, but, in competition and cooperation with state and independent universities, they have themselves become universities. With a vocational emphasis that is wanting in some other higher educational institutions, they have developed their own programs without much regard for the abstract ideas of legislators and philosophers. And in the process they have not only met the demands of the technological callings but have helped to develop new vocations that were not anticipated by the founders.

Never in any of the debates on the bills introduced by Morrill was it proposed that the land-grant colleges should prepare teachers. But by 1890 and 1900 several state and independent universities had begun to establish departments or schools of education. Many high schools were teaching manual training and shopwork, home economics, and agriculture, the very subjects in which the land-grant colleges were supposed to be expert and for which they might well have been commissioned to prepare teachers. Yet they did not actively enter upon this work until the twentieth century.

A slight beginning was made through the effort to secure increased income for their rapidly expanding work. The Nelson Amendment to provide further support was added to the 1907 appropriation bill of the Department of Agriculture. A proviso was inserted to permit a part of the money to be used for the preparation of teachers of agriculture and the mechanic arts. The effect of this would have been to draw the high schools into closer relations with the colleges. Actually not much of the new money was applied in preparing teachers. But a decade later the foundation was laid for a nationwide system of vocational education and the preparation of high school vocational teachers. Thus the land-grant colleges came to prepare teachers on a great scale. But before this came about the Congress developed a nationwide system of extension teaching. This action was directly influenced by the boys' and girls' club work.

RURAL CLUB WORK

Many parents knew long ago that young people on the farm take more interest in their work if they are given a calf, or colt, to raise as their own property; and it helps to make the youngsters not only better farmers but also better people. Parents often acted upon this principle, which involves some of the elements of club work.

Not only parents but also editors, railroad presidents, agricultural fair executives, superintendents of schools, and other community leaders sometimes acted upon the same principle. They may have been idealists or their aid to the youth may have been a skillful form of advertising. In either case the results were the same. Horace Greeley of the New York *Tribune* paid a prize of $50 to the teen-age winner of a New York corn growing contest. This was in 1856 and the yield of the measured acre was seventy-six bushels of shelled corn—very good for 1856. Similar contests were held in other states. Although these events lacked the scientific basis and the professional guidance of present-day club work, they grew from the grass-roots and were publicly and genuinely competitive.

A high proportion of the leaders of these competitions were rural school officers, and many of the activities were connected with the schools. We have seen that Arbor Day, school gardens, and the nature study movement all began in the latter half of the century. Liberty H. Bailey and his Cornell University associates were among the leaders. We shall mention a few of the school people who led in club work. A township superintendent,

A. B. Graham, in Clark County, Ohio, organized a boys' farm club in 1902. Many people had similar ideas, but he was certainly among the early ones. A rural county superintendent, O. J. Kern, was forming similar groups in Illinois. Both men secured help from their state universities and experiment stations. These institutions had a particular interest in the matter because they wanted to get plain dirt farmers to try fertilizers, seeds, kinds of tillage, and other experiments. Kern seems to have been more concerned to develop the interest of parents and children in the schools than he was in growing bigger crops. He tried to connect farm and school by drawing upon the farm work for problems in arithmetic and other school subjects. Kern also organized girls' clubs and campaigned for school gardens.

The true club requires the members to follow the most scientific procedure that can be applied and demands of every member a full account of all expenses, materials used, work done, and every pertinent feature. Everything is measured and stated in quantitative terms. The work is supervised by a competent leader. Prizes and recognition are given to the most successful. This club idea for farm boys and girls spread incredibly fast from state to state and took in more and more activities. In the South it was connected with Seaman A. Knapp's farm demonstrations; and it spread over the country with the county-agent idea.

As superintendent of schools of a Minnesota county, T. A. Erickson developed a program of educational and agricultural improvement similar to that of O. J. Kern in Illinois. In 1905 he used his own money to provide a number of boys with seed corn, the next year he added potatoes, and then settings of eggs. J. J. Hill of the Great Northern Railroad gave him a very modest sum for a prize. Erickson became rural school specialist of the state university and was commissioned to give aid to teachers in working out their agricultural problems.

In Georgia Joseph Stewart, professor of secondary education at the state university, in 1906 developed a system of corn and cotton growing contests. Those teen-age growers who won in their counties qualified to compete in the state contest. Stewart persuaded the State Fair Association to put up $500 for prizes. Georgia was the first state to declare a state corn champion. All this was a part of Stewart's work, which has already been mentioned, of developing high schools.

A similar kind of promotion was carried on by a county superintendent of schools in Oregon. In 1905 Louis R. Alderman organized a county children's fair. There were contests in gardening, cooking, woodworking, raising farm animals, and other activities. Alderman persuaded the Union Stockyards of Portland to provide a full-time man to travel over the state organizing these county children's fairs. This has been claimed as the origin of the 4-H Club movement in the Northwest.

The Department of Agriculture began to cooperate with the movement first in Iowa in 1912 and in half of the states by 1916. The land-grant colleges have also developed close relations with the 4-H Clubs, cultivating hand, head, heart, and health.

Farm demonstration work and the 4-H Clubs developed at the same time and there was work for both. Knapp found that lectures and bulletins are not enough and that farmers pay little attention even to demonstrations that are provided for them. They have to participate and risk their own land, time, and money in a project and then they do pay attention. Out of Knapp's work in fighting the boll weevil and doubling the Southern farmers' corn crop, there grew the work of the county agents. The first county agent was appointed in 1906 and the plan spread in the South and then in the North and West. The federal government began to aid this plan by making special appropriations for the purpose to the Department of Agriculture.

FEDERAL-STATE COOPERATION; SMITH-LEVER ACT

The idea of taking useful knowledge directly to the people was discussed in the meetings of the Association of Land-Grant Colleges in 1885, almost thirty years before the Smith-Lever Act was passed in 1914. When the time came to ask the government for regular and permanent support for extension teaching, Woodrow Wilson had just been elected President. He had never been identified with rural life and it fell to Walter Hines Page to explain to the President-elect the great value of farm demonstration work. Page's success was complete and agriculture was further reassured when David F. Houston became the new Secretary of Agriculture. In a period of three years Wilson approved three of the most important farm and agricultural education bills in the nation's history, the Smith-Lever Act (1914), the Federal Farm Loan Act (1916), and the Smith-Hughes Act (1917).

The Smith-Lever Act at last enabled the agricultural colleges to reach the working farmer and to help him directly with his problems. President Wilson called the law "one of the most significant and far-reaching measures for the education of adults ever adopted by any Government." The act was passed "to aid in diffusing among the people of the United States useful and practical information on subjects relating to agriculture and home economics, and to encourage the application of the same."

The cost of the program is shared almost equally between the federal government and the states. There is, however, for the first time, an element of federal control in a federal bill granting aid to education. The state program must meet standards set up by the Department of Agriculture; and the state director of agricultural extension represents both that department and the land-grant college. The element of federal-state cooperation and federal supervision was a departure from the *laissez-faire* policy of the Morrill Acts and its significance in this respect must not be overlooked.

The county agent, who is usually a land-grant college graduate, and who reports to the director at the state college, has been called "the key-teacher" of the extension program. He diffuses the knowledge that works, if any does work.

A few years fortunately were given the new extension service before the United States entered World War I. The difficulties and conflicts that arose between federal and state agencies were adjusted in a conference in 1916. In the war the service aided in producing, conserving, and distributing food, feeds, fertilizer, and seed, in the wise use of clothing and fuel, and in the preservation of health. The home demonstration agents were helpful in the 1918–1919 influenza epidemic. But military demands made it difficult to maintain the extension service and the losses had to be restored again after 1918.

COOPERATION, SECOND PHASE; SMITH-HUGHES ACT

The Smith-Hughes Act of 1917 was passed to foster the vocational education of youth aged fourteen or over, chiefly in high schools. The land-grant colleges were to prepare vocational teachers for the high schools; and these in turn broadened the vocational content of the high school program. The bill was intended to provide direction and financial aid for this expensive type of education.

The act called for a Federal Board for Vocational Education with the duty of annually apportioning to the states the federally provided funds. Each state was required to form or designate a state board of vocational education. The states accepted the plan with alacrity. Each state board submits its plan for vocational education to the federal board for approval. The power to approve or disapprove is obviously the power to exercise control. A similar scheme of national and local cooperation is used in England to maintain general education in primary and secondary schools. There the local education authorities submit development schemes to the office of the Ministry of Education in London. Whether such plans result in excessive centralization depends more upon the will of the people and the spirit of the administration than it does upon the letter of the law. Such a plan could be adapted to American needs if there is ever to be federal aid to general education.

The Smith-Hughes Act requires each state to provide for vocational education a sum equal to the amount that it receives for the same purpose from Washington. The money is to be used (1) to pay the salaries of teachers, supervisors, and directors of agricultural subjects; (2) to pay the salaries of teachers of trades, home economics, and industrial subjects; (3) to prepare teachers of all these subjects; (4) to study problems connected with the teaching of the same; (5) to pay for the administration of the law. The act includes a simple formula for determining each state's share of the annual appropriation. This formula is based upon the population census returns, and the rapid shifts from state to state and country to city that are taking place within the ten-year periods tend to create inequities that were not foreseen when the law was framed.

Table 10–1 shows the yearly amounts appropriated from 1917 to 1925 for each of the first four purposes that the law seeks to achieve.

TABLE 10–1
FEDERAL FUNDS APPORTIONED UNDER THE
SMITH-HUGHES LAW, 1917–1925

	Agric. Educa.	Home Ec. and T. and I.	Preparing Teachers of Agric., Home Ec., T. and I.	Research	Total Annual Federal Aid	Annual Increases
1917–1918	$ 500,000	$ 500,000	$ 500,000	$200,000	$1,700,000	
1918–	750,000	750,000	700,000	200,000	2,400,000	$ 700,000
1919–	1,000,000	1,000,000	900,000	200,000	3,100,000	700,000
1920–	1,250,000	1,250,000	1,000,000	200,000	3,700,000	600,000
1921–	1,500,000	1,500,000	1,000,000	200,000	4,200,000	500,000
1922–	1,750,000	1,750,000	1,000,000	200,000	4,700,000	500,000
1923–	2,000,000	2,000,000	1,000,000	200,000	5,200,000	500,000
1924–	2,500,000	2,500,000	1,000,000	200,000	6,200,000	1,000,000
1925–	3,000,000	3,000,000	1,000,000	200,000	7,200,000	1,000,000

The teaching for which the law provides must be on the secondary, not the college level. The pupils must be fourteen years of age or over. The courses may be provided for full-time or part-time pupils and they must be given in public schools. The Smith-Hughes teachers are attached to high schools and the law may be regarded as a high school law. From this standpoint its purpose is to expand the program of the public secondary school. The instruction is intended to prepare youth for agricultural, industrial, and home occupations of an immediately productive kind, and therefore the act is a vocational education law. While the agitation for such an act was in progress, there was a danger that a separate vocational education system would be established. Fortunately, this division of public education into competing systems was averted, but there are also difficulties in the administration of general and vocational education in the same school. There is a third consideration. The Smith-Hughes Act is a high school law and a vocational education law, but it is also a means of national preparedness. Food and technical skill are essential to national welfare under all conditions of peace or war.

COLLEGE GROWTH

Men have written of "the original conception" of the land-grant colleges as though these words could be made to stand for a clear and settled idea upon which people were agreed. But this is contrary to the facts. The founders and early promoters of the institutions did not agree upon any general plan, nor did their notions of means and ends remain unchanged through the years. The founders should be regarded as a quite miscellaneous group of politicians and creative social reformers trying to give expression to a set of abstract and only partially developed ideas. They were limited, as all reformers are, by the materials that were available for use. The materials with whom and with which they had to work were classically educated professors, poorly prepared students, inadequate funds, undeveloped sciences and methods, and an unresponsive public. Their "original conceptions" were indistinct and unstable, and they tried to make them clear and permanent by giving them expression in new institutions. And it was just this that favored the evolution of a new kind of college. The new institutions had to adapt themselves to a society already well supplied with colleges of older types. They had to be different.

One of the early and widely approved ideas was that the colleges were to be inexpensive, for otherwise farmers' and workingmens' children could not afford to attend. It was an "original conception" that the colleges should be free or low-cost schools. The lower schools and high schools that were in some states still collecting rates or tuition were made free in the period when the colleges were forming. The low fees of this new type of public schools, the land-grant colleges, were in harmony with the general trend of the time in public education.

In time in the administration of the colleges, this policy has been so modified or wholly abandoned that many people today do not know that it ever existed. The payments demanded of students grew slowly at first, reached fairly large annual amounts in the early years of the present century, and were doubled between World War I and the Great Depression. With the rise in operating costs have come both an increase in the number of fees and the requirement for students in public institutions to pay a rising proportion of the costs. The method by which these unjustifiable demands have been built up would often be the indirect one of piling one fee upon another in a series that might include matriculation, tuition, incidental, special, library, laboratory, athletic, health service, nonresident, and other fees. In one of the large state universities that contains the land-grant college, the students were asked to vote on the addition to their term-bills of a $5 fee to build a new student union. For obvious reasons, one being that most of the voters would not be payers very long, the measure was carried and the building is now in use; and this case was not unique. The state should erect and pay for state college and university buildings on state property. In some schools, professors have collected a book fee in their classes, and other abuses have grown up in connection with the student expenses in the public land-grant colleges. All this has a direct bearing upon the condition that for every student who is able to attend college there is another equally qualified prospective student who is kept away by the expense. It is hardly a sufficient answer to reply that the fees form only a fraction of the cost of a college education.

The growing college enrollment is a major reason for the increases in the fees. In a single year before the outbreak of World War II there were 20,000 students of home economics and 30,000 in agriculture. Although the numbers in veterinary medicine, forestry, and architecture were small, those in engineering and education were each over 100,000. The increasing size of the universities and colleges, especially of the public ones, is one of the phenomena of our time. And since every student costs the college several times as much as he pays, the larger the student body, the greater the funds that must be obtained from outside sources. The hard-pressed colleges do not wish to neglect any source of aid in balancing their budgets, such as the yield from new fees or of an increased tariff upon the old ones. But this is not in the interest of the student or of society if the social worth of a college education is what is claimed for it.

Many causes have promoted the increases in college attendance. Among these must be listed the development of new professions and callings, the acceptance of college-trained personnel in many business fields, the growth of cities that has drawn a larger proportion of the population to the vicinity of some college, the general prosperity, the very great changes that have occurred within the colleges themselves, and government aid for the education of veterans. All of these causes have affected enrollment in the land-grant colleges, but the internal development in these schools deserves special notice.

There has been a fundamental change in the general aims of the colleges. It is true that the sixty-nine institutions do not agree upon any single or closely similar statement of their aims, yet broad generalization from most of them is possible. The early colleges attempted to teach farming, housekeeping, and shop and trade practice to future practitioners. This is what the extension workers under the Smith-Lever Act and the Smith-Hughes teachers in the high schools, not the colleges, are doing now. The present colleges give more attention than they gave in early days to the basic sciences. Each student is usually asked also to choose a special field, such as dairy technology or clothing and textiles, and to study the applications of the sciences to it. The present-day colleges also give more attention than they formerly did to English, economics, sociology, and other humanistic and social subjects; in none do the curricula consist wholly of vocational subjects; in many the aim is to give a broad scientific and humanistic education with varied opportunities to acquire preparation in special fields.

The graduates become county agents, extension workers, teachers in high schools and in agricultural colleges. They engage in government service and in scientific research. Rural banking, the improvement, appraisal, and sale of land, the marketing of farm products, the management of estates, and farm journalism become the occupations of others. They build roads, design and manufacture machinery, and serve as operating and consulting engineers. They preside over good homes. All this is to say that the chief work of the land-grant colleges is not to prepare for general farming but rather to provide an education both cultural and useful. The broad aims and varied offerings of the colleges may be the most important of the reasons for the increased enrollments. This conclusion is supported by the fact that in the land-grant colleges, established to teach "agriculture and the mechanic arts," many of the students are in the division of arts and sciences. More are enrolled in the arts and sciences than in agriculture, or home economics. The colleges have become or are becoming universities. They are in more and more instances taking the name of university or state college.

The preparation of teachers has become one of the leading activities of the colleges. Instead of teaching the farmers themselves, as the founders had intended, they prepare teachers and county agents, and through these they reach thousands of present and future farmers and homemakers where the colleges could directly touch but a few. The close connection that has developed between the public schools and the colleges is significant. Pupils from the high schools go up to the state college and return to the high schools as superintendents, principals, teachers, board members, patrons, and taxpayers. The state college and the high school exert a mutual influence, each upon the other. And as a result the land-grant colleges have helped to enrich and diversify the program of public education of which they form an important part.

The broad constructionists of the original Morrill Act have gained a complete victory. The early effort to establish narrow trade schools never had any marked success, but the colleges began with directly practical goals. The act had, however, left a wide opening for the introduction of "other scientific" and even classical studies. This was a fortunate concession because the colleges discovered that scientific agriculture and engineering demand a sound general education as a prerequisite and foundation. The scientific vocations cannot be effectively taught to any who do not have a knowledge of English, mathematics, science, the use of books, and the art of study. Outside the colleges a vast urbanizing and technological change called for the broad, general education of millions who were no longer needed on the farm and of city-bred youth who were entering new vocations. As a result not only had the broad constructionists won, but the colleges were on the way to fulfill Morrill's dream, that of providing "all the learning demanded by any portion of the American people"; or, since the land-grant colleges do not teach law or medicine, it had better be said that the colleges and the universities together try to come as close to this vision as the realities of life permit.

SUMMARY

The land-grant college is a new type of institution, a vocational higher institution for the "industrial classes." The active period of its development may be dated from the opening of the Erie Canal in 1825 and the beginning of the railroads. The new transportation required more engineers, and the wasteful practices and isolation of the farmers required a new agriculture. There were many unsuccessful or temporarily successful attempts to establish schools of agriculture. From these efforts and a memorial to Congress in 1841, it seems probable, came the ideas of Morrill's Bill adopted in 1859 but vetoed by the president. The opposition to the bill was political, constitutional, and financial, and not to any great degree educational. Indeed, no one seems to have known just what educational results were intended. In 1862 a similar bill carrying a larger endowment and requiring military training in the projected colleges was enacted. And a supplementary bill to provide for current support, the second Morrill Act of 1890, required the establishment in the South of similar colleges for blacks. From these two measures sixty-nine land-grant colleges have resulted.

Several problems arose as a result of this legislation. First was the choice of a model for the organization of the colleges, and the choice fell out in favor of scientific rather than trade schools. The problem of regular support has been implied; and relief was obtained through the second Morrill Act supplemented by increasing appropriations by the states. The lack of scientific knowledge of agriculture was gradually overcome by the experiment stations that were aided by the Hatch Act. The failure to reach the working farmer and housewife was solved (1) by farm demonstrations, club work, county agents, and other extension work in the main brought under the terms of the Smith-Lever Act of 1914; and (2) by the teaching of agriculture, home economics, and trades and industries in the high schools under the Smith-Hughes Act of 1917.

The land-grant colleges have apparently been influenced by the state universities, which are older and reached relative maturity earlier. This is an excellent example of the "capture" of a groping institution by a more powerful one in the same "field"; and it was made easier by the union in many states of the state university and land-grant college. The land-grant college is less vocational and more general than it was. It offers an education that is both cultural and useful; and it prepares many teachers for the public schools.

QUESTIONS

1. Why did the land-grant colleges succeed although other attempts in the same field had failed? Discover reasons not mentioned in the chapter.
2. Compare the work of Hampton and Tuskegee with the early stages of the land-grant colleges.
3. In what ways did the earlier Rensselaer School anticipate land-grant college activities and problems?
4. Would an equal distribution of the public lands, in the same amount to each state, for the new colleges have served education more effectively than the method actually used? Why or why not?
5. What are the advantages and disadvantages of the separate land-grant college as compared with its union with the state university?
6. Consider the value of the land-grant colleges as cause and means for the development of the high schools. And compare this effect with the influence of the high schools upon the elementary schools.
7. How may one account for the difference between the present work and status of the colleges and the early ideas of what they should become?
8. What new activities should the colleges undertake?

BOOKS AND PAPERS

The magazine *Agricultural History*, the *Cyclopedia of Agriculture*, edited by Liberty Hyde Bailey, and the *Encyclopedia of Educational Research* have accounts of agricultural and vocational education, with bibliographies. The following list contains only a few of a large number of histories of individual land-grant colleges. On the plan of Mr. Meade of Virginia, which was to combine the ideas of Fellenberg and Amos Eaton, see the *American Farmer*, May 26, July 21, 1826, October 24, 1828, and October 1, 1830; and the *National Intelligencer*, September 29, 1830. Unfortunately, the plan was not put into effect.

BAILEY, J. C., *Seaman A. Knapp, Schoolmaster of American Agriculture*, Columbia University Press, 1945.

BLACKMAR, F. W., *History of Federal and State Aid to Higher Education*, Washington, U.S. Government Printing Office, Bureau of Education, Circular of Information, No. 1, 1890.

BLAUCH, LLOYD E., *Federal Cooperation in Agricultural Extension Work, Vocational Education, and Vocational Rehabilitation*, Washington, U.S. Government Printing Office, Office of Education Bulletin, 1935, No. 15, with bibliography.

BRUNNER, HENRY S., *Land-Grant Colleges and Universities*, Washington, D.C., U.S. Government Printing Office, 1962.

EDDY, EDWARD D. JR., *Colleges for Our Land and Time, The Land-Grant Idea in American Education*, New York, 1957.

ELIOT, CHARLES W., "The Achievements of the Democratic Party and its Leader Since March 4, 1913," *Atlantic Monthly*, October, 1916.

KANDEL, I. L., *Federal Aid for Vocational Education*. A report to the Carnegie Foundation for the Advancement of Teaching, Bulletin, No. 10, New York, 1917.

KLEIN, A. J., Director, *Survey of Land-Grant Colleges and Universities*, Washington, D.C., U.S Government Printing Office, Office of Education Bulletin, 1930, No. 9.

MORRILL, JAMES LEWIS, *The Ongoing State University*, University of Minnesota Press, 1960.

NEVINS, ALLAN, *The State Universities and Democracy*, University of Illinois Press, 1962.

PARKER, WILLIAM B., *The Life and Public Services of Justin Smith Morrill*, Boston, 1924.

POWELL, B. E., *Industrial Education and the Establishment of the University [of Illinois], 1840–1870*, University of Illinois, 1918.

PRICE, R. R., *Financial Support of State Universities in the Old Northwest Territory*, Harvard University Press, 1924.

RECK, F. M., *History of 4-H Club Work*, Iowa State College Press, 1951.

ROSS, EARLE D., *Democracy's College, the Land-Grant Movement in the Formative Stage*, Iowa State College Press, 1942; *History of Iowa State College*, 1942.

SMITH, C. B., and M. C. WILSON, *Agricultural Extension System of the United States*, New York, 1930.

STEMMONS, WALTER, *Connecticut Agricultural College, A History*, The College, 1931.

STEVENS, NEIL E., "America's First Agricultural School," *Scientific Monthly*, December, 1921. This excellent paper was mentioned in Chapter 4. The claim in the title may be arguable.

TRUE, A. C., *History of Agricultural Extension Work, 1785–1923*, Washington, D.C., U.S. Government Printing Office, 1928; *History of Agricultural Education, 1785–1925*, 1929; *History of Agricultural Experimentation and Research, 1607–1925; Including a History of the United States Department of Agriculture*, 1937.

WILLARD, J. T., *History of the Kansas State College of Agriculture and Applied Science*, Kansas State College Press, 1940.

WOODWARD, CARL R., "Woodrow Wilson's Agricultural Philosophy," *Agricultural History*, October, 1940.

Chapter 11

EDUCATION AS A PROFESSION

Whether there is a profession of education depends in part upon whether there is a science of education: the two questions thus connected are also partly distinct and independent of each other. There are no universally accepted answers. We shall examine the questions separately, considering first the existence of a science of education.

If there is such a science, it must deal with the nature of learning, the capacities and interests of pupils, the curricula, methods, administration and finances of schools, the educational needs of communities, and many other questions not unrelated to these. No one doubts that there is knowledge and intelligent opinion about these matters nor that teachers and administrators find this knowledge and instructed opinion useful and indeed necessary. Later chapters will provide a few illustrations of the development of such knowledge.

But is it science? The answer will depend upon the meaning given to science, a word of several meanings. There is a tendency, not the oldest tendency, to restrict the word to those branches that deal with matter and physical bodies. If we do this, we can distinguish the physical sciences, such as astronomy, physics, and chemistry, and the biological and medical sciences that are less exact but that can make probable predictions.

Education does not belong to either of these classes, but it uses some of the results of biological and medical studies; and it has a close dependence upon psychology, which is partly a biological and partly a social study. This brings us to a tendency, more recent than the one mentioned and contrary to it, namely, the tendency to stretch the word *science* to cover economics, sociology, politics, and anthropology, the social sciences. Many scholars resist this custom, but it seems to be growing. Education is certainly a social as well as a psychological study. If we are to recognize social sciences, education might well claim admittance into their circle.

There is, however, a special obstacle to this claim: education must take account not only of body and mind, biology and psychology, but also of

294

spirit and purpose. The teacher dare not use pupils as means. The physicist can do as he pleases with his material; the plant or animal breeder does not consult the welfare of his organisms; but the teacher cannot do as he pleases with his pupils and dare not for a moment disregard their welfare. Education is based upon ethics, as well as psychology and biology. It makes use of statistics, of history, of logic, and of general philosophy. It is, therefore, a practical study that draws upon all available knowledge that will promote the welfare of the pupils.

The oldest meaning of the word *science* has not been mentioned. In early times it meant nothing more than organized knowledge; and the root of the word signifies to know or to understand. Educators use a number of sciences, some highly developed, others largely empirical; and this composite may be called the science of education in the same way that we speak of the science of language, or the historical sciences. Like medicine, but to a less degree, education is a science; and to a greater degree it is an art. In speaking of the science of education, the qualifications mentioned in the preceding paragraphs should be remembered.

The educational calling includes many kinds of workers, from classroom teachers to superintendents of schools. When fully prepared they have the special knowledge and skill and the personal character and tact that the professions require. But many are not fully prepared, or remain in the work only temporarily. In public education they are government employees and lack the independence of the physician or lawyer; and there is little more freedom in private schools. The fact that many teachers are supervised and directed by a hierarchy of officials militates against their professional standing. The public also, which assesses the expertness of the physician and lawyer, does not consider the teacher as equally expert in his field. To the question whether there is an educational profession only a qualified affirmative can be given. But teaching is not a trade, and not a business. It is more nearly a profession.

EDUCATION AS A SCIENCE

The claim that education is a science was made by Johann Friedrich Herbart (1776–1841), but he spoke of it as a *Wissenschaft*, a broader term than the English word *science*, as this is now commonly used. As a realist, Herbart intended, at least, to develop both psychology and education into positive sciences. There is a connection between this purpose and his denial of the freedom of the will. The Scotsman Alexander Bain (1818–1903), a psychologist of the school of James Mill, chose as the title for a book the words, *Education as a Science* (1878). It has been claimed that William James drew heavily upon this book for his famous chapter on habit. *Education as a Science* presents a philosophical psychology and its bearings upon education, as well as some sections on educational values and methods of teaching. Despite its title it is not very scientific.

In the United States also the claim was made that education is a science. In 1885 William H. Payne published some of his papers under the title of *Contributions to the Science of Education;* but what he labeled science was humanistic and idealistic criticism. He translated Rousseau's *Emile*, Gabriel Compayré's *Histoire de la Pédagogie*, and other works. For his basic philosophy he went farther back into the past to the great systems of Plato and Aristotle, but what he presented, although stimulating, was neither science nor systematic philosophy, but criticism.

While Payne's book was still new, Wilhelm Dilthey (1833–1911), speaking before the Berlin Academy of Sciences, denied the possibility of a general science of education. He said the claims of Herbart and his contemporaries were an echo of the rationalism of their age when all institutions were to be explained by reason. But much had been learned since the eighteenth century, said Dilthey, namely, that institutions are historical. They are not planned; they grow, adapting themselves to time, and place, and people. Pedagogy alone, he claimed, is still in the arrested state in which it was left by the rationalists. Our system-makers still set up what they consider universal aims-according-to-nature. But no system of ethics has ever won universal acceptance; human nature has never been fully understood; and therefore, because education must be based upon ethics and psychology, it has to be tentative. Education must take account of its own past, out of which its present is growing, must take account also of the history of man and of the biology of the human organism. If the term *science* is to be applied to it we must understand that it has to be an inductive, exploratory, and tentative science, not a universal and dogmatic one.

Strange to say, these relativist views pleased the idealist philosopher Josiah Royce (1855–1916). He declared against the possibility of a real science of education. Although he cautioned the teacher against the danger of following fads, he recommended child study, object-teaching, and the appeal to children's interests. He thought the chief value of psychology lay in the guidance that it may offer to the teacher in the observation of her pupils. And even though education cannot become an exact science, the study of education is necessary.

As it happened, the study of education was pursued. Its students invented intelligence tests and devised educational measurements. Statistical methods were applied in some fields of educational interest. Even educational and, more frequently, psychological experiments were carried out. This further history suggests that the question raised by Dilthey and Royce had itself become antiquated. There is no universally valid system of government or medicine. We do not greatly miss the lack of such a system of education.

EDUCATION AS A BRANCH OF STUDY

The foundations of education as a separate study had been laid by Barnard, Mann, and their contemporaries. Further contributions were made in normal schools and universities, and by that new type of officer, the city superintendent of schools who conducted in-service training courses for his teachers. Of the latter group Edward A. Sheldon at Oswego was an active member. Much of the professional training of the time after the Civil War was still philosophical, but observation and experience also made their contributions. The work of Sheldon and G. Stanley Hall, the early stages of educational psychology, experience with the kindergarten, the industrial arts, and nature study, all made a contribution to the training of teachers and the practical study of education.

The topics to be considered in the present chapter are both theoretical and practical, and they will provide direct preparation for Chapters 14 and 15. Among those who had a part in developing the preparation for teaching as a profession were William H. Payne (1836–1907), a pioneer professor of education in a university, and William T. Harris (1835–1909), pioneer among superintendents of city schools. They represent the theoretical and the practical elements of the new study and may typify the large group of contributors who cannot be brought into one book.

It was a feature of the time that the main trunk of education as a professional study was dividing into special branches such as school management, methods of teaching, supervision, school law, educational psychology, and the history and philosophy of education. The universities began to offer different courses and sequences for academic teachers and school administrators and still others for teachers of such subjects as home economics, industrial arts, and agriculture. For a time it was possible for a single professor to teach all the education courses that a university offered, but these soon became more specialized. It is this early specialization that we are to consider. The specialization has gone to great lengths. The catalogue of a particular state college in 1955 listed fifty-nine education instructors and 127 courses, and this is, unfortunately, not a limiting case.

We may briefly return to the questions with which this chapter opens. Only qualified answers can be given. It will be admitted that some parts of the teaching vocation are professional. To answer the other question we inquired into the meaning of the word *science*. Like *Wissenschaft* today, it formerly meant knowledge, especially organized knowledge such as that of the "science of English grammar." It has been gradually broadened to include psychology, sociology, and anthropology. To the biological and behavioral sciences education belongs as we shall attempt to show in Chapter 14.

FACULTY PSYCHOLOGY

The system of ideas that forms what is called the faculty psychology is a philosophy of education, not a psychology only, although it employs psychological language. This philosophy was long dominant in America and Europe and maintained itself until 1900 and after. The concept of mental faculties is not, however, an American or a recent idea. It may be traced through the Scotch, the Germans, and in the Middle Ages through the Scholastics back to the founders of philosophy. Scotch immigrants, including John Witherspoon and many less known persons from various countries, brought it with them to America. It is not in good repute today, but it will be well not to speak too scornfully of it until we understand the nature of organism, mind, faculties, and training more fully than we do at present.

Mental faculties are supposed to be such capacities as the power to remember or to think or "to see a point." The notion has had a curious and disconcerting history. Whenever the science of psychology has expelled the faculties from its house, they have slipped in again and have become servants if not regular members of the family. Herbart, the arch-opponent of faculties, admitted that the words for them are very useful. The intelligence tests measure verbal, arithmetical, reasoning, and other abilities, and these are capacities, that is, faculties.

Some psychologists, after denying the existence of a faculty of memory, will assert that we have many memories. This is a way of getting rid of faculties by increasing their number. Others are willing to assume the existence of faculties if they are not regarded as sharply limited and separate. The matter of training is likewise troublesome. One must not speak of memory-training but of learning to remember by organizing materials serially or logically or otherwise into a system.

This account is not an argument for a return to the "faculty" psychology; and this is not the place to deal with these matters. They are considered in the books on psychology. We are here reporting the fact that the faculty psychology was the dominant philosophy of education in the middle of the last century and after. Francis Wayland (1796–1865) was an adherent of this school and he concluded his review of 1854 before the American Institute of Instruction with an outline of his views. Our faculties are, on the one hand, he declared, objective, giving us knowledge of the world around us, and on the other hand, are subjective, telling us of the energies and relations of the world within us. This is Locke's view. The object of education, Wayland continued, is to improve both classes of faculties, in a word, every power of the soul. So also said Pestalozzi and this aim was generally accepted. To improve the faculties was to train, discipline, or strengthen them; and in this process knowledge was to be acquired.

A Yale committee of 1828 had declared that "the two great points to be gained in intellectual education are discipline and the furniture of the mind; expanding its powers and storing it with knowledge." The faculties, so Wayland taught, can be strengthened only by exercise. All our studies should both increase our knowledge and improve our mental powers. We do not study one thing to strengthen the mind and another to increase our knowledge. Herbert Spencer agreed and called this an example of "the beautiful economy of Nature."

The next question concerns the order of the budding and flowering of the faculties. It was claimed that observation shows that the child does not have all the adult faculties; and the question was whether one, such as perception, develops before another, say, memory, or whether imagination becomes full-grown before the judgment. Wayland and his contemporaries were convinced that there is a serial development of the faculties; and that our system of education must recognize and follow that order. He wrote: "If there is an established succession in the development of the faculties, and if no faculty can be improved but by use, and if we can never use any faculty successfully until it has arrived at some degree of maturity, it will surely follow that the order of our studies must be arranged in conformity to the successive development of our faculties." We would do well to compare with this the principles of readiness of which we hear so much today.

Of the order in which our faculties develop, Wayland thought there could not be much doubt. The objective powers are the first to unfold. Hence the insatiable curiosity of little children about living and moving things and all that can be seen or heard. The powers of forming images and building an inner world develop somewhat later. And not until we approach maturity are we able to deal with higher generalizations and abstract truths and to observe our own nature and the nature of others. The memory accommodates itself to this development of the observing powers. At first it most easily retains the remembrance of sensory experience and of bare facts. "Hence the great power in youth of acquiring languages." As our capacity to deal with principles increases, that for acquiring languages declines.

The order of our studies, he continued, should obviously agree with the order in which our faculties appear and develop. Geography and many phases of natural science as well as languages should be taught early. Drawing is a great help in training the perceptive powers. If we could teach children to observe accurately we might, he believed, increase the number of able scientists, an idea that Charles W. Eliot was, much later, to dwell upon. Not until the third stage can we successfully introduce abstract subjects, such as logic, and subjects demanding taste, such as the books of the great creative authors. How shall we know when a pupil reaches the successive stages? There is an easy rule. It is to teach only what he understands. Wayland was doubtless correct in believing that lack of comprehension is a major reason for lack of interest in studies.

An early book that may be classed as an old-fashioned educational psychology is Wayland's *The Elements of Intellectual Philosophy* (1845). As in the address that has been reviewed, one of the chief themes is the order of the appearance and the growth of the faculties; but it also deals with their cultivation and improvement. Among the conditions of attention we must count health and hygiene. Proper diet, sufficient sleep, a moderate room temperature, and a reasonable limit to the time devoted to study, all will aid in maintaining one's attention. It will be aided also by the use of the pen, making analyses of books read, and writing on the subjects studied.

The book also treats the laws of association in the cultivation of the memory. The memory, we are told, may be improved more, and more quickly, than any other faculty. But Wayland did not distinguish between "strengthening" the memory and the judicious use of devices to aid retention and recall. Precise and definitive ideas and information when organized into a system are easily remembered, as the book clearly explains, but we are told by present-day science that, contrary to Wayland's view, this leaves the native tenacity of the mind unchanged. It is important to notice that this "native tenacity" of the psychologists, like their "native intelligence," is a theoretical construct like the "substance" of the philosophers.

Pages were given to the cultivation of the imagination and the reason, but Wayland took a moderate position on transfer of training. He favored the study of many varied subjects under an elective system, a most liberal and original policy in 1850. This view can be harmonized with transfer doctrines if it is supposed that the training effect is very general so that the serious study of any worthy subject will discipline the mind. This was what President Eliot of Harvard, a generation later, maintained, and it was what the Committee of Ten (1894) over the objections of a minority of its members taught.

The Herbartians, as will be shown in the following chapter, made a direct attack about 1890 upon the transfer doctrine. Burke Aaron Hinsdale read a notable paper on "The Dogma of Formal Discipline" before the National Council of Education in 1894. This was still mere philosophy; but William James had made a rather amateurish experiment in memory-training before 1890. Although the subjects in the experiment made a little improvement, the amount was so slight that some began to doubt the importance of transfer effects. This doubt was increased and spread by the slight transfer from specific habits in the more extended experiments of Edward L. Thorndike and Robert S. Woodworth (1901). In the last half-century a thousand or more transfer experiments have been carried out, and it has been indicated that the transfer may be very substantial if the learner realizes the similarity of the new situation to the one that has been practiced. Pupils who are ingenious, observant, and able to generalize from cases derive considerable benefits. It is to be feared that too many teachers and teachers of teachers are unaware of the present state of the old transfer controversy. This is unfortunate, for as Hinsdale saw, "the question is absolutely fundamental to the science of education." If there were no transfer, learning would be of little use because situations are rarely quite the same. Before we turn away from this topic we may recall that philosophers have declared that there is some truth in all the greater systems of philosophy.

GENERAL PRINCIPLES OF TEACHING

By general principles of teaching are meant those guiding ideas that apply to all, or to many, or at least to several subjects or situations. Special principles or methods apply to only one subject, such as arithmetic, or to a few related ones, say, arithmetic and algebra. The general principles that were considered in normal schools in the last century may be found in the textbooks on methods.

Between about 1840 and 1860 the nature of these books changed from the moralizing works of such writers as Samuel R. Hall and Jacob Abbott to the more empirical books such as Potter and Emerson's *The School and the Schoolmaster*, a work that may be considered to mark the first stage of the transition. Later and more advanced examples of the change are the psychological and practical books of Wayland, David P. Gage, William H. Payne, and Emerson E. White. All of these are still deductive and philosophical in nature. Among these books is the *Intellectual Philosophy* of Wayland, which has been analyzed.

A contemporary but more influential work than Wayland's was the *Theory and Practice of Teaching* (1847) by David P. Page, the first principal of the state normal school at Albany, New York. This book was in use by classes and reading circles of teachers for half a century. In 1885, forty years after publication, it was revised by the professor of education at the University of Michigan, W. H. Payne, who did not change a word of the text but added a number of passages. These serve a useful purpose today by indicating changes in opinion and practice that had taken place since 1847.

Fitness to teach, Page wrote, involves three kinds of qualifications: scholarship, skill and method in teaching, and understanding of the science of teaching. This science is based upon the principles of psychology, physiology, and ethics. To teach must be the teacher's primary purpose, not money, reputation, or preparation for another profession. The teacher is responsible partly or mainly for the morals, health, intellectual growth, and study habits of his pupils. He must teach pupils how to study intelligently, how to master the principles of a science instead of merely preparing for a recitation or covering a book.

The work contains skilfully illustrated chapters on "right modes of teaching," on ways "to wake up mind," and on school government. Page did not favor the use of corporal punishment, "the discussion of which in all our educational gatherings takes up so much time"; but he did not pronounce against all use of it. He considered the practical problems of school management, the daily time-table, the teacher's care of his own health, and his relations to the community, including those cases when "one part of the district is arrayed against the other." It is a historical fact of interest today that he thought there would be no objection to the teaching in public schools of the generally accepted Christian doctrines; but he did not indicate which doctrines he would include. Sectarian issues were to be referred to the family and the pulpit. Page was mistaken in thinking that there would be no objection to the direct teaching of religion.

In comparison with the brief vogue of most books on education, the Page text had a surprising career. This was because of its clear, practical instruction. It is readable today and those who discover it do, in fact, still read it. It is best read in the Payne edition of 1885; but it was revised several times by a number of editors.

METHODS AND MANAGEMENT

Many authors after 1860 prepared works on special phases of education in place of the comprehensive books that Page and his predecessors had produced. The day of the professional specialist was beginning. School management, methods of teaching, supervision, and educational psychology were now to be separately treated. The several phases of education could no longer be confined within the covers of one small book. Topics were treated that had not been thought of before. Such general titles as "theory and practice" or "the school and the schoolmaster" could no longer indicate the contents of the new books.

Specialized books to aid rural teachers in practical ways were written for use in normal schools. Resisting the temptation to write a general book that could be used in all professional courses, James P. Wickersham (1825–1891) prepared a special work on *School Economy* (1864). It contained nearly four hundred pages and treated the organization, grading, and government of schools. In a second, somewhat larger book on *Methods of Instruction* (1865) he dealt with the nature of the school subjects and "the methods of teaching them according to that nature."

Wickersham later became state superintendent of Pennsylvania and wrote a history of education in his state, published in 1885. It was one of the early books in the field and is still one of the better ones. Through his writing and speaking and his activity in the National Education Association, he acquired a very considerable reputation. At the time when he prepared his textbooks he was the principal of the newly opened normal school at Millersville.

In the *School Economy* he described the several kinds of graded schools and the effect of the numbers of the pupils upon the organization. This was a subject of current interest because in most states the grading of the schools was in its early stages. The evidence seems to indicate that the graded system was a native development and not copied from Germany, as has been claimed. Wickersham discussed the school plant including the playground and its equipment and urged the esthetic improvement of the schoolroom and the schoolyard. But for the most part the *School Economy* dealt with school routine. It was a conservative book but the author reported that it was used in nearly all the normal schools of its time, about a dozen in number.

The *Methods of Instruction* is mainly psychological. Reference is made to earlier and contemporary writers including Pestalozzi and Spencer. The usual order in which the faculties were supposed to develop was indicated, but Wickersham held that this was not entirely fixed. He held that perception, memory, recollection, imagination, understanding, and reason develop together but come to maturity in the order named. The suggestion is that the faculties are less distinct than had been claimed. This was a slight change in the old psychology.

Method is determined by the maturity of the faculties but also by the stage of the pupil's development, whether that of infancy, childhood, or youth, and by the nature of the branches of instruction. Wickersham in common with other writers of the 1860's dealt with object lessons. He was sufficiently Pestalozzian to propose the use of pictures, toys puzzles, and other constructions in addition to the usual objects from nature. He was sufficiently critical to condemn the random selection of "unworthy objects" when "all Nature" was available. And he deplored the verbalism that sometimes was the chief outcome of object lessons.

Numerous special books on object-teaching appeared. One of the early ones, *Object Teaching and Oral Lessons* (1860) by Henry Barnard, was composed of materials from his *Journal*. Edward A. Sheldon, the leader of the Oswego movement, wrote another. And a third was by Norman A. Calkins, the assistant superintendent in charge of primary schools in New York City. The office held by him is further evidence of the increasing specialization in education. His book was called *Primary Object Lessons, for Training the Senses and Developing the Faculties*. Published in 1870 it was in its fortieth edition in 1888. Included in the topics of this widely used book were form, color, number, drawing, and human anatomy, "the bones of the body." With "all Nature" before them, the educators of that period chose for little children isolated objects that could be used to represent abstract ideas. With the opportunity to introduce the children to an interesting natural world, they chose to train their faculties.

The *Normal Methods of Teaching* (1879) by Edward Brooks (1831–1912) was an exposition of special methods of teaching each of the common branches. The principles of arithmetic-teaching were illustrated by "model lessons." This was an addition to the pedagogical writing of the period. Brooks also included historical notes on the development of the school subjects, an idea frequently approved in later times. Other writers were also dealing with special methods.

A widely used series of books on education was prepared by Emerson E. White (1829–1902), at one time president of Purdue University. These were *The Elements of Pedagogy* (1886), which was the basic book; *School Management*; and *The Art of Teaching*, dealing with methods. White was highly critical of the extensive use of written examinations, not only the use made of them in the promotion of pupils but especially of their use as a basis for the comparison of schools and teachers. One may see here the faint beginnings of the survey idea already employed in Boston in 1845. Instead of giving heed to White's strictures, the profession went on to develop more effective instruments and to establish general norms.

The interest in the construction of school buildings was one of the earliest among the special interests that we are tracing. Horace Mann gave attention to the problem in his earliest reports; but the writings of Henry Barnard on this subject were more extensive and exerted a great influence that was long maintained. There were no professional school architects in those days and a book such as Barnard's *School Architecture* was needed.

A volume on *Country School-Houses* was prepared by James Johonnot (1823–1888). The author had some experience as a teacher of rural schools in his native Vermont and he wrote for those who had to build one-room schools and those who had to live and work in them. He treated every phase of the construction and use of such a school plant, the location and grounds, main and accessory buildings, their plan, cost, and construction, and the furniture and teaching apparatus. He gave special attention to the contribution that the physical conditions can make to the health, the moral conduct, and the aesthetic cultivation of the pupils.

Aesthetic cultivation is given a chapter in another book by Johonnot, his *Principles and Practice of Teaching*. This attention to proportion, unity, harmony, symmetry, and other aesthetic elements in education was an unusual emphasis in elementary education, but the topic had been introduced by Wickersham. Johonnot was interested most in the plastic arts but he stressed the importance of music also. He showed great interest in scientific subjects, and the educational reformers whom he admired most were Pestalozzi, Froebel, and Agassiz, especially the last. The sciences, he said, should be taught, as Huxley pointed out, because of their utility; and they should be studied by the direct observation of nature. The simplest equipment is often the best and may be borrowed from any farmer. Johonnot was a graduate of Page's old school, the state normal school at Albany, and the section of Page's book that Johonnot admired most was a lesson on an ear of corn, called "Waking Up Mind." Object lessons, he insisted, should be the gateways to science. Thomas E. Finegan of the New York State Department, who knew him well and admired his devotion to any cause that he advocated, called Johonnot a "radical," but he was merely a "progressive" born a little too early.

BROADER SPECIALTIES

A marked case of growing specialization is provided by a small book on the superintendency of schools. This work added a new province to the educational kingdom. Where separate one-teacher schools under the district system were visited by the minister or were managed by small committees of farmers, there was little practice and no theory of supervision; but education in the cities set new problems.

Several cities established the superintendent's office before 1840: Buffalo in 1837, Louisville and Providence in 1838, St. Louis in 1839. About twenty-five city school superintendencies had been created by 1860. The priorities are, as usual, debatable. The movement spread and by 1870 and 1880 even small towns had begun to employ a chief school officer. According to the small book mentioned, this was incidental to the grading of the schools and welding them into a system. The book bore the modest title of *Chapters on School Supervision* (1875) and was written by W. H. Payne, who at that time had the direction of the schools of Adrian, Michigan.

The subject of supervision occupied only a part of the space. Three chapters were devoted to the powers and general duties of the superintendent, "who is rather an officer of the Board than a member of the corps of teachers." Other chapters dealt with the admission and grading of the pupils, the organization of the schools, the examination and appointment of teachers, the curriculum, the schedule of classes, records, and matters of personnel management. It is, therefore, a work on school administration; and the author was not aware that any work of this special character had been published before.

This treatise of little more than two hundred pages laid a foundation for a new professional study. Judged by present doctrine its errors were few and its sensible answers to real problems were numerous. As we shall see, the author was a conservative critic of education, but in this book, which was based upon practical field experience, he made a positive contribution to what he considered the science of education.

How Sheldon managed and developed the small city superintendency of Oswego, we have seen; and we shall soon note the theory and practice of W. T. Harris in St. Louis. These men and their contemporaries were developing the office as it has come to be. As Burke Aaron Hinsdale explained in a report to the National Council of Education (1888), the American city school superintendency is an office not found elsewhere. The nearest analogy is with the inspectors of schools in Europe; but these are national rather than local officers.

The superintendent's duties were not defined by law, and this Hinsdale considered evidence that the office was not created but had evolved. After a term as superintendent of Cleveland, Hinsdale was somewhat pessimistic about the further development of the office. The big city superintendent would necessarily become a business manager, he thought, and only in smaller places could he remain an educator. Yet he also proposed to confine the work of the board to policy matters and to make the superintendent the executive agent of the board. Like Sheldon and Harris, he was concerned with the problem of securing good members of school boards, and he proposed their appointment for long terms by the mayor or the court. In this as in some other matters, history has not approved his insights.

Further knowledge of the state of education may be obtained from Payne's *School Supervision,* to which we return. He referred to "a graded-school of a thousand pupils and twenty teachers." This would not now be considered adequate staffing; but in the early 1950's enrollments increased so rapidly and teachers were so hard to secure in sufficient numbers that this ratio was no longer as unrealistic as it had seemed earlier.

The local high school seemed to Payne the best source of a supply of teachers. He thought every high school should have a normal class unless there was a municipal normal school such as the large cities maintained. A high school class "composed of pupils who proposed to teach, reciting twice a week and observing good models, using such a book as Page's *Theory and Practice,* may learn much about the art of teaching." In this way the superintendent could prepare his own staff. But times change. And at present, irrespective of the evils of "inbreeding" and meager preparation, this plan is no longer as effective as it was, for this supply of teachers has dried up at the source. In times of full employment at high wages, comparatively few city high school pupils are willing to consider teaching as an occupation. Greatly increased salaries and greatly improved working conditions in the city schools would increase the number of applicants.

The increasing proportion of women in the teaching force was for Payne a disturbing trend and he related it to the "emancipation of women," which was then agitating the public. He thought men were needed to render the staff more permanent, to make the science-teaching more effective, and to assure a "healthy discipline," and he did not mean corporal punishment. He referred to the idea of a single salary schedule but was not in favor of it. These ideas can be seen in their proper chronology and context if we remember that the states had only recently begun to pass laws giving women the right to own property, that they were still wives, mothers, and schoolteachers rather than persons, and that teaching was one of the very few professions open to them.

Boards should change textbooks only when this is in the interest of the pupils. Payne did not suggest that members might line their pockets at such times; but Hinsdale did not hesitate to consider this as a possibility. There is money in books, Hinsdale wrote. Publishers have done much good and some harm. They sometimes enter the political field to influence elections and corrupt the moral sense of teachers and superintendents through "largesses of various kinds." And then he unaccountably adds that the superintendent should have nothing to do with the selection of textbooks "unless he can be protected against foreign interference" (*Studies in Education*, pp. 286f.). Payne merely warned superintendents and teachers against selling to pupils any materials used in the schools.

The present good opinion of the quality of American schoolbooks was held, as we learn from Payne, as early as 1875. He said: "The American school-book has no superior. No class of books is subject to such vigorous and decisive criticism as this." And he praised the publishers for these conditions because they "have fostered and almost created the authorship of textbooks that are a credit to our age and country."

School administration and educational psychology became special branches of education at the same time. School administration was a broadened and more reasoned school management, a subject that had been touched upon by every writer since Christopher Dock. Educational psychology was cabined and confined by the doctrine of the faculties and the lack of experimentation and fresh observation. Book after book repeated the old formulas, and this in turn affected other branches, especially methods of teaching. A long step toward a new psychology and method was taken by G. Stanley Hall in 1880 when he studied, not faculties, but the "contents" of children's minds. Child study in taking this step achieved more than one value. Child study brought out the differences between the child and the adult, differences in bodily proportions, growth, play interest, dependence, lack of vocational drives, activity, and adolescent changes. Hall thought the principal use of child study was in directing the student to individual differences and personal traits rather than group averages and uniformities. All of these ideas had been considered by Locke and Rousseau, but few had seen very clearly what they implied for the work of the school. Study was required and several generations passed by before this knowledge was applied in the school, if it has been fully applied even now.

Ten years after Hall made his study, William James published his *Principles of Psychology* (1890) and almost a decade later his *Talks to Teachers* (1899). James took care to assure the reader that he did not volunteer but was asked to give the *Talks* and he did not place a high value for teachers upon a knowledge of his science. He wrote Hanus that he did not know "just what pedagogic psychology means except the habit, association, apperception, and attention chapters of common psychology." The *Talks* became an interesting book that may not have had much influence upon anyone's teaching. Another literary psychology whose style hardly needs to fear comparison with James was *Psychology and Psychic Culture* (1895) by Reuben Post Halleck. It was written for high school pupils and combines popular psychology with advice on mind-training. Concreteness and thoughtful self-study were the aims of Edward A. Kirkpatrick's *Inductive Psychology* (1895). The same author also prepared a widely used *Fundamentals of Child Study* (1903). These are only a few of the many attempts to make a knowledge of psychology valuable to teachers.

Those efforts met with only indifferent success. The results and values of child study did not immediately appear in the normal school classes. Pupils and teachers often felt that the psychology that was taught to prospective teachers had little bearing upon their future work. As late as 1911 Guy M. Whipple reported that teachers of psychology considered normal school students unable to profit from the usual textbooks in their field. The books were technical and lacked practical applications. The result was that the students memorized the words of the book without understanding. It was suggested that the students should carry on simple exercises—one would not call them experiments—in learning and teaching and should report the experiences in class discussion. Such a method would join educational psychology or child study with observation of children and practice teaching, a good idea.

It is appropriate to compare the difficulty of the psychology teachers mentioned with comparable episodes in the progress of education. The teachers of health and physical education have had to solve problems of selection of materials, clarity of presentation, and practical application and habit-building. A similar difficulty that was not solved in less than fifty years confronted the early teachers of agriculture. There would seem to be an obvious and important conclusion to be drawn from these and similar experiences: knowledge of the subject is not enough.

The work of Hall and his pupils in establishing psychological laboratories (the first at Johns Hopkins) and psychological journals, the child study movement, the *Principles* of James, and the Herbartian pedagogy made the nineties an active period in psychology. Educational psychology was the oldest form of applied psychology, but its most useful applications were the products, not of its earliest period, but of the twentieth century. Among these are the study of the changes in interests with age, readiness investigations, the search for the causes of failure in school, an understanding of the effect of knowledge of performance upon improvement, and tests of intelligence, performance, and aptitude.

A variety of other pedagogical branches gives further evidence of advancing specialization. Textbooks on school law began to appear before 1880. The opening volume of the International Education Series—a series that was edited by William T. Harris—was a translation by Anna C. Brackett of Karl Rosenkranz's *Philosophy of Education,* a Hegelian work. A one-volume general history of education (1886) by F. V. N. Painter and a volume on the history of education in the United States (1889) by Richard G. Boone were included in the same series. Payne translated the general history of education by Gabriel Compayré. Henry Barnard in 1855 began his monumental *American Journal of Education.* An excellent one-volume encyclopedia of education, edited by Henry Kiddle and Alexander J. Schem, had appeared in 1876. Nicholas Murray Butler established and for many years edited an important monthly educational periodical, the *Educational Review* (1891–1928).

The books and papers that have been mentioned here are only a small selection from the mass of educational publications, but they will serve the purpose of revealing some of the major specializations that were taking place. They show that education was more lively and active than it had ever been. They are evidence of the growth of a profession.

UNIVERSITY COURSES IN EDUCATION

There is further evidence. Early in the 1800's colleges had begun to contemplate offering courses in education, but not many did so until near the century's end. In some cases the marginal colleges made the first efforts. The faculty of Amherst, then small and in a thinly populated section, proposed such courses in 1826, but nothing came of this. Jefferson College at Washington in the mountains of southwestern Pennsylvania showed some interest. The infant New York University in 1831 even chose a professor, Thomas H. Gallaudet (1787–1851), but it is doubtful that he ever lectured. Brown University announced courses in the art of teaching in 1850.

The sparsely attended and precariously financed state universities of the Middle West began before, and continued for some time after, the middle of the century to offer normal courses for elementary teachers. Several of these universities had been set down in small country towns such as Bloomington, Indiana, and Columbia, Missouri. The growth of the towns and the invention of the automobile have changed matters, but in

1850 these isolated institutions had few students and these were poorly prepared for university studies. What was more natural than that such universities should offer to prepare teachers? This they did, maintaining both preparatory and normal departments.

When the high schools and normal schools became numerous, the state universities gave up the preparation of elementary teachers only to return after a generation to the preparation of secondary teachers. The State University of Iowa was something of an exception. From 1873 it had maintained a tripartite department of mental and moral science and didactics. Didactics was a weak member, and there were years when no work in that field was given. A separate "department of pedagogy" was organized in 1890 and a School of Education in 1907. Many universities in these years began to offer work for secondary teachers and administrators. The normal schools prepared elementary teachers. This arrangement tended to maintain the old separation between the schools for the common people and the secondary schools and universities—the schools for the directive and professional classes. In Chapter 6 it was explained that the elementary school and normal school tended to become a separate system, divided from the high school and university, which formed the other system. After 1900, when universities again undertook the preparation of elementary teachers and when from two to four years of college work became standard preparation for elementary teachers, the normal schools were driven to raise their standards and to become teachers' colleges. When this was achieved in fact, it helped to make the educational ladder a reality.

The University of Michigan in 1879 created a separate chair of the Art and Science of Teaching. The title is not definitive. The department was to help high school teachers, principals, and school superintendents, both prospective and those already holding positions. The action may be interpreted as a further measure to strengthen the alliance between the university and the high schools of the state, an alliance that had been forged by the university's accreditation policy and the decision in the Kalamazoo case. This was the interpretation placed upon the action by President James B. Angell, who had twice recommended it.

He pointed out to the Regents that many young graduates were at once appointed as principals of large schools or to superintendences of city schools. Before they went to their new duties, he thought they should have been taught something of the work of organizing, managing, teaching, and governing a school. "Experience alone can thoroughly train them. But some familiar lectures on these topics would be of essential service to them." It has been conjectured that President Angell's attention was directed to this matter through an address by Superintendent William H. Payne, and he was appointed to the new chair. The university gave as one of the uses of the new department that it would bring the secondary schools into closer relations with the university. The University of Michigan was thus becoming the head of the public school system of the state.

Other state and endowed universities and colleges followed the example of the University of Michigan. Columbia University and New York University became important centers. President Barnard of Columbia in 1881 produced an extended and able argument for professional instruction for teachers without knowing that Michigan had anticipated him in deeds, not words. Even then Columbia was not ready to follow his lead, but in 1889 a private institution, the New York College for Teachers, secured a charter. This school was rechartered as Teachers College in 1892, and affiliated with Columbia University in 1898. The chief leader in this movement was the young Nicholas Murray Butler, who was to become the twelfth president of Columbia University, an office that he held for almost fifty years. Teachers College has had great influence upon all institutions and phases of teacher education.

At Cornell University in 1886, at the University of Chicago in 1901, and elsewhere before and after the turn of the century scores of schools and departments of education and soon after bureaus of educational research were established. Richard G. Boone reported that in 1904, 250 colleges and universities out of 480 or 52 per cent offered courses in education. Although, as President Eliot said about 1890, the Harvard faculty had neither interest nor confidence in pedagogy, a department was established in 1891 at that oldest American college and thirty years later this was elevated into a Graduate School of Education in order, as one of its high officers reported, "to get our courses out of the control of a hostile faculty." This hostility was not confined to Harvard or to times long past. Instead it has shown itself with considerable virulence in recent times in several parts of the country including the Midwest.

The growth of a profession of teaching was furthered by the work of the universities but also by the leadership of the state and national organizations of teachers and superintendents. Ten state associations sent out a call in 1857 that led to the formation of the National Teachers' Association in that year at Philadelphia. This became the National Education Association in 1870 and gradually grew into a large and effective organization that currently has over one million members. Charles W. Eliot, Nicholas Murray Butler, and William Torrey Harris, as well as other distinguished men, became early presidents of the association, and the annual proceedings and addresses became a record of the thought and action of the educational leaders in the entire nation.

CITY SUPERVISION

The reputation of the schools of St. Louis for high achievement reached all parts of the United States at an early period in the growth of that city. This was owing in large part to the enterprise and administrative skill of Superintendent William Torrey Harris (1835–1909). The foundations had, however, been laid earlier. And the rapid growth of the city to which he had come by mere accident contributed to his opportunity. In little more than a decade from his arrival as a half-educated young man with empty pockets and a head filled with impossible projects, he became the city superintendent of schools (1868). At this time he was thirty-three years old. Eventually he was to be acclaimed as one of the most distinguished educators of his time and country.

St. Louis was a border city. The people had come from the North and the South; and, to the number of many thousands, also from Europe. Germans, numbering 60,000 or more, made up more than half of the European immigrants; and as always they were hard to assimilate. They wanted to have the schools conducted in their language; they opposed the use of textbooks; and the Catholics among them wanted to have a share of the public funds for their own church schools. The city was also on the border between the East and the West and a main depot for the westward-bound trains of emigrants, traders, and adventurers. Many of the people were therefore transients. The Civil War brought its own problems; and though the war was over before Harris became superintendent, some of the war problems remained.

Ten years before he was to become superintendent, Harris had begun to teach in the school system. This was still in its formative stages. Less than a decade had passed since Missouri had established the state school fund and since the city had levied its first school tax and opened a high school. The Lancasterian plan was still in use in the elementary schools, but the change to the graded system was accomplished before Harris took charge. School attendance long remained irregular. Missouri delayed to pass a compulsory attendance law until 1905. Children came and went and came back again at will. Many did not come back but left permanently when they reached the fourth or fifth grade. A great many did not come at all but spent their time on the streets until they were old enough to go to work.

The way had been well prepared for Harris. The graded system had been introduced, as has been indicated. The board of education was independent of the city council. Separate tax levies were voted by the citizens, and the board controlled its corporate funds and property without interference. Several capable superintendents had preceded Harris, who thus took over a healthy although immature system. One innovation that has been generally accredited to Harris, the practice of flexible and frequent promotion in the grades, had been introduced by his predecessor, Superintendent Ira Divoll. The irregular attendance of the pupils may have suggested this practice. While Harris was serving (1858–1868) as elementary teacher, principal of an elementary school, and assistant superintendent, he maintained close and friendly relations with pupils, teachers, parents, and the superintendent. The retirement of Divoll was partly because of ill health, and partly because of his desire to run for the state superintendency. Harris was his natural successor, had his active support, and succeeded to the place without competition. There were no wounds to be tended.

The practice of flexible promotion was continued, and Harris in his annual report for 1873 gave a detailed explanation and defense of it. The school year was divided into four quarters of about ten weeks each. Promotion and reclassification were carried out at the end of each quarter, and an effort was made to form sections of good, average, and slow pupils. This ability grouping was at one time regarded as a great discovery, but it has been practically abandoned in St. Louis; and the report of the St. Louis school survey of 1939 implied that it was based upon unsound assumptions. Others say that the results of the numerous scientific studies of homogeneous grouping are inconclusive.

The new administration did not lack for innovations. To make the system more compact, not to say rigorous, Harris early introduced a scheme of district supervision. Under the plan each of the principals of upper-grade schools served as the supervisor of those primary schools from which his pupils were drawn. Each supervising principal was to visit every school of his district once a week to consult with teachers and principals, observe the work, and report to the superintendent. The supervising principals were not to be entirely relieved from teaching in their own schools. Harris thought a principal should not allow himself to lose direct contact with pupils and classwork. Meanwhile, he did not spare himself. Even as the city grew, he continued to visit schools. When the board received his accounts of expenses for transportation, they decided to furnish him with what Americans of that day called a "rig." His organizing skill and the ability to secure the cooperation of those who worked with him were leading factors in the success of his administration.

The kindergarten was introduced in 1873, but Harris had been planning this step earlier. He had the help of Miss Susan Blow, an able young woman of means and social position. They moved slowly at first, but before Harris left St. Louis the city was supporting more than fifty public kindergartens. At that time (1880) only a very few cities had adopted the institution.

Other institutions were introduced during his administration. Schools with kindergartens for black children were added. Evening schools with vocational classes were formed. The city normal school, later to be named for Harris, was separated from the high school. Harris effected a closer grading of the children. Large building programs were completed to keep up with the growing population. Music, drawing, and gymnastics were added to the studies taught.

St. Louis, as we have seen, prepared her own teachers at first in the high school, then in the city normal school, later to be called the Harris Teachers College. But Harris also searched for special talent outside. For this he was criticized because St. Louisans, like others elsewhere, considered their own people the equal of any and also entitled to special consideration in their home town. Harris had set up a graded salary schedule, but when he found Anna C. Brackett teaching in South Carolina for less than $1,000 he paid her $2,000 to take charge of the St. Louis normal school.

There were some persistent problems and some new ones that arose from time to time. Classes in their own language were provided for the Germans but many parents were dissatisfied. They pressed for schools in which German should be the sole language of instruction. Harris reminded them that they had been admitted as citizens of a country of which English was the official and national language. Some took their children out of the public schools and entered them at private German schools. On the opposite side were many Americans who opposed the teaching of any foreign language in a public elementary school and agitated for the removal of all such instruction.

Religious issues in the St. Louis schools attracted widespread attention. There were many Catholic citizens and some, including priests and the supporters of a Catholic religious paper, demanded a share of the school tax dollar for the parochial schools. Attempts were made to effect changes in the Constitution of Missouri that would have allowed this division of the funds. In that city, political efforts were made by a Catholic faction to gain control of the board of education. Other religious factions on the Protestant side wanted to have the Bible in the King James version taught in the public schools. Harris took his stand upon the principle of the separation of state and church. He was in favor of maintaining the public school "as a purely secular institution without any religious instruction." These and other difficulties may have had some influence in leading Harris to resign in 1880 after a highly successful administration of twelve years. But it may be that he left the superintendency to pursue other interests. Some of these he had long been promoting along with his work for the schools; and some new activities were developing only in his last years in St. Louis. One of the latter was the compilation of a set of school readers for D. Appleton and Company, a task that in the course of years netted him a large amount in royalties.

The superintendency in America, as Harris explained, was undergoing a process of evolution. The early city superintendents had not been placed in charge of the education of children but only of the mechanics of a system. They were custodians of school property, they allocated supplies, kept records, and supervised building construction. Gradually they became educators and undertook to deal with the course of study and the methods of instruction. Some, such as Harris himself, thought it part of their function to inspire teachers with the spirit of self-culture, to counsel and advise the members of the board, and even to help in shaping the educational thought of the country.

The superintendent dare not neglect his historically earliest duties, so Harris believed. He must have at least "directive oversight" of the mechanics of the system. No merely theoretical superintendent can succeed. He must be informed concerning apparatus, salaries, finances, and legislation, and must devise and follow a policy in such practical matters. But these, he declared, are merely means to greater ends. His main function is to direct the education of children and youth for active participation in a democracy.

There are important duties contributory to the superintendent's main function. He must educate the members of the board and he must educate himself. One of Harris's own numerous ways of furthering his education was to visit city school systems. In 1872 he with F. Louis Soldan visited Cincinnati, Chicago, Cleveland, Oswego, New York City, and Boston.

In his own mind Harris divided board members into three classes, business and professional men, reformers, and politicians. It may be observed that these classes are not mutually exclusive. The superintendent, he said, must listen patiently and critically to the reformers and to parents, especially when they come with disciplinary problems. He must keep in close touch with the general public. And he must have genuine political skill or the reformers and politicians will combine against him and against the honest and conservative elements on the board.

In his efforts to educate the members of his board, Harris used the board meetings, private discussions with members, and his reports. Some of the topics in his reports were specific, such as grading, salaries, building plans, or German instruction in the schools; but he did not hesitate to consider the broadest topics of educational theory. He discussed the Pestalozzian system in comparison with the methods in common use in the schools; the relations of the public schools to the community and the nation under a democratic system; the teaching of science in elementary schools; and, becoming more practical, the evil tendency of boards of education in times of financial stress to cut and trim the educational budget and program. He thought both "the bulls and the bears" in education should be held in leash and not allowed to run wild.

During his connection with the St. Louis schools he edited the *Journal of Speculative Philosophy*, which he had founded in 1867 while he was a classroom teacher. During this period he was the pivot of the St. Louis movement in philosophy. Among the contributors to the *Journal* were such leading thinkers as William James, Josiah Royce, Charles S. Peirce, John Dewey, and G. H. Howison. During all these years and afterward, Harris developed his Hegelian standpoint, wrote books including *Hegel's Logic* (1890), and delivered many addresses. He and Francis W. Parker were for more than two decades nationally known educators and among the most eminent members of the National Education Association.

The Hegelian philosophy led Harris to emphasize man's cultural heritage and to consider its transmission as the main task of education. He would not have said that "the culture," in the present-day cant phrase, is more important than the child, but rather that only in a civilized society can the child grow mentally and become a moral person. Harris was not a "naturalist." His view that civilization is a primary fact for education led him to his figure of the five windows through which the child may look out upon the world and may also communicate with its human and subhuman denizens. The use of the word *windows* may tend to show that Harris held what Dewey was to consider a spectator theory of knowledge. Harris, however, was no mere spectator.

The five windows were (1) reading and writing, which by extension lead to communication and literature; (2) arithmetic, number, quantity, geometry, and the higher analysis; (3) geography, science; (4) history, society, government; and (5) grammar, languages, logic, and mental philosophy. These subjects show that Harris wanted to guard against any tendency to overemphasize a merely sensory and scientific education. Science is a field of mental activity, he said, perhaps following Bacon, so easy that all people may enter it successfully; and so practically useful that too many will want to do so. It does not follow that science should be permitted to usurp the place of the humane studies. The schools must not reduce all people to a level.

The school must be a community. Harris opposed the Herbartians because their system did not allow for the freedom of the will. Only free and independent persons can form a community. He quoted, with approval, Dewey's statement that "an interest is primarily a form of self-expressive activity"; but the later Dewey did not concede the transcendental freedom that Harris demanded. The fundamental difference between the two men lies in the fact that Harris sought to conserve and transmit, to conserve by transmitting, the achievements of the race. Dewey sought to use those attainments as instruments with which to investigate, discover, and apply ideas. Nicholas Murray Butler in *The Meaning of Education* (1902) said that education is "the gradual adjustment to the spiritual possessions of the race with a view of realizing one's own potentialities." This statement is in harmony with the general view of Harris.

After he resigned from the superintendency in St. Louis, he took part in the Concord School of Philosophy that Emerson had proposed and Amos Bronson Alcott had founded. He served as editor-in-chief of Webster's *New International Dictionary*. He became the general editor of Appleton's International Education Series and wrote the prefaces of more than fifty of those volumes. And for seventeen years (1889–1906) he rendered distinguished service as the United States Commissioner of Education.

Henry Barnard was the only predecessor (1867–1870) in that office whose attainments and contributions invite comparison with those of Harris. Barnard in his *American Journal of Education* and Harris in his official reports published extensive materials for the practical, comparative, and historical study of education. Neither Harris nor Barnard was successful as a politician in Washington. Even his long experience as a city superintendent had not fitted Harris to gain the attention of the Congress; but all educators except the promoters of vocational and agricultural education have had the same difficulty. We have the grateful testimony of Michael Sadler (later Sir Michael) that Harris's educational influence extended across the ocean. The Office of Special Inquiries and Reports, set up in England, was in part modeled upon the United States Bureau; and Sadler reported that upon application to Washington, Dr. Harris "gave full details on the working of the Bureau and other details of inestimable value."

In the first volume of the Special Reports this help was acknowledged in these friendly words: "Every student of education," wrote Sir Robert Morant, "is under a debt of gratitude to the United States Government for the work of the National Bureau of Education of the United States. Its volumes, published under the direction of Commissioner W. T. Harris, have probably done more than any other single agency to encourage a comparative study of the science and art of education, and of the various systems of educational administration now in force in different countries of the world."

If the number and quality of its professional publications were the sole criteria for the existence of a profession, then it could be pronounced that teaching had reached that status by 1900. Unfortunately, other criteria were not so favorable; and the shifting personnel of the lower and especially of the rural schools, as well as the low level of the general and special education of many teachers, deter one from calling them members of a profession. Many elementary and high school teachers, especially in the cities, deserved that classification. And to a lesser extent the same conditions obtain today and have been aggravated by the upsurge in attendance and the forced employment of insufficiently prepared teachers. How to adjust the supply of professional teachers to the shifting demands of an unstable society is an unsolved problem. And this is unfortunate if good teaching is as important to the individual and the society as it is claimed to be.

SUMMARY

Upon applying the usual criteria to teaching, one may infer that this occupation became more professional after 1860 than it had been. The increasing proportion of women who then came to fill teaching posts may not have had much effect upon this tendency toward professional status. It is probable, however, that salaries were kept low or that in some cases they declined as a result of the employment of a larger number of women. There was no thought of a single salary schedule at that time.

Special preparation for an occupation is one of the criteria of its status as a profession. The increased opportunity to secure this preparation is the chief subject of this chapter. Normal schools, universities, and superintendents were the chief agencies for direct teaching of educational branches. Most of the material was philosophical or at least theoretical. It gave opportunity for the disagreement that philosophical systems seem to invite.

The faculty psychology was the leading philosophy of education when the period began. The faculties were supposed to be separate from each other, to develop in a certain order, and to be improvable through training. Transfer of training meant that training of a faculty in one kind of material improved its performance when dealing with different material. There was also a belief in general mental improvement as a result of vigorous mental activity.

General principles of teaching dealt with teacher preparation and competencies, methods, curriculum theory, and similar broad topics. Early in the period books began to appear that dealt with specialized divisions of the general principles, such as teaching methods and school management. The subject of methods was also divided further into the methods of teaching particular branches, such as reading or object lessons. The planning and furnishing of school buildings became a division of school management. School management was also developed in the opposite direction to become school supervision and administration. Other specialties that developed in the 1870's and later were educational psychology, the philosophy and history of education, and comparative education.

The latter half of the century produced many writers on special educational topics and the rise of ideas that are still of practical importance. One of the hopes, not at once fulfilled, was that education would become scientific in the manner of medicine or agriculture. Criticism was also a leading task of the specialist writers. City school administration was one of the first areas of the whole field of education to become to a marked extent professional and in some measure scientific.

QUESTIONS

1. Why is transfer of training a matter of importance in educational theory and practice? Why did the older views upon the topic come under criticism from several quarters about the same time?
2. Why is it of interest today that some well-informed people in 1885

thought there would be no objection to the teaching in public schools of "the generally accepted principles of Christianity"?

3. Why, in the development of the literature on education, were the books at first general and only later to become more highly specialized? Would the reverse of this process have been more logical?
4. Collect evidence on the question whether the city superintendency is a native or imported office.
5. What are the several reasons for the care and expense devoted to the production of schoolbooks in the United States?
6. Collect the evidence for the early beginning of what was later called Progressive education.
7. According to Spencer, is the worth of knowledge intrinsic (valuable in itself) or extrinsic (valuable for what it will do or produce)? Was Spencer a pragmatist?
8. Why did the St. Louis schools acquire a great reputation under Harris? Was this reputation in your opinion fully deserved? Why or why not?
9. What were the historically earliest duties of the city superintendents in the United States? Compare with their duties and responsibilities today.

BOOKS AND PAPERS

The problems and the views of teachers at any given period may be studied in the addresses, periodicals, and books of the time. The proceedings of the Western Literary Institute and of the American Institute of Instruction and many of the addresses and discussions of national, state, and special subject teachers' associations have been published. Professional periodicals began to appear not far from 150 years ago and have been greatly improved in the latter half of this period. The *American School Board Journal*, *Educational Review*, *Pedagogical Seminary*, *Kindergarten Review*, *School Review*, and *Primary Education* were among those founded before 1900, and continuing at least to World War I. Only two of the many individual histories of schools of education are listed as examples.

ANDRESS, J. MACE, "Aims, Values and Methods of Teaching Psychology in a Normal School," *Journal of Educational Psychology*, Vol. 1, 1911, pp. 541–654.

BELTH, MARC, *Education as a Discipline*, Boston, 1965.

BOONE, R. G., *Science of Education*, New York, 1904. This was written when the measurement movement had barely begun.

BORROWMAN, MERLE L., *The Liberal and Technical in Teacher Education*, New York, Bureau of Publications, Teachers College, Columbia University, 1956.

BYERLY, C. L., *Contributions of William Torrey Harris to Public School Administration*, University of Chicago, 1946, with a bibliography that includes a list of sixty papers and addresses by Harris.

CALLAHAN, RAYMOND E., *Education and the Cult of Efficiency*, University of Chicago Press, 1962.

CHAMBLISS, J. J., *The Origins of American Philosophy of Education, Its Development as a Distinct Discipline, 1808–1913*, The Hague, 1968.

CORWIN, RONALD G., *Militant Professionalism*, New York, 1970.

DILTHEY, WILHELM, "On the Possibility of a General Science of Education," an address before the Berlin Academy of Sciences, *Transactions*, 1888, pp. 807–832.

DREEBEN, ROBERT, *The Profession of Teaching*, Glenview, Ill., 1969.

FRANK, LAWRENCE K., *The School as Agent for Cultural Renewal*, Harvard University Press, 1959. The Burton Lecture.

GOOD, H. G., *The Rise of the College of Education of the Ohio State University*, Columbus, Ohio, 1960.

HALLECK, R. P., *Psychology and Psychic Culture*, New York, 1895. Very popular with teachers although disowned by "real" psychologists.

HARRIS, W. T., "Elementary School Education," *Journal of Speculative Philosophy*, Vol. 3 (1869), pp. 181–190, a reply to E. L. Youmans' *The Culture Demanded by Modern Life* (New York, 1867). Harris took a social and idealistic view as opposed to the scientific-practical one urged by Youmans. "Division of School Funds for Religious Purposes," *Atlantic Monthly*, August, 1876; "City School Supervision," *Educational Review*, February, 1892.

JAMES, WILLIAM, *Talks to Teachers on Psychology: and to Students on Some of Life's Ideals*, New York, 1899. Reissued, New York, 1939, with an introduction by John Dewey and William H. Kilpatrick.

JOHONNOT, JAMES, *Country School-Houses*, New York, 1858; *Principles and Practice of Teaching*, New York, 1878.

KOLESNIK, WALTER B., *Mental Discipline in Modern Education*, University of Wisconsin Press, 1958.

LEIDECKER, K. F., *Yankee Teacher, The Life of William Torrey Harris*, New York, 1946.

LEWIS, F. C., "A Study in Formal Discipline," *School Review*, April, 1905.

LIEBERMAN, MYRON, *Education as a Profession*, Englewood Cliffs, N.J., 1956.

LOGSDON, J. D., *Development of Public School Administration in St. Louis, Missouri*, Chicago, 1946, a University of Chicago dissertation.

McCLELLAN, JAMES E., *Toward An Effective Critique of American Education*, Philadelphia, 1968.

PAGE, DAVID PERKINS, *Theory and Practice of Teaching*, edited by W. H. Payne, New York, 1885.

PATRICK, GEORGE T. W., *An Autobiography*, University of Iowa Press, 1947.

PAYNE, W. H., *Chapters on School Supervision*, Cincinnati, 1875; *Contributions to the Science of Education*, New York, 1886. Payne was also the translator and editor of Rousseau's *Émile* and other works.

PORET, GEORGE C., *Contributions of William Harold Payne to Public Education*, George Peabody College for Teachers, 1930, a dissertation.

ROBERTS, JOHN S., *William T. Harris, A Critical Study of His Educational and Related Philosophical Views*, Washington, 1924.

ROYCE, JOSIAH, "Is There a Science of Education?" *Educational Review*, January and February, 1891.

SILBERMAN, CHARLES E., *Crisis in the Classroom*, New York, 1970.

STINNETT, T. M., *Professional Problems of Teachers*, New York, 1968; *Turmoil in Teaching*, New York, 1968.

THURSFIELD, RICHARD E., *Henry Barnard's* "American Journal of Education," Johns Hopkins Press, 1945.

WESLEY, EDGAR B., *NEA: The First Hundred Years*, New York, 1957.

WHITNEY, ALLEN S., "The First Chair of Education in an American University," *School and Society*, March 1, 1941.

Part IV

ACHIEVEMENTS AND VISIONS

Preview

Part IV traces the achievements *of the American people in educating more people to a higher level of competence than any other nation has ever done in the twenty-five centuries of Western experience with organized education. Although the American system has not done its work perfectly, we continue to pursue our visions of an American National System of Education guided by the star of equality of educational opportunity for all children. As we plodded confidently ahead, we encountered many problems. But science, technology, and a government of the people, by the people, and for the people are gradually solving them.*

Chapter 12

EUROPEAN THEORIES
AND
AMERICAN EDUCATION

In earlier chapters references are made to the influence of European theorists upon American schools and schoolmen. We have already noted in some detail the influence of Pestalozzi. But there were others, both before and after Pestalozzi. In this chapter we shall briefly trace the seminal ideas that emanated from Europe and prepared the way for a new philosophy for American education.

A GREAT ENGLISH TEACHER

We shall begin far back in history with a great English teacher, Richard Mulcaster (c. 1530–1611), who lived in the reign of Queen Elizabeth I. Mulcaster proposed to have teachers as well as the clergy, doctors, and lawyers, prepared in the universities and thus recognized teaching as one of the learned professions. Mulcaster, one of the great but far too neglected English writers on education, was born on the Scottish border and attended both Cambridge and Oxford but received his degree from the latter. He taught at two famous schools, Merchant Taylor's for twenty-five years and St. Paul's for twelve years. One of his ideas was that children should learn the common words of the English language, and not the unusual ones that are seldom used, and he compiled a list of 8,000 common words as a spelling-list. In our own time, E. L. Thorndike made a list of 10,000 "commonest" words. The two lists largely duplicate each other, but it is doubtful that Thorndike knew about his predecessor. Mulcaster was one of the men who developed the interest of the universities in the lower schools and worked toward their unification into a single system.

JOHN LOCKE

In the next century, we come upon John Locke (1632–1704), who was to become very distinguished. Locke became a famous writer on education and psychology. Although writing about education is similar to discussing other equally loose and debatable subjects such as economics, politics, and religion, what Locke wrote has been carefully considered and has lasted better than most books of his time.

As a student at Oxford, Locke did not confine himself to philosophy, ethics, and politics, but also studied scientific subjects including chemistry and medicine. He became a bachelor of medicine but owing to a disagreement with the faculty he never received the M.D. degree. In the seventeenth century, this did not keep Locke from occasionally practicing medicine, and in prescribing for the Earl of Shaftesbury (1621–1683) Locke gained one of his most important and lifelong friends.

Another early friend of Locke was Robert Boyle (1627–1691), a notable physicist and chemist, who was to distinguish between elements and compounds and to discover the law, which now carries his name, that can be roughly stated as follows: the volume of a gas varies inversely with pressure. Boyle brought a chemist from Germany to lecture to students and the public at Oxford. Locke was one of the auditors. A fellow-student, who later became an opponent of Locke, complained that Locke would not take notes quietly like the rest but was "always prating and troublesome." This may only mean that Locke saw difficulties in the lectures and asked for explanations. Eventually, he became Boyle's literary executor. Locke was also a pupil of and an assistant to Thomas Sydenham (1624–1689) who is sometimes regarded as the founder of clinical medicine. But with all this association with scientists, Locke remained a philosopher and psychologist, a teacher of ethics at Oxford, and the author of a variety of books in different fields.

The most important of Locke's books and the one that made him the founder of an inductive philosophy was his *Essay Concerning the Human Understanding*. Locke was drawn to this subject by a question: "What is the mind capable of knowing?" which his friends raised in conversation. This started Locke upon an inquiry that was to last twenty years. In framing his answer Locke was drawn into logical and psychological questions, and his writing caused him to be considered as one of the founders of modern psychology. It appears that all through his life, although Locke wrote a number of books, he gave only his spare time to composition. Even the titles of his works, such as the *Essay, Letters on Toleration, Some Observations on Printed Money*, and *Some Thoughts Concerning Education* indicate that most of his works were tracts for the times. His last book, on the *Conduct of the Understanding*, which came out in 1706, after the author's death, shows that Locke believed in formal discipline and transfer of training. Many still do.

In addition to Locke's work on education, he spent three periods on the continent. First he was sent on a diplomatic mission to Brandenburg, Germany. For several years prior to 1690, Locke guided a student on a tour through France; it was in this period that he came close to the sphere of activity of Claude Fleury (1640–1723) whose views on education closely resembled his own as shown in Locke's *Some Thoughts*. The two men may never have met, and it is not certain that Locke ever read Fleury's *Choice and Method of Studies*. All similarities between the *Some Thoughts* and *Choice and Method* may have resulted from the use by both men of the same sources.

Locke spent a third period abroad in Holland where he and the Earl of Shaftesbury, his patron, were refugees for several years. The Earl used Locke in many services including his advice and care in the education of his son and grandson. Shaftesbury died in Holland in 1633 and Locke returned home in one of the royal vessels when William and Mary ascended the English throne. Several of Locke's books were written in the last decade of his life including *Some Thoughts on Education*, in which he made the remarkable claim that nine-tenths of a man comes from education and experience and only one-tenth from heredity. Although Locke was a man with an independent mind, he may have gained this notion from Descartes who also held that it is experience that forms a man; Descartes even held that by nature all men are about equal.

Early in his life, Locke prepared for himself a short guide to conduct. A man's proper business, he wrote, is to seek happiness and to avoid misery. The most lasting pleasures came through health, reputation, knowledge, doing good, and the hope of eternal happiness. "In life," he said, "I must carefully look that I cross not any of these great and constant pleasures." In a parallel passage of the *Thoughts* Locke listed health, virtue, practical prudence or wisdom, courtesy, industry, and knowledge.

Among these aims the controlling one is virtue. Locke wrote: "As the strength of the body lies chiefly in being able to endure hardship, so also does that of the mind; and the great principle and foundation of all virtue is placed in this, that a man is able to deny himself his own desires, cross his inclinations, and purely follow what reason directs as best, though appetite lean the other way." This is the real foundation of Locke's theory. He believed with Descartes that a man's reason can control his desires and stormy emotions and bring to a peaceful and rational end the conflict that otherwise rages between the good and evil forces of his inner life.

The great work of a governor [or director of children, according to Locke] is to fashion the carriage and firm the mind: to settle in his pupil, good habits and the principles of virtue and wisdom: to give him, little by little, a view of mankind, and work him into a love of what is excellent and praiseworthy, and in the prosecution of it, to give him vigor, activity, and industry. The studies that he sets him upon are but, as it were, the exercise of his faculties, and employment of his time, to keep him from sauntering and idleness, to teach him application, and accustom him to take pains, and give some little taste of what his own industry must perfect.

Locke speaks disparagingly of what may be expected of the boy's efforts. To be sure, we do not know his age but since his studies were to begin as soon as he was able to talk, what is said would apply to every age; and it prompts the question: what more can be expected? Plato, Aristotle, and Quintilian expect more from small children. "Information can be obtained," Locke said, "as needed, but of good breeding, knowledge of the world, virtue, industry, and love of reputation, he cannot have too much; and if he have these, he will not long want information." And yet "the wise Locke" devoted a third of his work to school studies.

In the selection of school branches, Locke followed his utilitarian principles, keeping his eye upon the main object, the education of a gentleman. The pursuit of studies is based upon curiosity as Locke says, but he does not seem to keep this in mind. Many of the studies that Locke prescribes do not seem to be such that the boy would select them. Indeed it is clear that Locke's philosophy of education does not hold together; he is inconsistent. He begins, naturally, with the alphabet, but it is doubtful that the boy had any great curiosity about that; he had never heard of it. Locke goes on to require most of the branches that custom approved; this was also the reason for their selection—custom approved, even demanded them. The languages had an important place in his scheme. Latin was essential but should be begun without grammar, which was to be gradually introduced as the boy progressed. French too was necessary but Greek would be omitted. We shall not repeat the long list of subjects that Locke proposed. Music was condemned because it takes too much time, but dancing and fencing were essential for a gentleman. And then some trade would be useful for exercise and as a background for the time when the boy became a man with an estate to manage. Locke finally chose gardening and carpentry as the trades that provided good exercise and useful knowledge for a gentleman.

ROUSSEAU

After a disobedient boyhood, Jean Jacques Rousseau (1712–1778) ran away from a master who demanded honesty and steady application to the engraver's trade. In his wandering a young man at Turin tried to teach him Latin but this like previous and later attempts was almost a complete failure. During his years spent with a demimonde, Rousseau read two popularly written books, one on mathematics and the other on science. The woman with whom he lived, Madame de Warens, tried to get a position for him; and she succeeded with one of the deMably brothers, Jean Bonnot, who was a high official in the government of Lyons. Rousseau was to teach two boys, one bright, one dull. At the end of a year he left a report, "Fragment of a Memorandum on the Education," of the two boys. This is noteworthy because it is entirely based upon Locke's theory and shows that in 1740 when Rousseau wrote it he had not formed an original view of the subject.

Many years were to elapse before Rousseau published his most extended version of his educational doctrine in a didactic novel, Émile, in 1762. This is one of the most original books on education, and although it may not be the best, it is worth examining. In the interval between the Memorandum and Émile, Rousseau wrote the Discourse of 1750, which won a prize offered by the Academy of Dijon, and a second discourse (1754), which did not win but that he said, was better than the earlier work. Rousseau was becoming known. He was writing articles for the famous Encyclopédie along with Voltaire, Diderot, and other famous men.

Both Locke and Rousseau were opposed to the doctrine of innate ideas, but this does not draw the two into agreement on the nature of the newborn child. Locke's view was that the infant is like a blank sheet of paper upon which experiences can write what it will; but Rousseau held that the infant is an organism that carries traits and capacities that will condition its whole life. Rousseau's view is the true idea. The child is not clay to be shaped as its parents and associates may desire.

One of those traits that conditions the infant's life and that continues into maturity is a sense of justice. Rousseau assured his readers that there is at the bottom of a man's heart an innate sense of "justice and virtue." In writing about this, Rousseau recalled a childhood whipping that he thought and continued to think unjust, and he became so excited that he could not write calmly about it. The essential point is that he believed in native, inborn traits that stay with us for life.

At the very beginning of Émile, (p. 6) Rousseau wrote:

All that we lack at birth, all that we need when we come to man's estate is the gift of education. This education comes to us from nature, from man, and from things. The inner growth of our organs and faculties is the education of nature, the use we learn to make of this growth is the education of man, what we gain by our experiences of our surroundings is the education of things.

This concept of three kinds of education came from Aristotle.

Five stages cover the twenty-five years from birth to manhood: infancy, until the child learns to speak; early childhood, later childhood, adolescence, and early manhood. One does not see the need for the two stages of boyhood. Rousseau does not clearly set forth the difference, but the situation is reversed in regard to adolescence, which is the author's great contribution to psychology. By the time early manhood is reached the inner fires have been dampened and peace again rules in the young heart. It is adolescence—adolescent psychology and secondary education—that became the great contributions to the five ages of man according to Rousseau.

A great upheaval in the boy's emotional life characterizes adolescence; he may weep, show sudden anger, contempt, and fear intermingled and without apparent cause. This leads Rousseau to introduce into his scheme some of the most unusual precautions, negative education, natural punishments, and isolation of the boy from society. Negative education meant "shielding the heart from vice, the mind from error," and to delay the maturing of the boy. He should be isolated from society as far as possible. He cannot understand moral lectures. He must be kept away from towns, parties, and society, especially of the opposite sex.

The social isolation has not always been accepted, but Rousseau may have understated—rather than overstated—the dangers; they have become much greater in modern times with the influences of cars, narcotics, liquor, and money on the young. The paradox of the good man destroyed by a bad society has become a fact and a condition so serious that in time civilization may be destroyed by it.

To protect Émile from the dangers of society, he was to be educated by a tutor who was to be a constant companion. This scheme is not closely followed because the boy, now and again, meets playmates, a juggler performing in public, a gardener, and others; but in general the boy and tutor are together alone. Rousseau learned a lesson from Locke who was troubled by servants in the boy's family. Social studies and history are excluded because a small boy can not understand them. Reading was to be postponed to the age of ten or twelve years, and *Robinson Crusoe* is the only book mentioned.

Nature is the proper field of study for a boy. Thinking begins with the excitement of the senses. By letting Émile handle objects he learns about size, weight, temperatures, shape, color, sound, and smell. Because we gain our knowledge of nature through the senses, Rousseau thought the senses should be trained; but he vastly overestimated the improvement gained therefrom and even more the usefulness of this improvement. He was impressed with the gain made in the sense of touch by the blind and thought that similar gains could be made in all the senses. His view of the gain in intelligence through sense-training was greatly exaggerated.

Geometry provided a good opportunity for sense-training, especially of sight. Rousseau's plan for the introduction of geometry was, therefore, inductive, a training of the eyes and touch. A boy who draws circles with a pencil and string will need no separate proof that the radii of a circle are equal, or that the three angles of a triangle fill the space around a point on one side of a straight line. But he was mistaken if he thought that this gave the boy the mental exercise of demonstration. The tutor, Rousseau said, will not teach the boy geometry, he will have him discover it. This is one of Rousseau's best ideas and is itself an educational discovery.

In Book III of *Émile* we find the main treatment of the teaching of science, the chief purpose of which is to develop a taste for science and not to cover the vast subject or prepare a scientist. Science, Rousseau claimed, is a fathomless and shoreless ocean; but it is of the greatest use in stimulating the mind. As motives for the pursuit of science, Rousseau selects curiosity, a present drive, and utility, a future value. As soon as the boy can distinguish between useful and useless studies, the teacher must lead him to see the need for theoretical studies. This too is of value, but Rousseau has the greatest difficulty in finding manageable studies. He flounders about in geography and astronomy, proposing problems that no boy with Émile's slight preparation can be expected to solve.

Geography offers a much easier introduction to science than astronomy. Rousseau proposes to have the boy study his familiar surroundings and to draw a map of the road from his family's townhouse to the country house where the family spends much of the summer. The problem selected is the drawing of the road connecting the two places, the intersecting roads, the neighboring residences, farms, and so on. This is a good idea but the idea leads to an exercise rather than a scientific problem.

To introduce the boy to the study of the sciences, Rousseau believes that physics and chemistry must be included, and he introduces a physical problem and a chemical problem concerning the adulteration of food and drink, but it is not very clear how the boy would attack either problem. At this point the discussion turns to the industrial arts, but this seems no easier for Rousseau than the sciences. The trouble, of course, is that Rousseau was almost completely ignorant of these essential subjects. Instead of preparation Rousseau read and reread "a hundred times" two books, by the popularizer Father Bernard Lamy, "Conversations" on the sciences and the "Elements" of mathematics. Rousseau like most nonmathematicians liked geometry better than algebra and took pains in his studies to provide geometric illustrations of algebraic equations such as $(a + b)^2 = a^2 + 2ab + b^2$; it seems clear that he was able to draw appropriate diagrams. But he simply did not know these subjects well enough to deal with the problems that arise in teaching them to children.

From the sciences and the manual arts we are instructed by Rousseau to turn to the languages in education. If Émile did not learn to read before he was ten or twelve years old, Rousseau was pleased. In this he gets a measure of support from those present-day teachers who have accepted "reading readiness" ideas and who carry on activities and conversations with the children. Another group of teachers puts a book into the hands of some precocious children when they are five, four, or even three years old. Some teachers hold the view that pupils who have trouble in learning to read need more practice and should have begun reading earlier. This view is also old. Quintilian said: "All that is learned early need not be learned later." Headstart is an example of one present trend, but it is not approved by everybody.

Although somewhat confused in his treatment of the study of reading, Rousseau is completely befuddled over the study of writing. It needs no study, he declared, the boy just writes. This is absurd. Languages are necessary for the understanding of literature. One must learn Latin to understand French. For poetry we need Greek, Latin, and Italian. Apparently Rousseau knew no Greek, and only some Latin and what Italian he picked up in a few weeks at Turin and the journey homeward. He eventually exercised great pains to acquire control of the language of France and Geneva, his native city. Rousseau returned to the Protestant Church and in the story of the Vicar of Savoy he accepted for himself faith in God, Freedom, and Immortality. Rousseau's shortcomings have been sufficiently stressed.

In summary of Rousseau's chief ideas, we should note that Rousseau differed from Locke in his account of inherited qualities; that there are three kinds of education; that negative education, delayed maturing, and sense training are overemphasized; that the boy will not be taught geometry but will discover and develop it; and that throughout, investigations, problem solving, and the inquiring mind are never forgotten.

BASEDOW

For reasons that are not clear, Basedow gave the name *Philanthropinum* to the new and expensive schools for boys that developed in the eighteenth century. He did not establish the first or the best of these schools, but his writing on the new education certainly increased his reputation and cemented his connection in the public mind with the new and expensive education for boys of the upper classes. Girls were frequently brought up like Rousseau's Sophy, but there were exceptions in families that employed a tutor.

In origin Basedow belonged to the working or small business classes; his father was a wigmaker. Johann Bernard Basedow (1724–1790) was employed in his youth to teach the son of a rich family and there a governess taught him to speak French. The head of the house advised Johann's father to give the boy an education. He attended a secondary school and at the University of Kiel obtained a doctor's degree with a thesis on the teaching of foreign languages. This is odd for he never acquired a good command of Latin, but many of his ideas were adopted by others. All this took place at least ten years before the publication of *Émile*. One of these ideas was that Latin and German should be pursued together in support of each other.

In 1768 Basedow issued a manifesto entitled A *Memorial to the Friends of Mankind and Men of Means on Schools and Studies and Their Effect upon the Public Welfare*. This document gained him wide notice and approval among the upper classes; and to this he attached a proposal to prepare a basic book for teachers or *Elementarwerk*. He secured support, selected a staff, and set them to work. Instead of working with them Basedow set himself to prepare An *Entertaining Arithmetic*. Basedow's defects are beginning to appear. After about four years, the *Elementarwerk* in four volumes was completed and, illustrated by a famous Polish artist and engraver, Nikolaus Chodowiecki, was put on sale at a price of twelve taler, too expensive for teachers. However, the book was an early landmark in visual education.

At the age of fifty, Basedow was unemployed, and an advertisement for employment brought only one response. This came from a small state, Anhalt-Dessau. Basedow agreed to establish and direct a school there with at first only three pupils and one teacher beside himself. The school did not come up to his expectations and he changed its name from Philanthropinum to a simple Institute. The school continued under different teachers but never came up to the founder's ideal.

The greatest of Basedow's several errors was his plan to put play in the place of work. "He proposed to have teachers teach and have pupils learn without intense effort," this was the opinion of a young teacher, Karl Pilger, who later became a famous writer under the name of *Spazier*, a word that might suggest a walk for pleasure. Basedow came without experience or training but became successful. He was favorably impressed by the physical and gymnastic exercises but soon discovered that they were the most important classes in the curriculum, more important than language lessons, which could be interrupted for an exhibition. Basedow approved of the chapel exercises but thought them too much directed to the heart and not enough to the head.

The philosopher Immanuel Kant (1724–1804) was deeply interested in the school of Anhalt-Dessau. This was, in part, because it was to embody the ideas of Rousseau's *Émile*. The day when Kant became immersed in this "dreambook" was the only day on which he missed his customary afternoon walk. Kant was deeply interested in Basedow's work because he thought that Basedow's work was to apply the theory of Rousseau. Kant held the idea that man's hidden nature might be revealed and perfected by better education that would tend to develop a generation and a whole race of men who were nobler and more perfect than those of the past. Kant used the analogy of cultivated plants that reveal perfections that are unsuspected in the wild state. Men who hope to improve education and consequently mankind must plan for the future. Such leaders must not depend upon the government that only uses men for its purposes, and does not plan for their perfection. Rulers care only for the state, Kant said, but we are to care for mankind. Actually Kant's vision was far broader and nobler than that of Basedow and the Philanthropinists.

PESTALOZZI

As we have noted in earlier chapters, several versions of the principles of John Henry Pestalozzi (1746–1827) combined with native American ideas changed schoolkeeping in the United States to teaching. We shall now summarize the life and views of Pestalozzi himself and the social conditions that led to their development. Pestalozzi was the great mediator through whom European theories were transmitted to American education.

After an attempt at farming that proved to be a failure, Pestalozzi and his wife Anna tried raising children—other people's children. They had a son of their own, a bright and clever boy, but they decided to take in and improve the neglected, the vagrants, and the pilferers. Others soon heard of the place and applied for admission. They were needy and shoeless, and could not be turned away. The idea of the Pestalozzis was that these children could be put to work to earn their own support even though they had never worked before. Some were feebleminded, but Henry believed that this condition could be cured. With more children, more help was needed, and administration of the school became a serious problem. The funds contributed by philanthropic souls were exhausted in about five years and the Neuhof institute had to be closed. Pestalozzi admitted his errors, but his best friends doubted that he could correct them if given another chance.

Pestalozzi's friends, Isaac Iselin, Henry Littlefoot, and others who had read some of his articles advised him to write. This he did and became famous for a short period. He wrote a novel called *Leonard and Gertrude, A Book for the People,* a pastoral and a problem novel combined. It was a successful book but Pestalozzi added Parts II, III, and IV with progressively decreasing interest on the part of the readers.

Pestalozzi also wrote *The Evening Hours of a Hermit* and other philosophical and religious books, but he is not numbered among the philosophers. He declared that the usual school curriculum was artificial and would not help people living in this century; much that was taught was confused as well as useless. He demanded a simple elementary course that would serve the simple innocent person at his work, in his family, and among his people. He, therefore, went beyond Rousseau.

The Economic Society of Berne offered a prize for the best essay on the place of luxuries in the trade of a simple economic state. Of the twenty-eight competitors, Pestalozzi and a Professor Meister divided the prize. Pestalozzi wrote on political freedom, and in 1782 he printed an essay to the effect that America had won its independence. Infant murder by unwed mothers was a problem in Switzerland and other countries. After an extended investigation, Pestalozzi wrote an important book on the subject. As a result of this investigation, he published his views on the proper treatment of criminals (*Swiss Paper*, May 30, 1782), including the state's duty to the children whose fathers are imprisoned. This indicates the kind of questions that were treated by Pestalozzi, but does nothing to indicate the humor and the friendly spirit that illuminate the lighter pieces in his *Swiss Paper*.

Pestalozzi's principles of teaching are referred to as "The Method." He wrote: "I am trying to psychologize the instruction of mankind . . . to bring it into harmony with the nature of my mind. . . . I start from no positive form of teaching but simply ask what I must do to give a single child all the knowledge and practical skill he needs. . . . I think to gain this end the human race needs exactly the same thing as the single child."

By no means, the present educator will say, is this all that is required; by no means is the mind of a child, any child, equal to that of another. This complicates the task of teachers and schools. The fact that Locke and Rousseau dealt with individual children concealed the fact that some are clever, others dull; but even if they had written about class-exercises they might not have hit upon the wide range of intelligence in any group. Pestalozzi at Neuhof even thought the feebleminded could with more effort learn the same lessons as the brilliant. The French psychologist Itard started out with this view but after five years gave it up. Even this experience did not lead Itard to write upon the general subject of individual differences.

We return to the passage quoted from Pestalozzi. One may well ask whether he realizes the vast differences in the scope of the ideas that he presents. To psychologize education, to bring it into harmony with his mind is the first purpose. The second is that of giving a single child all needed knowledge and practical skill; and thirdly, doing this we give the whole race what it needs. This is not to be accomplished at school; it requires the effort of a lifetime.

Pestalozzi wrote that all forms of instruction must be made to agree with those eternal laws by which the human mind is governed and is raised from sense impressions to clear ideas. He believed that sense impression of Nature is the only true foundation of human instruction. However, man also lives by ideals, by associations formed with other persons, in marriage, in clubs, "political" parties, financial groups, and religious affiliations. All of these are pretty far from the simple sensations and judgments with which instruction begins.

The conditions of Europe, at this time (1790–1815), during and after the great revolutions, greatly disturbed Pestalozzi. At the century's end, wars and rumors of further wars, devastation, and large numbers of hungry and homeless people, including many child refugees and associated social disorders seemed to him to be the results of bad education. The poor were ignorant and suppressed; the rich miseducated, greedy, and cruel; the schools and the want of schools together separated people into hostile classes; and everywhere there was a lack of Christian faith, charity, hope, and love.

The art of instruction, according to the Swiss master, should involve the use of speech, drawing, and writing, but also reckoning, and measuring. Both lists could be extended to include invention, making collections, classifying and describing along with forms of impression, sight, hearing, touch, and other senses as well as insight, weight, pressure, texture, colors, and melodies.

It was Pestalozzi's original idea to unite learning and labor, first at Neuhof and later in his *Leonard and Gertrude*, with the mother as the teacher of spinning and housework, the school arts, and manners and morals. But in the later parts of the novel he brought in a school perhaps because most mothers and families were not as he had pictured them. Family education could not become general. At Stanz he faced scores of unkempt children of various ages and conditions. Pestalozzi lacked equipment but he was able to develop cooperation and attention and to teach spelling. At Stanz he was forced to do a great deal with almost no equipment. At Burgdorf, for the first time he had the ordinary school equipment as well as assistance. Few people in educational history accomplished so much with so little.

Teachers point out that observation provides the materials of speech and that speech should precede reading. Teachers have made much of this sequence and have stressed the first two as preparation for the third. They tend to add mental maturity to the sequence and seem to delay reading longer than necessary.

In Pestalozzi's search for the elements of the art of speaking, he selected three that seemed to apply to all subjects: namely, language, form, and number (Letter VI of "How Gertrude Teaches"). Before one can speak of an object, one must learn the names that describe it. This was a mistake, and his three elements of speech are not universally applicable and are incomplete. A swarm of bees or a bank of clouds may be constantly changing. Color, if we include the grays, is more universal than form.

Even if all these criticisms are valid, and although others could be added, we must not miss the main points of Pestalozzi's quest. The three main points are that experiences must precede or accompany thought, speech, and action; that language is a means of thought and understanding; and that mere words without thought and experiences are only "chatter" that tend to interfere with real education. Here Pestalozzi succeeded in locating an important educational problem, namely, how much and what kinds of experiences should the school provide? His successors, Herbart, Froebel, and others, have worked at this task without reaching any final answers.

We have been considering the elementary curriculum that Pestalozzi promoted; but he with his fellow teachers also developed a more advanced course of study. This included work in geography, nature-study, music, arithmetic, the elements of science, the beginnings of the study of history, physical education, and others. Also included should be the education of girls in separate schools, including the preparation of girls to serve as teachers. As time went on, Pestalozzi's part in the conduct of his schools steadily declined, but he always conducted the daily prayers and religious services. His presence alone had a deep influence.

Early in his Burgdorf school Pestalozzi welcomed a vagrant boy, a homeless wanderer who was fleeing from some soldiers. He educated the boy, who was then growing into manhood and appointed him to teach classes. One day Pestalozzi was visiting his class when the young teacher lost his temper and slapped a boy. Pestalozzi left the room and closed the door not too gently. Later when he saw the young teacher, all he said was, "I thought we had gotten beyond that." When the boy grew up and later had a school of his own in Germany, he told the story about himself.

The teaching of geography and arithmetic was greatly affected by the ideas of Pestalozzi. Rousseau had begun to affect the teaching of geography. One recalls his having Émile, who was lost in the woods, find his way home and draw a plan of the roads and the natural conditions between his home and his summer home. Pestalozzi gave a new meaning to the subject: geography as the home and workshop of man. Karl von Ritter (1779–1859), sometimes considered the father of modern geography, claimed that he gathered the basic principles of the subject from Pestalozzi.

The Swiss leader broadened the scope of arithmetic to reach beyond business problems. All uses of numbers and measurements were to be included in arithmetic. Number problems were to be found in games, sports, crops, the growth of children in height and weight, in the measurement of time and of distance, and in many other fields. Pestalozzi had children calculate without pencil and paper. This led to a new branch of study called mental arithmetic. Until about 1900 American children often had two arithmetic lessons a day: written arithmetic on the blackboard and mental arithmetic "in the head."

About 1800, Pestalozzi had a government aided school at Burgdorf. He was no longer alone. His first assistant was Herman Krüsi a self-educated teacher who brought his flock to Pestalozzi to study and imitate his methods. Krüsi later became the head of a Swiss normal school at Gais, and his son, the younger Herman, came to the United States, taught at Oswego, and wrote a life of the great master.

At Burgdorf, Pestalozzi began to gain his European reputation. Many visitors came, perhaps only to see him, perhaps also to learn. It was largely through these American visitors that his ideas as modified by them influenced American education.

HERBART

A professional philosopher, Johann Friedrick Herbart (1776–1841), became an interpreter of Pestalozzi. He sympathized with the master's social goals and strongly approved of the idea that schools should provide experience instead of assuming that the pupils have already had experience. Herbart's attack upon formal discipline or transfer of training, although it had a useful effect upon practice, was not literally correct. It went too far. Experiment has shown that there is some transfer in many processes of learning and training, and that there may be a large amount in some cases.

But it was his doctrine of interest upon which Herbart laid extraordinary stress. One writer, W. E. Wilson, declared that until Herbart called attention to interest, it was a neglected subject even among psychologists. Herbart claimed that interest is a "stirring up" of the self, a vigorous mental activity; that it involves the absorption of the self in the object; and that it can so reinforce ideas that they will have practical effects upon conduct. Interest is the means to increased effort. Herbart further claimed that conduct is determined by the ideas that the individual has accepted. In this theory the self has no originating or controlling power. In taking these positions, Herbart was opposing the ethics of Kant, who in his ethics, had rejected all empirical influence. The agent who did right because it was beneficial, whether to himself or to others, would not, in Kant's view, be moral at all. Herbart postulated a will that would act in accordance with the acquired ideas. This made the self a pawn in the hands of the teacher, parents, and one who could get him to accept his ideas. The will postulated by Kant, on the other hand, could not be influenced at all by teachers or parents.

Herbartian psychology is essentially a schoolmaster's psychology, not the psychology of a growing, inquiring, experimenting child but the expression of a nation laying great emphasis upon authority and subordination, both in war and in civil life. It is not the psychology of a nation believing that every individual has the principle of authority within himself. But we are not compelled to follow either Kant or Herbart. We may instead either go back to Plato and Aristotle or forward to Hegel.

To Herbart it seemed irrational that Locke, the greatest of the social realists intended to prepare "men of the world." But Locke was planning the education of a country gentleman, one who was to live on his own estate, serve the local community, hold office and, perhaps, serve in Parliament. Herbart married an English girl but he never lived in England and confused men of the world with worldings, a class that applied more directly to Montaigne's prospective pupil than to Locke's. Americans knew little of Herbart's philosophy before 1890, and the slight knowledge that was possessed by a few had been supplied by German-Americans employed in the schools. Before 1880 G. Stanley Hall and Francis W. Parker had been exposed to the currents of educational theory in the German universities. At that time Herbart was in great favor in Germany. In 1876 the city of Oldenburg, where Herbert was born, held a centennial celebration of that event and dedicated a monument in his honor. But it was not Herbart's philosophy that attracted disciples. Philosophers were generally cool toward his metaphysics and critical of his ethical system. It was the educators and psychologists of Germany and Austria who became the professed Herbartians; this was also the case in the United States.

Other Americans became aware of the educational movements in Europe and entered German universities for the declared purpose of studying Herbart's educational doctrines. Charles De Garmo, Charles and Frank McMurry, and C. C. Van Liew were among the early ones, and they, with some who did not closely adhere to the true faith, formed the Herbart Club in 1892. This became the National Herbart Society and later the National Society for the Study of Education. The last-named body quickly forgot its parentage, but in attempting to found a science of education it followed closely what was indeed the central purpose of Herbart. If in his professional life Herbart can be said to have held more firmly to one purpose than to any other, it was to make education a science based upon ethics and psychology, just what Dilthey was to declare impossible.

The effect of the introduction of Herbartian doctrine was extraordinary. According to Francis W. Parker, no previous ideas had stimulated such a volume of educational discussion. B. A. Hinsdale also thought Herbartianism the most powerful stimulus that had ever acted upon educational thought in the United States. Similar testimony by others could be collected. There was an extrinsic reason for this: More teachers, schools, institutes, educational journals, and normal schools existed in 1890 than ever before. And all were eager to hear and publish the new ideas. More significant was the fact that in the controversial features, and even more in the real merits of Herbart's thought, there were intrinsic reasons for a discussion that was to continue for many years. The ancient arguments on mental discipline served to start this discussion.

When it is reported that the study of arithmetic has led to greater skill in dealing with numbers, discipline is affirmed. This kind of discipline is simple learning. Arithmetic, for example, disciplines the pupil in the use of numbers. One who has been thus disciplined shows the results in the performance of such skills as addition and subtraction. No one doubts the reality or the importance of discipline in this sense. But Plato in the *Republic* claimed that the study of arithmetic produces "quickness of apprehension." In this claim Plato was asserting what is now called transfer of training or formal discipline. For our purpose we may take these two phrases as synonymous. Formal discipline is the doctrine that the study of arithmetic, for example, makes the pupil expert not only in arithmetic but also in other abilities that may be only distantly related to arithmetic.

The speculative belief that the mind is made up of faculties was usually assumed as the basis of the doctrine of formal discipline. Scholars were not always certain about the number, scope, or order of development of the faculties. We have briefly reviewed one such scheme, that of Francis Wayland: his was a fairly widely accepted one, but there were others.

In the faculty psychology it was thought that selected branches of study were especially useful for training particular faculties: namely, mathematics for reasoning and classics for judgment. In the nineteenth century, when the sciences and other new branches were introduced, the teachers of the older studies had to relinquish a part of their ancient monopoly. Being unwilling to do this, they developed added arguments for their favorite studies. Bain declared that the disciplinary values of the classics were not emphasized whereas the ancient languages were necessary. In that period the practical value of the ancient languages attracted the students; but when the modern languages took their place, the claim was made and redoubled that the classics gave their devotees a uniquely valuable formal discipline, and in fact, a complete education.

A wholly new turn was given to the question by Herbart, who taught that the mind acts as a unitary organism, one without any separate faculties. This doctrine where it was accepted destroyed the faculty psychology and the formal discipline of the nonexistent faculties at one stroke.

FROEBEL

Two of the most famous modern educators—Rousseau and Froebel—had the misfortune to lose their mothers at birth or soon afterward. Froebel's father married again, and the boy's stepmother cherished him until she had children of her own but not afterward. There is a story of the young stepchild's being shut up in a basement and forgotten. The following day when he was discovered and was brought up into the family, he is supposed to have said that his mother had comforted him during the night. It could be and might be true.

Friedrich Wilhelm August Froebel (1782–1852) was born in a manse, and his father was the busy and often imperious pastor of a large parish, whose members brought their troubles and complaints to him. The recitals could not always be explained to a curious boy—nor should they have been. Religious worship and the hymns of the church were the daily concerns of every member of the family including the servants and the small boy. When Friedrich grew up, his religious views changed but always remained, as he thought, truly Christian.

A different and more wholesome influence developed for father and son from their life together out-of-doors. In the not-too-frequent periods when they were together in the garden the boy also played at gardening. His flowers bloomed and his beds required weeding, and the garden became his first school. His father was disappointed because Friedrich had great difficulty in learning to read. His father gave up the effort to teach young Friedrich and sent him to a girl's school because he had had a quarrel with the teacher of the boys. Word of the situation must have spread, and Friedrich's uncle invited the boy to come to live with him at Stadt-Ilm in 1792. This was good fortune. Friedrich attended a boy's school, played boy's games, and had a good time generally. He could take walks in the country and explore the surroundings, and became a real boy. He was allowed to stay at Stadt-Ilm until he was fifteen, five happy years. When he came home he was apprenticed to a forester who was to teach him the trade but neglected to do so. Left to himself, Friedrich studied the books on mathematics in the library. When he became nineteen (1801), he was brought home, although the forester offered to keep him and teach him. His father disagreed.

Froebel's next opportunity came at this time, at the University of Jena, perhaps the leading German university at that time. An older brother who was a student there, needed funds and Friedrich was to carry them. The language of instruction had been changed from Latin to German. In this post-Kantian era leading scholars taught there. Schelling had succeeded Fichte in philosophy, Schiller lectured on the arts, and Goethe was nearby at Weimar. Froebel is not likely to have heard these men. Instead he took the subjects to which he had already been introduced, elementary mathematics, mineralogy, botany and other natural sciences, and practical arts. He also overstayed the time for which he had funds but his family finally got him home, all bills paid. Froebel had studied at the University of Jena from 1799 to 1801.

The positive results of his studies did not come up to his estimate of them. He studied too many branches, about a dozen. He took up Latin but like Rousseau never mastered it. Later he also studied oriental languages, Hebrew and Persian. He was influenced by Professor Batsch, who taught that the human body structure is a model not only for mammals but also for birds and fishes, all built on the same plan.

Back home, Froebel helped his father whose health was failing and who died in 1802 when Friedrich was twenty. For advice Friedrich usually looked to his brother, Christopher, with whom he was in frequent touch by letter or during visits. Having a living to earn Friedrich looked around for opportunities. He began as a land-surveyor, followed with estate management, forestry, private secretarial work, and farm management. In the course of three years he worked for a number of employers including a Jena doctor of philosophy who introduced him to two of Schelling's works. It is possible and quite likely that this was Froebel's first introduction to this famous author. "When I reached Jena," Froebel wrote long after, "I was seized by the stimulating intellectual life of the place"; but this was a later memory and it does not mean that he studied philosophy at Jena; he may never have attended any of Schelling's lectures. This Jena graduate in philosophy whose farm Froebel was surveying gave him two of Schelling's books to read: *Of the World-Soul*; and *Bruno, or Concerning the Natural and the Divine Principle of Things*. It does not appear that Froebel ever read these books.

Giordano Bruno (1548–1600) was a sixteenth-century Italian philosopher who championed the Copernican theory and became an enthusiastic pantheist. For this belief he was convicted of heresy and was burned at the stake two centuries before Schelling used him in the title of his book. During that interval Kant had developed his philosophy and prepared the way for Schelling. Froebel, who never read Kant, lived in the world that Kant had prepared; and he agreed with the great German that the mind is spontaneously active in combining sensations and ideas into a unified consciousness. Froebel who never names any sources presents a Trinity of his own selection: God, man, nature. In the opening passage of his only book, *The Education of Man*, Froebel writes:

An eternal law pervades and rules all things. It is expressed in the external world of Nature, in the inner world of mind and spirit, and in life where these two are unified. It is clearly evident to the person who is convinced by temperament and belief that this must be so, as well as to him who has arrived logically at the view that our minds are revealed in our actions and that our actions are essentially the result of inner realities. Underlying this universal order of things is a living unity which is all-pervading, self-cognisant and everlasting. This unity too is known at all times by those who respond to it emotionally or who logically apprehend it, and so it will always be. This unity is God.

This conviction developed in Froebel's mind long before he wrote it in the *The Education of Man*, perhaps as early as the Jena period. By 1805 he had become dissatisfied with his work and its frequent changes. For a permanent vocation he selected architecture and decided to go to Frankfurt for the necessary training. Meanwhile he had to earn his living. At Frankfurt he met G. Anton Gruner, the head of a new Pestalozzian model school, who offered him a tentative appointment as a teacher. Froebel had never thought of teaching as a possible vocation but he had to earn his living and he accepted. He wrote to his brother Christopher for advice. His mind was not firmly made up but he claimed to be delighted. His appointment was confirmed and he got along well with his classes from 1805 to 1807. He then decided to go to Pestalozzi to learn how to teach.

After a month, he took a short vacation and hurried to Yverdon, where after a month of service he found that he knew more than the great master. Pestalozzi indeed showed him that it is not necessary to keep all pupils abreast. Promotion by subject is desirable. A given pupil may be put in Grade A in reading, Grade B in arithmetic, and Grade C in penmanship. But the great mistake was, Froebel declared, that although individual classes and subjects were well taught, there was no underlying foundation, no recognition of God, man, and Nature, and of "an eternal law" that "pervades and rules all things." After a few years Froebel was chosen to direct three boys of the Von Holzhausen family and after a short period took them to Yverdon where both he and the boys became pupils from 1808–1810. In the latter year Froebel resigned his charge of the boys and left Frankfurt for the University of Göttingen.

The extent of Froebel's change of mind was shown in a letter to a princess of Schwarzburg-Rudolstadt to suggest that she should consider the introduction of Pestalozzian methods in teaching children during their early or preschool years. The suggestion was inspired by an examination of Pestalozzi's *Mother's Book*. This seems to be the first hint anticipating the kindergarten; and more than twenty years were to pass before Froebel thought of the word *kindergarten*.

The class instruction provided an opportunity to hear and see what was happening at Yverdon, and Froebel went to classes with his boys. He seized opportunities to ask Pestalozzi's reasons for topics and methods, and he wrote on his impressions: "The powerful, manysided, and touching life in the instruction affected me strongly. Of course, I was not blind to the many errors and deficiencies but I was impressed by the general excellence of the work in many classes." The range of studies included reading, writing, music, drawing, arithmetic, geography, history, and others.

Froebel's view that a whole series of studies was needed to prepare children for history was not adopted. He thought the child could not understand history without first studying anthropology, psychology, physiology, and in general the nature of man. But it has been found that the study of history itself provides the best account of the nature of man. What man is may be seen in what he does.

To work in crystallography under Weiss, Froebel went to the new University of Berlin in 1812. For his support, he taught classes in the Pestalozzian school conducted by Plamann. But he was interrupted by the war with Napoleon. While in the army he gained two loyal collaborators,

H. Langethal, a scholar, and W. Middendorf, a capable teacher and a poet at heart. Returning from the army everything points to the conclusion that Froebel intended to prepare for a university career, but found that under C. S. Weiss he would be only an assistant.

Froebel suddenly changed his plans and established a school for three of his nephews at Griesheim, but soon moved to Keilhau. Other pupils came and his army friends, Langethal and Middendorf, came to join him, and by 1819 they had a school of over fifty pupils. In the Prussian reaction against liberal trends after the murder by a student of the playwright Kotzebue in 1819, the boys were withdrawn until only five or six were left. The school was taken over by G. Arnold Barop who gradually restored it. Froebel went to Switzerland but he still claimed Keilhau as his school although he no longer had any share in its management.

While still at Keilhau, Froebel wrote his book, *The Education of Man*. The first part details his religious views, but the greater part of its practical educational treatment is pure Pestalozzianism, a fact that is not mentioned. In the following period he developed plays, games, and songs for small children and hit upon the happy name of *kindergarten* for the "school" for children of four and five years. This was the most original of his efforts.

SUMMARY

The rationalism that the eighteenth century inherited from Locke was followed by romanticism in education. However it was a period of diverse trends in education. Humanism was still dominant but a young and vigorous Realism was opposing it. An early evidence of this was Mulcaster's recognition of the great and growing importance of the vernacular languages.

By an ironical twist, Locke who wrote for his own countrymen, was much more popular in Europe than at home. His book was translated into French, German, and other languages and was widely read. His more comprehensive aims, including physical, moral, social, and intellectual education and his direct methods of teaching by practical experience and self-training recommended his teachings to many. His realism was less bookish, literary, and esthetic than humanism. He was a utilitarian and influenced Basedow, but Rousseau although at first a disciple became his greatest critic.

Education is growth, Rousseau said, but growth is a biological term and education is a mental, moral, and spiritual idea. Men grow to maturity and stop growing, but they continue learning until they reach old age. In addition, education is a process of developing methods and goals and a pyramiding of results as in acquiring a fortune; but bodily growth is most rapid in infancy and declines year by year until it stops. Rousseau's stages of infancy, childhood, youth, and manhood are in harmony with his growth-idea; but the usefulness of his entire conception is doubtful.

Connected with the general notion are the ideas of natural punishment; the late appearance of the ability to reason; learning without lessons; and after the passing of years, the feverish activity of the adolescent period. The introduction of the idea of experiments, instead of observation only, into the study of nature is one of Rousseau's main contributions.

Rousseau's views, challenging existing and past ideas and practices, had the value of disturbing those who merely followed practice. They were based upon the false assumption that all customs were wrong and that he alone was wise. Their greatest fault was their neglect of the masses and especially of the poor; and this was exactly where Pestalozzi started.

When he was sixteen years old, Pestalozzi read the "dreambook," *Émile*, but many other influences prepared the way for him. For religious reasons, Luther and Comenius had implicitly favored universal education. For political and economic reasons, the rulers, kings and princes, the "benevolent despots" had done the same. Pestalozzi was influenced by both of these reasons but most of all by pity. He became an educator because he intended to reform society by reforming the school. He has sometimes been misunderstood. The reform of society, beginning at the bottom, preparing the poor to become members of the human family, was his aim. He began with the young underprivileged, teaching them how to live, to work, to worship, and to study. His methods were largely inductive and practical; his influence upon the teaching of arithmetic, geography, and music was helpful and was spread abroad by former assistants and disciples; but many did not see and, therefore, did not promote his larger aims.

Considerable stimulation came from the introduction of the teaching of Herbart on such topics as the mental faculties, pupil interest, and the processes of thinking. The curricula at all levels were broadened to serve wider constituencies. Efforts were made in college and high school as well as in the grades to cultivate student interest. The relations between teachers and students also became more friendly. In several ways the advanced schools became more like the elementary schools.

Froebel invented the kindergarten and thereby began the extension of schooling downward to the fourth and earlier years of children's lives. His followers used the new school for one of Pestalozzi's purposes, social reform, and introduced into schools many activities using tools and materials. We need not accept Froebel's pantheist and poetic philosophy in order to profit from reading Froebel's *The Education of Man*. One passage at the beginning of the second chapter—"the external world comes to the child at first out of the void—as it were, in misty, formless indistinctiveness, in chaotic confusion—even the child and the outer world merge into each other"—anticipated some well-known phrases by William James.

As we shall make clear in the next chapter, Dewey was the heir of an educational tradition that if not long before began with Rousseau, was continued by Pestalozzi, Herbart, and Froebel, and lasted for a century and a half. Dewey was the first philosopher who was competent and willing to deal with its ideas and to adapt them to American conditions.

QUESTIONS

1. What do you understand from the words, *mental faculties?* Why is the notion so persistent in education?
2. It has been said that Pestalozzi led a revolt against Renaissance principles by holding up the idea of an elementary school that would provide a liberal education. Do you agree? Why? What do you mean by a "liberal education?"
3. What relations can be made out between the new psychology and philosophy and the new methods of teaching?
4. Why, if the Realists had the complete truth, do the problems of language-teaching, language-learning, and the use of language occupy so large a place in educational discussion in all ages?
5. Why did Rousseau propose to have his pupil "educate himself?" Make a list of exercises, activities, and projects that would do this better than anything Rousseau suggested.
6. What ideas and educative proceses that may come from Rousseau have you noticed in education courses, such as philosophy of education or methods of teaching?
7. Can the statement that "the poor man has no need of education" be justified?
8. Is it true, that, as Rousseau seems to claim, indoctrination is always wrong? Give examples on either side or both sides.
9. Evaluate Basedow as an educational leader and promoter.
10. Compare Basedow and Rousseau on their attitudes toward memory work.
11. Is there a serious conflict between Pestalozzi's views on the nature and purpose of geography and history in education? Can it be resolved?
12. Why did Pestalozzi call *Émile* a "dream book?"
13. Why was Pestalozzi's program slowly and imperfectly assimilated in the United States?
14. How much of Pestalozzi's theory did Herbart accept; and, especially did he accept the democratic implication?

15. Why should Herbart, who denied the possibility of experiment in psychology be given some credit for the development of experimental psychology? (See E. G. Boring's *History*.)
16. In what did the originality of Froebel consist? Trace the evolution of the teaching of young and younger children from Pestalozzi and Froebel to Headstart.

BOOKS AND PAPERS

The following bibliography is not intended to be exhaustive but only representative of the thinkers and thoughts summarized in this chapter. More extended bibliographies will be found in the authors' *A History of Western Education*, New York, The Macmillan Company, 1969.

ADAMSON, JOHN WILLIAM, *The Educational Writings of John Locke*, New York, Longmans, Green and Co., 1912, 272 pp.

BORING, EDWIN G., *A History of Experimental Psychology*, New York, Appleton-Century-Crofts, 1957.

BOYD, WILLIAM, *The Minor Educational Writings of Jean Jacques Rousseau*, Glasgow, Blackie & Son, Ltd., 1910, 159 pp.

———, *The Educational Theory of Jean Jacques Rousseau*, New York, Longmans, Green and Company, 1911, 368 pp.

———, *From Locke to Montessori*, London, George G. Harrap & Co., Ltd., 1914, 271 pp.

CAMPAGNAC, E. T., ed., *Mulcaster's Elementarie*, London, Clarendon Press, 1925, 292 pp.

CHURTON, ANNE, *Immanual Kant, Education*, University of Michigan Press, 1960, 121 pp. It is mentioned here because Kant was greatly interested in Basedow's efforts.

DUNKEL, HAROLD B., *Herbert and Herbartianism*, University of Chicago Press, 1970.

FLETCHER, S. S. and J. WELTON, *Froebel's Chief Writings on Education*, New York, Longmans, Green & Co., 1912, 246 pp.

FOX BOURNE, H. R., *The Life of John Locke*, New York, Harper & Brothers, 1876, 2 volumes.

FOXLEY, BARBARA, *Émile*, New York, E. P. Dutton & Company, Inc., 1925, 444 pp. In the Everyman's Library. Complete translation.

FRITSCHE, THEODOR, *J. B. Basedow's Elementarwerk*, Leipzig, 1909, 3 vols., with the famous artist's engravings.

GREEN, F. C., *Jean Jacques Rousseau, A Critical Study . . .* , Cambridge University Press, 1955, 376 pp.

GREEN, J. A., *Pestalozzi's Educational Writings*, New York, Longmans, Green & Co., 1912, 328 pp.

———, *Life and Work of Pestalozzi*, London, W. B. Clive & Co., 1913, 393 pp.

HENDEL, C. W., *Citizen of Geneva, Selections from the Letters of Jean Jacques Rousseau*, New York, Oxford University Press, 1937, 405 pp.

JOSEPHSON, MATTHEW, *Jean Jacques Rousseau*, New York, Harcourt Brace and Company, 1931, 546 pp.

KOLESNIK, W. B., *Mental Discipline in Modern Education*, University of Wisconsin Press, 1958, a historical treatment.

LANGE, ALEXIS, *Herbart's Outlines of Educational Doctrine*, Annotated by Charles De Garmo, New York, The Macmillan Company, 1901, 334 pp.

MORLEY, JOHN, *Rousseau*, London, Macmillan and Company, Ltd., 1915, 2 vols.

MICHAELIS, EMILIE, and H. K. MOORE, *Autobiography of Friedrich Froebel*, Syracuse, New York, C. W. Bardeen and Co., 1889, 167 pp.

OLIPHANT, JAMES, *The Educational Writings of Richard Mulcaster*, Glasgow, J. Maclehose and Sons, 1903, 245 pp.

PAINTER, F. V. N., *Great Pedagogical Essays, Plato to Spencer*, New York, American Book Company, 1905, 426 pp.

PINLOCHE, A., *La Réforme de L'Education en Allemagne au dix-huitiene siècle*, Paris, 1889; also in German, *Geschichte des philanthropinismus*, Leipzig, 1896. A good account of Basedow by Spazier, at pp. 152 ff. in the French version and at pp. 131 ff. in the German version.

QUICK, ROBERT HEBERT, ed., *Mulcaster's Positions*, New York, Longmans, Green and Company, 1888, 309 pp.

——, *Some Thoughts Concerning Education* by John Locke, Cambridge University Press, 1895, 240 pp.

——, *Essays on Educational Reformers*, New York, D. Appleton & Company, 1907, 568 pp. The Essays went through several editions.

SILBER, KATE, *Pestalozzi, The Man and His Work*, London, Routledge and Kegan Paul, 1965. The German edition was published at Heidelberg, in 1957. The translation was made by the author.

Chapter 13

EDUCATION
FOR DEMOCRACY

In the preceding chapters we have noted the influence of European theories in the development of American education. Seeds scattered by Rousseau, Locke, Pestalozzi, Froebel, Herbart, and others had put down roots in the United States in the nineteenth century where they were cultivated by Mann, Emerson, Harris, Eliot, Parker, Dewey, and others. In addition seeds native to American conditions were sprouting. One such seed is represented by the word *democracy*, a word introduced occasionally by Eliot, and more frequently by Parker and Dewey.

For known reasons none of the founding fathers of this country proposed to educate youth for democracy. From Thomas Jefferson the young nation heard of an education to maintain liberty and civil rights, and Washington spoke of the need of an enlightened public opinion in a republic. Emerson, the unpolitical man, thought that Americans were too vain of their civil institutions as they indeed may be; but he considered that society has a duty to educate everyone for himself. Whether this could be done without political institutions or done better with a political institution other than the American type, he did not say. Horace Mann wanted to educate for morality and economic efficiency, and William Torrey Harris desired the school to transmit the fruits of civilization that were gathered up in the great institutions. But Francis Wayland Parker and John Dewey gave universal currency to a new word, *democracy*, and a new goal of education, a democratic society. The schools were to be democratic and to produce a democratic social order.

There is some difficulty in determining what Parker meant by democracy. He professed an "immense faith" in the possibilities of human growth and in man's capacity for self-government; but it is clear that with Parker democracy is no longer a merely political word. He asserted with Rousseau that children are "born good," but also that "the child is a born savage," evidently a good savage. When children grow up under conditions of freedom, their originally good natures will ensure a demo-

349

cratic society. But to freedom Parker added responsibility, and this constitutes a problem: How much freedom, for whom, and when?

Class education and social classes based upon family or property were heavily scored by Parker and held up for censure, and class education is linked with charity schools. Parker thought that there was a trend in cities to make pauper schools out of the public schools. It was in this connection that he gave the definition of democracy upon which he meant to stand. He said that democracy means living for others, the strong serving the weak. At this point he approaches John Dewey's idea that sharing is the essence of democracy.

Democracy in education as Parker interpreted it demands the joining of the school and the community. He considered the home as the natural link between the school and the public that sustains the school financially and morally. He encouraged parents' meetings and the use by teachers of home and community resources.

Teachers should understand the history of the common school. This school is the newest of all the great institutions that make for righteousness and is a mere neophyte. But its past growth and work show its capacity for growth and will encourage teachers to strive for the superior school of the future. Parker saw mighty forces working for that school of the future, the kindergarten mightiest of all. Other forces were the education of women, the normal schools, and the study of education in college. But the true history of the common school must show the dark thread as well as the bright one in its past. The common school has often been in a deplorable state. In the country districts the object has often been to provide schooling at the lowest cost without any regard to quality. Parker had personal experience of these conditions.

The charge has been made that Parker did not understand the economic and political forces of his day, gravely underestimated their strength, and consequently overestimated the power of the schools. It was his optimism, devotion to a cause, and strength of character that secured for him fame and an influence that few teachers who were young at that time completely escaped.

Two reasons or conditions help to explain why John Dewey became and continues to be the most distinguished American philosopher of education. This has come about not only by reason of his genius but also because of the period in which he lived.

One does not try to explain genius, but Dewey, born in Burlington, Vermont, on October 20, 1859, was not only the son of his parents but also the child of a new age of evolution, science, and psychology. He was born in the year when the *Origin of Species* was published and in the precise time when the kindergarten was being transplanted to America. Darwin's new book and Froebel's new school were to have great influences in making Dewey the new leader of a new American philosophy of education.

YOUTH OF JOHN DEWEY

The Dewey parents and three sons made up the entire family. The sons were Davis Rich, John, and Charles Miner. The family was Old American in both lines. The forebears had been public-spirited, active citizens. The father served in a Vermont regiment throughout the Civil War. The mother's ancestors had been the more distinguished and better educated. Her family name was Rich, and Davis Rich Dewey, who became a distinguished professor at M.I.T., was named for his grandfather.

The rural and small town neighborhood in and about Burlington, Vermont, where the Dewey family lived was homespun and socially democratic. General Grant, who grew up in a similar corner of southern Ohio, reported in his autobiography that in his youth everybody worked except the very poor who alone lived idle, thriftless lives. The Deweys were industrious but only moderately prosperous. The boys attended the New England public schools that were old-fashioned, with the furniture fastened to the floor, and as Dewey was to say, "made for listening." They learned much from people, nature, and private reading. The lessons in school were too simple. Life in the country and on the lakes was more interesting. On one trip to Canada the boys learned a little conversational French.

Some money could be earned by working on farms, carrying newspapers, and tallying shipments of lumber. With the money they bought what interests boys, including two sets of books, Chamber's *Encyclopedia* and the Waverley novels. If the *Encyclopedia* was a recent edition they may have learned about the *Vestiges of Creation*, a prescientific version of evolution.

The Dewey boys had access to other books and they were constant readers. John, the exponent of firsthand experience, continued this practice throughout his life. He was also bashful and self-conscious. Even when he had won his doctor's degree, the president of Johns Hopkins University advised him to mingle more with people, to be less immersed in his books.

Few boys from Burlington attended college, which at that time were small institutions. Davis Rich, who had lost time through illness, and John both graduated from the University of Vermont in the same year, 1879. They were the first of their father's near relatives to secure college degrees. Their class included only about a score of boys, most of them from the region around Burlington. John had graduated from high school at the age of fifteen and from college in his twentieth year.

The University of Vermont was even then seventy-five years old; it is one of the three or four oldest American state universities. About ten years before Dewey entered, the institution had received Vermont's share of the land granted by the Morrill Act, which had been promoted by Justin S. Morrill who was a Senator from Vermont. His bill had added departments of agriculture and engineering. These were patronized even less than the liberal arts college of the university, an institution that long remained mainly just that, a liberal arts college. For Dewey's development and life work, this is significant. His interest was in liberal education, even manual training in his program was a liberal subject. We do not know all that he studied in college but the sciences had come into the curriculum and we know that he learned about Darwin. A textbook on physiology written by Thomas Henry Huxley was used in one of his classes. From this course Dewey gained some knowledge of the doctrine of evolution and the notion of organism. Both concepts were later to form key ideas in his philosophy. Courses in zoology and in geology fitted into the same set of teachings.

There were loud outcries against such ideas in the churches and the religious press in various parts of the country. As late as 1920 a university dean in the American Southwest continued to hold out against evolution. The trial of John T. Scopes, who was accused of teaching Darwin's theory of evolution in Tennessee schools, was held in 1925, and in the mid-1960's a similar storm cloud hung temporarily over parts of the Southwest. But at the University of Vermont in 1880 evolution aroused no great opposition.

We may account for this difference, at least in part. An early president and professor of philosophy at the University of Vermont, James Marsh, who was influenced by Coleridge, had promoted liberal thought in university circles. There were fewer crusading sects in New England in 1880 than in the South in 1920. The general public gave less attention to what was said and proposed in universities, and state universities were privileged for they had no denominational ties. The professors in Vermont like the earlier ones at Yale doubtlessly tried to harmonize scientific and religious teaching. The desire for unity, agreement, and coherence is a universal quest in all fields. Both evolutionists and their opponents sought harmony, the former by interpreting the facts, the latter by denying or modifying their conclusions. But the state universities did not wholly escape the charge that they were "godless."

One must raise the question of the influence of youthful experience and college studies upon the mature Dewey. We shall see that college developed in him a strong interest in philosophy and that philosophy became for Dewey a means of harmonizing opposite or discordant views. All philosophers are peculiarly sensitive to the meanings of words, which are, after all, their tools. To a marked degree Dewey's method is based upon the defining and redefining or finding new meanings in words. He regularly shows that individual implies social, lack means power, imitation is originality, interest produces discipline, and so on.

From boyhood, Dewey, as we know, was a great reader. How does a child become a "bookworm?" There is no simple answer; some simply do.

How did potential bookworms differ from others before there were any books? Again, we do not know; but surely there must be differences in the nervous systems of those who love to make things, fish, hunt, and trap, gather and arrange collections, and those who read and read. Dewey was a reader and that may be the reason why he insisted upon activities for young children.

The Dewey family exchequer was not overflowing. Although they lived within walking distance from the University, and tuition costs were low, scholarships were sought to help with the boys' college expenses. Instead of hunting or fishing, the boys built boats, explored the lakes, and visited mills, kilns, and shops of various kinds. These were all small businesses, open to any chance visitor, and the Dewey boys could talk with the proprietor and workers. Did this help to lead Dewey to select construction and manufacturing activities for children in his Chicago school? We do not know whether it is the lack or the presence of something that guides later education.

The complete absence of organized sports from the story of Dewey's youth is a point to be noticed. According to one theory this should have led him to favor games, but his philosophy hardly deals with exercise, physical fitness, health-education, or sports. The competitive nature of organized games may have turned Dewey against them. We find him, on one occasion at least, watching football practice at the University of Michigan. His notice of Rousseau on physical activity is not enthusiastic. The present emphasis on physical education has developed since the days of Dewey's youth.

When Dewey in his old age looked back upon the scenes and activities of his youth, he was not charmed. He could not see why people spent their vacations in Vermont. Like Socrates in Phaedrus, he learned more from men in the city than from trees in the country. But for every positive there is a negative. When Dewey lived in Chicago he spent his vacations in the Adirondacks; when he lived in New York City he had a farm on Long Island.

AT JOHNS HOPKINS UNIVERSITY

The history of the university at which Dewey completed his formal education is important in American education and in the life of John Dewey. It was in several ways a new type of university in America, and in the story there will be occasion to speak of Daniel Coit Gilman, a great educator, and the first president and organizer of Johns Hopkins.

We should begin far back with the early European universities from which the American universities have grown. In the early centuries there were no laboratories or libraries and no systematic investigations in the universities of Europe. Their chief task was the transmission of what was known or accepted. When the spirit of inquiry arose during the Renaissance, many of the great discoverers worked independently of the universities, and it was in Germany rather than in England that university libraries were first opened and laboratories established for the use of professors and students.

Most early American colleges were established when English education was in a deep depression and they remained conservative until far into the nineteenth century. American medical students, the most numerous group who went abroad in the eighteenth century, saw no great light; but about 1820, George Ticknor, Edward Everett, and their successors discovered that European education was forging ahead. They came back full of enthusiasm for college reform but it was premature. Yale College had begun to develop the sciences, and Louis Agassiz (1807–1873) was soon to develop science-teaching at Harvard. But not until Johns Hopkins University was opened in 1876 did any American university make investigation a main object.

Johns Hopkins (1795–1873), a wealthy businessman of Baltimore, provided in his will an endowment that was large for the time, for a university, a hospital, and a medical school. Daniel Coit Gilman (1831–1908) set the pattern and organized the University. He had the medical school staffed with full-time teachers, which was something new.

Gilman has been celebrated as a genius in administration, but new institutions are never wholly new. He was a Yale graduate and became a member of its staff. He helped to change the library at Yale from a collection of books to an institution that was accessible to students. He taught geography, a subject not yet common at that time in college catalogues. He traveled, inquired, observed; he became President of the University of California. It is reported that when the Johns Hopkins Trustees were selecting a president for their new university, three university presidents—James Angell of the University of Michigan, Andrew D. White of Cornell, and Charles W. Eliot of Harvard—independently named Gilman as their first choice.

The frequent repetition of this story does not prove it true, but it may be one of those unusual facts that are stranger and yet more reliable than fiction. When Gilman, after twenty-five years retired as president, he presented a number of "eminent men, recommended by a committee of professors, for the degree of Doctor of Laws, honoris causa." He said: "Three of these scholars were friends and counselors of the Trustees before any member of this Faculty was chosen. They pointed out the danger to be avoided, the charts to be followed, and during seven and twenty years they have been honored friends by whose experience we have been guided, by whose example we have been inspired." The three whom he then named were the same university presidents—James B. Angell, Andrew

D. White, and Charles W. Eliot. This may be evidence for our story or it may have been the source of it. It is of interest that in their meetings with the Trustees, planning the future University, the same three men showed little foresight for the future course of higher education in America. They did not plan any such institution as the Trustees and Gilman created. The new Johns Hopkins University did not become a graduate school upon their advice, and President Eliot years later generously admitted this fact.

Johns Hopkins University was not absolutely new; it was only new in America, and Gilman was not the first to harbor the idea. Twenty years before, Henry P. Tappan of New York, later president of the University of Michigan, proposed that American universities should follow the German example.

In forming the Johns Hopkins University, Gilman showed a keen sense for research talent. His selections were mostly foresighted, young men who had begun to show their ability but who had not established great reputations. He chose Ira Remsen for chemistry, Henry Augustus Rowland for physics, Herbert B. Adams for history, and G. Stanley Hall for psychology. Basil L. Gildersleeve was brought from the University of Virginia for Greek. Gilman's sagacity is nowhere better exhibited than in his staffing of his Biological Laboratory: for physiology he chose a student of Thomas H. Huxley, H. Newell Martin, and for morphology a student of Louis Agassiz, William K. Brooks.

The institution was to be a graduate school but, from the first or nearly so, a few undergraduates were admitted. Not since Jefferson had planned the University of Virginia did an American organizer have a similar problem, so free a field and great an opportunity; but Gilman's field from which he could make his selections was much richer than Jefferson's, and he was also more successful in his choices. Research flourished. Gilman with a wry face once complained of the printer's ink used by the faculty, but he was proud of it. The list of learned journals founded to report faculty and student research would be a long one, and it witnesses to the amount and quality of the investigations.

When John Dewey in 1882 borrowed $500 and set out for Baltimore, the University was only six years old. For two years after he graduated from college, Dewey had taught school, rather languidly one gathers; but after that an early interest in philosophy firmly gripped him. W. T. Harris accepted three of his articles for the *Journal of Speculative Philosophy*, the only periodical in that field in America. A Vermont professor, H. A. P. Torrey, continued to direct Dewey's reading. Dewey knew that his interest was not to be in education but in philosophy in a country that had no technical philosophers. The investment of $500 was a speculation. Chance and circumstance drew him into education, another speculation.

One is justified in asking why Dewey went to Johns Hopkins, a university with one half-time professor of philosophy, whose first responsibility was to the University of Michigan. Also, President Gilman had a strong bias for science, history, and other fields that had positive, determinate content, and his interest in philosophy was only tepid; but this Dewey could not know at the beginning.

The half-time professor was George Sylvester Morris, who had been educated in Germany and had made an excellent translation of a famous work, the *History of Philosophy* by Überweg. Morris had a strong interest in history, and he and Dewey agreed on this; but Dewey's interest was not in the human pageant, not in the past, but in the future. History was the record of social and moral evolution. Dewey studied history with Adams, a social and educational historian, psychology with the wide-ranging and philosophizing Hall, and philosophy with Morris. Psychology threatened to become his primary subject but his record of psychological experimentation is slight. His dissertation for the doctor's degree in 1884 was entitled *The Psychology of Kant*, probably a philosophy of psychology, or the other way around. No copy of this paper is known to remain.

DILIGENT PROFESSOR

After Johns Hopkins, as after Vermont, Dewey experienced the pains of joblessness, but not for long in either case. In the fall of 1879, just out of college, Dewey was appointed to teach "a little of everything" in a small high school at a salary of $40 per month. He may have taught not ideas but subjects from textbooks and, hampered by timidity, he must have found it drowsily dull. Apparently he had endured similar lessons in school and college. This was the image that he presented and the condition that he attacked when he began to write on education. He professed to recall his schooldays as a series of listless lessons, read or quoted by teacher and pupils from a book. The picture may have been overdrawn but it was not totally false.

In the fall of 1884, upon the recommendation of his major professor, Morris, Dewey was appointed instructor in philosophy at the University of Michigan. Except for one year at the University of Minnesota, he remained there and rose grade by grade to become professor and head of the department until he went on to the University of Chicago in 1894. Michigan was one of the very few universities that had a separate department of education at that time. This arrangement placed that subject off-limits for Dewey. Except for this, Dewey might have offered education courses earlier than he in fact did. As it was, he published a few articles on the health of women students, a subject that concerned many men until women began to enter collegiate athletic sports. At Michigan, Dewey offered no regular courses in education but he found other ways to influence teachers. We shall return to this subject.

Some merely watch the world go by; many seek to exploit it; but others try to understand it and, if possible, to improve it. Dewey belonged to this third class and in this he resembled his mother, a woman of force and character. He was, however, mild and kind like his father, and was also like him in his lack of administrative genius. Dewey organized no new institutions; he was a man of the chair, platform, and writing-desk. At Michigan he taught classes and constantly worked with his pen. He was industrious.

In the work of Dewey as an author, three subjects—psychology, education, and philosophy—enlisted his interest, in this order of time and of importance. Dewey did not confine himself to these major professional subjects; he also wrote on a variety of questions including problems of war, the League of Nations, birth control, academic freedom, conditions in Mexico, China, and other countries that he visited, Teachers Unions, and many other subjects. But we must not allow these journalistic articles to divert our attention from his three main scholarly concerns.

His interest in psychology manifested itself at Johns Hopkins and lasted through the Michigan and Chicago periods. In the latter period his growing interest in education outstripped that in psychology. He also published a philosophical work dealing with Leibniz. By 1904, when he left Chicago, Dewey had finished twenty-five or more psychological publications, reviews, articles, and two books, one a book of four hundred pages entitled *Psychology* (1886), and part of a second book, *Applied Psychology, an Introduction to the Principles and Practice of Education*. Both were textbooks, and *Psychology* attained a third edition within a few years.

The primary author of the *Applied Psychology* was J. A. McLellan, Director of Normal Schools for Ontario, Canada, and an institute lecturer. During the Michigan years, Dewey also lectured at teachers' institutes and the two men may have met in this way. In the preface of *Applied Psychology* we are told: "The general mode of treatment in the part on mental science is that of Professor Dewey, whose work on psychology has been so well received by students of philosophy. . . . To Professor Dewey . . . I must express my obligations for most valuable assistance in the preparation of this work." The writer of this preface, obviously McLellan, considers himself the chief author; but Dewey's name also appears on the title page. An examination of the text will show that Dewey was the writer, or at least the source, of the first half of the book. At that point, page 164, the character of the book changes abruptly; it loses its scientific quality and becomes a manual of practice. There is no copyright notice and no date anywhere in the copy here examined, but it must be later than that of *Psychology* (1886).

To a young man and an innovator like Dewey, the only psychology worth studying was "The New Psychology." This was the title of one of his articles written in 1884 when he was twenty-five years old. Of psychology he said, "The least developed of the sciences, for a hundred years it has borne in its presentation the air of the most completely finished."

Innovators and dissatisfied people are almost by necessity bad historians, as is illustrated by the quoted sentence. Mills and Bain were ahead of Dewey's *Psychology* in their view of the self. Berkeley had shown that our knowledge of space is based upon the sense of touch. Astronomers regularly allowed for each observer's "reaction time." Beneke in 1833 reported mathematical studies of phases of psychology. Weber began the science of experimental psychology, and Fechner used the term *psychophysics* in 1860. Dewey cites all of these authors as well as Romanes on animal intelligence. Psychology had not stood still for a hundred years.

But what was new in psychology in 1884? Experiment was beginning to encroach upon introspection; biology and social studies were supplying useful information. Knowledge of the development of abilities and traits came from the study of children. Child study was soon to become a fad. Dewey himself reported upon children's vocabulary development and argued that the child's nouns really stood for verbs. How characteristic! It was his only original scientific observation in psychology. The French were studying mental defects. From defective persons one could learn about dullness, delusions, and depressions. Comparative psychology was still an infant, although as noted, Kant had made an observation. Lloyd Morgan came a little later than Dewey.

Wilhelm Wundt opened the first university laboratory of psychology in the year that Dewey graduated from college. Wundt's pupil, Hall, taught Dewey at Johns Hopkins. Another of Wundt's American pupils was J. McKeen Cattell, who acquired the mathematical and other methods of studying individual differences from Francis Galton in England. Psychology was indeed being renewed but it had been growing during the entire nineteenth century. Dewey incorporated the new results in his *Psychology*, but his only way of explaining the unity of the mental life is through the self, or the ego, which he leaves unexplained.

Two events transformed the new psychology of 1886 into a still newer psychology: the publication in 1890 of the *Principles* of William James and Dewey's growing involvement in education. After James, the theory that emotions begin in the bodily organs, the so-called James-Lange theory, engaged Dewey's attention; and mental and bodily activities were seen as phases cooperating in the same function. The entire organism became the self and the subject of study in psychology. Dewey became a functionalist.

What Dewey's psychology became can best be seen in his *Human Nature and Conduct* (1922), which was to be an "introduction to social psychology." Habit is called the key to social psychology; and the study of impulse and intelligence the means of access to individual psychology. But it is difficult to maintain this separation in action. The democratic process of proposition, debate, adjustment, and the vote clearly involves both factors. In theory, impulse should lead to the original motion but it is actually intellectual as well as spontaneous and impulsive. The theory of the stimulus-response leading to a new stimulus in Dewey's Reflex-Arc Concept (1896) is repeated in social as in individual psychology.

Human Nature and Conduct deals throughout with conduct. Like Dewey's first book, *Psychology*, it is in three parts, which in the later work deal with habit, impulse, and intelligence in conduct. The structural features of the earlier book are dropped and the entire work is functionalist in character. Nature, man, and society are seen as forming a superorganism; and each function can be understood only in relation to all the others.

We have called the young Dewey a diligent professor, but when he wrote *Human Nature and Conduct* he was no longer young, but still diligent. To close this section, which deals with Dewey's development as a psychologist, we shall return to the end of his University of Michigan period in 1894. In the decade ending at that time Dewey had published forty or more items of professional writing including three books and had coauthored a fourth. *Psychology* was in its third edition.

IN CHICAGO

Dewey became the first head of the department of philosophy, psychology, and pedagogy in the new University of Chicago in 1894. Although President William Rainey Harper (1856–1906) seems to have accepted Aristotle's view that philosophy demands a wisdom denied to the young, he was faced with a problem; three distinguished older men had declined his invitation for this position. It seems that Harper had not thought of Dewey who was in fact at the time young and not yet well-known. At this point a Chicago assistant professor, James H. Tufts, summond the courage to recommend Dewey to the President. Harper invited Dewey to visit the University and had him stay at the President's house. Dewey came and his demeanor and public address won the approval of Harper as well as general approval. Dewey came to Chicago in 1894 and served the University for ten memorable years.

Dewey himself later gave one reason why he was willing to come to Chicago; the department that he was to direct included not only philosophy but also psychology and education, the last a field that he had started to cultivate extraterritorially, as one may say, at Michigan.

Michigan had an established education department. Dewey could not teach education courses on the campus but he did speak at teachers institutes and collaborated with McLellan in producing a book for teachers. Even in *Psychology*, Dewey wrote on association, habit, apperception, interest, and other "education" topics, only briefly on habit, but exten-sively on association. The "Reflex-Arc Concept" was published in 1896 but its seeds were germinating earlier, and Dewey's functionalism was bound to lead him into education, ethics, politics, and other applications.

This is of the greatest interest to the student of educational history and philosophy. A few of the greatest philosophers, Plato, Aristotle, and Kant, had written on education, but philosophers in general looked upon the study of education with contempt, as a war not yet won or lost, even today. That Dewey should seriously concern himself with educational psychology, and with "pedagogy"—said with a sneer—was disturbing and ominous.

Dewey was also attracted to Chicago because, like Johns Hopkins, it had no ancient past to weigh it down. Its vigorous president was inter-ested in the public schools, in education of all kinds and levels, in the preparation of teachers, in the reorganization of the high school and college, and in other matters that led directly into the university study of education. The two men cannot have realized how far apart they were in some of their qualities. Harper was certainly a scholar and so lively a teacher of the Hebrew language that students elected his course to "get" Harper rather than his subject; but he was essentially an administrator, which is just what Dewey was not.

That was the time when the university study of education was begin-ning. The old normal departments and review courses were dead, except in backward institutions. Michigan had created the first separate collegiate department of education in 1879. Indiana followed in 1886, but allowed her department to lapse in 1894; in the twentieth century a school of Education was established at Bloomington. Iowa had a normal depart-ment, then a course or courses of education in the department of philoso-phy, and created a separate department of education in 1890. The midwestern state universities were not alone. An infant institution of doubtful viability was saved by Nicholas Murray Butler to become the Teachers College of Columbia University. President Eliot chose a professor of education for Harvard despite a hostile faculty, and he even persuaded William James, who thought psychology had no special value for teachers, to compose and deliver his *Talks to Teachers*. The oldest private univer-sities were establishing departments and colleges for teachers.

The University of Chicago's combination of philosophy, psychology, and pedagogy into one program greatly pleased Dewey; but that union was unusual even in 1894, and it was disappearing except in the small colleges. Harper and Dewey were in an eddy in this, not in the main stream. Dewey was also one of the few psychologists who continued to introduce his philosophy into a textbook on general psychology. We are even now required to study and try to solve life's fundamental problems before we undertake the practical problem of teaching a child to read; but we learn our philosophy of education, our history, economics, administration, and psychology of education in separate departments of great aggregations called colleges of education. The process had only begun when Dewey went to Chicago and he had no part in it.

The city of Chicago offered many opportunities for Dewey to meet stimulating people. Colonel Francis Wayland Parker (1837–1902) was the great progressive educator of the time. "When Dewey came to Chicago," wrote Robert McCaul, "he followed the Colonel's banner." Jane Addams (1860–1935), the noted social worker, founded the settlement Hull House in Chicago in 1899, and Dewey had spoken at Hull House while he was still at Michigan. She carried another banner that Dewey revered. His democracy led him to make common cause with civic leaders. He staffed his department with men such as James R. Angell (1869–1944) who was the son of President James Angell (1829–1916) of the University of Michigan, an eloquent fact. Young Angell, George Mead, Tufts, and Dewey soon formed a new "functional" school of psychology. Many other stimulating minds were on the university faculty. Gilman's advice to Dewey to look up from his books and to mingle with people seems amusing in retrospect; but who knows whether the advice may have been effective. On occasion it takes only a push to start an avalanche.

THE DEWEY SCHOOL

Only at teachers institutes did Dewey, while he was at Michigan, have much contact with experienced teachers; the old teachers institute made little provision for discussion. The days were filled with lectures and programs, and after the meetings, lecturers and audiences went their separate ways. At Michigan, Dewey taught undergraduates. His publications before 1894 do not reveal many connections with educational associations.

After Dewey moved to Chicago, all this was changed. Dewey undertook a heavy schedule including off-campus classes. Many of his students were professional teachers doing graduate work. His combined lecture and discussion method gave Dewey access to their opinions and problems. These opportunities and the opportunity to give graduate work were both reasons for Dewey's decision to go to Chicago.

Through the Dewey School of the University of Chicago, which was opened in 1896 and to which we shall refer again, he came into close contact with skilled teachers, parents, patrons, and the general public, including a segment of the university faculty. He also belonged to some study clubs. The ideas of all these people transformed by his own views were set down in a pamphlet entitled "Plan of Organization of the University Primary School," in which we have the first of the school's different names. We shall return to this "Plan."

A further, broader diagnosis of the health of the teaching profession was gained by Dewey from his membership and activity in associations quite separate from the University. The diagnosis led him to offer some suggestions for improvements. Three of these groups were the Illinois Society for Child-Study, the National Herbart Society, and the National Education Association. In the "Transactions of the Illinois Society for Child-Study" (1895) Dewey considered the effect of child-study when applied to education. His very important paper on "Interest Related to Will" (1896) was read before the National Herbart Society in Dewey's absence, and led to a discussion in which W. T. Harris was an enthusiastic participant favoring Dewey's conclusion. Dewey spoke to the National Education Association seven times between 1897 and 1902 and again in 1916. The long absence may be a result of Dewey's lack of interest in the subjects considered by the Association.

During his years in Chicago and later in New York, Dewey was busy writing and speaking. In 1899 he delivered the three lectures that were published in 1900 as *The School and Society*. It was reprinted several times for ten years or longer and sold in the neighborhood of 20,000 copies, not a large circulation for so celebrated a book. The book was dedicated to Emmons Blaine, one of the sponsors of the Dewey or University School. Mrs. Blaine was a daughter of Cyrus McCormick, inventor and manufacturer of agricultural implements, and she had endowed Francis Parker's Chicago Institute, formerly the Cook County Normal School. During these years Dewey, probably without yet being aware of it, was preparing to write his *Democracy and Education* (1916), which sums up his educational doctrines including all of the most important ideas of the speeches and books that had preceded.

We now return to the "Plan of Organization" of the new school. Dewey believed that human intelligence developed in the process of satisfying man's needs, and children learn in somewhat the same way as mankind had learned to find materials and to invent and use clothing, tools, shelter, and so on. It was a special version of the nearly 2,000-year-old theory of the culture epochs that Dewey now and then criticized. In his "Plan" he explained that occupations would take the place of school studies. The skills of reading, writing, and arithmetic were to be learned in use as needed in the occupations. The occupations were to be attacked by the method of inquiry and discovery, a process resembling the method of social evolution.

The "Plan" does not say what occupations were to be preferred but the ones actually employed had to do with the development of clothing and shelter. Dewey strongly preferred the use of the hands in grasping and manipulating, and in the invention and use of handtools to the use of the eyes in learning. He thought the report of the eyes was superficial but that the hand gave the child the feel of resistance and reality, and of the real nature of materials.

There was another factor. Instead of the mechanical occupations that were chosen, Dewey and the teachers might have selected the care of plants and animals and the processing of foods. These tasks were probably more basic and certainly more constantly required in primitive life than were the provision of clothing and shelter. This would have led to the study of chemistry rather than of physics and the use of fire, and to the study of organisms and evolution. In the "Plan" domestic work was not omitted but neither was it stressed.

A second great idea was added to or implied in the use of occupations: The school was to be a community. By living together in mutual helpfulness, the children were to learn what a good community should be like and how it could be made to grow. Even the parents were to form a part of a larger community that included the school. The aim was to have children discover and apply the principles that govern individual and social development. What was to be done with children and parents who would not cooperate?

The new school began in a dwelling house in January 1896, with two teachers and sixteen pupils. Six years later it had moved twice, its staff had grown to twenty-three teachers along with additional help from university students, and it had 140 pupils. Dewey was the administrator of the school, but he was also a busy department head and university professor. There is evidence, at least in the early years, that the school administration was quite loose, and before the school's existence came to an end, the administrative difficulties were compounded.

Officially, the school was known as the University Elementary School and was one of the structures that made up the University of Chicago. Ella Flagg Young called it the Laboratory School, and Dewey liked this name, pointing out that like more conventional laboratories it actively tried out a set of ideas guided by a philosophy. So it did, but a laboratory should also have a system of measurements; this was lacking in the Dewey School. Dewey was skeptical about psychological and educational measurements, and at certain moments he found intelligence tests amusing.

The historians of the school apply a very rough test to it. They say that the pupils of the University Elementary School succeeded very well in the schools they attended later. But this was someone's opinion and was perhaps only a remark. Nobody followed the school's children through their later education and lives. Frank N. Freeman made a study of this type with his gifted children who had high intelligence quotients and found that they were successful but not exceptionally so. There is unfortunately no accurate measure of the success of a teacher or a school.

The Dewey School was in operation for only a short time. The staff and student body grew so rapidly that it could hardly be considered the same school throughout its brief existence. The school was a partial embodiment of some of Dewey's ideas and became a kind of model or inspiration to other university schools and to the Progressive Movement. It may have also led to Dewey's resignation from the University of Chicago.

A small cloud had appeared over the school in 1898, when President Harper proposed to increase the size of the classes and the fees in the University Elementary School. Dewey agreed to the higher fees but "bluntly" refused to increase the size of classes. The sky became quickly overcast when Colonel Parker suddenly died in 1902. His death brought on the movement through which the University acquired the Chicago Institute. When Dewey became principal of its complex of schools, he said to Emmons Blaine; ". . . administration is not just my line." It was a confession that he often made.

The Chicago Institute and the University Elementary School with their different faculties, philosophies, and jealousies were to be combined. An administrator should have been appointed and given time and money for this purpose. Both Harper and Dewey, however, were too busy. Harper was already far overspending the University income and Dewey was living on a modest salary. No experienced administrator was appointed.

In 1903 Dewey's wife, Alice Chipman Dewey, became the school's principal. In agreeing to the appointment, Harper warned against the presence of husband and wife on the same faculty and payroll and said that the appointment was to be only temporary. His letter did not say it would be terminated in 1904, at the end of a year, but it is fair to say that Dewey often drew more difficult conclusions than this would have been; yet, when his wife was dropped as principal, Dewey resigned. His leave-taking was not quite as genial as one would expect from his customary manner.

Some might question the accuracy of Dewey's statement that his wife's failure to gain reappointment as school principal had no influence upon his decision to resign. It may, however, be entirely correct. He was shortly elected to a professorship of philosophy in Columbia University; and the timing of this action might suggest some speculation. It is even clearer that the management of a large and spreading department including subuniversity schools was, as Dewey said, "not just in his line." His books might not have been written if he had stayed at Chicago; administrators often do not have the time to write books. Even with the freedom of his new position, it was a decade before his *Democracy and Education* was completed.

BOOKS ON EDUCATION

Democracy and Education has been called the most important book on the philosophy of education ever written in America. But it is a universal book not merely a national treasure, and as a work in education it can well stand comparison with Plato's *Republic* and Rousseau's *Émile*, to both of which it is somewhat indebted. It is as original as either of these works, but differs from them in several ways, especially by entering into the classroom and directing the teacher and pupils at work. It is still a question of how much it has affected education and can still influence it. A practical book, and Dewey meant to be practical, has to be first understood and then applied. This book soon became widely known and was applied and misapplied in many places with various results.

The errors of its users led Dewey toward the close of his life to write a smaller book on the same subject but with a different title, *Experience and Education* (1938). It has been considered a criticism of progressive schools but that is not correct. This book is intended to make clear the real nature of good teaching for the information of those who had misunderstood him the first time. It does not in its essence change the message of *Democracy and Education*.

One may ask why people did not understand Dewey from the first book; it may have been the fault of the readers. It is easy for many people to misunderstand plain English. Dewey sometimes uses long sentences that seem to get a little longer with age—one sentence in this second book has ninety-three words—but this is beside the point and is not the real difficulty. The difficulty is that English, or any language, is not a precise instrument. All of the key words in Dewey's theory are subject to interpretation; there is always a "more or less" attached to such words as "freedom," "the democratic ideal," or "education is essentially a social process." *Freedom* and *democracy* are never wholly unqualified. *Experience and Education* was written to correct the misunderstandings of Dewey's other writings. In this, it was certainly helpful, but it still uses the same imprecise words and there is no help for this. This is why cadet teaching, teaching under guidance by "experts," or at least by persons of experience, is necessary in the preparation of teachers. One has to show and demonstrate good practice, always using words as well. Even medical graduates, after years of general and professional education, must serve an internship.

Others of Dewey's books dealing with education in one way or another appeared before *Democracy and Education*. We have already mentioned *The School and Society*, which was published at Chicago in 1900. In 1909 he prepared *Moral Principles in Education*. *Ethics*, prepared in collaboration with James H. Tufts, came out a year earlier and should perhaps be considered to deal with education. Plato and Aristotle would have thought so. *How We Think* (1910), an elementary logic or "method of inquiry," was widely used and was revised for a new edition in 1933.

When *Democracy and Education* was published, its author had been dealing with its problems in lectures, classes, and writings for more than twenty years. He had written over two hundred short or longer articles for

J. Mark Baldwin's *Dictionary of Philosophy and Psychology* and Paul Monroe's *Cyclopedia of Education*, the two tasks comprising a large and self-educative performance. In those decades, Dewey had become a recognized leader in education and philosophy; and *Democracy and Education*, as he several times remarked, remained for some years the most complete statement of his general philosophy. Dewey completed his *Reconstruction in Philisophy* in 1920, *Human Nature and Conduct* in 1922, and the important *Experience and Nature* in 1925.

DEMOCRACY AND EDUCATION

Education takes place, according to Dewey, only in experience; the two have a necessary relation to each other. A stone may be broken but it has no experience. All experience is both internal and external and results in changes in the organism. Events lead to experience only if they are known. Water lapping against the shores of an uninhabited island and the chemical processes in one's nerves and brain do not constitute experience. Experience involves the conscious interaction of a person and his environment, a stimulus and a response. This is the foundation of the doctrine of education through activities, in which person and environment act and interact.

Good education requires experiences having such qualities as clearness, vividness, pleasant feeling-tone and continuity, that is, the growing out of previous experience and leading to further experience. It must be related to the life and important institutions of the world. The teacher must promote the stimuli and reactions that will develop such experiences.

One thing that commends the education of experience is that it is in harmony with the democratic ideal. It permits individual choice of activities that aid the child's interests and purposes; and it enables pupils to cooperate with each other. These methods are also more humane than those of the autocratic school. We prefer democracy out of school; we should promote it in school.

Control in a progressive school resides not in the teacher but in the school that includes the teacher. Control is to be exercised in the same way as in a game in which the rules are agreed upon and the umpire calls the plays according to the rules; or in a well-regulated family where breaches of good order rarely occur and are settled with the guidance of father or mother in the best interests of the family when they do occur. Dewey usually has gentle, well-bred pupils and families in mind. He was hardly able to contemplate many of today's youngsters who cause violent clashes and wild upheavals in the classrooms, and who fight to win. This is a defect in the scope of his philosophy of education.

Progressive schools today sometimes labor under the difficulty that spoiled, unmanageable children are sent to them when they have been expelled from another school. Upheavals in such cases, Dewey said, are not evidence of weakness in progressive doctrine. Note that we have just now raised a doubt about this. It is a weakness in progressive practice, he said, when normal children become disorderly because the teacher did not prepare the program and materials beforehand. It is absurd, Dewey said, to suppose that the teacher is not to take the lead in a progressive school when he is the most mature and experienced member of it. He is the director but he should direct democratically not autocratically.

One of the advantages of the new schools is the freedom that they permit, freedom of movement and freedom of cooperation. This is necessary for the activities and for democracy, and some incidental noise does no harm. Dewey would excuse even an occasional failure in courtesy if it results from an eagerness to carry on the work in progress. There can be no greater mistake, than to treat freedom as an end in itself. It is the duty of teachers to make suggestions and give directions in the way that pupils should make use of their freedom.

The formal organization of subject-matter, developed in prescientific times, tends to hinder the effort to develop the steadily growing experience of children, and Dewey was not satisfied with it. He recommended a reorganization on scientific principles, but in *Democracy and Education* he still follows the old subject-lines to a great extent. And because in any class the children's past education and exposure to the world have been different, it is difficult to see how a rigid curriculum can be developed or that a uniform one should be developed.

In his effort to define education, Dewey uses various figures of speech. Education equals experience, life, and growth. These words are not synonymous in our common speech but in Dewey's philosophy they are reinterpreted. So *growth* means not maturity, not completed growth but growing, continuing and made more effective throughout life. Indeed it is life! A related word, *immaturity*, is reinterpreted to mean not a lack but a positive power to secure aid, cooperation, and love from nurses, parents, and all who care for the child. Dewey seems, in this interpretation, a little discomposed by his own boldness. In *Democracy and Education* (page 51) he wrote: "If it were said that children are themselves marvelously endowed with *power* to enlist the cooperative attention of others, this would be thought to be a backhanded way of saying that others are marvelously attentive to the needs of children. But observation shows that children are gifted with an equipment of the first order for social intercourse." This is a backhanded way of romanticizing the child, a process carried on by Rousseau and Froebel, and continued by Dewey.

When we turn to the text of *Democracy and Education*, we find that the first seven chapters deal with several conceptions of education and particularly with education as a "social need and function." When education is so broadly conceived, the entire natural and social environment becomes involved. The process may be regarded as a preparation for life, a renewal of life, the preservation of the race, guidance, growth, the unfolding of infolded powers, and so forth. In Chapter 7 we reach the summit of the series; and that summit is the democratic conception of education. This is the center to which all roads lead in Dewey's philosophy of education and from which one can directly reach every corner of its domain.

At the end of Chapter 7 we find the mention of the concrete conditions and results that are implied in the democratic conception. And then Dewey writes: "If these applications seem to be remote from a consideration of the philosophy of education, the impression shows that the meaning of the idea of education previously developed has not been adequately grasped." We may, and the authors do, take Dewey to mean that he has presented a new philosophy of education. And so he has. It is the philosophy of education "in a new key," to borrow a phrase; or, to copy one from the book, it is "the democratic ideal." But it was not entirely new; its antecedents can be traced in Comenius, Rousseau, Froebel, and others.

Democracy is based upon two principles. In a democracy, the people have a greater number and a greater variety of shared concerns and interests than the people in other types of society; and they look to increased sharing as the means to improve their democracy. In the second place, the people in any group of a democracy try to develop a freer interaction with other groups, to learn and to teach through such interaction, and so to pull down any walls of partition among them. "A democracy," Dewey continues, "is more than a form of government; it is primarily a mode of associated living, of conjoint communicated experience."

That "more" introduces the possibility of one of the dualisms that Dewey dislikes. It is evidently in a social domocracy, as distinguished from a political democracy, that the "more" is to be brought into the discussion. In Dewey's scheme, however, the social democracy includes the political democracy. Shared interests control the relations between citizens and all persons. Government by law and force ought to wither away, as it is presumed to do in communism, but Dewey does not spell this out. He was, however, some variety of socialist, although he was not a Marxist.

In much of his writing, Dewey employs history to show how existing conditions have come about. At Michigan he taught classes in the history of philosophy. One of his most interesting books, *Reconstruction in Philosophy*, may be the outgrowth of those courses. The contents of this book were first delivered as a series of lectures on his visit to Japan and the resulting book reads very much like a history of Western philosophy.

The estimate has been made by a professor of history, Thomas P. Neill of St. Louis University, that about one-half of Dewey's writing is historical. This may be correct but Dewey's history is intermingled with philosophy and with general opinion so that there is a wide margin of possible error in this calculation. And Dewey was not a historian in the usual sense; he was interested in history as a tool and he used the tool for his purposes. He did not praise historical knowledge for its own sake and simply as a contribution to knowledge. It was not the knowledge but the method of history that he valued; it could be used in argument for or against a proposal.

This conflict over the nature and uses of history is not very noticeable in *Democracy and Education* where history and geography are joined to form a single subject of study. That chapter comes after one, growing out of *The School and Society*, which he called "Play and Work in Education." In turning to the new subject, Dewey made one of the neat transitions for which he is noted. He said that geography and history are to be studied as an extension of the meaning of such primary activities as those that we carry on in play and work. Our experience may thereby be seen in a larger perspective. He called geography and history "the two great school resources" that extend the meaning of firsthand experience. He could have added science, the subject of the following chapter, and literature to the list of studies that broaden and interpret limited individual experiences.

Dewey praised intellectual history, but confined it to science, invention, and industry. We hold that it must also deal with literature, and Dewey does not disagree but he makes hardly any place for it; or for music. Poetry is to be a resource in the business as well as the leisure of life. That foreign languages receive no plaudits from Dewey is an example of provincialism in this wide-ranging philosopher.

The four chapters (14–17) on the course of study are followed by one on educational values that is an extension and refinement of the earlier treatment of aims such as utility, culture, mental discipline, and so forth. Some values, Dewey said, are absolute or intrinsic, and, we may add, unique. Such would be nourishment to a starving man, and, as Dewey declares, so would education itself. He wrote: "Since education is not a means of living but is identical with the operation of living a life which is fruitful and inherently significant, the only ultimate value which can be set up is just the process of living itself."

GROWTH AS THE END

In considering children in the family and especially in a farm family in the midst of all growing things, it was natural to hit upon growth as the end of education. Growth seemed like beauty, "its own excuse for being." As beyond space there is nothing but more space, so beyond present growth there seemed to be nothing but more growth, a true absolute in a relativist world. Growth needs no end beyond itself and could not have any, for it itself is to be endless.

Again, it is not strange that in Dewey's thinking about education the idea of growth should become an important concept, because he was greatly influenced by biological studies and the work of Charles Darwin. His emphasis upon movement, transition, continuity, and interaction between organism and environment are biological ideas. These were not recent notions. Aristotle had made growth one of the leading principles of biological science, along with assimiliation, reproduction, and the connection of function with structure. Among these Aristotle had also included the invariability of species.

Darwin released the objects of biology from the last-named of these principles and substituted for it the all-dissolving principle of an evolution based upon minute variations and the struggle for survival. This "law" enables us to view the growth of animal forms, from amoeba to man, as one continuous process. We shall not dwell upon the fact that experimental biology now considers the process to be less continuous than Darwin thought. But there is yet another obstacle in the way of using the word *growth* for the lifelong process of education. It is the fact that organisms reach maturity early and then stop growing. Dewey referred to John Fiske's *Meaning of Infancy*, which taught that man is able to progress and build up a civilization because, compared with other animals, man has a proportionately as well as an absolutely long period of immaturity and plasticity. But this was not enough for Dewey. He demanded continuing growth that would prepare for more growth. Upon consideration, Fiske's entire argument may seem to be self-defeating. One might have pointed out that if a long infancy promotes a more complex civilization, this will in turn require a still longer infancy for the mastering of it.

It was Rousseau, whom Dewey criticized, who introduced the idea that education should be a natural process of growth. But, as Dewey said, too great a dependency upon nature may tend to make foresight and insight seem unnecessary. This remark was not explicitly directed against Rousseau and does not altogether apply to him. Rousseau emphasized activity, contrivance, and discovery in education more than his predecessors and in a manner similar to that of Dewey himself. Both writers regarded the child as naturally curious, inquiring, exploring, and given to making things.

The identification or at least the comparison of education with the process of growth had been repeatedly made before Dewey adopted it. Such famous writers as Comenius, Rousseau, and Froebel had employed it; and actually the concept was a natural product of the speculation that accompanied the rise of science. One could find it even in Bacon, who praised the schools of the Jesuits. This would mean merely that Bacon was not consistent.

Those who adopted this naturalistic theory did not put their full weight upon such a teetering plank. Rousseau and Froebel, after claiming that education should be a natural process, also suggested a multitude of artificial exercises to promote the work of nature. The arrays of carefully contrived problems and exercises in Rousseau's *Émile* and in Froebel's *The Education of Man* are too long to quote.

Dewey also pointed out, as has been stated, that too great a dependence upon nature may tend to make foresight and insight seem unnecessary. And this, as with the principle of sharing, again brings up the question of how much of each. The simple truth is that education as growth, education according to nature, is only a figure of speech, a bit of persuasive rhetoric. If education is growth and the end of growth is more growth, then it follows that the end of education is more education.

In *Experience and Education,* Dewey considered that growth may take different directions. A burglar may grow to be a better burglar, a direction of growth that only accomplices, "fences," and makers of burglars' tools may approve. Here the objector will insist that growth is not a sufficient aim; we must also specify its direction and end. But Dewey disagreed. He said the question is whether the form of growth provides opportunities and stimuli for growth in other directions. He thought growth in the burglar's art probably would not. Society will stamp out asocial conduct. But the historical and contemporary facts are that democratic society has not been noticeably successful in doing this.

When Dewey occasionally became dissatisfied with growth as the aim of education, he substituted for it the continuous reconstruction of experience. This is similarly neutral in its bearing. Only if the reconstructed experience is better than the old experience can this formulation of the aim win approval. Such a statement, that any act or state is better than another, must be based upon a system of ethics, and in his ethics Dewey attempted to substitute statements of fact for statements of value. In the opinion of some he was unsuccessful. Furthermore, both of the efforts to propose a general aim of education were possibly inconsistent with Dewey's instrumentalism. It might have been better if he had remained true to another of his insights, namely, that no aim is suitable for all persons, at all times, and everywhere.

When Dewey came to deal with the means of promoting growth, he showed that he had not rejected the teaching of Herbart that ethics or, following Dewey, the principles of the good society will prescribe the direction that growth is to follow, but that psychology will have to supply the means. Dewey repeated this view in *The Sources of a Science of Education* (1929), claiming that there is agreement that the social sciences reveal what pupils are to learn, and that psychology deals with means and how they do and should learn. By learning Dewey doubtlessly meant experiencing, acting, creating, and thinking. Thinking was for Dewey the primary means of growth and of the reconstruction of experience as well. He was generally opposed to emphasis upon fixed instincts, rigid habits, and imitation, and he had little use for external standards or objective tests and measurements. He believed that the environment is the main source of problems and that in thinking the pupil should deal with a total situation. Thus he in a measure anticipated the "field theory" of problem-solving.

HOW WE THINK

Dewey held that we think when we must, and that thinking originates in a perplexity, an obstacle, or a doubt. Some have regarded this as a great discovery but it is in fact only a truism. If thinking is defined as the effort to find the answer to a problem or to resolve a perplexity, then, naturally, it cannot occur except in the presence of some difficulty. Like other truisms, however, this one is worth stating. It says that situations can be set up to stimulate thinking.

The sources and varied nature of pupils' problems are themselves problems that closely concern the teacher. Children are active by nature, "spilling over with activities," and from these practical concerns many problems arise. Getting out of his playpen is for the small child a problem that is about on a par with the problem of the cat in a cage. Rousseau and Froebel suggested many children's activities that involve problems, but they did not, like Dewey, consider the detailed ways in which the problems are solved by the children. Dewey suggests a few somewhat more intellectual but still simple problems. From *How We Think* everyone will remember the cases of the ferryboat with a white pole projecting from the front of the pilothouse, the soapy tumblers, and the problem in transportation.

Such examples are altogether appropriate as types of work for children; but they may lead the student to the notion that problems usually or always arise from external conditions. This is not true. Philosophers including Dewey have often gone out in search of problems because they enjoyed thinking. Problems do not always arise from circumstances nor do they have to be assigned by a teacher. It is a fact of history that science has been created largely by pure scientists—Galileo, Newton, Faraday, Darwin, and a host of others—who went out to look for problems and investigated them for the love of it.

Dewey was, of course, well aware of this and on some occasions he took it into account. He did so in explaining the history and usefulness of pure geometry (*The Quest for Certainty*, p. 150). Symbols for geometric objects and operations, he wrote, could "in no disrespectful sense be played with" and "treated from the standpoint of a fine art," and in this process geometry was developed as a science of ideas, not merely of particular things. But he retains his suspicion of all systems of ideas that cannot be concretely interpreted at once. Dewey added that "scientific conceptions are not a revelation of prior and independent reality." But scientists, Dewey should have reflected, do predict occurrences that they do not control. The astronomer who correctly foretells that future observation will verify his present calculation is not the superintendent of a celestial planetarium.

As we have seen, Dewey had faith in the capacity of pupils to learn to think, but he insisted that they must be taught. He held that thought results from "impeded habit," that is, from a difficulty; but the interest in solving problems must be nurtured lest it die. There are several ways of reacting to a problem. One may act impulsively, smashing the machine that does not work. One may turn away and take up something else. Mankind has shelved many unsolved problems, although one cannot know that this neglect will be permanent. Experience shows that in teaching it is wiser to deal with problems that can be solved or that can at least be clearly analyzed. This may be the reason why Dewey used simple mechanical and scientific problems to illustrate the process of thinking. The great social goals of democracy that Dewey has most at heart would pose extremely difficult problems.

In schools we must select problems that pupils will desire to solve, and we must encourage promising methods of attack. Dewey named three essentials of good method (*How We Think*, 1910, p. 30): a certain fund and store of experience and facts; ideas, insights, and theories; and consistent and orderly work upon the problem. The first of these, especially the body of facts, has a strange look in the context of Dewey's philosophy and in the second edition (1933) it was left out.

Some philosophers and some educators would have retained the body of experience and fact. As early as 1885 W. H. Payne and B. A. Hinsdale had noticed "the degradation of the memory" in schools. An experimental scientist, James B. Conant, who recently joined them, showed in *Science and Common Sense* (1951) that scientific experiment originates from a conceptual scheme or system of ideas. The scientist has to frame or master a system of ideas or theory before he can propose an experiment to test it. This evidently involves logical memory. Conant would call Dewey's examples and problems for pupils to solve instances of common sense, not science; Conant indicated his general view by devoting a chapter to "the alleged" scientific method.

Eliot also included memory in his formulation of the steps in scientific discovery. Five steps are included in the most elaborate of his analyses: accurate observation, correct recording and remembering, comparison and true inference, precise expression, and adherence to high ideals of truth and right. Eliot added that these processes may occur almost simultaneously. They are Eliot's version of a complete act of thought and may be compared with Dewey's list in the next paragraph.

The last of Dewey's three essentials, consistent and orderly work upon a problem, is the one upon which he puts the greatest stress. To this he comes back repeatedly, perhaps because teaching can be most helpful at this point. This leads him to his famous analysis of a complete act of thought. Dewey said that each unit of thinking begins in a perplexity and ends in a solution when completed. Reflection begins only as the problem emerges. Between the two limits, he distinguished five steps or stages: (1) suggestion in which may lie a possible solution; (2) explicit formulation or reformulation of the problem; (3) exploration by means of tentative hypotheses; (4) selection of the most plausible theory; and (5) testing of the theory by action, either overt or imaginative. In the common shorthand version of this analysis, the first and second steps are usually interchanged; and Dewey explained that the order of the steps may vary, that the problem may change as thought upon it proceeds, that two of the steps may be merged into one, and, in short, that the thinker should be ingenious. The analysis is a description, not a rule. Dewey offers numerous illustrations of the processes. He omits what Conant considers essential, namely, the system of ideas from which any scientific investigation must start.

This analysis of thinking was regarded by Dewey as a tool provided by psychology to aid the teacher. Psychology cannot do everything. It cannot provide the goals of education but it can often show the best way to achieve the adopted goals. In Dewey's view the true goals are democracy and growth, each of which requires thinking for its progressive attainment. The problem of the teacher is to find ways of training pupils to think "instead of following their instincts and impulses, or relying upon habits or imitation."

In the first edition of How We Think (1910) there was a section on "the formal steps of the recitation." There Dewey indicated his debt to Herbart for the idea of the analysis of thinking. Dewey said that little had been done to formulate a general method of conducting the recitation but that "one of these is of great importance and his probably had more and better influence upon the 'hearing of lessons' than all others put together," namely, the Herbartian five steps. Dewey thought that the Herbartian analysis was more useful to the teacher in preparing to teach a lesson than it was to the pupils. And it was a stroke of genius to turn the idea of the analysis endwise, as Dewey did, making it an analysis of the pupil's task rather than the teacher's. When the second edition of the book came out in 1933, the Herbartian movement had receded and the reference to it was omitted.

A COLLEAGUE AND DISCIPLE

We have noticed President Gilman who, by organizing a graduate university, had a great influence upon Dewey. We shall balance the account by noticing a student who was influenced by Dewey, who became his colleague at the University of Chicago, and who had an independent career as well. She was Ella Flagg Young (1845-1918), who also serves as a contrast to the philosopher.

Dewey had many disciples who may have been mistaken in thinking they understood him, perhaps without reading his books. The opposite of this was the case with Mrs. Young. She knew him well, studied with him, worked with him, and in Dewey's words sometimes seemed to understand him better than he understood himself. At least she seemed to see practical meanings and outcomes that had not occurred to him.

Before we repeat his estimate of her we should answer the question: Who was Ella Flagg Young? It has been over fifty years since she and her supporters routed the "Old Guard"—a term they resented—of the National Education Association by electing her the first woman president of that body. At the time she was Superintendent of the Schools of Chicago but in fifty years most people are well forgotten and many young teachers of today may never have heard her name.

Ella Flagg Young was born in Buffalo in 1845 during the Horace Mann period. Her parents were Scots with a Presbyterian alignment and background. The family was well-adjusted and Ella was allowed many amusements and was given *Mother Goose* and other children's books to read. Her health in childhood was delicate; she seemed frail in maturity, but she managed to do the taxing work of teaching and school administration. Even as a child she helped an overworked teacher with her busy schedule by hearing the class in Colburn's *Mental Arithmetic* while the teacher looked after other matters. After the family moved to Chicago, Ella passed the teacher's examination at age fifteen. Too young for an appointment she was enrolled as a pupil in the city normal school. She may have heard about nature study and Pestalozzi in those classes but it is almost certain that she did not learn about the kindergarten. The kindergarten was the only class in public schools that she did not teach. Wayland's *Mental Philosophy* was used in the normal school and she is supposed to have objected to the doctrine of mental discipline, but this must be a misplaced memory. Hardly anyone, much less a little girl, had that idea in 1860, for the arguments over formal discipline and transfer of training did not begin until the Herbartian period in the latter decades of the century.

In 1862, Ella was seventeen years old and became a teacher. Her first superintendent was the capable W. H. Wells, who established the first high school in Chicago. He was able to tell her what a young teacher needed to learn first.

Like other educational officers in similar positions at that time, Superintendent Wells had only limited powers. The boards both made the rules and saw that they were executed. City school boards had far too many members and, partly for that reason, too many axes to grind. Their outlook was political and they ran the schools at the dictation of politicians; teachers, principals and the superintendent were their servants; political odds were carefully calculated before the board adopted textbooks, selected school sites, or entered into any contracts. It was a good beginning school for one who was later to stop the "Old Guard" of the NEA, become a superintendent of schools in a large city, and interpret John Dewey. The city and the school board provided better preparation for teaching in such a situation than the normal school, for "Life educates."

Ella Flagg Young became "head assistant" in her school and she was soon appointed principal of a new practice department of the normal school. Her visit to Oswego, New York, where E. A. Sheldon was developing object-teaching on Pestalozzian principles proved a failure because at that time Sheldon was still keeping his secrets secret. That she knew about Oswego, wanted to go, and doubtlessly managed to have her expenses paid by the City of Chicago tells a great deal about her. She was then only twenty-one years old.

She continued her enthusiasm for teaching about nature and added literature as a second interest, if not the primary one. She organized study clubs with other teachers and held meetings outside of school hours. She moved up the city teachers' ladder until she became assistant superintendent of the schools of Chicago in 1887. On June 3, 1899, she resigned without consulting anyone because she disagreed with the policy of an incoming superintendent. She had no other position in view but wisely resisted all efforts to have her reconsider.

We have noticed her interest in liberal education, mathematics, nature study, and literature. When later in her life the state was pressed by employers to found a system of separate vocational schools for children of high school age, Mrs. Young vigorously opposed this class division of the school system. Such an "undemocratic" plan was followed in Germany. Georg Kerschensteiner, the head of the schools of Munich, was brought over for lectures explaining the German plan. Not only Illinois but Wisconsin and other states were interested. Dewey took an active part in the debate, opposing the separate vocational schools. He, like Mrs. Young, did not want to see children of fourteen years of age cut off from the study of literature, science, and other liberal arts, and he did not want schoolchildren separated into lower and higher social classes.

Mrs. Young almost faltered once in her steady endeavor to improve her own education, which was gained mainly while she was teaching. In 1894 Dewey had come to the new University of Chicago; the following year he offered an afternoon course in logic. He was thirty-six years old; she was fifty. Disconcerted by the youthfulness of the students who were enrolling for the course in logic, she turned to leave when a young man who recognized her offered to go for the required card of admission. She accepted the courtesy and continued to study with Dewey for four years, taking work in logic, ethics, the philosophy of Hegel, and other subjects.

Our reporter's opinion of Mrs. Young as a student in Dewey's class seems to have been judicious. Of Mrs. Young he wrote: "My impressions of her then were that she was a serious student, alert to what was going on, had opinions of her own, and was able to express them. In this latter respect I used to feel that she went too far; she seemed inclined to run things somewhat. I could see that she was acquainted with Dewey, and he let her have a great deal of rein—perhaps on account of their acquaintance. But she was not of the tiresome variety, who monopolizes things and rides over you [sic]. What she had to say was good. There were no indications of verbomania or the sort of egotism that bores you to death. It was, rather, if anything, a case of her and Dewey discussing Hegel to the neglect of the rest of us . . . she was giving her own views and not absorbing those of others."

At this time (1898), Dewey had practically outgrown Hegel, and it is a little surprising that he should have offered a seminar on him at that late date. One can be positive that Mrs. Young had few thoughts on the subject that were new to Dewey. He may have given her "a good deal of rein" because the discussion was more instructive to the class than his lecture or his "thinking out loud," his usual custom, would have been. His own report on Mrs. Young dealt with a situation externally different from the preceding but essentially similar; and one cannot help feeling that in speaking of her he was, in his customary manner, being very generous.

Long after the events and evidently in response to an inquiry, Dewey wrote: "It is hard for me to be specific," because in long and close association, "I was constantly getting ideas from her. In the reorganization of the laboratory school . . . her influence with that of Mrs. Dewey were [sic] the controlling factors. It was due to them that the laboratory school ran so much more systematically and definitely—free from a certain looseness of ends and edges—in its last three or four years." He ascribed the fault of the earlier "looseness," largely to his own "inexperience in administrative matters."

Dewey said Mrs. Young gained from philosophy both a point of view and a vocabulary to express the practical outcome of her experience. She was able to see the implications of his philosophy, he thought, better than he did! She saw what a doctrine would mean if put into practice. He continued: "It was from her that I learned that freedom and respect for freedom mean regard for the inquiry or reflective processes of [other] individuals." He evidently meant that students, for example, must not be driven or coerced to see things in the teacher's way. This was the way Mrs. Young is said to have actually treated her teachers when she was principal of the Chicago Normal School. If after discussion they could not agree with her view, they were privileged, indeed obligated, to continue to differ from her. Perhaps not many school administrators would carry this principle through to the end. Dewey and Mrs. Young apparently agreed that they should do so. It is well-known that some later professors interpreting Dewey have demanded the docile acceptance of their interpretation.

Dewey concluded:

I have hardly known anyone who made the effect of genuine intellectual development the test and criterion of the value of everything as much as she. I have known but one other person—also a woman—who so consistently reflected upon her experiences, digested them, turned them into significance or meanings for future use . . . I often think that [Franklin Delano] Roosevelt's knowledge of politics is the only analogue to Mrs. Young's knowledge of educational matters with which I am acquainted.

If we think about them, these remarks tell us about Dewey as well as about Mrs. Young.

In 1899, after reaffirming her resignation from her position in the Chicago schools, having been second in command since 1887, Mrs. Young was planning a trip to Europe. Just before she was to leave, President Harper of the University of Chicago offered her "a full professorship in the department," actually a subdepartment, of pedagogy. She objected that without having a degree herself she could hardly encourage students to complete their work. Harper then offered to "create for her on the spot" the position of "associate professorial lecturer in pedagogy" with the opportunity to work for her degree. She accepted.

The following year, perhaps after breaking a few rules in the process, she was awarded her degree and was appointed professor of education. It was at her suggestion that *pedagogy* was changed to *education* in the title. It is evident that her appointment could not have taken place without Dewey's approval, and probably not without his initiative. This is further evidence of Dewey's opinion of Mrs. Young's quality and his understanding that in her the department had one member who had firsthand knowledge of city school administration.

When Dewey resigned from the University in 1904, Mrs. Young also resigned and took the delayed trip to Europe. Upon her return, the superintendent of schools of Chicago asked her to serve as principal of the city normal school. The vacancy had occurred through the death of Arnold Tompkins, a Hegelian philosopher and educator, who had previously been on the faculty of the University of Illinois. Mrs. Young had met Hegelianism before in Dewey, as well as in William Torrey Harris, whose work in the St. Louis schools had been of great interest and help to her. At the Normal School she had the difficult task of reeducating the faculty to deal empirically and practically with real children in their infinite variety rather than the "pedagogical child" described by Tompkins.

When she was elected Superintendent of the Schools of Chicago in 1909, Mrs. Young became a national symbol of the self-made American in the teaching profession. Teaching has often been a stepping-stone on which future lawyers, doctors, preachers, and political leaders first found solid footing for a career, but Ella Flagg Young had succeeded in the teaching profession itself.

And she was a woman. Women had long formed the great majority of American teachers. In 1862 when Ella Flagg received her first appointment, male teachers were leaving for military service, and women forged ahead of men in teaching. In 1909, forty-seven years later, women teachers themselves formed a large army in which Mrs. Young had achieved high rank and conspicuous position. The women were irked that they were not given due recognition and place in the National Education Association and in state and local bodies. A movement, in which the teachers of New York City had a notable share, was started to elect Mrs. Young to the presidency of the NEA at the Boston meeting in 1910.

The nominating committee of twenty-four members, which included only three women, brought in its usual slate with a man at the head of the ticket. Katherine Blake, principal of an elementary school in New York City, presented a minority report and moved to substitute the name of Mrs. Young for the name reported by the majority. There was some parliamentary jockeying, but on the final ballot Mrs. Young won by a large majority. On her presentation to the Association as their first woman president she expressed her sense of the honor bestowed upon her, admitted that in one year the president of so large a body can do little, and then said, "I hope to assist in abolishing the distinction in membership between those who can and those who cannot pay comparatively high fees. This will never be a truly democratic organization while it shuts out from active membership the men and women who receive small salaries, teaching in a cramped environment where people have not yet learned the value of a teacher. . . ." She said the NEA should be able to interest all teachers in the education of all Americans, but, as she indicated, democracy sometimes grows all too slowly. If he had heard these words, John Dewey would have applauded them; and no doubt he would have been secretly gratified by her success.

PROGRESSIVE EDUCATION

The educational views and proposals of John Dewey and his disciples were the guide to a widespread progressive movement in the schools during the first half of the twentieth century. They were most closely followed in certain private and university schools but were also applied to a great or lesser degree in the public schools of some cities. They were preached more than practiced but they were also practiced.

Let us begin by summarizing the views that have guided this progressive movement. All pupils should have the freedom to choose for themselves, but unless there were materials and problems from which to choose this would be an empty liberty. To make real the opportunity for self-education, it was considered best to give the pupils teachers to counsel with and things to work with, such as shops, kitchens, gardens, studios, gymnasiums, and libraries. Under expert guidance and favorable conditions the pupils were to educate themselves.

This was the basis of the original principles of *Progressive Education*. In the first issue of the magazine of that name (April 1924) there is a statement of those principles under seven headings. It took the group weeks of labor to draw up the one-page program. The first topic was "freedom to develop naturally," and under it we read that the pupil should govern himself instead of being governed by arbitrary law; that he should have the free use of an environment that was rich in material things and a full opportunity for initiative and self-expression.

Other principles follow. Interest should be the motive of all work. The teacher should be a guide, not a taskmaster. Progressive teachers should encourage the use of all the senses and the study of life activities as well as books, and should promote the use of information to draw correct conclusions and express them forcefully and logically. The scientific study of child development, greater attention to health and growth, improved reporting upon school work, and cooperation between school and home in the interest of the children were demanded. The school was to be a laboratory, not controlled by "tradition alone," where new ideas "if worthy" were to be encouraged. This last sentence and the reference to the scientific study of child development should be noted.

This editorial statement, which now seems almost timid, was meant as a definition of Progressive—the capital P is significant—education. The most provocative sentence is the first one, on the pupil's choosing his own conduct, which might raise some questions about ages and the meaning of terms. But there is no Supreme Court to decide what the true sense of these principles is; later Progressives both reinterpreted them and added other principles.

Most of the ideas in the preceding analysis were the ideas of John Dewey, Francis Parker, and Charles William Eliot. The portrait of Eliot formed the frontispiece of the first issue of *Progressive Education*, and he was the honorary president of the Progressive Education Association (PEA) that had been formed in 1918 after consultation with him. In his letter congratulating the editor on the contents of the first issue of the magazine, Eliot remarked upon the rapidly growing numbers of the Progressive schools and predicted that they would be the "schools of the future in both America and Europe." This prediction has not yet been fully verified but the future still lies ahead of us.

One wing of the Progressives of that era was not recognized in the principles summarized but was fully represented in the magazine. The leader of this wing was Preston W. Search (1853–1932) who, while serving as a small-town superintendent of public schools, had begun to experiment with individual instruction before 1880. These methods were fully developed at Pueblo, Colorado, and became widely known as the Pueblo Plan. Search was not a man with just one idea. He was a many-sided educational liberal, as his book, *An Ideal School* (1901), proves, but he is best remembered for the Pueblo Plan. That individual instruction was considered an element in Progressive education is shown by the space given to it in the new magazine. Among the contributors to the first issue were Frederic Burk; Carleton W. Washburne; Helen Parkhurst (all three influenced by Search); John Eades, who described an English version of the Dalton School; and the famous Belgian educator, Ovide Decroly; all exponents of individual instruction.

It would not have been hazardous to predict the Progressive education movement at any time in the late Victorian period. It had been implied by Rousseau, Pestalozzi, and Froebel, and their general outlook had become familiar before 1900. Child study, the kindergarten, and manual training were spreading. Wealth, or at least economic well-being, and leisure were brought within the reach of a growing class by the urban and industrial revolutions. Educational experiments were being conducted. The humanitarian movement was freeing the last slave in Christendom, the child.

Several Progressive schools were named in 1901 in *An Ideal School*, but Search did not mention all of the existing ones nor did he go back into history to recall the schools of Alcott or those of the Englishman Rowland Hill. Even a quarter-century later the Progressive Education Association claimed only about forty American schools as embodying its teachings. Nearly all of these were private schools.

The period of most rapid expansion of the Progressive schools was just ahead, in the 1920's. After World War I a number of Country Day schools were founded in the environs of the large cities and most of them claimed the Progressive title. Being dependent upon fees for support and therefore upon good business conditions, many of them were closed in the depression. Some of the early Progressive schools were connected with universities. Such were the Laboratory School founded by John Dewey and briefly connected with the University of Chicago, the Lincoln School of Teachers College, and the school conducted by J. L. Meriam at the University of Missouri.

Through the teaching of Progressive ideas in the preparation of teachers in universities, and by means of books and lectures, the public schools of many cities were drawn into the movement. Few large school systems became entirely Progressive, but there were also few city systems that remained wholly uninfluenced. Among the general signs of this influence are the greater consideration given to the individual pupil's interests and aptitudes, greater flexibility of requirements, pupil activities usually including the school council or some form of self-government and participation in the management of school affairs, the use of community resources, and cooperation between school and home.

As Progressive education spread, it took on new and varied qualities until it became difficult to describe or define. Charles William Eliot, for example, was one kind of Progressive. He is known for his use of the elective system, his emphasis upon science and the cultivation of the senses, and his insistence upon good, even high, academic standards. It should be noted that he seemed to sanction the dichotomy between knowledge and power to think; this is one of the marks or the limitations of his Progressivism. His relation to the developing movement has been indicated.

At the opposite extreme of the movement a philosophy developed, or rather it was a compliant disposition that called out a protest from Dewey because it pressed restraints upon the teacher's plans and gave free rein to the desires and even the whims of the pupils. This was a form of the elective system that carried freedom of choice to an extreme. The little poem "Days" by Emerson might be taken for pertinent comment upon this hedonistic position. The "hypocritic Days" in the poem felt only scorn for one who was satisfied with the pebbles at his feet when he might have had diamonds by digging for them.

The question, then, arises whether children have the experience, wisdom, and self-control needed to choose wisely and to persevere in the chosen way. At what age do they acquire these abilities? Progressive, private schools are expensive and are patronized by people with good incomes who want to send their children to college. The second question must then be asked: Will Progressive methods prepare these children for the colleges that they wish to attend? A negative answer was given to this question by Ernest Cobb in a book *One Foot on the Ground* (1932). It was approximately this question that was investigated in the Eight-Year Study or the Thirty Schools experiment.

The Eight-Year Study (1933–1941), which was one of the most considerable achievements of the Progressive Education Association under its original name, gave a different answer. The study was organized to determine whether the customary college entrance requirements were essential to college success or whether pupils from a broader course in a Progressive school could succeed as well in college as the pupils from the college-preparatory course in the ordinary high school.

For the purpose of the study some three hundred colleges and universities agreed to waive their regular entrance requirements and to admit students from the participating schools without inquiring into the details of their preparation. In the evaluation, the work of 1,475 graduates of the participating schools was compared with that of an equal number of matched students from nonparticipating schools in order to determine whether the usual college entrance requirements were essential for success in college or whether core and other newer curricula would prepare pupils equally well. The experiment was directed by a commission of PEA chaired by Wilford M. Aikin. The results as measured by the evaluation staff of the commission under the direction of Ralph Tyler showed only a slight advantage—about 6 points in 250—in favor of the newer curricula and methods. Except in foreign languages, the subject marks of the Progressives were uniformly higher, but the advantage, as indicated, was so small that it is not considered statistically significant. In outside reading, music, debating, and other extracurricular activities, the records of students from the thirty Progressive schools were superior, and in some activities they were far superior. The experiment probably helped the trend toward more liberal requirements for college entrance.

In the Great Depression of the 1930's, Progressive schools lost some of their patrons. Opposition to the more extreme wing of the movement increased. Educators became critical of the extremist views and loose practices of some Progressives and of their failure to demand serious intellectual work and approved conduct from their pupils. This critical group was known as the Essentialists. The general public became concerned about the teaching of the fundamentals of reading, writing, and arithmetic, which they considered insufficient. They thought there should be more drill, and they wanted a stricter, more evident, discipline.

The Essentialists, led by William C. Bagley (1874–1946), emphasized these views and some even saw a connection between Progressive education and juvenile delinquency. One heard again the charge that was leveled against Hazelwood School in England a century before. The children, it was said, were arrogant and conceited and had been led to believe that hard-won principles of government and ethics were outmoded, that whatever is, is wrong, and that they could set it right at once by "the method of intelligence." Boyd H. Bode said that "the more prosperous element in society" who were the patrons of the Progressive schools would go only a little way with intelligence. They would not let it interfere with business. It was said that the Progressives favored both freedom and guidance, individualism and social cooperation; critics wanted to know how much of one and how much of the other. In 1944 the Progressive Education Association changed its name to the American Education Fellowship, but the name of the magazine *Progressive Education* remained unchanged. Later the Association restored its original name, but in 1955 it was dissolved because the dues-paying members had become too few to maintain the organization. The magazine was adopted by the John Dewey Society and continued publication under the name *Progressive Education*. It was discontinued in 1957.

Lack of direction and a frequent tendency to run to extremes have been charged against Progressive education. Although many absurdities have clung to the movement and have impeded true progress, a great deal of good has been accomplished. The old mechanical school is not extinct even now, but many people have learned that it should be.

In the second decade of the twentieth century Dewey was writing at almost the last moment in which he could have gained his great American and international support. Events rather than any new philosophy have been responsible for the decline in the Progressive movement. Two world wars, the discovery of atomic fission, space travel, technology, and the tension of international problems seem to require training in skill more than liberal education. Automation and peace may again alter the situation.

Meanwhile two educational movements, one to the right, the other to the left, are bypassing Dewey. On the right is the drive for "excellence" with emphasis upon technique, drill, and performance, including the ability to pass objective tests. On the left is the new and extreme permissiveness of the English Summerhill now introduced into the United States by Lewis-Wadham and other schools. According to this theory the school must fit the child who, whatever he does or fails to do, can do no wrong. Dress, hours, manners, conduct, "it is all up to him," or her. Dewey favored freedom, too much freedom many think, but not chaos. To the Scot, A. S. Neill, who founded Summerhill, and his disciples, Dewey would be a puritan. It is sagely predicted that schools such as Summerhill will prevent all wars forever. They have not yet become a great movement.

SUMMARY

The idea of a democratic school to educate youth for democracy was a relatively new idea when it was taken up by Parker and Dewey. The word *democracy*, which had referred to a political system, was now extended to include social and moral relations. Dewey made "sharing" the test of democracy, and this pointed toward a one-class society. The pioneer community in which Dewey grew up may have influenced his philosophy more than he was aware or more than his disciples recognize. Other influences were the evolutionary doctrine, the psychology of William James, and Hegelian philosophy.

The practical purpose of Dewey's theory is expressed in his definition, which states that philosophy is the general theory of education. This implies that the purpose of life and of education is human development or growth. And even if action, conduct, or practical application are to be the ends, thinking is the means to these ends. One of Dewey's main educational concerns was the teaching of thinking. Now thought, when it becomes general, becomes abstract; but it begins with concrete experiences of the old farm family and the self-sufficient family. These are also prime examples of the quality of the democracy that he praised and wished to see developed. Following the farm as a stimulus to thoughtfulness were the beginnings of industry. This idea, in which Dewey follows Eliot and Emerson, had received extended treatment in Froebel's *Education of Man*.

Thinking was for Dewey the primary means of growth. Thinking can be learned. It begins with a problem, and problem-situations can be set up. Dewey tended to select problems that lead to immediate action, but he was well aware that problem-situations may lead to play with ideas without reference to concrete application. Yet he retained his suspicion of truths that cannot be concretely interpreted at once. Whether Dewey's emphasis upon practical results will best promote the sciences is very much in doubt. Science seems to depend upon fundamental discoveries, the practical use of which may not become apparent for centuries. But the science that interested Dewey most was that which applied to the "real business of living" by making life safe, healthful, intelligent, active, and friendly.

Because the best means of education are not well understood, many educators have given children freedom to follow their interests in a stimulating environment. They try to encourage the growth of the individual and the promotion of cooperation in forming an ideal society. This is the attitude of Progressive educators who think of themselves as guides and counselors of children. They place great emphasis upon direct experience, problem-solving, and the cultivation of the intelligence. Progressives, however, do not agree in the details of their philosophy. From the beginning, the movement has been under attack from various quarters.

QUESTIONS

1. Why does educational progress frequently halt, retreat, and only later again go forward? By what means could steady or at least steadier progress in education be ensured?
2. How may the notion that all studies are equally educative be used to support the elective system? Might this notion be used in support of a narrow curriculum?
3. Why do students often work harder on work that they have selected?
4. Why did colleges in the nineteenth century raise both their entrance requirements and their demands upon the students during the college period?
5. Why was Eliot considered a Progressive educator? Was this title warranted?
6. How does it happen that people cooperate, form institutions, follow the leader, if "every individual has the principle of authority within himself?"
7. Do you accept Parker's definition of democracy? Why or why not?

How does his democracy differ, if it does, from Christian charity? From Dewey's definition?

8. Which philosophers, if any, form exceptions to the statement that not since Plato and Aristotle has a well-equipped philosopher maintained a deep and continuing interest in the problems of education? Consider John Locke, Immanuel Kant, G. W. F. Hegel, and perhaps others, presenting the evidence.

9. How thoroughly did Dewey understand children? Consider whether he underestimated their ability to look to the future, to deal with abstractions, and to accept authority cheerfully from those with wider experience than their own.

10. Try to work out in detail what Dewey seems to have meant by growth.

11. Can education become a science if it is based upon the shifting interests of those who are to be educated? Present evidence and arguments.

12. Critics have demanded that Progressive educators should tell how much freedom and how much guidance, how much individualism and how much social cooperation and sharing they favored. Can this or a similar question be so stated that it can be answered? How, or why not?

13. In your opinion, why have the results of the Eight-Year Study had so little effect upon college entrance requirements? Is this a result of the declining prestige of Progressive education? What policies, if followed early, could have moderated the decline in Progressive prestige? The student may wish to reject the opinion that Progressive education has lost prestige.

14. What is the meaning or meanings of the term *Progressive education?*

BOOKS AND PAPERS

Things worthy to be remembered and appreciations of Parker were published by W. T. Harris under the title, "Francis W. Parker and His Work for Education," in the *Report* of the Commissioner of Education, 1902, Vol. I, pp. 231–284. Parker's wide influence was largely personal. He wrote little besides *How to Study Geography*. His *Talks on Pedagogics* (title varies) and his addresses were reported. Some of his addresses may be found in the *Proceedings* of the National Education Association.

Jane M. Dewey's biography of her father was prepared for Paul Arthur Schilpp's edition of *The Philosophy of John Dewey*. See also George Dykhuizen in *Journal of the History of Ideas*, 1959, pp. 515–544, on Dewey in Vermont; 1961, pp. 105–116, Dewey at Johns Hopkins; and 1962, pp. 513–544, Dewey at the University of Michigan; for the decade at Michigan, see Axelrod; for Chicago years see the book by Mayhew and Edwards and the articles by McCaul.

On the educational movement of which Dewey was by many considered the leader, see Lawrence A. Cremin and the book by Dewey and his daughter;

and for a criticism of the movement, see Ernest Cobb, *One Foot on the Ground*, New York, 1932; and John Dewey, "Progressive Education and the Science of Education," *Progressive Education*, V (1928), pp. 197–204.

Dewey lectured in Japan, China, Russia, and other foreign countries. For sources see William W. Brickman, "John Dewey's Foreign Reputation as an Educator," *School and Society*, 70 (October 22, 1949), pp. 257–265.

AIKIN, WILFORD M., *The Story of the Eight Year Study*, New York, 1942.

AXELROD, JOHN A., "John Dewey, 1884–1894, a Decade of Ferment for a Young Michigan Teacher," *Michigan Education Journal*, May 1, 1966, pp. 13–14.

CAMPBELL, JACK K., *Colonel Francis W. Parker: The Children's Crusader*, New York, Teachers College Press, 1968.

CREMIN, LAWRENCE A., *The Transformation of the School, Progressivism in American Education, 1876–1957*, New York, 1961.

DEWEY, JOHN, *School and Society*, University of Chicago Press, 1900; *Moral Principles in Education*, Boston, 1909; *How We Think*, Boston, 1910, and the second edition, *How We Think, A Restatement of the Relation of Reflective Thinking to the Educative Process*, Boston, 1933; *Influence of Darwin on Philosophy*, New York, 1910; *Democracy and Education, an Introduction to the Philosophy of Education*, New York, 1916; *Experience and Education*, New York, 1938.

DEWEY, JOHN and EVELYN DEWEY, *Schools of Tomorrow*, New York, 1915.

ELIOT, CHARLES W., *Educational Reform*, New York, 1898; *More Money for Public Schools*, New York, 1903; *University Administration*, Boston, 1908; *A Late Harvest*, Boston, 1924, with a bibliography of nearly two hundred articles by Eliot.

FELDMAN, W. T., *Philosophy of John Dewey, A Critical Analysis*, Johns Hopkins University Press, 1934.

HAWKINS, HUGH, *Pioneer, A History of the Johns Hopkins University, 1874–1889*, Cornell University Press, 1960.

HORNE, H. H., *The Democratic Philosophy of Education*, New York, 1932.

KANDEL, I. L., ed., *Twenty-Five Years of American Education*, New York, 1929, Period; 1900–1925.

McCAUL, ROBERT L., "Dewey and the University of Chicago," *School and Society*, a three-part account in Volume 89 (1961), 152–157; 179–183; and 201–206. Also by McCaul, "Dewey's Chicago," *The School Review*, Summer, 1959, pp. 258–280, with notes and bibliography.

McMANIS, JOHN L., *Ella Flagg Young and a Half-Century of the Chicago Public Schools*, Chicago, 1916.

MAYHEW, KATHERINE CAMP, and ANNE CAMP EDWARDS, *The Dewey School, The Laboratory School of the University of Chicago, 1896–1903*, New York, 1936.

PATRIDGE, LELIA, *Notes of Talks on Teaching by Francis W. Parker*, New York, 1885; *Quincy Methods Illustrated*, New York, 1886.

SCHILPP, PAUL ARTHUR, ed., *The Philosophy of John Dewey*, New York, 1951.

TELLER, JAMES D., "Are American Schools Democratic?", *School and Society*, vol. 53, pp. 684–688, May 31, 1941.

WHITE, MORTON G., *Origin of Dewey's Instrumentalism*, Columbia University Press, 1943.

WILSON, W. E., "The Doctrine of Interest," *Educational Review*, March, 1896; and see many other articles in this decade in the *Educational Review*, in *Education*, and other journals on this general topic, in particular one by W. T. Harris on Dewey's doctrine of interest in the *Educational Review* for May, 1896.

WIRTH, ARTHUR G., *John Dewey as Educator, 1894–1904*, New York, 1966.

Chapter 14

SCIENCE AND EDUCATION

Both of the key words in the title of this chapter have several meanings. In Chapter 11 we noted the several senses in which the word *science* is used and traced the development of *education* as a profession with its own distinct body of knowledge. When the emphasis is on this store of knowledge, education can be treated as a discipline. This knowledge constantly increases and this increase is partly a result of the operations of a philosophy of education as it sharpens our values and objectives; partly a result of a science of education as it brings scientific method to bear on the solutions of problems of learning and teaching; and partly a result of an art of education as it applies knowledge to learning situations. In summary, education in these last three senses attempts to answer the cryptic question: "What should we do with what we have to get what we want?" *Philosophy of education* helps us to decide what we want; *science of education* tells us the nature of what we have to work with; and *art of education* guides us in what we do as teachers. This chapter emphasizes the development of education as one of the behavioral sciences and shows its relations to the other behavioral sciences, especially psychology, sociology, and anthropology. This development has been labeled "a scientific movement in education" and is closely related to what we have called "a Progressive movement in education," in Chapter 13.

The two movements developed together, and each influenced the other. There is no necessity for conflict between them. Some of the investigations of Horace Mann and Henry Barnard were positive and factual studies. The Boston school examination of 1845, which was devised by Mann and S. G. Howe, was an attempt to measure educational products. Child study held some of the purposes of scientific work, although its methods were often entirely unscientific. In the 1870's and 1880's the requirement of written work and written examinations in the elementary schools reached a height that some considered absurd. The attempt to improve school buildings and to make schools more healthful goes back to William A. Alcott, Horace Mann, and Henry Barnard. These men were both progressive and scientific.

The Progressive movement has emphasized selected lines of educational research. Its principles of 1924 called upon the schools to become educational laboratories for the study of pupil development. But there is no line separating studies of the pupil from studies of his environment. Statistics are used in the investigation of growth or learning but also in studies of salaries, building cost, or playground space. Historical research is a recognized pursuit in the study of education and it deals with many varied topics. Experimentation is a very important method of investigation. These few examples illustrate the fact that the field of educational science is a broad one.

RICE AS AN EDUCATIONAL SCIENTIST

The occasional gathering of objective information for use in education was not new in 1890; but a more investigative era began at that time. The well-known experiment by William Lowe Bryan and Noble Harter on the learning of telegraphy, published in 1897, was as much educational as it was psychological. The construction of scales to measure educational products and mental capacity began about 1900. It was Rice who took a first step toward the construction of an achievement scale, or rather a scheme of measurement, in 1894. His spelling investigation followed, and the results were published in 1897. This is often considered to be the beginning of the educational measurement movement in America.

The way in which Rice became an educational scientist forms the text of a surprising story. Joseph Mayer Rice (1857–1934) was educated as a physician and began to practice medicine in 1881. Undertaking a new career seven years later, he went to Germany to study psychology and education just as De Garmo and other early Herbartians were returning to the United States. Like them, Rice went to Jena and Leipzig, learned about Froebel, Herbart, and older writers, but did not become a pure disciple. Perhaps it was his medical education that led him to study European education directly by visiting schools.

When he came home he visited American classrooms and observed the work of 1,200 teachers in thirty-six cities from Boston to Minneapolis and from New York to Baltimore. The results were published in a series of articles in *The Forum* and then in a book, *The Public-School System of the United States* (1893). Rice's report was not entirely pessimistic but he found the teaching mechanical in most schools, the curriculum narrow and based upon textbooks alone, and the discipline repressive. One of his main theses was that when teachers are properly prepared for their work, the curriculum can be indefinitely broadened without detriment to the four

R's. Perhaps Rice had not read Pestalozzi, but he agreed with him that the school should be a pleasant place, teachers and children should be friends. To improve the city schools of the United States three things were necessary: to drive out the politicians, to train the teachers and keep training them in service, and to provide competent supervisors in sufficient numbers. He had clearly seen and learned some of these things in Germany.

The criticism did not make Rice popular. At the time he was only thirty-five years old and unknown. As Butler of Columbia said, school people "are to the last degree impatient of criticism and suggestion. They resent them as a reflection on their personal character. As one man, they rush to the defense. The better among them excuse the worse and the worse grow abusive." Horace Mann had experienced just such treatment upon returning from Europe fifty years earlier. Rice did not reply. Butler, with some reservations, endorsed Rice's criticism and said it was needed; and a few years later Butler took part in reforming the structure of the New York City school system.

This portion of Rice's life story is not often told. Most writers leave this part of the origin of the scientific movement unexplained. It seems that Rice was led to the measurement of educational results through his medical education, study in Germany, and his visits to schools. He saw that opinions about schools and teaching were only opinions, and that school men had few hard facts to support their judgments. The method that he had used in his tour to test the ability of children in reading at sight shows that he was trying to obtain objective evidence. One day in October 1894, the idea came to him that the results of the teaching of spelling could be determined with mathematical accuracy. The same day he selected fifty words and ultimately secured test results of 30,000 children who were being taught in different ways. By giving the same spelling test to all children he was able to make comparisons. Although his method was not perfect, it proved to be a fruitful experiment.

The spelling investigation marked the second period of Rice's educational activity. He also made extensive tests of the results of the teaching of arithmetic and language. In the 1890's and later, educators were much exercised over the question of "economy of time" in education. This was one of Eliot's themes, and a committee of the NEA worked on the matter. Rice, too, wanted to discover whether the great amount of time spent on spelling was well spent and necessary. He found that children's spelling ability was more closely connected with the quality of the teaching and the maturity of the pupils than it was with the time spent in spelling classes; this finding gave him the title of his report, "The Futility of the Spelling-Grind." His methods of investigation have been exhaustively reviewed and his results have been superseded, as may be conveniently learned from the article on "Spelling" in the *Encyclopedia of Educational Research*. Rice's importance is that of a pioneer, and it was his fate to be attacked and ridiculed by those leaders who "knew" that educational results could not be measured.

This testing venture changed one of Rice's opinions about education. From his study of city systems he had concluded that local politics was the great evil in the schools, and he proposed to cure or relieve this condition with state control. But he now came to believe that the chief difficulty was the inability to measure results. How is one to choose among such factors as different methods, topics, or time allotments without knowing which is better and how much better? This change of mind began the third period in Rice's work.

Always practical in his aim, Rice now undertook to interest the teaching profession in the measurement of educational results. Whether preceding or parallel activities in educational and psychological measurement had much effect upon him is an unanswered question. Others were at work on the same problems when Rice was making his spelling investigation, he was not as original as has been claimed. In 1902, Rice proposed that cities should appoint research assistants to the superintendent of schools; in 1903, together with twenty-four superintendents and others, he founded the Society of Educational Research. At that point the matter was taken out of his hands.

TOWARD A SCIENCE OF EDUCATION

The science of education, as it was understood by Alexander Bain and William H. Payne, employed little induction and no mathematics. Rice, although his methods were defective, introduced the quantitative idea into educational science. Others carried on. C. W. Stone produced a standardized achievement test in arithmetic in 1908 and S. A. Courtis produced another one the following year. E. L. Thorndike's handwriting scale appeared in 1910. Leonard P. Ayres constructed a handwriting scale in which legibility was measured by the rate at which the samples could be read. Scales in other subjects, such as spelling, composition, and language, quickly followed. Although the testing movement attracted the greatest attention, other studies were carried forward. There were publications on school law, taxation, and finance, studies of school building programs, and consideration of children's progress through the grades.

Investigation of this latter topic attracted wide attention and finally gained results. In 1901 P. W. Search presented statistical data on individual differences in growth, school abilities and performance, physical defects including defects in vision, and an age-grade table in a chapter on "the losses of the school." In his report for 1904 the Superintendent of Schools of New York City published a similar table and called attention to the number of "repeaters" in the schools. Retardation and elimination from school became schoolhouse words if not household words. Studies of this maladjustment of the curriculum to the children were reported by E. L. Thorndike (1907), Leonard P. Ayres (1909), and George D. Strayer (1911). In 1913 Ayres published *Laggards in Our Schools*, a widely discussed book.

The school survey movement began about this time. The studies of the schools of Montclair, New Jersey, by Paul H. Hanus in 1911 and of those of East Orange, New Jersey, by Ernest C. Moore in 1912 formed a beginning. The New York School Inquiry of 1911–1912 was the first large city survey and the first to make extensive use of an achievement test. S. A. Courtis gave his arithmetic test to about 30,000 children in this survey, which was conducted by Paul H. Hanus, one of the few educators of standing who had publicly commended the work of Rice.

The school survey movement spread so rapidly that it might be said to have swept the country. The schools of eleven cities and two entire states were surveyed between 1910 and 1913. This was only the beginning. Surveys were usually made by teams of professional educators who were brought in for that purpose. There have been many kinds of surveys. The United States Office of Education conducted a national survey of secondary education (1932). Some cities or single institutions conduct self-surveys or maintain a continuous survey of their operations.

Old-timers met the survey movement with derision, and dismay, and sometimes with angry denunciation. Some of these reactions were justified in special cases. Surveys have at times been instituted for the purpose of discrediting a school administration. This was a factor in the New York School Inquiry; and Hanus, who has told the story in his autobiography, had difficulty in securing the publication of his report without having it heavily censored. In fact, one section of his work was privately printed, another was not published at all. It is an obvious principle of school surveying that no part of the report may be garbled or suppressed. Such a requirement is now written into the usual survey contract.

This New York survey should not be dismissed without mention of the city's chief school officer, William H. Maxwell (1852–1920), whose name has been bracketed with those of William T. Harris, Andrew S. Draper, and other notable school administrators. Maxwell was a North Ireland boy who received a thorough education, taught briefly in his native land, and came to New York to follow the same vocation. Finding no opening because he was a foreigner, Maxwell engaged in newspaper work and in a few years became the managing editor of a Brooklyn daily paper. When he was twenty-nine Maxwell was at last accepted to teach history in the evening schools, and almost at once became assistant superintendent and then superintendent of the schools of Brooklyn. When the boroughs were consolidated in 1898, Maxwell became the first superintendent of Greater New York City and held that office for twenty years.

Educational organization in the metropolis was almost unbelievably un-developed at the close of the nineteenth century. Manhattan had only a seven-year elementary school, but the other boroughs each had eight-year elementary schools. There were local school boards, some of which con-trolled only a single one-room school, and borough boards as well as the city board of education. Classes in the primary grades were huge, often numbering seventy or more children. Many children were on part-time schedules or did not attend school at all. Public kindergartens and high schools were just beginning, twenty-five years after St. Louis had introduced them. The entire system was befogged by personal, religious, and partisan politics. Rice's first opinion that politics is the chief obstruction to good education was correct insofar as New York was concerned.

Four years after Maxwell became superintendent, the city charter was revised, the school administration was consolidated, and the superintend-ent was given power over education, not merely over school property. The School Inquiry of 1911–1912 was intended to upset the Maxwell regime but it misfired. In 1912 a great meeting was held in Carnegie Hall in recognition of the superintendent's twenty-five years in Brooklyn and New York.

Maxwell promoted junior high schools, trade schools, and industrial and physical education. He needed his great energy merely to keep up with the demands of the rapidly growing city. In his views on the preparation of teachers, which he favored, and on some other professional matters, he belonged to the nineteenth century. But he was a courageous, sufficiently combative, and generally wise administrator.

Surveys have a practical purpose: the improvement of educational prac-tice. The method of the survey and of educational measurement is in the main a comparative one. It seeks to determine, for example, whether the children of the fourth grade are able to spell as well as the fourth-grade children in other cities. Standards are derived from the better schools of those that have been tested. Sometimes there is little effort to apply the knowledge gained from a survey, so that the word itself has come to mean a mere gathering of information. Survey courses in college have acquired this same innocuous character.

Surveys are, however, intended to improve education, not to promote research, although they have occasionally done this incidentally. The desire to improve education leads to a philosophical question that asks what values are most cherished by the community. Do the people, for example, want their children to spend so much time in becoming very rapid calcula-tors and in gaining ability to spell hundreds of unusual words that they may not have time for current problems and controversy? Rice saw this point. He wanted to save time on the formal studies in order to enrich the curriculum. What use is made of educational science is determined by the philosophy of the people.

The early surveyors had few tools with which to do their work; the New York Inquiry consisted of only a single achievement test. But several thousand such tests in many school subjects and skills were developed within two decades after 1910. This was partly a result of the publicity that came from the surveys; partly of the demand that came from teachers, supervisors, and superintendents; and of competition among the commercial test manufacturers. The resulting tests varied in nature and quality. Some had only a limited application, some were imperfectly standardized, and many were not offered in a sufficient number of comparable forms for use in an effective testing program.

Many of the tests were prepared in university departments and bureaus of educational research. Such departments were opened at the universities of Oklahoma in 1913, Indiana and Iowa in 1914, and elsewhere in rapid succession after World War I. New methods and courses in educational research were developed in these departments.

Teacher's marks formed another of the areas of study. Walter Fenno Dearborn (1878–1955) published his study *School and University Grades* in 1910. Reports on the distribution and the unreliability of marks attracted wide attention. As in similar cases, the early interpretation of the facts was extreme. Marks can be made more reliable than the first investigators believed.

Index numbers were applied to the comparative study of state and city school systems. Leonard P. Ayres used ten sets of data, half of them financial, to compute educational index numbers for each of the states for the years 1890, 1900, 1910, and 1918. His early work on this problem was done in 1911 and the final results were published in 1920. Others have attempted improvements in the selection and weighting of data, and the method has also been applied to cities. The ranking of states or cities according to their educational performance may have some practical value in stimulating rivalry.

Rating scales or score cards for use in judging school buildings were developed early in the century and have been practically useful. A rating method was also used in developing handwriting and other scales. Scales for rating success in teaching have frequently been used. Rating methods, however, are not objective. They do not entirely eliminate the element of personal judgment. Their reliability can be increased by defining what is to be rated, by "educating" the users of the scale, and by pooling the scores of several raters. It is an awkward fact that there is no generally acceptable and exact definition of good teaching, and no accurate measurement of it.

Curriculum investigation has been one of the most popular types of research in education, but it is often criticized for its lack of objectivity. The methods that have been employed in curriculum study include job analysis, analysis of social needs, consensus of opinion, and study of school practices or previous curricula, of textbooks, and of pupil reaction. Boyd H.

Bode, who was one of the vigorous critics of these highly subjective and generally conservative procedures, denied the possibility of determining what should be taught from what is taught. It was important to have this said, but the application of the principle of social usefulness has produced important curriculum improvements, as, for example, in arithmetic. Many consider that the resultant pruning of arithmetic was extreme. But most people would agree that curriculum objectives and therefore curriculum content and method ultimately depend upon a philosophy; this was Bode's main contention.

At the same time science can make important contributions to the curriculum. It can, for example, determine the level of intelligence and the time that is required for the comprehension and learning of common fractions or other topics. It can test the results of teaching to determine when a process has been learned. This kind of knowledge has an obvious use in preparing a curriculum.

RESEARCH IN SPELLING INSTRUCTION

Children do not need to spell unless they are writing. This simple truth was hardly recognized by the old spelling book compilers, or at least it was ignored. It was customary to include some of the longest and most infrequently used words of the language in elementary spelling books. It should be remembered that the old spelling bee was a social event and to "spell down" the experts who competed in them some jaw-breakers were often needed.

Uniformity of spelling is not as important as many people believe, but this does not make the subject any less important in education. The primary reason that business will not tolerate errors in spelling carries the opinion of the general public along with it. The reason is a social one, and the school must teach what social use requires.

This principle is applied in selecting the words that are to be taught, namely, the hard words that are frequently written. The selection of these words was a basic step in scientific research in education. Very easy words that are in constant use will be learned without much teaching. The spelling of unusual words can be looked up in a dictionary if they should be needed. But between these two groups of words are several thousand words that are frequently written and that present spelling difficulties. These words had to be selected and they must be taught.

These words have been identified through word-frequency counts in such materials as personal and business letters, business papers, and school compositions. The extensive count for Thorndike's *Word-Book* was made from printed materials such as newspapers and the Bible. Later lists were drawn from manuscript sources. It has been shown that children at school use a somewhat special vocabulary that is derived from their studies. The word *minuend* from arithmetic is such a word. Each vocation, science, and sport uses a number of special words. *Touchdown* and *scholastic*, for example, are not found among Thorndike's 10,000 "most frequently used" words. This indicates that the frequency counts do not reveal all the words that should be learned. A judicious selection from the somewhat less frequent words should also be taught.

The methods of teaching spelling have been studied by investigators. Studies have been made of the relative difficulty of words and of the special points of difficulty in particular words. Attention has been given to the grades in which the selected words can be best taught. This is a comparatively simple problem of curriculum organization because each word presents discrete problems. The problems in arithmetic, science, or history are interrelated and attention must be given to the logic of the subject.

Should spelling be taught in connection with writing and reading as it may be needed, or systematically in spelling classes? The answer is not clear but there appears to be a place for both methods. Questions of motivation have been examined, and are of great importance to "poor spellers." Much has been learned about the teaching of spelling, but for the details the student must go to special sources. They do not belong here.

The first scientific spelling test was not J. M. Rice's casually chosen list of fifty words, but A *Measuring Scale for Ability in Spelling* (1913) prepared by Leonard P. Ayres. Further work was done on standard spelling scales by B. R. Buckingham and E. J. Ashbaugh. By means of these and later instruments a teacher can judge her success in teaching and can compare her results with those of other teachers.

SCHOOL ARITHMETIC

There is a parallel between the history of spelling and that of arithmetic as school studies. In each case, an early period of comparative neglect in the schools was followed by a period of overemphasis and, moreover, of emphasis upon the wrong phases of the subject. Later, common sense and philosophical consideration brought the teaching more into harmony with actual needs and also improved the methods. This third period prepared the way for a fourth, the present era of scientific investigation. It is to be noted that the scientific questions grew out of everyday experience.

In colonial times arithmetic was a vocational subject of commerce and the trades. This commercial arithmetic was also called common or vulgar arithmetic because it pertained to the common affairs of common people. It was taught in special writing and reckoning schools by special teachers of practical skills.

Before the Revolution, arithmetic was not included in Latin grammar school curricula. Upon the request of parents the schools excused pupils to take lessons in arithmetic from a writing and reckoning master. Until the latter part of the eighteenth century it was hardly unusual for a student to complete college without ever having received any instruction in arithmetic.

Many arithmetic textbooks appeared after the Revolution, displacing the English works that had been in use up to that time. One of the new books by Nicholas Pike was published in 1788. A later edition contained a section on the new decimal coinage that had been recommended by Thomas Jefferson. By 1800 arithmetic had become a frequently taught subject in common schools, and as public education expanded it occupied more and more of the time of the pupils.

The old arithmetic books often contained forty or fifty topics, each with a special rule and with numerous cases under each rule and topic. Six or more ways of calculating interest might be shown, including simple interest, the 6 per cent method, the sixty-day method, the cancellation method, exact interest with four or more cases, interest on promissory notes, annual interest, and partial payments. The subject of weights and measures was also extensive and complicated and much of it was useless to most of the pupils.

Arithmetic was often an individual study; the pupil began each year at the point reached the year before. When there was no printed textbook available, a manuscript ciphering-book was used. In the better schools the classwork consisted of writing solutions to problems on the blackboard and "explaining" them. There was little teaching. The application of common sense to arithmetic instruction was made by Pestalozzi, and Warren Colburn introduced his ideas of arithmetical analysis and primary arithmetic into the United States in 1821. This was the beginning of the third period.

The two movements for economy of time and for the enrichment of the elementary curriculum exerted strong pressure on the older subjects to gain a reduction in the time allotted to them. The pressure on arithmetic, which occupied so much of the school day, was especially heavy. Topics omitted from many textbooks by 1900 included circulating decimals, equation of payments, partial payments, gauging, tonnage, cube and square roots, unusual fractions, greatest common divisor, and least common multiple. The emphasis upon real life problems was growing. A. E. Winship of the *Journal of Education* in 1894 asked, "What can be eliminated from arithmetic?" and Frank M. McMurry in 1904, approaching the problem from the positive side, answered that only what has a clear relation to the needs of life should be included. This is the social use principle, which was to become the guiding principle of numerous investigations.

In arithmetic as in spelling, scientific research grew out of the practical problems of life and education. It was an effort to test unverified beliefs and to make vague and general statements more precise and specific. It is not correct to say that educational reform was begun by the scientific investigators. On the contrary, the investigators continued a trend that had already been set in motion. The student can conveniently verify this statement by examining books on the pedagogy of arithmetic published about 1900 or soon thereafter. David Eugene Smith in *The Teaching of Elementary Mathematics* (1900) and J. W. A. Young in *The Teaching of Mathematics* (1906) will supply evidence. It is to be understood that these authors were far in advance of the practice of their time.

Ordinary observation indicated that the old arithmetic of many rules, topics, and cases included much useless material. But this knowledge from ordinary observation was not sufficiently precise to guide the curriculum maker in applying the principle of social use. To do this efficiently, he needed a more exact and detailed knowledge of the arithmetic of daily life. This more accurate knowledge was to be gained by inquiry.

Surveys of the arithmetic concepts and practices needed in occupations appeared as early as 1900. A report to the National Education Association in that year included a digest of six hundred replies from businessmen to a questionnaire. Business colleges also gave attention to the problem. Educators were not satisfied, and further surveys of the concepts, skills, and degree of accuracy required were made. The search also became a phase of the job analysis effort of the 1900's, and a chapter in *Curriculum Construction* (1923) by W. W. Charters dealt with the problem.

The general conclusion was that only a small part of the arithmetic found in older textbooks was needed in business, and that the simplification that had been made before 1900 or 1910 had not gone far enough. Everybody agreed that pupils should learn to perform the four fundamental operations with the whole numbers and small fractions confidently, rapidly, and accurately; and that they should be taught to check their results. It was indicated by experiment that checking increased the initial accuracy. Some held out for complete accuracy as the ideal; but perfect agreement was not reached on this nor on the degree of speed or skill that would be acceptable. Norms were set, however, when in 1908 and 1913 standard tests began to appear. Some of the later tests were criticized because they included materials not used in business.

The important fractions, it was found, are halves, thirds, and fourths, with occasional use for fifths, eighths, and twelfths; but not for thirteenths, or any of the fractions with large denominators. The role of **decimals** was discovered to be a small one, confined to statistics and to factories making pistons or other products with tolerances of ten-thousandths of an inch. Also, and as early as sixty years ago, it was pointed out that the use of cash registers, automatic scales, calculating machines, interest and other tables, and formulas was narrowing the limits of the pencil-and-paper arithmetic needed in daily life.

The psychology of arithmetic has been extensively studied in order to improve the methods of teaching. H. V. Holloway carried out an experiment to determine the relative difficulty of the simple addition and subtraction combinations, $1 + 0, 1 + 1, 2 + 1 \ldots$ and $1 - 0, 1 - 1, 2 - 1 \ldots 9 - 9$. His results, published in 1914, interested other investigators, and ten years later F. L. Clapp also published lists of the relative difficulty of those combinations. Transfer of training experiments using the same combinations showed that pupils who are taught half of these combinations will complete the others without teaching. The transfer over this very small gap with second-grade pupils ranged from 70 to almost 100 per cent. Helping the pupils to generalize increased the amount of transfer.

STUDIES OF READING

Reading is more widely and frequently practiced than writing, spelling, calculating, drawing, or sewing. Yet many people cannot read and many more cannot read well. It is not surprising, therefore, that great efforts have been made to improve the teaching of this skill. Investigations of reading and of the teaching of reading outnumber those of any other school study; and each year sees the addition of from fifty to one hundred new reports on this topic. During the period from 1957 to 1968, the U.S. Office of Education alone has invested nearly $12 million in support of 257 separate reading research projects. The great need identified by Jeanne Chall in her intensive analysis and report in *Learning to Read: The Great Debate* (1967) is "to build a unified theory about the reading process."

We have already noted in Chapters 1 and 6 the conflict between the letter recognition and the word recognition methods of teaching reading. The theory that a reader perceives words letter by letter had deceived teachers including the astute Pestalozzi for centuries. Although word recognition methods of teaching had been developed by Joseph Jacatat and others, the resolution of the conflict was dependent upon studies of perception in reading. Such studies were made early, but the first noteworthy results were obtained about 1879 when Émile Javal of the University of Paris made the surprising discovery that the eyes of a reader do not advance smoothly along the line of print but move in sudden short sweeps, alternating with momentary pauses or fixations; that is, the motion is discontinuous. Since then these movements have been extensively studied by various means, but best by means of photography.

It was found that we recognize words only during the brief pauses while the eyes are at rest; and at such moments we recognize whole phrases and short sentences. William James pointed out that acquaintance with the structure of language contributes to this ability to recognize large sections of printed matter "at a glance." James was writing of readers who knew English grammar. One form of improvement in reading consists in learning to recognize such large sections rather than in attempting to change the eye movements.

Investigators found that the rapid reader is also the one who comprehends best and can report most fully upon what he reads. This is contrary to common opinion, which holds that rapid reading is superficial; and it is true that unfamiliar or technical matter must be read slowly to be comprehended. It was learned that reading such material increases the number of fixations. It leads also to regressive movements of the eyes, showing that parts of the reading material had been passed over without being sufficiently understood. By practice in increasing the eye-span, sharpening the attention, and other means, efficiency in reading can be so materially increased that business firms are willing to pay for the instruction of their staffs in reading, and colleges carry on remedial reading programs. Investigation has shown that many readers are inefficient because they have fallen into slovenly reading habits.

Other investigations have studied individual differences in reading, changes that come with age, as in the case of changing reading interests, and conditions that facilitate ease of reading or prevent harmful physical effects from reading. Some investigations have dealt with problems of fatigue and eyestrain, illumination, desirable type, near-sightedness, and other problems of the physiology and hygiene of reading. The differences between oral and silent reading have been explored. Francis W. Parker, who took no part in the scientific investigation of reading, nevertheless deplored the exclusive emphasis in schools upon oral reading. Incidentally, the spelling lesson was also an oral exercise at that time.

Other studies of reading have been concerned with the extent of people's reading and the influence that reading exercises upon the state of their information and opinions. This, as the founders of the American government explained, is especially important in a republic. Perhaps the most famous schoolbook author to share these sentiments was William Holmes McGuffey (1800–1873), who wrote his first reader at the age of thirty-six and at the time of his death had written six readers that sold 120 million copies by the beginning of the twentieth century. These books contained extracts from the world's great literature, Bible stories, ethical tales, and other stories that stressed patriotism, integrity, honesty, industry, temperance, courage, politeness, and other virtues. Recently these readers have been reprinted, and some school boards such as the one in Twin Lakes, Wisconsin, have voted to bring back the old texts to replace readers that tell about John and Jane's visit to the henhouse or Tom and Susan's trip to the zoo.

Admittedly, some could consider McGuffey narrow-minded, intolerant, or opinionated in selecting materials for his readers. A more scientific and more recent (1946) investigation directed by Henry C. Link showed that the amount of reading done by individual persons, like their incomes, intelligence, or education, varies between wide limits. Twenty-one per cent of the people questioned read 70 per cent of the total number of books that were read; and the upper half of those interrogated read 94 per cent of the books. This leaves only 6 per cent of the books that were read by the lower 50 per cent of the readers. About one-third of the homes that were canvassed claimed to have a hundred books or more, a surprising and perhaps incredible result.

The investigation showed that most people do not read many books. Efforts were made to learn what else they read. The first answer is that they read newspapers, many news weeklies, comic books, farm and trade papers, and sensational magazines. The large sale of good titles in paperback editions may lead some to conclude that the public literary taste has improved. According to reviewers, fiction is less popular than it once was but this may be a result of the lower quality of the new fiction. Link found that three-fifths of the books most recently read were works of fiction. There have been some successful examples of historical fiction in late years and of fictionized as well as more trustworthy biography. Some of the most popular novels and biographies have dealt with religion, and many books on purely religious subjects have found readers. During the period of the Link survey "the reading of the Bible was equalled if not surpassed by that of *Forever Amber* and *A Tree Grows in Brooklyn*." If the Bible is read so much one can only express surprise over the ignorance of its contents, which every investigator claims to have found. Some of these reports must be mistaken. Or are we to conclude that people remember almost nothing from their reading?

The first general report on scientific studies of reading was made in 1908 by Edmund Burke Huey (1870–1913), who proposed that children should learn from the beginning to get the meaning and not mainly to pronounce the words. That was a period when reading was still regarded as elocution. The numerous series of silent reading books that were published during the present century testify to a change in the teaching of reading. The summary by Huey, entitled *The Psychology and Pedagogy of Reading*, included brief accounts of Huey's own investigations, which had begun about 1898. He was not the first American to work in this field. James McKeen Cattell had previously considered some of its problems in the 1880's while he was student in Wundt's laboratory. Huey's interest was started by a question asked of him by Guy M. Whipple, a young fellow experimenter in the laboratory of Clark University, about the possibility of reading without inner speech.

The book contains a chapter on inner speech, but it deals further with all the current phases of reading research. After more than sixty years it still remains a useful resumé. It is divided into four parts. The first part is on the psychology of reading and the last part is on the hygiene of reading. The intervening two parts treat the history of reading and reading

methods, and the pedagogy of reading. The second part is entirely historical and necessarily considers the invention and development of writing and
reading as the two sides of the same coin. The third part is also historical
or, because it deals with contemporary practice, some may wish to call it
a comparative study. Parts Two and Three and the rest of the book are
also worth the attention of teachers and students of the history of education.

The first steps in learning to read and when they should be taken is one
of the topics of the book. Reading readiness was not a new subject in 1908.
Many writers, both ancient and modern, had treated it; and Rousseau had
expressed himself positively on both how and when children should learn
to read. Many others had acted as if they believed that whenever the child
came to school he should "take up his book," perhaps to read, perhaps "to
learn his letter." Rousseau, on the contrary, thought the age of twelve
was early enough to learn how to read, and that children at that age would
learn practically without any help from a teacher. Even a little teaching
experience should have shown him that this position was absurd. Rousseau's statement had no influence in America but it has the dramatic value
of showing that there is a problem to which science has not yet given an
explicit and complete answer. It may be that teachers who are recent
graduates of colleges of education tend to hold back bright children longer
than is necessary. Many children have learned to read at very early ages
without any apparent bad effects.

Other topics treated by Huey include the effect of memory limits on the
span of attention, the difference between perception and recognition, cues
used in word recognition, and many other problems that are still under
investigation today.

PSYCHOLOGY AND EDUCATION

During Huey's life American psychology became more of a biological
and an experimental science than a rational study exclusively. William
James is generally regarded as the founder of this "new" biological and
experimental psychology in America. As early as 1875 he was teaching
physiological psychology at Harvard and using a psychological laboratory
to facilitate his teaching. But not only was he a pioneer; according to one
of America's eminent psychologists writing in 1960, he is ". . . without
doubt the foremost psychologist this country has produced." What is the
secret of the greatness of William James as a psychologist?

James is great as a psychologist for the same reason that Galileo is great
as a physicist. James did not invent a "new" psychology any more than
Galileo invented a "new" physics. A completely "new" way of looking at
nature was at hand, and each seized the opportunity to look at a limited

part of nature in the "new" way. James is great because he did for psychology what his teacher Louis Agassiz was encouraging and training a generation of students to do for all the evolving branches of natural history, namely, to base biological instruction upon things rather than on words, upon nature rather than on books.

Not only did James apply the new method to the study of behavior but he attempted to show the place of psychology in teaching and learning as we have seen in Chapter 11. The publication of his *Principles of Psychology* in 1890 and his *Talks to Teachers* nine years later prepared the way for the development of an educational psychology, but it remained for one of his students to develop this new branch of psychology. This man was Edward Lee Thorndike (1874–1949).

We have already referred to Thorndike's experiments on transfer of training as well as in other areas. We now turn to show his influence on classroom methods and on educational measurement. After completing his studies under James at Harvard University, Thorndike moved to Columbia University just before the close of the nineteenth century. While at Columbia, Thorndike developed his Stimulus-Response or S-R Bond theory as an explanation of learning according to the laws of readiness, exercise, and effect, which was widely embraced by classroom teachers and textbook writers. The capstone of this activity was the publication in 1902 of his *Educational Psychology*, which was expanded to three volumes in 1913.

Thorndike's studies of learning showed him the significance of individual differences, and in attempting to measure these differences, he made his most important contribution to the field of educational measurement. This was a book on statistical methods, *An Introduction to the Theory of Mental and Social Measurements,* which was first published in 1904. It was the first work of its kind and it is perhaps significant that it remained the only book on the subject for more than ten years.

In addition to being one of the first scholars to apply statistics to the solution of educational problems, Thorndike produced a number of tests and scales in different areas including handwriting, drawing, and intelligence. Thorndike also guided many graduate students who added to the store of tests and scales while investigating specific learning problems. Among his early students were C. W. Stone, who studied arithmetical abilities; M. B. Hillegas, who attempted to measure quality in English composition; and B. R. Buckingham, to whose spelling scale we have already referred. Thus by his own efforts and those of his students, Thorndike gave impetus to the educational testing movement.

At an early meeting of research people, Thorndike, in striking words, laid down a kind of program for the general movement. He said, in effect, that whatever exists at all exists in some amount; whatever exists in any amount can be measured; and to know it thoroughly involves knowing its quantity as well as its quality. He hastened to admit that the measurement of some things might be difficult and might require fifty years or more. The movement begun by Thorndike is now more than sixty years old and a great many educational existents have not yet been accurately measured. One of the difficulties is that they are frequently hard to define in behavioral terms. Another difficulty is that most educational existents cannot be measured directly or at least have not been so measured. But in spite of such difficulties, much progress has been made; and the best evidence of this consists in the radical change in the entire character of educational writing and discussion since the times of W. H. Payne and W. T. Harris.

In addition to Thorndike and his students, many others contributed to the educational testing movement. We have already noted in Chapter 7, in our treatment of the child study movement, the work of G. Stanley Hall (1844–1924) and several of his students. Two of Hall's students played an important role in the development of the intelligence test. It was Henry H. Goddard (1866–1957) who in about 1908 translated into English from the French the original intelligence test of Alfred Binet and Théodore Simon, and it was Lewis M. Terman (1877–1956) who revised and improved it. Another student of Hall for a short time, James McKeen Cattell (1860–1944), first used the term *mental test* in an article written in 1890. The pioneering work of these men and others placed educational and psychological measurement on a firm foundation before World War I.

Terman's revision of the Binet test was published in 1916, revised again in 1937, and revised a third time in 1960. It is the most widely used and accepted intelligence test in the United States. However, it is an individual test that requires extensive training and practice to acquire the skill necessary in its administration. Both Thorndike and Terman had been experimenting with the adaptation of certain of the Binet and other types of tests to group testing. The entry of the United States into World War I in 1917 established the need for a group test of intelligence and enabled a group of psychologists under the leadership of Arthur S. Otis (1886–   ) to develop Army Alpha, the first extensively used group test of intelligence.

Concurrent with the wide use of intelligence tests, theories of the nature of intelligence were refined. In 1927 Thorndike published his book, *The Measurement of Intelligence*, in which he theorized that intelligence is not a single entity but is composed of a very large number of specific functions or factors. This is consistent with his S-R Bond theory, which hypothesizes that learning consists of forming bonds between specific stimuli and responses. Extensive research with these specific factors led to the development of a compromise theory by Lewis Leon Thurstone (1872–1956) which hypothesizes that intelligence consists neither of a single factor nor of many specific factors, but of groups of related factors. To discover these related factors, Thurstone developed a statistical technique called factor analysis. Following the publication of his book, *The Vectors of Mind*, in 1935, and its expansion in *Multiple-Factor Analysis* in 1947, many attempts were made to develop tests of these factors. Starting in 1938 with six primary mental abilities (verbal meaning, space, number, memory, word fluency, and reasoning) the number of factors continues to increase. One investigator, Joy P. Guilford (1897–   ) has developed a model of the intellect that postulates the possible existence of 120 factors.

Guilford's model of 1959 includes factors that he labels "divergent thinking" as contrasted with another group of factors called "convergent thinking." In the case of the former, thinking is less constrained and proceeds in different directions by different subjects. For example, a test such as Thurstone's "word fluency" might ask the subject to list as many words beginning with the letter s as possible in a limited period of time. Some have hypothesized that creative thinking may well be in this area. Many attempts have been made to devise tests of creativity, but it has been difficult to distinguish the concept of creativity from that of intelligence generally.

The results of the educational testing movement are known to every student and his parents. In 1964 the school and college enrollment in the United States was about 52,900,000. It is estimated that about 150,000,000 standardized tests, exclusive of those in nationwide testing programs, were used by schools and colleges in that year, or about three tests for each student.

As one would expect the movement has had its critics as well as its supporters. Some critics have claimed that such widespread use of tests stifles originality and encourages uniformity in learning and teaching. Others have been fearful that such national assessment programs of the type begun in 1964 by the Carnegie Corporation might lead to federal control of the curriculum. However, it must be recognized that progress in education is dependent upon comprehensive and dependable data. Statistics on numbers of schools, pupils, and teachers are not enough. We also need information on educational results. Objective, reliable, and valid instruments are necessary for an assessment of the effectiveness of learning and teaching. Thorndike's dictum is difficult to achieve, but teachers must be concerned with the quantity as well as the quality of all educational existents if they are to understand the individual differences of their pupils.

STUDIES OF EXCEPTIONAL CHILDREN

Although each student is unique, the majority of pupils in our schools are in the median or normal range in most of their abilities. However, some pupils are outside this range in respect to certain abilities. They may be exceptionally intelligent or mentally retarded; they may excel in physical skills or be physically handicapped; they may be emotionally well adjusted or maladjusted. Such children are referred to in educational literature as *exceptional* children. The development of a science of education and educational psychology has assisted in the identification and treatment of the exceptional child whether he is outside the upper end or the lower end of the middle range.

Whether the special preparation of experts and leaders is more necessary than the fundamental education of all is a question that has not always received the same answer. In early historical times the preparation of leaders received all the attention, and for a long period schools were not provided for the masses. In modern times this position was modified and two kinds of schools were maintained, one with a long course of special knowledge for the leaders, and another with a short course of common knowledge for the common people. About a century ago the United States developed a system that was to be open to all throughout its full extent from the primary grades through the technical and professional schools. Only lack of ability or enthusiasm was to hinder any from reaching the topmost rung of their ambition.

That this is an ideal not yet attained is recognized, but the mere entertaining of the ideal raised another question. Should the gifted children be selected and given special education or is the wide-open door sufficient and, indeed, best? This question has also received more than one answer. We may consider a few of them.

If gifted children are to have special consideration, ways of identifying and selecting these children must be found. Lewis M. Terman (1877–1956), a pioneer in the study of the gifted, used the Stanford-Binet Intelligence Scale for this purpose, and defined a gifted child as one with an intelligence quotient (IQ) of 140 or higher on this test. Leta S. Hollingworth (1886–1939) used the same scale, but required an IQ of 180 or above to define the gifted child. However, there are difficulties in using an IQ to determine who is gifted. Other measures that have been applied include achievement test results, school marks, activities records, teachers' judgments, reports of social and emotional balance and maturity, types and strength of interests, and family and personal history. Because none of these factors is completely objective or of a determined value, the selecting committee will have to use its best judgment; but an IQ of 140 or above, high marks, and a favorable history will in the absence of negative evidence convince most judges that the pupil belongs to the gifted class. Students have frequently found that gifted children have developed special talents and aptitudes at an early age. If tests of divergent thinking or "Creativity" prove successful, the definition of a gifted child may change.

Both acceleration and enrichment of the education of the gifted child have been tried and favored by different investigators. They are not mutually exclusive plans; the former is administratively simpler and a number of universities have accepted gifted youths at the completion of the tenth school year, that is, at the age of sixteen or earlier. Time has also been gained by proficiency examinations. President Eliot favored devices such as these long ago. Hollingworth claimed that acceleration works to the detriment of the normal development of children along both social and physical lines. Sidney L. Pressey (1888–1971) of the Ohio State University proposed a plan that included some acceleration and much enrichment.

The enrichment of the course by the introduction of special projects is a second way of improving the education of gifted children. There are some administrative problems in this plan because it involves increased individual instruction and guidance and, if the group is numerous, the formation of special classes.

The handicapped child as well as the gifted child should receive schooling appropriate to his capacities and needs. The physically handicapped do in fact receive more attention than the gifted.

Gifted and handicapped classes overlap. The same person may be both gifted and crippled, or deaf, or even deaf and blind, like Helen Keller. Charles Steinmetz was one of many examples of persons with a crippled body and great mental gifts. There have been composers who continued writing music after they became deaf, blind musicians, and blind poets. Francis Parkman (1823–1893), although nearly blind, became one of the greatest American historians.

A school for the deaf was opened in Hartford, Connecticut, in 1817 by Thomas H. Gallaudet (1787–1851), who taught the sign language and the manual alphabet. Later, methods of lip reading and voice production were introduced. All four skills were imported from Europe. Samuel Gridley Howe (1801–1876), husband of Julia Ward Howe, opened a school for the blind in Boston in 1832. Other schools for the deaf and the blind quickly sprang up. Howe did a great deal of promotional work. His most spectacular achievement, however, was the education of Laura Bridgman, a little girl who was both deaf and blind. This seeming miracle was accomplished by very simple, but not the best, means. The education of Helen Keller (1880–1968) is a more extraordinary case. Her teacher, Anne Sullivan (1866–1936), herself partially blind, was educated at Howe's school, and became a teacher of the highest genius. In Helen Keller she had a similarly gifted pupil.

It has been said that "Miss Sullivan began where Dr. Howe left off . . . By experiment, by studying other children, Miss Sullivan came upon the practical way of teaching language by the natural method. It was for this 'natural method' that Dr. Howe was groping, but he never got to this idea, that a deaf child should not be taught each word separately by definition, but should be given language by endless repetition of language that it does not understand. And this is Miss Sullivan's great discovery." These are the opinions of John Macy, the husband of Anne Sullivan, which were published in a book edited by him, *The Story of My Life, by Helen*

Keller (1903). It also contains some of Helen Keller's letters, reports by Anne Sullivan, and a short account by the editor. The book is an educational classic, one of very few thus far written in the United States.

The education of the handicapped in the public schools had hardly begun before the present century. The general purpose of this work is to fit as many handicapped children as possible to enter the regular classes and to become independent, emotionally stable, and self-supporting persons.

City schools teach lip reading and speech to the hard of hearing. Sight-saving measures aim to protect children with low vision from excessive and harmful use of their eyes, and to use touch and other senses as substitutes for sight. The deaf and blind must be taught in special schools or classes. Before World War I only a few of the largest cities provided corrective measures for stammering, lisping, nasality, and other speech disorders. In the next decade such teaching was rapidly extended and its spread has continued along with a great development in normal speech education. Crippled children often need expensive treatment and artificial limbs, braces, or other equipment. Rotary International, Kiwanis, and other service clubs have aided many schools in obtaining this equipment. Tubercular children need open-air schools that are now common in large cities.

SOCIOLOGY, ANTHROPOLOGY, AND EDUCATION

Although psychology was the first of the behavioral sciences to have its concepts and principles applied to the problems of learning and teaching, two other behavioral sciences have found applications in the study of educational problems, namely sociology and anthropology. Just as educational psychology emerged as a specialization within the field of psychology, so did educational sociology become a specialized study within the broad field of sociology. As cultural anthropologists turned to a concern with personality, learning, and character, anthropology began to exert an influence on education. Both of these developments were well under way by 1930.

Sociology studies group behavior using the methods and attitudes of science. The educational sociologist merely applies the concepts and methods of general sociology to education and its social systems. Such concepts as value systems, status, role styles, peer groups, leadership, and bureaucratic structures have been found useful in the study of educational problems. For example, the concepts developed for use in military and industrial situations by the Ohio State Leadership Studies have been applied in educational studies. Other examples of the use of these concepts by educational sociologists include those of James S. Coleman, *The Adolescent Society* (1961), and A. B. Hollingshead, *Elmtown's Youth* (1949). Many other studies have investigated education by using sociological methods. A survey of these have been made by Orville B. Brim, *Sociology and the Field of Education* (1958).

Even though it is a relatively new discipline, educational sociology has demonstrated that there is more to teaching than the transmission of knowledge. It has shown that the school as a society is a replica of the larger social order of which it is a part. It is important that teachers and administrators understand this and that they be given the tools to analyze the social forces in the educational environment.

An important group of sociological studies that have particular significance for education are those dealing with culturally and socially disadvantaged children. As with exceptional children, this term refers to a group of children who are deprived of what the average middle-class child takes for granted. The term includes children with widely varying characteristics. The deprivation may be economic, cultural, or social. Some children are hungry; some are without sufficient clothing; others lack parental care and attention; and still others are without books in the home. In *The Culturally Deprived Child* (1962), Frank Riessman presents a portrait of the underprivileged. Among other characteristics, the culturally disadvantaged preschool child is not ready to learn to read, tends to lack ambition, and is unfamiliar with schedules and time limits.

Perhaps the best known federal program for helping the preschool disadvantaged child is the Head Start program authorized under the Economic Opportunity Act of 1964. As the name implies, the purpose of the program is to provide culturally and socially deprived children with a "head start" through enriched preschool programs. The program aims to arouse curiosity, develop language skills, and develop the child's self-image. The children play together, sing songs, solve puzzles, explore nature, and in general share experiences that their advantaged middle-class counterparts have in the home. Other important educational aspects of this act were literacy programs for adults, part-time employment for needy college students, and the Job Corps to provide both basic and vocational training for school dropouts and potential dropouts.

Since about 1930 it has been recognized that anthropology has much to contribute to a science of education. Not all types of anthropological studies are relevant to education, but those concerned with cultural transmission and personality formation have a direct value to the teacher.

In the last 50 years many anthropologists have turned their attention to the relation of culture to the individual and to a consequent concern with learning and personality. Such a concern can be traced from the work of one of America's leading anthropological theorists, Franz Boas (1858–1942), through his students, Edward Sapir (1884–1939) and Ruth Benedict (1887–1948), and his grand student, Margaret Mead (1901–   ).

In 1911 Boas published his definitive work, *The Mind of Primitive Man*, which was the beginning of his opposition to all types of deterministic theories whether geographic, economic, or racial. He insisted on identifying the component elements of culture through objective observation and field work.

It was Sapir who stressed the need for relating individual and cultural behavior. In his writings from 1927 to 1934 and in his teaching, first at the University of Chicago and later at Yale University, Sapir delineated the relation between culture and individual behavior. Sapir also developed the idea that all cultural behavior is based on "meanings" shared and communicated among individual members of the culture. Many of the concepts that he applied to the study of cultural behavior are contained in his book *Language* (1921).

Using Sapir's insights, Benjamin Lee Whorf (1897–1941) concluded in 1940 that man's view of the world of events is determined by his language. Although anthropologists recognize the intimate relation between language and culture, most do not accept the Whorfian hypothesis that language "determines" culture in any comprehensive way. However, Whorf and Sapir stimulated the development of a science of linguistics that has important implications for educational research.

In a classic book entitled *Patterns of Behavior* (1934), Benedict developed a "typological" approach to cultural behavior. Using such concepts as *patterns, goals, orientations,* and *mainsprings,* she and her students studied not only the characteristic *patterns* of custom that were typical for normal behavior in the culture but also the personality development of individuals from infancy to adulthood.

The first anthropologist to make the individual the focus of her studies was Ruth Benedict's first graduate student at Columbia University, Margaret Mead. In 1927, Mead published *Coming of Age in Samoa* in which she attempted to show that the supposedly universal stresses of adolescence need not occur under certain conditions of child rearing. As a result of this book, child development became a concern for those seeking to understand cultural behavior. Mead's influence has been extensive in education and especially in child psychology.

Whereas Mead's approach to the individual in culture stressed the child, another anthropologist trained in the Boas tradition, Ralph Linton (1893–1953), applied the sociological concepts of *status* and *role* to studies of personality development in relation to cultural factors. In 1936 he published *The Study of Man,* which applies these viewpoints to anthropological materials. In this same year he was appointed to the professorship at Columbia University from which Boas had retired. In his teaching and writing Linton developed a theoretical scheme relating the individual, personality, culture, and society.

From such foundations as we have summarized, the field of educational anthropology has developed. More recent anthropological studies of education have been concerned with the description and analysis of classroom processes and with perceptions that condition pupil-teacher interactions. Several studies in the latter area were published in 1969 under the editorship of Stephen A. Tyler with the intriguing title, *Cognitive Anthropology*.

SUMMARY

In his Kappa Delta Pi Lecture of 1929, John Dewey concluded that the sources of a science of education are "any portions of ascertained knowledge that enter into the heart, head, and hands of educators, and which, by entering in, render the performance of the educational function more enlightened, more humane, and more truly educational than it was before." In reaching this conclusion, he warns that a science of education cannot be constructed simply by borrowing the techniques of the physical sciences. Nor will a science of education be found in books or laboratories or classrooms; it can only be found in the minds of those engaged in directing educational activities.

In this chapter we have sampled material drawn from psychology, sociology, anthropology, and other behavioral sciences. This material furnishes the content of a science of education when it is focused on the problems that arise in education. In our sampling we have neglected the contributions that might come from classroom teachers and those of other organized bodies of knowledge, such as economics and politics. To have broadened our sample into these areas would have extended this chapter into another book.

QUESTIONS

1. Compare the kind of influences exerted by Progressive education upon the school with those exerted by the scientific education movement.
2. Why should the organization of a school allow considerable freedom to teachers and pupils? How much freedom should be allowed, and in regard to what factors?
3. Why are manuscript sources considered better than printed ones in the determination of the most frequently used words, especially since the printed words were taken from a manuscript? Would you substitute a different word for *used* if you were framing this question?
4. Why do spelling investigations form a good starting point for a study of the history of the scientific education movement?
5. What changes in teaching methods did the "new" psychology bring about?

6. Do you agree with the quotation from Dewey concerning the sources of a science of education? Why or why not?

7. Is there a science of education? More fundamentally, can there be a science of education?

8. Select a textbook in educational psychology, one in educational sociology, and one in educational anthropology. How are they alike? How do they differ?

9. To what degree and in what ways can a philosophy of education be a source of the science of education?

10. Do you agree that classroom teachers can contribute to a science of education? If so, in what ways? If not, why not?

11. In what ways can Economics be considered a science? A behavioral science? An educational science?

12. If the scientific and Progressive movements were opposed to each other, as has been claimed, why did they develop together, often in the same school systems? Is the dispute mainly a jurisdictional one that makes little sense in a broad view?

13. Consider the statement that the early promoters of psychological and educational research were strongly influenced in their work by their past preparation and studies.

14. Select several educational questions that have been at least fairly well answered by the educational researchers and justify your selection.

15. Has research answered the question, At what age should schooling begin? In your answer evaluate "Head Start" programs for the poor and suggest other alternatives to early schooling.

BOOKS AND PAPERS

Bibliographies on several of the topics of this chapter may be found in the *Encyclopedia of Educational Research*, the various issues of the *Review of Educational Research*, especially Vol. 39, No. 5, December 1969, the *Handbook of Research on Teaching*, and the *International Encyclopedia of the Social Sciences*. The "Anonymous Critic" was of the abusive stripe mentioned by President Butler. For Butler's review of J. M. Rice's *Public School System*, in which the words quoted in this chapter occur, see the *Educational Review*, December 1893. Other periodicals reporting educational research are too numerous to list here. A few articles from these journals appear in the following references. Books cited in the chapter are usually not repeated.

ABELOW, S. P., *Doctor William H. Maxwell*, Brooklyn, 1932.

ALLEN, GAY WILSON, *William James*, Viking, 1967. Using unpublished papers, this is one of the best biographies of James.

[Anonymous Critic], "The Critic at Sea," *Education*, eight installments, May 1894 to February 1895. This is a review of J. M. Rice's *Public School System*. When the journal *Education* prepared its index of 1946 these articles were omitted, *spurlos versenkt*.

BELL, ROBERT R., *The Sociology of Education, A Sourcebook*, Homewood, Ill., Dorsey Press, 1962.

BORING, EDWIN G., *A History of Experimental Psychology*, New York, Appleton-Century-Crofts, Inc., 1957.

CALDWELL, O. W., and S. A. COURTIS, *Then and Now in Education, 1845–1923*, New York, Harcourt, Brace & World, Inc., 1925.

CALIVER, AMBROSE, *Literacy Education*, Washington, D.C., U.S. Department of Health, Education, and Welfare, June 1953, Circular 376.

CARROLL, J. B., ed., *Language, Thought, and Reality, Selected Writings of Benjamin Lee Whorf*, New York, 1956.

CASWELL, HOLLIS L., *City School Surveys*, New York, Teachers College, Columbia University, 1929; and Caswell and A. W. Foshay, *Education in the Elementary School*, second edition, New York, 1950.

GINZBERG, ELI, and DOUGLAS W. BRAY, *The Uneducated*, Columbia University Press, 1953.

GUILFORD, J. P., *The Nature of Human Intelligence*, New York, McGraw-Hill, 1967.

HOFFMAN, BANESH, *The Tyranny of Testing*, New York, Macmillan, 1962, one of the many challenges to the testing movement.

HOLLOWAY, H. V., *Experimental Study of the Elementary Number Combinations in Addition and Multiplication*, Trenton, N.J., 1914, a dissertation.

HUEY, E. B., *Psychology and Pedagogy of Reading with a Review of the History of Reading and Writing*, New York, 1908. Reissued at Cambridge, Mass., by the MIT Press, 1968.

HUNNICUTT, C. W., and W. J. IVERSON, eds., *Research in the Three R's*, New York, 1958.

LAMPORT, H. B., *A History of Beginning Reading*, University of Chicago, 1935, an unpublished dissertation.

LANDES, RUTH, *Culture in American Education*, New York, John Wiley & Sons, Inc., 1965.

LINK, HENRY C., and H. A. HOFF, *People and Books, A Study of Reading and Book-Buying Habits*, New York, 1946.

MONROE, WALTER S., *Ten Years of Educational Research*, Bureau of Educational Research Bulletin, No. 42, University of Illinois, 1928.

MOORE, RAYMOND S. and DENNIS R. MOORE, "The Dangers of Early Schooling," *Harper's Magazine*, Vol. 245, pp. 58–62, July 1972.

REEDER, R. R., *Historical Development of School Readers and Methods of Reading*, New York, 1900.

ROBINSON, R. R., *Two Centuries of Change in the Content of School Readers*, George Peabody College for Teachers, 1930; and on the McGuffey readers, see R. D. Mosier, *Making the American Mind*, King's Crown Press, Columbia University, 1947.

SCATES, DOUGLAS, "Fifty Years of Objective Measurement and Research in Education," *Journal of Educational Research*, December 1947, with bibliography.

SMITH, DAVID EUGENE, *The Teaching of Elementary Mathematics*, New York, 1913.

SUYDAM, MARILYN N., *An Evaluation of Journal-Published Research Reports on Elementary School Mathematics, 1900–1965*, doctoral dissertation, The Pennsylvania State University, 1967.

THORNDIKE, E. L., "Distribution of Education," *School Review*, May 1932.

TIDYMAN, W. F., "Critical Investigation of Rice's Investigation of Spelling Efficiency," *Pedagogical Seminary*, September 1915, with bibliography.

WRIGHT, GRACE S., *Core Curriculum in Public High Schools, an Inquiry into Practice*, 1949, Washington, D.C., U.S. Government Printing Office, Office of Education, Bulletin, 1950, No. 5.

YOUNG, J. W. A., *Teaching of Mathematics in the Schools*, New York, 1912.

Chapter 15

TECHNOLOGY AND EDUCATION

Chapter 14 traced the movement toward the development of a *science* of education. This chapter is concerned with the evolution of a *technology* of education. Educational technology is the systematic treatment of the results of scientific investigation and research in relation to educational problems. It is the application of the knowledge supplied by science to problems of learning and teaching. It is applied knowledge. A technology of education is the development of instructional techniques—of methods and procedures—by which the teacher facilitates the learning process of the pupil. A technique may or may not involve the invention and application of hardware, instruments, apparatus, or machines to the learning process. As we have shown, earlier instructional technologies such as those of Mulcaster, Locke, Rousseau, Basedow, Pestalozzi, Herbart, Froebel, James, Thorndike, and Dewey did not depend greatly upon the invention of new hardware. More recent technologies of instruction such as those employing science laboratories, teaching machines, audio-visual aids, and computers depend more heavily upon mechanical, electrical, and electronic inventions. However, since most advances in instructional technology have depended to some extent upon the invention of new materials or apparatus, we begin with this theme.

EDUCATIONAL INVENTION

The use of new and old apparatus in schools is a somewhat neglected phase of educational history. Newer aids such as television, language laboratories, and teaching machines may set new directions for many phases of schoolwork. Many older discoveries have also increased the power of schools to cultivate new skills, knowledge, and understanding. Examples of such powerful discoveries would include the art of writing, the improvements in the form of the book, and the invention of printing. Since the

416

new devices are only the latest additions to a large collection of inventions that have profoundly changed schoolwork, it will be appropriate to look briefly at a few of the old discoveries that have blazed trails for the new.

The school itself and subjects of study, arithmetic for example, had to be invented. Early man discovered the difference between one object and several of a kind. He learned to count by forming a one-to-one correspondence between objects and his fingers or other counters such as pebbles. Gradually, by developing names for the numbers, he formed an artificial and ever-ready set of counters. The decimal system grew from the use of the fingers in counting. The ingenious invention of the zero made in India somewhere about A.D. 800, furnished the vital step in a decimal notation for whole numbers and decimal fractions.

In time, the arts of writing and arithmetic calculation were joined in a permanent and happy marriage. The fruits of this union were calculation with the pen and written records of business transactions. These did away with notches on sticks in the vaults of the Bank of England and with knots tied in the strings of American Indian *quipus*. The counting-board or abacus could be discarded. The calculator was thus enabled to review his figures for errors, something that was impossible on the abacus. After many centuries the teaching of arithmetic was changed radically and improved.

Mathematics and science formed a second fertile union. The revival of science is one of the marks of modernity. The study of nature had never completely ceased but it increased rapidly in the seventeenth century. Scientific experiment with newly invented instruments became one of the reasons we call that a new age. Discoveries in optics and glassmaking led to the invention of the refracting telescope and microscope and, hence, many other discoveries. Galileo saw the moons of Jupiter, which then became an item in the Copernican theory; the sight of minute capillaries by Marcello Malpighi improved the older account of the circulation of the blood; Leeuwenhoek drew the outlines of bacteria he saw in a drop of water through his microscope. New sciences were born. Discovery led to inventions; new instruments led to new discoveries.

Science is an inductive process. Induction requires observation of natural objects. Such observations lead to the collecting and classifying of the objects. The product of this interest in collecting is the educational museum. One historian of the museum in America calls Louis Agassiz "the foremost museum collector of his day." Accordingly we shall use Agassiz to illustrate the movement to establish museums.

Agassiz's own collections in the United States became the nucleus of the Museum of Comparative Zoology at Harvard University in 1860, which was to become the school for a whole generation of museum workers. Practically all the students associated with Agassiz at the dedication of this museum later became heads of great museums. One of them, Albert Smith Bickmore (1839–1914), inspired New York to build the world famous American Museum of Natural History in 1869. Other students of Agassiz played leading roles in the development of Museums at Salem, Boston, Yale, and other places and universities. Not only did Agassiz exert an influence on the development of museums through his students, but he also influenced all museums through the principles he suggested for the arrangement of displays and exhibits to enable them to better serve as instructional aids.

Science created the laboratory to promote the scientific endeavor; first there was one type of laboratory, and then there were three: for research, demonstration, and class teaching. In the United States the teaching laboratory was developed by Amos Eaton (1776–1842) at the Rensselaer School of Troy, New York, just as the high school was taking its first deep breath. Eaton was a botanist and geologist, a collector and disseminator of information, who was most interested in the practical uses of knowledge. To lead his students, many of them college graduates, toward the frontier of the sciences underlying bleaching, tanning, and other industrial processes, he used a project method. He made little effort to devise original experiments, and no great discoveries are claimed for the school that he directed for years. Yet several of his students became investigators.

At the University of Giessen in about 1836, Baron Justus von Liebig (1803–1873) organized a chemistry laboratory that has been called the earliest successful effort to use original investigation as the main method of teaching. A drastic type of this method was used by Agassiz at Harvard. In this method the student is forced to observe, compare, and generalize for himself from collections of natural objects such as a half peck of bones of fishes of different species or a group of fossils. The English biologist, Thomas Henry Huxley (1825–1895) also developed a method of laboratory teaching for biology that is today widely used in the United States. Unlike Agassiz, Huxley did not use the laboratory to stimulate original investigation but rather to enable the student to verify what he had heard in his lectures or read in his textbooks.

Laboratories in chemistry and other sciences developed rapidly. Their general introduction into the colleges and high schools of the United States stems from German foundations, not from the Rensselaer beginning, and was accomplished after the Civil War. The laboratory is one of the most powerful instructional tools of the school. Like other versatile tools, it is a complex of many instruments and the result of many long series of inventions.

The psychology laboratory has achieved significant results in professional education. In its well-developed form it was, like the chemistry laboratory, founded in Germany. The founder, Wilhelm Wundt (1832–1920), created it at the University of Leipzig in 1879, and one of many early American students of this laboratory was J. McKeen Cattell (1860–1944). What has been called "the first psychological laboratory in America" was opened in 1882 at Johns Hopkins University by G. Stanley Hall (1846–1924) who had J. McKeen Cattell as his pupil for a short time. Cattell went back to Leipzig and took his doctor's degree under Wundt. This brief reference to the psychology laboratory has a special pertinence here because the teaching-machine to be discussed later is one of its products. The main thought of this section is that invention has made the school the powerful and flexible institution that it is, and may be renewing and remaking it before our eyes.

INDIVIDUALIZING INSTRUCTION

In the last decade the individualization of instruction has been one of the more important directions for innovation in American education. Both the scientific movement and the Progressive education movement stressed the significance of individual differences in learning and teaching. However, the design of an instructional technology to adapt teaching to the individual needs of each learner poses many problems as yet unsolved by the science of education. Proposals for reform consequently have taken many directions, some instructional, some curricular, and some admininstrative in nature; none has been widely adopted, many are mere fads; some are introduced into the usual graded school organization, others aim toward a nongraded or ungraded school; some use a generalist teacher, others stress the need for teams of specialists; some use little or no hardware, others depend upon expensive equipment. Of course, the important question to be asked of any proposal for the reform of an existing instructional technology is whether student learning is facilitated more under the "new" than under the "old." Concerning this question there is little research evidence to show the superiority of the "new" over the "old." This does not prove that the "old" is the best, but it does advise caution in extending innovative instructional technologies beyond the situations for which they were designed. A little knowledge of the history of instructional technology should temper the judgment of all innovators and reformers as the following paragraphs illustrate.

Some of the earlier innovations in instructional technology were administrative rather than curricular or instructional in their nature. Such was the St. Louis Plan (ca. 1865) in which pupils were reclassified every six weeks and the brighter ones were placed in advanced sections. F. W. Parker (1837–1902) used a coaching scheme at Quincy to keep the less able pupils in step with their classes.

At Batavia, New York, a coaching plan was developed that used two teachers in each room, one to help the pupils with their lesson difficulties, the other to conduct the class exercises. Apparently there was no connection between the Batavia Plan and the supervised study movement in the high schools in the early 1900's. In this movement the schools used a double period for each class meeting. One period was devoted to aided and supervised preparation, and the other to reports, discussions, recitations, and tests of the work done. The supervised study movement declined after about a decade; but schools that have abolished all homework assignments have sometimes set up a substitute, such as the introduction of additional study hours within a lengthened school day where the teachers can provide study guidance.

Some administrators have frankly conceded the impossibility of keeping every pupil in step. Some of these vary the amount of material to be studied by the slow, average, and fast groups of pupils. At Cambridge, Massachusetts, this double or triple track plan was in use for a short while. Some private schools and some public school systems have "X, Y, and Z classes."

The preceding plans were introduced into the usual class organization. Another plan to dispense with classes and group work except in such fields as music and physical education was promoted by Preston W. Search. Under his individual-study plan, each pupil worked by himself and at his own rate. Search began the plan in the teaching of bookkeeping at West Liberty, Ohio, in 1877, but he developed it more fully at other places including Pueblo, Colorado. His most effective disciple was Frederic Burk (1862–1924), the principal of the San Francisco State Normal School. From there Carleton Washburne (1889–   ) carried the ideas to Winnetka, Illinois. Under the Winnetka Plan a large part of the school day was given over to group activities, but individual methods were used in the more academic studies. The Dalton Plan devised by Helen Parkhurst (1887–1959) grew out of the work of Search and Burk, but it was also influenced by the Italian educator Maria Montessori (1870–1952).

The essence of the Dalton Plan was in the "job" or individual school work "contracts." Each pupil agreed formally to complete a carefully planned project or unit in a specified time, usually one month. This allowed the pupil to work in his own way at his preferred rate. Freedom with responsibility was the keynote. There usually was a daily session to plan work and to give counsel concerning difficulties. The Dalton Plan foundered on the difficulty that too many pupils accepted the freedom but neglected the responsibility.

The Dalton Plan spread not only in the country of its origin but also in England, on the continent, and even in Russia in the early years of the Soviet Union when the country seemed to be developing a liberal and popular form of government and education. Experience showed that the Dalton Plan had been praised far beyond its merits and it has been discontinued at home and abroad. It is a good example of an educational fad, but it is not the only such example among these plans.

A fad is a scheme or device that is advanced with exaggerated zeal. It tends to be accepted as a panacea without adequate evaluation. A fad wins a sudden and undeserved popularity because it is not noticed that it lacks the means to produce the promised results. The fashion collapses when people become aware that they have become victims of a delusion. But a fad may sometimes be of use in preparing for a successor of permanent value. It may not be a pure fake like the advertised memory systems or the methods of mastering a foreign language in only fifteen lessons.

The Lancasterian monitorial system was a fad. The means it employed were not fitted to achieve what was claimed for it, but it is believed to have promoted public education. Manual training was a fad. It may have aided the rise of industrial arts education but it certainly hampered the movement for vocational education.

Lists of educational fads do not agree in all cases. Jacques W. Redway (1849–1942), a specialist in geography, included the Quincy system and object-teaching among the fads. The inclusion of the Quincy system is curious coming from Redway who, with respect to the teaching of geography, was in the F. W. Parker tradition, and was joint author of a series of textbooks that followed Parker's ideas. Few people and no Progressives would consider the Quincy system a fad. Object lessons, said Redway, "are now [1896] mentioned only in derision." One may agree that object-teaching was a fad, but it must also be admitted that it aided the growth of nature study. Some would also include nature study among the educational fads. The decision would hinge, Redway thought, upon the way it was carried out.

In this connection, the reception of the instructional system of Montessori in the United States teaches a useful lesson. In the early decades of the twentieth century her rather mechanical system for teaching young children was dismissed as a fad by no less an authority than William H. Kilpatrick (1871–1965). Recently, however, there has been an upsurge of interest in the establishment of Montessori schools largely through the influence of the American Montessori Society, which was founded by Nancy McCormick Rambusch in 1956 in Greenwich, Connecticut. The Whitby School was founded in 1958 in Greenwich, Connecticut, and Xavier University in Cincinnati, Ohio, established a Montessori teacher training program in 1965 and is conducting research that could prove whether Kilpatrick was right or wrong.

Many innovations of the 1930's and 1940's were inspired by the scientific and Progressive education movements. They generally stressed "life-adjustment approaches to the development of an instructional technology. Following World War II, these approaches were criticised by Robert Maynard Hutchins, Mortimer Brewster Smith, Arthur Eugene Bestor, and others who favored intellectual training as the primary goal of education. As a result numerous innovations in the 1950's and 1960's centered about a rearrangement for instruction that would give the specialist in a discipline a larger role in the instructional process. These approaches are generally covered under the umbrella of "Team Teaching." The plans encompassed by this concept range from "turn teaching" (in which one elementary teacher agrees to teach science for another teacher if he will in *turn* teach mathematics for the first teacher) to more comprehensive programs. In all of the plans the objective is to utilize the specialized abilities of all members of the team to the fullest extent possible in the instructional process. Unlike the traditional departmental organization of the disciplines in the usual high school, team teaching in its more developed forms stresses cooperative planning by the specialized teachers for a given group of pupils.

Concurrently with the trend toward team teaching, innovations were proposed to break the lockstep of the traditional graded school in which pupils climb rung by rung (or grade by grade) up the educational ladder. These nongraded or ungraded plans have been proposed for both the elementary and secondary levels. All propose to be learner-centered and highly individualized.

Both team teaching and the nongraded school are in the frontiers of educational experimentation. Instructional theories and strategies must be further developed and tested in the 1970's. They both have much in common with the Dalton Plan, which time proved to be an educational fad Are they also fads or will they contribue to the further democratization of ed ıcational opportunity?

CURRICULAR INNOVATIONS

Illustrative of curricular innovations as the basis for an instructional technology, we shall summarize only four: unit-teaching, correlation, the core curriculum, and the discipline-centered approaches of the post Sputnik era. A coherent portion of the curriculum is currently called a unit, not, as it might be, a chapter, problem, subject, or world of discourse. Like these, a unit is supposed to have a unity that may be logical, historical, or psychological. Psychological unity is that which is developed in the process of an exploration or in the solution of a problem. Any locale such as a city or a valley has a unity that includes the events, people, and institutions that are connected with it.

Well-organized subjects such as arithmetic are somewhat intractable from this standpoint. Primary number and counting must precede, and the numerical solution of problems must accompany or follow the fundamental operations. It is, however, possible to have children "discover" the principles of arithmetic and science, and in that case they achieve a psychological unity. With loosely connected materials this is much easier. The problems of democracy, housing, safety education, or conservation have no preordained organization, and units may be formed to suit the purpose of the class or individual. The advantage of the unit in this sense is that it capitalizes upon the pupil's desire to work out things for himself.

Many of the special "plans" and Progressive education have used the term *unit*. It was also used by Henry C. Morrison (1871–1945), director of the University of Chicago High School. Morrison held that "assimilating lessons" does not educate. Education means adjustment and this always leads to an either-or situation: the pupil has made the adjustment or he has not. There is no middle ground. Each of the adjustments is achieved in a series of five steps that look and sound like those proposed by Herbart. Morrison began with a goal or desired adjustment that is approved by teacher and pupil and named the steps toward reaching that goal as follows: exploration, presentation, assimilation, organization, and adjustment. These are old ghosts brought to life again—or what seemed to be a living state.

The idea for which Morrison is best known was his demand for mastery and thoroughness. Everyone should approve his opposition to slipshod work. There is a great deal of such work, and there are many reasons for it. But complete and absolute mastery, thoroughness, and understanding are not within the range of human possibility. All men have their human limitations and no one ever understands anything perfectly. If one picks up a shell or reads a page, questions of meaning and value arise at every turn and line. Aside from the possibility of achieving mastery, there is the question of feasibility. The teacher has to see that the studies of the curriculum provide sufficient breadth and variety, and this precludes the mastery of a single course.

The real value of the unit idea is that it tends to break down subject lines. Information is where you find it. Pupils help to plan the units, and individual needs, interests, and differences are considered. A few schools make up the curriculum from day to day. All these processes must be carefully guarded or they become hindrances to education.

Curricula were long made by listing subjects and perhaps supplying some statements of objectives and methods. This old plan is still commonly used in curriculum-making. An investigator who examined 5,000 curricula reported that the overwhelming majority were of this kind.

Subject-matter curricula are criticized because, it is said, they have no plan. The subjects are like bricks lying scattered about, rather than arranged to form a house, a retaining wall, a walk, or some other structure that serves a purpose. Bricks lying scattered about serve no purpose and may be in the way. The analogy is not, however, accurate. The subjects, or at least some of them, have an internal organization that is lacking in a brick. Geography, history, and arithmetic are composed of related ideas that form a system.

An early effort to use this internal structure in the organization of a genuinely integrated curriculum was made by Herbart, who proposed to correlate the corresponding parts of two or more subjects. Correlation became an important educational idea even before 1900. Samuel C. Parker, in his *History of Modern Elementary Education*, which came out in 1912, said: "Correlation is now an important factor in the organization of courses of study in many places." He thought the report of the Committee of Fifteen (1895) may have been a cause of its adoption, but Paul Hanus of Harvard correctly pointed out that Harris, the chairman of the Committee of Fifteen, was opposed to Herbart and did not use the word *correlation* in Herbart's sense at all.

As used by Herbart, correlation meant the interlinking of the different subjects. Geography, for example, may be taken as dealing with the places, structures, and forces of the crust and surface of the earth; history deals with the purposes, actions, and institutions of men in the geographic environment. Not only can the two subjects be related, but they must be if either is to have much meaning. Arithmetic and industrial arts may easily reinforce each other in teaching and learning and so may all the communication skills, such as reading, writing, speaking, and some kinds of drawing and music. Each may be made to support any of the others. A dramatic exercise might easily require the use of all of these.

A core curriculum draws together from several subjects materials needed by all pupils. It is an extended and more fully developed form of correlation. Core lessons usually occupy more than one class period. The core is often given a title, such as *Democratic Living* or *Evolution of Civilization*. It may be planned and taught by more than one teacher, cooperatively. It is not always easy to distinguish between such forms as General Education, Integrated Program, or Unified Studies and the core curriculum. In all of these, as well, the work may be planned by teachers and pupils jointly.

The work of the core curriculum is usually organized in large units, each of which deals with an important problem. Each unit may be pursued by a group or committee with provision for integrating the work of the whole class at appropriate points, so that all pupils will benefit. Activities such as those of the homerooms or community studies or services may be included in the core program. Drills may also be practiced.

The unified studies curriculum may be merely an extended form of correlation and is likely to be the least radical of the core innovations. Other core curricula may be historical in organization. A common example is the development of civilization, which is likely to be a compound of English, history, geography, and the arts and sciences. A third type is called the contemporary problems core, which may have such titles as

Our City's Need for Water or *Good Neighbors in the Other Americas.*
Even the contemporary problems course may be largely historical. In
one school a study of collective security began with the ancient Greek
leagues and came by a roundabout way to the United Nations. Some
contemporary problems courses stay fairly close to the present; and these
sometimes break up into disassociated topics. One such so-called core consisted of a list of thirty separate topics including the following: preventing
accidents; spending money wisely; building a happy home life; and finding
the right job. We should note that each ends in *-ing* and is about doing
something. This is an example of the life-adjustment education that has
been described.

The core curriculum movement is related to several trends that developed a century or more ago. Herbart has been mentioned; Froebel's
emphasis upon pupil activities and child study must also be included. The
activities of the kindergarten in more mature forms worked their way into
all parts of the system. Child study and the work of the child development
investigations at such universities as Iowa, Yale, and Michigan have promoted the adaptation of schoolwork to the capabilities and needs of the
pupils. Handicrafts and industrial arts education, the project methods
introduced from agriculture, experimental schools, and new philosophies
have together overcome the hostility of the nineteenth century to pupil
activities.

In 1957 America's technological supremacy was challenged by Russia's
launching of Sputnik, the world's first space satellite. Within a year, Congress met the challenge with the National Defense Education Act, which
provided massive appropriations for educational reform. As a result, curricular innovations since 1960 have been dominated by the attempts of
authorities in the various disciplines, especially mathematics, and science,
to impose the logical order of the disciplines upon school subjects. Committees of subject-matter societies have published courses of study for
national distribution that stress the basic concepts, theories, and methods
by which the discipline is advancing. As an example of this trend, the
activities of the American Institute of Biological Sciences, a professional
society representing 85,000 biologists, can be cited. In January 1959, the
society established a Biological Sciences Curriculum Study with a steering
committee composed of college biologists, high school biology teachers,
and other educators. The committee recognized that various viewpoints
and approaches might be used in developing a technology for biological
instruction. To date, three such versions have appeared. All three versions
deemphasize authoritative content and stress the investigative processes
of science and their history. Financial support for the development and
testing of these materials has been provided by the National Science
Foundation. It is claimed that by 1963 over 1,000 teachers and 150,000
students participated in the tryout of these materials.

The discipline-centered approaches to curricular innovations have influenced science and mathematic teaching, in the elementary school as well as in the secondary school. An example of a project that has been concerned with the mathematics curriculum at both levels is the curriculum development activities undertaken by the School Mathematics Study Group (SMSG). This is a national organization founded in March 1958, by research mathematicians and classroom teachers of mathematics. Ten years later the group was able to report that over four million of their texts had been purchased. This group has also received support from the National Science Foundation.

What is the future of these curricular innovations? First, history teaches us that an established curriculum will not be easily changed and that change will be slow when it comes. Even the general curriculum shifts of great movements do not sweep everything off the board. Much of the medieval curriculum remained in the Renaissance, and the ideal of liberal education is effective in the present scientific and pragmatic age. The old professional studies of the Middle Ages and the new humanities flourished side by side in the Renaissance as the old and the new professional studies, the modern humanities, and the sciences do today. The general program of studies is cumulative, and those studies that satisfy the enduring needs of the human spirit are permanent elements of the curriculum.

Moreover, curriculum revolutions do not sweep everything before them for the reason that there are constituents that are essential to every curriculum, features that cannot be eliminated because without them there could not be a curriculum. Such are the closely related elements of the medieval trivium; namely language, logic, and rhetoric, because the need to speak, write, read, and persuade are universal. In the harsh period of the early Middle Ages the curriculum was stripped down to the bone and only these arts remained. All curricula and all teaching must use the arts of communication because without them teaching is impossible, and even society would be impossible. Also widely needed are number, order, quantity, form, and the concepts of mathematics; the ideas of right, good, and expedient and those of organization and administration—which belong to ethics and politics. Arts such as these are indispensable. Greek may not be essential but language is, and so are standards of value, measures of quantity, and forms of organization. They are universal curriculum elements.

Also, the earlier curricula of the schools were not carefully planned and they are not systematic or self-consistent now. They have been formed to meet the local conditions and temporary needs of place and time. Differences exist within the same school and to a degree must be permitted if teachers and pupils are to be allowed any individuality. Although schools, like plants, may be trained, trimmed, and cultivated, they must be allowed to grow. Too much restraint kills.

Under present conditions, a completely stabilized curriculum plan would be undesirable even if it were possible. There are too many genuine and important disagreements within the profession and too many quarrels on the outside to permit a general reconstruction, which would inevitably be an arbitrary one. But improvements are being made and new designs are being tried. Other plans are possible but a general and final solution of the curriculum problem is not possible. It is one of the persistent problems of education.

Lest anyone should think this unduly pessimistic, he should look at a few facts. The main fact is that the school and school people cannot control the social forces that beat upon them. The community may not allow the consideration of vital controversial questions; teachers have lost their jobs on such issues. Parents may want their children taught in the good old way, and vote the bond issues or reject them. Legislation may help or hamstring the school. In the long run, a better curriculum may affect community sentiment and turn it in favor of a still better curriculum. The wise course is to make improvements gradually and steadily.

SCHOOL AND LIBRARY

When instructional technology required the use of many books instead of a single textbook, a school library became a necessity. The connection of the library with the individualization of instruction and curricular innovations is evident. Frederic Burk recognized this when he said: "The place to study literature is in a library." This is true not only for literature, for the library serves the curriculum at all points. Even the work of the laboratory and the shop requires use of books. School library needs were not often recognized until the time of the educational awakening, and were not effectively met until long after that era.

The library of Harvard College was started with 370 volumes from the bequest of John Harvard. William and Mary College had no important collection for many years, and Yale College began with the few volumes donated by the founding ministers. As other colonial colleges developed, they slowly collected a few books. Teaching was carried on by means of textbooks and recitations and by lectures that were usually dictated.

College libraries were not open to the public, and the early conception of the function of a library, even one within the walls, was different from that which is held today. The library was supposed to preserve the books rather than to encourage and facilitate their use. This conception lasted far into the nineteenth century.

The University of Virginia was opened in 1825 and its library management conformed to the usual practice. At first, the librarian was required to receive and give out books for only one hour a week. Students were not admitted to the library building until the second year (1826), when the rule was relaxed and they were admitted by ticket. To consult a reference work students had to secure the written permission of the librarian. Library privileges were withdrawn if the students forgot themselves so far as "to violate the rule of silence." A $10 deposit was required to guarantee the payment of library fines, and the borrowing of books was hedged about with restrictions. This policy is the more surprising because the University of Virginia was in some ways an original creation, but her library followed the old tradition.

Much later, other colleges were still doing the same thing. Even after 1850 the students of the College of the City of New York could take out only one book at a time, and to do so they had to fill out a detailed form and have it countersigned by three members of the faculty. As in other cases, the library was open infrequently and only for a few hours at a time. Professors were treated more generously; they could take out six books at a time and tutors could take out three. The current view that the widest use of books is to be encouraged and that the cost of book replacements is a normal expense of effective operation is a recent attainment. The holdings of the colleges were still small in 1850. At that time there were only four college libraries in the country with more than 50,000 volumes and none with as many as 100,000.

Subscription, society, and other semipublic libraries were also started in colonial times. One of the most famous of these was that of the Library Company of Philadelphia, started by Benjamin Franklin in 1731 when he was twenty-five years old. The Philadelphia Library Company conducted a subscription library. The cost to subscribers, which was two pounds entrance money and ten shillings annually, was too much for poor people to pay. Merchants' and mechanics' associations and historical and scientific societies also founded libraries for the use of their members.

National and state libraries were another early species. The Library of Congress, established in 1800, is the most famous of these and has become one of the great libraries of the world. It was formed for the members of Congress, but in the services that it performs it has become a national public library. After the burning of the Capitol in 1814 it purchased the private library of Jefferson. State libraries were established early by New Hampshire, New Jersey, and Pennsylvania, and eventually by each of the states.

By about 1850, states began to pass laws permitting towns to create public libraries, but as in the case of public schools many town libraries were created without special legal warrant. In the nineteenth century the public library spread steadily, but the period of its most rapid development began about 1910. The city of Boston was in the field early, and its public library has celebrated the completion of its first century. Among the original promoters of the Boston public library were Edward Everett and George Ticknor, of whom Ticknor had the more liberal views. At a time when the future library was still only an idea, he wrote that a free public library "would be the crowning glory of our public schools." Ticknor wanted school children admitted upon the recommendation of their teachers. Against the judgment of Everett, he proposed to supply any good popular book in a sufficient number of copies so that many persons could read it at the same time. Ticknor insisted that the books must be allowed to circulate without cost, even though some might be soiled or lost. Only reference works and rare books were to be reserved for use within the library only. He began the practice of supplying forms upon which the public could enter the titles of books that they desired the library to purchase. Here in the early 1850's we seem to find some of the ideas of modern library management, but none of Ticknor's ideas was more important than that of cooperation with the public schools.

In the last century many of the large cities developed fine public libraries. Edward Everett's hope that they would serve the interests of scholars as well as those of the casual reader have been fulfilled, as best exemplified by the great New York Public Library. If libraries are educational institutions, and this they certainly are, then the history of the public library is a part of the history of public education. One kind of library, which is public in fact if not in everyday speech, is the library in the public school.

The early school libraries and the early free town libraries were begun about the same time, that is, about 1830. These pioneer efforts to provide collections of books for the use of schools were only partially successful. The plan seems to have been to serve the community as well as the schoolchildren. They were lending libraries, but because of a lack of trained librarians and good records, and because the schools were closed during the long vacations, many of the books drawn out of these libraries were never returned.

The states of New York, Massachusetts, and Michigan began to promote district school libraries in the 1830's. More than a dozen states followed their example. Governors and state school officials favored the plan, which seems to have originated with A. C. Flagg, state superintendent of common schools of New York. In 1835 the New York legislature appropriated $55,000 a year for books for district school libraries. The publishers, Harper and Brothers, prepared sets of uniformly bound volumes that were widely sold for use in libraries.

Horace Mann gave his approval to the New York idea and paid tribute to the state "whose enlightened and liberal care of the interests of education" he considered "entitled to the highest praise." Mann was concerned to keep works of fiction and other light literature as well as all books that might arouse religious controversy out of the school libraries. A firm of Boston publishers engaged several authors to write books for Massachusetts school libraries. These included Nathaniel Hawthorne, who was to prepare a volume of *New England Historical Sketches;* Jesse Buel, a work on agriculture; and Calvin E. Stowe, a *History of Education Both Ancient and Modern.* This last-named volume was not written.

All three of these states required each district to match the money received from the state. This plan produced considerable sums, and New York is supposed to have had 50,000 volumes in its district school libraries. Without state supervision and with a rapidly shifting body of teachers, the books were not easily preserved. The rural schools relapsed into the bookless condition from which governors and educators had tried to rescue them. Cities established their own school libraries, but for the towns help came from the expansion of the public library system.

The American Library Association was founded in 1876 and became the leader in library development and in library and school cooperation. Francis W. Parker had been invited to Quincy, Massachusetts, a year before and one of his chief sponsors, Charles Francis Adams, Jr. (1835–1915), was the head of the town library board. In a paper prepared for the teachers, Adams proposed that the schools and the town libraries should be joined together into "a people's college." This paper attracted attention, but cooperation between schools and libraries was not new in 1876. Another member of the same family, Brooks Adams (1848–1927), a brother of Charles, wrote on the introduction into the schools of good literature for free reading. This "new departure" was also calculated to make the school a vestibule of the public library. To make this possible there must be a public library within reach. As late as 1955 the head of the American Library Association asserted at its seventy-fourth annual meeting, that 27,000,000 Americans "had no access whatever to a local public library."

Public school and public library cooperation was not new in 1876. The new feature at that time was its greater feasibility through the growth and improvement of both institutions. About 1840, when S. S. Greene was superintendent of the schools of Springfield, Massachusetts, he developed a plan of cooperation between the schools and the library of the city. George Ticknor proposed similar relations in Boston at a slightly later time. In 1865, Superintendent Divoll of the St. Louis schools asked W. T. Harris to inquire into and to report upon the administration of the Boston Public Library and its service to the schools. Probably the statements of the two Adamses, particularly because they were prominent men, were copied by the newspapers. At least the cities of Chicago and Cincinnati explained that they already had such plans in operation, and there probably were many others. In 1876 the American Library Association devoted entire programs to the subject of books for schools. The importance of such cooperation will appear from the fact that at the present time students often make up more than half of the users of public libraries.

Schools handle their library problems in various ways. The pupils may go to the central public library or to a branch library. The library may place a loan collection in each school. State libraries provide traveling or package libraries, which may be obtained by rural as well as city schools. But these are substitutes for a school library that alone enables the school to teach its pupils how to use a library. The cultivation of this knowledge and skill may easily be one of the more important parts of the entire curriculum.

Some cities have a general public school library that serves all the schools. In Columbus, Ohio, the public school library was established in 1847 along with the first high school and the office of city superintendent of schools. This library served both the elementary and high school. In some cities each school has its own library, and collections from its stores may be placed in each classroom. This plan has evident advantages, but no library, not even the Library of Congress, is complete; and no plan possesses all the advantages without any defects. Those instructional technologies that emphasize individual investigations by pupils require a school library or convenient access to a public library.

In addition, these instructional technologies must give the teacher an efficient information retrieval system if he is to facilitate the learning of pupils by the independent study of printed media.

AUDIOVISUAL INSTRUCTION MOVEMENT

Thus far we have described educational innovations that were primarily administrative or curricular in nature, and that required only books and libraries for individualizing instruction. Other innovations were primarily instructional in nature and attempted to utilize a wide range of mechanical, electrical, and electronic inventions in the classroom. These include the phonograph, and other sound-recording devices, motion-picture projectors, radio, and television. The many attempts to incorporate these instruments either singly or collectively into the instructional process have been called the audiovisual instruction movement.

Good teachers have always used whatever visual aids were available. Quill pens were used until fifty years following the colonial period and were then replaced by steel pens. Horace Mann urged the introduction of blackboards in the schools of Massachusetts, and Edward Brooks strongly recommended the use of the abacus in the teaching of arithmetic. Louis Agassiz illustrated a course of lectures on "Glaciers and the Ice Period" with a stereopticon as early as 1864. In many of his lectures Agassiz either used specimens or chalked on the blackboard with illustrations "so graphic that the spoken word was hardly missed." The Keystone View Company of Meadville, Pennsylvania, published a guide to the use of its stereographs and lantern slides in 1906.

However, such early efforts toward visual education lacked a theoretical rationale to classify sensory impressions on a continuum from the most concrete to the most abstract and to guide their use in the instructional process. Such schemes began to appear as early as 1886 in the *Proceedings of the National Education Association* and finally culminated in Edgar Dale's "cone of Experience" in 1946 in which all experiences are represented in a triangle with "direct, purposeful experiences" at the base and "verbal symbols" at the apex with "motion pictures" and "radio, recordings, still pictures," and other experiences placed in intermediate positions in the triangle. Based on these concepts and similar theoretical variations, a new movement developed in American education shortly after World War I that at first was labeled "visual instruction" and later "audiovisual instruction." The National Education Association officially changed the name of its Department of Visual Instruction to the Department of Audiovisual Instruction in 1947. Dale's textbook describing the use of the "cone of experience" was titled *Audio-Visual Methods in Teaching*. This book contained suggestions for using the various audiovisual aids in the instructional process for different subjects; including models, dramatizations, demonstrations, field trips, exhibits, educational motion pictures, commercial films, photographs, slides, film strips, radio, recordings, charts, maps, blackboards, bulletin boards, comic strips, and books. Significantly, although the first commercial television sets appeared on the market at about the time of publication of Dale's book, he can only advise teachers to "begin to think now of this sight-and-sound miracle that promises to become an everyday affair."

Writing in the same year that Dale's book appeared, Dean Frank Freeman of the School of Education of the University of California deplored the fact that "comparatively little progress" had been made in using visual aids to increase the effectiveness of instruction in the more than quarter century since the aids became available to the schools. What was the reason for this lag? Dale blamed illiteracy, apathy, inertia, vested interests, and lack of money. In the last quarter century, textbooks, courses, and professorships of audiovisual education have proliferated in teacher education institutions, but the lag lamented by Freeman remains. The basic reason for the lag could be that the science of education has not yet provided the answers that are essential for the development of an instructional technology using audiovisual materials.

That such is the case is suggested by the fragmented nature of research related to the use of audiovisual methods. This is documented in the work of one of the pioneers in the scientific study of the use of both movies and radio in education, Werrett Wallace Charters (1875–1952). As Director of the Bureau of Educational Research at Ohio State University from 1928 until his retirement in 1942, Charters was eminently successful in obtaining financial support for his studies from various foundations, such as the Payne Fund of New York and the Rockefeller Foundation, and in stimulating his students, one of whom was Edgar Dale, to study the problems. The Payne Fund studies of the effects of theatrical films on the learning of children from 1929 to 1932 were the first comprehensive investigations in this area. Since many of the old Hollywood films evaluated in this project are being shown on television today, the twelve-volume report is still relevant with respect to the effects of television viewing on children. Another group of studies pioneered by Charters was the Ohio Evaluation of School Broadcasts Project from 1937 to 1943, which evaluated the effectiveness not only of school broadcasts but recordings as well.

Even though Charters and his students made a significant contribution to the instructional process, no grand design for a technology of instruction emerged from these essentially pragmatic studies. Charters himself recognized the "lag" between research and practice, and in one of his last articles written in 1952 he predicted an era in which "educational engineers" would develop an applied science of education. Thus, educational research results would be translated into action in the classroom. However the era of the educational engineer envisioned by Charters will not be realized until the audiovisual instruction movement converges with recent developments in theories and experiments concerned with social change, communication, social groups, and learning.

Despite these limitations of the audiovisual instruction movement, both instructional radio and instructional television have been widely used in the instructional process. Instructional radio expanded rapidly until the late 1930's and then began to decline. For example, the Ohio School of the Air began a weekly broadcast schedule in 1929 but it was disbanded for lack of funds less than a decade later. As radio instruction declined, instructional television expanded. Beginning in 1952 the Federal Communications Commission set aside 242 channels for the exclusive use of education and subsequently increased this number. The first educational noncommercial station was licensed jointly to the University of Houston, Texas, and the Houston Board of Education in 1953. By 1967 the number of educational television stations had increased to about 140 and reached a population of about 140 million persons. In addition, about one thousand closed-circuit television systems are now operating in educational, industrial, and service agencies. In 1959 a closed-circuit television project began in Washington County, Maryland, that served eight elementary schools in Hagerstown. In 1966 this system was enriching the school program for 84,000 students by offering such courses as art and music for the elementary schools, and advanced courses for gifted high school pupils. An important breakthrough in instructional television was the development of videotape for recording and immediate playback of television programs. This was first used in 1959 by the University of Texas for closed-circuit instruction.

The future for instructional television is not clear. Its use could decline, as did instructional radio, and it is sure to have competition from new technological developments that are more flexible and less expensive. As this is written an 8-mm magnetic sound projector is on the market. By means of a preloaded film cartridge this apparatus produces a sound color film that is sharper than television in daylight. In addition, it is much too early to draw fixed conclusions on the value of television education. Experience must determine the nature of that role and the changes that will take place in this teaching tool as new needs develop. The use of television in education will differ widely in the different studies in which it is used.

A good telecast fixes the students' attention, which is a great advantage. A second advantage is the selection of the best teachers for the studio lessons; all pupils come under their influence. The teachers are given time to prepare and perfect their presentations, a rare occurrence in the ordinary school. If television can also reduce the shortage of good teachers, this will be an added advantage.

Pupils, however, cannot review subject-matter that is not well understood or imperfectly remembered, and the pace of televised instruction cannot be varied to suit different pupils. Questions, if permitted, must be limited in large classes, and the intimacy of the give-and-take of a class in rapport with the teacher is lost in a televised course of study. The students miss another kind of contact: the opportunity to handle the material, to make mistakes, and to find out for themselves what a battery, an acid, or a frog can do. Television may not be a complete substitute for laboratory work and field trips. The student can see on a television screen only what is shown; some sensory impressions, those of touch, taste, and smell, are excluded. However, television has been used to increase the effectiveness of instruction in specific subjects, most notably language teaching.

LANGUAGE STUDY

A new era has begun in the study of languages in schools and colleges. A larger number of languages is being taught in the schools; the methods and purposes of language study have changed; new equipment, tapes, records, language laboratories, are provided; and the study of languages is being begun earlier and pursued for longer periods on the average. This description suggests radical change, not perhaps a revolution, but it may turn into one.

Languages have always been included in many curricula in American schools but never as large a part as in European schools. Many American high school language teachers and some college teachers of language have not had sufficient mastery of the language that they taught. Many teachers and students have aimed at a "reading knowledge" merely; grammar and translation methods were used, almost exclusively in some cases. The purpose of studying a language in high school was often merely to gain credit for two years of language study in order to satisfy college entrance requirements. The language requirements for the doctor of philosophy degree were of the same slender character. Language is the greatest medium of communication; it preserves knowledge and experience "to a life beyond life," as has been said of a good book. For these reasons it is one of the most useful means of teaching; too often it has been the only one.

The history of civilization explains why Greek, Latin, and Hebrew were so widely studied in Europe and early America. These languages were almost exclusively cultivated in early American secondary schools and colleges. Until 1850 even the formal study of English was not given much attention.

Modern foreign languages such as French, Spanish, and some others were offered in seaport towns in colonial times but primarily for commercial use. In multitongued communities such as New York, the study of modern languages may have served neighborly, religious, and other purposes. Aid from France in the American Revolution, the presence of French officers in American society, the word and example of Franklin and Jefferson, and the writings of Thomas Paine made the ideas of the French liberals and the French language popular for a time. The excesses of the French Revolution and American Federalism soon destroyed that popularity.

In the nineteenth century German was the modern language most studied in American schools and colleges. The large number of Germans who migrated to the United States, many of whom became prominent citizens, and the extraordinary number of Americans who studied in the German universities helped to promote the popularity of the language. This condition continued up to World War I.

A change in the study of modern languages took place in 1917. German was dropped, abruptly and everywhere, when the United States entered the war. Publicists, without avail, pointed out that knowledge of the language of an enemy had a very special importance. When the schools opened in the fall of 1917 many former teachers of German were placed in charge of classes in French, a fact that helps confirm what has been said about the prevailing standards of language instruction. In the following years, for both good and bad reasons, classes in Spanish multiplied. There was little "anti-German" agitation in the country in World War II, and since 1945 the German language has regained some lost ground in the schools, so that now three modern languages, Spanish, French, and German, are most widely taught in American high schools. In Europe, even a commercial course would require the study of one or more foreign languages, but in the United States many high school pupils study no foreign language at all.

The post-World War II period must be considered as a very important era in a discussion of language study. A sudden marked increased interest in languages was created by the fighting in Europe and in the Pacific, postwar military and diplomatic alliances, the United Nations, the cold war, and the space race. In earlier times people in most nations, especially the smaller ones, studied the languages of their neighbors and the great powers. The United States has now become a great power in a world in which all countries are neighbors.

Both the methods and the incentive for the intensive study of languages were developed in World War II. In 1941 a private foundation patriotically offered $50,000 a year for two years in order to set a new language teaching program into immediate operation. In the summer of 1942, forty-four courses in twenty-six languages were offered by eighteen universities. Over five hundred students completed their assignments in this program. The courses took up the entire working day of the students. They spent fifteen hours in class each week, the same amount of time being drilled by native speakers, and up to thirty hours of individual work —a work week of sixty hours. Two or more of these six-week training sessions, interrupted by short intervals of rest, were given to the study of a single language. For some languages, such as Chinese, Japanese, Turkish or Russian, there were textbooks, dictionaries, grammars, and even records; but for some of the less cultivated tongues the teaching aids were few or wanting, and competent native speakers were not easily found. Young American linguists were able to produce grammar books for some of these languages.

The results of "the Army way" of language teaching were remarkable and, according to some, "miraculous." Language specialists do not accept this extreme judgment. The results were good but they can be readily explained. The results were produced with small classes, by hard work, long hours, and powerful motivation, for these specially selected men knew that their lives might depend upon the knowledge obtained in the language-school. It is claimed that none of the methods used was new; all had been previously used in school, and if high school teachers could secure an equal intensity and urgency in their students they could gain comparable results.

The war experience with foreign language study has dramatized the study of languages in schools and colleges and has increased the emphasis upon the ability to speak the language and to understand it when it is spoken. This may, in some cases, have pushed the training in reading and writing too far into the background; but if the facts were known many more cases might be found in which the speaking and hearing of a language receive too little emphasis. The grammar and translation method has prevailed and will tend to persist; and the reading and writing of a foreign language, as of our own, is important. Even in speaking, the visual image of words plays a useful part.

The standard of acceptable achievement in language study is higher than it once was, and a longer period in the study of a given language than has been customary is now demanded. One or more foreign languages are taught in a significant number of elementary schools. Some elementary schools have been doing this for many years but others have joined the movement only in the last decade. Oral language instruction presents difficulties unless the elementary level teacher can provide a good model in pronunciation or unless a native speaker is available. Otherwise tapes and records with intervals for practice may be used. Good models of pronunciation are necessary, for a wrong habit is hard to correct later.

Some schools and colleges are developing language laboratories with individual booths and head-sets for practice, phonographs, sound moving-pictures, recorders, tapes, discs, and closed-circuit television. Many schools are equipped to teach French, Spanish, and German; if a fourth language is included it is usually either Russian or Italian. Cornell University is equipped to teach a dozen languages including Chinese, Czech, Rumanian, and Thai; the Institute of Languages of Georgetown University teaches an equal number including Arabic, Polish, Portuguese and Serbo-Croatian; and the Hartford Seminary Foundation offers no fewer than twenty-two languages some of which are certainly "rare" in American schools.

Language laboratories may be simple and inexpensive or large and fully equipped, providing for many students working at the same time, and costing thousands of dollars. With equipment a great part of the repetitive practice activities that are involved in the learning of a language can be carried on by the pupils themselves, or a single teacher may direct the studies of any number of students at one time. This will not dispense with teachers but may enable them to handle larger classes with satisfactory results.

The National Defense Education Act provides subsidies for the pursuit and promotion of language studies. Title VI of the Act deals with the need by the government, defense services, and business for persons with appropriate language skills. Many more students and teachers are needed, and the Act is concerned greatly with the preparation of language teachers. All languages are important, but among the so-called rare languages the highest priority is given Arabic, Hindu, Japanese, Portuguese, Russian, and Urdu, or Hindustani. The benefits of the Act are not restricted to the students of these or other "rare" languages. The Act offers fellowship stipends to students in graduate language and area studies who give "reasonable assurance" that they will either teach the language of their competence or will engage in public service. A number of language and area study centers have been developed at Columbia, Harvard, Johns Hopkins, Michigan, Princeton, and other colleges and universities.

TEACHING MACHINES

The teaching machines were not taken over from industry or the arts but, like the blackboard, were invented by school people for use in the schools. Unlike television, teaching machines are intended not to aid teachers but to eliminate some or all of them as unnecessary, perhaps even harmful. Spelling, for example, can be easily learned through work on a machine. Because machines do not teach in the usual sense, we might, except for the clumsiness of the phrase, have called them self-learning devices or aids. In any case, it is too late to change the name that has been selected.

We know that self-learning is a very common and useful activity in ordinary life and may be carried on without any aids or with improvised ones. Without preparation such learning may be casual and time-consuming. Teaching machines can make learning systematic, closely graded, and free from unnoticed errors. Their promoters have the fervor of a Comenius or a Rousseau, and the machines have the patience of Job or of Nature itself. The pupils who work on the machines are reported to share both the enthusiasm and the persistence of these personages.

Teaching machines are not completely new. The records of the United States Patent Office show that a few teaching machines were invented before 1820 and hundreds more since 1870. One of the inventors of a teaching machine was Maria Montessori, whose rather mechanical system for the teaching of young children has already been discussed. Her patent, obtained in 1914, was granted for a device intended to develop children's sense of touch.

Everyone who worked in psychological laboratories in earlier days is familiar with the tachistoscope. The word signifies a machine that provides a quick glance. This device exposed letters, figures, words, or drawings for brief measured intervals; for the purpose of testing and training attention, recognition, and perception. Anyone who has seen a tachistoscope has seen a primitive teaching machine with limited uses.

Leaders in the present movement maintain that the teaching machine is not a testing device, but obviously testing does take place and it is an essential element in learning. Without it how is one to know that he has learned? Every time a pupil is informed that he has or has not correctly completed a step on the machine he has been tested and the result has been announced. It would seem that there should be a historical connection, as there certainly is a logical one, between psychological instruments and tests, objective examinations, and teaching machines. Perhaps the line of descent has not been fully made out.

The present period in the history of the machines began about forty-five years ago when, in 1926, Sidney L. Pressey of The Ohio State University constructed a simple testing-teaching machine. One of it features was the immediate reporting of the student's success or failure, an essential feature of the present devices. Pressey and his students pursued their investigations and published their results but gained so little response that the inventor, although confident he was doing important pioneer work, renounced further effort along this line. After World War II, others re-entered the mine that Pressey had abandoned and have brought out the quantity of gold we now have.

Careful programming is the fundamental virtue of the teaching machine. Hence, the step from one question to the next must be very short and the novel element must be very simple. Not until the preceding question is answered correctly will the machine expose the next step. If an answer is wrong, the machine will so report, but it will not reveal the correct answer. There are other forms, and as the movement grows new ones will surely be developed.

We may compare the teaching machine to a carefully graded book with a question and answer device. The pupil must be restricted to each question until he answers it correctly. Such books are now in use in many schools. Illustrated feature articles published in local papers show pages of such paper and pencil self-teaching books. Each pupil works at algebra, or whatever, at his own rate. The results vary widely from pupil to pupil and resemble those results that were reported by Preston W. Search who had several enthusiastic followers even though his plan has not survived. The pupils show great interest in the machine exercises, which present a series of connected puzzles. Significant puzzles are among the important stimuli to learning. Will the puzzle-interest survive the growing familiarity with machine processes?

The teaching machine has challenged the interest of scientists and promoters. One of these is B. F. Skinner (1904–   ) of Harvard, who is known as a psychologist and a student of learning and conditioning. Pressey has become somewhat guarded in his estimate of the machine and points out that books and teaching machines are tools and guides to reality, not substitutes for it. Pressey also emphasizes the need for social experience. The machines may not be necessary; history will tell, but we must wait for its verdict.

The fully automatic classroom is not merely a dream by such men as James D. Finn who, as President of the Department of Audiovisual Instruction of NEA in 1960, was responsible for the book edited by Lumsdaine and Glaser and cited in the chapter bibliography on teaching machines. A fully automatic classroom, which has been in use at the University of Wisconsin since 1961, has projectors for slides, moving pictures, opaque materials, and television, a tape recorder, teleprompter units, and other equipment all electronically run and fully automatic, but under the control of a teacher. Thus the teaching machine is the entire classroom.

An automatic classroom requires the teacher to systematically and sequentially arrange the materials to be learned and determine the most effective methods for presenting these to the learner or, in the language of the teaching machine, to program the instruction. A digital computer with such a program can facilitate the teacher's control of the instructional process by storing vast quantities of information, retrieving it bit by bit on command, displaying retrieved material to the learner, recording his responses, and providing feedback on the accuracy of learning.

This scheme of computer-assisted instruction with its automatic classroom approaches the vision of the educational engineer as described by Charters. Such an approach to the development of an instructional technology tends toward a view of teaching as a man-machine system. In this system, machines, such as computers and audiovisual aids, do the tasks that they can do faster and more accurately; and the teacher does that which machines cannot do, namely, program the machines to accomplish his goals most effectively.

Such educational engineering must build upon a firm foundation of knowledge from all of the behavioral sciences, including the science of education, psychology, sociology, anthropology, and ergology, but especially as they study such specialized areas as learning, individual differences, evaluation, language, linguistics, communications, task analysis, data processing and information retrieval. In spite of the so-called knowledge explosion, we lack the research that is necessary to guide the educational engineer in building an instructional technology and we do not have the blueprint for designing such a system. As the Commission on Instructional Technology reported to the President and Congress of the United States in March 1970: "Instructional technology is more than the sum of its parts," and the many parts discussed in this chapter remain to be organized into a whole so as to achieve the American dream —equal opportunity for each individual to discover and develop his unique talents.

SUMMARY

We are living in an educationally innovative age. The existence of disagreement on educational questions and criticism of the schools is a favorable circumstance. It reveals the people's concern for education and a desire to promote a program that they can approve. The concern is caused, at least in part, by the magnitude of the problems that the schools must try to solve. The growth of the population, the technological and economic developments, and the international situation are only three of many conditions with which schools must try to cope.

What schools have been able to accomplish has always depended upon what tools were available for use. The earliest schools were much occupied with the art of writing and the brush, stylus, or other writing implement; the papyrus, clay, or other writing materials; and the tablet, or other product of the writer's art were the essential tools of a school. In the long history of education referred to in the introductory chapter, the school has increased its power by increasing the tools that it has adopted or created. In this chapter we considered some of the very remarkable new tools that are becoming available and are again transforming the school.

The revived study of languages is aided by an assemblage of new tools that form the language laboratory. The time when language was taught mainly from books to prepare the student mainly to use books is passing, and one must hope that it will not return. Speaking and understanding speech are the essences of a living language. This must not be read as an attack on books and the use of books. Books, including textbooks, are among the most useful tools not only of schools but of life. But one who learns to speak a language will also easily learn to read and write it.

Curricula have always been changing, usually slowly, but at some periods radically. Yet some basic elements must be included in all curricula. And curricular improvement is also conditioned by the social conservatism that holds the school in its grip.

A curriculum is no longer conceived as a selection of subjects. It also includes the activities, methods, and purposes of the school and indeed all that the school does to educate the children. It has become clear that in practice, the purpose, method, and content cannot be separated.

The newer school practices require not only space and machinery but also books. Every school should have a library or should have the use of a library with the needed books and trained library workers. One of the chief values of such a library is that it makes it possible to teach children how to use a library. This is an important part of a good school curriculum.

Special teaching plans have been a prominent phase of efforts to improve upon the dreary textbook recitations that plagued American education for so long. Two main features of these plans were the attempt to teach children how to read and study a given subject and to encourage children to work on problems related to a major curriculum topic. Given a skillful teacher, inquiring pupils, and classes that are not too large, the problem method is undoubtedly an admirable plan. These factors are not always present; and the fate of the Dalton Plan and similar plans have suggested that young pupils need supervision and a degree of pressure to produce good results.

Well-informed teachers have always used correlation to some degree, but following the Herbartian influence serious efforts were made to stress and improve it. The core curriculum is a current phase of these efforts and often stresses investigative methods and functional studies. It is not in general use, and it would be something more than a guess to say that the formal textbook recitation is more frequently used than the newer practices.

The current emphasis in educational innovation is to individualize instruction. But individualization means different things to different teachers. And even if we could agree on our goals, we would still lack a useful set of empirically validated principles of learning, to say nothing of an empirically validated theory of instruction. Consequently, in the light of these gaps in the science of education, a little knowledge of the history of instructional technology should advise caution before we attempt any large-scale general application of any innovative proposal.

QUESTIONS

1. What important innovations are omitted from this chapter? Where can one find adequate information on them?
2. It has been noted that new movements do not sweep away old conditions everywhere at once. How does this generalization apply to the audiovisual instruction movement in the United States? To the various movements to individualize instruction?
3. How has the use of blackboards affected instructional methods and types of learning? Instructional films? Sound recordings?
4. Do you agree that Amos Eaton used a project method? Why is the project method more strongly emphasized in modern than in earlier times?
5. What answer do you give to the question that concludes the section on "Individualizing Instruction?"
6. How did the oral character of schoolwork, that is, the absence of written work, affect the curriculum?
7. What are the fallacies in the claim that the schools should teach only, or mainly, what is widely useful? Explore the uses of the words *useful* and *practical*.
8. What correspondences can be traced between the development of schools and libraries? How can one account for them?
9. Which of the plans described in the text were administrative rather than curricular? How does one distinguish between the two?
10. Why should we classify any practices that had useful results as fads? May the use of this word be merely an expression of prejudice?
11. Why and how is a knowledge of curriculum trends useful in developing a new curriculum or changing an old one?
12. Read the article by Charters cited at the close of the chapter. Do you agree with his analysis of the reasons for the "lag" between research and practice? Why?

13. It has been hypothesized that a scarcity of books and writing materials fostered lecturing by teachers and memorizing by students. What instructional methods and types of learning would you predict will be fostered by the widespread use of radio in American classrooms? Educational television? Teaching machines?
14. It has been said that educational technology is either at a crossroad or at the threshold of a new era. Where would you place it today? Why?
15. Read McLuhan's book cited at the close of the chapter. What is the meaning of his well-known phrase "The medium is the message?" What are the implications of this theory for developing an instructional technology?

BOOKS AND PAPERS

At frequent intervals since its first volume in 1931, the *Review of Educational Research* has published curriculum bibliographies. The National Society for the Study of Education in its annual *Yearbook* has issued several curriculum studies including the following: "Adapting the Schools to Individual Differences" (1924); "Curriculum-Making: Past and Present" (1926); "The Activity Movement," (1934); "Theories of Learning and Instruction" (1964); and "The Changing American School" (1966). Almost all educational associations, the National Association of Secondary School Principals, for example, and most subject journals, such as *Industrial Arts and Vocational Education*, deal with curriculum problems.

Educational magazines and daily papers keep readers informed about what is new or projected in the schools. Educational journalism has become a profession, and like journalism in general tends to treat the unusual and sensational. On September 17, 1960, the *Saturday Review* began a monthly educational supplement of high quality, edited by Paul Woodring. *School and Society, School Review, Harvard Educational Review*, and the *Teachers College Record* are examples of excellent periodicals.

Use of the *Encyclopedia of Educational Research* (New York, The Macmillan Company, 1969), is recommended.

Topics treated or suggested in the chapter may be pursued further in the following list of publications. Books mentioned in the chapter are not repeated.

ALBERTY, HAROLD, *Reorganizing the High School Curriculum*, New York, 1953.

American Association for the Advancement of Science, Commission on Science Education, *Science, A Process Approach* (1965).

BEGLE, E. G. "SMSG, The First Decade," *The Mathematics Teacher*, Vol. 61, pp. 239–245, March 1968.

BESTOR, ARTHUR, E. *The Restoration of Learning, A Program for Redeeming the Unfulfilled Promise of American Education*, New York, 1955.

BORROWMAN, MERLE L., *The Liberal and Technical in Teacher Education*, New York, Bureau of Publications, Teachers College, Columbia University, 1956.

BRUNER, JEROME S., *The Process of Education,* Harvard University Press, 1960; *Toward a Theory of Instruction,* 1966.

CARLSON, THEODORA E., and CATHERINE P. WILLIAMS, *Guide to the National Defense Education Act of 1958,* Washington, D.C., United States Department of Health, Education and Welfare (1959).

CARPENTER, CHARLES, *History of American Textbooks,* University of Pennsylvania Press, 1963.

CECIL, H. L., *School Library Service in the United States,* New York, 1940.

CHARTERS, W. W., "The Era of the Educational Engineer" *Educational Research Bulletin,* Vol. 30, No. 9, pp. 230–237, 246, December 12, 1951.

CLEMENTS, ROBERT J., "Literature by Electronics," *Saturday Review,* July 6, 1960, p. 13 ff.

COLEMAN, LAWRENCE VAIL, *The Museum in America,* Washington, D.C., The American Association of Museums, 1939.

DALE, EDGAR, *Audio-Visual Methods in Teaching,* New York, 1954.

DOYLE, HENRY GRATTAN, "The Modern Foreign Languages. A Chronicle of Achievement," *Modern Language Journal,* October 1956, pp. 269–296.

ELSON, RUTH M., *Guardians of Tradition, American Schoolbooks in the Nineteenth Century,* University of Nebraska Press, 1964.

FAY, PAUL JOHNSON, *The History of Science Teaching in American High Schools,* unpublished Ph.D. dissertation, Ohio State University, 1930.

Fund for the Advancement of Education, Ford Foundation, *Teaching by Television,* New York, The Fund, May 1959.

FUNDERBURK, R. S., *History of Conservation Education in the United States,* George Peabody College for Teachers, 1948.

GOOD, H. G., "Invention and the Schoolbook," *School and Society* Vol. 33, pp. 815–818, June 20, 1931; other articles in this series on the general topic, "Invention and the School" deal with "the English Dictionary," "the Map," "School Arithmetic," and "the Student Laboratory" and appeared in *School and Society,* October 10, 1931; April 30, 1932; June 23, 1934; and September 21, 1935; respectively.

HOFSTADTER, RICHARD, *Anti-Intellectualism in American Life,* New York, 1963.

KOENIG, ALLEN E., and RUANE B. HILL, *The Farther Vision, Educational Television Today,* The University of Wisconsin Press, 1967.

LUMSDAINE, A. A., and ROBERT GLASER, eds., *Teaching Machines and Programed Learning,* Washington, D.C., National Education Association, 1960. A source-book.

McLUHAN, MARSHALL, *Understanding Media, The Extensions of Man,* New York, McGraw Hill, 1964.

National Education Association, Association for Supervision and Curriculum Development, *New Curriculum Developments,* 1965.

National Education Association, Project on Instruction, *Education in a Changing Society* (1963); *The Scholars Look at the Schools* (1962); and *Schools for the 60's* (1963).

OETTINGER, ANTHONY G., *Run, Computer, Run, The Mythology of Educational Innovation,* Harvard University Press, 1969.

PARRY, ALBERT, *America Learns Russian, A History of the Teaching of Russian in the United States,* Syracuse University Press, 1967.

PRESSEY, S. L., "Certain Major Psycho-Educational Issues Appearing in the

Conference on Teaching Machines," *Automatic Teaching, The State of the Art* (Eugene Galanter, ed.), pp. 187–198, New York, John Wiley and Sons, Inc., 1959.

Progressive Education Association, Commission on Secondary School Curriculum, *Science in General Education* (1938); *Reorganizing Secondary Education* (1939).

RICKOVER, HYMAN G. (Vice Admiral, USN), *Education and Freedom*, New York, 1959.

SAETTLER, PAUL, A *History of Instructional Technology*, New York, McGraw Hill Book Company, 1968.

SHERA, JESSE H., *Foundations of the Public Library*, University of Chicago Press, 1949.

SIEPMANN, CHARLES, *TV and Our School Crisis*, New York, 1958.

SKINNER, B. F., *The Technology of Teaching*, New York, Appleton-Century-Crofts, 1968.

SUPPES, PATRICK, "Computer Technology and the Future of Education," *Phi Delta Kappan*, Vol. 49, pp. 420–429, April 1968.

TELLER, JAMES D., "Humanizing the Teaching of Science by Using the Bulletin Board," *School Science and Mathematics*, Vol. 41, pp. 611–619, October 1941.

WASHBURNE, CARLETON W., and SIDNEY P. MARLAND, JR., *Winnetka, The History and Significance of an Educational Experiment*, Englewood Cliffs, N.J., Prentice-Hall, Inc., 1963.

WILSON, L. CRAIG, *The Open Access Curriculum*, Boston, 1971.

WOODRING, PAUL, A *Fourth of a Nation*, New York, 1957. A well-considered and imaginatively written work; *Investment in Innovation, An Historical Appraisal of the Fund for the Advancement of Education*, Boston, 1970.

Chapter 16

NEW DIRECTIONS
FOR SECONDARY
EDUCATION

Perhaps no institution reflects the American spirit of innovation and adventure better than the American high school, both public and private. It is this spirit that combines at once the elements of strength and weakness of American secondary education. Its contribution toward the development of the democratic system of education envisioned by John Dewey cannot be overestimated. The concept of a secondary school to embrace and provide meaningful educational experiences for all youth is an achievement of the twentieth century. Only forty years ago half of the boys and girls of secondary school age were not attending school. In the first three decades of the twentieth century the proportion of youth of high school age who were in high school increased from about one in ten to one in two. In this period high school enrollment doubled every ten years, and by 1970 more than 90 per cent of this age group was in high school, and three out of four now finish high school (compared with 1929 when three out of four never entered the ninth grade).

Of course, more students in school for longer periods does not necessarily mean better schooling. However, there is some evidence that students are learning more as a result of their longer exposure to schools. The U.S. Department of Health, Education and Welfare uses this evidence to conclude that ". . . American children in the sixties are learning more than their older brothers and sisters learned in the fifties."

Americans are justly proud of this achievement. Pointing to the substantial advances in education over these years, President John F. Kennedy said: "We are educating a greater proportion of our youth to a higher competency than any other nation on earth." This belief has been expressed by others and the statement may, indeed, be true.

The technological revolutions, which changed many of the ways by which material goods are obtained and the ways in which people lived, moved secondary education in new directions. They destroyed old vocations and created new ones. Men traveled faster, transported greater loads farther, and communicated with each other instantaneously over longer distances.

New knowledges and skills that are so technical that they have to be taught in schools and laboratories displaced former crafts. On a high level, education prepared the research scientist. Early inventors such as Morse, who worked on the telegraph, and Edison were amateurs without systematic training. Pure science today has become the foundation of invention, and the preparation of research workers has become the task of the universities.

On an intermediate level schools may teach expert workmen such as toolmakers, machinists, designers, draftsmen, and patternmakers. Machinery once installed has to be maintained and this requires the employment of highly skilled repair men. The human aspect of technology enlists personnel workers, physicians, nurses, and foremen.

The semiskilled and unskilled workers who operate machines or move goods require, like others, a general education including moral, civic, and prevocational schooling. Everyone needs training for health, thrift, social cooperation, family life, and all of those personal qualities that make life effective and happy.

In a broader sense, as technology has developed, education has been charged to deal with new social problems of citizenship, public health, labor organization, and recreation. In the small community one knew few people, but they were known intimately for a whole lifetime. In the great city one meets hundreds of people but rarely learns to know them well. Relations in church and school have tended to become similarly impersonal. Family life is changing, often breaking down and local government is becoming complex, a business for expert public servants. Modern life tends to standardize the individual, to assign him a number, and to employ him in a routine task. Outside of school hours youth is often left to fend for itself, and the juvenile delinquency rate is high and increasing. All this indicates that there is work for the school to do; but it is not fair to expect the school alone to do it.

The three decades after 1900 produced many great changes in secondary education. The vocational guidance movement began before 1910, the junior colleges multiplied, and the junior high school is usually dated from that time. Before 1920 the Commission on the Reorganization of Secondary Education made its report, and the Smith-Hughes Act was passed. The Progressive Education Association was organized at the same time. Few periods have seen so many important developments in secondary education.

Complementary to the rapid increase in numbers, and in part a cause of that increase, was the change in the high school curriculum. During the early years of the present century the high school changed from a school that was mainly academic and preparatory to one that is largely vocational and terminal. The Committee of Ten was formed to resist this change and did resist it but without success. Curricula and activities continued to multiply and methods and standards were adapted to the capacities of the pupils who were flocking to the schools.

The pupils of an earlier day may have suffered from the lack of physical activity and a complete absence of social life. Such defects were corrected. Social clubs now hold initiations and give dances and other clubs pursue special pupil interests such as photography or radio. Athletics, debating, and school publications had already been introduced into the early high schools. The vast proliferation of new activities gave teachers new duties or opportunities as advisers, sponsors, and chaperones. Americans are proud, but at the same time they are highly critical of their high schools. They deplore the frequently low standards and the slipshod and superficial work, especially in the weaker high schools. As the secondary school enrollment in past decades has increased, high school standards have been lowered in some schools, difficult topics have been omitted, and subjects that were formerly required have been made optional. Large high schools have many curricula, some of which require little intellectual work. These are only some of many criticisms of the American high school today.

Today we are again beginning to move in new directions. Scholars, scientists, officers in the armed forces, some parents, and some school-people say that academic standards should be raised. They are being raised in larger schools. Some want this done without depriving any pupils of the best education that they are capable of. This may be difficult to work out in a democracy in which the schools are controlled largely by local school boards. These boards might not agree to a general reorganization of the schools and their curricula and to a plan to divide pupils into slow and fast streams, as some have proposed, or to provide well trained and high salaried teachers for slow learners. Some of the critics, however, insist that ways must be found to educate the best minds in the best ways, to the highest degree of excellence, whatever the cost to the slow learners.

RISE OF THE JUNIOR HIGH SCHOOL

The junior high school began to spread after 1910 and spread rapidly after World War I. The figures, which have been compiled by different authors do not agree, but there may have been 2,500 such schools by 1940. Thus this type of school is far from being a universal one. Many 8-4 systems remain and there are other combinations of elementary and high school grades as well. Where reorganization has taken place, the 6-3-3 combination is most frequently found. There is a 6-6 combination that is intended to perform the functions usually proposed for the junior high school but without employing it as a separate unit. In Texas the 6-2-4 combination is common. Recently a Middle School concept using a 4-4-4 combination has been advocated by some. (See Figure 16-1.)

The functions proposed for the junior high school are abstract, armchair statements, but they notify the reader that the school was to be more than an administrative grade reorganization. The junior high school was

MAIN TYPES OF SCHOOLS

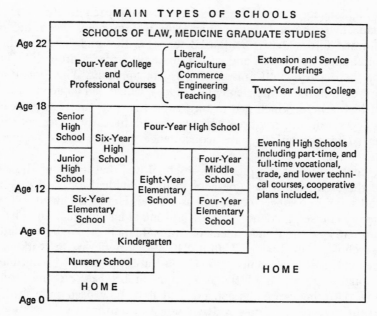

Figure 16–1

to bridge the gap between the elementary and high school, making the transition easier. It was to save time and retain pupils in school (1) by offering work that was more interesting and useful than the work of the upper elementary grades, and (2) by entering the pupils in a new school before the usual end of the compulsory attendance period of age fourteen. It was to offer some choice of studies, exploratory and orientation courses, individual instruction, and more expert guidance. Some thought the new type of school should be departmentalized, have a homeroom organization, and employ homogeneous grouping.

Like the normal school, which was proposed in 1789, fifty years before the first state institution was opened in 1839, the junior high school had been anticipated several years before it appeared. The Committee of Ten suggested the teaching of algebra, languages, and science at an earlier age than was customary. A number of other National Education Association committees, including particularly the committee on economy of time, supported this proposal. But the early beginning of these subjects was not new. Springfield, Massachusetts, had a curriculum that embodied some junior high school principles as early at 1867, but did not have a separate organization for the junior high school period.

The separate organization of the junior high school was not originally planned. Some cities set up new schools for the upper elementary grades to reduce overcrowding in existing buildings; but if this was all, the name junior high school was not justified. A closer approach to the later ideas was made in Richmond, Indiana, in 1896, where grades seven and eight were formed into a departmentalized school with some elective subjects, with promotion by subject, and with a homeroom organization. The necessity for the departmental organization is not apparent. This organization was, however, in use in the elementary grades, which had copied it from the regular high school, which had in turn copied it from the college. Even in the colleges this organization was not found in early times when any teacher could gain an adequate acquaintance with the entire program of studies.

The central idea of the junior high school was that at about the age of twelve the child clearly became adolescent, individualistic, and independent, and should no longer be treated as a child. Hence the introduction of exploratory courses, guidance services, and individual instruction. This idea was furthered by the development of a new branch of psychology, adolescent psychology. G. Stanley Hall (1846–1924) published a work in two volumes entitled Adolescence (1904), and also attempted to outline the educational applications of the new study in his Educational Problems (1911). Many books in this general field have now been published, and adolescent psychology is now widely studied in universities. The study has given direction to one of the chief functions of the junior high school, that of helping the family, church, and community in guiding children through the early adolescent period.

To measure the achievement of the junior high school is difficult. The school program is richer and more diversified than that of the upper grades in most elementary schools and this is an important gain. Elective courses are given and in some degree the schoolwork is adapted to the pupils' individual needs. As a negative outcome, it has been claimed that junior high school pupils do not acquire the fundamental school skills as well as those pupils who complete the eight grades. But many studies show that there is almost no difference between the two groups in their mastery of reading, writing, spelling, and arithmetic. A comparison between the marks earned in college by those who have graduated from the junior-senior schools with those earned by pupils from the four-year schools again shows no significant difference.

Because the junior high schools are located in many more sections of a city and therefore close to the homes of the children, they draw more pupils and hold them a little better than schools on the 8–4 plan. It does not appear that new studies and better methods have much influence in holding pupils in school. The reasons why pupils leave school early are as complex as society itself and include factors that the school cannot control, such as health, finances, conditions in the family, job opportunities, and many others.

The junior high school attracts more men teachers than the elementary school. This is probably of importance in the education of boys. Salaries paid in the elementary schools are less than those in the senior high schools. The junior high school teachers' salaries are a little higher than in the upper elementary grades but not much more. The expectations of those who thought the new junior high school would materially reduce cost have not been met. Nor has the school shortened the time required to complete the full school course. Youth still graduates from the secondary school at the same age as it has been doing for almost a century.

New York City is changing from the 6–3–3 combination to a 4–4–4 pattern, thus reducing the elementary school to four years; introducing a four-year middle school, and returning to the traditional four-year high school. Despite the arguments of those who favor such a middle school plan, there is a growing suspicion that the middle school concept represents an attempt to solve *de facto* racial segregation in large urban areas. The elementary school has been a neighborhood school reflecting residence patterns. Thus, the neighborhood schools of ghetto areas are predominantly segregated. Because the middle school can draw from a wider attendance area, racial integration is facilitated. Although one can give high priority to racial integration it would appear unwise to destroy the educational advantages of the junior high school concept in order to achieve it.

THE JUNIOR COLLEGE

The junior college is most frequently a two-year, freshman-sophomore school, as we saw in an earlier chapter, but there are variants to this plan. Four-year junior colleges may include the two upper high school years. Some junior colleges were born to this role, some grew to this status, and some had it thrust upon them through the decapitation of a four-year college. Some junior colleges choose to remain as they are, but others are biding their time in the hope of becoming four-year schools. A rapid increase in the number of college-going youth may provide such an opportunity for many current junior colleges.

The early origins of the junior college are not well understood. About forty junior colleges claim to be one hundred or more years old. Some of these are decapitants of four-year colleges. The Civil War interrupted the movement, but about sixty junior colleges were founded between 1870 and 1900 and about nine hundred were founded in the present century.

At the end of 1969 the five states with the largest junior college enrollments were California, New York, Illinois, Texas, and Michigan. Forty-nine states shared the total national junior college enrollment of nearly two million. Some of these schools are independent; many are public. Today many favor the development of junior or senior community colleges. It has been thought that the continued development of community colleges would do away with the existing independent colleges in the same way that the high school superseded the academy. This will probably not happen, if we may judge by the conditions in California, which has a full complement of state senior institutions, independent colleges including large ones such as Stanford University and the University of Southern California, teachers' colleges, and junior colleges. For the next decade the prospect is for large enrollments in all types of college institutions.

Rising standards of college education and the increase in the usual age of graduation from eighteen to twenty-two years is one reason for the junior college. So many years of life spent in preparation for life, keeping young men and women in school during years that should be productive, have seemed to some to be "too much college." Various palliatives have been proposed. A three-year college is an old idea; introducing preprofessional and professional work into the college course is another; and a third is the admission of bright students by examination before they have completed high school. None of these proposals has been useful to the great body of college youth.

For those who will not enter a learned profession but who need some schooling beyond high school, the junior college may provide a solution. The nearly two million students who attend such institutions are evidence of their value. Many of these students are acquiring preparation for a vocation. By attending a local institution a great deal of money is saved. If desired, the two-year college graduate may later attend a standard four-year college. Junior college work should be different from that of the upper division. Universities claim that they should not be burdened with the heavy weight of freshman and sophomore instruction, which is really a part of secondary education.

This last argument was used by William Rainey Harper (1856–1906), the first president of the University of Chicago who is sometimes called "the father of the junior college." He wanted to make the university a "real university" on the European pattern. But other early promoters of the junior college, such as Henry P. Tappan (1805–1881) of the University of Michigan and W. W. Folwell (1833–1923) of the University of Minnesota, had the same view. If this were accepted, schooling up to the age of twenty would be considered secondary, university work would begin at that point, and the four-year undergraduate college of arts and sciences would disappear from the American educational scene.

In 1970 the Carnegie Commission on Higher Education (composed of 19 industrialists, university presidents, economists, psychologists, and other citizens) proposed drastic changes in the traditional pattern of schooling as shown in Figure 16–1. The Commission would reduce the pressure on youth to spend more and more time in school while enjoying it less and less. They advocate encouraging restless youths to "stop out" after high school, obtain work experience, and enter college with this increased maturity. To achieve this result, the commission would have the federal government guarantee two years of college for everyone that could be put "in the bank" for later withdrawal at any age. Such a plan would require a great increase in community colleges.

NEW GOALS AND FUNCTIONS

The present high school has developed far beyond the ideas of 1890 and in a direction that diverges more and more from the European concept of the secondary school as a selective institution for the preparation of an intellectual elite. By 1910 the high school had come to the smaller towns and the automobile was facilitating the building of quality rural high schools; the junior high school was developing; the program of studies was still growing; and a broader, more democratic, and more practical education was gaining in favor. These trends were supported by the departments and schools of education, by the land-grant colleges and state universities, and by the social-educational philosophies of Francis W. Parker and John Dewey.

A reformulation of high school objectives was made by the Commission on the Reorganization of Secondary Education, which reported in 1918 under the title Cardinal Principles of Secondary Education. The Commission decided that secondary education should be based on the needs of society, the natures and capacities of the pupils, and professional knowledge of education. They pointed out that only one-third of the elementary school pupils reached the high school and that of these only one in nine remained to graduate. The Commission approved the junior high school and declared itself in favor of the comprehensive senior high school rather than one specialized along technical, commercial, college preparatory, or other particular lines. They proposed the following objectives: health, command of fundamental processes, worthy home membership, vocation, civic education, worthy use of leisure, and ethical character. As an aid toward the attainment of these aims, the Commission proposed that the curricula should be composed of constants—to be taken by all—variables, and free electives. The Commission declared that education in a democracy "should develop in each individual the knowledge, interest, ideals, habits, and powers whereby he will find his place and use that place to shape both himself and society toward even nobler ends." Whereas the Committee of Ten had made college preparation primary, in planning the work of the high school the Commission made preparation for life the primary purpose.

The responsibility of the high school principals to their pupils and communities frequently impressed the principals with the need for more power to resist unwholesome local interference. On the other hand, the old question of high school-college relations, which in spite of many efforts had never been settled to the satisfaction of the principals, was becoming more rather than less irritating as the high schools gained status. These two conditions were the chief reasons for the formation in 1917 of the National Association of Secondary School Principals. How urgent the latter problems seemed can be gathered from the proposal of one of the founders who said, "I believe in the principle of inspection so firmly that I would extend it even to the inspection of the colleges by the high schools. The colleges inspect us to see whether our product is good enough for them to work with. Now let us inspect the colleges to see whether they are good enough to have the care and direction of our boys and girls." And Jess B. Davis, a past president of the association, in a review of its history declared, "Twenty-five years ago the National Association of Secondary School Principals was conceived in rebellion." This rebellion began in the Middle West where the high school was most powerful.

One would expect to find extended consideration of the high school-college relation in the meetings of the association, but this did not happen. Instead this question was practically ignored and the Principals' Association dealt instead with problems of organization and administration, with the curriculum, student government, extracurricular activities, teaching problems, ability grouping, educational and vocational guidance, character development, the junior high school and junior college, and the function of education in a democracy. Although it may have been "conceived in rebellion," what really interested the association was the question of how the high school can best function as a higher common school. One of its important achievements has been the creation of a National Honor Society of high school students to encourage character development, leadership, scholarship, and service.

An important study was made by the association through its Committee on the Orientation of Secondary Education, of which Thomas H. Briggs was chairman. The committee began its work in 1932 and made its final report in 1935 during the tercentenary celebration of the founding of secondary education in the United States. The summary of the committee's findings is embodied in the ten "issues" and ten "functions" of secondary education that was formulated. These findings were submitted to forums of schoolmen throughout the country for their consideration and application. The functions are statements of the main tasks of secondary schools, a new and more elaborate set of "cardinal principles." Only once do these functions, even by implication, recognize that the high schools are preparing some of their students for college.

The ten issues, on the other hand, raise a whole series of questions, some of which are being answered by the trend of our history of the past fifty years. Whether public secondary education shall be given to all youth or only to some, whether the secondary school shall work for the welfare of both society and the individual, whether it shall provide differentiated curricula, whether it can offer vocational education, whether it shall be only concerned with knowledge or with attitudes as well, whether it has a distinct field of its own—these are hardly issues any longer. The answers that the history of the high school has given to these questions are now hardly in doubt, but the answers have certainly not yet been universally accepted, and they may need modification in the future. The purpose of the formulation was clearly to have them critically examined, especially by those of the profession who had not already accepted them.

The ninth issue asked, "Shall secondary education seek merely the adjustment of the student to prevailing social ideals, or shall it seek the reconstruction of society?" Clearly all education, even without an intent to do so, actually does something to reconstruct society. But since this question was asked during an economic depression, it was clearly intended to raise the alternative between the existing economic system and some degree of greater social control. In this sense it was a living issue.

The high school has developed as a public school, a local school, and a day school. These are among the most obvious as well as the most important of its institutional characteristics. It is a local, day school, not a state or national boarding school because it is intended to serve the great body of the people who cannot send their children away from home for purposes of education. The high school must, therefore, be located close to the homes of the children. As a result of this wide distribution, many high schools are small schools. A very large proportion of the smallest high schools are not accredited by their regional standardizing associations. President Conant's judgment on these smaller high schools can be seen in his report of 1959 (see the Bibliography). In the long run, the present condition of a school may be less important than the vigor and intelligence with which it is going forward and trying to improve its work. It was this view that led the standardizing associations to seek better ways of stimulating high school improvement.

The Cooperative Study of Secondary School Standards was carried out by a committee that began its work in 1928, but formally began its study in 1934. The committee was aided by advisory members from the American Council on Education and other bodies, and the study was jointly financed by the associations themselves and the General Education Board. Dissatisfaction with the rigid and mechanical standards that had come into use had been felt for some time. These standards usually covered such points as the amount of preparation that teachers had received, teacher loads, finances, the number of books in the school library, and laboratory and athletic equipment. The purpose of the study was to discover the characteristics of a good school, the best means of evaluating these characteristics, and the best methods by which a school can be stimulated to improve.

By a process of formulating evaluative criteria, trying these experimentally in a number of schools, and criticizing and reformulating them in the light of the experience gained, a definitive scheme for the cooperative evaluation of secondary schools by the staff with the help of external committees was perfected by 1940. The scheme of evaluation uses both judgments made by teachers and competent investigators and objective measures obtained from the use of tests and scales. More than a dozen phases of the school and its work are covered in a complete evaluation, and a definite program for improvement is the finest result of this plan. Among the phases covered by the plan are the school's philosophy of education, the pupils and community, the program and courses of study, pupil activities, the library and its use, guidance, instruction, the staff, the plant, the administration of the school, and the outcomes of the school's work. Evidently a survey of a high school made on these broad bases will be more qualitative than an inspection that uses the older quantitative standards. Because the evaluations are made cooperatively by teachers, administrators, and outside experts, they serve an important purpose as means for the professional reeducation of the staff and the improvement of the work and services of the schools. The stimulus that such an evaluation can give may be far more valuable than its standardizing function.

Secondary education was deeply affected by the depression of the 1930's. Because there were fewer jobs, many young people who would have preferred to work remained in school. The codes of the National Recovery Administration (NRA) in 1933 set a minimum employment age of sixteen years, or higher in some instances. When the NRA was declared unconstitutional, child labor increased but never reached its former peak. Thus the 1930's became notable for a rapid increase in high school attendance. The increase in numbers and costs and the financial depletion of the high schools in those years led to a number of studies.

The American Youth Commission (AYC) of the American Council on Education began its work in 1935. Several motives may have operated in the Council to lead it to create the AYC, the simple desire to alleviate the evils suffered by youth was one. The depression was calling attention to the inadequacies of the schools. Also, many believed that there was a danger of youth being regimented by national agencies. It was believed that a voluntary agency such as the AYC would serve youth without partisanship. How far these opinions were correct is a matter of opinion.

Before the AYC could consider solutions, it seemed necessary to secure accurate information on the condition and needs of youth. One extended investigation made along these lines was reported by Howard M. Bell in *Youth Tell Their Story* (1938), and in more popular form in *How Fare American Youth?* (1937) by the director of the commission, Homer P. Rainey, and others. A scientifically chosen sample of the 250,000 persons between the ages of sixteen and twenty-four years living in Maryland was studied for these reports.

Although the investigation did not reveal many totally new facts, it provided quantitative and current data, and showed that more than half of the pupils leaving high school did so for economic reasons, and another quarter left for scholastic or disciplinary reasons. The latter group did not care to learn or were unable to learn what the school was teaching, or they did not fit into the routine and regimen of the school.

The report showed that the pupil with the poorest chance of finishing high school was a Negro boy from a large but broken family whose father was an unskilled worker. The pupil with the best chance was a white girl from a small family with educated parents in good economic circumstances. It appeared that the children with a poor likelihood of becoming well educated would have children with a similarly unfavorable outlook. Racial and economic factors were both considered to be very important.

Although this was not a wholly new discovery, the report put it into concrete terms somewhat as follows. The occupation of a youth's father profoundly affects the amount of the youth's schooling. This in turn affects the kind of job that the youth will later have and the income that he will earn. Furthermore, the youth who leaves school early is likely to marry early and have a large family. This closes the economic-scholastic circle and makes it very difficult to break up the pernicious class structure; the poor and poorly educated will tend to become a permanent mudsill of society.

The report also dealt with youth and the church, youth at work, and youth at play. The investigators seemed surprised to find that the church was a living influence. Three-quarters of the youth studied claimed to have church connections. The investigators proposed the creation of community youth centers and believed that the demand of social recreation was the most significant revelation of their study. They praised the work of the youth-serving agencies.

Teachers may not generally be adequately acquainted with the great youth organizations for which America is and deserves to be famous. Many of these groups agree with the schools in some of their aims and principles and the schools should make common cause with them. To do this effectively teachers must know about these organizations and must take an interest in their work.

Such acquaintance could begin with a study of another survey made for the AYC by M. M. Chambers and reported in his *Youth-Serving Organizations* (1941), which provides information about more than three hundred national but nongovernmental associations that spend all or part of their efforts in advancing the welfare of youth. Examples of these are the Junior Red Cross, Boy Scouts, Girl Scouts, Camp Fire Girls, 4-H Clubs, and the American Friends' Service Committee. There are also a great many Catholic, Protestant, and Jewish youth organizations.

GENERAL OR SPECIAL HIGH SCHOOLS?

Although the Commission on the Reorganization of Secondary Education under the leadership of Clarence D. Kingsley advocated a comprehensive senior high school, David Snedden and other critics of the report believed that specialized vocational schools were essential. Kingsley argued that vocational education should be a part of the comprehensive high school. Both points of view have found application in American secondary education. The comprehensive or general high school is an American development. It comprehends several and often many kinds of curricula, liberal and vocational, preparatory and terminal. It is a school with many purposes. The special high school has a narrower field. It may be a commercial, technical, or even a classical school, as in the case of the oldest secondary school in America. The first high school had a single curriculum that emphasized English and mathematics. The promoters of that school had a practical end in view, namely, to prepare boys for business. In this general sense it was a vocational school but it did not prepare its students for a definite vocation. A number of cities began to build special schools in the early years of the high school movement, but they later turned to the comprehensive type. When the commercial, manual training, and agricultural curricula were developed, special vocational or prevocational schools were being founded, but in time many of these also became comprehensive. Evidently "there is something that does not love a wall" in American education and that particularly disapproves of the separation of general education from special education.

The phrase *vocational education* is defined in the Smith-Hughes Act as education that is of "less than college grade" and that is given to pupils, who are at least fourteen years old, for the purpose of fitting them for "useful employment" or to render them more efficient in it. This language is not entirely precise, but it does set limits and thereby excludes several kinds of education that might be confused with vocational education, such as professional education and general industrial arts. It also excludes general education that has only incidental applications to vocations and all merely exploratory courses. On the other hand, the language of the definition would cover high school commercial education that fits pupils for useful employment but is not named in the act because the act did not provide any funds for this branch of vocational education.

The Smith-Hughes Act and the federal laws that were passed to supplement it provide support for the teaching of agriculture, homemaking, trades and industries, and the distributive vocations. These, together with commerce, may be called the Big Five among the vocations for which the high schools prepare their pupils. But there are many other vocations including journalism and commercial art that do not receive federal aid. Many vocations are also taught in evening schools, corporation schools, correspondence courses, and other public and private, part-time and full-time institutions. All of these will be excluded from a detailed consideration under the present topic.

The comprehensive high school is the typical American public secondary school, but there are exceptions other than the vocational schools. One exception that is usually omitted because it is not recognized as an exception is the very small school. There are many schools that can offer only one curriculum and very few electives. These are in effect special schools even though it is their purpose to provide a general education.

Not all vocational work is done in purely vocational schools. Many comprehensive schools provide complete vocational curricula. By making appropriate selections, pupils may graduate in a course in which a vocational certificate may be earned.

Private trade schools were opened in New York in 1881 and in several other cities before the end of the nineteenth century. Cities soon began to open public trade schools, which were usually designed with narrow restrictions, but together with continuation evening schools they were the direct precursors of the vocational high schools of today. The vocational high school is only sixty years old at the earliest and one can hardly speak of a vocational high school movement before 1920.

Since trade, vocation, profession, and technical activity are words that are often confused, a few simple definitions and typical examples will serve a useful purpose. Professional education in such fields as engineering or law is usually distinguished from vocational education, which includes mainly trade or technical preparation. A trade demands skill and special knowledge but usually not much scientific or literary preparation. In addition to skill, a technical occupation involves scientific preparation and good judgment in applying such knowledge in the arts. Surgery is a profession as well as a highly technical occupation, but the latter term is more commonly applied to such work as television mechanics or electronics. Ordinary carpentry and house painting are trades. Many vocations combine a considerable variety of skills and a considerable range of knowledge. Such vocations as farming and caring for a home and family are partly trades, partly professions, and partly ways to achieve independence. Much depends in all cases upon the level at which the work is performed.

Professional education that is carried on in colleges, universities, special institutes, and seminaries will not concern us here. Vocational education in many fields is provided in high schools as well as in college in many cases. Vocational high schools may be specialized along one or a few lines, or they may be almost as comprehensive as the schools that have that title. Thus, as mentioned before, we have here an illustration of the tendency of special schools to become broad and general.

Vocational education is one of the growing points of the school system.

There is no necessary conflict between vocational and liberal education. In a working society, manual, technical, and professional workers are also citizens, neighbors, consumers, and potential leaders, that is, people. All need both a broad and liberal education as people and a specific education as workers. Some of this may be best given in school, some on the job.

INTRODUCING VOCATIONAL EDUCATION

Before the industrial revolution, skilled workmen were prepared by apprenticeship, but with increasing specialization this system of training declined. Immigration, by bringing in many highly skilled craftsmen, also dealt a severe blow to the apprentice system. Immigration has now been reduced to small numbers, and American industry cannot depend upon Europe to prepare its skilled workers. However, many such men are still needed. The machinists in railroad shops and the loom-fixers in textile mills are examples of the many highly skilled and highly paid industrial workers. The low point in apprenticeship training was reached in about 1900; today many industries are again training their craftsmen by apprenticeship.

Apprentice standards are set up by industry and labor jointly, but there are also standards set by law, and the National Association of State Approving Agencies, which is largely composed of representatives of state education departments, is also involved in this function. An old struggle is going on between the state departments of education and labor with respect to apprentice standards. The unions, on one hand, naturally desire to protect the interests of labor, to prevent an oversupply of trained workers, and to maintain high wages. The state departments of education, on the other hand, try to inject academic requirements into the training and reduce the length of the apprenticeship. Thus, recently the state education departments attempted to require that those who supervise apprentice training programs must have bachelor's degrees.

For a century men have also argued over vocational education in the public schools, usually against it. Common school leaders in vocational education had to exercise great tact and skill to secure support for their cause, since free vocational education could easily be made to appear as an offer of special privilege to a few.

There were practical difficulties in the providing of vocational education in schools such as the high cost of this program, the difficulty of obtaining teachers who were both well educated in school learning and skilled in trades, and the question of what to teach and how to teach it.

There were also theoretical difficulties such as the formal discipline philosophy. It said that the academically well-educated man would easily solve any problem. In that case the man with a good general education should have been an effective vocational teacher. Although it was evident that such men were not capable in that field, it was not often noticed that this conflicted with the theory. Another difficulty was the notion of many teachers that the practical and useful skills and knowledge were in some way opposed to the high ideals of truth, goodness, and beauty. Teachers, like others brought up on books and employed in the work of communication, had little firsthand knowledge of industry and felt some antipathy to it. Until 1870 it was widely held that no vocational knowledge should be taught in the schools.

It was in 1878 that Emerson E. White (1829–1902) called attention to the growing demand for industrial education by taking what was for the time a liberal position. He proposed to have the elements of vocational knowledge taught in public schools, and he added that the industries should build upon this foundation in their own vocational schools. This was as wise a statement on the subject as had yet been made at that time, and it did not deserve the criticism that White received for making it.

The principle of White's solution is accepted today. Schools do in fact teach those features of vocational knowledge and skill that are of general application and usefulness. The employer takes the pupil at that point and completes the training under ordinary operating conditions. Manual training came into the schools soon after White's pronouncement, and was often regarded as a form of vocational education. This mistake was not made by John D. Runkle at the Massachusetts Institute of Technology, for he was not preparing craftsmen but engineers. Manual training gave his students some understanding of tools and materials, which was all that it was intended to provide. But the unfounded faith of others in manual training delayed the introduction of true vocational education into the schools.

General vocational education, such as manual training was supposed to be, has only a limited sphere of applications. Vocations are distinct and have to be learned separately like languages. As in the case of languages, there are common elements. Such topics are shop mathematics, drawing, and science, all of which are useful at least to the machinist, electrician, and others, but have much less relevance to the commercial artist. It was also seen that the schools cannot provide complete preparation for many vocations; mastery has to be acquired in actual production.

School people hesitated so long before organizing vocational schools that businessmen became impatient. The state of Massachusetts provides an illustration. An investigating commission on the need for vocational education was appointed by Governor Douglas and made its report in 1905. At this time Paul H. Hanus fortunately returned from a sabbatical year in Germany where he had studied Georg Kerschensteiner's system of vocational education in Munich.

When the state legislature, upon recommendation of the Douglas commission, created a state commission on industrial education, Hanus was appointed its chairman. In 1906 the commission undertook to explain the provision of the legislation for the institution of vocational education either in separate public vocational schools or in special departments in regular high schools. Both employers and employees had to be persuaded, one that the education would have practical value, the other that the pupils would not be employed at low wages or serve as strikebreakers. The state Board of Education was not merely unconvinced but it actively opposed the work of the commission. George H. Martin, who was the secretary of the Board of Education, the position first held by Horace Mann, pursued a dog-in-the-manger policy, it has been said, because he thought the state board should have been placed in control. In 1909 both the commission and the state board were abolished and a state Department of Education was established to supervise both general and vocational education under public auspices.

The increased interest in vocational education early in the twentieth century is shown by the numerous studies of the problem made at that time. The New York State Department of Labor made a report on the vocational education needs of that state. The National Education Association had a Committee on the Place of the Industries in Public Education. Under the leadership of Charles R. Richards and David Snedden, the National Society for the Promotion of Industrial Education was formed in 1906. Six years later the society declared itself in favor of a system of public vocational schools separated from the regular high schools. Wisconsin had already passed such a law (1911), creating a state board and local boards of industrial education and a system of vocational schools parallel to the high schools.

A similar movement was progressing in Illinois, where the legislature petitioned Congress for federal aid for vocational training. Chancellor Samuel Avery of the University of Nebraska, President James H. Baker of the University of Colorado, John Dewey, and other prominent educators spoke against separate educational systems. The author of the Illinois plan was Edwin S. Cooley, former superintendent of schools in Chicago, who replied to Dewey's heated argument that his own plan would not interfere with the regular system but would supplement it by creating a vocational school for youths who would otherwise leave school. The Cooley plan failed; but the framers of the Smith-Hughes Act did not put the vocational system into the hands of the local high schools without some degree of external control over its administration. This has been shown in Chapter 10.

PRIVATE SECONDARY EDUCATION

Thus far we have been concerned primarily with public secondary schools. However any discussion of new directions in secondary education cannot ignore the instruction provided by nongovernmental agencies such as charitable organizations, trade unions, philanthropic foundations, churches, and other nonpublic enterprises.

The American national system of education is not a federal system or even a public system. At all levels—federal, state, county, and local—both public and private agencies engage in educational activities. Public tax-supported schools are important, but they do not constitute the entire national effort in education. Nonpublic secondary schools, both church-related and nonchurch-related, are very numerous. One school guide lists about two thousand of the many nonpublic secondary schools in the United States.

It is not compulsory for a child to attend a public school. An Oregon school law of 1922 provided that all children between the ages of eight and sixteen years had to attend the public schools whenever these were in session. The effect would have been to close all private elementary and junior high schools in the state. The Supreme Court in 1925 declared that "the Act of 1922 unreasonably interferes with the liberty of parents and guardians to direct the upbringing and education of children under their control. . . . The child is not the mere creature of the State. . . ."

The court in the so-called Oregon Case, 268 U.S. 510, held that the Oregon law violated the Fourteenth Amendment and denied the right of the states to prohibit private schools, although the states could inspect and reasonably regulate these schools. The decision declares that the Fourteenth Amendment requires the states to permit private and public schools to continue. Only autocracies such as Nazi Germany and Communist Russia have found it necessary to prohibit private schools.

It has been estimated that one in ten secondary school pupils attends a nonpublic school. Enrollment figures are not completely accurate or complete, but the National Center for Educational Statistics of the U.S. Office of Education reports that in 1966–1967 nonpublic secondary schools enrolled 1,364,522 pupils. Over 1.2 million of these students were enrolled in church-related schools, whereas less than 200,000 were enrolled in nonchurch-related schools. The great majority of the students in church-related schools attend parochial schools maintained by the Roman Catholic Church, although many attend schools supported by Protestant, Jewish, and other religious denominations.

The earliest types of Catholic secondary school were imported from Europe. Schools for girls were finishing schools maintained by the religious sisterhoods and boys' schools were attached to colleges. Usually the numbers of students in the parochial schools were much larger than those in the colleges. Many of these preparatory schools have now been separated from the colleges or closed. Another type of secondary school evolved from the parish schools in the way in which public high schools grew out of elementary schools.

The third type of nonpublic secondary school is the diocesan or central high school, which draws its pupils from several parishes and is controlled by a board under the bishop as chairman. The first such school was a boys' school that was opened in Philadelphia in 1890; in 1912 a similar school for girls was opened in the same city. The boys' school, called the Roman Catholic High School of Philadelphia, opened with three curricula, Latin-scientific, commercial, and manual training. These were the most popular curricula in the public schools of that time and this parallelism has been fairly well maintained. The original idea was that the central high schools should include religious training but should provide for the education of Catholic laymen and that they should be organically connected with the parishes rather than the colleges that were training priests. This is still the plan, and yet most of these schools also prepare pupils for college and many of their graduates attend state and private universities.

Although Protestants as a group have not used parochial schools as a general solution to the problem of religious education, they support the right of all denominations to establish and maintain church-related secondary schools. However, Protestants have usually resisted attempts to divert public funds to the support of these schools. As a result, a relatively small per cent of students in church-related secondary schools are in schools supported by denominations such as the Lutherans, Seventh-Day Adventists, Episcopalians, Baptists, and Mennonites.

As with the Protestants, Jews have not used parochial schools generally to provide religious education. The number of Hebrew day schools is relatively small, and these are concentrated in large metropolitan areas, especially New York City.

The future of church-related secondary schools in the United States is unclear. It is generally conceded that to continue their present standards these schools will require a tremendous increase in income. With the American tradition of strict separation of Church and state, it will be difficult if not impossible to obtain these funds from public sources. In addition, a substantial body of opinion, Catholic, Protestant, and Jewish, questions the desirability—or even the necessity—of continuing these church-related secondary schools. On the other hand, many citizens believe that both public and nonpublic secondary schools are essential to the advancement of American civilization.

A second large class of nonpublic schools is formed by the 2,000 or 3,000 institutions that are usually called private secondary schools. These have now chosen to call themselves independent schools, but the old name still clings to them. They are independent of state control but some have close connections with a church—Methodist, Episcopal, Catholic, or some other.

The class of new academies, established in most cases after the Civil War and mentioned in Chapter 5, belong to the independent schools.

One of these, St. Paul's School of Concord, New Hampshire, was founded in 1855. This Episcopal school has claimed, somewhat too broadly, that "a new trend was given to education in America in the establishment of St. Paul's. It was the first of the church schools to appeal to the new class that was rapidly acquiring wealth from water-power, textile mills, and the exploitation of the continent."

Some of the independent schools are much older than St. Paul's and were originally church schools, and in fact were country academies that had low tuition rates. Such a school was Phillips Academy, located at Exeter, New Hampshire, and founded in 1783. It is a comparatively large independent school. The other Phillips Academy is at Andover, Massachusetts, and is a little older than Phillips Exeter. Another old Massachusetts school is the Deerfield Academy, which was founded in 1797. Like the colleges, the older independent schools often boast about their age. The Governor Dummer Academy, founded in 1761, considers itself "the oldest boarding school for boys in the United States." Recently founded independent schools do not mention the dates of their origin.

Noted independent schools are most numerous in the New England states especially in Massachusetts, in the states of New York and California, and in the environs of great cities. They are generally expensive, as we have already suggested. What do parents of boys in these schools get for their money? The most famous of the independent schools have small classes and good teachers, although, as in public schools, they are sometimes more highly skilled in Latin than in the teaching of it. Many of these schools have splendid buildings that are elaborately equipped and appointed. Swimming pools, horseback riding trails, and courts and fields for all kinds of games are provided. Many of these schools prepare pupils for college, and in some cases these are pupils whom the public schools might not succeed in getting into college. One thing that parents buy in these schools is "class" or prestige. It is also a fact that some children have educational needs that the local public school cannot satisfy. Schools whose chief merit is their exclusiveness may seem to be undemocratic, but to suppress them would also be undemocratic. The principle is comparable to Voltaire's comment on free speech: "I detest what you say but I will defend to the death your right to say it."

For some children, boarding schools seem to be necessary. There are private schools for slow learners, and military academy and ranch and mountain schools may render necessary services that public schools do not offer. There are also schools for homeless children and some schools for possible or actual delinquents.

Nonpublic schools have contributed much to the diversity of secondary education. Unhampered by the legislative and administrative controls over public education, they have been free to pioneer innovations in curricula and teaching methods. They have cherished the American ideal of freedom of choice, which is inherent in our pluralistic society.

GUIDANCE AND SECONDARY EDUCATION

Guidance is a concept that is intimately related to the American dream of equality of opportunity. As we have seen, increased attention was given to this concept with the establishment of the junior high schools. However, guidance did not become an instrument of national policy until the Soviet Union succeeded in putting two satellites or Sputniks into orbit in 1957. Public Law 85–864, the National Defense Education Act of 1958, declares that "the security of the nation requires the fullest development of the mental resources and technical skills of its young men and women." Thus, Congress recognized that even in this age of atomic power the nation's most creative power is its manpower. The law provided appropriations to educate guidance workers to spearhead a national effort to continuously discover and develop the abilities of American youth.

Fortunately, this national emphasis upon guidance had a firm foundation on which to build. As early as 1908 Frank H. Parsons (1854–1908) had organized the Boston Vocation Bureau with financial support provided by Pauline Agassiz Shaw, the daughter of Louis Agassiz.

Events followed rapidly, showing that this had been a timely step. Upon the death of Parsons, the direction of the bureau was taken over by Meyer Bloomfield, who was in turn followed by John M. Brewer, the author of *The Vocational Guidance Movement*, an early account. Vocational guidance was introduced into the schools of Boston (1909) and of Cincinnati (1911). City-wide vocational guidance services in the schools were created in Grand Rapids, Michigan, in 1912 and in Des Moines, Iowa, in 1914. Helen T. Woolley and Jesse B. Davis were among the new leaders of guidance in the Midwest.

The two World Wars both had considerable influence upon the growth of interest in guidance. The army's use of intelligence tests and its personnel system stimulated an extraordinary degree of interest and research activity among the country's psychologists who developed new kinds of group and individual tests of aptitudes, achievement, interests, and personality.

In the United States vocational guidance is often given by high schools and colleges. This is appropriate, for vocational guidance implies vocational education. In the last half-century guidance has been systematically given. The growth and specialization of industry and the rise of new skilled and technical occupations have increased the need for guidance.

However, in his 1967 follow-up study of a 10 per cent sample of 2,000 medium-sized (enrollment between 750 and 2,000 students) comprehensive high schools, James B. Conant found only about 32 per cent of the sample had a ratio of one counselor to 349 or fewer students, although in his original study (1959) he had recommended a ratio of one counselor to 250 to 300 students.

The spirit of vocational guidance is one of its significant characteristics. The counselor does not command the pupil or make decisions for him. He does not determine the student's future job nor even the curriculum that will prepare him for it. The young person and his family must make the decisions and bear the responsibility. In much of Europe the opposite course is followed. In many countries the government sets up employment bureaus in the departments of labor or the interior. The purpose of these bureaus is not to help the individual but to help the nation make the most effective use of its manpower. Under a dictatorship no man can leave his job and choose another. It is in the democracies that vocational education and vocational guidance have been linked together to promote individual as well as national welfare.

Knowledge of the individual and of occupations and wisdom in applying this knowledge to cases are leading requirements of effective guidance. This knowledge is often difficult to obtain and apply. The instruments of guidance are: (1) the cumulative record of the pupil's interests, attitudes, and achievements in school, home, and social life; (2) batteries of tests of traits and abilities; 3) vocational experiences on the job or in school shops; (4) occupational information; and especially (5) the interview. Teachers who take part in extracurricular activities learn a good deal about the pupils in their groups, but studies show that the regular high school teachers often have only a small part of the knowledge needed for effective counseling. Yet the best school guidance systems make use of the regular staff, and it becomes one of the tasks of the school counselor to guide the teachers in obtaining the needed information and developing the skill required for guidance counseling.

PERSISTENT PROBLEMS

The high school was created for a society and an era that was very different from our own. The cold war, the armaments race, the great cities and increased population, the growth of technology, and the contraction of all space on the earth and beyond make ours a different world from that of 1871 or even 1971. Education must take account of these changes, but many of the smaller or even larger high schools have not done so.

Some persistent problems have become more urgent under present conditions. Many pupils do not know how to study or lack the needed interest in study. Home and community conditions may be unfavorable to hard work, and excessive devotion to athletics by a pupil, by a school, or by an entire town can interfere with schoolwork. Teachers resign because of the confusion and disorder caused by unruly pupils. Large and some small high schools suffer from a shortage of the classrooms, equipment, and teachers needed to serve large enrollments. The schools are sometimes blamed for the high rate of juvenile delinquency among the pupils.

The fault of the school may not lie in Progressive education, as has been charged, but in the school's imposition of an academic curriculum, filled with difficult words, upon boys who cannot handle abstractions, do not read well, would choose to read only sports and comics, dislike all writing, hate arithmetic, play truant, and, when interviewed, ask only to be allowed to quit school. They dislike school because they do not succeed in school work, because as one boy said: "I am always left behind."

Not only delinquents or probable delinquents but also a significant proportion of the children in our schools are in this nonacademic group. In some states, if these youths cannot obtain working-certificates they must remain in school until they are eighteen years old. Some of these older pupils, many of them retarded a year or more, become leaders of disturbance, instigators of ludicrous or malicious incidents or serious disorder. In these ways they satisfy their hunger for leadership and show their contempt for school and its demands.

All countries have a secondary education problem. The United States long ago, and the Soviet Union quite recently, both entered upon the apparently laudable experiment of educating all youth in the humanities, languages, mathematics, sciences, and the arts. Other countries had assumed that only a minority of youth is capable of such education and developed two parallel systems, one for the academically gifted and another for the larger group that does not thrive on such fare. In 1944, England, France to a certain degree, and West Germany all began to turn toward a system of universal secondary education while the Soviet Union, after giving this plan a trial, has been definitely turning away from it since 1958 and is putting nonacademic youth to work at an earlier age.

The high school has made considerable efforts to meet the needs of youth. At any rate, some high schools deal with problems of health, moral conduct, family life, citizenship, consumer education, dating, dress, table manners, and recreation and at the same time offer excellent guidance services; and yet a large proportion of the youth either do not enter high school or drop out during the course. This condition has given rise to the demand that the high school provide a program composed entirely of such applied knowledge. Except for only the "tools of learning," all academic subjects are to be omitted from this "life adjustment education."

The term *life adjustment education* has come into use since World War II and particularly since the adoption of the Prosser Resolution at an educational conference in Chicago in May 1947. The resolution, offered by Charles Allen Prosser (1871–1952), stated that 60 per cent of American youth are not properly served by the present high schools because the high schools do not attract them or because they do not hold them, or finally, because many who remain have to engage in educational activities that are so unrelated to the everyday needs of the students' lives that when the students graduate they are not well adjusted to life. The resolution declared that this large body of boys and girls is entitled to life adjustment training as citizens, and called upon leaders in vocational education and school administration to formulate a plan for educating all American youth in school up to the age of eighteen.

Committees of educators have repeatedly favored this plan as a general policy, but states that have extended their compulsory attendance period to that age grant work permits at age sixteen. Even so there are still complaints about the unwilling pupils in the schools. One question that has been raised is whether the program of the Prosser Resolution would make these pupils more willing to remain in the schools.

There are really two propositions: to extend the compulsory age for school attendance and to introduce life-adjustment education. There is no scientific conclusion with regard to either proposition and the advisability of either would depend upon many changing social factors. It may even be undesirable that all children be retained in school to the same chronological age by force of law.

The number of small, inefficient high schools that are not acceptable to their regional associations nor otherwise accredited is a difficult problem in education. Among the public high schools the weak greatly outnumber the strong, and the deficiencies of the weak schools are usually the result of the poverty and limited population of the supporting districts, but they are sometimes also caused by the limited understanding of the people.

The early districts were too small to provide even a good elementary school. The school consolidation movement began in New England, where the district system had begun and was spreading over the Middle West by 1900. The consolidation effort and a new interest in agricultural education led to the formation of rural combined elementary and high schools that were much admired fifty years ago but are now regarded as inadequate. Not many years later many states under the leadership of the United States Office of Education began to combine school districts into larger units and to close the weakest high schools. Great progress has been made in a scant generation. Small high schools are far more numerous than large ones. The number required for an acceptable high school is debatable. James Bryant Conant holds that one high school that graduates fewer than one hundred students annually is too small, and would require an enrollment of four hundred or more in a three-year school and five hundred and fifty in a four-year high school. Such estimates are somewhat precarious because retention rates vary.

For many years, teachers have known that a great proportion of high school pupils do not elect the more difficult academic courses such as advanced mathematics, chemistry, physics, or languages. Since the excitement raised by the Russian Sputniks of 1957, attention has been called to the large number of small high schools that do not even offer these courses. In the larger schools, the majority of students follow a vocational or general course of study, partly as a matter of individual choice or economics, but partly because the pupils are not able to do advanced mathematics or complete even two years of study of a foreign language.

As a consequence of the changing character of the school population, enrollments in academic subjects did not keep pace with the increasing high school attendance. Some of the academic subjects have as many enrollees across the country as ever, and yet comprise a much smaller fraction of the total enrollment than they formerly did; some academic subjects have lost in actual numbers of pupils or have been dropped from the program. This decline, whether relative or absolute, in the popularity of academic subjects is much influenced by the increased offerings of the high school and the mass attendance. When the high school program was almost entirely academic, there was no escape from mathematics, science, and foreign language. When the high school introduced vocational and activity studies and opened its doors to the vast body of youth, many chose the newer studies in preference to the old ones. Whether this flight from academic studies was avoidable and whether the trend can be reduced are momentous questions of modern educational policy.

The relative decline in the popularity of academic studies is a matter of public concern for several reasons. The maintenance of a complex economic system is directly involved. Agriculture, industry, engineering, business, and the entire American economy depend upon languages including the English language, mathematics, and the sciences. Both practical scientists and research scientists are needed to provide a growing population with the means of maintaining an adequate and, if possible, a rising living standard. The entire economy is also the base upon which the nation's system of defense must rest. Furthermore, the United States is committed to a policy of collective security and needs strategic materials and international markets. In peace and war, for trade and the arts, the United States must understand her allies as well as her actual and potential enemies. If ignorance of the languages, history, philosophy, and resources of the countries of the world were ever permissible, that day is past. Isolation is both undesirable and impossible in the present world. High school and college students must study mathematics, sciences, and languages more diligently than they have done in the past and far more diligently than they are doing now.

The need for mathematicians, scientists, engineers, and persons skilled in languages is great. Excellence in these areas comes only after years of preparation that must begin at the high school level and even earlier. Under present conditions national survival may well depend upon a sufficient number of both original investigators and skilled technicians in these fields. This is one of the chief concerns of James Bryant Conant and Admiral Hyman G. Rickover, and it explains in part their pleas for larger and better high schools.

Important though these disciplines are, it is necessary to remember that there are areas of human life and endeavor in which they play a secondary part. The older professions, law, medicine, and the ministry, and callings such as teaching (except for teachers of pure and applied mathematics and science), politics, journalism, nursing, and literature are comparatively nonmathematical. Those preparing for such vocations should study mathematics and the sciences as a necessary part of their general education but not as the specialties that they are for professional scientists and engineers. Perhaps one year of college-level mathematics and one of a physical or natural science would suffice for most; and preparation for this work has to be made in the lower schools. The speech of home and street may not be good and the standards of the community may not lead the pupil to improve his use of language. All pupils study English throughout the high school course; those who go to college take additional freshman English courses. Yet many do not learn to write well. Classes are too large, are likely to become larger, and each teacher has too many class-hours. College students have been known to report that they were not required to write a single theme in high school. Perhaps their memory was no better than their use of language. Finally, English teachers are said to be inadequately prepared.

The rapid learners may be most important of all and it is not always true that they will take care of their own development. They may be bored and may drop out of school. A large, well-prepared faculty and a guidance staff concerned with finding gifted youngsters and directing them into proper channels early are of first importance. High schools have sometimes attended to individual differences and rare gifts, but too many have not. Individual instruction is old but not general practice in American schools. Recently schools have developed advanced placement programs for gifted children who will go to college. Enriched programs are offered; creative writing is encouraged; science experiments are worked out, demonstrated and written up; and college-level courses are introduced into high schools.

All of these and numerous other opportunities require a well-prepared faculty that is not so overloaded with classes, committees, and reports that they cannot attend to special problems. For some unfathomable reasons the American college instructor teaches three classes a day and the high school teacher teaches five or six classes, supervises a study-hall, and directs the band or other student group. The difference between the needs of the high school senior and the college freshman is not very great.

There is a deep concern today that youth shall be better prepared to deal effectively with questions of public policy and the problems of democracy. It is altogether probable that people will be more deeply concerned with foreign policy in the future. Social studies have long been emphasized in the high school and in college. Almost one-third of the college students whose records were examined in the Thirty Schools experiment specialized in these fields, whereas the next most popular fields of English and the physical and mathematical sciences each attracted less than one-half as many students. But whereas the social studies are popular, there is great disagreement on what should be taught in this field and how it should be taught. There are still those who think that the schools should "teach the facts" and the "known truth" of history and economics, avoiding controversial questions; others who would indoctrinate the pupils in what they regard as the best answers; and a third group who doubt whether high school students can think to any purpose about such issues as the tariff, sovereignty, and the relations of capital and labor. But if young people who have been in school for twelve years, do not have the knowledge and training to deal with public questions by the age of eighteen, then it is difficult to see where and how they will be equipped to perform the duties of citizens in a democracy. This applies particularly to that large group whose schooling ends with high school graduation. The Social Studies Investigation, which was sponsored by the American Historical Association between the years of 1929 and 1933, the *Fourteenth Yearbook* (1936) of the Department of Superintendence, and a library of volumes by individual authors have all dealt with this problem. Although no final solution to the problem of teaching social studies has been found or will probably be found, it is reasonable to hope that the teaching of social studies is becoming more effective in developing political and economic understanding among high school students. This is certainly an urgent need. The high school must learn to teach democracy by democratic processes. As one phase of this task, it must establish closer contact with its local community; as another phase, it must teach its pupils to read, to handle evidence, and to think independently.

The depression of the 1930's taught us much about the sad dilemma in which youth in an industrial society find themselves in such a period. The high school of the future will give more attention to vocational guidance and to vocational education. It is not enough to provide courses that describe occupations and to supply occupational guidance through counselors. The school must provide work experience in school and in the community. It must teach working skills and attitudes, both as bases for the choice of an occupation and preparation for the pursuit of the occupation that is finally selected.

In these and other ways the high school of the future must be closely related to its community if it is to be effective in teaching citizenship, vocations, and economic cooperation. It must use the educative resources of its community more fully than it has done, and it must also aid the continuing education of the parents and other adults of its locality and serve as an effective agency for the improvement of community life. By taking advantage of these and other opportunities to serve, the high school as a still young and adaptable institution has before it the promise of extended development and usefulness.

SUMMARY

The twentieth century, dominated by the complete success of the industrial revolution, has seen many great changes in secondary schools and secondary education. More money, more people, and increased demands for skilled and professional services have caused the development of more and larger high schools. The first two decades of this century saw the rise of six movements that were of first-rate significance to secondary education.

People became aware that it was too difficult for the child to get to the city high school, and that after the child arrived it was too hard for him to get in and stay in the course. Efforts were made to bridge the gap between elementary schools and high schools, and the junior high school was created for this purpose. A large number of functions was assigned to the new school, of which the exploratory and orientation courses, attention to the individual, and guidance were probably the most important. Studies of adolescent development aided in the achievement of these aims. It does not seem that the junior high school was as great an improvement as was predicted; but generally it has not been abandoned wherever it has been established.

Vocational and educational guidance have both experienced a rapid growth since 1908. Many universities prepare high school counselors, and the larger schools are equipped to provide the kind of education that is needed to adapt pupils for their indicated careers.

— The comprehensive high school provides both preparatory and terminal courses, and, using a different classification, both liberal and vocational courses. It is the typical high school but it cannot be maintained in small communities.

Vocational education is still carried on by apprenticeship methods. Educators are attempting to raise the academic standards of the apprenice teacher and supervisor, but they meet some resistance from labor unions. The arguments of both sides of this question may have some merit.

Public school men were lacking in interest in vocational education or hostile to it. This was partly a result of the formal discipline philosophy, and the movement was delayed many years. The federal Smith-Hughes law prevented the establishment of the proposed separate vocational educational system. There are now many vocational high schools, some of which are double-purpose schools and may become comprehensive schools. Many of these great schools have grown from very modest trade and continuation schools, a remarkable development of the last forty years.

The independent schools with their variety of forms, facilities, and functions supplement the public schools at many points, but high fees put their services out of reach of the middle and low income groups. Many of these schools, such as the church-related high schools, tend to be conservative in their curriculum policy and keep their standards high. At the opposite extreme in these two respects is the life adjustment education proposed in the Prosser Resolution of 1947. Neither among educators nor in the public mind is there agreement on curricula or standards in secondary education.

QUESTIONS

1. Why are small high schools relatively ineffective, if they are, as compared with the larger ones? In what respects may the smaller schools be more effective? Is there an ideal size? And could it be realized?

2. Why did so many new departures in secondary education originate in the years between 1900 and 1920?

3. If the junior high school movement is considered as an educational experiment, what conclusions can be drawn from the results of this experiment? What new problems has this movement raised?

4. Why should the student counselor be well educated in several fields, and in which fields outside his specialty should he be educated?

5. In what ways is the definition of vocational education in the Smith-Hughes Act lacking in precision?

6. Why do state departments and labor unions disagree in matters relating to apprentice-training? What are the underlying factors behind this dispute? Compare this dispute with the disagreement in 1909 in Massachusetts between the Commission on Industrial Education and the state board.

7. Extend the comparison requested in question 6 to the struggle between conservative public school leaders and the promoters of vocational education. What conclusions do you draw from the studies suggested in questions 6 and 7?

8. Consider the pros and cons of public aid in support of church and independent schools. In dealing with this topic it should be remembered that such aid was traditional in earlier times in America and that England finds no insuperable difficulty in giving such aid.

9. Whether or not aid is given to church and independent schools, should not all schools be inspected by public agencies?

10. After reading the articles by Kingsley and Snedden cited in the following list, summarize the arguments for comprehensive and vocational high schools. Which do you favor? Why?

11. If further efforts are to be made to provide schooling for the least intelligent pupils, would it not be logical to provide increased incentives and direction to the most intelligent pupils? If so, how can this be done?

12. Unruh and Alexander in the book cited in the following list expect "widespread change" during the 1970's in American secondary schools because of the innovations that these authors describe. Do you agree? Why?

BOOKS AND PAPERS

The *School Review* was founded in 1893 by Jacob Gould Schurman and C. H. Thurber, a university president and a principal of a private secondary school, respectively. There are other secondary school magazines, and some special-interest magazines, such as *School Science and Mathematics*, that deal largely with problems of secondary education. The articles and bibliographies on secondary education in the *Encyclopedia of Educational Research* cover fifty pages and the index locates much additional material. Many journals and serials are named in the list of publications used by the *Education Index*. Few of the articles thus found are historical in intention but they become historical as soon as the ink dries on them. Some of the references listed for Chapter 8 can be used for this chapter and are not repeated in this list.

BEREDAY, GEORGE Z. F., and L. VOLPICELLI, eds., *Public Education in America*, New York, 1958.

BLAUCH, LLOYD E., *Federal Cooperation in Agricultural Extension Work and Vocational Rehabilitation*, Washington, D.C., U.S. Government Printing Office, Office of Education Bulletin, 1935, No. 15, with bibliography.

BUCK, PAUL H., *General Education in a Free Society*, Harvard University Press, 1945, commonly known as the "Harvard Report."

BURNS, J. A., and BERNARD J. KOHLBRENNER, *A History of Catholic Education in the United States*, New York, 1937.

CONANT, JAMES BRYANT, *The American High School Today*, New York, 1959; *The Comprehensive High School: A Second Report to Interested Citizens*, New York, 1967.

DONAHUE, J. L., "The Gap between the Secondary and the Elementary School," *School Review*, November 1902; and a contemporary report of professional opinion on the same subject in E. L. C. Morse, "From Grammar School to High School," *School Review*, October 1902.

EVERETT, SAMUEL, ed., *Programs for the Gifted, A Case Book in Secondary Education*, New York, 1961. Fifteenth yearbook of the John Dewey Society, in a new key.

FAY, PAUL JOHNSON, *The History of Science Teaching in American High Schools*, Unpublished Doctoral Dissertation, Ohio State University, 1930 xiv + 517 pp.

FISHER, BERENICE M., *Industrial Education: American Ideals and Institutions*, Madison, Wisconsin, 1967.

GREELY, ANDREW M., and PETER H. ROSSI, *The Education of American Catholics*, Chicago, 1966.

HANUS, PAUL H., *Adventuring in Education*, Harvard University Press, 1937. Deals with industrial education in Chapter Eleven.

INGALLS, ALBERT, "The Amateur Scientist," *Scientific American*, July 1954, on training young scientists at Milbrook School, New York State.

JONES, GALEN, *Extra-Curricular Activities in Relation to the Curriculum*, New York, Teachers College, Columbia University, 1935.

KELLER, FRANKLIN J., *The Double-Purpose High School: Closing the Gap between Vocational and Academic Preparation*, New York, 1953.

KINGSLEY, CLARENCE, "Cardinal Principles of Secondary Education," *School and Society*, pp. 19–20, July 5, 1919.

MAYS, A. B., *Concept of Vocational Education, 1845–1945*, Bureau of Educational Research Bulletin, No. 62, University of Illinois, n.d.; *Essentials of Industrial Education*, New York, 1952.

McCLUSKEY, NEIL G., ed., *Catholic Education in America: A Documentary History*, New York, 1964.

MICHAELS, WALTER C., "The Teaching of Elementary Physics," *Scientific American*, April 1958.

NEA, Commission on the Reorganization of Secondary Education, *Cardinal Principles of Secondary Education* (U.S. Bureau of Education, Bulletin No. 35, [Washington, D.C., 1918]).

NIETZ, JOHN A., *The Evolution of American Secondary School Textbooks*, Rutland, Vt., 1966.

PARKER, W. R., "Foreign Languages and Graduate Study." A paper at the meeting of the Association of American Universities, *Journal of Proceedings*, New York, 1953.

PILCH, JUDAH, ed., *A History of Jewish Education in America*, New York, 1969.

RICKOVER, HYMAN G., *Education and Freedom*, New York, 1959.

ROSENBAUM, E. P., "The Teaching of Elementary Mathematics," *Scientific American*, May 1958.

SIMON: LADY SIMON OF WYTHENSHAWE, *Three Schools or One? Secondary Education in England, Scotland, and the United States*, London, 1943, a pamphlet.

SIZER, THEODORE R., *Secondary Schools and the Turn of the Century*, New Haven, Connecticut, 1964.

SNEDDEN, DAVID, "Cardinal Principles of Secondary Education," *School and Society*, pp. 522–523, May 3, 1919.

SPIERS, E. F., *The Central Catholic High School*, Catholic University of America, 1951, a dissertation.

TOMPKINS, ELLSWORTH, *The Activity Period in Public Schools*, Washington, D.C., U.S. Government Printing Office, Office of Education, Bulletin, 1951, No. 19.

United States Office of Education, *Life Adjustment Education for Every Youth*, Washington, D.C., U.S. Government Printing Office, Office of Education, Bulletin, 1951, No. 22.

U.S. Department of Health, Education, and Welfare, Office of Education, *The Education Professions*, Washington, D.C., U.S. Government Printing Office, 1969.

UNRUH, GLENYS, and WILLIAM M. ALEXANDER, *Innovations in Secondary Education*, New York, 1970.

WATSON, FLETCHER G., "Crisis in Science Teaching," *Scientific American*, February 1954; and with others, *Critical Years Ahead in Science Teaching*, a report of a conference held at Harvard University, 1953.

Chapter 17

ADVANCES IN
HIGHER EDUCATION

For two centuries there was only one type of institution for higher education in the United States—the college. A few medical and law schools were founded, but their standards were such that their work cannot be regarded as higher education, and after 1825 a few engineering schools began to appear. After the Civil War the state universities at last came to life and the land-grant colleges were established. The latter have already been described in this book. Professional schools began to establish entrance requirements, first requiring high school graduation, then some college education, and finally the completion of a full college course.

Graduate schools, of which Johns Hopkins University was the pacemaker, became the professional schools for college teachers. Universities and colleges began to prepare teachers for the lower schools. Women's colleges and coeducation developed. Teachers' colleges and junior and community colleges, with some notable exceptions, are products of the twentieth century. Diversity among institutions became one of the characteristics of American higher education.

Diversity among functions within many of these institutions became another characteristic. The old college was a simple establishment. It taught several branches but it had no departments, no deans or other personnel officers except the president, little property, and small budgets. It was to higher education what the one-room school was to elementary education. As they developed, the universities added new colleges to the college of arts, including colleges of business, engineering, and others. Each college was organized into departments and the departments were in turn organized into areas. Each area, department, college, division, and the university as a whole acquired an administrative staff. On and off the campus the universities undertook to teach, investigate, advise, and furnish practical services to private individuals, corporations, as well as to local, state, and national governments.

No other institutions of precisely this scope and kind are found elsewhere, and a comparable diversity of functions is beginning to develop in teachers' and junior colleges, although it has not yet progressed significantly. Such diversification also seems to be a long-time trend in high schools. It is a development that is severely criticized, and some of the critics would refuse to give the title of university to the complex new institutions.

The American university is governed by a board of external trustees, who are frequently businessmen. The board president is the executive officer of the board rather than a member of the faculty as the old college president was. The board is a policy-making body that does not normally concern itself with administrative detail. It is more concerned with public opinion and is sensitive to it.

BEGINNING OF UNIVERSITIES

A brief history of higher education will give a better view of the evolution of the American type of university than a general statement could offer. The colonial colleges, which were described in Chapter 2, were small, their humanism was brittle, the teaching was formal, and although the religious life was often sincere, the religious teaching was dogmatic. Divinity was taught from the first; and from the eighteenth century onward, schools of medicine and law were attached to some colleges but were not controlled by them. This was, however, the beginning of the university as an assemblage of colleges, the name university came into use before 1800. The standards of some of the proprietary medical schools that were conducted for the profit of the professors were at times so low that men who were hardly literate were allowed to matriculate. The reasons for this are evident.

State legislatures granted college charters freely and without any test of the fitness of the recipient boards to exercise the conferred powers. Although several hundred colleges were established and more were projected prior to 1860, less than two hundred of these are still in existence today. This indicates that the college mortality was high; and it was. Most of the surviving colleges continued in the old ways, but a few older Eastern schools and a few of the state universities had begun to broaden their curricula before 1860.

After the Civil War science instruction in the colleges was increased and laboratories were established; libraries were enlarged, and their collections were made accessible to the students. The modern languages, which had been introduced earlier, were given a more prominent place; English, which had been neglected if not excluded from the curriculum was introduced; and American history, economics, and political science were taught. As the scope of instruction was broadened, the number of college departments increased and specialists were appointed to the faculties. Economics was no longer taught by a historian or sociology by a political scientist. Even these fields were subdivided until the American historian who dealt with the colonial period felt unable to teach a course on the Civil War and Reconstruction; and the professor of banking had only general ideas about the tariff or insurance.

In the late nineteenth century, college programs were sometimes expanded too rapidly for the available college resources. New types of institutions were established, as we have seen, and the standards of professional education were raised. Preprofessional courses were introduced and the attention given to liberal studies was thereby reduced. The elective system and the course-credit scheme brought into the college the idea of interchangeable parts that had been so useful in industry. Its use in education has not always been applauded.

The expansion of research and advanced study led to the organization of graduate schools with their deans, secretaries, and committees, a college within the college. The heart of the American university had begun to beat. The graduate school became a professional school, preparing university teachers and research workers. The other professional schools were gradually brought under university control. Students came to the undergraduate departments in growing numbers from private and public high schools; and money, both philanthropic and public, was provided in ever-increasing sums.

When ambitious colleges lacking the library, laboratories, and trained staff for such work began to confer masters' and doctors' degrees, a standardizing agency, the Association of American Universities, was formed about the turn of the century to recognize and maintain the quality of graduate work. Only those universities that had an adequate graduate school were admitted. Fourteen universities were members at the beginning, only three of which were state universities. Fifty years later the association had thirty-five members, a majority of them state universities.

The training of college and university instructors and investigators has been one of the chief functions of the graduate schools. The doctorate of philosophy was until recently a teaching degree, which it still is to a great extent. This advanced work has done much to raise college scholarship. Whether it has also improved college teaching is more doubtful; and it is claimed that some training in public speech, psychology, and education would help to put the beginner on the road to teaching success. The holders of doctorates disagree on this problem, but it may receive more attention as college enrollments swell and the number of young instructors grows.

Higher standards in academic fields made the improvement of professional education possible. The change spread to all professions but was particularly significant in medical instruction. A whole series of evils had grown from the fact, already noted, that the medical schools were proprietary institutions, that is, they were not controlled by the university boards but by groups of doctors who were teaching in them.

Until 1910, when the Carnegie Foundation for the Advancement of Teaching published, in what is called the Flexner Report, the results of its investigation of medical education, there was a scandalous lack of both facilities and standards in many medical colleges. State laws were lax and there were and still are no national laws governing medical school standards. As a result of the Flexner Report, the public, led by the American Medical Association and the American Public Health Association, effected the closing of the most inadequate, and sometimes even fraudulent, schools of medicine. In twenty years the number of schools was reduced from 160 to 80. Standards were raised, money and clinical means were secured, and research was promoted, until American medical education attained the high rank in the world that it now holds. A French authority, for example, has recently called the American schools of medicine "peerless" because they fuse teaching, research, and hospital care and administration instead of "fragmenting" them. He had undoubtedly seen some of the better examples; but medical education in the United States is generally considered to be in a healthy state. One frequent criticism holds that the number of physicians prepared in the United States is inadequate to meet the country's needs. Sixty years ago when the medical school standards were low there was an oversupply of doctors, but many were poorly prepared. Largely as a result of the control exercised by the American Medical Association, all three conditions have been reversed; but ways may now have to be found to provide more well-trained doctors.

COEDUCATION

A radical break with academic tradition and one in which the United States was a pioneer and has since maintained a prominent position was the provision of higher education for women, an opportunity that was quickly grasped. One hastens to say that it was not an offer made by men but mainly an achievement by the women themselves. The Middle West opened the first door to women. The declaration of Theodore Parker (1810–1860) that no New England college had in forty years favored any great reform may have been extreme, but that they long kept their doors closed against women is true.

The way was prepared by the academies; and the normal schools were already coeducational. It is, therefore, surprising that the first coeducational colleges should have been severely attacked, as they were, by Mrs. Grundy. This was the penalty inflicted upon Oberlin College, which began as a coeducational school in 1833, admitted women to its degree course in 1838, and graduated four women bachelors of arts in 1842. Antioch in 1853 was opened as a coeducational college under Horace Mann. But it was not mainly the independent colleges but the state universities and the land-grant colleges that most generously opened their doors to women students.

Out on the frontier of that time, the State University of Iowa and the University of Wisconsin admitted women to degree courses in the middle 1860's. The University of Wisconsin, under a president who was opposed to coeducation, made some attempt to institute a women's division, but when a new executive came into office the plan for coeducation was abandoned. The University of Michigan, the University of Maine, and Cornell University, half land-grant college, half endowed university, all became coeducational in the early part of the 1870's. About that time the other institutions of this class were swept into the same strong current.

State universities and land-grant colleges were young schools in need of students and lacking the large and conservative alumnal bodies of the older colleges of the East, which made no concessions to women. Meanwhile, separate women's colleges such as Elmira, Wells, Mount Holyoke, Vassar, Smith, Wellesley, and Bryn Mawr were being formed, and came in time to oppose coeducation as much as Princeton or Yale. Perhaps these are merely examples of a natural conservatism in people or of the reluctance in institutions to change a policy that has been successful.

Some of the men's colleges that refused to adopt coeducation began to create affiliated women's colleges. President Barnard of Columbia College, having discovered that college enrollments were lagging, startled his faculty by proposing that Columbia admit women. The college fathers, after a long decade, found a way out of their dilemma. In 1889, Barnard's last year as president, they created a women's college with a separate board and an independent budget. This school was made an affiliate of Columbia, and was named for the retiring president. At Harvard some professors began to give private lectures to women in the year of Barnard's first pronouncement. This became the Harvard Annex, and in 1893 was constituted Radcliffe College under a separate board. Tulane, Brown, Western Reserve, and other universities adopted similar plans. Like the land-grant colleges, the early colleges for women conducted preparatory departments because the applicants for admission were not prepared for college work.

The University of Mississippi admitted women in 1882, but in most of the Southern states, including Mississippi, separate state colleges for women were opened in towns remote from the state university. Florida, for example, had a state university for men at Gainesville and a state college for women at Tallahassee. Both of these schools have since become co-educational. The former continues to be known as the University of Florida, but the latter in the state capital has been renamed the Florida State University. Confusing nomenclature such as this is unfortunately common in the United States, both North and South. The state college for women was a Southern institution.

By slow stages, coeducation overtook some of the oldest colleges and universities. The University of Pennsylvania, step by step, admitted women to premedical work, to teachers' courses, to the graduate school (1885), and finally to all departments. Many institutions, which have kept the arts college as an exclusive men's preserve, have admitted women to other divisions, especially to the graduate school. The doors of the graduate schools were opened to women in about the following order by New York University, Brown, Yale, Harvard, Columbia, and in 1907 by Johns Hopkins. The medical school of Johns Hopkins University was coeducational from its beginning in 1893. The Woman's Medical College of Pennsylvania had been chartered as early as 1850. Today most medical and dental schools are open to women and men on equal terms. Occasionally a woman graduates in veterinary medicine or engineering, and many women graduate in law.

The old issues have not all been closed. Some still hold that since men and women, boys and girls, mingle in the family and in business, in love and in war, they should be allowed to mingle on the campus. Others argue that just for this reason the sexes should be separated in school. The economic factors favor coeducation; Catholic practice and ancient custom and tradition are against it; but then the most ancient custom is against all education for women. The arguments are no longer heard that study will impair the graces of women or that they will be unable to compete with men for college marks.

A determination of what courses are most appropriate for women is still a problem. More than ever before, women are planning twofold careers, in the home and outside of it. For outside occupations women tend to select certain professions more than others. They are active in politics, several have been ambassadors to foreign countries, and two women, Frances Perkins, and Oveta Culp Hobby have held cabinet appointments. Men, including university presidents, continue to lecture on the education of women but they do not claim to know the only true and complete answer, nor do women themselves.

UNIVERSITIES BREAKING OLD BONDS

Colleges and universities long confined their efforts to the campus teaching of academic subjects. Now they carry out research, render services to students and to the public, and on and off the campus teach many occupational and welfare subjects as well as academic ones. Many of the old bonds have been broken by the colleges and universities.

Private or independent institutions sometimes anticipated the public ones in breaking these bonds. Schools of business, for example, did not arise in state universities or land-grant colleges. The Wharton School of the University of Pennsylvania, which opened in 1881, was the first university school of business. Suggestions along this line had been made earlier by General Robert E. Lee (1807–1870) when he was president of the institution now named Washington and Lee University. Engineering education was developed at Rensselaer, Yale, and the Massachusetts Institute of Technology before the public institutions became widely active in the field; a little later all the practical studies were much cultivated in the state universities and land-grant colleges. The University of Michigan made an early beginning in engineering. These institutions, because of their close relations to the public elementary and secondary schools, were among the first to prepare teachers for those schools. It was especially in the latter half of the nineteenth century that both the universities and the public high schools broke their bonds. This coordinate development of secondary and higher public education can be explained by the connections between them, their common social environment, and their relations to the state.

The idea of extramural teaching came from mid-Victorian England. A group of young women wishing to become teachers asked an Oxford professor for help in acquiring the desired art. Like Socrates the professor disclaimed the power to teach this, but instead offered them lessons on astronomy. He thought the ladies might learn some pedagogy by observation. History does not say what the outcome of this was, but the professor's lectures became the starting point of university extension.

In the United States the movement toward extension teaching created great excitement. Melvil Dewey of the New York State Library, and Herbert B. Adams, history professor at Johns Hopkins, became leading promoters. An American Society for the Extension of University Teaching was formed (1890), and university credit for the courses was arranged. About 1890 and after, lectures were given for some years in a hundred centers, chiefly by professors from Eastern universities. Interest in this, the third notable type of adult education, declined even more rapidly than in the cases of the lyceum and the Chautauqua movement. College instruction in history or science had only a limited and temporary appeal to persons who in many cases had neither the preparation nor the time to pursue them with profit. College lecturers were not always able to gauge the difficulties of their listeners. Every new movement has to catch its second wind before it can become a lasting success. This the early extension movement was not able to do, and it practically disappeared soon after 1900.

A new era in university extension which was more vocational in nature, began in about 1906. One phase in this era was the agricultural extension aided by the Smith-Lever Act (1914). Teachers' classes were held in towns within the university orbit and classes in economics and business were taught. And the universities began to take a part in the newly rising movement of adult education. Many administrative questions arose, questions about funds, rate of pay, size of classes, professors' teaching schedules, college credit, and library and field materials.

Summer schools, now almost universal in the large universities, are little older than university extension. Agassiz conducted a summer session at Penikese in 1873. Chautauqua and Martha's Vineyard followed. Each of these programs enrolled many teachers, and some universities allowed credit for work done at Chautauqua. Many universities opened their own summer schools before 1900. The University of Chicago was opened in 1892 and adopted an all-year plan in which the summer school occupied one of the four regular quarters. This eliminated the troubles that other universities had with fractional courses, special contracts for instructors, a special administrative staff, and other irregularities. It also disposed of the difficulty found in many institutions where some departments do not open and some courses are not staffed in the summer. The quarter-plan has not been generally adopted; but even where only a part of the university is open, the summer enrollments have become large. There is no longer any question of shutting down huge university plants for one-fourth of the year.

Home study or correspondence departments are maintained by some of the largest universities. From the advertising circulars it is clear that attracting students to the campus is one of the aims of these departments. Some of these courses offer high school as well as college level work. After an examination, usually proctored by someone appointed by the university, credit may be allowed for mail courses; and a certain proportion of such credits may be used to meet college entrance or degree requirements. It is true that such courses have certain advantages, but they also have some disadvantages in comparison with courses taken in the classroom. The exclusive dependence upon books and the lack of needed books are examples of these defects. But it is a fault of the overall situation rather than of the individual courses that many students do not complete the correspondence work that they undertake.

Technical services are rendered by state and private universities. They make building surveys for city school systems, help in city planning confer and advise with industries and governments, or test the purity of city water or commercial products. Law schools offer certain limited kinds and amounts of legal advice, and accounting teachers interpret income tax laws. Sixty years ago such services were known as the "Wisconsin idea" but they have now been widely spread.

The enlarged scope of their instructional program is a mark of the difference between the early colleges and the present universities. Some professional instruction, especially in divinity, was given in the first colleges. Before 1850 several schools of science and engineering had appeared. From these simple and meager beginnings the numerous and extensive engineering courses of the present evolved. A similar proliferation has occurred in business education.

Schools of social administration prepare those who would help in dealing with poverty and crime and the other diseases of the social order, and in bringing relief to the young who have been deserted and to the aged who have been defeated. There are schools of nursing, hygiene and public health, education, physical education, and general education. The graduate schools occupies the topmost floor of the building that has displaced the early college. The old college, like the farmer with his flock of sheep, spinning wheel, and loom, produced excellent products in limited quantities. The same kind of change has overtaken both the college and the domestic industries.

We shall omit the large business and administrative features of the educational leviathan; but one of the further differences is found in the student activities. The college restrictions on student conduct have been modified. Food is plentiful, there are no more diet riots, and organized activities have been developed to fill the vacuum formed by the ending of the student feuds.

The new student activities are often educative. Even a century ago some students testified that they learned more from the exercises of the literary societies of those days than from their courses. Some activities have been listed by Stephen Leacock, an unfriendly critic of the colleges. Concerning the gay collegians, he said: "They sing, they dance, they act, they run mimic newspapers and make-believe elections." The last item should not receive too much stress. American students pay too little rather than too much attention to political issues, less than the students of many other countries. Yet political education is of primary importance in a democracy. Otherwise, Leacock's list is only the beginning of an index of student activities and leaves out even athletics, the most hotly pursued and most controversial of all student activities.

Since Leacock wrote, campus unrest and political involvement have accelerated. In 1970 student protests and strikes hit more than eighty educational institutions. Four students were killed at Kent State University in Ohio by National Guard fire, and two were killed at Jackson State College in Mississippi by the State Highway Patrol. Classes were suspended on some campuses and normal operations ceased at several institutions. A Presidential Commission on Campus Unrest, headed by William W. Scranton, former governor of Pennsylvania, recommended that college administrators more clearly define the limits of dissent and the penalties for violent and unlawful acts.

Football, the national collegiate game, has been especially troublesome. Attacks are directed against the time it consumes, the emotions it arouses, the injuries and even fatalities caused by the competitive fury and physical contacts of the players, and the moral evils that grow out of the public interest in these contests. Many attempts have been made to develop a safer game, but the complaint is heard that if football is made safe it will become tame. Great improvements have, however, been made in the rules of football.

There was a time when slugging, gouging, and other criminal violences were encouraged, when players had to be "warned" and could not be penalized for a first offense, and when team captains uniformly instructed their men "to take their warning." Conditions were also bad in the secondary schools. Bills to outlaw the game of football were introduced into state legislatures. College presidents and a President of the United States, Theodore Roosevelt, wanted the game saved and urged the adoption of uniform eligibility rules to eliminate the "bruisers" who were not genuine students. Physicians, trainers, coaches, and officials who are alert and fearless have done much, but even today few if any squads go through a season without serious injuries.

Collegiate football was saved to become a big business, a multimillion dollar industry. In no other country do universities invite temptation by engaging in a gigantic amusement enterprise. The first college football stadiums were built in the opening years of the twentieth century, and the larger ones, able to accommodate 80,000 or more shouting fans, were built after World War I. To exclude all commercialism and gambling from college football would be difficult; but by 1950 there were cases of corruption in both college football and basketball that shocked the moral sense of the nation. Scandals that will be long remembered occurred at the United States Military Academy, at the College of William and Mary where the athletic authorities were involved, and in several colleges where basketball players were convicted of "throwing" games for money. That public opinion condemned these lapses is also a part of the story.

CRITICISM OF UNIVERSITIES

The critics to be considered in this section are not the impartial investigators who usually deal with limited phases of higher education. Examples of these are E. C. Elliott and M. M. Chambers, who studied the charters, basic laws, and court decisions of the colleges and universities in a series of publications starting two decades ago. The *Encyclopedia of Educational Research* (1950) names many objective studies, some giving only the apparent facts and others containing the writers' interpretation. But the criticisms to be considered here are sweeping indictments of universities that are based upon personal philosophies and experience, and not upon research.

A prominent example of this kind of writing was furnished by Thorstein

Veblen (1857–1929), who in his *The Higher Learning in America* (1918), maintained that a university must be completely devoted to the satisfaction of intellectual curiosity. Veblen presupposes a complete, and it would seem impossible, separation of the university from business influence. J. E. Kirkpatrick (1869–1931) in *The American College and Its Rulers* (1926) also proposed to dispense with boards of trustees, which were usually composed of businessmen, and to have the faculty control the university. There are historical examples of this kind of university government. A later study by H. P. Beck, *Men Who Control Our Universities* (1947), reported the economic composition of the boards of thirty universities and showed the preponderance of businessmen on them. It may be admitted that boards composed of businessmen may be inclined toward economic and social conservatism, but at least they will not isolate the institution from social reality. The history of such boards and of the politically appointed boards needs thorough study.

We now turn to two critics whom we have accused of composing sweeping indictments based upon personal philosophies. These are Abraham Flexner (1866–1959), whose *Universities, American, English, German* appeared in 1930, and Robert M. Hutchins (1899–   ), who, in numerous addresses, collected and published in *No Friendly Voice* and *The Higher Learning in America*, both in 1936, and in a more recent volume, *The Conflict in Education in a Democratic Society* (1953), has dealt with the universities and with education in general.

Some of the criticism of universities lacks a consistent philosophical foundation. This seems to apply particularly to Flexner's strictures. Flexner's limits to what a university may do appear to be arbitrary. He rejects some activities because, although they are proper in themselves, do not belong to university work, and others because they are worthless or harmful in themselves. But the bases upon which Flexner makes these judgments are obscure. He declares that he will consider whether American universities "now discern and discharge their special functions or whether they meddle with functions that do not constitute their proper business." "Very well," the reader may reply, "but how can he tell? By what principles is this to be determined?"

Flexner, who made the highly effective report on medical education, had no doubt that it is the function of universities to transmit, and by research to increase, higher learning, and to prepare men for the advanced professions. As an undergraduate of the Johns Hopkins University in its early and greatest period, Flexner acquired high respect for science; when he writes about research he has the laboratory sciences in mind. He also lays great weight upon good teaching and names Friedrick Paulsen of the University of Berlin and Michael Foster of Cambridge University as preeminent professors, although they were not original thinkers. He does not find that originality and research are in conflict with good teaching.

Although the universities are to constantly renew the higher professions, Flexner doubts that originality, research, and good teaching can develop any of the lower vocations into professions. He opposes vocational education in universities, and he would disallow all merely technical, vocational, and popular instruction in the university. There should be no schools of business, journalism, domestic "science," or library "science." Flexner maintains this last-named exclusion in the face of the world's admiration and imitation of American library administration as it is taught in some of the most respected universities. Even engineering is to be barred, apparently because the German universities do not include it.

The school of education barely escapes a similar sentence. Flexner had himself been a successful teacher in Louisville before he became an investigator, and the German universities offered lectures on pedagogy. But he would prune the too luxuriant growths of the school of education—perhaps not a bad idea—and he ridiculed some of the efforts in educational research. The university was not to engage in any secondary school work and this interdict might also extend to campus experimental schools. Finally, no home study or off-campus course or service work was to be offered.

On university athletics, Flexner and Hutchins agree. The position of Hutchins was stated in a sentence: "The social and athletic character that large numbers of students have given the universities has done more than most things to prevent them from being universities and to debase the higher learning in America." Flexner had, in effect, said this earlier and added that only courage is needed "to place athletics where everyone perfectly well knows they belong." This is too sweeping and too optimistic. Except for professionals, few people seem to know their own minds on this question or remain of the same mind very long.

The Carnegie Foundation for the Advancement of Teaching, as a result of its investigation of college athletics in 1929, favored "not more law but a more genuine regard for existing law," honesty, and better sportsmanship. It did not, as has been thought, propose the abolition of college athletics, and it did not justify the sentence quoted from Flexner. It did say that colleges do not make sufficient effort to secure the educational results that could be derived from sports, and it severely attacked commercialism and came out in favor of intramural games. The report, which cost a great deal of money and started a nationwide discussion in newspapers and magazines, does not seem to have had any great influence.

In his condemnation of vocationalism, Hutchins is even more extreme than Flexner; and although Hutchins does not define the term he seems to oppose all vocational education. And because of this absolute disapproval, Hutchins hardly seems willing to admit professional schools into the university. It is not surprising, therefore, that he attacks teacher preparation. He wrote: "Vocationalism has suffered no more single defeat than the abolition of our School of Education [at the University of Chicago] and the creation of the University Committee on the Preparation of Teachers." This is not very different from the Ford Foundation's attempt to turn back the clock of teacher education to prenormal school days.

Hutchins accepts the research function of the university, but by this he means mainly philosophical reflection, with logic as the main instrument. He is lukewarm if not hostile to the gathering of facts. This seems to take him back to the Platonic ideas and intuition. Furthermore, Hutchins claims that research and teaching conflict with each other. Such a conflict may exist in some cases, but it is certain that this is not inevitable. Research should serve to improve teaching and often does so.

The best reply to the criticism of Flexner and Hutchins is to be found in history rather than in logic. Briefly, the relevant history is as follows: The scientific revolution began to change the American college into a university. The industrial revolution, which resulted from the scientific revolution and in turn also promoted it, caused a further transformation of the infant university. This so-called industrial revolution included a series of constituent revolts in manufacturing, transportation, and communication, and likewise in labor organization, government, family life, and many other areas. It is in this new social world that the American university is to function. Like all living institutions, it has been improvised, added to, and subtracted from, and in trying to solve its problems it has become thoroughly American. It must be judged partly by the standards and traditions of the past but not by those alone. It is following an old tradition, but is also creating a new one; and the new tradition must be judged by its results.

The ambiguity about the nature of higher education in American society is related to the conflict between the German idea and the English idea of a university. American universities borrowed both ideas without resolving the dilemma.

The German idea of a university is that of a higher institution of instruction and research in the arts and sciences and the three old professions. Applied sciences are taught in another type of institution called the *Hochschule*, literally High School, but actually an institution of university grade.

Freedom of teaching and study was a reigning idea of the German universities at the time when they influenced America. Professors were free to lecture on any subject and generally to say what they thought. There was some ostentatious German boasting about this freedom but it was never absolute. A student also was free to attend any lecture, study any subject, and migrate from one university to another in order to hear the greatest scholars in their special fields. The custom of moving from university to university was one of the admirable gifts from the Middle Ages. This student freedom was sometimes abused, leading to waste of time, but it should not be condemned without consideration of the advantages conferred by it.

A small book on *University Education* by Henry P. Tappan, who later became president of the University of Michigan, was published in 1851. It gave home-staying Americans some account of the European universities; and James Morgan Hart (1839–1916) in 1874 in his *German Universities* gave a fuller one. Hart anticipated the major premise of Flexner and Hutchins, and defined "university," as they do, in terms of his own experience and liking. Only the German are real universities, he declared, and although it required a long period of time, he eventually discovered that the German universities did not pretend to give "a so-called general education." Because Oxford and Cambridge do this, neither, Hart declared, "is a university in the true sense of the term." Specialist education is one main characteristic of the German university, he claimed correctly, and freedom is the other. On freedom he wrote this admirable sentence: "The university is a law unto itself, each professor is a law unto himself, each student revolves on his own axis and at his own rate of speed."

Many American students in those universities, beginning with George Ticknor and Edward Everett in the first quarter of the nineteenth century, became professors upon their return to the United States and influenced the institutions where they taught. A few Germans, Charles Beck and Francis Lieber, for example, who taught in American colleges may also have had some effect. But when Johns Hopkins University, organized by Daniel Coit Gilman, was opened in 1876, the country was furnished with a living example of a university on the German model. Thus was introduced and emphasized the idea of research, discovery, and the advancement of knowledge, not merely its transmission. Research, however, implies specialization. Professor Teufelsdröckh existed only in Carlyle's imagination. There is no research into things-in-general.

Although great administrative changes had occurred in the American college, the English idea of general or liberal education and character formation remained its academic base until the German influence entered. With the development of universities the idea of academic freedom, research, and specialization became prominent. Now, after a century, the English idea has regained new vigor. There is no intention of neglecting specialized research, but there is also an almost universal emphasis upon general education.

John Henry Newman (1801–1890) gave the classic statement of the English *Idea of a University*. According to Newman, knowledge may be its own end. A university may cultivate all sciences and professions, but it is "formally based" upon the liberal arts, and its primary purpose is to make men rather than scholars, surgeons, or engineers. It is this liberal knowledge that is its own end. The second end of learning should be the training of good members of society, who are "fit for the world." Both the nearer end of knowledge for its own sake, that is, for the love of it, and the further end of fitness for the world can be best attained in collegial living and the free and intimate conversation of studious youth.

Two recent critics of the American university, Jacques Barzun (1968) and Harold Taylor (1969) exemplify this conflict between the German and English ideas of a university when they accuse the university of over-emphasizing research and ignoring their teaching responsibility.

TREND TOWARD GENERAL EDUCATION

Despite similarities, general education is more than the old liberal education without the old subjects. And the old subjects, the Greek and Latin classics in translation, may be included in substance along with any others that are not by nature specialized and technical. General education is analogous to the core idea in the high schools, and like the core it may be based upon a group of associated subjects or it may try to dispense with all subjects and try to organize the work under problems.

A main purpose of general education is that of developing a body of common knowledge and understanding to draw people together in devotion to the public welfare. An effort is implied to develop college rather than university or specialized education. This movement may be traced from the period of World War I and became full-grown after World War II.

Attempts to define the trend have not been entirely satisfactory. A Columbia University committee declared that all studies that contribute to the art of living, as distinct from direct preparation for making a living, belong to general education. This distinction is certainly not new, but the implied separation of nonvocational from vocational studies would be difficult to maintain and would be undesirable. A Harvard University committee held that general education is to prepare people to live as citizens, enjoying, maintaining, and promoting a common culture. The social emphasis of this statement supplements the preceding neutral definition. Both imply the supplement of specialized and technical education.

Opposition to individualism had been building up for half a century. The introduction of the Hegelian philosophy by Harris is one piece of evidence. Hegel's conservative idealism derived its norms from the institutions and culture of society. Arnold Tompkins (1849–1905), who was thoroughly Hegelian, had a loyal following among educators. Even John Dewey from individualistic Vermont, although he discarded his early Hegelianism, maintained a strong social emphasis. From where we stand today it appears that the elective system was the belated expression of a declining individualism.

The social trend has continued. Columbia University in 1919 established a required course in contemporary civilization, and two other general courses in the humanities and in science were soon added. World War I had only recently ended and perhaps Columbia's measures were war-connected. This was certainly true of the proposal of a Columbia professor, John Erskine, who was moved by his experience in providing educational opportunities for American soldiers at Beaune, France, and by his observation of their educational deficiencies. Erskine proposed a system of universal training for peace and war, which was to be administered by the army and was to prepare men for national service, citizenship, and the art of living, as well as training for making a living. The scheme was pretentious and hardly sufficiently worked out. Few, also, would support Erskine's choice of the army as the educator of a free people. Erskine's proposal was immature, and judging from present trends, it was certainly premature.

Erskine had another general education idea, education through "great books." He gave such a course at Columbia and the plan has been followed at St. John's College, Maryland, and elsewhere, including many adult education centers. Some prominent institutions employ the idea but limit the books to be read to a small number. To read books such as Plato's *Republic*, Aristotle's *Politics*, or Locke's *Essay* at the rate of one book a week results in general distraction rather than general education. A slower pace with the preparation of essays and sufficient discussion may provide one kind of general education.

At the University of Wisconsin a widely discussed Experimental College was in operation between the years 1927 and 1932. The plan was devised by Alexander Meiklejohn (1872–1964), at one time a controversial figure as president of Amherst College. The freshman year of the Experimental College was given over to a study of ancient Greek civilization in all its phases. The sophomores then used their results to compare the Greek with the present American civilization. Only men were enrolled in this college, which was maintained in a coeducational university. They lived in collegiate style in a separate building that was reserved for them. The plan was expensive. These and other administrative features caused the university to end the experiment after five years.

The general education movement was reinforced by the scarcity of jobs and the urgency of many social problems in the great depression, by closer contacts with England, and after World War II, by the international outlook of that era. During the war, colleges were trying to foretell the future and to prepare for the "postwar world." The so-called Harvard Report was prepared at that time.

This report, entitled *General Education in a Free Society* (1945), was issued after two years of work by an interdepartmental committee of Harvard professors, and deals with both secondary and college education. It is impossible to say how much effect the report has had but it has been read; in five years, 50,000 copies of the report were sold. After an experimental period the recommended plan became a permanent program at Harvard in 1949.

The report represents an effort to interpret the words of Harvard President James Bryant Conant, that the chief concern of American education is "the infusion of the liberal and humane tradition into our entire educational system." The committee took this to mean the training of men in (1) effectively thinking, (2) communicating clearly, (3) making relevant judgments, and (4) discriminating among values. The courses and methods that they chose will fit only students of high talent who have had good formal preparation. For this reason the plan has been labeled academic.

Six courses, out of 16 required for graduation from Harvard College, are to provide general education, but not only these, one hopes. These courses take the place of the old distribution requirement instituted by President Abbott Lawrence Lowell (1856–1943) of Harvard in 1909. Three of the courses are "elementary" and must be taken in the first two years of college, and the other three come in the upper years. Within these limits they may be fitted into any schedule at the student's convenience. This avoids the block programming of most general education schemes and solves a problem that is mentioned again. In teaching and in evaluating the work of students the plan employs student essays instead of, or in addition to, quizzes and discussion. Possible topics would be: Did Joan of Arc receive a fair trial? Is Tawney's account of the rise of capitalism acceptable? and similar questions demanding both knowledge and evaluation.

The three elementary courses lie in the areas of the humanities, the social sciences, and the physical and natural sciences. There are several parallel forms of each of the courses. The three areas named are the ones most frequently included in general education in all colleges because they are less technical than statistics, languages, or physics, and because they involve the consideration of questions of values.

To fit abstract physical science into a program of general education presents difficulties that have not yet been solved. The Harvard science courses in general education seem to be about science rather than ordinary courses in science. There is a course on the principles of physics, one on the evolution of physics, another on the patterns of research; and finally there is one on the influence of technology upon civilization, which should come very close to being a social study.

A very different plan, one devised by the American Council on Education for the armed services of the United States, is called a Design for General Education. It describes problem-type courses in four areas, as follows: personal and community health, problems of social adjustments, marriage and family adjustment, and vocational orientation. We should never forget that, if they are to be functional, different plans are needed for different people. But these two examples, the Harvard Report and the American Council Design, may be taken to mark the limits at either end of the general education scale.

None of this should be taken as a criticism of necessary specialization. We have been dealing mainly with the college, but higher education in the

United States extends beyond the college level to the upper limit of regularly organized schooling. Its three upper phases include the work of (1) graduate schools, (2) professional schools, and (3) the research activities of the university staff and students. These three phases are not independent of each other.

The first American university to grant the doctor of philosophy degree for original investigation was Yale, which did so in 1861. Yale advanced to this preeminence through the work of a chemist, the second Benjamin Silliman (1816–1885), who was taught by his father, a leading scientist and teacher of that day. Harvard soon began research work, but the great leader in the field of pure graduate study was Johns Hopkins University. Today, pure and applied research, much of it subsidized by the government, is one of the major facets of most large universities.

The second of the services of universities is the preparation for practice in one of the major professions. Some of the less technical professions, as in some of the fields in teaching, nursing, or social administration, may be studied in college as major components of the four- or five-year college course. This is not true of the old professions, or of all newer ones. The professional schools of medicine, theology, and law, and some of those of education, nursing, and business administration require a college education and degree for admission. This is a rather recent development.

The Office of Education has issued a survey of about thirty leading professions; there are many more if subdivisions and specialized vocations commonly listed as single professions are included. To the schools, low and high, is committed the task of preparing those who will serve the people through expert knowledge and skill, and through public service as men and citizens. That the good architect, sailor, or farmer must also be a good man is a piece of the most ancient wisdom. That specialists should know the whole of the vocation to which their specialty belongs is a part of the same ancient insight. Those who guide higher education know that education for the professions must be based upon a sound general education. The responsibilities laid upon those who practice in the professions justify these high requirements.

PREPARATION OF TEACHERS

Courses in education have been under severe attack by university professors and promoters of liberal education, who charge that the best young people do not prepare for teaching because of the heavy load of professional courses—"methods courses." These courses, according to the critics, are "stuff," "chaff," "flummery." Such abusive terms are not creditable to those who use them or to the magazines that print them.

The states require different kinds and amounts of professional study for teachers; in many states the required subjects include psychology, methods of teaching, class and school management, and, frequently, philosophy or history of education, or educational sociology. The average total requirement in all these courses is about twenty semester-hours or one-sixth of the course requirements for a bachelor's degree. This is not excessive.

These courses are a genuine addition to a liberal education. Plato and Aristotle dealt with the philosophy of education, although some of their successors have not followed their example. The history of education is as much an element of our general culture as is the history of the church or of industry. Courses on teaching methodology involves a reexamination of the subjects to be taught, and if well-conducted, may, for the first time, open the student's eyes to the real character and meaning of his major subject. "Methods" courses are partly psychological, and psychology is an accepted subject in a liberal education. This does not include the course in class and school management or school administration, which, whether liberal or not, is of immediate practical value to the teacher.

Professors disagree on the general issue of teacher training. In its *Recommendations for the Training of Teachers of Mathematics, A Summary* (January, 1961) the Mathematical Association of America, after outlining courses in mathematics for teachers of elementary and secondary schools, lists (p. 14) five "curriculum-study courses" and adds: "Such topics," namely, the objectives and content of mathematics courses, the relative merits of different teaching procedures, proposals for change in curricula and methods, "the literature of mathematics and its teaching," and so on, "are properly taught in 'so-called' methods courses." The report adds that only those who know the subject of mathematics can be permitted to deal with the teaching of mathematics. One may admit that, as matters stand, this note of caution is a necessary one.

The young prospective teacher must also serve an internship or do student teaching. At present this adds another five semester hours or more to the preparation of the teacher. Everyone approves of student teaching; it is sometimes claimed that it is not always well-conducted, but then only a few courses are always well-taught, and well-received by all students who must take them.

The way in which the two sets of liberal courses, academic and professional, are to be related to each other is an unsettled question. Educators often prefer to have some professional work begin in the freshman year and to have it parallel the study of the major and minor courses of study throughout the college courses. Some academic people would postpone the professional training to the senior year and, if possible, to the last half of that year.

The Fund for the Advancement of Education, based on a proposal of Abraham Flexner, instituted a program to test the idea that academic and professional education should be kept separate. The view seems to be that they are, or should be, entirely different, that professional education should be purely vocational, and that there is no place in a university for vocational education.

The Fund's test consisted in setting up a program beginning in 1953 in Arkansas. Following the completion of a four-year academic education, the program adds a fifth year of actual teaching and part-time professional reading and study. In some of the participating institutions only elementary level teachers were enrolled under the plan. Of this program as a whole, I. L. Kandel has said that it is a return to the apprenticeship method of preparing teachers, and Paul Woodring in his historical appraisal of the Arkansas Program says "it failed in its primary purpose of establishing a new program of teacher education for all the teachers in the state."

This account should not lead to the conclusion that all is well in the colleges of education. They have been content to meet state requirements although some have gone beyond the minimum. In the academic or teaching fields the state requirements have often been too low. At present great efforts to raise these standards are being made.

Most states now require beginning teachers to have completed a four-year college course, which is a great improvement over the situation that existed a few decades ago. Some states with many small, rural schools will accept teachers who have only completed one, two, or three years of college work. The states discriminate among elementary, secondary, and special positions. Teaching positions are to be filled, if possible; and, if necessary, a state will issue temporary or emergency teaching certificates; the number of holders of the latter is quite large at the present time.

A considerable number of states has been raising requirements in the teaching of English, foreign languages, mathematics, science, and social studies. A good deal of this improvement was begun in 1958 and has been attributed to the effect of the Sputniks, but some states, including Pennsylvania and Connecticut, began to improve their schools earlier. Connecticut raised her requirements in all these subjects, and even doubled requirements in science and social studies. The changes made in some states in teaching requirements have been far reaching and extensive. Kentucky raised the requirements for the provisional elementary certificate to a full college course at a time (1959) when two-thirds of her teachers did not meet this standard. Georgia took the same step in 1960 although 5,000 of her teachers did not meet the new standard. No doubt the new standard applies only to those teachers who will enter the system in the future. Richer states, such as New York and California, whose standards already were high found it easiest to raise them still higher.

Teachers in public schools must hold valid certificates before they can legally draw their salaries. The requirements for certification are established by law and tend to follow the recommendation of the state department of education, which can be expected to consult teachers, school administrators, certification officials, and perhaps others before making its recommendations. Teachers' salaries cause problems. If the Congress or the state legislature increased salaries materially, the certification requirements could be raised further. In the poorer districts and states both salaries and requirements should be raised, and the requirements in the different states should be made more nearly uniform.

The Summer Institute Program of the National Science Foundation has been an important factor in improving the subject-matter competence of both high school and college teachers of biology, chemistry, mathematics, physics, and general science. The Foundation has conducted these institutes for several years; in 1959 it was able to provide stipends and travel allowances for 18,000 teachers attending its institutes for periods of from five to eight weeks. It also provided funds for study by a limited number of teachers during the regular college year.

Scientists and scholars are giving far more attention than ever before to an improvement in methods of teaching, the very subject that they have for years been criticizing as a waste of time in teachers colleges. The National Academy of Sciences education committee considered the problem of disseminating scientific knowledge among the people, and especially the best ways to present such material to students. In September, 1959, the National Academy held a conference at Woods Hole on Cape Cod, which was called to examine the psychology of learning and the process of learning, the role of intuition and experiment in thinking and learning, and cognate topics. The Academy tried to ask critical questions and to explore their ramifications. The report by Jerome S. Bruner is listed in the bibliography for this chapter.

The report cannot be discussed here but one point may be mentioned. It stressed the "structure" of science; we might say, the principles, or the meaning of fact and idea. Children are to discover the implications of what they learn. This heuristic principle is also stressed in the various experiments on the teaching of mathematics, such as that conducted at the University of Illinois and elsewhere. One of the questions concerns the kinds and amounts of practice and concrete information that children of several levels of intelligence must have before they will be able to draw specific conclusions.

ADULT EDUCATION

The two words of our subhead must not be taken literally. College and graduate students are adults extending their education; but adult education usually refers to part-time study that is not pursued for credit toward an academic degree. There is also confusion at the other end of the scale, for mere listening, viewing, or unsystematic reading should not be counted as adult education although it cannot be denied that such activities may produce changes in the opinions and information of those who engage in them. We venture an approximate definition; adult education is planned part-time study systematically pursued by persons who are at least eighteen years old. This sentence contains some undefined terms and has other deficiencies. We shall not hesitate, therefore, to add that such study is usually directed by a teacher, or leader, or planned cooperatively by a group of students.

Adult education has been carried on in America from early times, as for example, in the colonial evening schools. The nineteenth century was enlivened by at least four adult education movements. Early in the nineteenth century the education of skilled workmen was carried on in the mechanics institutes. The plan was imported from England. A few examples of these early institutes remain such as the Rochester Athenaeum. The American Lyceum of 1826 and later, and the Chautauqua, which was developed after the Civil War, were native adult education institutions. About 1890 university extension classes, following an English model, were introduced in the United States. The University of Pennsylvania and the state universities of Wisconsin, Minnesota, and California were active in this movement. William Rainey Harper (1856–1906), an active leader in the Chautauqua movement, had long been engaged in taking learning to the people; and he brought the University of Chicago, of which he was president, into the university extension movement. Economic conditions at the end of the nineteenth century and the failure of university professors to adapt their instruction to the needs and the educational level of the students caused the decline of this first form of university extension. It was soon to be revived in a more practical and less academic form.

A new era in adult education began with World War I. The Smith-Lever Act of 1914 provided farmers with instructional services that were directly useful in growing, processing, and marketing their crops. As a result, today there are county agents, home demonstration specialists, and advisers on family life, health practices, child care, and cultural activities working with farm families. Federal aid is one of the reasons for the extraordinary success of rural adult education, as it makes possible the training of the leaders in the land-grant institutions and contributes to the support of those leaders in their work.

Most people, however, no longer live on farms, so that most adult education is provided for the urban population. Some of the reasons for its popularity are the shorter work week allowing more free time, improved communications, easy access to libraries, less expensive books, and the increased proportion of older people. The percentage of the population over forty-five years old is double what it was a century ago and is still increasing. This partly leisured class accounts for some of the heavy enrollments in adult education classes. Students under forty-five must, in many cases, study to meet changes in their vocations or to prepare for new ones. Technological changes in industry is another reason for the growth of adult education, and the lack of jobs for many people during the great depression led to new forms of adult education: the Works Progress Administration, the National Youth Administration, and the Civilian Conservation Corps. Some think that the last of these should have been maintained on a permanent basis.

General organization came to adult education after World War I. Until then each form of adult organization had its own name as university extension, evening high school, literacy education, and so forth. In 1924 the NEA Department of Adult Education was formed. In the same year Frederick P. Keppel (1875–1943), the new president of the Carnegie Corporation, returned from Europe where he had been studying various forms of adult education. Two years later the American Association of Adult Education was formed and the Carnegie Corporation began and, for a quarter of a century, continued to contribute very materially to its support including its extensive publication activities. Since there was a good deal of duplication in the work of these two bodies, they were combined in 1951 to form the Adult Education Association of the United States. The AEA publishes a monthly, *Adult Leadership*, and a quarterly *Adult Education*. It has received support from the Fund for Adult Education created by the Ford Foundation. The Kellogg Foundation has also long supported the movement and maintains two Centers for Continuing Education, one at the Michigan State University and the other at the University of Georgia. Some special organizations are also involved in adult education including the National Association of County Agents, the University Extension Association, and the National Association of Public School Adult Educators.

Adult education is, to a great extent, carried on by volunteers. Lawyers teach classes on "law for the layman," and physicians deliver weekly lectures on health topics. Leaders direct discussions on the "Great Books." The number and variety of subjects undertaken are infinite. A list of the forms and areas prepared by UNESCO contains twenty-six main titles ranging from "agricultural" to "worker's education." England has had an active Workers' Education Association that maintains serious courses, many of which are literary or scientific in character. American workers' or labor adult education is more likely to deal with the problems of organized labor or is directed to the preparation of labor leaders. After World War I, a Workers' Education Bureau, modelel upon England's W. E. A., was established near New York City and for a period maintained a resident school called Brookwood College. Colleges and universities maintained summer school courses for organized labor; Bryn Mawr and the University of Wisconsin are examples. The International Ladies Garment Workers Union has long maintained an educational program for its members as have other unions.

One of the rapidly growing phases of adult education in the United States is that of the public evening school. Evening elementary and evening high schools are carried on in cities throughout the country and teach thousands to learn to read English or complete work toward a high school diploma after their children attend the day schools. University extension enrollments are also growing rapidly, but the private correspondence schools, although still large and important, seem to be losing patronage. Although the desire to learn is not universal, it is in many people inexhaustible and so, fortunately, is their capacity.

Numerous investigations into the growth, problems, scope, and health of adult education are frequently made and reported in the journals. A comparative study of adult education in Europe was made by Frederick P. Keppel, as noted above, in 1924. In 1940, Isaac L. Kandel devoted the *Educational Yearbook of the International Institute of Teachers College* ... to reports on adult education in fifteen countries, not including the Soviet Union, which could have provided an example of adult political education as indoctrination. The impression one gains from these and other studies is that of a worldwide desire for knowledge, ideas, intellectual opportunity and growth, and of haphazard efforts to understand and meet the need. We shall not quote the figures on enrollments found in books and magazines. It will be sufficient to say that at least as many persons are involved in adult education schemes in the United States as there are in all regular, full-time school and colleges from kindergarten to graduate school. But the figures are not comparable. The adult education students are involved for unequal periods, a half-year, a month, or for a few lectures or discussions. Although these statistics are suspect, the movement for adult education is vast and highly important in education and to the American people.

PUBLIC MONOPOLY OF HIGHER EDUCATION?

Uncertainty and foreboding mark the administration of higher education in our time. Higher education, seen as a national interest, is lacking in central direction and organization. State institutions compete with each other and with private colleges within their own state boundaries and beyond.

Higher educational institutions are variously enumerated, but there may be about 1800 such institutions and more if we include the junior colleges. Aside from universities and small colleges there are also state colleges formerly known as teachers colleges, technological schools, theological schools, and women's colleges, some of which are highly selective and distinguished. An interesting chapter in the history of higher education could be written on the various origins and transformations of the different institutions. Some junior colleges have become four-year colleges. Normal schools became teachers colleges, which in turn became state colleges with a diversified program of which teacher training is only a part. All colleges try for university status. To imitate one of Robert Frost's famous lines, there is something in American education that does not love a barrier.

There is a particular something that does not love the barriers of sect and class. Let us look at the record. Private elementary schools have declined under public pressure; private secondary schools have become a small fraction of all secondary schools. Private colleges and universities, however, still far outnumber the public colleges and universities, although there is a creeping tendency working in favor of increasing public education. A strong movement for public elementary schools was under way by 1850, for public secondary schools by 1890, and current enrollment figures in higher education point in the same direction.

Public higher institutions are only a small minority of all colleges and universities, but many of these are large and the tide is running in their favor. The sixty largest public institutions have almost a million students; the sixty largest private universities, including the famous ones, Columbia, Yale, Harvard, Pennsylvania, Chicago, and New York University have little more than half as many.

Another ship on the waves of time shows how the tide is running. Students in private institutions outnumber those in public ones only in the older parts of the country: New England and the eastern parts of the Middle Atlantic States. Public enrollments exceed the private in the Middle West, Southeast, and Southwest; they are three times as large as the private in the Rocky Mountain and Pacific Coast states. The rapid growth of the population of the West is to be noted. In Hawaii and Alaska, the two newest states, less than 7 per cent of the college students are in private universities.

Some private universities are in a strong intellectual and financial position. They count their endowments in large figures but endowments must be replenished constantly. The entire public has more money than the wealthiest alumni body and the richest local constituency. The states do not yet tax themselves very heavily for higher education; they may need to expand their junior college and state university systems to accommodate all the worthy students. The private colleges will also have full classrooms. At present, all colleges of value are needed.

Small colleges are in distress because the cost of educating every student is more than he pays in tuition, even though the tuition and fees have been raised to the highest practicable level. The student in the small college is likely to be poor and finds it difficult to pay college costs and the rising expenses of living away from home in a college town. Many small colleges are located in small towns where students cannot easily find part-time work to earn their way. Less than a century ago private academies were changed into public high schools in times not altogether unlike the present. A second factor in this problem is the gradual eastward advance of the junior college, which grew in the West and Southwest and is now invading states east of the Mississippi. Students may draw their own conclusions from these facts, but should not be absolute or too extreme. A slowly rising tide is running in favor of public higher education; but the private institutions will be needed for some years.

EXCHANGE OF STUDENTS

In all ages, students in pursuit of learning or adventure have traveled from university to university and country to country. Cicero and less famous young Romans studied in Greece; the wandering students of the earlier Middle Ages prepared the way for groups of students to form the "Nations" in the universities of a later period; during the Renaissance, all Europe wished to study in Italy and many did; but, with the growth of nationalist feeling, the crossing of frontiers became emotionally and politically more difficult. The Germans continued to circulate among the universities of their own lands, but the English student, once settled at Oxford or Cambridge, remained there.

In England, the early Americans could obtain a more advanced education than their country or colony afforded, and this was most especially true of those from the South where schools were few and often of poor quality. Some of those young Americans attended English public schools or one of the British universities, read law in the Middle Temple, or studied in Roman Catholic schools in Belgium or France. But soon American patriots, jealous of the success of their experiment in republican government, began to frown upon foreign study. They feared lest the young migrant should become, if not an expatriate, then, at any rate a lukewarm republican. Even in our own time a director of the Institute of International Education "decided that exchanges should be limited to students who had already secured their national education, that is, had their baccalaureate degree."

In the nineteenth century the German universities attracted foreigners, as Athens had once drawn the Romans, or Florence, Padua, and Naples the eager youth from the North. In 1810 the national university, as one may say, of Berlin was opened and other German universities also developed an extraordinary enthusiasm for the advancement of learning. For a brief period it seemed that Germany might become a democratic country. The doctor's degree from a German university soon became a mark of distinction for the young scholar returning to the United States. This migration continued for almost a century and ended with World War I.

The German Universities were not the only universities that attracted Americans in the nineteenth century. A few studied in Scotland, some in

Vienna, and a number in France. Charles Astor Bristed, who wrote a once well-known book, *Five Years at an English University*, is proof that England was not entirely overlooked; but the English universities were expensive and the degrees that they conferred were no different in title, however superior they may have been in quality, from those that could be obtained at home. But many Americans turned to Oxford when the Rhodes scholarships were made available.

Cecil Rhodes (1853–1902), who made his fortune in diamonds, established a series of scholarships at Oxford University for students from the British dominions, Germany, and the United States. Rhodes was an empire-builder who was eager to promote the union of the English-speaking peoples, to prepare young men for public service, and to promote international peace. In the nineteenth century England had become, in Bismarck's words, a "satiated nation" with a world-spanning empire. That empire Rhodes wished to preserve, but he lived to see the Boer War (1899–1902) foreshadow the growing attack against colonialism. International peace has not been attained. Perhaps the desire to draw the English-speaking peoples together has, of all of Rhodes' aims, had the greatest success.

Whatever influence the Rhodes scholarships have had in the United States must have been favorable to general education and international education. The holders of these scholarships, which became available early in the present century, have usually been graduates of an American college. The scholars in residence live the collegial life of Oxford and devote the best hours of the day to study and the rest to talk and sports. There are no paid coaches, but everybody plays intensely and without much of a gallery. Talk occurs at breakfasts, lunches, coffee-hours, and dinner at High Table. There are club meetings and debates. In all of these and other ways the American student learns what Newman meant when he made conversation between men in the same and in different fields of study a major means of education in a university.

The American student is somewhat disturbed to learn that there are no courses to be taken and that hearing lectures is not thought to be of great value. He has to do the work himself. He is assigned to a tutor who suggests topics to explore, books to read or master as the case may be, and subjects for regular essays. Everything depends upon what in the United States are called final and comprehensive examinations, which are prepared to test not only the student's knowledge but also what he can do with it. The aim is to develop the power to think, write, and work independently.

If he is sufficiently well prepared and industrious the Rhodes scholar can earn a doctorate in three years. The university year is short, only 24 weeks. The purpose of the long vacations is to allow the students time to get their work done. The students go in small groups to quiet places where there will be no teas, parties, games, or other interruptions. They are not spoon-fed and it is not possible to cram for the examinations.

Vacations leave some time for pleasure, such as travel on the continent or in Scotland. The Rhodes scholar will learn about England and its people. In term-time he will make friends with his fellow students, some of whom come from far places in the English-speaking world. It has been said that when he returns to the United States, the Rhodes scholar will be a better internationalist than he was before he left—a result that does not win universal approval in a divided world.

The influence of the Rhodes scholars is difficult to determine. No canvass of their views on general education is available, but some recent developments suggest English influence. Such are plans used in many colleges of "reading for honors" and the comprehensive examinations for graduation. The essential elements of an honors system were set out by Frank Aydelotte, (1880–1957), long president of the Association of the American Rhodes Scholars, as follows: (1) selection of the best students, (2) provision of a rigorous course of study, and (3) greatest possible freedom of work consistent with adequate supervision. Aydelotte reported in 1925 that ninety-three colleges were offering honors work. This number has probably shrunk since then.

Where honors work and comprehensive examinations are used they modify the American course-credit system. Tutorial work has been introduced into many institutions, but it also is difficult to combine with course work. Where classes are small the professor can serve as a tutor and combine the two plans as far as a single course is concerned. The scope of the Oxford tutor's work is, however, far wider. Some of the wealthier American universities have built residence halls or "houses" on the English pattern to domicile students in small groups, with a housemaster as guide, counselor, and friend. The purpose is to create the collegial living conditions and to encourage the intellectual conversation of Newman's "Idea." A book on *Comprehensive Examinations in American Colleges* (1933) by Edward S. Jones has a short section summarizing a comparison of the English and American systems by American Rhodes scholars; but apparently the term *general education* does not occur in it.

As a result of the efforts of a Rhodes Scholar, Senator J. William Fulbright, the 79th Congress in 1944 enacted Public Law 584, commonly known as the Fulbright Act. In the first twenty years of the Act, a total of about 37,000 students, teachers, investigators, and technical specialists have received Fulbright aid to enable them to continue their studies abroad. Private foundations, such as the Rockefeller, Guggenheim, and Ford foundations, also make arrangements for the exchange of educators and students. Other scholarships; such as the Woodrow Wilson and the Danford enable students to pursue graduate studies in American universities.

The eastward flow of the student migration was complemented by another moving in the opposite direction, and in the school year of 1915–1916 almost 4,000 foreign students were studying in the United States. At that time the largest numbers came from Asia and Europe. These factors have been changed by the world wars, the increased national prestige, and advances in American education. In 1961, more than 53,000 foreign students were in the United States. They came from Canada, Latin America, the Far and Near East, and the Islands of the Pacific Ocean; every quarter of the globe and a hundred countries were represented.

Upon the signing of the armistice in 1918, the Carnegie Endowment for International Peace decided to organize an Institute of International Education. The first director of the Institute was Professor Stephen P. Duggan (1870–1950), who served for thirty years. His annual reports and a book, *A Professor at Large* (1943), contain accounts of the work of the Institute in supplying information, counsel, and direct help to universities and exchange students, both those who plan to go abroad and those who hope to come into the United States. International understanding and peace, as well as the dissemination of learning, were the objectives of the Institute under Duggan.

The securing of scholarships for exchange students was one means by which the Institute hoped to promote its aims. In the United States the scholarships for incoming students were supplied from university funds, but in Europe such money was supplied by governments.

Early in its history the Institute rendered a special service to students fleeing from the Russian Revolution. A special fund was collected to place six hundred of these fugitives in American universities where they were able to complete their studies. Most of the money has been repaid and the recipients have become American citizens.

Between these "displaced" students from Russia and the ordinary foreign students there are many similarities and also great differences. The most important difference is that the students normally do not remain in America; after one or more years they return home carrying a report upon the treatment they received and the opportunities they enjoyed. They come in many cases to study engineering and other technical and professional subjects, but they do not come for formal education alone. They also want to see the United States and to experience its business, political, and domestic life. Often they come with impressions derived from American films. It is important that they become acquainted with another America.

The distribution of the foreign students has much to do with the achievement of this goal. The foreign students are distributed unevenly among many colleges, universities, and technical and vocational schools. Some of these schools have only a single foreign student, many have fifty or more, and the number of foreign students in the 12 largest American colleges and universities is about one-fourth of the whole number.

Universities with large groups of foreign students supply counselors and provide organizations and plans to welcome, house, and entertain the students and introduce them to various features of American life. Where the numbers of foreign students are small, these services are performed more informally, but not all the advantages are found in the large institutions. In the smaller schools the visitors are almost completely absorbed in the life around them. In either case they may be made to feel welcome and may be invited to homes, games, meetings, and churches. There is even a national voluntary association, the Committee on Friendly Relations Among Foreign Students, which aids in laying the foundation for real friendship between the foreign students and the American people. The committee, which publishes the annual, *Friendly Ambassadors,* was founded by John R. Mott and others, and has headquarters in New York City. Many foreign students need the opportunity to improve their use of English, and this can be provided upon either a formal basis or, without cost, upon an informal basis. Many of the foreign students are poor or at least their funds are limited, and to help them to live comfortably at moderate cost is a great service.

Good will and helpfulness form the only solid base of international education. Both the educational and the humane and social aspects of the American residence of these "unofficial ambassadors" depend upon the spirit of their school and community. This is usually admirable but there have been exceptions. The chief criticism of America, and it is often harsh, comes from Asians, Africans, and Islanders, against whom the color bar has been raised. This results in international miseducation. Tolstoi said that "the most important thing in life is for man to unite with man, and the worst thing in life is for men to go apart from one another." For a half-century now, men have been driven apart by wars and hatred. The exchange of students may do something and should be helped to do all it can do to draw mankind together in peaceful emulation.

SUMMARY

The college in the United States offers liberal or general education, and the university is a complex institution with professional and vocational colleges built around the original liberal college. Some of the professional colleges require a bachelor's degree for admission. Universities developed in the last century and especially in the later decades, when the idea of specialization and research was introduced from Germany. State and national governments do little to regulate higher education, and this leaves a wide field for private and church initiative and helps to explain the wide variety and great number of institutions. Progress in higher education has often been made through surveys and reports; one famous example is the Flexner Report in 1910 on medical education.

Coeducation and women's colleges also developed in the nineteenth century and the former was furthered by the state universities and land-grant colleges. The older schools had grown conservative and their alumni could not allow changes in alma mater. Affiliated colleges and separate colleges for women, and in the South even state colleges for women, were established. Many of the old men's colleges and some of the state colleges for women are becoming coeducational. The "best" education for women, if there is a best one, has not been discovered; this is a problem that exercises the minds of some educators.

The growth in numbers of students and the need for many kinds of preparation have caused higher education to come down from her ivory tower and into the market place. Conservatives hold up their horrified hands without avail. Courses multiply, and are given in places remote from the campus, and universities maintain hospitals, experimental farms, and service departments. Summer schools are maintained by all but a few of the large institutions and by many small ones. Student activities and especially athletics have developed to gigantic proportions, and various devices are employed to regulate student participation.

Just this expansion has been the cause of sharp criticism of universities. Some of the critics seem to favor a return to the past. Others, who may admit that there are excesses, refuse to accept the past as a criterion for the present. Although all must learn from experience, this latter group insists that universities must deal with present problems. History proves that history alone is not a safe guide. For the present, the view that universities and schools should build a new social order is no longer frequently expressed. At least the collectivist social order is not often praised; and one reason may be the assault upon freedom of teaching by legislative investigation. This is politics in education rather than the objective study of education.

There are many reasons for the renewed emphasis upon general education. Some of these are the need for a broader and sounder base for specialization, the desire to provide a greater measure of education common to all students, the effort to stress values and ideals, and the purpose to relieve the overproduction of narrow specialists. England has always placed great emphasis upon general education and may have influenced the new American emphasis that has increased since World War I. The Harvard Report outlines one type of general education but there are many others.

The thousands of students who come to the United States from other parts of the world may be taken as evidence that American universities have won widespread approval. And it is to be noted that many come to study medicine, public health, library administration, agriculture, engineering, and other vocational and technical fields. But they come also because the obstructions and destruction of war have reduced European opportunity, and because they want to see America. Whatever the reason for their coming, American colleges and universities welcome them.

QUESTIONS

1. After examining appropriate yearbooks and guides to gain a view of the many types of colleges and universities in the United States, consider the question: Why does the United States have so many and so great a variety of these institutions in comparison with France or any other selected country?
2. Why, in your opinion, has coeducation been more widely followed in the United States than elsewhere? Look up De Tocqueville for one possible lead on this question.
3. How does the university in its evolution resemble the development of the high school and how do they differ? Is it true that elementary, secondary, and higher schools are developing the same social outlook and comparable purposes?
4. Compare the educational theories implied in the Rhodes scholarships and the research fellowships awarded by the Du Pont Company.
5. Why is it difficult for people to come to universally acceptable conclusions about education, and especially difficult with respect to higher education?
6. What are the chief contributions made by higher education in America?
7. Does the large number of foreigners studying in the United States prove the excellence of American colleges and universities?
8. How small may an excellent small college be without impairing the quality of its education? How large may the large university become?
9. What materials, books, pamphlets, and the like, can you locate that would help a prospective student and his family to select a college?
10. Why is the humanistic thread in college work important? Compare the functions of collegiate and specialized vocational studies.
11. It has been said that historical movements grow out of incidents. Do you see any movements growing out of any of the recent incidents of student unrest and violence on American college campuses?
12. It has been noted that new movements do not sweep away old conditions everywhere at once. How does this generalization apply to the movement toward the introduction of Afro-American studies in American colleges?

BOOKS AND PAPERS

For current ideas and changes the *Journal of Higher Education,* the *Bulletin* of the American Association of University Professors, *School and Society,* and the Conference *Proceedings* of the Association for Higher Education, NEA, are useful. There are many books on higher education and many histories of individual colleges but no good general history of higher education in the United States. Of those mentioned, Thwing devotes too much space to the colonial period, and Earnest devotes too much space to the Ivy League colleges. Wills has prepared a useful outline but it is only that. There is nothing like the work of Paulsen on the German universities or that of D'Irsay on the French universities.

BARZUN, JACQUES, *The American University*, New York, Harper & Row, 1968.

BLAUCH, LLOYD E., ed., *Education for the Professions*, Washington, D.C., Government Printing Office, 1955; *Accreditation in Higher Education*, Washington, Government Printing Office, 1959.

BOAS, LOUISE S., *Women's Education Begins*, Wheaton College Press, 1935.

BORROWMAN, MERLE L., *The Liberal and Technical in Teacher Education*, New York, Teachers College, Columbia University, 1956.

BOWLES, FRANK H., *How to Get into College*, Revised, New York, 1959. A guide by the president of the College Examination Board; also published as a paperback.

BRICKMAN, WILLIAM W., and STANLEY LEHRER, eds., *A Century of Higher Education*, New York, McGraw Hill, 1962.

BRUBACHER, JOHN S., and WILLIS RUDY, *Higher Education in Transition, An American History, 1636–1956*, New York, 1958.

BRUNER, JEROME S., *The Process of Education*, Harvard University Press, 1960.

BUTTS, R. FREEMAN, *The College Charts Its Course*, New York, 1939.

COLE, A. C., *A Hundred Years of Mount Holyoke College*, Yale University Press, 1940.

CONANT, JAMES B., *The Education of American Teachers*, New York, McGraw-Hill, 1963.

CURTI, MERLE, and RODERICK NASH, *Philanthropy in the Shaping of American Higher Education*, Rutgers University Press, 1965.

DUGGAN, S. P., *Professor At Large*, New York, 1943.

EARNEST, ERNEST, *Academic Procession, An Informal History of the American College, 1636–1953*, Indianapolis, 1953.

ERSKINE, JOHN, *My Life as a Teacher*, Philadelphia, 1948.

FLEXNER, ABRAHAM, *Universities, American, English, German*, Oxford University Press, 1930.

FOLWELL, W. W., *University Addresses*, Minneapolis, 1909. In this address, President Folwell's inaugural delivered in 1869, the state university is ranked as the highest of the public schools.

GOODSELL, WILLYSTINE, ed., *Pioneers of Women's Education*, New York, McGraw-Hill, 1938.

GRATTAN, C. HARTLEY, *In Quest of Knowledge, A Historical Perspective on Adult Education*, New York, Association Press, [1955].

HART, A. B., "New Attack on American Universities," *Current History*, February 1931.

HAVEMANN, ERNEST, and PATRICIA SALTER WEST, *They Went to College, The College Graduate of Today*, New York, 1952.

HOFSTADTER, RICHARD, and WALTER P. METZGER, *The Development of Academic Freedom in the United States*, Columbia University Press, 1955.

JOHNSON, WALTER, and FRANCIS J. COLIGAN, *The Fulbright Program, A History*, University of Chicago Press, 1965.

JONES, E. S., *Comprehensive Examinations*, New York, 1933.

KIRKPATRICK, J. E., *The American College and Its Rulers*, New York, 1926.

KNIGHT, E. W., *Fifty Years of American Education*, New York, 1952.

KOTSCHNIG, WALTER, *Unemployment in the Learned Professions*, London, 1937.

MORISON, S. E., *Founding of Harvard College*, Harvard University Press, 1935; *Harvard College in the Seventeenth Century*, ibid., 1936; and ed., *Development of Harvard University, 1869–1929*, ibid., 1930.

NORTON-TAYLOR, DUNCAN, "The Business Schools: Pass or Flunk?" *Fortune*, June 1954.

PENTONY, DEVERE, ROBERT SMITH, and RICHARD AXEN, *Unfinished Rebellions*, San Francisco, California, Jossey-Bass, Inc., 1971. (Issues underlying campus unrest at San Francisco State College.)

RUDOLPH, FREDERICK, *The American College and University, A History*, New York, Knopf, 1962.

SCHMIDT, GEORGE P., *The Liberal Arts College, A Chapter in American Cultural History*, Rutgers University Press, 1957.

SELDEN, WILLIAM K., *Accreditation, A Struggle over Standards in Higher Education*, New York, 1960.

SINCLAIR, UPTON, *The Goose-Step*, Pasadena, California, 1923.

STICKLER, W. H., ed., *Organization and Administration of General Education*, Dubuque, Iowa, 1951.

STORR, RICHARD J., *The Beginnings of Graduate Education in America*, University of Chicago Press, 1953.

TAPPAN, H. P., *University Education*, New York, 1851.

TAYLOR, HAROLD, *Students without Teachers, The Crisis in the University*, New York, McGraw-Hill, 1969.

THOMAS, RUSSEL, *The Search for A Common Learning, General Education, 1800–1960*, New York, McGraw-Hill, 1962.

THWING, C. F., *History of Higher Education in America*, New York, 1906; *The American and German University*, New York, 1928.

VEYSEY, LAURENCE R., *The Emergence of the American University*, University of Chicago Press, 1965.

WECHSLER, JAMES, *Revolt on the Campus*, New York, 1935.

WESTLEY, WILLIAM A., and NATHAN B. EPSTEIN, *Silent Majority*, San Francisco, Jossey-Bass, Inc., 1969.

WILLS, E. V., *Growth of American Higher Education*, Philadelphia, 1936.

WOODRING, PAUL, *Investment in Innovation: An Historical Appraisal of the Fund for the Advancement of Education*, Boston, Little, Brown and Company, 1970.

Chapter 18

GOVERNMENT
AND EDUCATION

Like their English ancestors, the American people originally regarded education as a proper function of home and church and not of government, either federal or state. Gradually, however, in the period preceding the Civil War, after attempting to extend education to larger numbers through private institutions and philanthropic agencies, the American people began to recognize education as a proper function of local government and to a lesser extent of state government. This chapter traces this developing awareness of education as a legitimate function of government, and of the many attempts to differentiate the responsibilities for education of the various levels of government (local, state, national, and international) as well as of the different branches of government (legislative, executive, and judicial).

It is not always easy to classify American schools because there are many varieties and the differences among them are not always seen by the untrained eye. One may identify a number of levels from the kindergarten to the professional schools and research institutes; there are liberal, technical, professional, and vocational schools of many types; schools for both sexes or for only one; for all races or for one; public schools that may be municipal, state, or national in scope and control; and nonpublic (private) schools of most of the varieties mentioned. Finally, the preceding classification includes overlaps and other logical defects.

Our basic differentiation in this chapter is that between public and nonpublic schools. The Constitution guarantees to individuals and associations the right to maintain and patronize nonpublic schools, either parochial or independent. In some countries the latter are called free schools, that is, free from government control. The Catholic church has many schools, the Lutherans have some, and other denominations, a few; but the movement for church-connected education is growing. Some of the old and famous private secondary schools are church schools and some have no such connection. Many private schools offer services and opportunities that are seldom or never found in the public schools. All the church schools provide religious training that public schools are not allowed to give.

Church and other private or independent schools are not tax-supported, but in other respects they are not far removed from the public schools. They prepare citizens; they prepare their pupils for life in the United States; in their methods and curricula they do not greatly differ from public school practices. Pupils transfer from one type of school to the other without great difficulty.

After World War I an unsuccessful effort was made in Oregon to abolish all private elementary schools. Had it succeeded the prohibition might have been extended to all private education. The Supreme Court in the Oregon case held that this would have been a denial of the right of parents to direct the education of their children; it would also have been an interference with one of the freedoms inherent in real democracy. A democratic government may, however, set up standards that apply to all schools on matters of sanitation, morals, and civic instruction; and the states should do this more effectively than they do.

Public education began in colonial times. During the struggle for independence, the states included provisions on education in their new constitutions and began to enact laws on education. The people in the states took an active part in promoting public schools. Under the Articles of Confederation the general government adopted the ordinances of 1785 and 1787 in support of township schools and in order to promote "religion, morality, and knowledge." Slowly but unmistakably the cooperation among the people in the districts, the states, and the government in Washington has tended toward the development of a local-state-federal public school system. The student should have a copy of the national Constitution at hand in reading the following section.

EDUCATION AND THE CONSTITUTION

This section is not called "Education *in* the Constitution" because the Constitution does not mention schools or education. This does not mean that no position is taken on the subject of education. The people have established the public schools and direct and maintain them in accordance with state and federal laws enacted by their representatives and with the decisions of the Supreme Court. We inquire how a people of various opinions, each a citizen not only of the nation but also of one of the fifty states has established, maintains, and directs its schools; and, incidentally, what is the nature of the instrument that they have created.

All of the public institutions in the United States, including those developed by the states, are agencies of the people; all public officers are agents and representatives of the people. Although the people are the sole source of governmental powers, these are variously distributed and assigned by the federal and state constitutions. In making the fundamental distribution of powers, the Constitution of the United States says: "The powers not delegated to the United States, nor prohibited to the States, are reserved to the States, respectively, or to the people" (Amendment X). Since no educational powers are overtly delegated to the United States, this amendment reserves the power to educate "to the States, respectively, or to the people." This may have been one of the aims of the authors of this language; we do not know for certain that it was. The federal government has, however, acquired power to influence education in the states, by virtue of a broad construction of the federal Constitution.

Other provisions of the Constitution may seem to affect education. The Tenth Amendment is supplemental to Article I, Sections 8, 9, and 10, which deal, respectively, with the "powers granted to Congress," the "powers denied to the Federal Government," and the "powers denied to the State Governments." There is no direct reference to education in these sections but also no word denying the government the power to promote education or to provide for schools. The government had already begun and continues to do both as we shall show.

Congress is empowered by Section 8, to "provide for the common defense and general welfare of the United States," but the context does not suggest that, to the minds of the authors, education had any particular relation to either defense or welfare. In the twentieth century this relation is seen to be direct and vital. The National Defense Education Act is based upon this section.

A closer approach to an educational implication may be found in a later clause of Section 8, which grants to Congress "the power . . . to promote the progress of science and the arts," by means of patents and copyrights; but again there is no indication that the Convention considered the relation between school education and progress in science and the arts. Today, most significant inventions are not products of the shops of mechanics, but rather of the laboratories of research scientists. The implements of war and diplomacy, as the National Defense Education Act of 1958 implies, are fashioned by those who have an advanced education.

One further provision of the Constitution may be cited as having a possible application to the relation between the government and education. Article IV, Section 4 provides: "The United States shall guarantee to every State in this Union a republican form of government . . ." The context of this language indicates that this is intended as an assurance against invasion or subversion by a foreign power; but it could also be applied to subversion and perversion of a state government through the dictatorial conduct of a governor and a compliant state legislature. It may appear, and many have believed, that republican government without free and general education would be impossible. Why the Constitution is silent on education and how the federal government has come to the aid of education in the states are topics to be kept in mind in reading the following section; but the major topic is education in and by the states.

When the Constitution was being prepared, the people feared tyranny as would be exercised by a strong government far more than they feared anarchy under a weak one. The Convention, composed of practical men of affairs and skillful dialecticians, wisely undertook the framing of a federal government that was stronger than that under the Articles of Confederation, but not so powerful that the people in the states would reject the Constitution. At the Convention, education would have been controversial in at least two ways: many states had included articles on education in their constitutions, and thereby, to a certain extent, preempted the field; and some churches maintained their own schools and the relation of religion to the government was a delicate subject. Under these circumstances, the new Constitution guaranteed the freedom of religion and made no mention of education. Even a hint that the federal government might favor one kind of school over others would have been resented.

Two years before the drafting of the Constitution, the Congress of the Confederation had passed the Ordinance of 1785, which provided for a survey of the western lands that were recently ceded to the United States, and initiated the sixteenth-section grants of land for the support of schools, thereby recognizing the townships as school districts. In 1787 the same Congress granted two townships to the Ohio Company for a university, "to be applied to the intended object by the state." The institution thus endowed is Ohio University at Athens. In the same year the Congress declared through the Northwest Ordinance that "schools and the means of education shall forever be encouraged." Only a permanent institution such as a state could honor that "forever"; and to "encourage" meant, then more often than it does now, to give financial support especially if, as here, the government was called upon to do so. Through these actions the United States, the states, and the townships were involved in educational functions and duties. The pattern set here was continued and school and university land grants were made regulaarly as new states were formed out of the public domain.

During those years an unsuccessful effort, renewed more than once, was made to create a national university. The Congress established a number of national schools in various parts of the country and could have established a national university in Washington or elsewhere. The fear of federal aid to education is a later development.

Educational institutions and education are not mentioned in the Constitution. The national government, however, can and does promote education in various ways. Congress may provide for the general welfare or the common defense (Article I, Section 8) by encouraging education. It may also aid schools by exercising the implied powers that grow out of powers expressly granted by the Constitution. The doctrine of implied powers was expounded by Chief Justice John Marshall in *McCullough v. Maryland*. Using either the general welfare clause or the doctrine of implied powers, the government may, can, and does appropriate money to the states for educational purposes; it may do so if its action does not interfere with the powers reserved to the states.

Congress has made and does make such appropriations, releasing large sums for improvements in the teaching of various vocational subjects and for further research in these fields. The Morrill and Smith-Hughes Acts, to which we shall return, are examples of such legislation. Educational purposes are also served by aid to vocational rehabilitation, and to school lunch and school milk programs, and by the distribution to schools of surplus federal property such as microscopes.

Other policies are related to the appropriation of federal funds to the states for use in education. One principle that has gained fairly general acceptance only within the present century is the doctrine that federal money appropriated for use in the elementary and high schools shall be administered by the state board of education rather than by federal agencies. This applies particularly to vocational education funds. Complementary to this is the approval given by the White House Conference on Education (1956) to the view that the states may be required to give an accounting of the use made of federal appropriations, and that this requirement does not constitute interference in a state educational program. The purpose of this accounting is to prevent the misapplication or inequitable distribution of federal funds. This is an opinion and is not the law.

THE STATES AND PUBLIC SCHOOLS

The states have each adopted a state constitution with provisions on education and, through their legislatures, have secured the enactment of school laws in conformity with the constitution. Schools controlled by a state government or any of its agencies are called public schools. The central state educational agency is the state education department. In most states this department is made up of a state board, a chief state school officer, and a large staff of technically skilled persons who deal with the specialized problems of school finances, child accounting, or teacher qualifications. The powers of the education department are delegated and are usually extensive but not destructive of district initiative. The education department carries out the distribution of state and federal funds to support the schools, to supply school lunches, to improve education, and to supplement the funds of the poorest school districts.

In 1942 the Council of Chief State School Officers, a private association, undertook a study of the proper functions of the state education department and its relations to other governmental agencies. The council came out in favor of a small board of lay persons who were chosen for long staggered terms without regard to political parties. The members of the board were to serve, without salary, as a policy-making body and were to select a "professionally qualified person" as chief state school officer. Another important conclusion was that the members of the board were to be elected by the people to represent them.

Many political scientists hold that education should be a function of the politically chosen state government coordinate with the state constabulary or the highway department. The judicial department might seem to offer some embarrassment to the political science theory, for judges are supposed to be free from political entanglement. But in spite of this anomaly, many political scientists continue to hold that, in a democracy, education should be part of the "democratic process" and that to separate it from other parts interferes with proper administration. They would have the governor appoint the chief state school officer to serve at the governor's pleasure.

Educators object to this procedure because it would lead to political control of the schools. It has been tried but only four states now permit the governor to appoint the state school head. Perhaps the answer to the political scientists' argument is that there are many checks and balances and many blocks in the American governmental system, some the result of historical circumstance, and others inserted on purpose; and also that most people hold that the danger of party favoritism, demagoguery, and indoctrination in the schools can be best avoided by nonpartisan control and that this is more important than consistency in a political theory.

The 51 separate school systems of the states and the district of Columbia are similar in form but differ in many matters of great substance. Some of the differences are of national and even international significance. Control of the schools in some states is much more highly centralized than in others, and academic standards vary from state to state as well as within a given state. The states differ in their institutions: for example, the public junior college is widely distributed in California and other states, but is less often found in the East. The junior college adds two years to the period of free public education. Because it is a local school the expenses of the students are relatively low. The great pressure to get into college may lead the eastern states to establish new junior colleges.

Greater uniformity in institutions and standards throughout the country would be desirable. This might require the redistricting of the states in order to enable them to assign to each school the number of children and the amount of tax support needed for the efficient and economical operation of the schools. Today, pupils who are educated or largely uneducated in any state have free access to education in any other state because they are citizens of the United States.

School districts vary in population and wealth from the greatest cities to small patches of land with a one-room school, or in some cases, strange though it seems, without any school at all. The local school districts are not without powers. The state permits each district to elect a school board that selects the superintendent and teachers and, under state law, operates the schools. When the district is too small, the district's schools become unnecessarily expensive, the curriculum too narrow, and the local people may become meddlesome. Small districts may lack leadership. Nearly all states have a number of small districts, and in the most rural states most districts may be undersized.

School district lines do not always conform to the boundaries of political units, and the functions of the districts vary. Some districts are attendance areas but not taxing areas. Each high school district may contain several elementary school districts; supervising districts may extend over several kinds of units.

Both efficiency and economy require a reduction in the number of school districts. This has been known from the beginning of public education, but the public is either apathetic or hostile to the idea; yet progress has been made. In 1900 the United States had about 150,000 school districts. The National School District Reorganization Study helped point the way, and, as we have seen, by 1957 the number had been reduced by more than two-thirds to about 45,000, largely as a result of state action.

Further reduction in the number of school districts is needed but the people in the small districts will not lead. The states have made the districts, or at least have given them legal status, and history shows that the states must consolidate them. England went through such a surgical operation. As a standard for the size of a school district, the English law of 1944 took the population, resources and area that are able to provide a complete system of elementary, secondary, and vocational education at a reasonable cost.

It has been calculated that, to be operable at reasonable cost, a complete system would need at least 2,000 pupils and one of 3,000 would be preferable. But in 1957 only 2,000 districts had at least 3,000 pupils, and only 6,000 had 1,200 pupils or more; that is, 39,000 of the 45,000 districts had fewer than 1,200 pupils.

We must not miss the point that this is a historical question. There was a time when a knowledge of reading and simple arithmetic was thought to be sufficient for the ordinary boy. As the curriculum expanded the school had to be graded, and classes with only two or three pupils in the upper grades made teaching expensive. The high school and vocational education increased costs at a rapid rate and to a high level. The junior college took another step in this process. Before the proper size and wealth of a school district can be determined, the curriculum, equipment, and methods must be decided upon. Future needs may require larger districts; but there may also be an upper limit to the proper size of a district.

The districts have powers that have not been mentioned. They may issue bonds voted by the people, levy school taxes, employ architects, locate and erect buildings, engage school nurses and physicians, and may, in general, do whatever is necessary and reasonable. State law puts a "floor" under such items as salaries, subjects taught, length of terms, and finances, but will allow great freedom above the minimal demands. In legal disputes over the conduct of schools the courts have generally followed their own concept of what is "reasonable." The intricate and extensive subject of state school law is discussed at length in one or two references listed in the bibliography.

Local freedom will not always remain at its present pitch. The cold war and international competition in many fields are placing higher values upon speaking skills, rather than mere reading knowledge, in modern languages, and upon science and technology. High schools will urge a wider election of these subjects and will require higher levels of achievements in them. A recent study showed that, in many states, more than half of the subjects required for graduation from high school are electives. Some states are taking away the charters of the weakest high schools and are transporting the pupils from these schools to better schools.

State authority over the school districts is absolute. The districts are created and may be abolished by the state. Each state controls many other features of its school system including the preparation and certification of public school teachers. In other areas, state authority is restricted by decisions of the Supreme Court. One of these decisions is concerned with racial segregation in the schools and is the subject of the next section.

RACIAL SEGREGATION

The education of black children no longer concerns black children only; the questions reach out into matters of citizenship, national defense, and international relations with those who are using the issue as a stick with which to beat the United States. The space to treat these topics is limited but they should be kept in mind.

As applied to the American black, the word *race* carries the heavy load of centuries of slavery and second-class citizenship. Without proper education or opportunity to develop his abilities, the black was believed inferior by nature; the early group tests of intelligence were used to "prove" this. We now know that the scores strongly reflect the experience and schooling of those who were tested. The treatment for slow-learners of the two peoples showed a strong contrast. White children who made low scores were often placed under the care of skillful teachers, specially trained for their work and provided with expensive equipment; not so for the black children.

A general outline of the education of blacks is presented in Chapter 9. After Reconstruction, 17 states demanded the separation of white and black children in school. The laws of four other states permitted the districts to decide this question.

The Supreme Court, looking for an example to illustrate a point, gave its blessing to the practice of segregation in schools in the case of *Plessy v. Ferguson,* decided in 1896. The question presented to the court was whether the Louisiana law requiring blacks to ride in special railroad cars violated the civil rights of those so compelled. The Court decided against the plaintiff and in one of its "dicta" declared that "separate and equal" facilities did "not necessarily imply the inferiority of either race"; the high court added that "separate schools for white and colored children" were the most common instance of this. Apparently the Court had not learned that white passengers did not ordinarily ride in "Jim Crow cars" nor did they send their children to black schools. In a dissenting opinion, Justice John Marshall Harlan declared that "the Constitution is color-blind," a statement that has become historic.

The Berea College case came about a decade after *Plessy v. Ferguson.* Berea College in Kentucky taught both white and black students in the same classes since the date of its inception in 1855. A state law of 1904 forbade this practice, and in 1908 the Supreme Court affirmed the right of the State of Kentucky to insist upon segregation in its schools. When the Kentucky law was later amended in 1950 to permit segregation, Berea returned to its original unsegregated teaching.

In the South, under segregation, separate schools for black have generally not been equal to those for white children. Some of the facts are found in Chapter 9. After the blacks were completely deprived of political power they could no longer help themselves, and many white people were unwilling to help them. Even after the Peabody, Slater, Jeanes, Rosenwald, and other benefactions were applied, a wide gap remained between the two sets of schools. In 1920 only 15 out of every hundred black children progressed beyond the fifth grade; and only 1 per cent of the 2,500,000 children enrolled in high school at that time were blacks. Black teachers were poorly paid; many of them still are. That the blacks were poorly prepared for their work was not at all their own fault. Progress has been achieved but it is not apparent that the black schools are gaining on the white schools.

Although not in accord with the facts, the doctrine of "separate and equal" was accepted in law until 1935. As in the earlier period, the areas of higher and professional education in the border states were most vulnerable. Under the skillful direction of the National Association for the Advancement of Colored People (N.A.A.C.P.), the attack was first directed against the exclusion of blacks from the Law School of the University of Maryland at Baltimore. In 1935, Donald Murray, black, applied for admission to that school and his application was rejected but he was offered the tuition costs at an out-of-state law school. He argued that this was discriminatory because it involved a great increase in his other expenses of obtaining a legal education. The state court of appeals upheld his contention and ordered him to be admitted to the Maryland Law School from which he was duly graduated.

A similar case arose in Missouri in 1938. The state law school refused to admit a black, Lloyd Gaines, and his complaint was taken to the United States Supreme Court, which reversed the decision of the state court, rejected the legal basis for out-of-state scholarships, and demanded equal treatment for all applicants. The high Court continued to honor its "separate and equal" doctrine of 1896 but began to indicate that it would demand equality. To the South these cases, and others in Oklahoma and Texas, were the handwriting on the wall. The states of that section began to spend larger proportions of their income on schools for blacks. In some locations these schools, because they were newer, came to be even better than the white schools. It was, however, too late; Southern states would have to spend unprecedented percentages of their income to build and maintain everywhere, especially in the rural counties, two parallel systems of equal quality.

Meanwhile, the undergraduate colleges of the state universities had not yet been required to admit black students. The Negro land-grant colleges were supposed to provide "equal" facilities for them, but it is clear that these institutions have been starved from the first. They are inferior to the white land-grant colleges and even more so to the state universities in terms of their libraries, curricula, equipment and buildings, capital assets, faculties, and the standing of their alumni. The educational opportunities that they can offer are not equal to those of the corresponding white institutions.

In 1948 nine states signed an agreement to consider the establishment of regional university-centers for professional education including the fields of medicine and dentistry. These centers were to admit students of both races from the contracting states. More states accepted the plan and it was carried out on a permanent basis under the Southern Regional Educational Board. This agency and the entire plan were challenged in 1949 when a black girl was refused admission to the School of Nursing in the University of Maryland because under the regional plan she could enter the Meharry Medical College for Negroes in Nashville, Tennessee. As in the Murray case the Maryland court of appeals ordered her admission to the University of Maryland.

Other state universities began to admit black undergraduates, and by

1953 only five states were holding out: South Carolina, Georgia, Florida, Alabama, and Mississippi. In the winter of 1960–1961, the University of Georgia admitted two blacks. The only large contingents of students of both races are found in border states including West Virginia and Tennessee, which have modified their segregation laws. Many private colleges have been desegregated and many former all-black colleges now admit white students.

Because of pressure from its members, but somewhat against the judgment of its lawyers, the N.A.A.C.P. in 1952 brought five cases from different states and the District of Columbia to the Supreme Court asking for the desegregation of public elementary and high schools. On May 17, 1954, the Court in the landmark case of *Brown v. Board of Education of Topeka, Kansas,* announced its now historic decision, unanimously declaring that segregation of the races in public education at any level is unconstitutional. The opinion, read by Chief Justice Earl Warren, included a synopsis of the reasoning of the tribunal.

The Court explained that only by considering public education in its full development and present importance in American life was it possible to determine whether segregation "deprives these plaintiffs of the equal protection of the laws." In the judgment of the Court: "Today, education is perhaps the most important function of state and local governments. . . . It is required in the performance of the most basic public responsibilities, even service in the armed forces. It is the very foundation of good citizenship." Even if the grounds, buildings, books, and teachers were equal, segregation would still have a bad effect because it is "interpreted as denoting the inferiority of the Negro group." The Court held the opposite view in *Plessy v. Ferguson.*

Finally, the Court said in 1954: "We conclude that in the field of education the doctrine of 'separate but equal' has no place. Separate educational facilities are inherently unequal . . . the plaintiffs and others similarly situated . . . are . . . deprived of the equal protection of the laws guaranteed by the Fourteenth Amendment."

For the South, and some localities in the North, the Brown decision marks an end of the epoch, and a new era has begun. The decision promises the ultimate disappearance of the parallel educational systems that have separated the races and overburdened the taxpayers. To many, both black and white, it seems an application of simple democracy; to others, an interference with state rights.

The claim has been made that if desegregation had been pressed in 1954 there would have been little resistance. It is impossible to give a conclusive verdict on this "if," and the other "ifs," of history. But the South had a year of grace to think things over, to form White Citizens Councils, to conduct political campaigns based upon a policy of massive resistance, to bring in "rabble rousers," and in some instances to help local elements defy the Court. At the end of the year, in 1955, the Supreme Court asked only that the states and districts should proceed to desegregate their public schools with "all deliberate speed."

The riots of 1957 against the admission of blacks to the high schools of Little Rock, Arkansas, were noted everywhere. The high schools of that city were closed in 1958–1959, but were reopened in the following year. In the school year of 1960–1961, 11 blacks were attending the high schools without any disturbance. In the election of 1960, Arkansas voted three to one against an amendment to its Constitution that would have abolished the public schools to avoid desegregation.

Desegregation, interrupted by the events in Little Rock and elsewhere has proceeded. It began first, and proceeded most rapidly, in the border-state counties, which had few blacks, and in large cities in the same areas. Louisville, Wilmington, Baltimore, and Washington set good examples. By 1958, over one-fourth, or 764, of the almost 2,900 school districts in the South, which enroll children of both races had desegregated some of their schools. This does not mean that all of the 764 districts in question were fully desegregated, but only that each had some mixed schools within its territory. In 1958–1959, for example, some black pupils were admitted without incident into white schools in Alexandria, Virginia, but the state as a whole made no concessions. In the fall of 1960 all of the 21 public schools of Prince Edward County, Virginia, in which there were 3,200 school children, were closed for the second year in order to avoid compliance with a court order to desegregate. White people maintained classes for which they paid tuition in churches, homes, and public buildings. Some black children received aid from the Society of Friends and other groups to attend schools outside the county. Those children of either race without money or friends received no schooling. Some leaders in the county hoped to make the present arrangement permanent, taking the county back to the conditions of 1860 and earlier when families provided the educational opportunities for their own children and those without means did without schooling.

These are only examples of the many schemes and devices intended to evade the order of the Supreme Court. The federal courts have become increasingly critical of such schemes. However, it was not until May 1968 that the Supreme Court itself lost patience with the slow pace of desegregation, and in a major ruling demanded immediate abolition of separate school systems in Mississippi.

The degree of school integration required by the Constitution has been a major source of controversy. As late as 1970 President Richard Nixon interpreted the constitutional mandate to require only the elimination of segregation that exists *de jure*, that is, by law or manipulation of public authorities; segregation that exists *de facto*, as a result of housing patterns, whereas undesirable, he held does not violate the Constitution. In addition, the President favored that desegregation be effected at the local level rather than be imposed from Washington, and that primary consideration be given to preserving the ideal of neighborhood schools. He further opposed busing a child out of his own neighborhood to foster integration.

However, in various integration plans Federal District Judges have ordered busing, redrawing school districts, establishing white-to-black ratios, and other devices to achieve integration. One such plan concerning the schools of the Charlotte and Mecklenburg area of North Carolina reached the Supreme Court. In a landmark unanimous decision of April 20, 1971, written by Chief Justice Warren Burger (President Nixon's appointee to the Court), the Court ruled that student busing, flexible quotas, and other devices are legitimate tools for federal courts to order toward the elimination of *de jure* segregation. The decision did not affect segregation that exists *de facto*.

SUPREME COURT DECISIONS

Of all recent federal dealings with education, those of the judicial department have received the greatest attention. This is in part a result of the *Brown* decision on school segregation, and of decisions in other cases in which the Court has been heatedly accused of unconstitutional intervention in state educational affairs. The Court decided at least forty educational cases in the first half of the twentieth century as compared with only nine in the entire nineteenth century. It should be recalled that we have mentioned a number of education cases dating back to 1908 when Berea College was enjoined from teaching black and white students in the same school. Frequently, the decisions of the Supreme Court have turned upon the interpretation of the Fourteenth Amendment and of the First Amendment as applied to the states by the Fourteenth.

Laws to Americanize the recent immigrants were sometimes connected with teachers' loyalty laws. Like the loyalty laws, the immigration laws were intended to repress German Kultur and Communism and to promote national unity. The teaching of English and the prohibition of modern foreign languages, particularly German, were chosen as means. Between 1917 and 1921, 31 states passed laws that contained one or more of the following propositions: all schools to be conducted in English, certainly a salutary proposal; no German to be taught in public elementary or, in some states, in any elementary schools; no modern foreign languages to be taught in one or either type of elementary schools. After 1921 still other states joined the group.

This type of legislation provoked immediate opposition. Attempts to have the laws declared unconstitutional by state courts met with no success. In 1923 the matter was adjudicated by the Supreme Court in *Meyer v.*

Nebraska, in which the Court held that the Nebraska law, and by extension similar laws, invaded the liberty guaranteed by the Fourteenth Amendment. The mere knowledge of German, the Court said, is not harmful, and the right to teach that language is "within the liberty of the Amendment."

Many of the cases deal essentially with civil rights and only incidentally with education, and this has troubled the Court. The Court has shown reluctance, on more than one occasion, to interfere with the state management of schools. This can be understood for some decisions are restrictive: they limit what the state law may require of the public schools and their boards, officers, and pupils. The decisions in the segregation cases of 1954, and in *Meyer v. Nebraska,* and the Oregon case are of this character. All three turn on the Fourteenth Amendment, and the decisions in each case place restrictions upon state law and practice. The student should have the language of the First Amendment and the first paragraph of the Fourteenth clearly in mind and a copy of the Constitution at hand for reference.

In the decisions of the Nebraska, Oregon, and many other cases, the Supreme Court makes it clear that the general power of the states to legislate for the public schools is not questioned. The public schools of each state are created by the people acting through the legislature of the state. State laws on schools are numerous and deal with almost every conceivable kind of educational question. As interpreted by the state courts they are authoritative. Each state has its own school system and it is, in each instance, quite independent of the school systems in other states. Only when a state law or court action seems to conflict with federal law are cases under state law carried to the United States Supreme Court. In the cases cited, the Supreme Court ruled that school authorities, parents, and pupils have powers and rights that the state is not permitted to invade. It should be noted that the laws that were declared unconstitutional had been enacted in a time of grave social unrest resulting from World War I.

A Tennessee law of the same era similarly illustrates the general fact that in periods of widespread alarm, state legislatures are more likely than the Congress to enact extreme and even absurd legislation. The Tennessee law in question led to what is known as the Scopes Case or, in disrespect, the "monkey-trial," one of the most widely known education cases in American history. The state court decision was not appealed to the Supreme Court, but the court in November, 1969, struck down a similar Arkansas law forbidding the teaching of evolution in the public schools of that state, which contained the same basic issue as the more famous Scopes Case.

The Scopes case developed as follows: Scopes, a young teacher of high school biology, and who was also the football coach, deliberately transgressed a Tennessee law that prohibited the teaching of the doctrine of evolution 66 years after Darwin's *Origin of Species* was published. It was another odd circumstance that the biology textbook, furnished by the state, contained the usual account of evolution. Religious fundamentalism was an important factor in the attitude of the public and may have affected the procedure in the case. The presence of William Jennings Bryan, a three-time Democratic candidate for president of the United States, for the prosecution, of Clarence Darrow, a famous criminal lawyer, and Arthur Garfield Hays of the American Civil Liberties Union, for the defense, as well as other learned and famous men raised the public interest in the proceedings. Reporters and photographers from near and distant cities, including H. L. Mencken, were present. Mencken is said to have written reports that were so "vitriolic" that the defense persuaded him to leave.

The law was clear and the facts were admitted: Scopes had taught the banned subject. The judge directed a verdict of guilty but the highest state court voided the decision on a technicality. We may add that the legislature clearly had the right to determine what was to be taught in the schools. The state court said that the school could discontinue the teaching of biology if it was considered worthless without the doctrine of evolution, and advised that the legislature had the real remedy. Thereupon, the six other states that were considering similar anti-evolution laws quietly ceased to consider them.

School cases that raise religious and sectarian issues have frequently been before the Supreme Court in the twentieth century. In 1930, in *Cochran v. Louisiana State Board of Education*, the Court upheld a Louisiana law that allowed the state to furnish free schoolbooks without regard to the nature of the schools. This was done with the view that the state was benefiting children and not the school; it has been surmised that if parochial schools had been named in the law the Court would have declared it unconstitutional. A similar decision was handed down in 1947 in a school bus case, *Everson v. Board of Education*, in which the local school authorities were allowed to transport parochial school pupils along with pupils going to public schools. The law did not permit the public school bus to change its route to accommodate parochial school children, but, however, permitted the board to reimburse the parents of children, Catholic and others, who had to use a tram or streetcar. This, like the Cochran case, comes under the "child benefit doctrine." The Court was almost evenly divided and the dissenting opinions were vigorous.

Two flag salute cases were brought before the Supreme Court: *Minersville School District v. Gobitis* (1940), and *West Virginia Board of Education v. Barnette* (1943). In the *Gobitis* case the Court sustained the ruling of a school board requiring the participation in a salute to the flag as a requisite for attendance at school. It was in reading this decision that Justice Felix Frankfurter remarked that the Court, by attempting to decide the growing number of educational issues, was in danger of becoming "the school board for the country." Three years later, in a similar case from West Virginia, the Court reversed itself. In the interim it had been decided that, by merely standing at attention with bared head while the salute was given, a boy was showing full respect to the flag. The religious significance of the cases may not be apparent. It arose from the fact that the complaints were brought by members of the sect of Jehovah's Witnesses who see in the flag ceremony a transgression of the Ten Commandments in which the worship of images or symbols is forbidden. Only God may be worshipped.

In a noted case, *Illinois ex rel. McCollum v. Board of Education* (1948), it was held that religious instruction on "released time" is contrary to the First Amendment if the teaching is done on public school premises; but in *Zorach v. Clauson* (1952), the court ruled that such instruction is constitutional if carried on outside the school property. The Court was divided on this case, and Justice Frankfurter expressed "the hope that in future variations of the problem which are bound to come here" the principles applied in the McCollum case will again be applied. One of the principles to which Frankfurter referred is the conclusion drawn that there must be a separation not only of state and church, but also of state and religion. The Court took occasion in the *Zorach* case to cite the prayers offered when the Congress convenes and other examples of cooperation between state and religion. A peaceful, friendly spirit pervades the opinion in the *Zorach* case in contrast with the cold legality of the *McCollum* opinions. Constitutional experts seem to disagree on whether state and religion must be separated.

The *Dartmouth College* case (1819) is sometimes called the first educational case decided by the Supreme Court, but this may be a mistake in classification. It had little enough to do with education although the fate of a college charter was involved. The issue was whether a charter is a contract and, therefore, not liable to annulment. The decision, that a charter is a contract and irrevocable, is important in business affairs but students are still debating its influence upon education.

Another case decided by the Supreme Court concerned the apportionment of school funds in cases where some districts were wealthy through land grants in which other districts did not participate. The problem was one of the equal distribution of school aid. Several Supreme Court cases have also dealt with teacher tenure and retirement allowances, with loyalty oaths and free speech, and with compulsory military training in state land-grant universities. All of these cases and others arose from laws and practices in the states and local districts.

The Justice who referred to the Supreme Court as almost a national school board must have been speaking in a humorous vein. The United States does not, like France, have a national school system; it does not, like England, have a national official with power "to promote, control, and direct education" in the states; there are no national laws on education in the states; the federal government has no power to form a school district, extend the compulsory attendance period, or fix the salaries of teachers in the schools of all states or of any one state. The Office of Education in the federal government has performed many useful functions since its creation under another name in 1867, but it is not a national school board. Even elevating the office of the Commissioner of Education to Cabinet rank would not give him the power to control and direct education in the United States as the Ministers of Education do in France and England. We have reviewed some important Congressional appropriations and Supreme Court decisions that have had pronounced effects upon certain phases of education carried on in the states. These appropriations were accepted and administered by the states.

Although the powers of the federal government are limited, whenever education has become highly important to the national defense or to the general welfare, the Congress has not refrained from passing laws affecting education everywhere. Whenever state laws deprive persons of the equal protection of the laws, the Supreme Court will not refrain from deciding that such laws are unconstitutional and therefore void. The United States does not have a national school system but in emergencies the nation may act as if it had such a system. Although this is confusing, this is the way it is. The confusion results from the existence of states with "states rights" and "sovereignty" in some states: smaller nations within the Nation, an historical inheritance from the unhistorical eighteenth century.

FEDERAL SUPPORT OF EDUCATION

A fourth act in the developing drama of federal aid to education was initiated in the name of national defense several months after Russia put the first satellites into orbit in 1957. In the first act that long preceded Sputnik, the government made grants of land for the support of township schools and state universities. The donations to Ohio inaugurated a policy; each new state received similar or larger grants, and for a time federal aid to all levels of schools may have seemed assured, but matters turned out otherwise.

The second act was put on in 1862, when Congress provided for grants of land on a large scale to endow the systems of state colleges of agriculture and mechanic arts. By that time the emphasis upon states rights and the emphatic silence of the Constitution about education served to check all thought of federal aid to elementary schools. The heat of the Civil War and Reconstruction threatened for a time to change the national policy in the South but the fire burned out without result. The country continued to support public higher education in the second Morrill Act of 1890 and in regular appropriations to the state colleges, which steadily expanded their programs to become, in fact, a second chain of state universities.

Since the federal government had undertaken the support of higher education, it was natural that the third act in the drama should deal with the high school. The Smith-Hughes Act of 1917 and supplementary legislation form this third phase in the history of federal aid. These laws aided only vocational education in the high schools and the preparation of vocational teachers. This arbitrary separation of vocational from general education cannot be fully maintained, and the new laws clearly affected the development of secondary education. The law of 1917 also created a Federal Board for Vocational Education and gave it powers not far removed from federal direction of vocational education in the states.

Strong pressures developed to have the federal government cross the line that was supposed to separate vocational from general education; and, also, to provide federal aid for salaries, buildings, and other needs of both elementary and secondary schools. The time for this step seemed favorable. The record of the Wilson era in educational legislation, the excitement and industrial expansion of the years of World War I, and the draft boards' revelations of the educational deficiencies of the recruits gave strong impetus to this movement.

Seventy education bills and resolutions had been introduced for Congressional action by 1920. The most extreme group of these proposed the establishment of a Federal Department of Education to have "power to shape national policy." The United States was not ready for so radical a change in its attitude. Most Americans who have desired federal aid for education have wanted it without any federal control at all.

Many questions have divided the public on this subject: aid to private and church schools; the division of funds between the races; the matching of federal subsidies by the states; the appropriating of funds to the richest as well as to the poorest states; and on the educational standards required in order to qualify for aid. The Eisenhower administration was more or less willing to subsidize building construction but not salaries; but if a city is relieved from the necessity to build school buildings it will have that much more money to raise teachers' salaries.

Tradition is a great force against the movement for federal aid to education. Many oppose it for no other reason than the tradition is against it; but tradition is not impregnable. Many fear national control of education without realizing that state control can be equally obnoxious. Catholics oppose all federal subsidies in which parochial schools do not receive a share. Representatives from Southern states refused to vote for a bill that requires the equal distribution of funds to blacks and whites. We do not have the space for a thorough discussion of all the issues.

As an example of one of the seventy education bills considered by the Congress before 1920, we shall discuss the Smith-Towner bill in detail because it was the first fully developed proposal. This bill, introduced in 1919, was designed to create a Department of Education and the Office of Secretary of Education, to provide federal aid to general education in the states, and to erect standards that the states were to meet in order to participate in the financial benefits. The bill proposed the appropriation of $100,000,000 annually, a very small sum by present standards. The funds were to be applied to five objects: the removal of illiteracy, Americanization, salaries of teachers, physical and health education, and teacher preparation. These were modest goals and some of the need for the first two has disappeared in the intervening time.

The standards required by the bill were the matching of federal funds by the states, a school term of twenty weeks with compulsory attendance, the use of English as the language of instruction. Aid was to be given only to public schools. The last item was the first to be attacked. Parochial school interests demanded a fair share of the proceeds and Catholic organizations have persistently fought this and similar bills. Many public school people opposed the very slight controls of the bill and the matching principle, both of which were in the Smith-Hughes law. The bill was called a war-emergency measure designed to gain votes. After 150 years of local and state effort, to turn to a nationally supported and directed system exposed to all the storms of national politics was felt to be a momentous change, indeed a denial of the American past.

Those who shuddered at that prospect may not have considered all the personal, local, church, and business politics that normally affect local school policies. The record of the local school boards is not spotless. The bills that have been before Congress would not have materially affected local control of the schools or, with one exception, the state systems. The exception is the equal distribution of funds between the races. If the bills were enacted into law, they would not nationalize or socialize the schools. History can supply confidence. The land-grant institutions are not suffering from increasing national controls. History would place more emphasis upon present conditions and needs than upon tradition. Uncriticized tradition obstructs progress.

In the fourth act, tradition was shattered by the National Defense Education Act (NDEA) of 1958. The law did not provide funds for teachers' salaries or school buildings but did affect the equipment, curricula, and teaching in the lower schools. Its major purpose was to improve instruction in mathematics, science, engineering, and modern foreign languages. Before World War II language instruction would not have been subsidized by a defense act, but that conflict started a new tradition.

The law provided for about $1 billion worth of services, chiefly to college and university students, to be spread over four years. The money was appropriated annually to the states on the familiar matching principle: each state must add from its own funds an amount equal to the federal appropriation. The combined sums provided loans to college students and fellowships to graduate students preparing to become college teachers; they gave aid to improve facilities and instruction in schools below the college level, in science, mathematics, and languages; they offered means to improve pupil guidance, to study the educational uses of television, radio, and other devices, to equip laboratories including language laboratories, and to promote the vocational education of technicians in such fields as electronics, drafting, design, and practical chemistry.

The act also provided for the expansion and improvement of statistical and information services by the state education departments. The original Bureau, now the Office of Education in Washington, was especially charged to collect and disseminate information about the schools in the United States. This has always been one of its services but it has never been possible to make this information available when it would be most useful. The President's Commission on Education Beyond the High School deplored "the astounding lack of accurate, consistent, and up-to-date facts," and the resultant ignorance of the nation about "the vital and expensive educational enterprise in contrast with what it knows, in great detail, about agriculture, industry, labor, banking, and other areas." This is an old story retold but the act provided some funds for improved reporting and earlier publication.

The NDEA was extended in 1962, expanded in 1963 and 1964, and revised again in 1967. During this period the specific controls on federal aid to education increased at an unprecedented rate. Gradually the American people began to question the wisdom of these piecemeal responses by the federal government to specific educational crises. Old objections to federal aid to education were reexamined and compromises were developed. From 1963 to 1967 two Congresses, responding to this change in the attitude of the American people, passed more than thirty acts relating to education. Although this legislation is regarded as a breakthrough in the long controversy over federal aid to education, it is categorical, strings-attached aid to education as opposed to general federal aid to education as proposed in the Smith-Towner bill.

An example of this type of legislation is the Elementary and Secondary Education Act (ESEA) of 1965. Although this act is probably the most significant federal aid to education program ever enacted by the Congress, and although it accounts for more than one-third of all federal appropriations to education, each of its titles is so restrictive as to raise the specter of "federal control" over education. Title I money must be spent to meet the needs of educationally deprived children; title II money can be used for instructional materials that have some degree of permanence as compared with those that are consumed in use. The situation is similar for the other three titles of the act. However such requirements are an intrinsic part of categorical aid for elementary, secondary, or higher education.

One important feature of these acts was a reconciliation of the Church-State issue on the basis of a pupil benefit theory, which maintains that public money can be channeled through public educational agencies for the use of individual pupils whether they attend public, private, or church-related schools. If this theory is upheld by the courts, it is possible that general federal aid to education will be a reality before the end of the present decade.

GOVERNMENT AND EDUCATION IN EMERGENCIES

Two world wars and a deep and prolonged economic depression have forced both state and federal governments to play a more active role in education. During a war, men are conscripted for the military services, steel and labor are allocated, food is rationed, and marginal land is ploughed up to grow more wheat. Older children leave school for work, school attendance declines, school supplies are hard to obtain, terms are shortened, and some schools may be closed. School improvements that were painstakingly developed are dropped, and classes and school services are reduced or abolished. Men leave the classrooms for war work or the battlefield, and standards of teacher preparation have to be lowered because men and women can earn higher wages in war industries.

Two contrasting periods of prosperity and depression span the twenty years between the two world wars. The financial crash of 1929 divides this period into two nearly equal parts. Prosperity was promoted by the automobile industry, road construction, the electrical and radio industries, and a building boom that created new suburbs and changed the skyline of the cities. This development was not spread evenly. Agriculture, coal, textiles, and some other industries were less prosperous. Labor and "the little man" did not gain the increased purchasing power needed to maintain the expanded production. High-pressure selling, excessive installment buying, uninhibited stock speculation, loose banking practices, and stock market manipulations brought on an economic depression.

World War I began in September, 1914, and continued for three and one-half years before the United States entered the conflict. Prior to its entry in the war, the United States served as the granary of the combatants, but a critical food problem arose when the American Army was expanded to 4,000,000 men. The state colleges and the Departments of Agriculture and of Labor worked to enlist school youth for farm work. A few young men were given preparatory training at state colleges, but most began working on the farms without any previous knowledge or experience. The program was continued, and in 1918 a quarter-million workers were reported in the United States Boys' Working Reserve.

Where this program was in effect, schoolwork naturally suffered. Schools closed early in the spring and opened late in the autumn. As usual in such cases, claims were made that farm work had educational value. Although, it no doubt had the moral value of all honest work performed in the public interest, to give credit in algebra or Spanish for pulling weeds or cutting corn, as was actually done, had no better justification than that others were also doing it. Many states, however, placed limitations on the giving of such credits.

War gardens that were to be worked evenings and Saturdays by school-children formed a second phase of the food-raising effort. There was for-tunately no question of school credits or shortened terms for this work. The school garden movement had started about 1890. At that time it was intended to serve educational purposes; but the war gardens were intended to produce beans and potatoes, which they did. President Wilson spoke in favor of this effort, and it was reported that 1,500,000 children partici-pated in this program. A national director of the United States School Garden Army was appointed, and the departments of home economics of the state colleges gave help in conserving the very substantial harvests.

Military training in schools, although not widely practiced, had been fostered long before by Alden Partridge. Private military academies were in operation, and some public high schools maintained a voluntary cadet corps. It has been estimated that only a few thousand cadets were in mili-tary schools when the war broke out. The preparedness agitation along with strong urging by the War Department increased this number to 100,000 in 1918. The National Defense Act of 1916 had provided for a Junior Reserve Officers' Training Corps in high schools, but the regular army officers assigned to train the units were withdrawn when the nation entered the war. Some cities and state legislatures encouraged military drill in schools. New York made it compulsory for boys aged sixteen and up and in 1919 substituted physical education for drill. With the return of peace the interest in military training in secondary schools declined and World War II did not greatly revive it.

School people and especially the directors of physical education have usually been critical of the claim that military drill provides good physical and health education or a discipline that is appropriate to civilian life. The American Physical Education Association favored athletics, the activities of the Boy Scouts, Girl Scouts, Camp Fire Girls, and similar organizations, but "strongly disapproved" of military drill. The National Education Asso-ciation called for physical education and opposed military drill in schools.

Within three years after the armistice, half of the states had adopted compulsory physical education laws. Behind these remarkable actions there was a remarkable reason. It had been revealed that one-third of the Army recruits suffered from physical defects that temporarily or permanently unfitted them for military service. Physical and health education was intended to prevent many of these disabilities and to teach athletics and recreational skills suitable for the maintenance of health. These efforts were not highly successful. Qualified teachers of physical education were not always available and public interest declined. The recruits of 1941 had almost as many physical defects as those of 1917.

The United States was involved in World War I for only 19 months, but the farms and factories had actually become engaged much earlier in the war effort, and by 1918 a serious shortage of teachers had developed. Four million men were in the army and millions of women were working in factories at jobs that were much easier and paid much better than teaching. Newspapers described a grave situation of discontinued or overcrowded schools in different parts of the country. In New York City eight hundred classrooms were without teachers and the pupils swelled the numbers in other classes. In New England only one-half or fewer of the high school teachers who had served in the Army in the spring of 1918 returned to their schools in the autumn. When thousands of teachers were leaving the schools, the press declared that "the public knows the reasons perfectly well, namely low salaries, uncertain tenure, and arbitrary administration." This was not a complete analysis. The shortage of teachers continued for years and emergency certificates were granted to many who could not meet state requirements. The period after World War II was to see an even greater decline in teaching standards and in the condition of school buildings.

The colleges suffered the greatest disorganization during World War I. Colleges for men almost ceased to exist in their usual state. The ill-planned Student Army Training Corps (SATC) was introduced in the autumn of 1918 to save higher education, but would have injured it almost irreparably if the war had continued. The colleges were turned into armed camps and professors had to carry passes and take orders from students in uniform. Entrance requirements were reduced and classes were interrupted or canceled for drill. The severe influenza epidemic of 1918 also interfered with the success of the program. The government, however, paid for the use of private property and its money helped colleges over the financial difficulty caused by the loss of student fees. In the official report on SATC, recommendations were made for the collegiate Reserve Officers' Training Corps, which had been begun in 1916, but was given up for the SATC, and which was now to be permanently established.

World War II affected the high schools in several ways. In the first two years of American participation in the war, high school enrollment declined by 17 per cent. Many pupils were close to the draft age and others were at or above the employment age. Some enlisted, some engaged in war work, and many who remained in school were disturbed in mind and unable to concentrate on their work.

The war also reflected the state of education in high school. Examinations by the armed services produced results that at least confirmed earlier reports. Two-thirds of the college freshmen in a large number of colleges failed the arithmetic test for admission to the Naval Reserve Officers' Training Corps; most of the failures were not "near misses," but were far below the passing mark. Only one-fourth of these 4,000 freshmen had taken more than one and one-half years of high school mathematics, and only four hundred or 10 per cent had studied trigonometry. The best marks in arithmetic in the entire United States were made by students from Troy, Brooklyn, and Buffalo, New York, all school systems that operated under the often-maligned Regents.

To promote the active participation of youth in community war work and to prepare them for induction after graduation, a Victory Corps was set up (1942) in the high schools. The Corps provided a plan to be followed in high schools in which all pupils could join. The plan emphasized physical fitness and vocational studies and activities that had a bearing upon the war. Increased attention was also given to the study of mathematics, science, and English. Social studies were broadened to include the study of foreign countries and areas and thus called attention to the meaning of the struggle to the world as a whole.

In World War II the armed services profited, although too slowly, from some of the mistakes of 1918. They gradually instituted plans of deferment for college students who were preparing themselves in fields that served the national health and safety. A formula was also worked out that permitted draft boards to grant occupational deferments. Even so, many serious shortages of scientific and technical manpower developed. The services in this war also used the specialists on the faculties and the facilities of the universities in the Army Specialized Training Program (ASTP). In a global war men who were fluent in Russian, Chinese, Japanese, and other languages were needed. The armed services introduced foreign language classes that worked every day under native speakers together with experts in language analysis. The remarkable success of these classes was the result of intensive work and powerful motivation guided by proper techniques. No lives are wagered upon the success of high school languages classes and this is one reason why these classes are less successful.

Many other defense programs were conducted in the universities. Geographers, meteorologists, and many kinds of engineers taught recruits or rendered direct help to the military forces. The Office of Strategic Services was staffed by men from the universities, and many faculty men also left the campus for work in the armed services or in civilian jobs with the government.

College attendance declined rapidly after the attack on Pearl Harbor on December 7, 1941. Men enlisted or were called into service, and both men and women engaged in war industry. Classes dwindled to half or less of their former numbers. Many girls, however, remained and some men's colleges became coeducational in the early years of the war. Colleges that were accepted for one of the specialized training programs profited in their enrollments. Otherwise, the men who remained in college were 4F's, boys below the draft age, and a few veterans who had been discharged because of wounds or shock. A few men who were deferred because they were engaged in vital war work also found time to take college work. All of these together left some colleges, especially the small liberal arts schools, with sharply reduced enrollments and in financial difficulties.

As the end of World War II came into view, the Army and Navy began to eliminate their specialized training programs. The colleges, which were already in a critical state, were hardly in condition to survive a further cut in their income. A resolution in the House of Representatives on June 21, 1944, proposed a study of "means by which such effects might be alleviated." That summer, partly to help the colleges but more to help the veterans make up the losses from their interrupted education, Congress passed the GI bill (P.L.346). Soon veterans flooded college campuses, forcing colleges to set up temporary housing for them, to expand their faculties, and to increase class size. The college enrollment of 1946 was 45 per cent above that of 1944; and in the peak year of 1947 more than one million veterans were enrolled in college. In 1952 the educational and other benefits were extended by legislation to include veterans of the Korean conflict who served from 1950 to 1955. In 1966, Congress passed and in 1967 liberalized a permanent GI bill extending these benefits not only to veterans of the war in Vietnam but also to all men and women who had been honorably discharged after six or more months of service in the Army, Navy, Marine Corps, Air Force, and Coast Guard since the original GI bill expired on January 31, 1955. The cost of this new GI bill amounted to about $2 billion in the five-year-period from 1966 to 1971, a substantial investment by the federal government in education for democracy. In only five years, the 2.4 million veterans trained under the new bill already exceeds the 2.3 million veterans trained in the 14 years under the Korean conflict GI bill. The GI bill and ESEA together are without doubt the most significant federal aid to education programs.

Between World War I and World War II, the United States suffered a deep and prolonged crisis that is properly called the depression of the 1930's. A Citizens' Conference on the Crisis in Education was called by President Hoover in January, 1933. One of its resolutions urged the states to reorganize their school districts into larger units that would be both economically and educationally sound. Partly as a result of further investigation by the Office of Education of ten state systems, some reorganizations were effected but not nearly enough. These efforts did not go far in solving depression problems, but the depression called attention to an administrative problem.

Each of the early depression years saw a further decline in school efficiency. The chairman of a national commission on the emergency, John

K. Norton of Columbia University, declared in 1935 that the three years immediately preceding had been the most disastrous in educational history. He said the educational opportunities of millions of children had been impaired or denied. There were no easy solutions, but the commission favored resort to state and federal support instead of the prevalent local and property taxes. Large and well-knit teachers' associations with means to reach the public were needed, it was thought, to counteract the propaganda of selfish interests and the negations and despair of the fainthearted. Unfortunately, the national organizations that were concerned to keep down taxes had many more propaganda dollars than the teachers.

At the beginning of the New Deal, before President Roosevelt had been in office quite a month, Congress authorized a program of emergency conservation work, otherwise called the Unemployment Relief Act of March, 1933. The Civilian Conservation Corps (CCC), with 2,600 camps at the peak of its development, was part of this program. The Corps seems to have been the President's own idea, having grown out of his interest in reforestation and land utilization. Suggestions by Louis Howe and Secretary of Labor Frances Perkins were incorporated, and in the interest of dispatch the latter proposed to put the Army in command because it had available tents, cots, blankets, dishes, and cooking facilities. She admitted in the New Republic (June 21, 1954) that this was "a desperate suggestion."

Young men who were in need voluntarily joined the Corps and maintained it at full strength, about 300,000, by filling vacancies as they opened. They enrolled for a six-months period and were permitted to re-enroll if their need continued. The War Department, aided by other executive branches, was placed in charge of the construction and maintenance of the camps, of the feeding of the men, and of discipline in the camps. The men were well fed and many gained in weight and health, but it was mistakenly thought that they would be "tough guys" requiring military discipline.

The object of the Corps was to relieve distress by providing jobless and destitute men, aged from eighteen to twenty-five years, with work in improving the national forests and parks and thus promoting both the rehabilitation of men and the conservation of resources. Foresters directed the work of planting trees, removing fire hazards, reducing erosion, and laying out and building paths and roads. The men worked forty hours a week and received a small stipend for themselves and their families in addition to maintenance.

The work was of national importance and was well performed, but the education of the men was to a degree a missed opportunity, and was in fact an afterthought. There were no educational advisers at the camps during the first nine months of operation. And according to Secretary of the Interior Harold L. Ickes, when the advisers were added this step was taken "in spite of the Army." The educational advisers in some camps felt that the Army officers were opposed to their work. Also, as in other cases when the government has engaged in education, it largely bypassed its own Office of Education. The Commissioner was allowed to appoint the educational advisers but they served under the War Department.

The general director, appointed by the President, was a labor organizer, not a forester. He banned from the camps a pamphlet that contained ideas on labor and industry of which he disapproved. The Association of American University Professors protested the ban. But it must be remembered that every phase of the New Deal was under constant criticism by one or another faction of either party. Like other New Deal installations, the plans for the Corps were drafted hurriedly on the theory that the depression would quickly yield to the measures taken. In the short run, education was not considered important.

Under difficult conditions the educational program was gradually expanded. George F. Zook, United States Commissioner of Education, had a better idea of the need than the War Department. He pointed out the opportunity to teach botany and zoology, forestry, surveying, English, and citizenship. Many of the men had had little schooling; others were ready for college and except for the Depression would have been in attendance. The courses named by Zook together with certain semivocational ones became popular when they were introduced to the Corps members.

The classes were relegated to evening and other spare hours when the men were often fatigued. Books were usually scarce or lacking. Some camps had no assembly hall or any good classrooms. One camp in southern Michigan was described by Henry S. Curtis, well-known educator, who in 1935 found that on rainy days the men of this camp had to stay in their bunkhouses. There was no recreational organization, and only one room was set apart as a classroom, which had three tables and ten chairs. Classes met wherever room could be found.

Even under these conditions 60 per cent of the men were enrolled in classes and 50 per cent attended. The camps probably provided real relief to the men, gave them good food, a wholesome environment, and useful work that they respected and the doing of which gave them self-respect and confidence; but the educational program was not as good as the work and relief programs.

Many kinds of opinions were expressed outside the camps. Some thought the Corps was a good start for a national system of adult education. Others, perhaps influenced by the theory of William James that "a moral equivalent of war" was needed, thought of the work as a desirable form of national service. This implied that it should be made universal and permanent. On the other hand, Agnes E. Meyer, a well-known liberal connected with the *Washington Post*, feared just this, that the CCC and similar New Deal agencies might become permanent. She had this fear because she thought students and teachers kept on a dole would certainly be regimented. Many condemned the Corps solely on the ground that it was an expensive part of the New Deal. The cost figures will no longer seem as large as they appeared to be in the depression.

Relief needs declined after the war broke out and the CCC was abolished in 1942. About 2,500,000 young men, or really boys since most of them were under nineteen, had been furnished work, food, shelter, and some education. The total cost was short of $3 billion and the value of the work accomplished has been estimated at half of that amount. In addition to its direct benefits the experiment provided lessons on conservation and on vocational and adult education that may prove valuable in prosperity as well as in adversity.

The National Youth Administration (NYA) was a relief agency set up in 1935 under the Works Progress Administration (WPA) to aid young people of both sexes living at their homes rather than in camps. To enable the young to stay in school was one of its purposes and it helped millions to do so. The Depression was one of the causes of a rapid increase in high school enrollment at that time, and after leaving school it was the young men who felt the deepest discouragement. The numbers of those who could not find employment were far beyond the capacity of the CCC, which was at times unable to accept more than two out of five applicants. The Depression was hard upon parents but often harder upon the young; and there were so many of them. One-third of all the unemployed were under the age of twenty-four. The Depression raised in them the soul-destroying feeling that they were not wanted.

The program of student relief was begun by the Federal Emergency Relief Administration, one of the early New Deal agencies. This program was given over to the newly organized National Youth Administration. Together the two administrations gave work relief to more than 1,000,000 young people in high school and college. The three requirements for receiving NYA aid were that the student could not remain in school without financial help; that he must be certified as a person of good character; and that he must have good academic ability. The amount that could be earned by the student was at first limited to $15 a month. The work might be clerical, bibliographical, research, or other, at the discretion of the instructor in charge.

The NYA aided 125,000 college students in 1936–1937 out of a total college enrollment of 1,500,000. But the amount paid to the individual was so small that only those who were almost able to finance themselves could take advantage of the plan. Those who most needed help could not maintain themselves in school with what could be earned in this program.

The plan was not always carried out in good faith. Some of the work was "made-work." Some students interpreted "ability to remain in college" to cover the ability to pay sorority or fraternity dues. Some of the work to be done required specialized preparation, such as an ability to read Spanish or to give psychological tests, and care was not always taken to make reasonable assignments. Some colleges refused NYA money because acceptance of it "might be taken to mean approval of the New Deal extravagance." A group of professional educators called NYA "just another propaganda mill for the New Deal"; and they added, with reason, that it should have been administered through the Office of Education and the several state departments of education. This has come to be a frequent criticism of several of the educational activities of the federal government. Naturally there was also the argument that there were "too many young people in college anyway" and the fear that the NYA was a step toward federal control of higher education. The NYA, like the CCC, was closed in 1942. A full history with documents of these institutions should be prepared for the guidance of the future.

Other emergency legislation provided funds for schools and college buildings and extended relief with employment to teachers, musicians, writers, and artists who had lost their positions. The government, for a short time only, paid for the maintenance of nursery schools, kindergartens, and a variety of adult education classes. Workers' education, vocational education, citizenship classes, the Federal Writers' Project that produced the series of illustrated state travel guides, WPA orchestras, and murals in public buildings are other examples of the effort to help cultural workers through the Depression.

U.S. OFFICE OF EDUCATION

A step looking toward the development of a more truly national system of education in the United States was made by the creation of the United States Office of Education (USOE). This office was created as a "Department of Education" by the Thirty-ninth U. S. Congress on March 1, 1867, in the administration of President Andrew Johnson. As aid-to-education bills have been enacted by the Congress, the significance of this office has increased. A century after its founding, in the fiscal year ending June 30, 1967, USOE channeled about $3.9 billion into the American educational enterprise.

The USOE has functioned in three different federal agencies: from 1869 to 1939 in the Department of the Interior; from 1939 to 1953 in the Federal Security Agency; and since 1953 in the Department of Health, Education, and Welfare (HEW). Its designation has changed from "Department" to "Office" to "Bureau" and then from 1929 to the present back to the "Office of Education."

Despite these many changes in its organization the functions of the USOE have remained primarily educational research; educational services to local, state, national, and international agencies; and the administration of federal educational grants. In fiscal year 1970, its bureaus supported all levels of education as well as vocational, adult, and special education, embracing about one hundred separate programs at a cost of about $4 billion. In addition to its bureaus, divisions, and branches in Washington, D. C., there are regional offices in various geographical areas of the United States from Boston, Massachusetts, to San Francisco, California.

The head of the USOE is the United States Commissioner of Education, appointed by the President with consent of the Senate. The pioneering activities of the first commissioner, Henry Barnard, who served from 1867 to 1870 and the fourth commissioner, William T. Harris, who served for 17 years from 1889 to 1906, have been mentioned previously. This pair is without doubt the most famous of the 19 USOE commissioners who were appointed from 1867 to 1970.

A definitive history of the USOE remains to be written. The data for such a history is contained in the *Annual Reports* of the Commissioner published from 1868 without interruption through 1917 (except for 1869). These reports have recently been reprinted in a Centennial Edition of the Annual Reports of the United States Commissioner of Education. Beginning with the 1918 *Report*, the form was changed to a single volume containing brief summaries of the activities of the USOE. In addition the office issues many bulletins a year and publishes a monthly magazine. Its *Biennial Survey of Education* is a primary source on education in the United States for each two-year period, and it also prepares and publishes many studies of education in foreign countries.

The USOE is not the only educational activity of the federal government. The Smithsonian Institution and the Library of Congress are also national educational agencies. Many of the departments of the government such as the Department of Agriculture and the Department of Defense carry on extensive educational activities. The Department of Defense operates the United States Military Academy at West Point, the Naval Academy at Annapolis, and the Air Academy at Colorado Springs, which are national schools. Finally in 1972 the Congress established a National Institute of Education to enable the federal government "to provide leadership in the conduct and support of scientific inquiry into the educational process."

INTERNATIONAL EDUCATION

International education may be regarded as the spread of ideas, any ideas, across national frontiers; or as the spread of educational ideas across such boundaries; or as the attempt by educational means to promote peace and mutual cooperation among nations. In the first of these definitions, education is defined in the manner of Thorndike as the production of change in people. The content of the ideas that are spread need not come into question. The transmission and borrowing of economic or military ideas would in this primary sense be examples of international education.

International education may also be regarded as the spread of ideas about education and about educational services from nation to nation. This second interpretation of the phrase is the one commonly adopted, and it is the one used by William W. Brickman of the University of Pennsylvania, editor of *School and Society,* in an article entitled "International Education," in the *Encyclopedia of Educational Research.* As interpreted in this manner, the title covers comparative education, teacher and student exchanges, the international influence of the views of John Dewey, for example, and perhaps even the study of foreign languages. Many topics in earlier chapters of this history, including Franklin's plan for an academy with its numerous quotations from European educators, the Lancasterian schools in America, the Rhodes scholarships, and study in German universities by Americans, come under this interpretation.

A special type of associations that is covered by this second interpretation is the international educational organizations. The "educational commission" proposed in 1817 by Marc-Antoine Jullien (1775–1848) was to be such a body. It was to collect and distribute information on education from and to the nations of Europe. In his draft of a plan, written in 1817, Jullien uses the term "comparative education," and he may have invented this now familiar phrase. Jullien's proposal was not immediately put into effect, but over the years hundreds of international organizations to promote education have been created. The International Kindergarten Union (1873), the Institute of International Education (1919), and the World Federation of Education Associations (1923) are examples of these organizations. The International Institute of Teachers College, Columbia University (1923), under the direction of I. L. Kandel, was founded to promote Jullien's idea; the volumes published by the Institute have been of high interest and great value.

With regard to scope, the three definitions are placed in a descending order. The third is the narrowest. It defines international education as the effort to promote peace and mutual cooperation between nations by educational means. This makes international education a form of propaganda, good propaganda we may hold, but still a proposal to secure agreement upon a policy. It is a policy to prevent wars and abolish isolationism. This is an effort to initiate a new epoch in history.

The United Nations (UN), in contrast with the League of Nations, has recognized the international functions of education. Thus the United Nations Educational, Scientific, and Cultural Organization, or UNESCO, is an agency of the United Nations. Both the UN and UNESCO were created in 1945 but not all of the countries in the United Nations are members of UNESCO. The United States adheres to both.

There were two views on the formation of UNESCO. Those who won out created a body to serve, not as an arm of the government or foreign offices of the member nations, but as a representative of the educational, scientific, and cultural associations in those nations. In the United States, Congress provided for a National Commission of one hundred, sixty of whom are named by private associations of scholars and educators and forty by the Department of State. The National Commission selects the voting delegates of UNESCO. The first general conference of UNESCO was held at Paris in 1946, with delegates from 28 nations in attendance. The present member-nations number 125.

The preamble of the constitution of this unparalleled organization begins with the now celebrated words that "since wars begin in the minds of men, it is in the minds of men that the defenses of peace must be constructed." It rejects the idea that peace can be maintained if it is based exclusively upon political and economic arrangements. Peace, it claims, must be founded "upon the intellectual and moral solidarity of mankind," and this solidarity is to be attained by the "wide diffusion of culture," the universal application of "the democratic principles of the dignity, equality, and mutual respect of men," and education "for justice and liberty and peace." All nations, the preamble declares, have the sacred duty to promote these means to the intellectual and moral solidarity of mankind.

A comparision of these ideas with those expressed at other great moments of history, such as the American and the French revolutions, would be an educative exercise. That these principles have not always, or perhaps often, been followed and that the peace has not been kept does not condemn the effort. The failures of one period often prepare the way for success in the next. Isaiah, Kant, and many others have had visions of perpetual peace that may and, if the human race is to endure, indeed must become reality.

UNESCO attempts to promote knowledge and understanding of nations by nations, with special attention to the use of the radio, motion pictures, and textbooks. Textbook revision had been begun between the two world wars. UNESCO is particularly interested in the rectification of textbooks in history, the social studies, and literature. These books together with songs, ceremonies, and patriotic ritual have been used in schools over the world to promote chauvinism and the spirit of aggression and revenge. Related to textbook revision are the surveys of national school systems, fundamental education, the removal of illiteracy—for illiteracy retards progress among half of the people of the world—adult education, and the education of teachers. These along with others are among the many interests of UNESCO.

In pursuing these interests, UNESCO uses specialists from its member states either by bringing them together in international conferences to advise on worldwide problems, or by sending them out in the field to tackle a variety of missions such as improving the quality of the environment, eliminating pollution, and preventing industrial fallout. In 1969 and 1970 UNESCO held 233 meetings to advise on such problems. In this same period seventy missions were sent to assist member states in developing educational planning.

As a result of world surveys into the state of education made by UNESCO, and to mark the twenty-fifth anniversary of the UN, 1970 was designed as International Education Year (IEY) by the General Assembly of the United Nations. Its purpose was to promote concerted action by individual countries to improve education. IEY will provide a valuable stimulus for many educational activities in the decade of the 1970's.

In addition to UNESCO, the United States participates in numerous other international educational programs. Space permits brief descriptions of only two of these, the Peace Corps and the Agency for International Development (AID).

One of the most effective international programs of the United States is the Peace Corps. It was established in 1961 by Congress at the request of President Kennedy "to assist other nations toward their legitimate goals of freedom and opportunity." In the Peace Corps we have a modern governmental application of the ideals of service and sacrifice that have motivated private missionary organizations serving overseas. The programs of the Peace Corps are tailor-made to meet the requests that come from about sixty foreign countries, primarily newly independent nations. Among the more than 15,000 Peace Corps volunteers sent to meet these demands are carpenters and doctors, mechanics and home economists, draftsmen and architests, and many other trades and professions. The largest single profession represented is teaching. The historian Arnold J. Toynbee on the occasion of its first birthday expressed his belief that "in the Peace Corps, the non-Western majority of mankind is going to meet a sample of Western man at his best."

In addition to contributing over 30 per cent of the budget for UNESCO and supporting the Peace Corps, the United States annually spends billions of dollars on other foreign aid programs. Since 1961, the nonmilitary part of these programs has been administered by the Department of State through the Agency for International Development (AID). Although its projects encompass a wide spectrum of activities in more than seventy countries, many are in the field of education. AID assists underdeveloped countries to help themselves in such areas as education, health, and agriculture. AID technical advisors train teachers and direct programs aimed at eliminating diseases.

UNITY THROUGH COOPERATION

The opportunity for schooling for most of those who settled America was merely individual good fortune and was of little interest to the community or the government. The Supreme Court said in the Brown decision of 1954: "Today education is perhaps the most important function of state and local governments. . . . It is required in the performance of the most basic public responsibilities, even service in the armed forces. It is the very foundation of good citizenship."

The National Defense Education Act of 1958 declares, in effect, that the safety of the nation depends upon advanced schooling for which elementary schooling is preparatory. The United States government, through the support it has given the land-grant colleges and through the Smith-Hughes law, declares that practical education is essential to the welfare and material prosperity of the nation. This will suggest to students a comparison between the ideas of the seventeenth and the twentieth centuries that we do not intend to pursue.

We shall instead look at a few steps in the long journey from the past to the present. To the founders of the nation, general education was a national goal, indispensable in a republic. They did not, however, as practical statesmen, see how they could attain it. Success came only after a strong effort or as Ellwood Cubberley chose to say, after a series of battles. Even the common schools, the base of the system, were established after prolonged opposition through the efforts of dedicated pioneers who did not constantly count the cost to themselves.

The lack of an understanding of the nature of public education and the want of an acceptable and adaptable plan were great obstacles. Existing practice favored schools that were supported and controlled by their patrons and were free to those who could not pay, namely, pauper schools. These were not generally acceptable nor adaptable.

Thomas Jefferson tried to solve the problem, and in 1779 hammered out an instrument that would have provided a very elementary school free for three years, and under local control. There were to be scholarships in secondary school and college for the "best geniuses"; but the "rubbish" was to be discarded. This scheme, although unworthy of the author of the Declaration of Independence with its bold words about human freedom and equality, was too advanced for the State of Virginia.

Fifty years later, in 1829, a generation of great Americans was preparing to institute the public elementary school with a still narrow but expanding curriculum, and the education of teachers in state normal schools. The district system was the Achilles heel of their plan. By 1879 there was a public high school in every progressive city and the state university and land-grant college was about to receive annual grants of either state or federal support or both together. All three of these institutions had begun to disseminate modern knowledge and give vocational and professional education to masses of people who would have been kept out of college and indeed from the high school under the narrow opportunities and limited educational institutions of 1800 or 1850.

The great ideas and practical achievements of the twentieth century included Progressive education, educational measurements, school surveys, the junior high school, the rebirth of the senior high school, the junior college, federal aid, and the great effort to provide equal and not separate education for the proud descendants of the pioneers, and founders, and the black, the Mexican, the Puerto Rican, and the stranger within our gates. Equal opportunity and the full development of every talent through the cooperation of the community, state, and nation is a worthy goal that has not yet been attained.

SUMMARY

Again and again the federal government has come to the aid of education. Each time education, at home or abroad, has been confronted by a major crisis, the federal government has been appealed to, and each time it has responded with help. This has happened in war and peace, in depression and prosperity, and never without controversy and compromise.

In wartime, schools suffer from shortages and retrenchment, and the services most recently added are among the first to be discontinued. The schools became involved in the war propaganda, the drives to sell war stamps and Liberty Bonds, and the effort to increase the food supply. Those educators who disagreed and who had the courage to go on record spoke against this diversion of the schools from their normal functions and this integration of children into a war system. The military training that the war brought into the schools disappeared when peace returned. The hastily organized Student Army Training Corps of 1918 also disappeared, fortunately, before it ruined the colleges. World War II led to the permanent establishment of the Reserve Officers Training Corps and to the passage of the GI Bill.

The period of adversity was marked by many attempts in state legislatures to police the minds of teachers. Both wars and the Depression contributed to this policy. There were laws against evolution, socialism, and communism, as well as laws to promote Americanism without, however, defining it. Related to these laws were the legislative attempts to revise the history textbooks, a task for which legislatures are not well equipped. Many states forbade the teaching of foreign languages in elementary schools. Twenty years later there was a great revival of foreign language instruction in the elementary schools.

The Depression had many destructive effects. Teachers' salaries were reduced and often remained unpaid for months and even years. Many teachers left the profession. School enrollments rose and there was a building shortage. The curriculum was often emasculated, terms were shortened, and the graduates in great numbers were unable to find work. The public did not realize the depth and severity of the crisis, and they were misled by the past history of business reverses, which had been relatively short. For this reason, among many others, the measures taken to fight the depression were inadequate.

This last fact carries over into the measures taken to aid the destitute and discouraged young people. Although mistakes were made in its organization and administration, the Civilian Conservation Corps did useful work and gave the country experience that may have future application. Other organizations, both public and private, did important work with youths. Many schoolmen were prejudiced against government activity in this field, regarding it as propaganda for statism. Federal funds for school buildings and for the maintenance of unemployed teachers and other cultural workers were provided. Parallel with these positive efforts there were many surveys of youth problems and secondary education. Along with emergency measures one should also consider the great permanent youth aiding organizations, such as the YMCA and YWCA, the Boy and Girl Scouts, and many others.

The founding of the United Nations led to the establishment of a new, unprecedented organization to promote international education, UNESCO, which is unprecedented in the scope of its purpose and activities. UNESCO is particularly concerned with the development of international understanding through the promotion throughout the world of education, science, and culture, making them more available to all peoples. The theory seems to be that although "wars begin in the minds of men," their minds are not unresponsive to good physical conditions. Peace depends upon knowledge, wisdom, and good will, but also upon relief from oppression, depression, and hunger.

In the world of today and tomorrow, education must be an instrument of United States policy, both domestic and foreign. Not only must we constantly improve our national system of education—local, state, and federal, private and public, informal and formal—we must also assist developing nations to do the same in the spirit of the Peace Corps.

QUESTIONS

1. Is state control of education to be preferred to federal control? Why?
2. What is meant by democratic control of education? Why is it to be desired?
3. Which should be most jealously preserved, local control or state control of education? Why? What does history have to say about the defects of each type of control?
4. Should private schools be abolished as intended under the Oregon Law of 1922, rigidly controlled as in France, or allowed considerable freedom as in most states?

5. What educational provisions are found in the constitution of your state?
6. Why in your opinion is there no direct reference to education in the United States Constitution?
7. What is the reasonable position in the debate between military training and physical education in the schools? Consider high schools and colleges separately.
8. Why, in all probability, did the Ku Klux Klan favor the Oregon law? Compare this with the reason why Justice Holmes dissented from the majority decision of the Supreme Court.
9. If another CCC or similar agency were needed, what modifications of the 1933 plan would you propose?
10. If, instead of NYA, the federal government had provided funds for the existing private youth organizations to expand their work, would youth have been effectively served? How would such a plan be administered?
11. Why should pupils be taught about the background and origins, the purposes, and the achievements of the United Nations and UNESCO? What obligation is implied in this question?
12. How are comparative education and the studies made by UNESCO related to each other and to the history of education?
13. As a result of its many decisions on educational issues, the Supreme Court has been accused of becoming "a National School Board." Is this a proper function of the Court, and why?

BOOKS AND PAPERS

Some of the large city newspapers that reported the events of the wars and the Depression as they occurred are indexed. Among the educational journals that gave attention to the adversities of our time may be mentioned *The Nation's Schools, The American School Board Journal, School Review,* and *School and Society.*

A *Bibliography on Education in the Depression* (1937) was prepared for the Educational Policies Commission, NEA, by Jesse B. Sears.

A sheaf of illustrated articles on UNESCO with facsimile copies of related documents is to be found in the *School Executive* for October 1946. More recent books, pamphlets, and films can be obtained from the UNESCO Publications Center, New York, N. Y. Some of these are listed in a booklet entitled *Introduction to UNESCO* prepared in 1970 for the twenty-fifth anniversary of the United Nations, and published in the NEA journal, *Education Today* for October 1970.

The monthly education supplement of the *Saturday Review* beginning September 17, 1960, will provide a critical examination of educational policies and trends for the decade of the 1960's and 1970's.

The Harvard Center for Law and Education is an interdisciplinary research institute established by Harvard University and the United States Office of Economic Opportunity to provide study and reform of governmental policies affecting equality of educational opportunity. It publishes *Inequality in Education* six times a year. The first number appeared October 10, 1969. Recent numbers deal with school financing and the fourteenth amendment, Title I of ESEA, student rights, integration and American Indian Education.

ACKERLY, ROBERT L., *The Reasonable Exercise of Authority*, Washington, D. C., The National Association of Secondary School Principals, 1969. (Highlights State and Federal court decisions on such issues as freedom of expression, right of petition, behavior codes, and dress codes.)

BELL, HOWARD M., *Youth Tell Their Story*, Washington, D. C., American Council on Education, 1938.

BOWERS, C. A., *The Progressive Educator and the Depression, the Radical Years*, New York, Random House, 1969.

BRICKMAN, WILLIAM W., and STANLEY LEHRER, eds., *Religion, Government, and Education*, New York, Society for the Advancement of Education, 1961.

BRUBACHER, JOHN S., *The Courts and Higher Education*, San Francisco, Cal., Jossey-Bass, Inc., 1970.

CHAMBERS, M. M., *Youth-serving Organizations, National, Nongovernmental Associations*, Washington, D C., American Council on Education, 1941.

CHANIN, ROBERT H., *Protecting Teacher Rights, A Summary of Constitutional Developments*, Washington, D. C., National Education Association, 1970.

CORDASCO, FRANCESCO, ed., *The Annual Reports of the United States Commissioner of Education, 1867/8–1917*, New York, Rowman and Littlefield, 1967.

CROWELL, BENEDICT, and R. F. WILSON, *Demobilization, Industrial and Military, 1918–1920*, Yale University Press, 1921.

EDWARDS, NEWTON, *The Courts and the Public Schools, The Legal Basis of School Organization and Administration*, University of Chicago Press, 1971.

EPC, *Education for all American Youth*, Washington, D.C., Educational Policies Commission, 1944; and a second edition, revised, and subtitled, *A Further Look*, 1952.

FRASER, STEWART, *Governmental Policy and International Education*, New York, John Wiley and Sons, 1965. (The exchange of students between different countries.)

GATEWOOD, WILLARD B., Jr., *Preachers, Pedagogues, and Politicians, The Evolution Controversy in North Carolina, 1920–1927*, University of North Carolina Press, 1966.

HAMILTON, ROBERT R., and PAUL R. MORT, *The Law and Public Education, with Cases*, Chicago, Foundation Press, 1941.

HUMPHREY, HUBERT H., ed., *School Desegregation, Documents and Commentaries*, New York, 1964.

ICKES, HAROLD L., *Secret Diary of Harold L. Ickes, 1933–1936*, New York, 1953. Contains a number of entries with educational interest.

KANDEL, I. L., *The Impact of the War Upon American Education*, University of North Carolina Press, 1948.

KIZER, GEORGE A., "Federal Aid to Education, 1945–1963," *History of Education Quarterly*, Spring 1970, Vol. X, No. 1, pp. 84–102.

LANNIE, VINCENT P., *Public Money and Parochial Education*, Press of Case Western University, 1968.

MASSIALAS, BYRON G., *Education and the Political System*, Reading, Massachusetts, Addison-Wesley Publishing Company, 1969.

PITKIN, STANLEY ROYCE, *Public School Support in the United States During Periods of Economic Depression*, Brattleboro, Vermont, Stephen Daye Press, 1933.

SCOPES, JOHN T., and JAMES PRESLEY, *Center of the Storm, Memoirs of John T. Scopes*, New York, Holt, Rinehart and Winston, 1967. (Both a Broadway play and a movie, "Inherit the Wind" are based on events described in the book.)

SPURLOCK, CLARK, *Education and the Supreme Court*, University of Illinois Press, 1955.

TODD, LEWIS P., *Wartime Relations of the Federal Government and the Public Schools, 1917–1918*, New York, Teachers College, Columbia University, 1945.

ULICH, ROBERT, *The Education of Nations. A Comparison in Historical Perspective.* Harvard University Press, 1961.

UNESCO Statistical Yearbook, 1969, N. Y., Unipub, Inc. (Data from some two hundred countries on population, education, libraries, museums, science and other subjects.)

U. S. DEPARTMENT OF HEALTH, EDUCATION, AND WELFARE, OFFICE OF EDUCATION, *The Education Professions, 1968*, Washington D.C., U.S. Government Printing Office, 1969. (First annual assessment of the state of the education professions required by the Education Professions Development Act of 1967; also see subsequent report for 1969–1970.)

WILLEY, M. M., *Depression, Recovery and Higher Education*, New York, 1937.

WILSON, HOWARD E., *United States National Commission for UNESCO*, New York, 1948.

INDEX

Abacus, 31–32, 431
Abbott, Edward, 262
Abbott, Jacob, 178–79, 262, 301
  The Teacher, 183
Academic subjects
  decline in popularity of, 470–71
  need for persons skilled in, 470–71
Academician, The, 177, 118, 163, 165
Academy, the, 67–71, 106–13, 464–65
  academy movement, 106–13
  county academies, 109–10
  curriculum of, 111–12
    in Franklin's plan, 69–70
  defined, 68
  girls' and coeducational, 108–109, 110
  life span of, 110–11
  New York standards with regard to, 107
  number and distribution of, during se-
    lected periods (1775–1870), 107–
    108
  Philadelphia Academy, 63, 65, 68, 70
  problems of, 110–13
  vs. public high school, 110, 111, 112, 234
  Young Ladies' Academy (Philadelphia),
    65
Achievement tests, 392, 393, 395
Adams, Brooks, 430
Adams, Charles F., Jr., 430
Adams, Herbert B., 355, 356, 484
Adams, John, 54, 87, 90–91
  author of educational sections of Massa-
    chusetts Constitution, 84–85
  on education as public policy, 87–88
Adams, Samuel, 88
Adams Act (1906), 281
Addams, Jane, 361
Adler, Felix, 195, 198–99
Adolescent psychology, 450
Adult education, 484, 485, 498–501
  defined, 499
  history of, 499–500
  lyceum movement as form of, 118, 484
  organization support for, 500
  public evening schools, 501
Adult Education Association of the United
  States, 500
Aesop's Fables, 29
Agassiz, Elizabeth C., 210

Agassiz, Louis, 165, 305, 354, 355, 404, 431
  influence of, on development of mu-
    seums, 417–18
  laboratory investigation and, 418
  at Penikese, 485
  role of, in nature study movement, 209–
    10
  on superficiality, 206
  teaching methods of, 209
Agency for International Development
  (AID), 544
Agricultural high schools, 235, 238
Agricultural schools, 122, 269–92. *See also*
  Land-grant colleges
  early, 271–73
Air Academy at Colorado Springs, 541
Alabama, 522. *See also* South, the
Alcott, Bronson, 170–72, 316
  difficulties of, in Temple School, 171–72
Alcott, William A., 171, 179, 390
Alderman, Edwin, 262
American Annals of Education, 117, 165
American Council on Education, 455, 456
  Design for General Education, 494
American Education Fellowship, 383. *See
  also* Progressive Education Associa-
  tion
American Institute of Biological Sciences,
  425
American Institute of Instruction, 118, 168,
  182
American Journal of Education (first), 117,
  145, 164–65
American Journal of Education (second),
  169, 309
American Journal of Science, 117
American Library Association, 430
American Lyceum, 118, 499
American Medical Association, 481
American Missionary Association, 257, 258
American Montessori Society, 421
American Museum of Natural History, 210,
  418
American Philosophical Society, 68–69
American Public Health Association, 481
American Society for the Extension of Uni-
  versity Teaching, 484

American Spelling Book, The (Webster), 29
American Youth Commission (AYC), 456
  investigation by, 456–57
Angell, James B., 310, 354–55
Angell, James R., 361
Anglican schools in America, 35–36
Annapolis, Naval Academy at, 541
Anthropology and education, 409, 410–12
Antioch College, 482
Apprenticeship, 25–27, 460
Arithmetic, 535. *See also* Mathematics
  Colburn's influence upon, 175, 398
  First Lessons in Arithmetic on the Plan of Pestalozzi (Colburn), 28, 175–76
  Pestalozzi's influence upon, 337, 398
  textbooks, 32, 64
Arithmetic instruction
  during the awakening, 175–76
  early methods of, 31–33, 397–98
  research in, 398–400
  use of abacus in, 31–32, 431
Arkansas: educational legislation in, 256
Armstrong, Samuel C., 258, 263–64
Army Specialized Training Program, 535
Ascham, Roger, 7, 53
Ashbaugh, E. J., 397
Association of American Universities, 480
Association of American University Professors, 538
Athletics, university, 486–87, 489
Attendance, compulsory, 469
Audiovisual instruction, 431–34
  instructional television, 433–34
  studies on, 432–33
Automatic classroom, 439–40
Awakening, educational, 162–88. *See also* Pestalozzi
  books for teachers during, 182–85
  educational journals and, 163–66
  elementary schoolbooks of, 174–76
  reports on foreign schools, 166–67, 182
  role of Henry Barnard, 168–70
  role of Horace Mann. *See* Mann, Horace
  teachers' associations and, 168
  teaching reading during, 172–74
  useful knowledge made interesting, 176–79
Aycock, C. B., 262
Aydelotte, Frank, 505
Ayres, Leonard P., 392, 393, 395
  spelling scale prepared by, 397

Bache, Alexander D., 182, 220
  organization of high school by, 229
Bacon, Francis, 162, 316
Bagley, William C., 383
Bailey, Ebenezer, 226
Bailey, Liberty H., 212, 213, 283
Bain, Alexander, 295, 392
Barnard, Frederick A., 199, 311, 482
Barnard, Henry, 116, 117, 168–70, 194, 223, 231, 232, 238, 297, 303, 316–17, 389–90
  American Journal of Education, 169, 309
  School Architecture, 304
  as U.S. Commissioner of Education, 316–17, 541
Barnes, Earl, 196
Bartram, John, 24, 69
Bartram, William, 24
Barzun, Jacques, 492
Basedow, Johann B.: profile and theories of, 332–34
Batavia Plan, 419–20
Bateman, Newton, 147
Battledore, 28
Bay Psalm Book (1640), 3
Beard, Charles and Mary: on Dartmouth College decision, 94
Beck, Charles, 491
Beck, H. P., 488
Beecher, Catherine, 109, 110, 184
Bell, Andrew, 129
Benedict, Ruth, 410, 411
Bestor, Arthur E., 421
Bible Commonwealth, 12
Bible-reading in schools, 9, 13, 27, 28, 144
  conflicts in New York City and Philadelphia, 130–31
  court decisions, 131
Bickmore, Albert Smith, 210, 418
Binet, Alfred, 197, 405
Biological Sciences Curriculum Study, 425
Blackboard: introduction of, 156, 181, 431
Blacks. *See also* Racial segregation
  colleges for, 263–65, 521
  creation of Freedmen's Bureau for, 258–59
  schooling of, after end of reconstruction, 261–62, 520
  schools for freedmen, 257–59
Blair, Henry W., 256
Blair Bill, 247, 256, 261
Blindness. *See* Handicapped children
Bloomfield, Meyer, 466

Blow, Susan, 195, 313
Board of Regents of New York State, 107, 127, 137–38
creation of, 136
Boas, Franz, 410–11
Bode, Boyd H., 395–96
Bond, Thomas, 69
Books. *See also* Textbooks
to make useful knowledge interesting, 177–78
for school libraries, 429–30
for teachers, in the educational awakening, 182–85
Boone, Richard G., 309, 311
Boston
English High School in, 224–26
school examination of 1845, 389
Boston Latin School, 32, 50, 224, 226
change from classical to realist theory in, 60
curriculum of, 53–54
Boston Public Library, 428–29, 430
Boston Vocation Bureau, 466
Bowditch, H. P., 197
Bowdoin College, 91
Boyle, Robert, 7, 326
Brackett, Anna C., 309, 314
Brainard, John, 200
Brewer, John M., 466
Brickman, William W., 542
Briggs, Thomas H., 454
Brim, Orville, 410
Brinsley, John, 7, 8–9, 11
Brooks, Charles, 156
Brooks, Edward, 31–32, 151, 304, 431
Brooks, William K., 355
Brown University, 55, 58, 309, 482, 483
Bryan, William Jennings, 526
Bryan, William Lowe, 390
Buchanan, James: first Morrill bill vetoed by, 275
Buckingham, B. R., 397, 404
Buel, Jesse, 430
Bureau for Refugees, Freedmen, and Abandoned Lands. *See* Freedmen's Bureau
Burk, Frederic, 381, 420
Burlamaqui, Jean J., 82
Burrowes, Thomas, 223
Business education, 486
Business schools, 484
Busing, 524, 526

Butler, Nicholas Murray, 200, 309, 311, 316, 360, 391

California, 450, 451, 499
early history of state school system, 144–45
Calkins, Norman A., 303
Cambridge University, 5, 9, 56, 199, 491
Carnegie Commission on Higher Education, 452–53
Carnegie Corporation, 406, 500
Carnegie Endowment for International Peace: Institute of International Education, 506
Carnegie Foundation for the Advancement of Teaching
on college athletics, 489
on medical education, 481
Carter, James G., 148–49, 167
Carver, George Washington, 265
Cattell, J. McKeen, 358, 402, 405, 419
Chall, Jeanne, 400
Chambers, M. M., 487
Charters, Wallace W., 399, 432, 433, 440
Chautauqua movement, 484, 485, 499
Cheever, Ezekiel, 13, 40, 51, 53
Chicago, 430. *See also* University of Chicago
Chicago Institute, 364
Chief of state school system, 146–47. *See also* Superintendency of schools
Child labor in the colonies, 24–27
Child study, 192, 195–98, 307, 308, 358, 381, 389, 425
Chipman, Nathaniel, 88
Cincinnati, 430
Civilian Conservation Corps (CCC), 500, 537–39
Clapp, F. L., 400
Classical education, 52–54, 60
vs. realist education, 59–62
Classroom, automatic, 439–40
Clinton, George: on disadvantages of the academy, 112–13
Clinton Academy, 107
Clubs, rural, 283–85
Cobb, Ernest, 382
Colburn, Dana P., 165
Colburn, Warren: *First Lessons in Arithmetic on the Plan of Pestalozzi*, 28, 175–76

Coleman, James S., 409
College Entrance Examination Board, 184, 240
College of Philadelphia. See University of Pennsylvania
Colleges, 479–80. See also State Universities; Universities
  accreditation of high schools by, 239–40
  agricultural. See Agricultural schools; Land-grant colleges
  attempts of states to take over private colleges, 92–94
  black, 258, 265
  colonial, 46, 51, 55–59, 479
    charters of, 58
    connection between Latin grammar schools and, 52–53, 58
    curriculum of, 56
    entrance requirements of, 52, 54
    foundation dates of (1636–1769), 55t.
    instruction in, 59
    relation of, to churches, 57–58
    size of, 58–59
  community colleges, 451–52
  of the early national period, 90–92
    foundation dates of (1782–1800), 91t.
  engineering education introduced, 271
  failure of agriculture in academic colleges, 271
  in first century of settlement, 11
  GI bill and enrollment in, 536
  junior colleges. See Junior colleges
  land-grant. See Land-grant colleges
  language laboratories in, 437
  libraries in, 354, 427–28
  military training in, 276, 534, 535, 536
  opposition to, 90–91
  post-Revolutionary War interest in, 78
  trend toward more liberal requirements for entrance to, 383
Colles, Christopher, 64
Colonial America. See also English settlements; Middle Colonies
  apprenticeship in, 25–27
  children and the four R's in, 27–33
  children and manual labor in, 24–27
  early attempts in vocational education, 19
  educational laws in, 26–27
  life in, 17–24
    home manufacturing, 19–20

Colonial America [cont.]
  newspapers in, 21–23
  oral methods of teaching in, 31
  schoolbooks of, 28–30, 32, 33
  teachers in, 33, 35, 37, 39–40
  transportation in, 20
  types and systems of schools in, 33–39
  upper schools and colleges of, 45–73. See also Academy, the; Colleges: colonial; Latin grammar schools; Practical schools; Private schools
  usefulness of children in, 21
Colorado Springs, Air Academy at, 541
Columbia University, 55, 58, 92, 199, 411, 437, 482, 483, 492–93
  Teachers College of, 199–200, 311, 360
  International Institute of, 542
Comenius, John Amos, 6, 8, 9, 60, 62, 162, 196, 370
Commission on Instructional Technology, 440
Commission on the Reorganization of Secondary Education, 453, 458
Committee of Fifteen, 424
Committee of Ten (NEA), 240, 300, 449
Community colleges, 451–52
Comparative education, 542
Computer-assisted instruction, 440
Comstock, Anna B., 213
Conant, James B., 373, 455, 467, 470, 494
  on larger and better high schools, 471
Concord School of Philosophy, 316
Conference for Education in the South, 262
Consolidation, school, 469–70
Constitution of the United States: indirect influence of, upon education, 82–83, 513–16
Constitutions, state: education in, 82, 83–85, 516
Cooley, Edwin S., 462
Coram, Robert, 77, 89, 90
Core curriculum, 424–25
Cornell, Ezra, 279
Cornell University, 211, 212–13, 279, 283, 311, 437, 482
Corporal punishment, 154, 302
Correlation between two or more subjects, 423–24
Correspondence courses, 485
Cotton, John, 12–13, 28
Country day schools, 110, 381
County academy system, 109–10
Court cases. See also Supreme Court

Court cases [*cont.*]
on Bible-reading in schools, 131
on establishment of high schools, 228, 235–36
Scopes case in Tennessee, 525–26
Courtis, S. A., 392, 393
Cousin, Victor, 143, 166, 220
Curricula, 441
in the academies, 111–12
in Bronson's Temple School, 171
colonial, 27–33
in colleges, 56
in private schools, 62–66
in English High School of Boston, 225, 226
in Franklin's plan for an academy, 69–70
in Gardiner Lyceum, 272
in Jefferson's proposed law, 85
in Lancasterian schools, 219
in land-grant colleges, 277, 289
in Latin grammar schools, 52–54
Mann's views on, 150–51
in Philadelphia Central High School, 229
in Rensselaer School, 272
studies of, 395–96
Curricular innovations, 422–27
core curriculum, 424–25
correlation, 423–24
discipline-centered approaches to, 425–26
unit-teaching, 422–23
Curry, J. L. M., 260, 262
Curtis, Henry S., 538

Dabney, Charles W., 249, 262
Dabney, Robert L., 249
Dale, Edgar, 432, 433
Dalton Plan, 420–21, 422
Dame schools, 28, 30, 34, 172, 224
Dane, Nathan, 104, 108
Darrow, Clarence, 526
Dartmouth College, 55, 58, 279
lawsuit over control of, 93–94, 527
Supreme Court decision, 94
Darwin, Charles, 196, 370
Davis, Jesse B., 454, 466
Deafness. *See* Handicapped children
Dearborn, Walter F., 395
Decroly, Ovide, 381
Deerfield Academy, 465
De Garmo, Charles, 339

Delinquency, 468
Democracy and Education (Dewey), 364, 367–69, 371
Dewey, Alice Chipman, 364
Dewey, Davis Rich, 351
Dewey, John, 123, 194, 315, 316, 349–85, 412, 446, 453, 462, 492, 542
debt to Herbart, 374
Democracy and Education, 364, 367–69, 371
Ella Flagg Young and, 375–78
on growth as the aim of education, 369–72
ideas on progressive education, 380
philosophy defined by, 384
psychological writing of, 357–59
on thought process, 372–74
at University of Chicago, 359–64
University of Chicago Elementary School founded by, 361, 362–64
youth of, 351–53
Dewey, Melvil, 484
Dickinson, John, 93
Dickinson College, 91
Dictionaries, 29
Dilthey, Wilhelm, 296
Dilworth, Thomas, 29, 172
Disadvantaged children, 410
Discipline-centered approaches to curricular innovations, 425–26
District system of schools, 38–39, 40
Divoll, Ira, 312, 430
Dix, Dorothea L., 119–20
Dock, Christopher, 65–66, 68, 307
Dove, David James, 65, 70
Downing, Elliot Rowland, 211
Draper, Andrew Sloan, 139, 147, 393
Drawing instruction, 200, 299
DuBoise, W. E. B., 264
Duggan, Stephen P., 506
Du Pont de Nemours, Pierre S., 77, 89
Dury, John, 8, 9
Dutch schools in America, 32, 34–35
Dwight, Edmund, 153, 156, 167
Dwight, Timothy, 91, 109

Eades, John, 381
Eaton, Amos, 122, 418
Eaton, John, 258
Economic Opportunity Act (1964), 410
Edgeworth, Maria, 163
Edgeworth, Richard, 163

Education
  anthropology and, 409, 410–12
  as a branch of study, 297
  comparative, 542
  democracy and, 366–69
  departments of, created in universities, 360
  federal aid to, 140–41, 256–57, 261–62, 274–75, 276, 286–87, 528–32
  government and, in emergencies, 532–40
  immigration and problems in, 105
  influence of U.S. Constitution upon, 82–83, 513–16
  international, 541–44
  preservation of liberty and, 77–101
  progressive, 379–84. *See also* Progressive education
  psychology and, 403–406
  as a science, 294, 295–96, 392–412
    dispute over, 296
  sociology and, 409–10
  specialties in, 305–309
  in the state constitutions, 82, 83–85, 516
  technology of, 416–45. *See also* Technology of education
  university courses in, 309–11
Educational awakening. *See* Awakening, educational
Educational measurement, 390–412
Educational problems, 467–73
Educational psychology, 307–309, 403–406
Educational Review, 309
Educational testing, 404–406. *See also* Intelligence tests
Eggleston, Edward, 21, 143
Eight-Year Study on preparation for college, 382–83
Elementary education, 191–218
  American kindergarten. *See* Kindergarten
  child study movement, 192
  handwork, preparation of teachers in, 198–200
  nature study, 205, 208–14. *See also* Nature study
  object-teaching in, 202, 203–206, 303. *See also* Object-teaching
  Quincy methods, 206–208
  science-teaching trends, 214–15
Elementary and Secondary Education Act (1965), 531
Eliot, Charles W., 151, 240, 299, 300, 311, 354–55, 360, 382, 391, 408
  ideas on progressive education, 380
  on steps in scientific discovery, 373

Elliott, E. C., 487
Elocution, 173
Emerson, George B., 156, 172–73, 175, 183, 184, 240
  as principal of English High School, 225
  The School and the Schoolmaster, 184, 201, 301
Emerson, Ralph Waldo, 4, 170, 316
  educational theory of, 122–24, 133
Engineering education, 484
  beginnings of, 271
Engineering schools, 122, 486
England
  early civilization of, 4–5
  schools in, 7–10
  science in, 7
  social classes in, 7–8
English, teaching of, 8–9
  in colonial schools, 33, 65
  by Puritans, 13
English High School (Boston), 224–26
  curriculum of, 225, 226
English idea *vs.* German idea of universities, 490–92
English settlements, 10–14
  attempts to establish colleges in, 11
  early failures in colonization of, 10–11
English universities, 504–505
Erasmus Hall, 107
Erickson, T. A., 284
Erskine, John, 493
Ethical Culture Society and schools, 195, 198–99
European universities, 55–56, 59, 353–54, 490–92
Evening schools, 501
Everett, Edward, 156, 157, 354, 428–29, 491
Exceptional children. *See also* Gifted children; Handicapped children
  defined, 406
  studies of, 406–409
Exchange students, 503–507
Extension teaching, university, 285–86, 484–85, 499

Faculty psychology, 298–301, 340
Federal aid to education, 140–41, 256–57, 261–62, 274–75, 276, 286–87, 528–32
Fellenberg, Philipp von, 183
Fellenberg manual labor system, 165–66, 271

Finley, Samuel, 49
Finn, James D., 439
Fisk University, 265
Fiske, John, 370
Fitch, John, 64, 105
Fithian, Philip, 50
Flagg, A. C., 429
Fleury, Claude, 327
Flexner, Abraham, 496
  criticism of universities, 488–89
  report on medical schools, 481, 488
Florida, 482–83, 522
Folwell, W. W., 452
Football, 486
Ford, Paul L., 28
Ford Foundation, 500
Foster, Michael, 488
4-H Clubs, 284–85
Fowle, William B., 175
Fox, George, 29
Frame of Government (Penn), 61
Frankfurter, Felix, 526–27
Franklin, Benjamin, 23–24, 32, 33, 63, 65,
    80, 428
  American Philosophical Society orga-
    nized by, 68
  early writings on education, 32, 33–34
  Proposals of, for an academy, 68–70
Franklin and Marshall College, 91
Free School Society (later, Public School
    Society) of New York City, 128–31
  Lancasterian system used by. See Lancas-
    terian schools
Freedmen's Bureau (Bureau for Refugees,
    Freedmen, and Abandoned Lands),
    247, 258–59, 264
Freedom of speech and press, 22–23
Freeman, Frank, 432
Friends, Society of, 7, 9, 523
  schools of, 34, 40, 51–52
Froebel, Friedrich W., 169, 177, 183, 192–
    94, 198, 305, 370, 381, 425
  The Education of Man, 342, 344
  profile and theories of, 340–44
Fulbright, J. William, 505
Fulbright Act (1944), 505
Fund for Adult Education, 500
Fund for the Advancement of Education,
    496–97

Gallaudet, Thomas H., 120–21, 167, 181,
    309
  school for deaf opened by, 408

Gardiner Lyceum, 122, 183, 271–72
Garrison, W. L., 119
General Education Board, 235, 260, 263,
    455
General education in universities, 492–95
Geography, 299
  Pestalozzi's influence on teaching of, 337
  Rousseau's ideas on teaching of, 331
  teaching and textbooks of the awakening,
    174–75
Georgetown University: Institute of Lan-
    guages of, 437
Georgia, 522. See also South, secondary
    education in
German Hochschule, 490
German Realschule, 69, 220, 229
German idea vs. English idea of universities,
    490–92
German universities, 503
Germantown Union School, 65
Gesell, Arnold, 196
GI bill (1944), 536
Gifted children. See also Exceptional chil-
    dren; Handicapped children
  advanced placement programs for, 471–
    72
  selection and education of, 407–408
Gilbert, William, 7
Gildersleeve, Basil L., 355
Gilman, Daniel C., 353–56, 374, 491
Girard College, 259
Girls, education of, 45, 65, 68, 152, 463,
    464. See also Women
  girls' and coeducational academies, 108–
    109, 110
  girls' high schools established, 226, 227
Goddard, Henry H., 196, 197, 405
Godfrey, Thomas, 63–64, 69
Goodrich, Samuel G., (Peter Parley), 178
Graduate schools, 478, 480, 486, 495
  opened to women, 483
Graham, A. B., 284
Grammar in early schools, 33
Graydon, Alexander, 65
Greeley, Horace, 117, 283
Greene, S. S., 430
Greenwood, Isaac, 32, 64
Grew, Theophilus, 63
Griscom, John, 164
Gruner, G. Anton, 342
Guidance in school, 466–67
Guilford, Joy P., 406
Guyot, Arnold, 165, 175

Hale, Benjamin, 272
Hall, G. Stanley, 297, 307, 339, 355, 358, 405, 419, 450
 child studies by, 196–97
Hall, Samuel R., 148, 178, 183, 301
 Lectures on School-Keeping, 148, 182
Halleck, Reuben Post, 308
Hamilton, Alexander, 54
Hamilton, Andrew, 22
Hampden-Sidney College, 91
Hampton Institute, 212, 257–58, 263–64, 265
Handbook of Private Schools (Sargent), 110, 223
Handicapped children
 establishment of classes for children of low intelligence, 121
 establishment of schools and classes for the deaf and blind, 120–21, 408–409
Hanus, Paul H., 393, 424, 461
Harlan, John Marshall, 520
Harper, William R., 359, 360, 364, 452, 499
Harris, William T., 168, 195, 201, 209, 297, 306, 309, 311, 349, 393
 "five windows" theory of, 316
 as interpreter of Hegel, 315–16
 as superintendent of St. Louis schools, 311–16
 as U.S. Commission of Education, 316, 541
Harris Teachers College, 313
Hart, James Morgan, 491
Harter, Noble, 390
Hartford Female Seminary, 109
Hartford Seminary Foundation, 437
Harvard Report (1945), 493–94
Harvard University, 51, 55, 57, 58, 61, 64, 87, 91, 92, 354, 360, 418, 427, 437, 482, 483, 493–94, 495
 early entrance requirements of, 52, 54
 Graduate School of Education, 311
 Museum of Comparative Zoology at, 417
Harvey, William, 7
Hatch Act (1887), 281
Hawley, Gideon, 137, 139
Hawthorne, Nathanial, 13, 430
Hays, Arthur Garfield, 526
Hazelwood School (England), 183, 272, 383
Head Start program, 410
Hegel, Georg W., 315–16, 376, 377

Hegelian philosophy, 492
Herbart, Johann F., 295, 423, 424
 profile and theories of, 338–40
High schools, 222–40, 453, 454, 455. *See also* Secondary education
 accrediting system for, 239, 455
 advanced placement programs in, 471–72
 agricultural, 235, 238
 commercial courses in, 238
 comprehensive or general, 453, 458
 Conant and Rickover on larger and better schools, 471
 court cases concerning, 228, 235–36
 decline in popularity of academic subjects, 470–71
 English Classical School, 224–26
 evolution of, 222–23
 inefficient, 455, 469–70
 legislation for establishment of, 223, 228
 life adjustment training in, 469
 for manual training, 238
 in Massachusetts, 227–28
 in the Middle West, 231–33
 military training in, 533
 parochial, 463–64
 in Pennsylvania, 228–31
  Central High School of Philadelphia, 228–30
 percent of population, 14–17 years of age, enrolled in, 236, 237t.
 in the South, 233–35
 specialized vocational, 458–59
 spread of, 222, 228–40
 standards for, 238–40
 vs. the academy and private schools, 110, 111, 112, 234
 vocational education in, 286, 287
 World War II and, 534–35
Higher education. *See also* Colleges and Universities
 advances in, 478–511
Hill, Frank A., 237–38
Hill, Thomas W., 183
Hillegas, M. B., 404
Hilo Manual Labor School (Honolulu), 264
Hinsdale, Burke A., 300, 306, 307, 339, 373
Hoar, George F., 256
Hoar Bill, 247, 256
Hobart College, 271
Holbrook, Josiah, 118, 181
Hollingshead, A. B., 409

Hollingworth, Leta S., 407, 408
Holloway, H. V., 400
Holmes, Ezekiel, 272
Home and Colonial School Society, 203
Home economics in colleges, 280
Hoole, Charles, 8, 9
Hoover, Herbert, 536
Hopkins, Johns, 354
Hornbook, 28
Howard University, 265
Howe, Samuel G., 121, 154–55, 389
  school for blind opened by, 408
Howison, G. H., 315
Huey, Edmund Burke, 402, 403
Hull House, 361
Hus, John, 15
Hutchins, Robert Maynard, 421
  criticism of universities, 488, 489–90
Huxley, Thomas H., 355, 418

Illinois, 462. See also Chicago
Illinois Society for Child-Study, 362
Immigration, 16, 65, 105
Indian words in modern English, 3–4
Indiana: early history of state school system, 143–44
Indiana University, 98
Individual instruction, 381, 419–22
Industrial Education Association, 199–200
Institute of International Education, 506, 542
Intelligence: theories of, 405–406
Intelligence quotient (IQ), 407
Intelligence tests, 197–98, 296, 405, 407. See also Testing
International education, 541–44
  defined, 541–42
  organizations for, 542–44
International Education Year (1970), 544
International Institute of Teachers College, Columbia University, 542
International Kindergarten Union, 542
Iowa
  academy movement in, 110
  high schools in, 232–33
Iowa State University, 280, 310, 482
  School of Education of, 310

Jackman, Wilbur S., 211
Jackson State College, 486
Jacotot, Joseph, 172, 400

James, William, 295, 300, 308, 315, 358, 360, 400, 403–404
James-Lange theory, 358
Jardine, George, 163, 164
Javal, Émile, 400
Jay, John, 88
Jeanes, Anna T., 260
Jefferson, Thomas, 32, 54, 77, 81, 117, 183, 252, 269, 271, 349, 355, 398
  on Dartmouth College case, 94–95
  educational views of, 85, 86–87
  Virginia bill of, for more general diffusion of knowledge, 85–87
Job Corps, 410
John Dewey Society, 383
Johns Hopkins University, 308, 419, 437, 478, 483, 491
  graduate study at, 495
  organized by Daniel Gilman, 354–55
Johonnot, James, 304–305
Jones, Edward S., 505
Jones, Margaret, 204
Jones, Thomas P., 178
Journals, educational: of the awakening, 163–66, 166t.
Jullien, Marc-Antoine, 542
Junior colleges, 241, 451–53, 517
Junior high schools, 448–51. See also Secondary education
  central idea of, 450
  teachers in, 450–51

Kalamazoo case, 235–36, 310
Kandel, Isaac, 497, 501, 542
Kansas State College, 280
Kant, Immanuel, 333–34, 338, 342
Keagy, John M., 165
Keller, Helen, 408–409
Kellogg Foundation, 500
Kennedy, John F., 446
Kent State University, 486
Keppel, Frederick P., 500, 501
Kern, O. J., 284
Kerschensteiner, Georg, 376, 461
Kiddle, Henry, 309
Kilpatrick, William H., 421
Kindergarten, 381
  American-type, 192, 194–95
  criticism of Froebel's theory, 193–94
  development of, in St. Louis, 195, 313
  training schools for kindergartners, 194
Kingsley, Clarence D., 458

Kirkpatrick, Edward A., 308
Kirkpatrick, J. E., 488
Knapp, Seaman A., 235, 263, 284, 285
Knox, Samuel, 77, 89
Kriege, Matilde, 194
Krüsi, Hermann, 337–38
Krüsi, Hermann, Jr., 165, 204, 205, 211, 338

Labor unions
  high school and, 221
  public education favored by, 114–15
  vs. state departments of education, on apprentice standards, 460
Laboratories, 418–19
  psychological, 308, 358, 418–19
  for research, demonstration, and class teaching, 418
Lamb, Andrew, 64
Lancaster, Joseph, 129, 132
  conflicting views about, 132
Lancasterian (or monitorial) schools, 128–32, 312, 421
  curriculum of, 129
  in Detroit, 142
  failure of, 130–31, 132
  faults of, 129
  Horace Mann on, 149
  in New York City, 129–31, 164
  in Philadelphia, 131–32
  spread of, 132
  teaching system in, 219
Land-grant(s)
  mismanagement of, 279
  size of, in first Morrill Act, 276
Land-grant colleges, 270, 482. See also Agricultural schools; Morrill Acts
  admission of women, 280, 482
  aided by experiment stations, 281
  black, 263, 265, 521
  extension teaching by, 285–86, 485, 499
  formation of, 277–79
    problems in, 278–79
  growth of, 288–91
  military training requirements in, 276
  problems encountered by, 279–81
  schools of science, 278
Langethal, H., 344
Language study, 434–37, 542
  during World War II, 436, 535
  history of, 434–35
  importance of, 470, 471, 535

Language study [cont.]
  language laboratories, 437
  post-World War II, 436–37
  Supreme Court decision on, 524–25
Lathrop, John H., 272
Latin grammar schools, 45
  change from classical to realist theory in, 59–60
  close connection between colonial college and, 52–53, 58
  curricula of, 52–55
  in the Middle Colonies, 51–52
  in New England, 50–51
  origins of, 46–48
  in the South, 48–50
Leacock, Stephen, 486
League of Nations, 542
Lectures on School-Keeping (Hall), 148, 182
Lee, Robert E., 484
Libraries, 185, 427–31
  American Library Association, 430
  college libraries, 354, 427–28
  cooperation between schools and, 430
  national and state, 428
  school libraries, 429–31
  semi-public and public, 428–29
Library of Congress, 428, 541
Lieber, Francis, 491
Liebig, Justus von, 418
Life adjustment education, 469
Lincoln, Abraham, 104, 275
  on education of the blacks, 250
Lincoln, Levi, 157, 164
Linguistics, 411
Link, Henry C., 401–402
Linton, Ralph, 411
Little Rock: riots in, 523
Locke, John, 8, 9, 28, 61, 69, 82, 162, 298, 307, 339
  on English grammar schools, 47–48
  Essay Concerning the Human Understanding, 326
  profile and theories of, 326–28
"Log-College," the, 52
Lord, Asa D., 232
Lowell, Abbott L., 494
Lowth, Robert, 33
Luther, Martin, 60
Lyceum, the, 174, 176, 177, 484
  description and function of, 118
  role of, in advancement of public education, 118

McGill University, 269
McGuffey, William H.: readers of, 28, 401
McIver, Charles D., 262
McLellan, J. A., 357, 359
Maclure, William, 121, 163
McMurry, Charles, 339
McMurry, Frank, 339, 398
Madison, James, 54, 88
  national university favored by, 89
Mann, Horace, 117, 121, 133, 147, 148–
    57, 168, 172, 174, 181, 182, 191,
    200, 208, 297, 304, 349, 389–90,
    431, 482
  on conditions in Massachusetts schools,
    150
  controversy with Boston masters, 154
  creating public interest in public educa-
    tion, 152
  on education in colonial Massachusetts,
    149
  influence of, 156
  religious controversy, 155
  on school libraries, 429
  on schools in Germany, 166–67
  teaching of music recommended by, 175
  on value of normal schools, 156, 167
  views of, on curriculum, 150–51
Manual training, 121–22, 381, 421, 461
Manual training high schools, 238
Marcet, Jane H.: books written by, 177–78
Marsh, James, 352
Marshall, John, 516
Martin, George H., 462
Martin, H. Newell, 355
Maryland, 277
Mason, Lowell, 165, 175
Massachusetts, 251, 278, 431
  admission of girls to district schools, 152
  attacks upon the normal schools, 153
  compulsory school attendance in, 157
  control of academies in, 108
  district school libraries in, 429, 430
  early history of state school system, 147–
    57. See also Mann, Horace
  education law of 1642, 26
  establishment of state normal schools,
    153
  high schools in, 227–28
    English High School, 224–26
  Latin grammar schools in, 50–51
  prohibition of sectarian teaching, 155
  1647 school law (old deluder Satan law),
    37, 50, 51, 133, 135, 149

Massachusetts [cont.]
  town schools in, 37–38
  vocational education in, 461–62
Massachusetts Institute of Technology,
    278, 461, 484
Mathematical Association of America, 496
Mathematics, 470, 471, 535. See also Arith-
    metic
  in colonial period, 32
  early teachers of, 63–64
  School Mathematics Study Group (SM-
    SG), 426
Mather, Cotton, 6, 15, 60
Maxwell, William H., 393–94
Mayflower Compact, 11–12
Mead, George, 361
Mead, Margaret, 410, 411
Measurement, educational, 390–412
Medical schools
  admission of women to, 483,
  control of, 481
  early, 479, 481
    closing of, 481
Meiklejohn, Alexander, 493
Mental retardation. See Handicapped chil-
    dren
Meriam, J. L., 381
Meumann, Ernst, 197
Miami University (Ohio), 98
Michigan, 251, 277
  district school libraries in, 429, 430
  early history of state school system, 142–
    43
Michigan State Agricultural College, 279
Michigan State University: Center for Con-
    tinuing Education, 500
Middendorf, W., 344
Middle Colonies, the, 14–17. See also Co-
    lonial America; English settlements
  education in, 16–17
  Latin grammar schools in, 51–52
  sects, nationalities, and languages of, 14–
    16
Middle school plan, 448, 449 fig., 451
Middlebury College, 91
Military Academy at West Point, 270–71,
    487, 541
Military schools, 110, 219, 533
Military training
  in colleges, 534, 535, 536
  in high schools, 533
  in land-grant colleges, 276
Milton, John, 8

Minnesota, 499
Mitchel, Ormsby M., 271
Monitorial schools. *See* Lancasterian schools
Montessori, Maria, 420, 438
Montessori schools, 421
Montessori teacher training programs, 421
Moore, Ernest C., 393
Moravians, the, 15–16
Morehouse College, 265
Morrill, Justin S., 273–74, 275–76, 278, 281, 282
Morrill Acts, 257, 285, 351, 516. *See also* Land-grant colleges
  first Act (1862), 275–77, 528
  first bill vetoed (1859), 275
  second Act (1890), 263, 281–83, 528
Morris, George S., 356
Morrison, Henry C., 423
Mott, John R., 507
Mott, Lucretia, 106
Moving School, the, 38, 145
Mulcaster, Richard, 7, 8, 9
  profile and theories of, 325
Murray, Lindley: grammar book of, 28
Museum of Comparative Zoology at Harvard University, 417
Museums and schools, 210, 417–18
Music in elementary schools, 175

National Academy of Sciences, 498
National Association for the Advancement of Colored People (NAACP), 520–21, 522
National Association of Secondary School Principals, 454
National Council of Education, 300
National Defense Education Act (1958), 425, 466, 514, 530–31, 545
  promotion of language studies by, 437
National Education Association (NEA), 196, 240, 311, 315, 362, 375, 379, 449
  Committee on the Place of the Industries in Public Education, 462
  Department of Adult Education, 500
  Department of Audiovisual Instruction, 432
  formation of Committee of Ten. *See* Committee of Ten
National Herbart Society, 362
National independence and education, 77–101

National Institute of Education, 541
National School District Reorganization Study, 518
National Science Foundation, 425, 426
  Summer Institute Program of, 498
National Society for the Study of Education, 339
National Teachers' Association (later, National Education Association), 311
National university, idea of, 89–90
National Youth Administration (NYA), 500, 539–40
Nature study, 205, 208–14, 330
  growth of movement in, 211–14
  role of Agassiz in, 209–10
  role of Cornell University in, 212–13
Naval Academy at Annapolis, 541
Navigation: results of advances in, 6–7
NEA. *See* National Education Association
Neef, Joseph, 121, 163
  as a Pestalozzian teacher, 163, 176
  Sketch of a Plan and Method of Education, 163
Neill, A. S., 384
New and Complete System of Arithmetic (Pike), 64, 77
New England
  connection of government, church, and school, 36–37
  Latin grammar schools in, 50–51
  town schools in, 37–38
    decline in, 38
New England Primer, The, 28, 29, 155, 177
New Hampshire, 428
  early history of state school system, 145–46
New Harmony community, 115, 121, 163
New Jersey, 428
New York City, 199
  middle school plan in, 451
  School Inquiry of 1911–1912, 393, 394, 395
New York Public Library, 429
New York State, 462
  Board of Regents, 107, 127, 137–38
    creation of, 136
  control of academies in, 107
  district school libraries in, 185, 429, 430
  early history of state school system, 136–39
New York University, 309, 311, 483
Newman, John Henry, 491
Newspapers
  freedom of the press and, 22–23

Newspapers [*cont.*]
   relation of, to education, 21–22, 117
   role of, in pre-Revolutionary debate, 23
Nixon, Richard M.: on school integration, 523–24
Nongraded school, 422
Normal schools, 167–68, 259, 260, 481
   city normal schools, 201
   first state normal school opened, 153
   Mann's estimate of value of, 156, 167
   Oswego Normal School, 202, 206
   promoted by Gallaudet, 120
   recommended by Carter, 149
   spread of state normal schools, 200–201
   teaching of drawing compulsory in, 200
North Carolina. *See also* South, the
   academy movement in, 109
   educational progress in, before Civil War, 251–52
Northwest Ordinance of 1787, 85, 103–104, 515
Norton, John K., 536–37
Norwich University, 271

Oberlin College, 45, 482
Object-teaching, 202, 203–206, 296, 303, 421
   books on, 303
   criticism and controversy over, 205–206
Office of Education, U.S., 393, 469, 528, 536, 540–41
   creation of, 540
   functions of, 540
   support of reading research projects, 400
Ohio, 251, 277–78, 515, 528
   early history of state school system, 140–42
   high schools in, 231–32
Ohio Evaluation of School Broadcasts Project, 433
Ohio State University
   Bureau of Educational Research at, 432
   Leadership Studies, 409
Ohio University, 98, 515
"Old field" school, 34
Oral methods of teaching in early schools, 31
Oratory, 173–74
Ordinance of 1785, 140–41, 515, 528
Ordinance of 1787, 85, 103–104, 515
Oregon case, 136, 463, 525
Oswego, New York, 306, 376

Oswego, New York [*cont.*]
   object-teaching in, 202, 203–206, 210–11
Oswego Normal School, 202, 206
Otis, Arthur S., 405
Owen, Robert, 119
   New Harmony colony founded by, 115, 121
Owen, Robert Dale, 115
Oxford University, 5, 9, 56, 491, 504

Page, David P., 306
   Theory and Practice of Teaching, 182, 201, 301–302, 305
Painter, F. V. N., 309
Palmer, E. Laurence, 213
Parker, Francis W., 168, 206, 207, 208, 211, 315, 339, 349, 350, 361, 401, 419, 421, 430, 453
   ideas on progressive education, 380
Parker, Samuel C., 424
Parker, Theodore, 481
Parkhurst, Helen, 381, 420
Parley, Peter. *See* Goodrich, Samuel G.
Parochial schools, 34, 219, 314, 463–64, 530
Parsons, Frank H., 466
Partridge, Alden, 271, 273, 533
Pastorius, Francis D., 15, 51
Paulsen, Friedrick, 488
Payne, William H., 168, 199, 296, 297, 301, 305, 306–307, 310, 373, 392
Payne Fund of New York, 432–33
Peabody, Elizabeth, 194
Peabody, George, 259
Peabody Fund and Board, 259–60
Peace Corps, 544
Peake, Mary L., 257
Peirce, Charles S., 315
Peirce, Cyrus, 157
Penmanship: teaching of, 30, 67
Penn, William, 8, 9, 51
   educational opinions of, 61–62
Penn (William) Charter School, 32, 51–52
   two-course plan of, 60
Pennsylvania, 251, 277, 428
   control of academies in, 108
   early history of state school system, 139–40
Pennsylvania Society for the Promotion of Public Schools, 118, 140
Perkiomen School, 15
Perry, William, 29

Personality development, 411
Pestalozzi, Johann H., 30, 79, 162, 177, 196, 298, 305, 338, 343, 381
  profile and theories of, 334–38
Pestalozzianism, 163–64, 165–66, 167, 169, 202, 203, 204, 303, 342, 343, 344
  criticism of, 179–80
  in the teaching of arithmetic, 175–76
  in the teaching of music, 175
Peters, Richard, 65
Petty, William, 8
Phelps, Almira L., 109
Philadelphia: diocesan high schools in, 464
Philadelphia Academy, 63, 65, 225
  founding of, 68, 70
Philadelphia Central High School, 228–30
  School of Pedagogy, 233
Philadelphia Library Company, 428
Philanthropic societies: establishment of schools by, 128. See also Free School Society; Lancasterian schools
Phillips Andover, 106, 465
Phillips Exeter, 106, 465
Physical education, 533–34
Picket, Albert, 117
Picket, John W., 117
Pierce, John D., 143
Pierce, Sarah, 109
Pike, Nicholas: New and Complete System of Arithmetic, 64, 77, 398
Plato, 86, 191
Poor, John, 65
Postal service
  development of, 23–24
  education and, 24
Potter, Alonzo: The School and the Schoolmaster, 184, 201, 301
Practical schools, 46
Preparatory schools, 219–20
Presidential Commission on Campus Unrest, 486
President's Commission on Education Beyond the High School, 531
Pressey, Sidney L., 408, 438–39
Primer, the, 28, 172
Princeton University, 55, 58, 437, 482
  early entrance requirements of, 54
Private schools
  colonial, 62–67
    curricula in, 62–66
    teachers in, 63–67
  in secondary education, 462–66

Private schools [cont.]
  Supreme Court decision in Oregon case, 136, 463
  vs. public high school, 234
  weakness of, 111
Professions, 495
Progressive education, 379–84, 419, 468
  individual instruction, 381. See also Individual instruction
  schools connected with universities, 381
  scientific movement in education and, 389–90
Progressive Education Association, 380, 381, 383
  Eight-Year Study of, 382–83
Proposals Relating to the Education of Youth in Pennsylvania (Franklin), 68–70
Prosser, Charles Allen: Prosser Resolution and, 469
Protestant Reformation, 5–6
Psychological laboratories, 308, 358, 418–19
Psychology
  adolescent, 450
  education and, 307–309, 403–406
  faculty, 298, 340
Public education movement, 102, 127. See also Public schools; State school systems
  definition of public education, 134–35
    by court decision, 135
  favored by labor unions, 114–15
  influence of the lyceum and other societies upon, 118–19
  influence of the press on advancement of, 117
  opposition to, 116
  social reforms and, 119–20
  Southern opposition to, 248–50
Public School Society (formerly, Free School Society) of New York City, 128–31
  Lancasterian system used by. See Lancasterian schools
Public schools
  need for greater uniformity in, 517–18
  state control of, 516–19
Pueblo Plan, 381, 420
Pugh, Evan, 277, 281
Puritanism, 7, 8, 9–10
  influence of, on education, 12–14, 37
Puritans, the, 16

Puritans, the [*cont.*]
harshness of, 12–13
Purnell Act (1925), 281

Quakers, the, 10, 12, 14, 15, 16, 131. *See
also* Friends, Society of
Quill pens, 30, 431
Quincy, Josiah, 156, 226
Quincy (Mass.) methods of teaching, 206–
208, 421

Racial segregation, 519–24. *See also* Supreme Court
decision outlawing (1954), 522
Little Rock riots, 523
middle school concept and, 451
Richard Nixon on school integration,
523–24
schools closed in Prince Edward County,
Va., 523
Radio, instructional, 433
Rambusch, Nancy McCormick, 421
Randolph, Virginia, 260
Raymond, Henry J., 117
Reading
in colonial times, 30, 172
public speaking and, 173–74
studies of, 400–403
teaching of, in the educational awaken-
ing, 172–74
word recognition in, 172, 400
Reading readiness, 403
Realist education, 8–9, 60–61
proposed by Benjamin Franklin, 69–70
vs. classical education, 59–62
Reconstruction and education, 255–56
Redway, Jacques W., 421
Reflections and Maxims (Penn), 61
Reforms
educational, 120–22
social, 119–20
Religion in education, 28, 34, 36–37, 56–
58, 68, 130, 144, 155, 171–72, 302,
314, 464, 479
court cases involving, 131
Protestant-Catholic conflicts, 130–31
Remsen, Ira, 355
Renaissance, the, 5
Rensselaer School (later known as Rens-
selaer Polytechnic Institute), 122,
271, 418, 484
Reserve Officers' Training Corps, 534

Reynard the Fox, 29
Rhodes, Cecil, 504
Rhodes scholarships, 504–505
Rice, Joseph, 390–92, 393
criticism of American schools, 390–91
Society of Educational Research founded
by, 392
spelling investigation by, 391
Richards, Charles R., 462
Rickover, Hyman G.: on larger and better
high schools, 471
Riessman, Frank, 410
Rittenhouse, David, 20, 24, 32, 93
Roberts, Isaac, 212, 280
Rochester Athenaeum, 499
Rockefeller, John D., Sr., 262
Rockefeller Foundation, 433
Rosenkranz, Karl, 309
Rousseau, Jean, 4, 162, 196, 307, 333, 370,
381, 403
profile and theories of, 328–32
Rowland, Henry A., 355
Royce, Josiah, 296, 315
Ruffner, William H., 249
Runkle, John D., 461
Rural clubs, 283–85
Rush, Benjamin, 32, 65, 77, 88
federal university proposed by, 89
Russell, William, 117, 145, 164, 173
American Journal of Education, 164–65
Rutgers University (formerly, Queen's Col-
lege), 55, 58, 279

St. John's College, 91
St. Louis Plan of instruction, 419
St. Louis schools, 430
William T. Harris as superintendent of,
311–16
St. Paul's School of Concord, New Hamp-
shire, 465
Sapir, Edward, 410–411
Sargent, Porter: *Handbook of Private
Schools*, 110, 223
Schem, Alexander J., 309
Scholarships, 504–506
School administration, 305–307, 314–15
School buildings: construction of, 304
School consolidation movement, 469–70
School districts, 141, 143, 518–19
powers of, 519
redrawing of, to achieve integration, 524
reduction in number, 518

School management, 303, 304
School Mathematics Study Group (SM-SG), 426
School and the Schoolmaster, The (Potter and Emerson), 184, 201, 301
School surveys, 393–95
Schooling: patterns of, 448–49, 450, 451
  Carnegie Commission on changes in, 452–53
Schools
  cooperation between libraries and, 430
  superintendency of, 305–306, 314–15
Schwenkfeld, Caspar, 15
Science
  books to add interest to, 177–78
  trends in teaching of, 214–15
Sciences, the, 176–77, 305, 470, 471
Scientific movement, early, 7
Scopes case in Tennessee, 525–26
Search, Preston W., 380–81, 392, 420, 439
Sears, Barnas, 259, 260, 261
Secondary education
  American *vs.* European, 220
  Commission on the Reorganization of Secondary Education, 453, 458
  Cooperative Study of Secondary School Standards, 455
  decline in popularity of academic subjects, 470–71
  definitions of, 219–20
  high schools. *See* High schools
  National Association of Secondary School Principals, 454
  new directions for, 446–77
    goals and functions, 453–58
    guidance, 466–67
    junior college, 451–53
    private schools, 462–66
    rise of the junior high school, 448–51
  percent of population, 14–17 years of age, enrolled in, 236, 237t.
  persistent problems, 467–73
Segregation, racial. *See* Racial segregation
Self-education, 24
Self-government of students, 183
Sewall, Samuel, 13
Shaler, Nathaniel S., 210, 211
Shaw, Pauline Agassiz, 466
Sheldon, Edward A., 202–204, 206, 208, 297, 303, 306, 376
Sheridan, Thomas, 33
Silliman, Benjamin, 117, 278
Simon, Theodore, 405

Skinner, B. F., 439
Slater, John F.: Slater Fund and, 260
Slavery and education, 119, 254
Small, Walter H., 51
Smith, Adam, 19
Smith, David E., 399
Smith, Mortimer B., 421
Smith, Samuel H., 77, 89
Smith, William, 70, 92
  A General Idea of the College of Mirania, 71
Smith-Hughes Act (1917), 235, 286–87, 289, 458, 462, 516, 529, 530, 545
Smith-Lever Act (1914), 285–86, 289, 485, 499
Smith-Tower bill, 529–30, 531
Smithsonian Institution, 541
Snedden, David, 458, 462
Social studies: teaching of, 472
Society of Associated Teachers of New York, 114, 118
Society of Educational Research, 392
Society of Friends. *See* Friends; Quakers
Society for the Propagation of the Gospel in Foreign Parts, 34, 35–36, 40, 49
Sociology and education, 409–10
Soldan, F. Louis, 315
South, the. *See also individual states*
  Conference for Education in the South, 262
  educational aid from Peabody and other funds, 259–60, 263
  educational progress in, before Civil War, 250–53
  opposition to public education, 248–50
  reconstruction and education, 255–56
  schools for freedmen, 257–59
  secondary education in, 233–35
  slavery and education, 119, 254
  special schools for blacks, 263–65
  toward universal education in, 261–63
South Carolina, 522. *See also* South, the
Southern Education Board, 234, 235, 260, 262–63
Southern Regional Educational Board, 521
Spearman, Charles, 198
Spelling books, 9, 29–30
Spelling instruction: research in, 396–97
Spelling investigation by Joseph Rice, 391
Spencer, Herbert, 151, 299
Stanford-Binet Intelligence Scale, 407
Stanton, Elizabeth Cady, 106

State colleges, 270. *See also* State universities
State constitutions: education in, 82, 83–85, 516
State control of public schools, 516–19
State school systems, 135–36, 516–19. *See also* Public education movement; Public schools
in California, 144–45
chief official (superintendent) of, 146–47
in Indiana, 143–44
in Massachusetts, 147–57
in Michigan, 142–43
in New Hampshire, 145–46
in New York, 136–39
in Ohio, 140–42
in Pennsylvania, 139–40
state constitutional provisions for, 135
State universities, 482. *See also* Colleges; Universities
admission of black undergraduates, 521–22
efforts to transform private colleges into state institutions, 93–94
first nine to be chartered (1785–1819), 95
Stewart, Joseph, 284
Stimulus-Response Bond theory, 404, 405
Stone, C. W., 392, 404
Stowe, Calvin E., 118, 166, 167, 182, 430
Straight, Henry H., 205, 210–11
Strayer, George D., 393
Student Army Training Corps, 534
Subscription schools, 34, 40
Sullivan, Anne, 408–409
Sullivan, James, 77, 88
Sully, James, 197
Summer schools, university, 485
Summerhill, 384
Sumner, Charles, 156
Superintendency of schools, 305–306, 314–15. *See also* Chief of state school system
Supreme Court of the United States. *See also* Court cases
decisions on education, 524–27
Dartmouth College case, 94, 527
dealing with teaching of evolution, 525
dealing with teaching of foreign languages in elementary schools, 524–25

Supreme Court [*cont.*]
on flag-saluting in schools, 526–27
Oregon case on private schools, 136, 463, 525
on public provision of textbooks and transportation to private school children, 526
on teaching religion on "released time," 527
decisions on racial segregation
on admission of blacks to public higher institutions, 521
Berea College case, 520
Brown v. Board of Education of Topeka declaring segregation at any level of public education unconstitutional, 522, 524, 525, 545
enforcing desegregation, 523
Plessy v. Ferguson, 520, 522
on student busing, 524
Survey Ordinance of 1785, 140–41, 515, 528
Swett, John, 145, 147
Swift, Joseph G., 271
Symms-Eaton School, 48

Tachistoscope, 438
Taine, Hippolyte, 196
Tappan, Henry P., 452, 491
Taylor, Harold, 492
Taylor, J. Orville, 117
Teacher, The (Abbott), 183
Teachers, 534
in academies, 112
associations of, 168
average monthly wages (about 1847), 150*t.*
books for, during educational awakening, 182–85
colonial, 33, 35, 37, 39–40
boarding 'round of, 40
in private schools, 63–67
information for, 168
in junior high schools, 450–51
preparation of, 208
current, 495–98
disagreement about, 496
in elementary education, 198–200
high school as factor in, 238
inadequate, 471
in land-grant colleges, 290
in New York, 137, 138

Teachers [*cont.*]
in normal schools, 168. *See also* Normal schools
state requirements, 497–98
for universities and colleges, 480
university courses in education, 309–11, 495–98
for vocational education, 283, 286, 287
salaries of, 150, 498
textbooks for, 301, 302–304, 308–309
union organization of, 114
Teachers College of Columbia University, 199–200, 311, 360
International Institute of, 542
Teaching
general principles of, 301–302. *See also* Teaching principles
methods of, 302–305
Teaching aids, 31, 416. *See also* Audiovisual instruction; Teaching machines
abacus, 31–32, 431
in the awakening, 180–81
blackboard, 156, 181, 431
introduced by Lancaster, 129, 181
for language study, 437
Teaching machines, 419, 438–41
automatic classrooms, 439–40
history of, 438–39
Teaching principles, 162–86
educational journals of the awakening, 163–66, 166*t.*
reports on education in foreign countries, 166–67
Team teaching, 422
Technology of education
audiovisual instruction movement, 431–34
curricular innovations, 422–27
individualizing instruction, 419–22. *See also* Individual instruction
laboratories, 418–19
language study, 434–37
museums, 417–18
school and library, 427–31. *See also* Libraries
teaching machines, 438–40
Television, instructional, 433–34
Tennessee, 522. *See also* South, the
academy movement in, 110
Tennyson, Alfred, Lord, 4
Terman, Lewis M., 196, 197, 405, 407
Testing, 392, 393, 395, 404–406. *See also* Intelligence tests

Textbooks, 307. *See also* Books
of colonial period, 28–33, 64, 398
authors read in Latin grammar schools, 53–54
in elementary schools of the awakening, 174–76
McGuffey's readers, 28, 401
for teachers, 301, 302–304, 308–309
Theory and Practice of Teaching (Page), 301–302, 305
Thirty Schools experiment, 472
Thomas, Isaiah, 22, 29, 177
Thorndike, Edward L., 197, 300, 392, 393, 404–405
Stimulus-Response Bond theory, 404, 405
Thurstone, Louis L., 198, 405
Ticknor, George, 354, 429, 430, 491
Tompkins, Arnold, 492
Torrey, H. A. P., 355
Trade schools, 459
Transcendentalism, 170–72
Translation, double, 53
Transylvania University, 91, 279
Tufts, James H., 359, 361, 365
Turner, Jonathan B., 273
Tusculum College, 91
Tuskegee Institute, 264, 265
Tyler, Stephen A., 412

UNESCO, 542–44
Union College (Schenectady), 91
Unit-Teaching, 422–23
United Nations, 542
International Education Year (IEY), 544
United States Boys' Working Reserve, 532
United States military academies, 270–71, 487, 541
United States Office of Education. *See* Office of Education, U.S.
United States School Garden Army, 533
Universities, 478–511. *See also* Colleges; Medical schools; State Universities
affiliated women's colleges, 482
aid to students and, through National Defense Education Act, 530–31
Association of American Universities, 480
attendance drop during World War I, 535–36
beginning of, 479–81

Universities [*cont*.]
  campus unrest and political involvement at, 486
  coeducation in, 481–83
  correspondence courses, 485
  courses in education, 309–11
  criticism of, 486, 487–92
  education departments created in, 360
  European, 55–56, 59, 353–54, 490–92, 503–505
  exchange of students, 503–507
  expansion of curricula and activities, 483–87
  extension teaching, 285–86, 484, 499
  formation of, in Middle Ages, 56
  German idea *vs.* English idea of, 490–92
  GI bill and enrollment in, 536
  graduate schools, 478, 480, 483, 486, 495
  national university idea, 89–90
  organization of Johns Hopkins University, 354–55
  preparation of university teachers and research workers, 480
  Presidential Commission on Campus Unrest, 486
  progressive schools connected with, 381
  public *vs.* private, 502–503
  student activities, 486–87
    athletics, 486–87, 489
  summer schools, 485
  technical services rendered by, 485
  trend toward general education, 492–95
University of Chicago, 211, 311, 356, 485, 489–90, 499
  John Dewey at, 359–64
  University Elementary School (Dewey School) of, 361, 362–64, 381
University of Chicago High School, 423
University of Connecticut, 278
University of Georgia, 91, 95, 235, 522
  Center for Continuing Education at, 500
University of Iowa, 425
University of Leipzig, 418
University of Maine, 482
University of Maryland, 521
University of Massachusetts, 278
University of Michigan, 97, 199, 239, 356–57, 360, 425, 437, 482, 484
  department of the Art and Science of Teaching, 310
University of Minnesota, 356
University of Mississippi, 482
University of Missouri, 381

University of North Carolina, 91, 95–96, 97, 251
  early years of, 96
University of Pennsylvania (formerly, College of Philadelphia), 55, 57, 58, 70, 483, 499
  temporarily made a state institution, 92–93
  Wharton School of, 484
University of South Carolina, 97
University of the State of New York, 92, 95
University of Tennessee (formerly, Blount College), 91, 97
University of Texas, 433
University of Vermont, 91, 97, 351–52
University of Virginia, 86, 95, 97, 183, 234, 252, 355, 427–28
University of Wisconsin, 439, 482
  Experimental College at, 493

Van Liew, C. C., 339
Van Rensselaer, Stephen, 272
Vaux, Roberts, 118, 140
Veblen, Thorstein, 487–88
Vermont, 278
Virginia, 252. *See also* South, the
  bill for more general diffusion of knowledge (1779), 85–87
  early schools in, 48–50
  high schools in, 234
  schools of Prince Edward County closed, 523
Vives, Juan Luis, 53, 60
Vocational education, 421, 458–62
  defined, 458
  early attempts in, 19
  Federal Board for Vocational Education, 286, 529
  in high schools, 286, 287
  introduction of, 460–62
  Massachusetts law on (1642), 26
  opposed by educators, 461
Vocational guidance, 466–67
  instruments of, 467
Vocations, 458–59
  big five among, 458

Wadsworth, James, 183, 185
  district school libraries in New York and, 185
Wallin, J. E. Wallace, 196

Warren, Earl, 522
Washburne, Carleton W., 381, 420
Washington, Booker T., 262, 264
Washington, George, 87, 89
Washington College, 91
Washington and Lee University, 91, 107, 484
Wayland, Francis, 298–300, 301, 340
Webster, Noah, 77, 172
  dictionary of, 77
  speller, grammar and reader of, 28, 29, 173
Weiss, C. S., 344
Wells, William H., 232, 375
West Point, Military Academy at, 270–71, 487, 541
West Virginia, 522
Western Academician and Journal of Education and Science, 118
Western Literary Institute and College of Professional Teachers, 118, 168, 182
Wharton School, 484
Whipple, Guy M., 308, 402
White, Andrew D., 354–55
White, Emerson E., 301, 304, 461
White House Conference on Education, 516
Whorf, Benjamin L., 411
Wickersham, James P., 302–303
Wilbur, H. B., 205
Wilder, Burt G., 211
Wiley, Calvin H., 252
Willard, Emma, 109, 175
William and Mary College, 11, 48–49, 55, 86, 92, 93, 427, 487
Williams, Nathaniel, 53
Williams, Roger, 15, 16
Williams College, 91
Winnetka Plan, 420
Winship, A. E., 398
Winthrop, John, 32
Wisconsin, 462, 499
Witchcraft delusion, 13

Witherspoon, John, 96
Woman's Medical College of Pennsylvania, 483
Women. See also Girls, education of
  admitted to land-grant colleges, 280, 482
  graduate schools opened to, 483
Women's colleges, 482
Women's Educational Association, 110
Woodbridge, William C., 117, 165, 166, 171, 175
Woodring, Paul, 497
Woodworth, Robert S., 300
Woolley, Helen T., 466
Worcester, Samuel, 172–73
Workingmen's Party, 114–15
Works Progress Administration, 500
World Federation of Education Associations, 542
Writing lessons in early schools, 30
Wundt, Wilhelm, 358, 418

Xavier University: Montessori teacher training program at, 421

Yale University, 55, 57, 58, 92, 278, 354, 425, 427, 482, 483, 484
  early entrance requirements of, 54
  first American doctor of philosophy degree granted, 495
Young, Ella Flagg, 375–79
  John Dewey and, 375–78
  as president of the NEA, 379
  as superintendent of the schools of Chicago, 378
Young, J. W. A., 399
Young Ladies' Academy (Philadelphia), 65

Zenger, Peter: case against, 22–23
Zook, George F., 538